SPECIAL EDITION

USING

Adobe®

GoLive 6

Brian Dunning

Allyson Knox

Lori Becker

201 W. 103rd Street
Indianapolis, Indiana 46290

SPECIAL EDITION USING ADOBE GOLIVE 6

International Standard Book Number: 0-7897-2727-7

Library of Congress Catalog Card Number: 2001099273

Printed in the United States of America

First Printing: September 2002

05   04   03   02   4   3   2   1

Trademarks

Warning and Disclaimer

Executive Editor
Candace Hall

Acquisitions Editors
Lloyd Black
Loretta Yates

Development Editors
Laura Bulcher
Sean Dixon

Managing Editor
Thomas Hayes

Project Editor
Natalie Harris

Production Editor
Benjamin Berg

Indexer
Mandie Frank

Proofreaders
Kay Hoskin
Abby Van Huss

Technical Editor
Alan Hamill

Team Coordinator
Sherry Lee Gregory

Interior Designer
Kim Scott

Cover Designer
Dan Armstrong

Page Layout
Susan Geiselman

CONTENTS AT A GLANCE

Introduction   1

I   Overview of Adobe GoLive

1   Introducing GoLive 6.0   11
2   GoLive Essentials   23

II   Web Site Basics

3   Introduction to Sites   37
4   Working with Sites   49

III   The Work Area

5   GoLive Interface Elements   75
6   Setting Preferences   91
7   Customizing GoLive   111

IV   Setting Up Pages

8   Creating and Saving Pages   121
9   Working with Code   139

V   Standard Page Layout

10   Working with Text   159
11   Using Graphic Elements   183
12   Working with Links   201
13   Page Extras   217

VI   Advanced Page Layout

14   Working with Frames   229
15   Working with Tables   239
16   Creating Forms   255
17   Styles   279

VII   Movement, Multimedia, and Interactivity

18   Using the JavaScript Editor and Inserting Java Applets   303
19   Working with Layers and Floating Boxes   315
20   Animation, Audio, and Video   341

VIII   Integrating GoLive with Other Programs

21   Smart Objects   369
22   Integrating with Photoshop, Illustrator, and LiveMotion   383
23   GoLive Plug-Ins   419
24   Lasso Studio for Adobe GoLive   431

IX   Wireless and Collaboration

25   Developing for Wireless Devices   467
26   The WorkGroup Server   481

X Using Dynamic Content

27 About Dynamic Content   495
28 Using Dynamic Content   505
29 Custom Merchant   539

XI Viewing and Managing Web Sites

30 Streamlining Site Construction   561
31 Publishing Your Site   571

XII Appendixes

A What's on the Companion CD   585
B Palette Definitions   589
  Index   451

CONTENTS

Introduction 1

I Overview of Adobe GoLive

1 Introducing GoLive 6.0 11

Welcome 12

Code 12

Productivity 14

Integration 17

Site Management 18

Dynamic Development 20

Standard and Emerging Web Technologies
20

Extensibility 20

Troubleshooting 21

Going Live 21

2 GoLive Essentials 23

Getting Your Bearings 24

Getting Started 25

The Site Window 26

The Page Window 26

The Inspector 27

The Palettes 28
   The Objects Palette 29
   The Color Palette 29
   The History Palette 30
   The Table Palette 30

   The Source Code Palette 31
   The Transform Palette 32
   The Align Palette 33

Troubleshooting 34

Going Live 34

II Web Site Basics

3 Introduction to Sites 37

Creating a New Site 38
   The Site Wizard 38
   Creating a Blank Site 38

Importing a Site 40

Site Templates 43

The Site Window 45
   Anatomy of a Site Window 45
   The Files Tab 46
   The Extras Tab 46
   The External, Colors, and Font Sets
   Tabs 46
   The Errors, FTP, and WebDAV Tabs 47

Troubleshooting 47

Going Live 48

4 Working with Sites 49

Site Design Basics 50
   Creating a Site Design 50
   Using the Site Design Window 51
   Anchoring a Design 52
   Defining a Design Section 53
   Adding Pages and Subsections 54
   Adding and Editing Pending Links 55
   Moving Pages 56
   Annotating a Site Design 57
   Managing Annotations 57

Submitting a Site Design to a Site **58**
About Recalls and Updates **58**
Grouping Design Items **59**

Filenames **59**
Changing Filename Constraints **60**

Site Diagramming **61**
Solving a Site Hierarchy **64**

Site Management **65**
Site Views **66**
The Links View **66**
The Navigation View **66**
Magnifying and Reducing the View **67**
Spotlighting Page Groupings in
Navigation View **67**
Variations in Orientation **68**

Using Panes **69**

Site Reporting **70**

Troubleshooting **71**

Going Live **71**

III The Work Area

5 GoLive Interface Elements 75

The Toolbar **76**

Page Window **76**
Layout View **76**
Frame View **79**
Source Code View **79**
Outline View **79**
Layout Preview **79**
Frame Preview **80**

Inspector 80
Setting Page Properties: The Page
Inspector **80**
Creating Links: The Link Inspector **80**
Grappling with Graphics: The Image
Inspector **81**

The Palettes **82**
Objects Palette **82**
Color Palette **84**
Transform Palette **84**
Align Palette **85**
History Palette **86**
Table Palette **87**
Markup Tree Bar **88**
Source Code Window **88**
In & Out Links Window **89**

Troubleshooting **90**

Going Live **90**

6 Setting Preferences 91

About Preferences **92**

General Preferences **93**
General Preferences **93**
URL Handling **94**
User Interface **95**
Images **95**
Invisible Elements **96**
Cache **96**

Modules **97**

Fonts **97**

Encodings **98**

ColorSync **98**

Script Library **98**

Site Preferences **99**
Filename Constraints **99**
Status **100**
Clean Up Site **100**
Export **101**
Upload/Sync Times **102**
Design Colors **102**
Link Type **102**

Browsers **103**

Find Preferences **103**
    Regular Expressions **104**

Spell Checker **104**
    Regular Expressions **104**

Network Preferences **105**
    Network Status **105**

Source Preferences **105**
    Browser Sets **105**
    Font **106**
    Colors **106**
    Printing **107**

JavaScript Preferences **107**
    Font **107**
    Colors **107**
    Printing **107**

Dynamic Content **108**

QuickTime **108**

Troubleshooting **109**

Going Live **109**

7   Customizing GoLive   111

A Space of Your Own **112**

Examining Your Workflow **112**
    Establish Your Role **112**
    Trace Your Steps **112**
    Beat the Clock **113**

Customizing the Desktop **113**

Using Custom Palettes **114**
    Custom Color Palette **114**
    Custom Objects Palettes **115**

Setting Keyboard Shortcuts **115**

Troubleshooting **116**

Going Live **117**

IV   Setting Up Pages

8   Creating and Saving Pages   121

Creating a New Page **122**

Reusing Pages **124**

Choosing the Dimensions of Your Page **125**

Page Margins **127**

Using the Grid **128**
    Placing a Grid **128**
    Sizing a Grid **128**
    Optimizing a Grid **129**
    Resizing Grid Squares 129
    Snap and Visibility **129**
    Aligning the Grid **130**
    Adding a Background Color **130**
    Adding a Background Image **130**
    Using Multiple Grids **131**
    Placing a Grid Within a Table **131**
    Copying a Grid **131**

Layout Rulers **131**

Selecting Page Colors **132**

Background Images **133**

Saving Pages **134**
    Saving a Page as a Template **135**
    Saving a Page as Stationery **135**

Troubleshooting **137**

Going Live **137**

9   Working with Code   139

Breaking the Code **140**

Source Editor **140**
    Line Breaks **142**
    Drag and Drop **142**
    Source Editor Preferences **143**
    Browser Sets **143**
    Font **143**

Colors **143**
Printing **143**

Using the Source Split View **143**

Source Code Palette **144**

Markup Tree **145**

Outline Editor **145**
Expanding and Collapsing Tags **146**
Selecting Elements **147**
Adding and Modifying Elements **147**
Viewing Images **147**
Outline Editor Toolbar **147**

Highlight Palette **149**

HTML Element Find & Replace **150**

Adding Head Tags and Scripts **151**
Adding Scripts to the Header **152**

Generating XHTML Code **153**

Troubleshooting **154**

Going Live **155**

V Standard Page Layout

10 Working with Text 159

Text on Your Pages **160**
Entering Text **160**
Editing Text **161**
Special Characters **163**
Checking Your Spelling **164**
Finding and Replacing Text **164**

Jazzing Up Your Text **166**
Formatting Text **166**
Font Sets **166**
Font Size **167**
Font Style **169**
Font Structure **170**
Text Color **171**

Putting It All Together **172**
Formatting Paragraphs **172**
Headers **175**
Alignment **175**
Line Breaks **176**
Lists **178**

Troubleshooting **180**

Going Live **181**

11 Using Graphic Elements 183

Easy on the Eyes **184**

Adding Images **184**
About Web Images **184**
Using Images in GoLive **185**

Horizontal Lines **186**

Manipulating Images **186**
Resizing an Image **187**
Positioning an Image **187**
Aligning an Image **187**
Creating a Border **187**
Including Alternative Text **188**
Editing Images **189**
Transform Palette **189**

Arranging Objects **190**
The Objects Toolbar **190**
Creating Space **190**
Align Palette **191**

Using a Tracing Image **192**

Creating Image Maps **194**
Creating Image Maps in GoLive **194**
Applying Actions to a Hot Spot **197**

Creating Rollovers **197**
Rollover Options **198**

Troubleshooting **199**

Going Live **199**

12 Working with Links 201

Linking Up with the World **202**

Adding Navigational Links **202**
    Point-and-Shoot (Fetch URL) **202**
    Link Field **203**
    Browse **205**
    Menu Options **206**
    Creating Text Links **206**
    Creating Image Links **207**

Using Anchors **208**
    Placing Anchors **208**
    Naming Anchors **208**
    Linking to Anchors **209**

Creating URL Pop-up Menus **209**

Managing Links **210**
    Gathering Addresses From Your
    Pages **211**
    Adding Addresses Manually **211**
    Gathering Addresses from a
    Browser **211**
    Organizing and Editing Links **212**
    In & Out Links Palette **213**

Troubleshooting **213**

Going Live **214**

13 Page Extras 217

Adding Value with Extras **218**

Adding Comments **218**

Creating a Marquee **221**
    Resizing a Marquee **221**
    Other Marquee Options **222**

Creating Date and Time Stamps **223**

Viewing Document Statistics **224**

Previewing Pages **225**
    Layout Preview **225**
    Frame Preview **225**

Troubleshooting **226**

Going Live **226**

VI Advanced Page Layout

14 Working with Frames 229

Using Frames **230**

The Frame Editor **231**
    Set Versus Variable Frames **232**
    Resizing Frames **232**
    Frame Names and Target Frames **233**
    Scrolling **233**
    Preview **233**

Previewing Frames **234**

Using a Table of Contents Frame **234**

Displaying Two Frames from One Link **234**

Troubleshooting **236**

Going Live **236**

15 Working with Tables 239

The Ubiquitous Table **240**

Creating Tables **240**
    Adding and Deleting Rows and
    Columns **241**
    Merging Cells **242**
    Resizing Tables, Rows and
    Columns **244**
    Creating Borders **244**
    Cell Padding and Cell Spacing **245**
    Setting Background Colors **245**
    Setting a Background Image **246**
    Alignment **247**
    Creating Captions **248**

Table Palette **249**
    Setting Table Styles **249**
    Sorting Table Content **250**

Creating Nested Tables **251**

Converting a Table to a Grid **252**

Troubleshooting **252**

Going Live **253**

16 Creating Forms 255

About Forms **256**

Form Elements **257**
  Creating a New Form **258**
  The Form Tag **258**
  Creating Buttons **260**
  Form Input Image **262**
  Labels and Text Fields **262**
  Checkboxes and Radio Buttons **266**
  Pop-up Menus and List Boxes **269**
  Setting Up a File Browser **270**
  Hidden and Disabled Form
  Elements **272**
  Read Only Form Elements **273**

Form Navigation **273**
  Tabbing Chains **273**
  Defining Access Keys **275**

Troubleshooting **277**

Going Live **278**

17 Styles 279

About Styles **280**

Cascading Style Sheets **280**
  Browser Compatibility **281**
  External and Internal Style Sheets **281**
  Element, Class, and ID Selectors **282**
  Inheritance and Precedence **282**

Implementing CSS in GoLive **283**
  Class and ID Styles **288**
  ID Styles **289**
  Snippets **290**
  Components **291**

Stationery and Templates **294**
  Creating Templates and Stationeries in
  GoLive **294**
  Creating Pages from a Template or
  Stationery **296**
  Modifying a Template or Stationery **296**

Troubleshooting **298**

Going Live **298**

**VII Movement, Multimedia, and
Interactivity**

**18 Using the JavaScript Editor and
Inserting Java Applets 303**

About Java and JavaScript **304**

The JavaScript Editor **304**
  Overview of JavaScript **304**
  Creating a Simple JavaScript **306**
  Checking for Syntax Errors **310**

Inserting Java Applets **311**
  Java Accessibility **312**

Troubleshooting **312**

Going Live **313**

**19 Working with Layers and Floating
Boxes 315**

Layers, Floating Boxes, JavaScript, and
DHTML **316**

Using Floating Boxes (Layers) in
GoLive **316**
  Managing Floating Boxes **320**

JavaScript and DHTML **321**

Applying Actions in GoLive **321**
  Reading the Actions Palette **325**

Executing Actions Based on the Page's
Events **326**

Common JavaScript Applications (Uses of GoLive Actions) **328**
Generating Pop-Up Windows **328**
Form Validation **329**
Detecting a Loyal User with a JavaScript Cookie **332**

Advanced Actions and DHTML **334**

Troubleshooting **337**

Going Live **338**

20 Animation, Audio, and Video 341

Pizzazz on Your Pages **342**

Animation with DHTML **342**
Creating a Floating Object **342**
Animating a Floating Object with the Timeline Editor **343**
Showing and Hiding a Floating Box **346**
Triggering Your Animations with Actions **346**
Managing Multiple Floating Boxes **346**
Using Scenes **349**

SWF and SVG **350**
Shockwave Flash (SWF) **350**
Scalable Vector Graphics (SVG) **351**

Audio and Video Clips **351**
RealMedia Files **351**
QuickTime Movies **353**

Editing QuickTime Movies **354**
Setting the Mode for a Video Track **362**
Creating Streaming Movies **363**

Troubleshooting **364**

Going Live **365**

VIII Integrating GoLive with Other Programs

21 Smart Objects 369

About Smart Objects **370**

Inserting a Smart Object **371**
Creating a Bitmap **372**
Creating a SVG File via an Illustrator Smart Object **377**
Changing the Export Settings **380**
Opening the Original File from Within GoLive **380**

Troubleshooting **380**

Going Live **381**

22 Integrating with Photoshop, Illustrator, and LiveMotion 383

About Inter-Application Integration **384**

Building Mockups **384**
Which to Choose: Photoshop, Illustrator, or LiveMotion? **385**

Slicing a Photoshop Mockup **386**
Photoshop's Integration Features **386**
Using Illustrator to Slice a Pages **396**
Slicing in LiveMotion **405**

Using a Photoshop or Illustrator File as a Tracing Image **409**

Adobe Support for Scalar Vector Graphics **410**
Embedding an SVG Element in an HTML Page **410**
Opening an SVG in Adobe GoLive **411**
Creating SVGs **412**

Troubleshooting **413**

Going Live **415**

23 GoLive Plug-Ins 419

Extending GoLive with Plug-Ins **420**

Downloading and Installing Existing
Extensions **420**

Creating Your Own Menu Items **423**

Troubleshooting **429**

Going Live **430**

24 Lasso Studio for Adobe GoLive 431

About Lasso Studio **432**

Installing the Lasso Suite **432**
    Installing Lasso Studio on Windows **433**
    Installing Lasso Studio on
    Mac OS X **435**
    Installing FileMaker Pro **436**
    Configuring Lasso **437**

Scoping Out the Functionality **439**

Creating Your Databases **439**
    Making the Databases Accessible to
    Lasso **441**
    Lasso Studio for GoLive **443**
    Creating the Membership Registration
    Screens **446**
    Creating the Genres Page **451**
    Building the Member Search **456**
    Creating Navigation **461**
    Lasso Studio Wrap Up **462**

Troubleshooting **462**

Going Live **463**

IX Wireless and Collaboration

25 Developing for Wireless Devices 467

Wireless: A Growing Market **468**

WML, XHTML-Basic, and CHTML **468**
    Planning Your Development **469**
    Palettes and Preferences **469**
    Previewing with an Emulator **470**

Developing in WML **470**
    Building a Basic Deck **470**
    Entering Text **472**
    Using Images **473**
    Anchor Navigation in WML **473**
    Form Elements **474**
    Events in WML **475**
    Timers in WML **476**
    Variables in WML **477**

Developing in XHTML-Basic and
CHTML **477**
    Planning Your Site **477**
    Customizing GoLive's Environment **478**
    Finishing Your Site **479**

Troubleshooting **480**

Going Live **480**

26 The Workgroup Server 481

Playing Nicely with Others **482**

Web Workgroup Server Administration **482**
    Creating a Workgroup Site **485**
    Converting an Existing Single User Site
    to a Workgroup Site **486**

Interacting with the Workgroup's Site
Window **486**
    Changing the User and Passwords **489**

Publishing Workgroup Sites **490**

Troubleshooting **490**

Going Live **490**

X Using Dynamic Content

27 About Dynamic Content 495

The Dynamic Web **496**

How Dynamic Web Sites Work **496**

Using GoLive to Build a Dynamic Web Site **497**
  ASP **497**
  JSP **498**
  PHP **498**

What GoLive Provides **498**
  Dynamic Content Module **499**
  Custom Merchant **501**
  EasyHost **502**
  Preconfigured Servers **502**
  PageGenerator **502**

Troubleshooting **503**

Going Live **504**

28 Using Dynamic Content 505

Overview of Dynamic Content **506**

About Web Applications **506**
  About ASP **507**
  About JSP **507**
  About PHP **508**

About Data Sources **508**

The Dynamic Content Tools **509**
  Dynamic Content on the Objects Palette **511**

Building the Dynamic Site **514**
  Preparing the Servers **515**
  Starting and Stopping the Servers **515**
  Preparing the Databases **516**
  Building the Prototype Site **517**
  Converting the Static Site to Dynamic **521**

Adding the Dynamic Elements **526**

Security **536**
  GoLive Dynamic Site Security **536**

Troubleshooting **536**

Going Live **537**

29 Custom Merchant 539

About Custom Merchant **540**

Implementing Custom Merchant **541**
  Add the Custom Merchant Data Source **541**
  Building an Add to Cart Button **542**
  Viewing the Cart **545**
  The Check Out Screen **549**
  The Ship To Page **551**
  The Ship Via Page **552**
  The Review Page **554**
  The Receipt Page **555**

Troubleshooting **556**

Going Live **557**

Part XI Viewing and Managing Web Sites

30 Streamlining Site Construction 561

Optimizing and Troubleshooting **562**

The Site Window **562**

Keeping Files Clean **568**

Troubleshooting **569**

Going Live **570**

31 Publishing Your Site 571

Publishing Overview **572**

Setting Up FTP and Internet Access **572**

Connecting to an FTP Server **574**

Transferring Files **575**
  GoLive's FTP Browser **577**

WebDAV Server **578**

Publishing Workgroup Sites **580**

Troubleshooting **580**
  Going Live **581**

XII Appendixes

A What's on the Companion CD **585**

The Companion CD **586**

Lasso Professional 5 Evaluation
Edition **586**

Lasso Studio for Adobe GoLive **586**

Evocative's ProCart Live **586**

CatalogIntegrator Cart from
eCatalogBuilders **587**

digital.forest Coupon **587**

B Palette Definitions **589**

ABOUT THE AUTHORS

Brian Dunning is the author of several books, including the *Master Class* series on Web development and the novel *Strapping Young Lads.* He has trained hundreds of Web developers in dynamic site creation. A technical editor at *FileMaker Advisor* and *ISO FileMaker* magazines, Brian also reviewed Lasso Studio for GoLive for Adobe's Web site. References to Brian's volleyball jump serve appear in Norse Sagas dating as far back as 600 A.D. You can find Brian at `http://www.briandunning.com/`.

Allyson Knox is a freelance graphic artist and Web developer who has been using Adobe GoLive to design professional Web sites since its original inception as GoLive Cyberstudio. She considers herself a whole-brain thinker, and her direct involvement in every aspect of Web site creation makes her uniquely qualified to discuss the product from the varied perspectives of designer, programmer, and site manager.

With more than three years experience as a server administrator, she understands Web site design from a comprehensive technical viewpoint. Allyson is also a skilled FileMaker Pro database architect and Lasso programmer who has participated in panel discussions on networking and the integration of online databases. She has written countless technical articles and given lectures on the basics of Web design.

A Liberal Arts education—she holds a bachelor's degree in English and another in French literature—provided the context for her to live for extended periods abroad. She studied for a full year in Paris and spent another year working and traveling from her flat in Exeter, England. She currently makes her home in Minneapolis.

With a background in marketing, *Lori Becker's* first encounter with Web development technologies occurred in June of 2000 when she joined WestLake Internet Training as a Web development Instructor in Washington, D.C. Since then, Lori has worked as a teacher, course author, and developer and has consulted with charities, non-profits, and private companies to include the Kennedy Center and the World Bank.

Lori holds an undergraduate business degree from the College of William and Mary and is pursuing her MBA as a member of Goizueta Business School's (Emory University) class of 2004.

ACKNOWLEDGMENTS

Brian Dunning would like to thank our friend Lloyd Black, who was our original acquisitions editor on this project but did not have the opportunity to see it through to its thrilling climax.

To Patrick Rigney of Evocative, who came through just at that moment when he was needed most.

A third most special thanks to the folks at Adobe, for creating such great products; not only GoLive, but all the rest in their fine stable. We're certainly not the first to express this appreciation, as most of the civilized world relies heavily on San Jose's finest.

A second most special thanks to my very good friend Bill Doerrfeld, president and CEO of Blue World Communications, without whose input this project would never have left the ground.

But the biggest thanks can go to none other than my wife Lisa and kids Andrew and Erika, who put up with an abbreviated dadless family for much too long, and deserve all of the credit for my contribution to this volume. Until you've tackled a project of this size, your perception of "perseverance" is only a shadow of the real thing. And once you have, it's still nothing compared to what your family goes through. Thanks crew!

Allyson Knox would like to thank: Brian & Lisa, my parents & the entire Ryan-Alex clan, Zen dog Eddie Boyle and the gang at Half Price Books, Cory Zerwas, Chris Moyer, Pete Mayers, Noah Polk, The Old 97's, Josh Joplin Group, Colby Falk, Erik Dunn, Bill Duncan, Jimmy McConnell, everyone at Davis-Kidd Booksellers, Stephanie Marks-Ryan, Michael Parrish, Acuity Marketing, Paula Southgate, Nashville Creative Forum, Jeff & Todd at CDS, everyone at Adobe & Que Publishing, Jimmy Stewart, Dr. Seuss, and the SETI at home project. This book is dedicated to the memory of Michael Brandon.

Lori Becker would like to thank: first and foremost my parents, who believe in everything I do; Glenn Fleishman, the e-friend I had without knowing it; my fantastic colleagues (friends and teachers) at WestLake Internet Training; all those who kept me company late nights (both in thought and in practice); and last, but not least, Oscar.

April, 2002

TELL US WHAT YOU THINK!

As the reader of this book, *you* are our most important critic and commentator. We value your opinion and want to know what we're doing right, what we could do better, what areas you'd like to see us publish in, and any other words of wisdom you're willing to pass our way.

As an executive editor for Que, I welcome your comments. You can fax, email, or write me directly to let me know what you did or didn't like about this book—as well as what we can do to make our books stronger.

Please note that I cannot help you with technical problems related to the topic of this book, and that due to the high volume of mail I receive, I might not be able to reply to every message.

When you write, please be sure to include this book's title and author as well as your name and phone or fax number. I will carefully review your comments and share them with the author and editors who worked on the book.

Fax: 317-581-4666
E-mail: feedback@quepublishing.com
Mail: Candace Hall
Que
201 West 103rd Street
Indianapolis, IN 46290 USA

INTRODUCTION

IN THIS INTRODUCTION

About This Book   2

Why Adobe GoLive?   2

Our Audience   3

How This Book Is Organized   3

Conventions Used   7

CD/Web Resources   7

ABOUT THIS BOOK

As technology races forward to reveal new opportunities for communication, commercial success, and creative expression across the Internet, Web designers and programmers require more powerful and sophisticated tools for their trade. Project managers and Web teams need ways to control their workflow with greater efficiency, particularly as Web sites grow in complexity, so that the workload may be shared by developers in different departments or even different cities. End users are smarter, increasingly tech-savvy and demanding, and won't be satisfied with the same old static pages of the past. We all want to push boundaries, attempt the untried, and interact with the world around us. Adobe GoLive 6.0 is the ideal application for doing just that.

With a wealth of new tools intended to simplify site management, lay out eye-popping pages incorporating the latest in multimedia design, edit HTML and customize scripts, publish to wireless and handheld devices, interact with databases, and integrate with other Adobe applications, Adobe GoLive gives administrators, designers, and developers the ultimate in organizational and creative control. But even a great tool is limited by one's ability to use it.

Welcome to *Special Edition Using Adobe GoLive 6*. In clear, concise language, accompanied by extensive examples, screen shots, and other visual cues, we offer the most complete and easy to use GoLive guide available. This book appeals to a broad range of GoLive users: Those who have some knowledge of the Web, but are not yet fluent in most of GoLive's features; as well as those who bought the book to advance their knowledge and use the tool to the best of their ability.

To help you accomplish these goals, we offer well-organized chapters and thorough explanations covering every aspect of the program. We show you, step by step, how to take advantage of the latest tools and technologies. What's more, we provide an indispensable index, countless cool tips and tricks, and a friendly attitude that'll have you reaching for this reference again and again.

WHY ADOBE GOLIVE?

With more than 300,000 registered users, Adobe GoLive already has a proven wide-range appeal among Web professionals of all types. Put simply, GoLive has it all. As a comprehensive building tool, it handles every aspect of the Web construction process. GoLive facilitates page design both from a visually oriented standpoint and from a hard-coding perspective. GoLive not only assists in laying out individual pages; it enables users to plot the architecture of an entire site. It also simplifies ongoing site maintenance with tools for updating or expanding the site, uploading files to the server, and tracking updated files.

GoLive is completely cross-platform. In fact, with the use of a WebDAV server, it provides the perfect team environment, enabling diverse groups to collaborate on a single project, update pages simply via local or remote access, and track usage so that a page can only be updated by one person at a time. The new features for integration and collaboration, both with other Adobe products and with outside software, now enable users to migrate naturally between GoLive and other programs, allowing them to work smarter and make more efficient use of their time and their tools. Given the additional features of version 6.0—particularly its exciting new compatibility with mobile devices, improved integration with databases, and team-building advances in the area of workgroups—Adobe GoLive clearly demonstrates its ability to meet the needs of an ever expanding and changing market.

Now, with version 6.0, Adobe GoLive is better than ever. Some of the more notable of its myriad new features include native support for JSP and PHP in the Dynamic Content module; a true Nokia XHTML-Basic emulator for developing wireless applications; a full suite of WML tools for developing even more wireless applications; new collaboration tools such as the Web Workgroup Server, versioning, and synchronization; new diagramming and site architecture tools; a veritable Camelot of wizards; and the tightest integration yet with Adobe Photoshop, Adobe Illustrator, and Adobe LiveMotion.

OUR AUDIENCE

Intended for use by a more technically skilled audience, our book takes the reader beyond the basics, expanding on the manual in a simple, no-nonsense way that will improve user fluency and increase efficiency in no time. This book assumes each reader already possesses a good understanding of Internet technologies and a general knowledge of HTML and its capabilities. Many users may already have experience with the fundamental aspects of Web design as well, and are most likely familiar with other products within the Adobe family, such as Photoshop or LiveMotion. With that foundation in place, we aim merely to build on the reader's current body of knowledge and expand his or her existing skills.

Designers who are familiar with the intuitive Adobe interface and accustomed to page layout applications such as Adobe PageMaker or Quark Xpress will progress naturally into the online world. Now it's easier than ever to bring your graphics to life on the Web, explore new possibilities in multimedia, and make changes to existing pages using the brilliantly integrated features in the Adobe family.

Programmers who enjoy the challenge of hand-coding their HTML will still benefit from our discussion of GoLive's convenient source code editing features.

Project managers and administrators who oversee group projects and would like to understand more about efficient site management using GoLive will save valuable time, money, and energy by reading our sections on WebDAV and Workgroup Server.

Developers who prefer to customize and extend GoLive to meet their own needs and take the software beyond its current capabilities should find plenty of new ground to cover in our chapters on scripting, actions, elements, customization, and extensibility.

Whole-brain thinkers who resist established labels and prefer the challenge of integrating art and technology will feel at home here. The Web continues to be driven forward by self-taught Renaissance men and women, and we're proud to be surrounded by such good company.

HOW THIS BOOK IS ORGANIZED

As with any course of learning, we begin with a general overview of the GoLive program and then proceed to more detailed and complex tasks. This not only assists new users in establishing a firm foundation, but also serves to ensure that everyone begins on the same page, so to speak, that we share a common language as we move into foreign territory.

Part I: Overview of Adobe GoLive

Chapter 1, "Introducing GoLive 6.0": Here we talk specifically about what's new with this upgrade. Lots of new material to cover.

Chapter 2, "GoLive Essentials": This is intended as an overview of Sites, Elements, and Standard Features. You might find this helpful as a preparation for GoLive or as a review.

Part II: Web Site Basics

Chapter 3, "Introduction to Sites": Covers the principles of Web site diagramming and management. This chapter could be of particular interest to those planning new sites or overseeing a total project or existing site.

Chapter 4, "Working with Sites": Dives into the details of GoLive's Site Management tools. It covers creating a new site, working with site windows, using the various site views, using panes, designing sites, site reporting, using site templates, planning your page hierarchy, and following file naming conventions.

Part III: The Work Area

Chapter 5, "GoLive Interface Elements": More specific information about the Page Window, the Inspector, and all the various Palettes used in creating Web pages.

Chapter 6, "Setting Preferences": This describes various options for personalizing your GoLive experience via Preferences. Have it your way.

Chapter 7, "Customizing GoLive": This covers options for customizing your Desktop and setting up your own keyboard shortcuts, among other things.

Part IV: Setting Up Pages

Chapter 8, "Creating and Saving Pages": This shows you how to lay out Web pages from a graphic perspective. It covers window sizes and page margins, the Grid, Layout Rulers, color selection, background images, the History Palette, and viewing options.

Chapter 9, "Working with Code": For those of you who prefer to go behind the scenes, this chapter is for you. It concentrates on the different ways GoLive presents the HTML code and lets you work with it. It covers using the Source Code Palette and Source Window, using the Markup Tree Palette, working with 360 Code, re-writing source code, searching and replacing HTML elements, adding unknown elements, adding head tags and scripts, using text macros, saving code fragments, and generating XHTML code.

Part V: Standard Page Layout

Chapter 10, "Working with Text": In the beginning was the word. Here we'll talk all about putting the printed word online, everything from entering and arranging text to special formatting requirements.

Chapter 11, "Using Graphic Elements": A picture's worth a thousand words. In this chapter we'll spice up your page with images and other visual cues, and discuss some of the basics of a good layout.

Chapter 12, "Working with Links": Links are what hold the Web together. Here we'll talk about various navigational options, both traditional and more exciting.

Chapter 13, "Page Extras": This gets down to the nitty-gritty of date and time, document statistics, and keeping track of your pages.

Part VI: Advanced Page Layout

Chapter 14, "Working with Frames": GoLive makes it easy to set up a site with frames. We'll look at how this is done and some good uses for frames.

Chapter 15, "Working with Tables": Tables have gotten a whole lot more interesting and more manageable over the years. Here we examine the Table Palette, various styles, and effective sorting of data.

Chapter 16, "Creating Forms": This chapter deals exclusively with all the details of a good form. Covers form elements, navigation, and more.

Chapter 17, "Styles": One of the best aspects of GoLive is that it enables you to create something once and use it as many times as you like. In this chapter we'll discuss the efficient use of Cascading Style Sheets, Stationery, and other reusable components.

Part VII: Movement, Multimedia, and Interactivity

Chapter 18, "Using the JavaScript Editor and Inserting Java Applets": The uses of Java and JavaScript are limitless. In this particular chapter we show you some of the most common uses: Rollovers and Java Applets.

Chapter 19, "Working with Layers and Floating Boxes": Discusses your page in three dimensions. We cover Floating Boxes, W3C Object Control, and using Actions.

Chapter 20, "Animation, Audio, and Video": The world of multimedia is right at your fingertips. Discover how to integrate animation, audio, and video clips into your Site. We also provide advice on editing your own QuickTime movies.

Part VIII: Integrating GoLive with Other Programs

Chapter 21, "Smart Objects": Why can't we all just get along? Adobe takes full advantage of a technology that enables files to get along from one app to another. Here we talk about Smart Objects and their uses.

Chapter 22, "Integrating with Photoshop, Illustrator, and LiveMotion": Move files quickly and easily between Photoshop, Illustrator, LiveMotion, and GoLive for greater efficiency in your workflow.

Chapter 23, "GoLive Plug-Ins": Here we discuss how to push the envelope even further using Adobe's Online Xchange and the GoLive SDK.

Chapter 24, "Lasso Studio for Adobe GoLive": In this chapter we cover the integration of GoLive and Lasso Studio for creating dynamic, database-driven sites.

Part IX: Wireless and Collaboration

Chapter 25, "Developing for Wireless Devices": Here we discuss emerging technologies such as WAP and iMode devices. Covers the WML language and WML tools in GoLive, as well as optimizing your site for WAP and iMode.

Chapter 26, "The Workgroup Server": Playing nicely with others. The Workgroup Server opens new doors in collaborative Web creation. Here we discuss the how-to's and the advantages.

Part X: Using Dynamic Content

Chapter 27, "About Dynamic Content": Everything you need to know about server requirements and compatibility issues, security, and user interface creation.

Chapter 28, "Using Dynamic Content": Topics in this chapter include configuring a new site, adding databases, adding dynamic content, using dynamic tables, and creating links to dynamic pages. Applying formatting filters and previewing dynamic pages are also covered.

Chapter 29, "Custom Merchant": Explore how to create an eCommerce site and a Web-based front end using Adobe's complete Custom Merchant system.

Part XI: Viewing and Managing Web Sites

Chapter 30, "Streamlining Site Construction": This chapter presents how to optimize and troubleshoot GoLive Sites. Also learn how to publish Web sites and understand Site Designer.

Chapter 31, "Publishing Your Site": Walk through the finer points of connecting to a Web server via FTP and WebDAV. This chapter helps you understand uploading, updating, and downloading a site as well as using the WebDAV Browser. You'll also take a look at the Network Status Window, keychain security, and customizing Internet access.

Part XII: Appendixes

Appendix A, "What's on the Companion CD": An overview of material available to support your use of this book in learning GoLive.

Appendix B, "Palette Definitions": A guide to all the toolbars, icons, buttons, widgets, and gizmos found on GoLive's innumerable screens, windows, and palettes.

CONVENTIONS USED

Special Edition Using Adobe GoLive 6.0 uses a number of conventions to provide you with special information. These include the following elements:

Tips and Notes give advice on how to do things a little easier or more efficiently, or provide additional information on a topic or feature covered in one of our chapters.

Caution

Cautions warn you of potential problems and pitfalls and help you avoid them.

Keyboard Shortcuts

Throughout the book we will provide instructions that include keyboard shortcuts for both Mac and PC. To help distinguish between the two, we will feature the Mac shortcuts in parentheses (Mac) and use a hyphen for key combinations (Mac-combo), while the PC shortcuts will be shown in brackets [PC] and use a plus sign for key combinations [PC+combo]. Both shortcuts will be provided for any given task, as in the following example: To create a new page, select New Page from the File menu or press the (Cmd-N) [Ctrl+N] keys.

Most keyboard shortcuts easily translate from one operating system to the other if you keep the following equivalents in mind:

Mac	PC
Mouse click	Left mouse click
(Ctrl)	Right mouse click
(Cmd) or (Apple) or ([cl])	[Ctrl]
(Option) or (Opt)	[Alt]

CD/WEB RESOURCES

As the book proceeds from fundamentals of page layout and site management to more highly skilled techniques, the CD-ROM provides visual examples to accompany the text. Thus readers can witness the building of a GoLive Web site from the ground up, with our sample site expanding and growing in complexity as it demonstrates more advanced aspects of the program. Examples on the CD-ROM include

- **Web Site Basics (companion to Chapters 3 and 4)**—This section demonstrates planning and diagramming techniques for a typical Web site. Here we introduce a site proposal for a fictional company, Rooftop Records, and show diagramming options.

- **Standard Page Layout (companion to Chapters 8–13)**—Here we display a simple Web page for our sample site, Rooftop Records, which features formatted text and graphics, navigational links, anchors, head tags and scripts, date and time, and other basic page elements.

- **Working with Frames (companion to Chapter 14)**—Here we show a variation of the Rooftop Records Web page that was created using frames.

- **Working with Tables (companion to Chapter 15)**—Tables prove to be quite effective for displaying featured artist names, albums, and song titles on our Rooftop Records site, as we show with this additional page.

- **Creating Forms (companion to Chapter 16)**—View a completed online form that enables users to contact Rooftop Records and request additional information about a particular artist.

- **Styles and Stationery (companion to Chapter 17)**—Several additional pages are added to the Rooftop Records site using Cascading Style Sheets, Stationery, and Reusable Components. Our examples not only demonstrate GoLive's ease of use and timesaving techniques, but also show how the pages maintain a consistent appearance throughout the entire site.

- **Movement, Multimedia and Interactivity (companion to Chapters 18–20)**—Readers can see first-hand how these advanced elements truly bring our Web site to life. Images from the original pages are improved using image maps, creating new navigation and display options for our sample site. The appearance of our basic navigation is improved again through the use of JavaScript rollovers. We also show how a simple Java Applet can spice up a page. Additional pages include the use of Layers, Floating Boxes and Actions, animated gifs, audio and video clips, and QuickTime movies, all within a real-world example. Rooftop Records now has a much more interactive and exciting environment that shows off the artists to the best of their abilities.

- **Integrating with Other Programs (companion to Chapters 21–26)**—This section demonstrates how graphics may be exchanged and manipulated using other software in conjunction with GoLive. Readers can see several versions of our sample site here, and how each of the new graphics would appear in a browser.

- **Integrating with Lasso Studio (companion to Chapter 24)**—Since Lasso enables users to perform such a wide variety of functions, we cannot possibly demonstrate them all here. We will attempt to show how our sample site could be enhanced with some of Lasso's features, namely by creating an eCommerce site for selling records and showing readers their options in this area.

- **Using Dynamic Link (companion to Chapters 27–31)**—Our Rooftop Records site is expanded with the addition of a database, which turns our basic table of artists and albums into a dynamic inventory and sales tool. This in turn drives our new eCommerce Site, which enables our sample company to sell its records online.

OVERVIEW OF ADOBE GOLIVE

IN THIS PART

1   Introducing GoLive 6.0   11

2   GoLive Essentials   23

INTRODUCING GOLIVE 6.0

IN THIS CHAPTER

Welcome   12

Code   12

Productivity   14

Integration   17

Site Management   18

Dynamic Development   20

Standard and Emerging Web Technologies   20

Extensibility   20

Troubleshooting   21

Going Live   21

1

WELCOME

Welcome to Adobe GoLive, an incredible program offering robust features for designing, building, and managing your Web sites from start to finish. Whether you're a print designer making the jump into Web development, a sophisticated hand-coder looking for a package that streamlines your development process, or simply curious about what GoLive has to offer, we're confident you'll walk away with knowledge of the features and capabilities that set GoLive apart from its competitors.

As you already know, Adobe GoLive is a leading software package designed to cut down on your production time, manage your site assets, and enhance your ability to provide a personalized and professional Web site to your target audience. But as you proceed, you'll find that GoLive 6.0 in particular offers enhancements that build upon the successes of GoLive 5.0, ensuring your success as an efficient and effective Web developer.

CODE

First and foremost, GoLive 6.0 enhances the streamlined code integration already available in GoLive 5.0. Avid HTML coders can still rely on the source editor to make simple modifications or to build an entire page from scratch. In addition, the source can be viewed according to your individual preference: in the Layout Editor, Source Editor, and the Outline Editor.

- Layout Editor (see Figure 1.1): Shows an approximation of what the page looks like in a browser. This feature is an approximation simply because different browsers interpret and render the same code slightly differently.

Figure 1.1
GoLive's Layout View shows an approximation of how the page might appear in a browser.

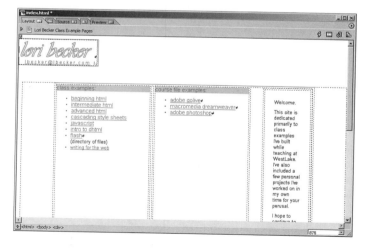

- Source Editor (see Figure 1.2): Provides direct access to all the code in the page. Any changes you make in the code will automatically transfer over to the Layout View.

- Outline Editor (see Figure 1.3): Provides a hierarchical view of the code. You can navigate through the structure and even make changes to the code within this hierarchy. Especially useful for novice coders, the hierarchy provides a means to dig through the code for the pieces you want to change without running the risk of making accidental changes elsewhere in the code.

Figure 1.2

GoLive's Source Editor lets you delve into the code at your own free will.

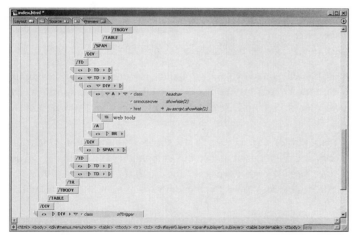

Figure 1.3

GoLive's Outline Editor features a hierarchical representation of the page's code.

The coding features, however, do not stop there. New in GoLive 6.0 is the Split View feature (see Figure 1.4), in which code can simultaneously be examined as you view the page's development in the Layout Editor.

As recently as a year or two ago, standard HTML was the only language most page designers needed to be concerned with. Web browsers have historically allowed a certain amount of leeway to your code, permitting some sloppiness in your code, but still rendering it correctly. But this is decreasingly true. As pages are continually deployed in more languages specific to a particular purpose (WML for Wireless devices, XHMTL for future browsers, SMIL for media purposes, and so on), developing compliant, well-formed, and valid code will be crucial to ensuring that all of your users can access the information available within your site. GoLive 6.0's Syntax Checker can automatically validate your page's code against a DTD (Document Type Definition) declared within the page, and can lead you to any discrepancies via the Outline Editor and new Highlights palette. GoLive holds internal requirements for each of the standard DTDs, and can then verify that your page's code is compliant with the specifications set by that DTD. For example, GoLive's Syntax Checker can verify that the code in a particular page is WML valid, well-formed, and therefore accessible via a wireless device.

Figure 1.4
GoLive's Layout View now incorporates a split view. As you modify the page, you can watch the code develop. Likewise, if you change the code by hand, the Layout View automatically updates.

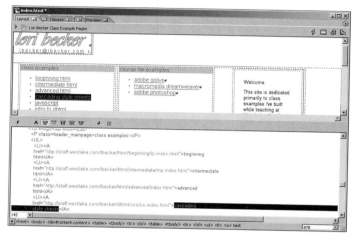

Other additional coding features include GoLive's JavaScript shell, in which developers can hand-code and test out custom JavaScripts without leaving the GoLive interface. More specifically, the JavaScript shell provides a means for writing sophisticated JavaScripts without leaving the Layout View.

Furthermore, GoLive 6.0 offers support for XML editing. XML, the next evolution of HTML, allows each developer to write their own language based on a set of tags that describe the data nested inside. Many XML languages have already been developed, including the SVG (Scalar Vector Graphic) language. GoLive offers support for viewing and coding Scalar Vector Graphics within GoLive.

As you can see, GoLive has become much more than a simple graphical user interface (GUI) for writing Web pages. In addition to providing the ability to generate the code for you, GoLive offers a number of features that let you dig directly into the source code. Whether a novice HTML coder or a sophisticated XML developer, GoLive offers the code-editing capabilities that will prove useful to your efforts.

> GoLive automatically creates a DTD when you create a new XHTML file, new SMIL file, new WML file, and so on, all available from selecting File, New Special, ... from the command menu. When you simply create a new HTML page, no DTD is declared.

PRODUCTIVITY

But let's be honest. As fantastic as the integrated coding features are, you're just as interested in GoLive for its coding abilities—the coding that GoLive can create for you. GoLive 6.0 offers more extensive coding capa-bilities and writes far cleaner code than its predecessor. Whether inserting a rollover onto the page, using a table for page layout, or building a site based on dynamically generated content, GoLive 6.0 offers greater and superior GUI options than the previous versions.

To begin, GoLive 6.0 includes multiple wizards for quickly and easily starting Web pages and Web sites with the click of a few buttons and by answering a few questions. Each step is detailed, pro-viding beginners a handy way to jump into a site's development without first suffering a steep learning curve. These wizards walk you through the process of setting up a single-developer site, or a site that will be worked on by a team and managed through a Web server. In either case, the wiz-ards cut down on the administration and logistical issues that must be taken care of before begin-ning or working on a site.

In addition, you'll find that Adobe has increased the number of options available through contextual menus. Contextual menus are those that appear when you right-click (Windows) or CTRL-click (Mac) an object within the page. An example of a contextual menu is shown in Figure 1.5. Depending on the object, the contextual menu will give you any number of options specific to that object. To make the development process easier for you, Adobe has increased the number of features available via such contextual menus in its latest version.

Figure 1.5
Adobe GoLive's contextual menus provide more thorough options than previous versions of the software.

The GUI builds upon that of GoLive 5.0, but offers greater flexibility and customization. Interface lay-outs can be customized and saved so that when you return to your computer, all of the palettes are available in the locations you prefer. The addition of palette stashing (see Figure 1.6) provides a means for organizing the palettes along the edge of your window, storing them so they're easily accessible without sacrificing too much of your screen real estate. Even dual-monitor configurations are supported by GoLive 6.0.

Furthermore, GoLive's SDK (Software Development Kit) means that sophisticated developers can actually code and add in their own windows and palettes using JavaScript and CSS.

Other enhanced features increase GoLive's flexibility and power as well. If you're familiar with GoLive 5.0, you've most likely already fallen in love with GoLive's Layout Grid, the robust feature that allows you to design your pages without having to deal with the technicalities of visualizing that complicated HTML table. In GoLive 5.0, even tables could be (after the fact) converted into the

Layout Grid. GoLive 6.0 takes this feature further: Not only can tables be converted to Layout Grids, Layout Grids can be converted back into tables. In addition, this inter-feature capability has been enhanced so that nested table designs convert to a single Layout Grid for ease of managing and updating. Last but not least, you have the option to build cleaner, more browser-compliant code by replacing the proprietary spacer files supported by Netscape Navigator for the purpose of holding table cells with transparent gif files, supported by all major browsers.

Figure 1.6

New to GoLive 6.0, the option to stash your palettes along the edge of the window ensures that you can maximize your screen real estate for the purpose at hand.

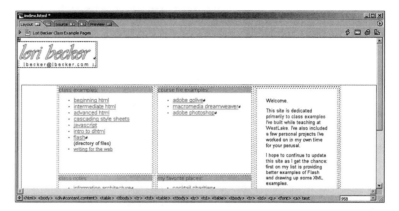

As if that weren't enough, GoLive's Hints palette provides clues to buttons, icons, and tabs available throughout the program. Simply hover your mouse over an item in question with the Hints palette open, and the Hints panel will dynamically update with information about that particular feature, thereby lessening the time you'll have to devote to learning the ins and outs of the program. Figure 1.7 shows how the Hints palette helps you figure out what a particular tool is meant to do without fishing through the help files. In this case, the Hints Palette is displaying the definition and purpose of the Show in Browser icon on the Toolbar.

Figure 1.7

GoLive's Hints palette dynamically updates based on what you've hovered the mouse over on the page.

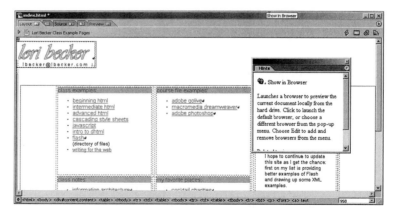

A handy new feature is GoLive 6.0's Accessibility Reporter, included as part of the program's Site Reports. Based on the government's 508 Accessibility requirements, the Reporter can provide handy information about which pages are 508 compliant and which pages are not. More important than just complying with government standards is the idea of ensuring that all users have user-friendly access to the site's information, making the Accessibility Reporter a great added feature to Adobe's Web editor.

GoLive 6.0 also includes an increased number of pre-written JavaScripts, HTML Styles that allow you to create and store standard styles to use across pages in a site, and many other smaller, but no less powerful, options integrated into GoLive's 6.0's GUI.

INTEGRATION

One of Adobe's greatest strengths stems from its long-term commitment to building award-winning solutions for publishing enterprise solutions. From its start as the leader in print production to its evolution into the realm of the Web, Adobe's products have captured designers and continuously innovated over time to stay abreast of its competitors. With this commitment comes Adobe's powerful integration from program to program. Whether you're building a file in InDesign and exporting it as XML; creating images in Photoshop, ImageReady, or Illustrator; or animating movies using Adobe LiveMotion; Adobe GoLive integrates remarkably well with each of these programs, offering the most streamlined and simple means for managing files from program to program.

For example, once in GoLive, Adobe's Smart Objects feature allows you to insert a non–Web-compliant format into the Layout View, and then to create a Web-compliant version from that format without leaving GoLive's interface. Essentially, this means you can optimize that file for Web display without ever exiting GoLive's interface, cutting down on the time you'll devote to the logistical process of juggling multiple programs. Furthermore, Adobe's programs maintain a virtual link from the virtual file to the Web version, meaning that any change made to the original version will automatically update the new format. No longer do you have to juggle multiple formats and concern yourself with which files need to be updated and changed—GoLive takes care of this for you.

In addition to offering integration with these programs once inside GoLive's interface, each of these programs offers remarkable integration features with Adobe GoLive. Create mockups in Photoshop and Illustrator, and export the HTML tables that reassemble smaller sliced image pieces into a cohesive page. Or, use Illustrator or LiveMotion to generate .swf animation movies. Perhaps while in ImageReady you want to create the image rollover effects that add a dynamic and interactive spark to your page. Just about any feature you implement in any Adobe program integrates with GoLive, enabling you to focus on the inspiration of Web development, not the logistics of file management.

Finally, the latest and greatest versions of each of these software programs support increased variable support, enabling even your graphics to be data-driven. Rather than modifying the original file, you simply modify the text variable in the image and the change will automatically cascade throughout GoLive. Variables that you can define include text, visibility, links, target, object color, style, or texture, and all can be changed without actually changing the original source file.

As you can see, GoLive's integration with other Adobe products puts it head and shoulders above the competition.

SITE MANAGEMENT

GoLive 6.0 also implements additional features with regard to site management and site creation. To begin, the process of blueprinting and implementing a site from its first concoction to its final implementation can all be achieved within GoLive's interface.

For example, begin by defining the site's structure and architecture: how the pages will relate one to the other with GoLive's View, as shown in Figure 1.8. Use the structure developed in Design View to collaborate with team members about the site's architecture or garner client's approval. In addition to displaying the structure of HTML pages, a standard in architecture mapping programs, GoLive 6.0 offers additional objects, including objects symbolizing technologies such as ASP, JSP, PHP, PDF, databases, SWF, DIR, SMIL, SVG, and so on.

Figure 1.8
Use Adobe GoLive's Design View to build a site map and define the site's architecture and organization.

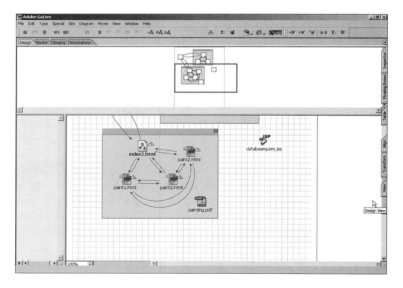

Furthermore, Design View supports the use of native artwork from other programs, so that you can customize the blueprint with your own look and feel, particularly useful when handing it off for client approval.

Even if you need to add a new section to an existing site, GoLive's Design View promotes a hierarchical structure that can be anchored to an existing section of the site, making sure that the pages' creation, development, and deployment can be accomplished in an organized, well-thought-out manner rather than in a haphazard way.

All of the site management features available in GoLive 5.0 still exist in GoLive 6.0. Move files; rename files; add in existing files; and manage external links, color sets, and fonts; all from within GoLive's versatile Site Window. As GoLive tracks the files in any given site, changes made to a

New to GoLive 6.0 is the inclusion of icons specific to a certain file type. For example, in this demo, notice the visual indicators for a .pdf file and .jsp file.

page's name or location automatically update all instances of a link to that file, so you need not worry about returning to the other pages and making changes. In addition, if for some reason you want the versatility of moving or renaming a file without the pages changing the links to that page, GoLive offers that capability as well.

Although Adobe GoLive has always proved a powerful means for creating and managing Web sites, never before has the power extended to a collaborative environment. Adobe GoLive 6.0 supports Adobe's Web Workgroup Server, which serves as a central repository for storing a team's site files, notes, maintenance updates, and archived versions. Included in the Adobe Workgroup Server is a Web-based Server Administration tool, shown in Figure 1.9. Using this administration tool, you can create new sites, add users to a particular site, control users' access to the works-in-progress, and monitor which users currently are working with specific files. In addition, the administrator can recover files and formulate the publishing process.

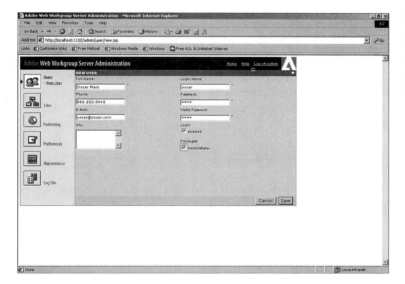

Figure 1.9

Using a browser-based administration tool, you can control users' access to files, set up and administer sites, monitor log files, and so on.

The Adobe Workgroup Server provides a means for users to check out and check in files from a central location, making sure a streamlined source of communication for the workflow of files exists. All users share the view of the same Site Window, customized to show which files have been checked out and which files coworkers have pulled from the ranks. Meanwhile, any user is allowed to download a local version of a file so that all may view and plan for the necessary changes. However, because only the individual who checked out the file may check that file back in, you need not worry about one individual accidentally overriding someone else's changes. Furthermore, in the event that an accidental revision is implemented, the Workgroup Server stores previous, archived versions of the site's files. Simply restore the pre-existing file from which you would like to work, and begin. Meanwhile, a site's administrator can control how many iterations of the files are saved and given what parameters, allowing you to control the server's resources and therefore its efficiency. No doubt, this streamlined collaboration increases your team's speed of production, and avoids the painstaking mistakes that push a project past deadline and budget.

DYNAMIC DEVELOPMENT

Completely new to GoLive 6.0 is the addition of building dynamic content with GoLive's GUI. Gone are the days where static, generic content will capture your end user's attention. Instead, using customized information dynamically driven by that user's preferences and interests ensures a better user experience and a more loyal customer. GoLive 6.0 offers dynamic content driven by ASP, PHP, or JSP. Instead of learning the language to build your e-commerce site, you can rely on GoLive 6.0 to do the work for you, writing the code that pulls information from a database, XML document, or e-commerce server. In addition, GoLive can write code that updates the source data, and allows you to publish the site either as a set of dynamic pages (for sites that change frequently) or as a set of static pages (for sites that need updating every so often, but not by the hour).

In addition, for those developers without access to an application server (a server that can fetch and deliver dynamically-driven content), GoLive's installer includes an integrated application server complete with PHP and JSP modules for quick, simple setup and access.

In addition to behind-the-scenes programming, Adobe has worked out a partnership providing you a huge head start in developing e-commerce applications via GoLive's Custom Merchant. By integrating the software of Adobe's partners into the GoLive program, you can quickly set up an e-commerce site without having to fight through the intricacies of that particular vendor's programming code. In essence, you can set up a merchant account with half of the work usually required already complete for you.

STANDARD AND EMERGING WEB TECHNOLOGIES

Finally, the latest edition of GoLive illustrates Adobe's commitment to supporting and promoting emerging Web-based technologies. Whether authoring the W3C's Synchronized Multimedia Integration Language (SMIL) for the production of interactive audiovisual presentations, Wireless Markup Language (WML) for the display of content on handheld PDAs and cellular phones, or eXtensible Markup Language (XML) for the purpose of creating data-driven documents in multiple formats, GoLive continues and will continue to support and integrate the array of emerging technologies into its GUI.

Adobe GoLive 6.0 supports authoring of WML, either visually via new Objects in the Objects palette or by hand; XHTML Basic with an integrated simulator of how the page will look on supporting handhelds (Windows only); SMIL, including a preview module that allows for visual layout and time-line controls; and XML authoring support, to include support for emerging XML languages such as SVG (Scalar Vector Graphics).

EXTENSIBILITY

Perhaps the most powerful component of GoLive is its flexibility. Perhaps your team has a task it must carry out repeatedly: A number of options for completing specific tasks exist, including the use of code snippets, components, stationeries, and templates. In addition, in the event that one of the pre-built shortcuts does not fit the bill for your particular task, GoLive's SDK (Software Development Kit) supports JavaScript-based exchange actions and extensions. No need to worry if you are not a sophisticated JavaScript editor yourself: Many actions and extensions made by others in the GoLive community are available to you at www.AdobeXchange.com. You'll find it very useful to explore what others have already created and made available to you before plunging into your own code. If you're still in need of a starting ground for writing your own JavaScripts (perhaps for the purpose of writing a custom extension), check out Chapter 19 for a brief introduction to the client-side scripting technology.

As demonstrated, Adobe GoLive 6.0, in addition to offering many of the incredible and powerful features previously brought forward in its preceding versions, offers incredibly powerful streamlining processes.

TROUBLESHOOTING

Like all software applications, you will run into quirks and potential bugs along the way. While we have done our best to point out the bugs we encountered in version 6.0 throughout this book, you'll also find it helpful to pay attention to Adobe's Web site for additional information and bug fixes. Keep in mind that Adobe has provided a lengthy manual and online help, which, when thoroughly searched, will usually provide the answers you need.

As an added round of ammunition, consider joining a mailing list or participating in an online forum about Adobe GoLive and Web design. Particularly if you're new to Web development, you'll find that the available resources of others with more experience in the technology can be an invaluable (sometimes even a client-saving!) resource.

Best of luck.

GOING LIVE

Throughout this book, you'll find sections like this at the end of each chapter where we humbly endeavor to provide some real-world advice for using the features just discussed. If you're having trouble, at least one of the authors has probably been in your shoes before, and we make a point any time we encounter a pitfall into which you may have tumbled.

Perhaps the best "real-world advice" to heap upon you at this stage is to reiterate the suggestions from the Troubleshooting section. No GoLive user is alone, and if you're having difficulty figuring out how to make something work, start by knowing that there is a way and somebody else has probably already figured it out. If you can't find any helpful reference in Adobe's online help, the documentation, or this book, you almost certainly will in an Internet mailing list or forum. A good place to start is Adobe's own Community section at http://www.adobe.com/support/forums/main.html. Or just go to your favorite Web search engine and look for "golive help", "golive discussions", "golive mailing list", or some such resource. I promise you will find all the help you can use.

So without further ado, let us dive headlong into the pool of Adobe GoLive 6.

GOLIVE ESSENTIALS

IN THIS CHAPTER

Getting Your Bearings   24

Getting Started   25

The Site Window   26

The Page Window   26

The Inspector   27

The Palettes   28

Troubleshooting   34

Going Live   34

GETTING YOUR BEARINGS

All right. You're convinced that Adobe GoLive is the extraordinary wonder-tool you always believed it to be—exactly the application a person like you needs to help you build and maintain your extraordinary Web sites. You're ready to break new ground. Well, in this book, we'll demonstrate how to construct an entire sample site, from blueprints to rooftop, using all the powerful features in the GoLive repertoire. But before we begin, let's take a moment to review the essentials.

Based on the sheer complexity of the program, Adobe GoLive can often prove a little daunting at first glance. At any given time, there are multiple aspects all working together to produce the final product, and while this wide variety of options grants you immense power and flexibility, it may also appear somewhat overwhelming until you've mastered all the gears and gadgets. Thankfully, the traditional Adobe graphic interface is highly intuitive and intelligently organized, with plenty of icons and helpful indicators to assist you in this learning process.

If you already feel confident in your overall knowledge of GoLive's assorted elements and features, or if you would prefer to concentrate on a particular area of the program, you may opt to proceed directly to one of the following chapters.

To see the sites, try

- Chapter 3, "Introduction to Sites": This chapter covers the principles of Web site diagramming and management. This chapter could be of particular interest to those planning new sites or overseeing a total project or existing site.

- Chapter 4, "Working with Sites": This dives into the details of GoLive's Site Management tools. It covers creating a new site, working with site windows, using the various site views, using panes, designing sites, site reporting, using site templates, planning your page hierarchy, and following file naming conventions.

To explore the Work Area, try these:

- Chapter 5, "GoLive Interface Elements": Here's where you'll find more information about the Page Window, the Inspector, and all the various palettes used in creating pages.

- Chapter 6, "Setting Preferences": This chapter describes various options for customizing your GoLive experience via Preferences...so you can have it your way.

- Chapter 7, "Customizing GoLive": This chapter covers options for customizing your Desktop and setting up your own keyboard shortcuts, among other things.

To proceed directly to page making, check these out:

- Chapter 8, "Creating and Saving Pages": This shows you how to lay out Web pages from a graphic perspective. It covers window sizes and page margins, the grid, layout rulers, color selection, background images, the history palette, and options for how you want to view your pages.

- Chapter 9, "Working with Code": For those of you who prefer to go behind the scenes, this chapter is for you. It concentrates on GoLive's many options for viewing your source code. It covers using the source code palette and source window, using the markup tree palette, working with 360 code, re-writing source code, searching and replacing HTML elements, adding unknown elements, adding head tags and scripts, using text macros, saving code fragments, and generating XHTML code.

For the rest of you, who'd welcome a refresher course on the GoLive Essentials, look no further. You have arrived.

GETTING STARTED

Despite your enthusiasm for creating Web pages, the first step you need to take when using Adobe GoLive is figuratively a step backward. You need to see the big picture, view the site as a whole panorama, rather than as a series of smaller scenes. This vantage point ultimately leads to a better organized, more consistent, and more professional-looking Web site. Used in conjunction with other tools that GoLive offers, it makes your job a whole lot easier overall.

If you'd rather not be forced to choose an option each time you start GoLive, you can simply check the box that says Don't Show Again, or you can adjust your General Preferences to do the same. Then, to create a new site manually, you'll need to select New Site from the File menu or press (Option-Cmd-N) [Alt+Ctrl+N].

Proper planning is the key to any successful project, and with this in mind, GoLive starts you on the right track as soon as you open the program. Immediately a window pops up, requiring you to make a choice in your actions: Do you want to create a new page, create a new site, or open an existing file? (If you prefer, you can also choose to eliminate the opening dialog box.)

If you turned off this auto-prompt option seen in Figure 2.1 and wish to restore it, select Edit, Preferences and then choose Show Intro Screen from the At Launch pull-down menu in General Document Preferences. Your other options here are Do Nothing—which keeps the dialog box from appearing—or Create New Page, which is the most common option.

⇨ *To gain more power over your GoLive Preferences, see Chapter 6, "Setting Preferences."*

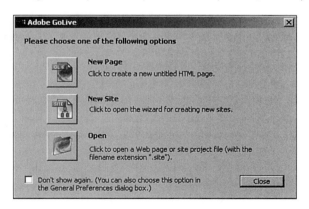

Figure 2.1

These are the options you're presented with on the Intro screen.

THE SITE WINDOW

Whenever you begin a new Web site, your first step in GoLive should be to create a new Site. This leads you through a simple wizard, and then creates a brand new project folder for you, with the name and the location you provide. From this moment forward, GoLive keeps track of every page you create, and stores them all in one convenient place, together with all the other elements you'll need to keep your pages connected and functioning happily as a unit.

Once you establish your site, the sky's the limit. You can diagram the site, create new pages or delete them, change page names or positions within the site, check your pages for broken links or errors, update pages en masse, share the site with others in a workgroup, upload and download the site to and from your server...you can easily and effectively fulfill every aspect of site architecture and management from within one application. It also helps to establish efficient work habits, builds organizational skills, and keeps your desktop tidy.

When you set up a new Site, the new file that's created on your hard drive—called the Site Document—can be viewed and controlled via the Site Window, as seen in Figure 2.2. You can easily identify the Site Document by its `.site` file extension. It is automatically set up to contain a new default page, called `Index.html`, plus the necessary folders for storing any extras and settings your pages may need. Any new pages you create for this site will also be stored in the Site Folder, and linked together relative to each other.

Figure 2.2
All your Site's elements reside within the Site Window.

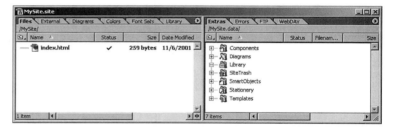

Chapters 3 and 4 discuss the specifics of Site Management, so we won't delve too deeply into that here. All you really need to know for now is that a home page has been established for you, and that all the pages of your site will be housed in the Site Folder from now on.

THE PAGE WINDOW

Now let's open up the home page and take a gander at your canvas for page creation. Double-click on the `Index.html` file within the Site Folder, or select it via File, Open from within GoLive as you would with any file. Up pops a blank page, ready for you to design as you choose.

The Layout mode displayed by default enables you to create a page graphically. If you prefer, you could select the Source tab near the top of the Window in order to type HTML code directly, or choose the Preview tab to see what your page will look like in a browser. You also have tabs that enable you to create or preview pages with frames, and an Outline Editor for better control over your source code. In addition, there's a toggle switch at the bottom left of the window that enables you to view the page graphics and source code simultaneously—the perfect situation for you whole-brain thinkers. If you simply want to add code to the header of your document, such as meta tags to be used by search engines, there's a toggle at the top left to open a window specifically geared toward editing information in the head section. (All these window options are discussed in more detail in the next few chapters.)

The rest of the icons at the top of the Page Window correspond to other palettes, windows, and tools used in conjunction with the Page Window. Examine Figure 2.3 to see what each icon opens.

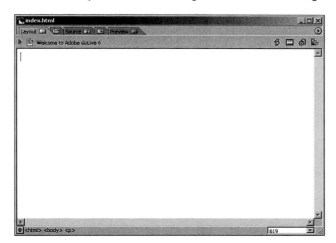

Figure 2.3
The Page Window is where each page and all its contents are presented and edited.

For additional information about the Page Window icons, **see** *Appendix B, "Palette Definitions."*

Generally, a good way to begin the page creation process is by double-clicking on the Page icon in the top left to display your Page Properties in the Inspector. Here you can change the title of your new page from *Welcome to Adobe GoLive 6* to something more appropriate to your particular site. This is also where you can set things like size, background, and colors, the basic parameters of your page.

The circled arrow at the top right of the Page Window leads to an assortment of pull-down menus that offer you a whole range of new alternatives, including one that controls what appears in the Status Bar below the page. Again, see Figure 2.3 or Appendix B for details.

THE INSPECTOR

Think of the Inspector as a spy, a super-sleuth who chooses to disguise herself according to what best suits the situation. This aspect of the Inspector—the fact that it's an adaptive palette—makes it the ultimate all-purpose desktop tool. Yet this convenient feature can also be confusing. Its appearance shifts with each object you click on or each new tool you try, offering entirely new options at every turn. Until you become accustomed to her dynamic nature, you may find yourself wondering what happened to the palette you just saw. Don't panic. Simply select the tool you wish to use or the object you'd like to adjust, and the Inspector will knowingly provide the appropriate options or prompt you for the necessary details.

2

Like a spy, the role of the Inspector, shown in Figure 2.4, is to obtain information: What's the title of your page? Where does that image file reside? To which file are you establishing a link? The Inspector asks all the right questions to help you control all the individual elements on your page. Once you fill in the blanks or provide the specifics it needs, it passes that information to other parts of the program and creates the source code necessary to make your Web page operate as instructed.

If something on your page isn't functioning as expected, you can also use the Inspector as your own private eye and investigate problems that stem from human error, such as typos or misnamed files. Since you need only glance at the blanks instead of searching through all your code, it can be a time-saving troubleshooter.

Figure 2.4

The Inspector is the palette of a thousand faces.

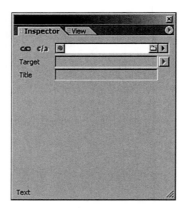

THE PALETTES

What Adobe GoLive terms *Palettes*, as the name colorfully suggests, are tools that display your options for creating on the Web canvas. Each palette covers a different aspect of the page designing process; therefore, some are absolutely essential to every page while others you may rarely find an occasion to use. It all depends on your own role in the project (whether you're the graphic designer or the programming guru) and the work style that suits you best.

As with other Adobe applications, you can customize your workspace by re-arranging the palettes and grouping them as you see fit. Simply click on the tab of any palette and drag it to the desired location. You can place a palette alone or drag it on top of another palette to combine them. In addition, the palette windows may be docked: Grab onto the palette edges and drag them nearer to each other, and they automatically align vertically or horizontally and click together to form a panel of palettes. Like any window, you can resize them by dragging the lower-right corner, or roll them up like a window shade by double-clicking on the top bar.

To access a palette that is not visible, select the name of the palette from the Window menu, or use the appropriate keyboard shortcut. Items in the Window menu are grouped according to which palettes are normally grouped together in a window (for example, Objects and Color share a window). If you select a palette whose window is already on your desktop, it will approach the forefront and the proper tab will be selected for you. This is particularly helpful when many overlapping palettes are being used and screen real estate is scarce.

To restore palettes to their original states, select Window, Workspace, Default Workspace. This replaces the Restore command used in previous versions.

The Objects Palette

Look around you, wherever you are. Whether you're in an office, at home, or someplace else, chances are good that you're surrounded by identifiable objects. Desks are cluttered with stuff, walls are decorated with objets d'art, and shelves are stocked with a whole assortment of things. Everything can be broken down into basic pieces, in what amounts to a childlike name game: Cat. Tree. House. Sand Castle. Hydroelectric Dam.

Similarly, your Web page is composed of objects, and this palette serves as a kind of toy box for them all. Want to insert a new image? Click on the Image icon and drag it to the proper location on the page. Need a text box? Just click and drag. Every element you use to construct your page is essentially an object, a piece that contributes to the whole. The concept seems simple enough, yet it's GoLive's display of intuitive icons and ease of use that make the Web game feel like child's play and set it head and shoulders above other programs of this type.

The Objects Palette keeps Web design on a purely graphic level, enabling visual thinkers to assemble all the desired elements in a language they already understand, without worrying about knowing code. Simply point the mouse at what you want to use, and pull it to your page. Once it's placed, the Objects Palette works in conjunction with the Inspector to help you set up the specifics about that object.

There are 12 different types of objects that you can control with the Objects Palette. Basic objects, as you can see in Figure 2.5, include icons for text boxes and images as well as more advanced elements like multimedia or JavaScript. In addition, there's a more detailed set of icons dedicated to using QuickTime. Smart Objects are those used in conjunction with other Adobe applications such as Photoshop or Illustrator. There are objects specific to creating Forms and Frames, placing code in the Head of your document or using WML elements, managing your site, adding site extras and site diagramming essentials, using dynamic content, and storing elements in your Library.

Figure 2.5
The Objects Palette provides icons for nearly all elements that you will ever drop into your pages.

The Color Palette

Just as the name implies, the Color Palette, shown in Figure 2.6, helps you add color to your pages. You can mix colors according to your own preferences using tools to select Grayscale, RGB, CMYK, HSB, or Web colors. It also provides several options for displaying Web-friendly colors, enabling you to select them based on sight, by color name, or by hexadecimal code. You can customize the Color

Palette by adding your own assortment of palette colors, or store colors specific to a particular Web site within the palette for convenient frequent use. Simply click on the icon of the color selection method you'd like to use, and its window becomes available.

Figure 2.6
The Color Palette allows you to select the color for any selected object.

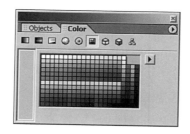

The History Palette

The History Palette, despite its glorious claims to mastery over time, more closely resembles a glorified Undo tool. As you can see in Figure 2.7, the History Palette operates much as it does in other Adobe applications, recording each action you take when constructing a page and enabling you to retrace your steps. Each action is named automatically so that you can follow along and see your work, or click on an action to proceed directly to a particular point in the creation process. In this way, it is a form of time travel. The page reverts back to the way it looked at that stage of the game, frozen in the evolutionary process like a fossilized Pterodactyl. This tool, which arrived in the previous version of GoLive, can be absolutely indispensable for correcting human error, comparing alternate versions of a page, appeasing an indecisive boss or client, or simply reviewing your work.

It's important that you realize the default number of actions recorded is 20—so if you're anticipating a lot of changes to the page, you may want to up this number. To do this, click on the small arrow in the upper-right corner of the palette and select History Options. This opens a dialog box that allows you to enter a number between 0 and 1600 to serve as your Maximum History States. Use the lowest number of states you feel comfortable with, as this feature eats up a huge amount of memory.

Figure 2.7
The History Palette shows all the recent actions, and lets you click on any one of them to restore your page to that previous condition.

The Table Palette

Tables have long been used to assist in the alignment of text and images on a Web page, or to present spreadsheet or numerical data in neat rows and columns. Nearly any object can be inserted into a table cell, including text, images, QuickTime movies, and even other tables. Used in conjunction with the Layout Grid, tables grant you a high level of control over the placement of objects on your page.

While you must first create a table using the Table icon in the Objects Palette (it's a Basic object), and you still control certain aspects of table construction via the Inspector, the Table Palette, shown in Figure 2.8, facilitates the arranging of data within your table, and helps you control the look and size of your table and its cells. The palette itself is broken down into two distinct parts: Select controls the cell content, while Style controls cosmetic changes.

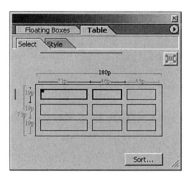

Figure 2.8
The Table Palette lets you manage the rows and columns of your tables.

Within Select mode, you can highlight individual cells, entire rows, or entire columns, and manipulate the data within them. The Sort feature enables you to perform multi-level sorts on data, in ascending or descending order, by row or by column.

The Styles mode makes it easy to change the color, cell size, and spacing of your tables. There are 10 built-in styles to choose from, ranging in mood from Just the Facts to Seventies, plus you can import and export styles or create your own new styles to suit any page you can dream up.

The Source Code Palette

True to its name, the Source Code Palette, shown in Figure 2.9, enables you, the user, to view the code behind your graphic document, to take it apart and see what makes it tick. Grouped conveniently with other code-driven palettes such as In & Out Links, Site Navigator, and JavaScript Shell, it enables programmers to tinker directly with the HTML and see instantly how code changes affect the appearance of the page.

Figure 2.9
The Source Code Palette provides a window dedicated to displaying your source code.

Identical in purpose to the Source View or even the new Source Split View built in to the Page Window, the Source Code Palette has the distinct advantage of remaining mobile, which may be the reason it's been retained despite its seeming redundancy. As a separate window, it can be positioned anywhere on the user's desktop, even arranged for viewing on a second monitor, a viable option which some Web professionals choose in order to expand their workspace. It also permits a designer or programmer to see the entire page layout while simultaneously viewing code, an option otherwise lost using only the Source Views within the Page Window.

Additional viewing options include Local Mode (which zeroes in on a particular line or section of code), Word Wrap (places soft returns at the ends of lines to keep lines of code in full view), Display Line Numbers, and Dim When Inactive. These can be checked or unchecked by clicking the arrow in the top-right corner of the palette and selecting each from the pull-down menu.

The Transform Palette

Adobe GoLive enables you to position objects precisely on your Web page and size them according to your own specifications using a variety of methods. You can resize and reposition objects by dragging. The toolbar enables you to resize, reposition, and group objects. The Transform Palette, seen in Figure 2.10, provides all of these options. In addition, it also enables you to change the stacking order of items that overlap, such as hot spots, an image map, or tracks in the QuickTime Movie Viewer. (You can't change the stacking order of floating boxes.)

Objects must first be placed on the layout grid before they can be repositioned or grouped. To reposition an object, enter new values for the x and y coordinates of the object's upper-left corner, and press Enter or Return after each. The object will automatically migrate to its new home. Resizing works much the same way: Simply insert values for the height and width of the object in pixels, or enter one of these and check the box to constrain the ratio. When you press Enter or Return, the object will transform itself to fit the new dimensions.

Grouping enables you to move several elements as a single unit, thereby maintaining the proper spacing established between them. To group elements, select one by clicking on it, and then Shift-click to select the others. In the Transform Palette, under Grouping, click the icon on the left to group, or click the icon on the right to ungroup. Similarly, to change the stacking order of overlapping objects, select an object then click the appropriate Bring to Front or Bring to Back icon under Z-Order. The objects should respond accordingly.

Figure 2.10
The Transform Palette makes it easy to reposition and resize elements.

The Align Palette

Using the Align Palette, it's easy to arrange objects precisely on a Web page. You can objects in relation to their parent, such as the document window or layout grid. To do so, first select the object or group of objects you wish to align. Then under Align to Parent, click a horizontal or vertical alignment button. The buttons in the Align Palette are identical to those on the toolbar, and enable you to align left, center, or right horizontally, and top, center, or bottom vertically.

You can also use the Align Palette, shown in Figure 2.11, to align and distribute objects in relation to each other.

Figure 2.11
The Align Palette provides tools for aligning objects on your page relative to one another.

First, select the objects by clicking on the first one and Shift-clicking on each additional object. Then, under Align Objects, click a horizontal alignment button (left, center, right) or a vertical alignment button (top, center, bottom) .

- Align Left aligns the objects along the left vertical axis of the object furthest left.
- Align Center aligns the objects along the vertical center axis between them.
- Align Right aligns the objects along the right vertical axis of the object furthest right.
- Align Top aligns the objects along the top horizontal axis of the highest object.
- Align Center aligns the objects along the horizontal center axis between them.
- Align Bottom aligns the objects along the bottom horizontal axis of the lowest object.

To distribute items in relation to each other using similar guidelines, first select the items to be distributed, and then under Distribute Objects, click a horizontal distribution button or a vertical distribution button. The affected items will become more evenly spaced.

Now that you have a clearer understanding of the GoLive essentials, you're ready to tackle the tools yourself. Proceed to the next chapter on working with sites, if you need to construct a Web site from the ground up. Go to Chapter 5, "GoLive Interface Elements," if you already have a site in place and would like to begin designing pages. Chapter 5 covers the work area in much greater detail and allows you to see our sample Web site as a work in progress, each step of the way.

TROUBLESHOOTING

Locating Missing Windows and Palettes

I can't find the window or palette you mention.

All the windows and palettes are available under the application's Window menu. Often, the palette you seek may be a different pane of one of the palettes already open. These can be accessed either by locating the open palette and clicking on a tab to activate your desired pane, or by going to the Window menu and selecting the palette you want.

Fixing the Appearance of Windows and Palettes

I found the window, but it looks different from the picture in the book.

Many of the windows and palettes change their contents contextually. Selecting an element in your Web page and viewing its properties in a palette may drastically change the appearance and options available in the palette. The appropriate and possible options are always made available, so have no fear.

GOING LIVE

You can control the location and size of all these palettes. After a time, you'll find that some of them are more useful to you than others, and this is often different from one developer to another.

You can drag their bottom-right corner a certain amount to resize some of the palettes, but they all have a minimum size that they won't shrink beyond. If your screen space is limited, sometimes you'll find that you absolutely have to stack one window on top of another. Some of the palettes will expand when a certain tab is selected, and then shrink back when another tab is clicked, so you can't always depend upon the neat tiling you may be able to achieve by dragging them into place. Be sure to take the time to find the arrangement that matches the way you work.

WEB SITE BASICS

IN THIS PART

3	Introduction to Sites	**37**
4	Working with Sites	**49**

3

INTRODUCTION TO SITES

IN THIS CHAPTER

Creating a New Site   38

Importing a Site   40

Site Templates   43

The Site Window   45

Troubleshooting   47

Going Live   48

CREATING A NEW SITE

The best way to create your new Site is to use the Site Wizard. Unless you've disabled it with the Don't Show Again check box, GoLive presents you with the option to start a new Site when you launch the program.

If that option box doesn't appear, or if you want to manually launch the Site Wizard at any other time, simply go to the File menu and select New Site. Right away, you're into the Site Wizard, and are about to dip your first toe into the pool of GoLive site development.

The Site Wizard

The Site Wizard, shown in Figure 3.1, offers a variety of options to accommodate Workgroups and more advanced users as well, making it a useful tool for any level of expertise. Let's walk through the process step by step so that you can see for yourself how easily it sets up any site. We'll opt to take the Single User route since Workgroups will be covered in greater detail later in the book.

Figure 3.1
The Site Wizard first presents you with the option to create a Single User or Workgroup site.

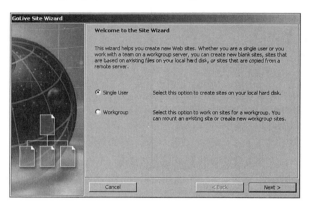

For more on Workgroups, **see** Chapter 26, "The Workgroup Server."

As the Site Wizard opens, select Single User and click Next. Your options when creating a New Site, shown in Figure 3.2, include beginning completely from scratch with a new Blank Site, Importing a Site either locally from your hard drive or remotely from a server, or choosing a Site Template from the Templates Folder with GoLive. We'll explore each of these options separately.

Creating a Blank Site

Creating a blank site means that you're creating a brand new root directory for your site. Whenever you create a site, GoLive assembles a complete package with all the things you'll need for that site. The site folder automatically contains a generic home page called Index.html. The data folder contains empty subfolders for future elements of your site. The settings folder will hold specifications for your site. And the site document itself—identified by the site extension—opens to reveal the hierarchy of your site within a Site Window.

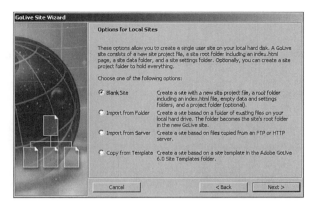

Figure 3.2
This next screen of the Site Wizard lets you choose the origin of your site's material: whether it's a new original site, or is being imported from an existing source.

➡️ *For more detailed information about the Site Window, see "The Site Window" in Chapter 3, "Introduction to Sites."*

To create a new blank Site, complete the following steps:

Choose Blank Site from within the Site Wizard.

1. To access the Site Wizard, select File, New Site from the menu, or press (Opt-Cmd-N) [Alt+Ctrl+N] on your keyboard. Establish yourself as either a Single or Workgroup User and choose Blank Site. Click Next or simply hit Enter/Return on your keyboard to proceed to the next step.

2. Name your Site. Type your site name into the space provided.

   For our example, we'll be creating a Site for Rooftop Records, a fictional record shop; therefore our site will be called Rooftop, as in Figure 3.3. (For more information on file naming conventions and restrictions, see "File Naming," later in this chapter.)

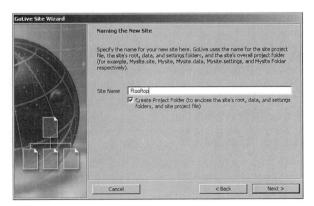

Figure 3.3
On this screen, you can give your new Site whatever name you choose. This name will not appear in the finished Web site; it's only a reference for how your GoLive files are named.

Optionally, you may choose to create a single project folder here that contains all your site-related files, and will be named accordingly. For instance, if you name the site Mysite, the umbrella folder will be called Mysite Folder. Check the Create Project Folder box on this screen if you'd like to take advantage of this option.

3. Choose a location to store your site. Click Browse, navigate within your system until you reach the appropriate folder, and select it, as shown in Figure 3.4.

4. Click Finish. As you can see in Figure 3.5, your new site opens automatically in a Site Window.

Figure 3.4
Use this screen to tell GoLive where to put your files. If you're testing the Site from a local server, it's best to store the files inside the server folder so you can test them directly.

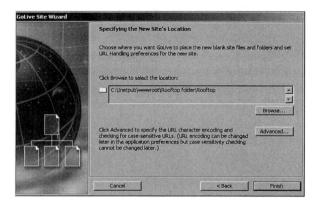

Figure 3.5
The finished Site Window shows all the components and folders that GoLive has created for your site.

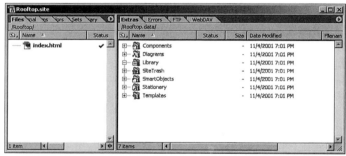

IMPORTING A SITE

You may choose to create a site by importing an existing one. The site can be located either locally or in a folder on a remote FTP or HTTP server. Either way, the process of importing will create a new Site Document and new site-related folders.

For a local import, the root folder of the imported Site becomes the root folder of the new Site. From a remote server, the root folder of the remote Site is downloaded to become the root folder of the new Site. For both options, page links remain the same, and the Site's navigational hierarchy is built from these.

When you import from a remote server, the imported files may be copied to a project folder for the site. However, if you wish a locally imported site to have a project folder, you'll need to create that folder arrangement before you import the site. To do so, create a new folder and name it according to the naming convention for your site. That is, if you plan to name the new site Mysite, name the folder Mysite Folder. Next, copy the folder you plan to import to the umbrella folder. This means you will actually import the copy. Finally, rename the copied folder, if necessary, giving it the name of the new site you are creating.

To import a site from a local folder, complete the following steps:

1. Choose Import From Folder from within the Site Wizard. This is another of the options on the first screen of the Site Wizard.

   To access the Site Wizard, select File, New Site from the menu, or press (Opt-Cmd-N) [Alt+Ctrl+N] on your keyboard. Establish yourself as either a Single or Workgroup User and choose Import From Folder. Click Next or simply hit Enter/Return on your keyboard to proceed to the next step.

2. Select the site to import.

   Click the upper Browse button, seen in Figure 3.6, and navigate to the root folder of the desired site (not the project folder, if you have created one).

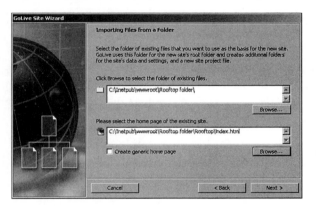

Figure 3.6
Use this screen to select the existing site files on your computer or network, and also to specify which is the home page. This allows GoLive to build the site hierarchy.

3. Select a home page.

   Either click the lower Browse button and navigate to the established home page of the site you're importing, or check the box below to create a new generic home page. If you select the first option, the Wizard will alert you with an error if you select a home page that is outside the selected root folder.

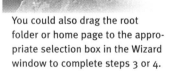

You could also drag the root folder or home page to the appropriate selection box in the Wizard window to complete steps 3 or 4.

4. Click Next or hit Enter/Return on your keyboard to proceed to the next step.

5. Choose a location to store your site. Click Browse, as shown in Figure 3.7, navigate within your system until you reach the appropriate folder, and select it.

   You also have an alternate option. You can click the Advanced button to set up URL Character Encoding and Case Sensitivity Checking.

6. Click Finish. Your new site opens automatically in a Site Window.

   If the Site contains any orphans, broken links, or missing items, error indicators appear in the window to alert you of these problems.

Figure 3.7

This screen lets you specify where GoLive should place the new Site containing the imported material. If you want, it is permissible to use the exact same location as the existing material.

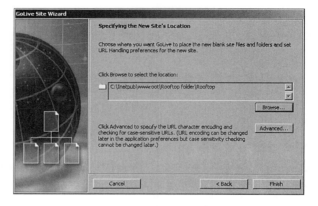

To import a site from a remote server, complete the following steps:

1. Choose Import From Server from within the Site Wizard.

   To access the Site Wizard, select File, New Site from the menu, or press (Opt-Cmd-N) [Alt+Ctrl+N] on your keyboard. Establish yourself as either a Single or Workgroup User and choose Import From Server. Click Next or simply hit Enter/Return on your keyboard to proceed to the next step.

2. Select which type of server you'll be accessing. Click Next or simply hit Enter/Return on your keyboard to proceed to the next step.

3. Enter the appropriate access information.

   For FTP, as shown in Figure 3.8, you'll need to provide valid account information, such as the server address, directory, and your username and password for login.

Figure 3.8

Use this screen to enter the location and password, if any, to access your existing site via FTP.

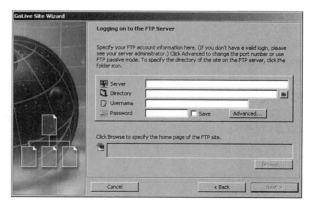

For HTTP, you'll need a valid home page URL. Type this information into the spaces provided in the next screen of the wizard, seen in Figure 3.9.

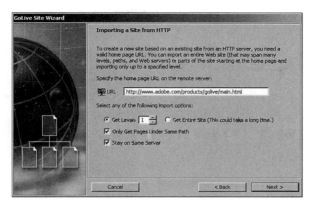

Figure 3.9
Use this screen to enter the location and password, if any, to access your existing site via HTTP.

4. Click Browse to initiate the server connection for either type of server.

   Navigate to the home page of the site and click OK to select it. Click Import.

5. Name your site. Type your site name into the space provided.

   The site will share the same name as the folder that contains it. For our example, we'll be creating a site for Rooftop Records, a fictional record shop; therefore our site will be called Rooftop.

   ⇨ *For more information on file naming conventions and restrictions,* **see** *"File Naming" in Chapter 3.*

6. Choose a location to store your site. Click Browse, navigate within your system until you reach the appropriate folder, and select it.

   This will be the umbrella folder if you have created one. You may also choose to create a new folder to contain the new site. For our example, we've chosen to save our imported Rooftop site in a newly created Rooftop folder on the desktop.

7. Click Finish. Your new site opens automatically in a Site Window.

   If the site contains any orphans, broken links, or missing items, error indicators appear in the window to alert you of these problems.

SITE TEMPLATES

Using a Site Template is one convenient way to streamline the site creation process. When you create a site by copying a Site Template, you simply copy its root folder and all Site-related folders. Each of the Site Templates within GoLive has a home page and a few pages linked to it in a simple navigational hierarchy. The pages have navigation bars for easy movement, and these bars are components for easy updating. The templates use different cascading style sheets and differ in their page layouts. Their pages make use of various features, such as floating boxes, layout grids, tables, anchors, and images. This means you save time in the design process but still end up with a professional-looking Web site.

Once the template is copied, you can replace the images and text with images and text of your own. Images such as buttons that you may want to customize are Photoshop smart objects, which makes them easy to work with. In addition, each of the template pages is based on a stationery page. This means if you use these stationery pages for layout changes, you can use your changes on any new pages you create.

Keep this tip in mind: Customize a Site Template to serve as the starting point for a Template of your own. This is particularly convenient for Web sites being developed by teams. When you design a template for the Site, each team member can start with the same basic layout and navigation. This helps save time and maintain consistency throughout the project.

To create a new Site using a Site Template, complete the following steps:

1. Choose Copy From Template from within the Site Wizard.

   To access the Site Wizard, select File, New Site from the menu above, or press (Opt-Cmd-N) [Alt+Ctrl+N] on your keyboard. Establish yourself as either a Single or Workgroup User and choose Copy From Template. Click Next or simply hit Enter/Return on your keyboard to proceed to the next step.

2. Select a Site Template from the list, as shown in Figure 3.10.

   Examine the layout and structure thumbnails provided with each template to help you determine which one you would prefer to use.

Figure 3.10
If you elect to create a new Site using one of GoLive's templates, use this screen of the Site Wizard to choose the template and a name for your new Site.

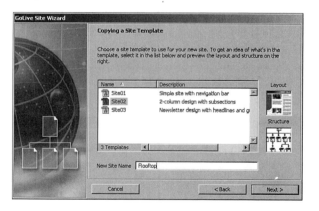

3. Name your Site. Type your Site name into the space provided.

   The Site will share the same name as the folder that contains it. For our example, we'll be creating a Site for Rooftop Records, a fictional record shop; therefore our Site will be called Rooftop. (For more information on file naming conventions and restrictions, see "File Naming," later in this chapter.)

⇨ *File naming conventions and restrictions are covered in greater detail later in this chapter.* **See** *"File Naming," in Chapter 3.*

4. Choose a location to store your site. Click Browse, navigate within your system until you reach the appropriate folder, and select it.

   The Site Template that will be copied already has a project folder; you don't need to create it, but you still retain the option to create new folders.

5. Click Finish. Your new site opens automatically in a Site Window.

THE SITE WINDOW

Now that you've created a Site, GoLive keeps track of every page you create, and stores them all in one convenient place, together with all the other elements you'll need to keep your pages connected and functioning happily as a unit.

Now you've got a world of options. Figure 3.11 shows the Site Window with all its components and folders that the Site Wizard automatically generates.

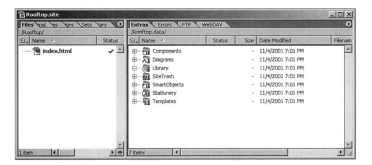

Figure 3.11
When you finish the Site Wizard, you're presented with the Site Windows containing all the folders and documents in your site.

Anatomy of a Site Window

The very first time you open a site document (the site file), you can view its contents in the tabs of the Primary Site Window. This window has a total of ten tabs, split into two panes, with six tabs in the left pane and four tabs in the right. Each of these tabs also corresponds to an option in the Pane Menu, a pull-down menu accessed by clicking on the small arrow in the top right corner of the Site Window.

To display tabs in a Secondary Site Window, select the Navigation View or Links View command from the Pane Menu. Alternately, choose Site, View, Navigation or Site, View, Links from the Site Menu. These commands, in effect, form the eleventh and twelfth Site Window tabs.

For the most part, the Site Window tabs behave like palettes. You can click and drag any tab just as you would a palette, to mix and match them in new windows, alone or in groups, in whatever arrangement works best for you. Your customized desktop of tabs and site windows will return the next time you open its Site Document. You can have more than one Site Document open at the same time, but dragging tabs from one site into the Site Window of another site is forbidden.

The Files Tab

The Files tab lists the page and media files in the Site Folder. If a page contains anchors, they're listed here under the page. If your site groups its pages and media in folders, the Files tab retains that folder structure.

The Files tab operates exactly like a regular folder would elsewhere on your computer. You can open, close, or delete files, drag files to other folders, copy to the clipboard, even spell check any HTML files you may have open. For each file, the tab lists particulars such as name, size, and date modified by column, just as you might see in a normal list view.

In addition, there are symbols specific to GoLive that indicate more details about the status of a file. These are located within the Errors tab.

- In the Status column, a check mark symbolizes that the file is free of errors, and that all files referenced in it have been found.
- In the Filename Status column, an "error" symbol indicates that the name of the file violates some filename constraint.
- In the Locked column, a padlock indicates a locked file in Mac OS or a read-only file in Windows.
- A pencil indicates a locked workgroup file.
- In the Used column, a number indicates the number of links to the file from other files at the site. The links can be hyperlinks or references.

With these clear symbols, you can troubleshoot and manage your site files at a glance.

The Extras Tab

The Extras tab lists files in the Data folder: Components, Diagrams, Library, Site Trash, Smart Objects, Stationery, and Templates. Most of these are self-evident, and contain reusable design elements for the Site. Exceptions are

- The Components folder contains source files for components of pages that update when the source file is edited.
- The Site Trash folder contains files you have deleted in Adobe GoLive but have not yet deleted on your hard disk—that is, not moved to the Recycle Bin (Windows) or to the Trash (Mac OS).

The External, Colors, and Font Sets Tabs

The External, Colors, and Font Sets tabs list items that are stored in the site file, and assist in the storage of certain layout details.

External lists URLs and e-mail addresses that are available to use as links on site pages. Simply point and shoot to insert one of the URLs or addresses on a page in a document window.
Colors indicates which colors you can use on site pages. To use a color, drag it from the tab onto selected text or a selected object on a page in a document window.

Font Sets lists the available font sets for the site pages. Those listed will appear on a menu in the document window. You can also drag a font set onto selected text on a page in the window.

The Errors, FTP, and WebDAV Tabs

The Errors, FTP, and WebDAV tabs list files that are not stored within the site. Instead, these assist with Site Maintenance and Troubleshooting.

Errors lists missing and orphaned files, such as broken links or misplaced files.
FTP and WebDAV are used in uploading the site files to a Web server. Although FTP is still a more common form of file transfer, the advanced WebDAV connection uses file locking to enable Workgroups and other teams to collaborate effectively on projects.

With your site created and securely in place, you now have a firm foundation and a world of options. In the next chapter, Chapter 4, "Working with Sites," we discuss other tools GoLive offers to assist you with site design, diagramming, and overall management. There are many different ways to view your site and understand how all the pieces fit together within a larger structure. This will become increasingly important as your site grows in size and complexity. Chapter 4 also covers site reporting, which provides feedback from your site, helping you to troubleshoot and continue to make your site better and better.

TROUBLESHOOTING

Launching the Site Wizard

The Site Wizard you mention doesn't automatically pop up when I open GoLive. How do I create a new Site?

To activate the Site Wizard and create a new Site, select New Site from the File menu or type (Option-Cmd-N) [Alt+Ctrl+N].

To instruct GoLive to launch the Site Wizard each time you start the application, select Edit, Preferences and then choose Show Intro Screen from the At Launch pull-down menu in General Document Preferences.

Creating a New Site from a Local Folder

I'd like to import a local Site into a new project folder, but the Site Wizard doesn't give me this option. How do I make this happen?

To place a locally imported Site into a project folder, you'll need to create that folder arrangement before you import the Site. Simply create a new folder and name it according to the naming convention for your Site. That is, if you plan to name the new Site Mysite, name the folder Mysite Folder.

Next, copy the folder you plan to import to the umbrella folder. This means you will actually import the copy. Finally, rename the copied folder, if necessary, giving it the name of the new Site you are creating.

GOING LIVE

Customize a Site Template to serve as the starting point for a Template of your own. This is particularly convenient for Web Sites being developed by teams. When you design a template for the Site, each team member can start with the same basic layout and navigation. This helps save time and maintain consistency throughout the project.

1. Choose Copy From Template from within the Site Wizard.

2. Select a Site Template from the list.

3. Adapt the template to meet your specific needs by changing the graphics or other elements.

4. Save your new customized template in its new location, and use it to build consistent pages throughout your Site quickly and easily.

3

4

WORKING WITH SITES

IN THIS CHAPTER

Site Design Basics 50

Filenames 59

Site Diagramming 61

Site Management 65

Using Panes 69

Site Reporting 70

Troubleshooting 71

Going Live 71

SITE DESIGN BASICS

Every Web site begins with a concept. You and your Web colleagues not only need to create the site; you also need to be able to discuss it conceptually. Ask yourself some tough questions: Who is this site's audience? What is the purpose of the site? What is the most effective way to present this site to its target audience?

The answer to these questions relies on both the graphic appeal of the page layout and the ease of use for those visiting your site. Even a visually stunning site will fail if viewers find it difficult to navigate. Therefore the concept of your site depends on an intelligently planned structure to bring it to life.

GoLive understands that you're not working in a vacuum; you need to effectively communicate your ideas for the site, express yourself in a way that's clearly understood by all parties involved, and be able to make changes quickly and easily if the site requires it. GoLive simplifies that whole creative process by allowing you to create a site design.

A site design is a kind of work-in-progress that serves as a prototype for your entire site or for a piece of your site. It is constructed of HTML pages that show actual content and links, thereby conserving your time and energy: Create your site here in a Site Design, and when the design is completed to your satisfaction, you can simply move it to a live site as is.

Creating a Site Design

For each site design, you need to follow the same basic setup process:

1. Open your Site.

2. Create and name the design.

3. Open a Design view.

4. Anchor the Design View in the Site itself.

5. Create a Design Section to create an area in which to manage files.

Let's begin by creating a design for our sample site, Rooftop Records:

1. Open the Rooftop Records site.

2. Click the Diagram tab in the Site window.

3. From the menu bar, choose Diagram, New Design Diagram. A new design appears in the Diagrams tab of the Site window with its filename already highlighted. In the Extras tab, a folder for the design appears within the Designs folder, and another file is created here.

4. Type a new name into the highlighted area of the new design in the Diagrams tab, as shown in Figure 4.1. The folder in Extras automatically adopts the same name.

Figure 4.1
When you create a site design, it shows up in the Diagrams tab of the Site Window.

Using the Site Design Window

To open the Site Design window, double-click on the design within the Diagrams tab.

The Design window, shown in Figure 4.3, contains four different tabs to assist you, each of which corresponds to a stage in the design process:

- The Design tab features the actual Design view. It acts as the canvas you use to develop and display your design. Items you place here can later be submitted to the Site.

- The Master tab is new to GoLive 6.0. Items you place on the Master tab show up on all the other pages of your diagram, but are not part of the actual design. You might place a title or a version number into the Master tab to identify all the pages.

- The Staging tab lists the HTML files contained in the design, grouping them according to the stages each has reached.

- The Annotations tab lists any additional notes for the design by subject.

Figure 4.2
The Diagram pane of the Objects Palette provides all the tools needed to create a Site Design.

After you create a site design, you can use the tools on the Diagram window of the Objects Palette to lay out your design. Use the same techniques for adding pages that you would use to build up the navigational hierarchy of a Site as discussed in the previous chapter "Introduction to Sites," adding child and sibling relationships between the pages. Additionally, in the Design view, you can also treat the pages and link lines as strictly visual elements, repositioning the pages, bending and unbending the lines, and so on.

4

Figure 4.3
The four tabs in the Site Diagram window provide an interface to manage the design and flow of your Site.

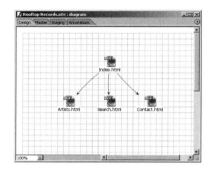

You arrange the design pages here both logically and visually. Logically, you arrange them in a hierarchy and connect them with pending links. Visually, you move pages around by clicking and dragging, place them into appropriate positions, align and distribute pages, and bend or unbend the lines linking them by dragging the handles that appear on the link lines.

Anchoring a Design

When you submit a design, it must be anchored to a page in the site's navigation hierarchy to become part of the Site. That means it can become a *live* part of the Site; in other words, pages that actually become accessible to users once submitted. If you submit a design without anchoring it, its pages become scratch pages, which are stored in the Site for potential later use, but not uploaded.

You can add an anchor to an unanchored design you have already begun work on. But if you know how you will be using a design before you begin the Site, it's best to anchor the design as soon as you start it. If you intend to start a complete Site using a design, create a blank Site and anchor the design to the Site's default home page. If the design is a subtree of an existing Site's current navigational hierarchy, anchor the design to the page the subtree descends from.

To anchor a new design to an existing page in a site, follow these steps:

1. Display the page that will anchor the design in a Site window, either in a navigation view, a links view, or the Files tab.

2. Open the Site Design window for the design.

3. Make sure that both windows are accessible, moving one or both windows if necessary.

4. Drag the page that will anchor the design from the Site window to the Design view. The page appears in the Design view with an anchor icon. It is also listed in the Anchor Pages group in the Staging tab.

> Using a navigation view gives you the best idea of how the design will be anchored, since you get a good overall visual of the Site.

To anchor the design of a complete new Site, follow these steps:

1. Create a blank Site.

2. Follow the procedure for anchoring to an existing page, using the home page of the existing Site as the anchor.

To add an anchor page to an existing unanchored design, follow these steps:

1. Follow the procedure for anchoring the design to an existing page in the Site, but drag the anchor page from the Site onto an existing page in the design.

2. The anchor page will appear in the design with a link to the existing design page.

Defining a Design Section

A *section* is a hierarchy of design pages, usually a subtree, that you group together to simplify site management. The pages in a section have the same base filename, and you can put them in their own folder and give them their own stationery (see Chapter 17, "Styles," for more on stationery). Sections can contain sections (subsections).

Creating a design section is the concluding step in setting up the design. (If you create subsections of the section, it is during the development of the design.) Creating a section creates a *section page*—the page at the top of the section hierarchy. During the final setup step, you have the option of adding any number of child pages to the section page. Strictly speaking, you begin development of your design when you specify these pages.

To define a design section, follow these steps:

1. Open the Site Design window for the design by selecting it from the Diagram menu.

2. Click the Design tab of the Diagram window, and click the Diagram pane of the Objects Palette.

3. Drag a Design Section icon from the Site tab of the Objects Palette to the Design tab. The icon changes to a section page, identified as such by its boldface label.

4. Click the section page to select it.

5. Do either of the following in the Object tab of the Section Inspector:

   ■ Provide a design name for the page in the Name text box. This name appears as the label for the page in the Design tab only if Design Name is selected in the View Controller. Otherwise, the label will be its filename or page title.

   ■ Change the default page title from Welcome to Adobe GoLive 6.

Dragging the anchor page to a Design view shows it in the view and lists it in the Design folder. However, it does not move or copy the page to the site folder or place an alias (Mac OS) or shortcut (Windows) there.

Page hierarchy is described in terms of "family relationships." Each page can be described as a *parent*, *child*, *previous sibling*, or *next sibling*. These terms don't necessarily refer to specific links, but rather to logical groupings of your pages. A parent page can have many children, and those children are siblings of one another. Adjacent children can be described in terms of previous and next.

4

There is probably no reason to change the default filename `index.html`. Even if the home page for the Site has the same filename, the two `index.html` files will have different paths because the section has its own folder.

6. Click the Section tab of the Section Inspector.

7. Do either one of the following using the Section tab of the Inspector:

   ■ Provide a base filename for the child pages you will place in the section (and their descendents in the section). The filenames will be provided automatically. For example, if you are developing a section on hiking, provide the base filename Hiking, and the filenames will be `Hiking.html`, `Hiking1.html`, `Hiking 2.html`, and so on.

   ■ Specify a target folder for the child pages in the section (and their descendents in the section). It should be a subfolder of the root folder, either an existing one or a new one that will be created for the purpose. When the design is submitted, the pages will be placed in this folder. For example, if you're designing the hiking section of a recreation site, you might specify the new folder Recreation/Hiking as your folder. In this case, the folders Recreation and Hiking will be created upon submission. If you don't specify a target folder, either the root folder or the folder for generated items you have specified in site preferences will be used.

   Specify stationery for the pages, if desired (see Chapter 17 for more on stationery).

8. If you want to add child pages to the section page at this time, do both of the following:

   ■ Choose the types of parent and sibling links you will generate between the section page and its children.

   ■ Type the number of child pages to add to the section page in the Count text box.

9. Click Create New Pages.

Adding Pages and Subsections

Pages can be added to a design with any relationship to any other page in the design. If the page you link to is part of a section, your new page will become part of that section too.

If you are adding a set of child pages to an existing page, they can become a new subsection of the existing page's section.

To add a single new page to a section, follow these steps:

1. Select a page in the section to add the page to.

2. Choose a new page, next page, previous page, or parent page from the toolbar or the Design menu, depending on what relationship you want your new page to have to the existing page.

To add new pages or a subsection containing several new pages, follow these steps:

1. Select a page in the section to add the pages or subsection to.

2. Choose Design, New Pages.

3. Specify the number of pages to create, the filenames, and the types of links to generate.

4. If you want the selected page and the child pages you are creating to be a new subsection, select Make Parent a Section.

5. Click Create. The child pages are created. If you selected Make Parent a Section, the page you selected is turned into a section page and identified as such by a boldface label.

Adding and Editing Pending Links

You normally define a page's pending links when you create the page. However, you can add pending links between pages, and you can change links between pages from one type to another. Link types are named by the family relationships, representing a page's position within the hierarchy of the design flow. The link types you can define when you create a page are child to parent (Parent), parent to child (Child), previous sibling to next sibling (Next), and next sibling to previous sibling (Previous) .

The type of newly added links is Hyperlink—a link to a location external to our Site, such as another Web page. You can change a pending link to any of these five types and also to the type Tour. Tour links connect a series of pages, not necessarily adjacent siblings, in a sequence that could be realized as a page-by-page tour of some subject area.

Link types are editable. You can change the color of a type or add a new type with a new color and name.

To add a pending link of the type Hyperlink from one page to another, follow these steps:

1. Select the source page. A point-and-shoot button appears on the page.

2. Drag from the point-and-shoot button to the target page. A new line with the link type Hyperlink is created.

To add additional pending links between already linked pages, follow these steps:

1. Either select two pages linked to each other, OR select two or more pages linked in sequence, starting with the first page in the sequence.

2. Choose a link type from the Add Design Line submenu of the context menu. Ordinarily, you add a type that matches the current link type. For example, you add a Child link (parent-to-child) to a Parent link (child-to-parent).

To change a link's type, follow these steps:

1. Display the Inspector.

2. Click a link line to select it. The line shows a grab handle, and the source and target pages are highlighted.

3. If necessary, select other lines. If multiple lines are selected, their source and target pages are not highlighted.

To select any page or line after the first page or line selected, Ctrl-click (Windows) or Shift-click (Mac OS). Ctrl-clicking or Shift-clicking again deselects the page or line.

4. Choose a new link type in the Link Inspector. Normally, you would choose only Hyperlink or Tour because the family link types (Parent, Child, Next, and Previous siblings) are more easily changed by dragging one of the linked pages onto the other one.

If you want to use your own scheme for categorizing links, you can create your own link types and give them your own colors. You might do this if you've invented some crazy new navigation scheme that can't quite be represented by GoLive's default link types. To add or edit link types, follow these steps:

1. Choose Site, Settings, Link Types.

2. You must check Site Specific Settings to add your own link types or edit the default ones. Do one of the following:

   - To change the color of a link type, select the type, click the color field, and provide a new color.

   - To add a link type, click New, provide a color, and type a name.

3. Click OK.

Moving Pages

You can treat a page simply as an object in a drawing program and drag it to position it wherever you like within your site design. Alternatively, you can drag a page onto another page as you do in a navigation view, to create a new family link in the logical hierarchy.

You can select a number of page objects by Shift-selecting them or dragging a selection box around them, and then drag them all at once. However, a better method for this purpose is to group the pages and then drag the group.

To move a page without changing position in the logical hierarchy, drag the page to any new location. If you drag a page near another page or partially over it, the other page will also move (to avoid a collision) when the drag is completed.

The link lines connected to the page you drag move with the page. However, descendents of the page do not move with the page as they would if you were moving the page into a new hierarchical position. When you move a page, the lines connected to it move with it.

To move the copy of a page to a new position, follow these steps:

1. Begin dragging the page.

2. Hold down Ctrl (Windows) or Option (Mac OS). A plus appears next to the pointer.

3. Continue dragging to the new position. A copy of the page is created at the position. If the original page is annotated or connected to lines, the annotations or lines are not copied.

> If you drag a page on top of another page and a line appears to the top, bottom, left, or right of the other page, you have dragged the page too far into the center of the other page. Decrease the overlap until the line disappears.

Annotating a Site Design

Annotations consist of a subject line and text. You can add an annotation to the design as a whole or annotate individual design items or lines. Annotations appear in the design as an icon, and you can also display their subject or text. The Annotations tab lists all the annotations to a design by subject. You can place the icon on a page, on a link line, or in any area of the Design view. Annotations added to items stay with the item when it is moved.

To add an annotation to a design, follow these steps:

1. Display the Inspector and the Objects Palette.

2. Drag a Design Annotation icon from the Site tab of the Objects Palette to the design.

3. Continue dragging to a page, a line, or some other location.

4. Type the subject and annotation text in the Annotation Inspector.

5. Do either of the following in the Annotation Inspector:

    - If you want the subject to appear in the design, select Display Subject.

    - If you want the text to appear in the design, select Display Text. If you select both Display Subject and Display Text, the text appears under the subject.

6. If you select Display Subject or Display Text (and if necessary), change the position of the subject or text relative to the annotation icon.

Managing Annotations

The Annotations tab for a design shows you the subject and text of all the annotations to the design. You can also use the tab to delete a design or change its subject.

To view the subject and text of an annotation, do either of the following:

- Click the Annotations tab and view the annotation's subject and text there.

- Select the annotation and view it in the Inspector.

To move an annotation, drag the annotation to another position.

To copy an annotation at another position, follow these steps:

1. Begin dragging the annotation.

2. Hold down Ctrl (Windows) or Option (Mac OS).

3. Continue dragging to the new position.

With designs intended for presentation, displayed subjects are useful as captions for key features. This helps communicate the purpose and flow of your Site to others.

To change the subject of an annotation, do either of the following:

- Select the annotation in the Annotations tab and type a new subject.

- Select the annotation in the Design tab and type a new subject in the Annotation Inspector.

To edit the text of an annotation, do one of the following:

- Select the annotation in the Design tab of the Diagram window.

- Edit the text in the Annotation Inspector.

To delete an annotation, select the annotation in the Design tab of the Diagram window or the Annotations tab of the Inspector and press Delete.

Submitting a Site Design to a Site

You can make a design live by submitting it. When you submit a design, the following changes take place:

- Its pages move from the Design Pages group to the Live Pages group in the Staging tab, where they are also displayed with a Live Page icon in the Diagram view.

- Its pages are moved from the Design folder in the site data folder to the target folder in the root folder and appear in the Files tab. Its pages appear in the Navigation view. If they are anchored, they appear in the central pane in the same hierarchy they form in the Design view. If they are scratch pages, they appear in the Scratch pane.

A submitted design can be *recalled* at any time. A recall reverses the submission action, and restores your live site to the way it was, yet retaining the design.

To submit a design to a site, follow these steps:

1. Open the design in a site design window and click the window.

2. Click the Submit Design button on the toolbar, or choose Design, Design Staging, Submit Design. You can submit a design for the first or only time, submit a design you have recalled for further development, or submit a design to update a previous submission of the design.

To recall a design from a site, follow these steps:

1. Open the design in a site design window and click the window.

2. Click the Recall Design button on the toolbar, or choose Design, Design Staging, Recall Design. The changes to the pages of the design made when you submitted it are undone. That is, they move back to the Design Pages group, they move back to the Design folder in the Site Data folder, and they disappear from the Navigation view.

About Recalls and Updates

You often submit a design with the intention of recalling it after you have examined it in a live context. For example, you submit a design in progress to examine it in context and then recall it for further design development. Or you submit one of two alternative designs and recall it so that you can submit the other and choose between them.

In fact, you don't need to recall a design to work on it further. You can submit an unfinished design, leave it live, and work on the design further in a site design view. Submitting the same design again updates the live site.

Updates involving substantial design changes can sometimes produce confused results. If this happens, try recalling the updated design, checking and fixing it, and resubmitting.

Grouping Design Items

A *design group* is a rectangle that encloses a number of design items (pages or other groups) and permits you to treat them as a unit. You move, copy, or delete them by moving, copying, or deleting the group.

Groups are not defined logically. The items in a group need to be located within the group rectangle, but they don't need to be in any particular logical relation with one another.

To group selected pages, select the pages and choose Edit, Group. A group rectangle encloses the selected pages. If unselected pages would be enclosed by the rectangle, they are automatically moved outside its border. To ungroup grouped pages, click the group and choose Edit, Ungroup. To create an empty group in a particular location, drag a Design Group icon from the Site tab of the Objects Palette to an appropriate location in the Design view. If there are pages in or near this position, they will move out of the way automatically.

Do one or both of the following if necessary:

- Resize the group by dragging one of its corner handles.

- Reposition the group by dragging its title bar or border.

To add pages to a group, drag pages into the group. If the group is too small to hold the pages you drag into it and Auto Resize is selected in the Group Inspector, the group will enlarge automatically. If you don't select Auto Resize, the pages will still go in but you might not see all of them.

FILENAMES

Adobe GoLive contains a kind of play book of filenaming rules that ensure cross-platform compatibility. When it encounters a filename that violates one of these rules, the Site window and the File Inspector indicate this for you. The File Inspector even lists the rule itself so that you understand exactly how to correct the naming error.

The default set of filenaming constraints is the one that applies to your own file system, either Windows 98/NT/2000 or Mac OS. Other sets you can choose include Unix, DOS/Windows 3.1, GoLive standard, GoLive small caps, and GoLive strict. The three GoLive sets are described in Site Filename Constraints preferences.

For more information on setting filename constraints, **see** *"Filename Constraints," p.99*

Changing Filename Constraints

For those of you who refuse to play by the rules, you're in luck; your kindred rebel spirits at Adobe have given you the power to make your own rules, at least where filenaming conventions are concerned. In GoLive, you have the freedom to examine, modify, delete, and add filenaming constraint sets as you see fit.

Figure 4.4
Use Site Settings to change filename constraints for just the specific Site you're working on.

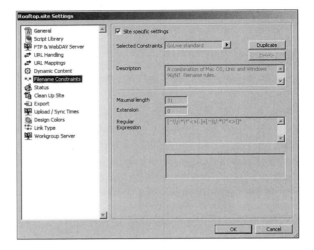

To modify filenaming constraints for a particular Site, follow these steps:

1. Click the Site Settings button on the toolbar, choose Settings from the Site menu, or press (Opt-Cmd-Y) [Alt+Ctrl+Y] on your keyboard.

2. Click Filename Constraints in the left panel and check Site Specific Settings.

3. Choose another constraint set from the Selected Constraints menu, as shown in Figure 4.4.

4. Click OK.

To modify filenaming constraints for all Sites, you follow a similar sequence of steps:

1. In Preferences, expand Site in the left pane and click Filename Constraints in the left panel.

2. Choose another constraint set from the Selected Constraints menu.

3. Click OK.

To add a new set of constraints for a particular Site, follow these steps:

1. Go to Site Settings.

2. Click Filename Constraints in the left panel and check Site Specific Settings.

3. Click Duplicate. This creates an identical new set, which you can edit or delete. (You can't delete the original.)

4. Type a name for the new set in the Selected Constraints text box.

5. Click OK.

To add a new set of constraints for all Sites, follow these steps:

1. In Preferences, expand Site in the left pane and click Filename Constraints in the left panel.

2. Choose another constraint set from the Selected Constraints menu.

3. Edit the set in the other text boxes as you prefer.

4. Click OK.

To delete a filenaming constraints set for a particular Site, follow these steps:

1. In Site Settings, Click Filename Constraints in the left panel and check Site Specific Settings.

2. Choose the constraint set you want to delete from the Selected Constraints menu.

3. Click Delete.

4. Click OK.

To delete a filenaming constraints set for all Sites, follow these steps:

1. In preferences, expand Site in the left pane and click Filename Constraints in the left panel.

2. Choose the constraint set you want to delete from the Selected Constraints menu.

3. Click Delete.

4. Click OK.

SITE DIAGRAMMING

When starting a new Site, you could just start building pages one at a time; but a more structured alternative is to use Navigation view. First you lay out the site's structure by creating empty pages in a hierarchy of unresolved pending links generated to and from the home page. Later, when the pages have content, these pending links can be resolved naturally by creating hyperlinks that reflect them. It's the equivalent of drawing dotted lines so that you can trace the proper paths when the time comes.

Two types of generic pages are used for building within the Navigation view. *Pages* contain unresolved pending links, whereas *scratch pages* have no pending links of any kind. Pages are blank HTML pages that appear in the view with an empty-page alert to indicate that proper links are not yet in place. Scratch pages are added only as placeholders to facilitate linking pages to the hierarchy at a later time.

To add an empty parent page with pending links, follow these steps:

1. Open a Navigation view of the Site. Either choose Site, View, Navigation from the top menu, choose Navigation from the pull-down menu in the top right corner of the Site folder, or click the Navigation View icon in the toolbar.

2. Select a page in the view.

3. Click the New Parent Page button (a page with a line above it) on the toolbar or choose Diagram, New, Parent Page.

This inserts a page between the one you selected and its former parent page. The new page is the child of the former parent page and the parent of the selected page. All three pages are connected by "to child and back" links—pending links from parent pages to child pages and from child pages to parent pages.

To add an empty child page with pending links, follow these steps:

1. Select a page in Navigation view.

2. Click the New Parent Page button (a page with a line below it) on the toolbar or choose Diagram, New, Child Page.

This creates a new page with "to child and back" links from the selected page.

To add an empty next sibling page with pending links, follow these steps:

1. Select a page in Navigation view.

2. Click the New Next Page button (a page with a line to the right of it) on the toolbar or choose Diagram, New, Next Page.

This inserts a next sibling page with "to adjacent siblings" links from the selected page—that is, a pending link from the selected page to the new sibling page and a pending link from the new sibling page to the selected page.

To add an empty previous sibling page with pending links, do the following:

1. Select a page in Navigation view.

2. Click the New Previous Page button (a page with a line to the left of it) on the toolbar or choose Diagram, New, Previous Page.

This inserts a previous sibling page with "to adjacent siblings" links from the selected page.

To add a group of child pages with pending links, do the following:

1. Select a page in Navigation view.

2. Choose Diagram, New Pages from the top menu.

3. Type the number of pages to create.

If the home page is selected in Navigation view, your only option is to create a new child page. Click the New Child Page button or choose Diagram, New, Child Page.

4. Name your file. Type a filename in the blank provided. Otherwise, the page will simply be tagged *unidentified*.

5. Select the appropriate types of links from the Parent and Sibling pull-down menus to create pending links.

6. Click Create, as shown in Figure 4.5.

This creates new pages and new unresolved pending links. A pending link between two pages can be resolved by adding a hyperlink from the source page to the target page that reflects it.

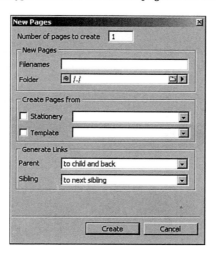

Figure 4.5
Use the New Pages screen to create a group of new child pages in Navigation view.

4

To add a pending link from one page to another, follow these steps:

1. Position the pointer over the source page of the desired link.

2. Hold down the (Command) or [Ctrl-Shift] keys. A point-and-shoot icon appears next to the pointer.

3. Click and drag to the target page to create a new pending link.

The source and target page for a link can be any two pages. They do not need to have a family relationship.

To remove a page from a Navigation view, do the following:

1. Select the page. If the page you select has descendents, they will automatically be moved to the Scratch pane after you remove the selected page.

2. Click the Delete Selected Item button (trash can) on the toolbar, choose Edit, Clear from the menu above, or press the Delete key.

A warning dialog box appears before you delete a page, so that you can't delete one accidentally. Also remember that when you delete a page, the page moves to the Site Trash, not directly to your desktop Trash or Recycle bin.

You may also opt to move the page to the Scratch pane without deleting it by choosing Diagram, Move to Scratch from the top menu.

To move a pending link and its descendents to another position in the site, follow these steps:

1. Position the pointer over the page you want to move.

2. Click and drag this page until it rests above the target page—the page to which you want it to be linked.

3. Release the moving page over the top, bottom, or sides of the target page to establish the type of relationship the pages will have.

In tall orientation

■ Drag to the *top* of the target page to make the page you're dragging its *parent*.

■ Drag to the *bottom* to make the page its *child*.

■ Drag to the *left* to make it the *previous sibling*.

■ Drag to the *right* to make it the *next sibling*.

In wide orientation

■ Drag to the *left* of the target page to make the page you're dragging its *parent*.

■ Drag to the *right* to make the page its *child*.

■ Drag to the *top* to make it the *previous sibling*.

■ Drag to the *bottom* to make it the *next sibling*.

A line at the top, bottom, left, or right of the target page appears to show you where to drop the page, as shown in Figure 4.6. These indicator lines correspond to the New Page buttons in the tool-bar.

Solving a Site Hierarchy

When you import a Site, its hierarchical structure is constructed automatically. This initial structure is based on both the arrangement of hyperlinks that exist on the Site pages as well as the hierarchy of the root folder's subfolders. In addition to the actual hyperlinks, the initial structure contains pending links; that is, it retains a record of every possible parent-child or sibling-sibling relationship within the actual hierarchy.

This hierarchy should be rebuilt if you have made changes in your Site outside Adobe GoLive, or if you want to change its navigational structure. For example, if you have provided your site with all the hyperlinks it needs, you could eliminate pending links from the hierarchy. You could also decide to base the structure entirely on hyperlinks rather than taking the subfolder structure into account.

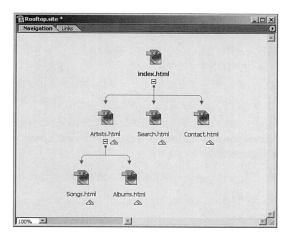

Figure 4.6
Move a pending link page by dragging it. Watch carefully where the bold black line appears; it should appear below the target parent page.

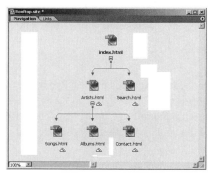

To resolve the site hierarchy, do the following:

1. Open the Site in its Site window.

2. Open a Navigation view of the Site. Either choose Site, View, Navigation from the top menu, choose Navigation from the pull-down menu in the top right-hand corner of the Site folder, or click the Navigation View icon in the toolbar.

3. Select a page in the view.

4. Choose Diagram, Solve Hierarchy from the top menu.

5. Choose Links or Hierarchy as the basis for your site structure by checking or unchecking the proper boxes here.

6. Click OK.

SITE MANAGEMENT

GoLive offers a variety of views and tools for effectively overseeing your Site. Using site views you can check the links, navigation, and file hierarchy at a glance and make corrections wherever necessary. With Site Reporting, you can keep track of your live Site's performance on the Web, troubleshoot problems, and see which pages are in demand.

All these options give you more power over what you've created by providing Site information at your fingertips, enabling you to be a better site manager.

Site Views

Site views are visual indicators of a site's pages and the links that connect them. They help you to quickly identify the relationships between the pages that comprise your site. There are three different views, each displaying a slightly different aspect of the Site:

- The *Links view* shows the Site's pages and all the hyperlinks between them.

- The *Navigation view* shows the Site's navigation hierarchy. This is the treelike structure that underlies the hyperlink web.

- The *Structure view* shows the Site's file hierarchy. This is the structure of folders and the files they contain.

The Links View

The *Links view* of a Site is the view that maps out the hyperlinks of a Site (see Figure 4.7). It begins by displaying the Site's home page file (`Index.html`). From there, you can expand the view to show both the incoming links (those linking to the Site) and the outgoing links (those linking from the Site to other Sites). An individual file could potentially appear several times in this view if it contained links going in both directions.

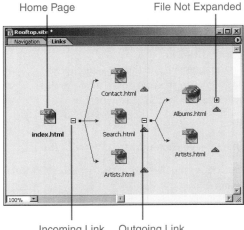

Figure 4.7
The Links view shows all the links in a Site.

The Navigation View

The Navigation view (Figure 4.8) shows the structure of the site much like a family tree, all descending from one common ancestor, the home page. Initially, this view shows only the home page. You then build the structure of the site by creating new empty pages and establishing a hierarchy based on the relationships of the pages to each other and to the home page.

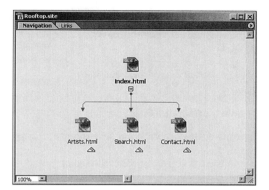

Figure 4.8
The Navigation view = shows the family hierarchy of your Site.

Magnifying and Reducing the View

A pull-down menu of magnification percentages is available for zooming in and out of the entire view, or you can click to zoom in on a particular area. In either case, you work separately on the main central pane or on any of three peripheral panes: Scratch, Reference, or Pending. You can also use a slider for precision magnification control of the central pane.

To magnify or reduce the view with a Zoom menu, click the button at the bottom-left corner of the central or peripheral pane and choose a magnification level from the menu that pops up.

To zoom in on a particular area

1. Hold down Shift [Windows] or Option (Mac). If the pointer is in a pane you have not already zoomed in on, it changes to a plus. Otherwise, it changes to a minus.

2. Click in the desired area of either the central pane or a peripheral pane. The magnification increases 200% the first time you click, and 100% more each time thereafter.

Alternatively, you can draw a rectangle defining the area and release. The area enlarges to fill the pane. You can do this repeatedly, until the magnification reaches 500%.

To magnify or reduce the view with the Site Navigator, choose Window, Site Navigator. Then, click the Zoom In or Zoom Out button. Alternatively, you can drag the zoom slider or enter the percentage of magnification or reduction you
want, and press Enter or Return.

Spotlighting Page Groupings in Navigation View

Spotlighting a navigation view is similar to centering it, but provides the advantage of being able to focus on specific pages without removing other pages from the view.

You can use the Site Navigator both for focusing the view on a particular area and for magnifying it. This has the same effect as zooming it.

You can spotlight several types of page groupings:

- *Family* spotlights a selected page, its parent page, and its children.

- *Incoming* spotlights any page containing the source of a hyperlink to the selected page.

- *Outgoing* spotlights any page that is a hyperlink destination from the selected page.

- *Pending* spotlights all pending links in the Site.

- *Collection* spotlights all pages in the Site within a selected group of pages.

> You can also spotlight with the View window. In the Inspector, click the View tab, then the Navigation tab, and select your spotlight choice.

To spotlight groups of pages in a Navigation view, follow these steps:

1. Expand the Navigation view as necessary to show the pages you want to spotlight.

2. Select a page and choose Spotlight Family, Spotlight Incoming, or Spotlight Outgoing from the Navigation tab menu.

3. Select another file to move the spotlight.

Alternatively, you can choose another spotlight command to change the type of spotlight.

Variations in Orientation

Navigation views and Links views can appear in both wide and tall orientation. Wide orientation is shown in Figure 4.9. Refer to Figure 4.8 to see an example of tall orientation. Your choice depends on your personal preference, and how your particular design fits best on the screen.

Figure 4.9
This shows the Navigator in "wide" orientation; notice that everything is sideways from the more familiar "tall" orientation.

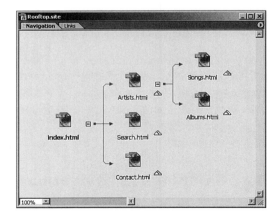

Both views use the four directions to indicate types of links.

Changing the Orientation of a View

When you first view a site, its Navigation view has a wide orientation, and its Links view has a tall orientation. To change the orientation of a view, click the Toggle Orientation button on the toolbar.

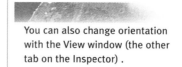

You can also change orientation with the View window (the other tab on the Inspector) .

USING PANES

Site views are used to help visualize the relationships between the pages that comprise your site. Two views are available: a view of the actual hyperlinks (Links view) and a view of the hierarchy of pages underlying the web of links (Navigation view).

Each view contains a central pane and peripheral panes that provide specialized views: the Panorama pane, Pending pane, Reference pane, and Scratch pane.

Panorama pane   Main pane

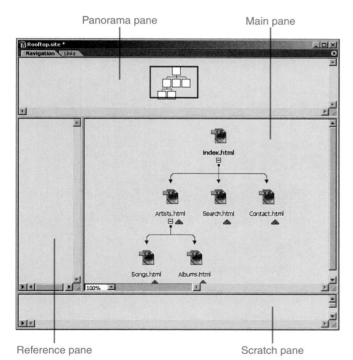

Reference pane   Scratch pane

Figure 4.10
Each peripheral pane provides a specialized view.

The Panorama pane provides a bird's-eye view of the entire site or site design. It contains a view box that corresponds to the current view in the Main pane. By moving the box, you can move the main view around the Site. You can do anything with the Panorama pane that you can do with the Main view—for instance, you can select a page or drag a page to another page in a Navigation view to make it that page's child or parent. The Panorama pane is available in all views.

The Scratch pane displays two kinds of files that are stored in the root folder and listed in the Files tab of the primary site window: HTML pages that aren't part of the Site's navigation hierarchy and media files that aren't referenced on any HTML page listed in the Files tab. The Scratch pane is available only in Navigation views.

You can drag HTML pages from a Navigation view's Scratch pane to its central pane, You use a Navigation view's Scratch pane as you would its central pane, dragging a page to a target page in the central pane and positioning it so that it becomes the parent, child, or sibling of the target page. Similarly, you can build up partial trees in the Scratch pane and drag them to target pages.

The Reference pane references the files containing the media objects embedded in HTML pages. As you move the selection from page to page, you can easily view the embedded objects. The Reference pane does not show media files hyperlinked to the HTML page, only those embedded in a page. The Reference pane is available in all views.

SITE REPORTING

The Site Reports tab of the Find dialog box allows you to search for files using a wide range of criteria. To display the Site Reports tab, open a Site or bring to the front a Site already open; then choose Site, Site Report or Choose Edit, Find, and click the Site Reports tab.

You define a site query on one or more subtabs of the Site Reports tab. Follow these steps:

1. Display the Site Reports tab.

2. Provide your site report criteria on one or more of the Site Reports subtabs shown in Figure 4.11.

Figure 4.11
The sub-tabs on the Site Report window let you specify just about any parameter you can imagine.

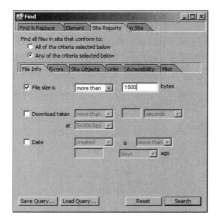

3. Save the query for reuse or generate a report based on the query for viewing.

To view a site report, follow these steps:

1. Open a Site or bring to the front a Site that is already open.

2. Display the Site Reports tab.

3. Either define a new query or load an existing one.

4. Click Search.

5. View the report on one or more of the following tabs:

- The Files Tab creates a table of the files that conform to the query, with one file per row. The columns are similar to those in the Files tab of the Site window—Name, Status, Size, and so on.

- The Navigation Tab gives you the same graphical view of the site provided by the regular Navigation view, but here the files that conform to the query are spotlighted, and the view cannot be edited. You can make further refinements in a report by viewing it in the Navigation tab and filtering the view.

- The Structure Tab displays the file hierarchy of your site using only those files that conform to the query. Also shown are folders and subfolders that contain the conforming files. The root of the hierarchy is the site folder.

To edit a page shown in a site report, follow these steps:

1. Select a page in the Report tab. Report tabs allow you to select pages but not open them.

2. Open a Navigation view or Links view of the site. The page you selected in the report tab will be selected.

3. Open the selected page in a document window to edit it.

TROUBLESHOOTING

Changing the View on Your Site

I don't like the way my site design looks. How do I change the appearance?

The View Palette, shown by default as a tab in the Inspector, controls the way your design looks. To access the View Palette, select Window, View from the menu; press [Cmd-9] on your keyboard; or with your design open, simply click the View tab in your Inspector.

Within the View palette, you'll find additional tabs labeled Design, Display, and Grid, which allow you to adjust grid size, the appearance of design icons, and the orientation of panes, among other things.

GOING LIVE

Because GoLive makes site diagrams so easy to create and edit, you no longer need to map out your Site structure or present your ideas using other applications. Print out diagrams directly from GoLive or impress clients in the early stages of Site development by providing a digital presentation of their proposed Site. As they suggest changes, you can update the Site structure before their very eyes. This type of dynamic presentation may also work effectively in communicating ideas to a supervisor or to other team members on a project.

THE WORK AREA

IN THIS PART

5 GoLive Interface Elements   **75**

6 Setting Preferences   **91**

7 Customizing GoLive   **111**

5

GOLIVE INTERFACE ELEMENTS

IN THIS CHAPTER

The Toolbar **76**

Page Window **76**

Inspector **80**

The Palettes **82**

Troubleshooting **90**

Going Live **90**

THE TOOLBAR

The toolbar rests just below the menu bar at the top of your screen, slim and sleek and ready for action. Like other elements you'll see in GoLive, it's context sensitive and changes its appearance according to what tools are most needed at the time. As you see in Figure 5.1, the toolbar contains mainly tools for formatting text, lists, and links, much like a word processing program. Yet it changes its face according to the object or mode of the moment. Depending on which window you are working in, and which mode, the tools available on the toolbar change automatically to those functions that are relevant to the currently active window.

Figure 5.1

The toolbar shows a context-sensitive set of tools, depending on which other GoLive palette and windows are in the foreground.

PAGE WINDOW

In Part II, "Web Site Basics," you saw that GoLive creates a home page automatically whenever you start a new site. Let's open up that home page now and take a look at your canvas for page creation. Double-click on the `Index.html` file within the Site folder, or select it by choosing File, Open from within GoLive as you would with any file. Up pops a blank page, as shown in Figure 5.2, ready for you to design as you choose.

Alternatively, you could simply start with a blank new page, free and unattached as yet to any site. Choose File, New Page from your menu bar for this option, or press (Cmd-N) [Cmd+N] on your keyboard to begin. Whichever method you choose, you should see a blank page like the one shown in Figure 5.2.

The Layout mode displayed by default allows you to create a page graphically. If you prefer, you could select the Source tab near the top of the window to view and edit your source HTML code directly, or choose the Preview tab to see what your page would look like in a browser. You also have tabs that allow you to create or preview pages with frames, and an Outline view for better control over your source code. Let's examine each of these page view options in greater detail.

Layout View

The Layout view is intended to resemble a typical page layout program, such as QuarkXpress or Adobe PageMaker. The familiar appearance makes designers and visual thinkers feel at home in this environment, where they can lay out elements just as they might do for a printed piece. In this book, we will concentrate on designing in the Layout view more than with other views because this is where most designers can be most productive, and where all your work can be immediately evaluated visually.

Generally a good place to begin the page creation process is by clicking on the Page icon in the top left of the Page window to display your Page Properties in the Inspector, shown in Figure 5.3. Here you can change the title of your new page from Welcome to Adobe GoLive 6 to something more appropriate to your particular site. This is also where you can set the basic parameters of your page, such as size, background, and colors. (See Chapter 8, "Creating and Saving Pages," for more on this.)

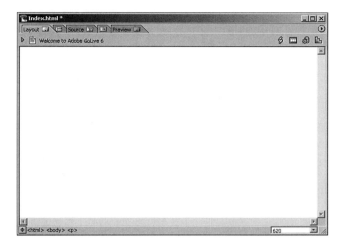

Figure 5.2
The Page window is your main editing environment in GoLive.

Figure 5.3
The Inspector is a context-sensitive window with options for setting the properties of whatever item you have selected in any other window.

The toggle just to the left of the Page icon opens a mini-window specifically geared toward editing information in the head section.

To learn more about this option, **see** *"HTML Element Find & Replace," p.150.*

The rest of the icons at the top of the Page window correspond to other tools we'll explore later in the book:

- The Scrolling Script icon opens the JavaScript Editor, where you can write and edit your own JavaScripts, which can be added directly to your page or stored for later use. Read more about the JavaScript Editor in Chapter 18, "Using the JavaScript Editor and Inserting Java Applets."

- The Filmstrip icon opens the DHTML Timeline Editor, which allows you to create animation using floating boxes and multiple layers on a page. To find out more about this option, see Chapter 19, "Working with Layers and Floating Boxes."

- The Gold Star Cookie Jar icon opens the Content Source Editor, a new feature that makes it easier than ever to work with dynamic content. Read more about this in Chapters 27 and 28 covering Dynamic Content.

- The Stair Step icon opens the CSS Editor, where you can create Cascading Style Sheets. Chapter 17, "Styles," discusses this feature in more detail.

If you're a GoLive veteran, you might notice a few more changes to the appearance of the Page window. In this version, Adobe concentrated on making the user interface as friendly and intuitive as possible while offering a greater number of options than ever before. To accomplish this twofold task, Adobe added toggles and pop-up menus in new places, including here on the Page window.

Click on the circled arrow in the upper right-hand corner to reveal a new cascading menu filled with a number of new options. The first two choices apply to new Source Code options. DocType allows you to choose between different HTML versions, whereas Markup lets you convert the entire document into XHTML if you want. Template enables you to apply a template to your page, an option that could save you time and provide greater site consistency. The Template option here also enables you to lock or unlock the page to prevent it from being edited, a new safety feature for those working with multiple pages simultaneously. Finally, the menu allows you to customize the status bar beneath the Page window and determine what will be displayed there. Your choices for display are Source Split view, Window Size Popup, Line Break Mode, and Markup Tree. You may check or uncheck each option separately, as you see fit and see changes immediately at the bottom of the window.

The following are descriptions of the new status bar features:

- Source Split View —A toggle switch in the bottom left corner of the status bar enables you to view the page graphics and source code simultaneously—the perfect situation for you whole-brain thinkers. Many designers who are comfortable with HTML source code work in this mode nearly all the time, as it provides easy and immediate access to the source code generated by GoLive when editing in the page view.

- Markup Tree palette —Notice some HTML code in brackets like so:

  `<html> <body> <p>`

  This is the new and improved Markup Tree palette. It functions the same as its former incarnations, but now works in conjunction with the Source Split view by selecting blocks of source HTML when you click on an element in the Markup Tree.

- Line Break Mode —This option controls the visibility of the line break arrow in the lower-right corner of the status bar. When visible, this arrow displays the Switch Line Break Mode popup menu, which allows you to choose what type of line breaks will be used on the page. These are based on the handling of line breaks in different operating systems.

- Window Size Popup menu —In this menu you can size your page to fit standard window resolutions. You also would select a tracing image (see Chapter 11, "Using Graphic Elements") or change default window settings in this menu.

All the items in the new status bar are visible by default, so you must use the menu to hide them. One option that seems to have strangely disappeared in this version is the Ruler icon, which used to reside in the top-right corner of the Page window. The rulers are now only accessible via the View menu. Activating the rulers shows your precise cursor position, and that of selected elements.

Frame View

In this view, you're actually arranging the frameset, choosing the quantity, location, and size of the frames rather than laying out the pages contained within them. After your pages are named and linked to the frameset page, you still need to open each in the Layout view to design it. In fact, it is preferable to design the individual pages before creating the overall frameset. This and other issues will be addressed in Chapter 14, "Working with Frames."

Source Code View

The Source Code view allows you to create your Web pages using the old-school method of typing HTML code directly onto the page. For some, this is quicker and easier than using the Layout view. Another advantage is that it allows you to see and control exactly what is happening on the page. Even the best of page layout programs can still generate quirky code from time to time, particularly if a page gets updated frequently, and it's easier to troubleshoot a problem when you can understand what's going on behind the scenes.

Of course, this is more than just a text editor. With a whole range of features to help you write code more quickly, accurately, efficiently, and consistently, GoLive serves as an invaluable resource even for those who don't need the graphical interface to create pages.

Outline View

The Outline view, like its neighbor the Source Code view, mainly appeals to those who prefer to create with code. It may be used in conjunction with the Source Code view to quickly assess a page. By providing an overview, the Outline view allows troubleshooters to take a step back and see the page from a new perspective. It also helps those who are less code savvy glance behind the scenes without becoming overwhelmed.

Layout Preview

The Layout Preview window allows you to preview what your page would look like in a typical browser and allows you to check the appearance of a page within several different browsers quickly and easily. Just open your page and select the Layout Preview tab to see the results. By using the pull-down menu in the View window, you can select from a range of viewing options, including an estimation of how your page would appear within a Web-enabled Nokia cell phone. See Chapter 25,

5

"Developing for Wireless Devices," for more information on developing for platforms other than computer Web browsers (basically wireless devices like mobile phones and PDAs).

Frame Preview

The Frame Preview functions identically to the Layout Preview but can be viewed only if frames are present on the page and you are using GoLive on a Mac. In the Windows version, framed pages are viewed with the regular Layout Preview.

INSPECTOR

Think of the Inspector as a spy, a super sleuth who chooses to disguise herself according to what best suits the situation. This aspect of the Inspector—the fact that it's an adaptive palette—makes it the ultimate all-purpose desktop tool. Yet this convenient feature can also be confusing. Its appearance shifts with each object you click on or each new tool you try, offering entirely new options at every turn. Until you become accustomed to the Inspector's dynamic nature, you may find yourself wondering what happened to the palette you just saw. Don't panic. Simply select the tool you want to use or the object you want to adjust, and the Inspector will knowingly provide the appropriate options or prompt you for the necessary details.

Like a spy, the role of the Inspector is to obtain information: What's the title of your page? Where does that image file reside? To which file are you establishing a link? The Inspector asks all the right questions to help you control all the individual elements on your page. After you fill in the blanks or provide the specifics it needs, it passes that information to other parts of the program and creates the source code necessary to make your Web page operate as instructed.

The following sections look at some of the roles the Inspector plays and the duties it performs.

Setting Page Properties: The Page Inspector

Clicking on the Page icon in the top-left corner of the Page window reveals your basic page parameters within the Inspector. In this mode, the Inspector is called the Page Inspector; but it's basically still the same friendly palette: keep in mind that its contents are context sensitive. The Page Inspector is the ideal place to start when beginning a new page. Here you can title your page, set colors for text and links, select a background color or image, and indicate the height and width of your page margins. Additional Page Inspector tabs provide control over HTML page tags and JavaScript functions as well as your ColorSync settings.

Creating Links: The Link Inspector

When a linkable element (text, a graphic, and so on) is selected, the top section of the Inspector contains link information, and is called the Link Inspector. In the top-left corner of the Link Inspector appears an icon that looks like a chain. Click on this to create a new link. (After a link has been established, a broken chain icon lights up as a possibility, enabling you to remove a link, so these two effectively serve as a toggle.)

Naturally, you'll need to establish which items should be linked together. Select the hot item on your page where the link will originate. You can create a link from text, a full image, or an image map. Highlight the appropriate text, and the Text Inspector automatically changes, ready to create a link. Click on an image to select it, or create an image map, and the Image Inspector contains a Link tab for this express purpose.

     For more information on image maps, **see** *"Creating Image Maps," p.194.*

Next locate your linking destination, the place you'll be linking to. The Link Inspector provides several options for this step:

- Point and Shoot—Beside the Link icons (or the URL check box, in the case of an image map) you'll find a small spiral that looks like a coiled-up rope. This unique innovation lets you lasso your link like a cowboy after a wayward calf. Just click on the coil and drag to extend the rope directly to the file that's the link destination. The name of the file appears instantly in the Inspector's link field, along with path information to that file. Keeping your Site window open lets you zap files and create links quickly in this manner.

- Link Field—If you know the name and location of the linking file, you can simply type the path and filename directly into the space provided, and GoLive will find the file based on what you've typed. For some, this can be the quickest and most direct method for setting up links, but beware, the margin for human error widens whenever extra typing is involved. A safer method might be to copy and paste filenames into the field.

- Browse—Click on the Folder icon to the right of the link field to browse throughout your system and locate the files you need. Again the name and path to the file you select appear in the link field.

- Menu Options—Click on the small arrow to the right of the folder to view commonly used link options. Within this menu, you can choose to make your links relative or absolute, edit the path and parameters of a linked file, or choose from recently selected HTML files or miscellaneous URLs in the list.

GoLive assumes that your link destination is a non-frames page, but you can also choose a new target frame in the Link Inspector from among the options in the pull-down menu (Top, Parent, Self, and Blank are constant options plus your custom names appear in the menu if you've created your own frame names). Similarly, you can choose a title for your frame pages here.

Grappling with Graphics: The Image Inspector

When you place an image on your page, the Image Inspector assists you in linking to the image file and controlling the way the image appears on the page. Much like the Link Inspector, you can choose to lasso your image file using Point and Shoot, type the path and filename into the field provided, browse to locate the image, or select from various menu options to obtain your image.

When your image is positioned on the page, use the Image Inspector to adjust the height and width, align the image using the grid, add or eliminate a border, or add alternative text to describe the image for visually impaired users or text-only browsers.

Click on the More tab within the Image Inspector to select a low-resolution image, reserve horizontal or vertical space around the image, create an image map, or use the image in conjunction with a form.

The Link tab lets you establish a link from the image, plus specify a ColorSync profile for the image. A ColorSync profile is only needed in high-end situations where a specific profile is needed to properly display the colors in the image.

The Rollover tab allows you to create mouseover and mousedown effects easily by specifying links to alternate image files and providing text messages. You can also check a box to preload these images. Select a mouseOver image to briefly display this image in place of the original whenever the mouse is passed over it; select a mouseDown image to display this image whenever the original image is clicked on.

If something on your page isn't functioning as expected, you can also use the Inspector as your own private eye and investigate problems that stem from human error such as typos or misnamed files. Because you need only glance at the blanks instead of searching through all your code, it can be a time-saving troubleshooter.

THE PALETTES

Adobe GoLive *palettes* are, as the name colorfully suggests, tools that display your options for creating on the Web canvas. Each palette covers a different aspect of the page designing process; therefore, some are absolutely essential to every page, whereas others you may rarely find an occasion to use. It all depends on your own role in the project (whether you're the graphic designer or the programming guru) and the work style that best suits you.

As with other Adobe applications, you can customize your workspace by rearranging the palettes and grouping them as you see fit. Simply click on the tab of any palette and drag it to the desired location. You can place a palette alone or drag it on top of another palette to combine them. In addition, the palette windows may be docked: Pull them by their perimeters nearer to each other, and they automatically align vertically or horizontally and click together to form a panel of palettes. Like any window, you can resize them by dragging the lower-right corner, or roll them up like a window shade by double-clicking on the top bar.

To access a palette that is not visible, select the name of the palette from the Window menu, or use the appropriate keyboard shortcut. Items in the Window menu are grouped according to which palettes are normally grouped together in a window(for example, Objects and Color share a window). If you select a palette whose window is already on your desktop, it will approach the forefront, and the proper tab will be selected for you. This is particularly helpful when many overlapping palettes are being used and screen real estate is scarce.

To restore palettes to their original states, choose Window, Workspace, Default Workspace. This replaces the Restore command used in previous versions.

Objects Palette

The Objects palette, shown in Figure 5.4, serves as a kind of toy box for all the many different objects and elements a Web page can be composed of. Want to insert a new image? Find the Image icon here and drag it to the proper location on the page. Need a new text box? Just click and drag. Every element you use to construct your page is essentially an object, a piece that contributes to the whole. The concept seems simple enough, yet it's GoLive's display of intuitive icons and ease of use that set it head and shoulders above other programs of this type.

Figure 5.4
The Objects palette is separated into a number of tabs, each featuring a group of icons representing types of elements that can be dragged into the Page window.

The Objects palette keeps Web design on a purely graphic level, enabling visual thinkers to assemble all the desired elements in a language they already understand, without worrying about knowing code. Simply point the mouse at what you want to use and pull it to your page. After it's placed, the Objects palette works in conjunction with the Inspector to help you set up the specifics about that object.

The Objects palette has panes for 12 different types of objects, accessed by clicking the icon for each:

- The Basic tab features elements generally found in the main part of your layout. These include Layout Grid, Layout Text Box, Floating Box, Table, Image, Plug-in, SWF, QuickTime, Real, SVG, Java Applet, Object, Line, Horizontal Spacer, JavaScript, Marquee, Comment, Anchor, Line Break, and Tag.

- Smart Objects are those used in conjunction with other Adobe applications. They include Smart Photoshop, Smart Illustrator, Smart LiveMotion, Smart Generic, Component, Rollover, Modified Date, URL Popup, Body Action, Head Action, and Browser Switch.

- The Forms tab contains all the elements pertaining to forms: Form, Submit, Reset, Button, Form Input Image, Label, Text Field, Password, Text Area, Checkbox, Radio Button, Popup, List Box, File Browser, Hidden Key Generator, and Fieldset.

- The Head tab controls those elements found in the Head of your document: Isindex, Base, Keywords, Link, Meta, Refresh, Tag, Comment, Encode, Script.

- The Frames tab features 15 different arrangements for framesets that you can use.

- The Dynamic Content tab covers elements assisting in the retrieval and display of dynamic content: Content Source, Container, Hide Content, Repeat Content, Repeat Rows, Repeat Cells, Show Next Record, Show Previous Record, Show Details of Current Record, Bound Image, Submit Action, Button Action, Image Action, Bound Label, Bound Text Field, Bound Password, Bound Text Area, Bound Checkbox, Bound Radio Button, Bound Popup, and Bound List Box.

- The Site tab contains elements relevant to sites: Generic Page, URL, Address, Color, Fontset, Folder, URL Group, Address Group, Color Group, and Fontset Group.

5

- The Site Extras tab contains nothing by default but allows you to store certain reusable elements such as Stationery, Components, Library, and Templates.

- The Diagram tab includes a wide array of elements for use in diagramming: Page, Section, Group, Annotation, Box, Level, AASP Element, Atmosphere Environment, CGI Script, Database, DIR, Form, iTV, Java Applet, JSP Element, Multiple Pages, PDA, PDF, PHP Element, Secure, SMIL, Static Page, SVG, SWF, Video, Wireless cHTML, and Wireless Xhtml-Basic.

- The WML Elements tab contains exactly that: Card, Template, Do, Onevent, Postfield, Go, Prev, Refresh, Noop, Setvar, Input, Select, Option, Optgroup, A, Fieldset, Anchor, Img, Timer, and Pre.

- The QuickTime tab includes all the makings of a QuickTime production: Movie Track, Video Track, Color Track, Picture Track, Generic Filter Track, One Source Filter Track, Two Source Filter Track, Three Source Filter Track, Mpeg Track, Sprite Track, SWF Track, 3D Track, HREF Track, Chapter Track, Text Track, Sound Track, MIDI Track, Instrument Track, Streaming Track, and Folder Track.

- The Library tab is a place to store custom objects, or any chunk of content you've created that you might like to reuse.

Color Palette

As the name indicates, the Color palette, shown in Figure 5.5, helps you add color to your pages. All color decisions, whether as part of the background, text, links, and so on must be handled with the assistance of the Color palette.

Figure 5.5
The Color palette provides a quick way to choose a color for whatever object you have selected.

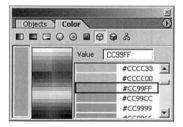

The various sections within this palette, accessed via the row of icons represent different methods for selecting color. Select from Grayscale, RGB, CMYK, HSB, or Web colors. You can select Web friendly colors based on sight, by color name, or by hexadecimal code.

In addition, a special Custom Color palette allows you to hand-pick your own assortment of palette colors or store colors specific to a particular Web site within the palette for convenient frequent use.

Transform Palette

Adobe GoLive enables you to position objects precisely on your Web page and size them according to your own specifications using a variety of methods. You can resize and reposition objects by clicking and dragging them. The toolbar allows you to resize, reposition, and group objects. The Transform palette, shown in Figure 5.6, provides all these options. In addition, it also enables you to change the stacking order of items that overlap, such as hot spots on an image map or tracks in the QuickTime Movie Viewer. (You can't change the stacking order of floating boxes.)

Figure 5.6
The Transform palette gives you precise control over the position and size of a selected element.

Objects must first be placed on the layout grid before they can be repositioned or grouped. To reposition an object, enter new values for the x and y coordinates of the object's upper-left corner and press Enter or Return after each. The object automatically migrates to its new home. Resizing works much the same way: Simply insert values for the height and width of the object in pixels or enter one of these and check the box to constrain the ratio. When you press Enter or Return, the object transforms itself to fit the new dimensions.

Grouping allows you to move several elements as a single unit, thereby maintaining the proper spacing established between them. To group elements, select one by clicking on it; then Shift-click to select the others. In the Transform palette, under Grouping, click the icon on the left to group and click the icon on the right to ungroup. Similarly, to change the stacking order of overlapping objects (called Z-Order), select an object and then click the appropriate Bring to Front or Bring to Back icon under Z-Order. The objects should respond accordingly.

Align Palette

Using the Align palette (shown in Figure 5.7), it's easy to arrange objects precisely on a Web page. You can align objects in relation to their parent, such as the Document window or layout grid. To do so, first select the object or group of objects you want to align. Then under Align to Parent, click a horizontal or vertical alignment button. The buttons in the Align palette are identical to those on the toolbar and allow you to align left, center, or right horizontally, and top, center, or bottom vertically.

You can also use the Align palette to align and distribute objects in relation to each other.

First, select the objects by clicking on the first one and Shift-clicking on each additional object. Then under Align Objects, click a horizontal alignment button (left, center, right) or a vertical alignment button (top, center, bottom). The alignment options perform as follows:

- Align Left aligns the objects along the left vertical axis of the object farthest to the left.

- Align Center aligns the objects along the vertical center axis between them.

- Align Right aligns the objects along the right vertical axis of the object farthest to the right.

- Align Top aligns the objects along the top horizontal axis of the highest object.

- Align Middle aligns the objects along the horizontal center axis between them.

- Align Bottom aligns the objects along the bottom horizontal axis of the lowest object.

To distribute items in relation to each other using similar guidelines, first select the items to be distributed; then under Distribute Objects, click on a horizontal distribution button or a vertical distribution button. The affected items will become more evenly spaced.

Figure 5.7
The Align palette permits precise position of one element relative to another.

History Palette

The History palette, despite its claims to mastery over time, more closely resembles a glorified Undo tool (see Figure 5.8). It operates much as it does in other Adobe applications, recording each action you take when constructing a page and allowing you to retrace your steps. Each action is named automatically so that you can follow along and see your work, or click on an action to proceed directly to a particular point in the creation process. In this way, it is a form of time travel. The page reverts back to the way it looked at that stage of the game, frozen in the evolutionary process like a fossilized Pterodactyl. This tool, which arrived in the previous version of GoLive, can be absolutely indispensable for correcting human error, comparing alternate versions of a page, appeasing an indecisive boss or client, or simply reviewing your work.

The default number of actions recorded is 20, so if you're anticipating many changes to the page, you might want to up this number. To do this, click on the small arrow in the upper right-hand corner of the palette and select History Options. This opens a dialog box that allows you to enter a number between 0 and 1600 to serve as your Maximum History States. Use the lowest number of states you feel comfortable with because this feature eats up a huge amount of memory.

Figure 5.8
The History palette shows a list of the recent actions you've taken, making it possible to revert to a previous state.

Table Palette

Tables have long been used to assist in the alignment of text and images on a Web page, or to present spreadsheet or numerical data in neat rows and columns. Nearly any object can be inserted into a table cell, including text, images, QuickTime movies, and even other tables. Used in conjunction with the layout grid, tables grant you a high level of control over the placement of objects on your page.

Although you must first create a table using the Table icon in the Objects palette (it's a Basic object), and you still control certain aspects of table construction via the Inspector, the Table palette facilitates the arranging of data within your table and helps you control the look and size of your table and its cells. The palette itself is broken down into two distinct parts: Style, shown in Figure 5.9, controls cosmetic changes, whereas Select, shown in Figure 5.10, controls the cell content.

Within Select mode, you can highlight individual cells, entire rows, or entire columns, and manipulate the data within them. The Sort Table dialog box, shown in Figure 5.11 and accessed by clicking the Sort button in the Table palette, allows you to perform multilevel sorts on data, in ascending or descending order, by row or by column.

The Styles mode makes it easy to change the color, cell size, and spacing of your tables. There are 10 built-in styles to choose from, ranging in mood from Just the Facts to Seventies, plus you can import and export styles or create your own new styles to suit any page you can dream up.

Figure 5.9
The Style tab of the Table palette provides an easy way to control the cosmetic styling of a table.

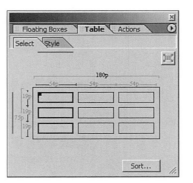

Figure 5.10
The Select tab of the Table palette makes it easy to visually select entire rows, columns, or cells of a table.

Figure 5.11
Click the Sort button in the Table palette to reorder a table's contents.

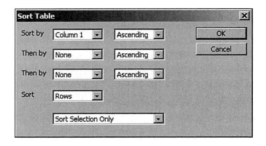

Markup Tree Bar

The Markup Tree Bar (see Figure 5.12), which is that line of tags along the bottom edge of the Page window, translates your HTML source code into an easy-to-follow outline so that you can quickly locate and select pieces that might otherwise get lost in the shuffle. When you click on something in the Markup Tree Bar, it becomes simultaneously highlighted in the Layout mode as well as the Source Code palette if it's open. These speed up your troubleshooting and updating efforts by a long shot and will be especially appreciated by anyone who's ever tried to select an invisible GIF.

Figure 5.12
The Markup Tree bar is a row along the bottom the Page window that shows you where in the hierarchy of the page's tags the currently selected element resides.

Source Code Window

True to its name, the Source Code window (see Figure 5.13) enables the user to view the code behind your graphic document, to take it apart and see what makes it tick. Grouped conveniently with other code-driven palettes such as In & Out Links, Site Navigator, and JavaScript Shell, the Source Code window allows programmers to tinker directly with the HTML and see instantly how code changes affect the appearance of the page.

Figure 5.13
The Source Code window can be positioned anywhere on screen as a way to view the source of whatever's going on in the Page window.

Identical in purpose to the Source view or even the new Source Split view built into the Page window, the Source Code window has the distinct advantage of remaining mobile, which may be the reason it's been retained despite its seeming redundancy. As a separate window, it can be positioned anywhere on the user's desktop and even arranged for viewing on a second monitor, a viable option that some Web professionals choose to expand their workspace. It also permits a designer or programmer to see the entire page layout while simultaneously viewing code, an option otherwise lost using only the Source views within the Page window.

Additional viewing options include Local Mode (which zeroes in on a particular line or section of code), Word Wrap (places soft returns at the ends of lines to keep lines of code in full view), Display Line Numbers, and Dim When Inactive. These last two options can be checked or unchecked by clicking on the arrow in the top right-hand corner of the palette and selecting each from the pull-down menu.

In & Out Links Window

The In & Out Links window (see Figure 5.14) earns its name by displaying all links in and out of any selected element. If a page is selected, it shows all the other elements included on that page, plus all the pages to which that page is linked. If another object (such as a graphic) is selected, it displays all links to and from that object. Links to the chosen element appear on the left, whereas links from it take their leave on the right.

What's truly remarkable about this palette is that it allows you to see all the links, both internal and external, even those embedded in PDF or multimedia files. And as if that weren't amazing enough, it even permits you to update these links. Any link you see can be edited and its destination switched, by simply inspecting that page or address and then using point and shoot to attach a new address.

This feature proves beneficial when troubleshooting or repairing broken links. When an empty reference appears, you know you've got a problem link, and you can correct the problem immediately, right inside the palette. Overall it serves as an invaluable tool in the GoLive repertoire.

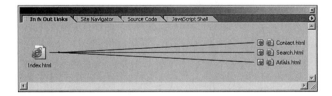

Figure 5.14
The In & Out Links window shows all the links into and out of the current page.

Congratulations! You've now completed a full tour of GoLive's interface elements.

If you want to dig a little deeper and discover how to set preferences and otherwise customize your experience with the application, go to Chapter 6, "Setting Preferences," and Chapter 7, "Customizing GoLive."

If you're ready to get started creating a page, proceed to Chapter 8.

TROUBLESHOOTING

Locating Palettes, Windows, and Other Tools

I don't see the palette you mention. How do I make it appear?

If a palette you need is not visible, it could be closed or simply obstructed by another window on your screen. In either case, opening the palette will bring it to the foreground. From the Window menu, select the name of the palette, or press the appropriate shortcut on your keyboard.

The Window menu displays a check mark next to the palettes that are already open. If the desired palette is supposedly open but still cannot be located, select it in the Window menu once to close it, then again to re-open it. The palette should appear in the foreground.

This problem often occurs when many palettes fill the desktop simultaneously, when the palette windows have been rolled up using windowshades, or when the desktop has been customized so that palettes have been combined in uncommon ways.

GOING LIVE

While getting to know the interface elements or when sampling new tricks of the trade, you may find it helpful to create a dummy Site simply for research and development. This way you can experiment fearlessly, pulling assorted objects onto the page and manipulating them without any serious repercussions. Check out the Inspector in all her various disguises, note how the Toolbar changes in different situations, and view your pages in other layouts. Natural curiosity and hands-on exploration go a long way when it comes to mastering an application.

5

6

SETTING PREFERENCES

IN THIS CHAPTER

About Preferences 92

General Preferences 93

Modules 97

Fonts 97

Encodings 98

ColorSync 98

Script Library 98

Site Preferences 99

Browsers 103

Find Preferences 103

Spell Checker 104

Network Preferences 105

Source Preferences 105

JavaScript Preferences 107

Dynamic Content 108

QuickTime 108

Troubleshooting 109

Going Live 109

ABOUT PREFERENCES

It's all about options. Consistent with the rest of the Adobe family of products, GoLive 6.0 offers you full range of motion when it comes to expressing your own style. In this arena, the individual rules, and you can have things just the way you want them—provided, of course, that you know how to ask for what you want. This is where preferences come in.

Many users don't even realize what a plethora of choices the application offers. In this chapter, we'll lead you through the entire Preferences panel and show you just how far your bounds of power extend.

Before we begin, keep in mind a few things concerning preferences or any kind of customization settings you apply:

- Although most changes made in Preferences will be reflected immediately in GoLive, some may require that you restart the application before they take effect. If you discover to your disdain that no updates appear to have been made, try closing and reopening the document you're working on. If you still see no changes, try quitting and relaunching GoLive. To avoid any confusion, it's generally best to update preferences without any documents open.

- Remember that changes you make today will affect only the way GoLive behaves from here forward; documents created in the past will still reflect the old settings until you bring them into GoLive and update them. (For example, checking the box for Write "Generator Adobe GoLive" means that all new pages will include this statement, but any pages created before the change will not. To retain sitewide page consistency, you'd still need to open and update the old files.)

- When working in teams, make sure to discuss preferences and settings up front and agree to a set of standards for the project. Many organizations maintain consistent standards on all their projects, and it is important that you become aware of such policies before you begin any work. In circumstances where multiple users share files or even share the same machines (as with a workgroup server or in a school environment, for example), you might want to restore the application to its default settings when you finish. This is merely an exercise in collegial courtesy.

- While the Preferences window is open, you are prohibited from doing anything else within the application. You cannot access other windows or menus, nor can you even quit until you click Cancel or OK within the Preferences dialog box.

6

The bulk of your customizing tools are grouped for convenience at the bottom of the Edit menu. Here you'll find controls for your Web Settings, Adobe Online Settings, Servers, Keyboard Shortcuts, and Preferences. Of course, additional, more specific controls are located throughout the program, but for now we'll concentrate on the applicationwide set of preferences.

To access your GoLive 6.0 preferences, choose Edit, Preferences or press (Cmd-K) [Cmd+K] on your keyboard.

In an attempt to make keyboard shortcuts even easier to recall, you'll find in this version that several shortcuts have been updated so that similar processes share similar keystrokes. For example, the shortcuts for all kustomizing (sic) tools in this area contain the letter K. This replaces the Y used for both Web Settings and Preferences in the previous version of GoLive.

Although we sympathize that these changes may prove frustrating for old-school users, this is consistent with Adobe's commitment to making the interface as user friendly as possible. The interface throughout version 6.0 shows substantial improvements over previous incarnations. Oh, and if you're curious, the former Preferences shortcut (Cmd-Y) [Cmd+Y] now toggles a split Page window, if one is open. If no window is open, nothing happens at all, so there's no harm if you forget and use the old shortcut by mistake.

GENERAL PREFERENCES

When open, the Preferences panel reveals a handy table of contents on the left side for easy reference and a quick hop directly to the preference you want to update. To conserve space, certain types of preferences are grouped together. Click the arrows to the left of these to display a complete list for each. For simplicity's sake, we'll cover all the preferences from top to bottom here. Consult individual chapters or the book's index for customization details specific to a particular aspect of the application.

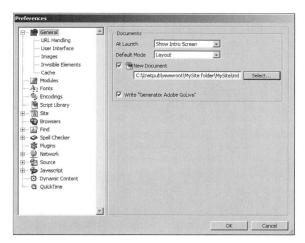

Figure 6.1
The General Preferences tab lets you set some of the fundamentals of the program.

General Preferences

General preferences, shown in Figure 6.1, include a variety of different choices all on the first panel. These include At Launch, Default Mode, New Document, and Write "Generator Adobe GoLive".

At Launch

When you launch GoLive initially, a dialog box opens, requiring you to make a make a decision: Do you want to Create a New Page, Create a New Site, or Open an Existing File? You can choose one of these actions, click to close the box, or check the "do not show" box to banish the opening dialog box into oblivion.

Users who choose the latter option and want to restore it can select Show Intro Screen from the At Launch pull-down here. Other options are Do Nothing, which keeps the dialog box from appearing, or Create New Page, which automatically opens a new blank page for you each time you launch the application. Simply select one of these from the pull-down menu to determine how your GoLive experience will begin.

Default Mode

The Default Mode option refers to which kind of Page window you generally prefer to use. Pull-down menu choices include the same view types as the tabs at the top of the Page window. Here's what each selection allows you to do:

- Layout —Lay out pages graphically
- Frames —Lay out pages graphically using frames
- Source —Create pages by writing source code
- Outline —Create pages using source code in outline form
- Preview—View pages as they would appear in a browser
- Frames Preview —View frames pages as they would appear in a browser

Simply choose the type of Page window you prefer to use, and this tab opens in the forefront the next time you create or open a new page.

New Document

The New Document option allows you to specify where any new pages you create will automatically be saved. Check the box to take advantage of this option; then browse to find the appropriate folder and select it. This is particularly efficient when generating many pages for the same Web site at one sitting.

Write Generator

Check the Write "Generator Adobe GoLive" box and GoLive automatically includes "Generator Adobe GoLive" in its source code for every new document. Although it's blatant self-advertising, it does actually help in the coding process as well. It makes one fewer line to type each time, plus it helps others to better understand the code by knowing which program's standards were used. The `Generator` tag is among the `Meta` tags in the head of the document that search engines use to locate your site.

URL Handling

URL Handling preferences, shown in Figure 6.2, provide several choices for how you'll deal with URLs.

The first option, Check URLs case-sensitive, will make sure the case of URLs is maintained, as required by some servers. URL encoding can be set to either UTF 8 or %HH escaping, which are two different formats, and your Web server may require one or the other. Check your Web server's documentation to see if either of these options are needed.

You can set GoLive to automatically add `mailto:` to email addresses, so that they become instant links. If you check Make new links absolute, then the full absolute pathname for URLs will be used instead of the relative pathname, when available. A *relative pathname* is only that portion of the full pathname that differs from the current page's location.

When you cut URLs after a certain character, such as ?, everything from that character on will be truncated. For example, if you link to a page that contains name/value pairs for a dynamic application server, such as `http://www.mysite.com?login=yes&id=12345`, checking this option will cause that URL to be truncated down to just `http://www.mysite.com`.

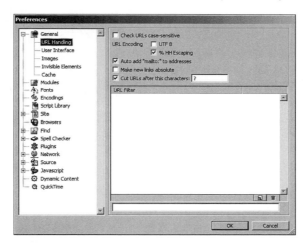

Figure 6.2
Use URL Handling to instruct GoLive how you want URL codes dealt with in the code.

User Interface

Check the box to launch other applications to edit media files, and then it will be possible to launch Adobe Photoshop, for example, to edit a certain element. When this box is unchecked, such integration will not be automatically launched.

The size knobs area just lets you make relatively subtle adjustments to the appearance, size, and color of your size knobs, also known as grab handles, that appear on the corners and edges of resizable elements.

Images

In the Images window, shown in Figure 6.3, you can select your import folder for images by clicking on Select and searching for the appropriate folder. You can also choose what format the images will be saved in, or select Ask User, which allows you to decide on a case-by-case basis. You have choices about your Low Source images here as well, including where to store them, whether they'll be generated automatically, and whether the images will be black and white or color. Low Source images are like previews that load quickly, while the actual graphic takes longer to load in the background. Low Source images are generated by whatever program is used to create the images, and in this case, GoLive can create them for you. They are useful when you have lots of large graphics and expect low bandwidth connections.

Figure 6.3
Use the Images pane to tell GoLive how and where you want images saved that it creates when you import them.

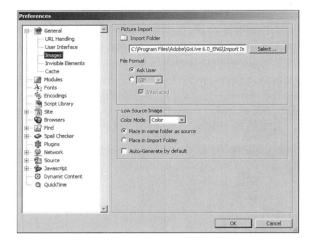

Invisible Elements

Invisible Elements (shown in Figure 6.4) is a new preference, intended to give you more control over the appearance of certain page elements. You can select from a list of various document markers and global settings and choose to make them hidden or visible. This helps eliminate clutter on your layout while still providing the option to see elements for troubleshooting.

Figure 6.4
The Invisible Elements pane lets you specify which code icons will appear, and which will be invisible.

Cache

Another new preference, Cache, is shown in Figure 6.5. This screen allows you to set up a cache folder and indicate a maximum size or clear the cache. You might choose to store the cache on a separate scratch disk if you're low on space or if you have a particularly fast drive for such purposes. GoLive will use as much cache space as it needs, up to the maximum you specify here. The default of 32MB is generally enough for all but the largest sites.

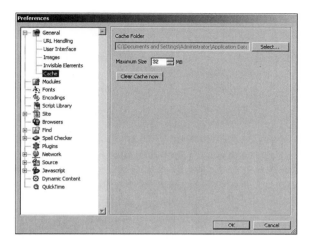

Figure 6.5
Use the Cache pane to set the size of GoLive's RAM cache.

MODULES

The Modules preference, shown in Figure 6.6, displays a list of available modules and extend scripts and allows you to check or uncheck those you want to use. Modules and extend scripts do expand GoLive's capabilities, but if there are some you're not using, it's best to deactivate them. Fewer active modules and extend scripts means a sleeker, more streamlined application that will launch sooner, respond faster, and require less memory to be productive. For example, if you're not going to do any WML development for wireless phones, turn the WML extend script off.

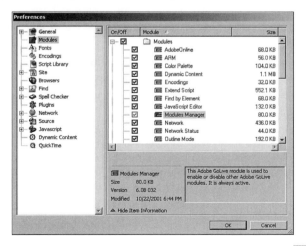

Figure 6.6
The Modules pane lets you enable and disable all of the different modules within GoLive.

FONTS

In Fonts preferences, shown in Figure 6.7, you indicate your choices for typefaces and sizes in assorted font situations:

You will need to restart GoLive after adjusting the Modules panel for changes to take effect.

proportional and monospaced, serif and sans serif, cursive and fantasy. Simply choose from the list of fonts available for your machine.

When GoLive displays your page for you, it needs to use a font. The default fonts are often set as the default fonts on most browsers, so to see what most users see, it's best to leave this preference alone.

Figure 6.7
Use the Fonts pane to determine which fonts GoLive will use to display text on your pages, much like you would in a browser.

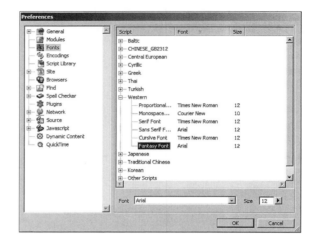

ENCODINGS

The Encodings preference defines which type of encoding will be used and cooperates with the Fonts and the URL Handling preferences. The default is Western, but a new Multilingual option has been added, with three types of Unicode available.

Unless you're developing for a non-Western language, you generally will not need to change this preference. To use a different encoding, your computer will need the proper system resources and fonts for this setting to make any difference.

COLORSYNC

ColorSync is a color management system used by Adobe. Generally, you'll only need to select this if you are developing a high-end graphics site, and you have ColorSync profiles for your images, which is not the case for most Web developers. If you select ColorSync, you can also select Default RGB as the color profile to be used when your image tag does not specify a particular profile.

When you open graphics files created without using ColorSync, other Adobe products such as Photoshop will provide you with the option to convert your colors at that time.

SCRIPT LIBRARY

JavaScripts can be either embedded within the code of a page or referenced in external files. In the Script Library preference pane, you can choose to embed all your scripts into your pages, or else select the name of your Script Library, which contains the scripts that will be available for referencing from your pages. Scripts are not added to your library here; this screen merely decides which folder will house them.

As with many preferences, this is overridden by any site-specific settings changes you make in your Site Settings screen for a site you're working on. The preferences here only affect all new pages and sites not yet created.

SITE PREFERENCES

Site preferences, shown in Figure 6.8, is where you set some overall rules for site file management, such as home page name, file extension and folder location of new items, how to handle deleted files, and several others. It's important to look at this group of preferences carefully before beginning a project because it affects so many areas of your site. These settings only affect new sites. Sites that have already been created retain their current settings.

Reparsing files will cause GoLive to go through and reformat the source code upon the events that you check. Spring-loaded folders, familiar to Macintosh users, are pretty cool: Dragging a document in the Site window over a folder will cause that folder to "spring" open so you can see its contents and drop the document somewhere inside. Most of the other settings on this screen are self-explanatory, but if you have any questions, consult the GoLive documentation. The settings on this screen are not critical, you can change them at any time without affecting your pages.

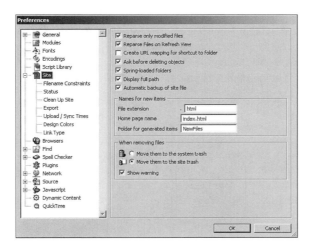

Figure 6.8
Use the Site preferences pane to tell GoLive how you want it to deal with Sites and Site files.

6

Filename Constraints

Adobe GoLive contains several built-in sets of filenaming rules to ensure cross-platform compatibility. When GoLive encounters a filename that violates one of these rules, the Site window and the File Inspector both indicate this for you. The File Inspector even lists the rule itself so that you understand exactly how to correct the naming error. The Filename Constraints preference screen, shown in Figure 6.9, allows you to define these rules.

Figure 6.9
Use Filename Constraints to ensure that GoLive only creates filenames that comply with any special naming convention rules that you may choose to enforce.

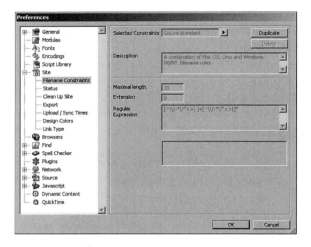

Each constraint consists of a set of rules concerning the length of the name, length of a filename extension, and illegal characters. GoLive provides sets specific to all popular operating systems, and also one called GoLive Standard that's a combination of all of them. You can't go wrong with GoLive Standard. All you really need to do here is ensure that you're enforcing rules to make your filenames compatible with any platform that is likely to be used with your files, including at least your development computer and the machine to be used as the server.

To modify filenaming constraints for all sites, simply choose another constraint set from the Selected Constraints menu and click OK, or click Duplicate to duplicate the currently selected set, edit the set and rename it, and then click OK. Sets that you have created may also be deleted simply by selecting them from the pop-up menu and clicking Delete. (You may not delete the original GoLive constraint sets, however.) See "Filenames" in Chapter 4, "Working with Sites," to learn about setting filename constraints for a particular site.

Status

The Status preference helps you establish a personal color-coding system to group similar files and organize them by priority. Here you can create a new *status*—that is, a new set of criteria by which to label your files—and select a color to represent each new type of file. Later files of similar status can be easily rounded up without having to isolate them inside a separate folder.

Clean Up Site

The Clean Up Site utility (located under the Site menu) keeps track of all the files, colors, font sets, and external references used within a particular site so that you can easily group the essential files together and remove those that are superfluous. This is particularly handy for managing large sites or sites that have undergone multiple updates.

In the Clean Up Site panel, shown in Figure 6.10, you can select precisely what types of files to add or remove when taking advantage of the Clean Up Files utility. You can also request that GoLIve rescan the root folder or show an options dialog box when performing a clean up.

The options in the Add Used section will caused the selected elements to be added into the site folders when a clean up operation happens. By default, all of these are checked, and it's generally a good idea to leave these alone.

The options in the Remove area, however, cause any unused items in your site folder (items that are in your site folder but not actually used on any pages) to be permanently deleted. Use this feature with caution, and only if you know for sure that you don't have valuable items locked away in your site folder that you may potentially want to reuse.

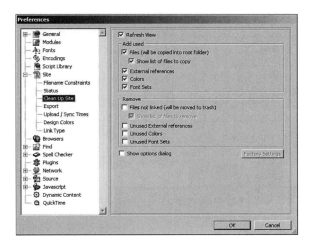

Figure 6.10
The Clean Up Site pane allows you to manage the automatic deletion and cleanup of trashed and unused elements in your site.

Export

In the Export preferences, shown in Figure 6.11, you can provide specific instructions for exporting site files. You can set export conditions, tell GoLive how to arrange the site hierarchy, and instruct GoLive to strip the HTML code under certain conditions.

The choices in the Export Conditions section determine which files will be exported. You can choose only those which are marked to be published, or by unchecking these options, you can export all files and folders whether they're intended to be published or not. You can also choose to export only those files that are within the site, and not externally referenced files.

The Hierarchy section specifies the folder structure that will be created upon exporting your site. The choices are to use the same structure in your GoLive site, flatten everything into a single folder, or separate everything into folders that contain all the media files and all the pages.

The bottom section lets you choose to strip GoLive-specific data from your site. This is up to you; it will not affect the function of the exported site, but it will cause that material to be unavailable if you ever import the newly created site into GoLive.

It's a good practice to leave Show Options Dialog checked, to give yourself a chance to double-check these settings when you perform an export.

6

Figure 6.11
The Export pane gives you control over the way GoLive exports a Site.

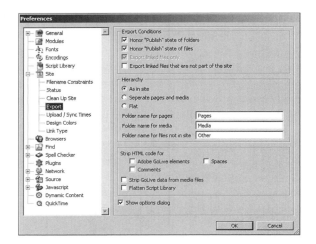

Upload/Sync Times

In the Upload/Sync Times preferences, you provide specific instructions for uploading site files. This is similar to the Export panel in that you can choose to honor the "publish" state of files and folders, send linked files only, and strip HTML code. The difference is that this controls what happens when you sync or upload the site, rather than what happens when you choose the manual Export option.

Design Colors

Just to brighten your spirits, GoLive enables you to select the background colors for all your view panels and panes, items, and links, as shown in Figure 6.12. Choose from Factory Settings (white backgrounds, colored links) and Pastel Settings (a range of pastel-colored backgrounds, dark links) or update either of these by clicking on a color swatch. This invokes the Color Picker, where you can select any color you prefer and click OK to add it as a background color. Whatever colors you choose here will not affect your site itself in any way; the colors simply serve as a quick indication of which view you're in as you switch from one to the next. It also makes site layout a little easier on the eyes.

Link Type

Link Type is another color-coding scheme, this time to help you instantly recognize and categorize the link types on your site when in design mode. You can select new colors for the default link types or even create your own types, as shown in Figure 6.13.

6

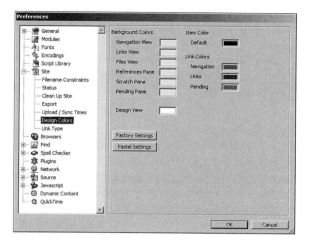

Figure 6.12
The Design Colors pane lets you choose your favorite colors for certain elements in GoLive, including the background colors for many of the palettes.

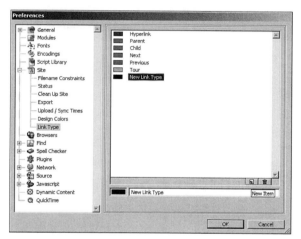

Figure 6.13
The Link Type pane lets you create and manage custom link types for use in the Site Design module.

BROWSERS

Click Find All in the Browsers preference pane to locate all the browsers installed on your computer; then check the boxes for those you want to show up under the Show in Default Browser toolbar menu. You can check multiple browsers to preview your site in a variety of browser situations.

FIND PREFERENCES

Customize your searches by instructing GoLive what to do when a match is found and whether to consider text files when searching in a site. You can choose to have GoLive automatically open the document in which it found the search string, or simply mark it in the Site window but leave the search dialog in front.

Regular Expressions

This preference allows you to define your find expressions, create new expressions or replacements, or return to factory settings if you choose. It's also helpful as a guide to refer to when constructing a search and you need to figure out the right wildcard characters, for example.

SPELL CHECKER

Set your personal dictionary here to check spelling in your documents. Select from American or British spelling standards.

You can also add or remove words to this dictionary using the Add and Delete buttons in the bottom right of the window. This is useful when you use unique terms on your site, such as product names that might not appear in the dictionary.

Regular Expressions

Here you can define your expressions for items such as URLs, email addresses, or other commonly used patterns the spell checker may flag. Defining a term here, such as the URL term that is defined by default, examines the structure of the term, verifies that it is a valid URL, and will not mark it as a spelling error.

Plugins

The Plugins preference screen, shown in Figure 6.14, lets you assign a plug-in to any of the media types listed, and add your own media types. To view media with a plug-in using GoLive, you need to install the plug-in into GoLive's Plugins folder, and then use this screen to find the MIME type for that kind of media, and assign it to the plugin.

If you're unfamiliar with the MIME types needed for a particular plugin, consult the plugin's manufacturer for the correct information.

Figure 6.14
The Plugins pane allows you to properly configure plug-ins to permit GoLive to play back media that require plug-ins.

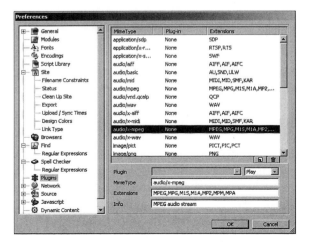

NETWORK PREFERENCES

Save time and hassle by storing network information here. You can choose to import the necessary fields from the Internet Control Panel, or type in specifics for an FTP proxy or HTTP proxy in this panel.

Typically, all the information here is going to be the same as your computer's Internet settings, so it's usually best to just check the Use Always box for Internet Control Panel. Only if you need to access a different Internet gateway for your Web development would you ever need to make any changes here.

Network Status

This Network Status panel gives you the option to track Warnings and Status Messages in addition to the Errors normally tracked to the Network Status window, plus choose the maximum number of items in this status list.

SOURCE PREFERENCES

The Source preferences, shown in Figure 6.15, contain a number of customization options for the viewing of source code, making it easier to read, share, dissect, and troubleshoot. You can check boxes to enable text dragging, set HTML tags in bold, auto-indent and set tab size, and use line numbers or word wrap.

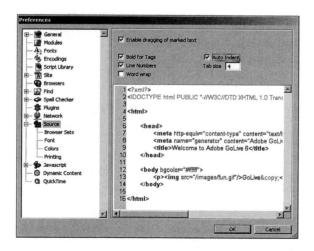

Figure 6.15
The Source pane lets you manage the way GoLive displays HTML source code.

Browser Sets

Because each browser is set up to interpret source code in a slightly different manner, you can choose from various browser sets to check compatibility. Select from a range of Netscape Navigator or Internet Explorer versions or create your own customized combination set, as shown in Figure 6.16.

It's good development practice to make sure that your code works on most, if not nearly all, of the browsers you expect to be used to access your site. You can check your site's server log to find out what the most common browsers all, and then you may want to create a browser set that covers all of those. Develop to that standard, and you can't go wrong.

Figure 6.16
When developing for certain types of browsers, use the Browser Sets pane to define groups of browsers that you can validate your code against.

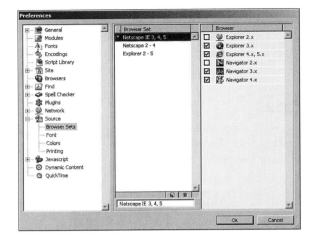

Font

Here you can set the typeface, size, and style of the font used for your source code, and even view a sample of what it will look like onscreen.

Colors

Select colors for the coding of regular text plus links, media, and particular types of tags, as shown in Figure 6.17. This allows you to keep code more organized and troubleshoot at a glance.

Figure 6.17
The Source Code Colors lets you tell GoLive what colors to use in displaying the different types of tags in HTML source code.

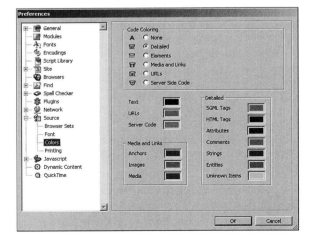

Printing

Because onscreen and printed appearance can differ so greatly, especially if you have a cheesy printer, GoLive allows you to create separate specifications for the printing of code. In Printing preferences, you can check printer-specific settings plus set a font name, size, and style used only for printing.

JAVASCRIPT PREFERENCES

Your JavaScript preferences, shown in Figure 6.18, are set up almost identically to the Source Code preferences, containing various customization options intended to make code easier to read, share, dissect, and troubleshoot. You can check boxes to enable text dragging, use auto-indent and set tab size, and use line numbers or word wrap.

Use the large preview window in this panel to see what your settings look like.

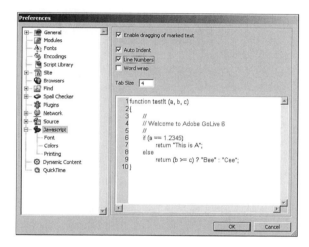

Figure 6.18
The JavaScript pane gives you a place to tell GoLive how to format the text in the JavaScript Editor.

Font

In the Font preferences, you can set the typeface, size, and style of the font used for your source code, and even view a sample of what it will look like onscreen.

Colors

Select colors for the coding of regular text plus links, media, and particular types of tags on the Colors panel, shown in Figure 6.19. This allows you to keep code more organized and troubleshoot at a glance.

Printing

Because online and printed appearance can differ so greatly, GoLive allows you to create separate specifications for the printing of code, just as it does in the Source section above. Code may need to be printed for use in troubleshooting, publication, manual distribution, educational instruction, or any number of other reasons. In the Printing preferences, you can check printer-specific settings plus set a font name, size, and style used only for printing.

Figure 6.19
The JavaScript Colors pane lets you color different types of JavaScript code elements for clarity when using the JavaScript Editor.

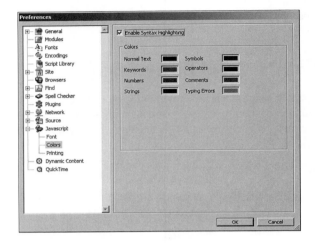

DYNAMIC CONTENT

The Dynamic Content preference allows you to set certain specifications concerning the Web server, including the number of seconds before timing out and how cached responses will be handled.

When developing a Dynamic Content site, you're often the only one using the test server, and consequently it should respond very quickly. You may want to set your HTTP timeout to a low number, like 5 seconds, to avoid wasting time when developing.

The use of cached responses means that the page will not be regenerated when you make a subsequent request with exactly the same URL parameters. For this reason, it's often recommended to use cached responses when offline only, since you generally want to see the actual results of any changes you just made while in online mode.

You can choose how long to keep cached responses. Again, if you're doing live development, you probably don't want to use cached responses at all. But if you do, you may not want to keep those cached for more than a day or so.

QUICKTIME

The QuickTime panel enables you to choose a movie scratch volume plus set up specifics for your layout grid, such as color, style, and distance between gridlines.

A scratch volume is useful to speed up QuickTime development if you have a separate faster drive, as many QuickTime developers often do, or if you're running out of space on your application drive.

The options in the Layout Grid section affect the QuickTime editing window. Using layout grids can assist you with the placement of objects when you're using GoLive's advanced QuickTime development functions to assemble a QuickTime movie from scratch elements.

For those interested in intriguing Easter Egg types of things, here's a cool trick. Because you cannot quit the GoLive application while the Preferences panel remains open, you can go directly to the QuickTime preference from any other preference screen by pressing (Cmd-Q) [Ctrl-Q] within the Preferences window.

TROUBLESHOOTING

Making Your Changes Stick

I've changed the preferences but I don't see any difference.

Try closing and re-opening the document you're working on. You may even need to quit and re-launch GoLive in order to see changes in your preferences. (See the beginning of this chapter for complete details.)

And of course, though it may not be necessary to state the obvious, make sure you click OK when finished adjusting the preferences, and not Cancel. Stranger things have happened.

GOING LIVE

For those of you who prefer your HTML tags in all caps, you may find the choices in GoLive's Source preferences a bit limiting. If using color, bold, or indentation doesn't differentiate the code quite enough for your liking, take advantage of GoLive's 360 degree coding and fix it yourself. Select the entire page in Source layout and copy it to any HTML editor that allows you to change all tags to uppercase. Once the tags have been converted, select all, copy, and paste the new code back into your GoLive document, replacing the original code. Once you re-save the page, your source code will be stored in all caps.

6

7

CUSTOMIZING GOLIVE

IN THIS CHAPTER

A Space of Your Own   112

Examining Your Workflow   112

Customizing the Desktop   113

Using Custom Palettes   114

Setting Keyboard Shortcuts   115

Troubleshooting   116

Going Live   117

A SPACE OF YOUR OWN

Perhaps it's all part of the effort to improve the overall user interface...to keep loyal customers happy and coming back...to create the best possible programs for the creative, by the creative. Perhaps it's how some of the cleverest ideas are developed, as open minds share secrets for setting up the perfect desktop, a better way to work. Whatever the reason, it's clear that Adobe GoLive is all about customization.

By learning early on how you can create a workspace uniquely your own, you'll likely feel more in control and master the application more quickly, boosting your overall productivity by leaps and bounds.

Plus it's fun. This is part of what makes GoLive so enjoyable to use. The sheer versatility means you'll never need to work in a rut. You can build on the system that works for you, and begin to collect and develop pieces that make your job easier and reflect your own experience and insights.

EXAMINING YOUR WORKFLOW

Let's face it: Screen real estate is in high demand. Why waste even one precious pixel on a tool you never use? Your workspace is like an artist's studio or a carpenter's shop, where all your tools can be laid out in a way that suits your particular style of working. This is your space; your palettes should reflect that. Before you can truly customize your space, you need to ask a few questions of yourself. Take a moment to take stock.

Establish Your Role

What do you do? GoLive is an enormous, complex program. It's highly unlikely that any one person uses all the tools it provides. Creating a Web site can prove to be an equally complex challenge, which is why Web teams have grown in popularity. Usually each person contributes his or her unique piece to the whole rather than attempting to master the universe. If you're a programmer, concentrate on that. If you design, that should be your focus. That doesn't mean you can't ever cross over or learn a new skill; it simply means that the tools you use should reflect the work you do. Streamlining your desktop to concentrate on the job at hand enables you to work much more efficiently. Remember: Work smarter, not harder.

Trace Your Steps

What tasks do you regularly perform? Let's say you're purely a designer. You know you should focus on the graphical layout and can ignore those issues concerning the source code. Now take this idea one step further, and examine which activities absorb most of your time during the page creation process. Use your imagination to follow yourself through a typical day, noting which aspects of the site you worked on and which tools you used along the way. You might even want to keep an actual record of all the steps you took in the course of bringing a site to life. Look back at the History Palette to see which actions you've taken repeatedly. It's easy to get so engrossed in your work that you can't accurately recall everything you've done in a day, but make an attempt to start paying attention. It can only help you in the long run. Familiarizing yourself with your own habits is the first step in arranging the palettes, setting the preferences, and creating workspaces.

Beat the Clock

Once you've given some thought to exactly which aspects of GoLive hold the most value for you, and which tasks you need to accomplish, examine the creation process again, this time as a chrono-logical conundrum. When you begin a new project, what's the first thing you do? What comes next? Are you working strictly on a single project, or on several different projects at once? How is your time divided? The goal of this exercise is to figure out your natural workflow. Perhaps certain tasks may be combined, saving time by multitasking or eliminating unproductive gaps, or possibly you should specialize even further instead and give a task your undivided attention to do it more effi-ciently. Only you can answer these questions.

By following this line of questioning and examining your own work habits, you become better equipped to make decisions about how your GoLive workspace could be laid out most suitably. This kind of self-assessment is absolutely necessary before effective customization can begin.

CUSTOMIZING THE DESKTOP

Now that you've ascertained which palettes you use regularly, in what order and in what combina-tion, designing a palette scheme that's ideal for you should be a breeze. First, gather those palettes you find indispensable, and close the rest. These are your tools.

To access a palette that is not visible, select the name of the palette from the Window menu, or use the appropriate keyboard shortcut. Items in the Window menu are grouped according to which palettes are normally grouped together in a window (for example, Objects and Color share a win-dow). If you select a palette whose window is already on your desktop, it will approach the forefront and the proper tab will be selected for you. This is particularly helpful when windows overlap.

With the proper collection of tools laid out in front of you, you're ready to arrange them into a cus-tom placement that works for you. Like any window, you can resize them by dragging the lower-right corner, or roll them up like a window shade by double-clicking on the top bar. Determine the best sizes for each and whether all windows should remain open, or whether some should roll up temporarily. Next, try to combine palettes in ways that complement your designated workflow. You can do this in two ways: by grouping palette windows and docking them, or by dragging tabs from one window to another. Pull palettes nearer to each other by dragging their edges, and they auto-matically align vertically or horizontally and click together to form a panel of palettes. This is called *docking*. To pull tabs, simply click on the tab of any palette and drag it to the desired location. You can place a palette alone or drag it on top of another palette to combine them. In time, with a bit of trial and error, you'll soon establish a combination of windows and tabs that works best for you.

Once you've set up your workspace exactly as you like it, remember to save it for later use. You may even opt to save multiple workspaces for use with distinct tasks.

7

To save a new workspace, follow these steps:

1. Select Window, Workspace, Save Workspace to open the Save Workspace dialog box, seen in Figure 7.1.

2. To create a brand new set, name this workspace and click OK. To edit an existing one, select it here from the list and click OK.

Figure 7.1
Save Workspaces on this screen to store a particular customization.

To manage workspaces, these steps are needed:

1. Select Window, Workspace, Manage Workspaces to open the Manage Workspaces dialog box, as you can see in Figure 7.2.

2. Select a workspace from the list and click OK.

Figure 7.2
All the customized workspaces you have saved are accessible here on the Manage Workspaces screen.

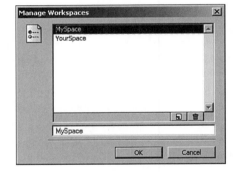

USING CUSTOM PALETTES

Some palettes contain more specific customizing features within them as well, and you should take advantage of these where applicable. Our favorites include the Color Palette and the Objects Palettes.

Custom Color Palette

One of the many options in the Color Palette is the capability to create your own Custom Palette. To do this, select the submenu on the Color tab, and then choose Custom Palette, as shown in Figure 7.3. A blank palette appears, ready for you to fill with your own favorite colors. Do this by switching back and forth between this palette and others, selecting colors in the established palettes (or mixing your own!), and then dragging each color into place on the Custom Palette. There are places to hold 36 hand-selected colors.

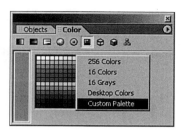

Figure 7.3
When you choose a Custom Color Palette, you can drag in all your favorite colors, or just the colors you've defined for a particular site.

Custom Objects Palettes

Several of the tabs within the Objects Palette allow for the storage of custom objects, which can be accessed by other pages, even other sites, for later use. Thus, you can create an object once and use it a multitude of times, saving you time and headaches in the long run, and ensuring site consistency. Figure 7.4 demonstrates the library effect of a customized objects palette.

For more details on using the Library and Site Extras tabs, **see** *Chapter 17, "Styles and Stationery."*

Figure 7.4
This view of the Library, a Custom Objects Palette, shows a couple snippets of text and HTML and a graphic. Drag stuff in here for convenient repeated access.

SETTING KEYBOARD SHORTCUTS

Having trouble remembering all those crazy keyboard shortcuts? Now you don't have to. Do away with all the guesswork and memorization and just create your own! Once you get started with this customizing tool, you'll agree it's one of the coolest critters around.

Follow these steps to create a new keyboard shortcut:

1. Select Edit, Keyboard Shortcuts or press (Shift-Option-Cmd-K) [Shift+Alt+Ctrl+K] to open the shortcuts window. Here you can store multiple sets of shortcuts, so you can create your own and still retain the GoLive factory defaults, or store multiple sets for use in different circumstances.

2. Click on New Set.

3. Name the new set. When you click New Set, a dialog box pops up allowing you to type a name for your new set of shortcuts. Then it actually copies the shortcuts from whatever set you specify, and enables you to edit the copy.

4. Click OK.

7

5. With the copy set active, begin to make your changes. Open each menu by clicking on the arrow to expand it and view its contents, as you can see in Figure 7.5.

Figure 7.5
Set Custom Keyboard Shortcuts
on this screen.

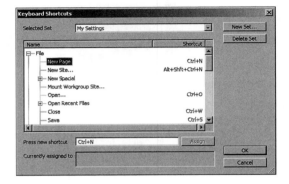

6. Select an item you'd like to update. When its current shortcut appears in the line below, delete it and press the key combination that you want to replace it with. Click Assign (or Replace, if it was previously assigned) to make it official.

Keep in mind that as you press potential new key combinations, the dialog lets you know if this shortcut has already been assigned elsewhere. You can then choose to create a different shortcut or override the original and assign your new one anyway. You can change the original item's shortcut to something else as well. Continue this way down the list until you've reassigned all the shortcuts you wish to change. The new shortcuts appear instantly beside the appropriate menu items.

TROUBLESHOOTING

Restoring the Desktop to Its Default

Once my desktop has been customized, how can I reset it to the way it was originally?

From the Window menu, choose Workspace, Default Workspace, and GoLive will restore itself to its own factory settings.

Using a Keyboard Shortcut That's Already Taken

The keyboard shortcut I want to use for a particular function says it's currently assigned to something else. What can I do?

Locate the function to which your desired shortcut has already been assigned, and either create a new shortcut, or delete the shortcut for this function. This frees up that keystroke combination to be used for the function you wanted.

GOING LIVE

Use the Custom Color Palette option to store all your colors for a particular Site. This way you can keep track of all background and text colors, plus note the colors used in logos and other graphics, making your Site easier to maintain over time.

Use the Custom Objects Palette in the same way, placing reusable components here for easy access throughout the Site. Storing items here within the application keeps you from having to search all over tarnation for the pieces you need to use.

Then store these settings in a custom workspace, and if you ever need to work on the same Site again, all the original tools will be right there and everything will be optimized for your project.

7

SETTING UP PAGES

IN THIS PART

8 Creating and Saving Pages   **121**

9 Working with Code   **139**

8

CREATING AND SAVING PAGES

IN THIS CHAPTER

Creating a New Page   122

Reusing Pages   124

Choosing the Dimensions of Your Page   125

Page Margins   127

Using the Grid   128

Layout Rulers   131

Selecting Page Colors   132

Background Images   133

Saving Pages   134

Troubleshooting   137

Going Live   137

CREATING A NEW PAGE

Visual thinkers everywhere appreciate the way Adobe GoLive makes page layout for the Web as simple and straightforward as assembling a page for print. Those accustomed to using programs such as Adobe PageMaker or QuarkXpress will find the same familiar tools and standards here, making the transition to online design even easier. Those without a design background can still see the benefits of GoLive's user-friendly layout interface, where tools like the ruler and the grid offer precision and help you set up your pages exactly as they appear in your mind's eye.

In this chapter, we'll be discussing the nuts and bolts of creating a new page. Even before you add content such as text or graphics, you should understand your options in terms of the page itself. Much like their cousins in print, Web pages can vary in size, color, and other attributes. Thus GoLive gives designers freedom of control over the dimensions and specifics of each page.

At this point, we'll assume that you already understand the basics of GoLive well enough to create a new Site and maneuver your way through the interface. The Page Window, Inspector, and various palettes should all be familiar to you. If at any time you need to review these aspects of the application, see Chapters 3 and 4 to learn more about Site building or Chapter 5 to investigate the interface elements.

We strongly recommend that you begin by creating the Site before constructing the individual pages, and always create and open your pages from within the Site Window. That way, your pages are readily established as part of a Site. Links and updates are easily managed, saving changes is a breeze, and your files stay organized. See Chapters 3 and 4 for more specifics.

To open an existing local page

1. Open the appropriate Site Window. This window lists all the documents indexed within the .site file.

2. Select the Files tab, located on the left side of the Site Window, if both sides are open.

3. Locate the page file you want, and open it as you would any file, either by double-clicking its listing in the Site Window or by clicking the Open icon in the Site Toolbar.

If the page is one you've opened recently, you could also retrieve it by choosing File, Open Recent Files and selecting the page from the list. The Recent Files list shows the most recent sites you've had open at the top, followed by all the individual pages you've recently worked on.

To open a page via the Workgroup Server, choose File, Mount Workgroup Site to initiate logon. See Chapter 30 for more information about the Workgroup Server.

To create a new blank page, select File, New Page or press (Cmd-N) [Ctrl+N] on your keyboard. The new page will not be connected to any site until you name and save it as such. See "Saving Pages" later in this chapter for more information.

You also have several New Page options under File, New Special. Here is a brief description of each possibility:

- **New Page From Template**. Allows you to choose from available templates and create a new page based on one of these. If no templates yet exist, this option is grayed out and cannot be used. See "Reusing Pages" later in this chapter for more details.

- **New Page From Stationery**. Allows you to choose from available stationery and create a new page based on one of these. If no stationery yet exists, this option is grayed out and cannot be used. See "Reusing Pages" later in this chapter for more details.

- **HTML Page**. Creates a new blank page written in HTML. The default code for a new page is HTML, and the only difference in the code between creating a New Page and selecting the HTML option here is that the HTML Page includes an extra comment line to introduce the document type. The document type, specified by the DocType tag, defines what specification of code the document conforms to for example, HTML 3.0, HTML 4.0, XHTML Basic 1.0, any flavor of XML, and so on. DocType is listed as HTML 4.01 Transitional by default. Read more about all your source code options in Chapter 9, "Working with Code."

- **XHTML Page**. Creates a new blank page written in XHTML. DocType is listed as XHTML 1.0 Transitional.

- **XHTML-Basic Page**. Creates a new blank page written in XHTML. DocType is listed as XHTML Basic 1.0.

- **WML Deck**. Creates a new blank page written in WML. Layout is designed specifically for WML, not for a graphical layout, so the page bears a slightly different appearance. DocType is listed as WML 1.3.

- **Generic XML Document**. Creates a new blank page written in XML. Again, this page is not intended for graphical layout, and appears different than the normal page window. See Chapter 9, "Working with Code," for more details.

- **Cascading Style Sheet**. Opens the window enabling you to create a new style sheet. See Chapter 17, "Styles," for more details on using Style Sheets.

- **QuickTime Movie**. Opens the QuickTime Editor, allowing you to create a new QuickTime Movie. See Chapter 21, "Smart Objects," for more details.

- **SMIL Document**. Creates a SMIL Document (Synchronized Multimedia Integration Language).

- **Text Document**. Creates a new blank text document. This is handy for keeping notes or comments to yourself as you create, or for copying and storing text without leaving it on the clipboard or opening third-party software.

- **Java Script**. Opens the JavaScript Editor. See Chapter 19 for more details.

- **Perl Script**. Opens the Perl Script Editor. See Chapter 19 for more details.

REUSING PAGES

8

Creating Stationery and other reusable elements not only maintains a consistent, professional appearance throughout your Site; it also saves you time and eases your workload. Think of this as a great way to work smarter, not harder. With your model pages prepped and ready, it's a snap to create more pages in their image.

To create a new page from a Template, follow these steps:

1. With your Site Window open, select File, New Special, Page from Template, as shown in Figure 8.1.

2. From the list of Template pages, select the one you'd like to use. Click Show Preview if you need help remembering what each page looks like. When you've made your selection, click OK.

3. A dialog box asks if you'd like to modify the Template page or create a new page. Click Create to begin a new page.

4. Rename and save the new page in the Root Folder of your Site.

Figure 8.1
Select Page from Template from the New Special menu to bring up the list of templates to use to start your new page.

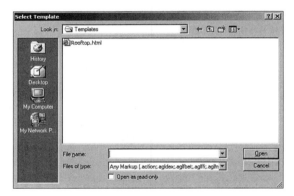

To create a new page from Stationery, follow these steps:

1. With your Site Window open, select File, New Special, Page from Stationery, as shown in Figure 8.2.

2. From the list of Stationery pages, select the one you'd like to use. Click Show Preview if you need help remembering what each page looks like. When you've made your selection, click OK.

3. A dialog box asks whether you'd like to modify the Stationery page or create a new page. Click Create to begin a new page.

4. Rename and save the new page in the Root Folder of your Site.

Figure 8.2

Select Page from Stationery from the New Special menu to bring up the list of templates to use to start your new page.

CHOOSING THE DIMENSIONS OF YOUR PAGE

Whatever method you choose, whether you create a brand-new page or open an existing one, you should arrive at a Page Window approximating the one shown in Figure 8.3. This is the default index page created by GoLive. See Chapter 5 for complete details on all the icons, toggles, and available options within this window. For now we'll concentrate on setting up the basic dimensions of our page.

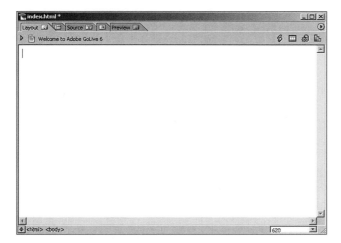

Figure 8.3

Here is a new blank page shown in the Page Window.

The Window Size pop-up menu, located in the lower-right corner of your Page Window, lets you to automatically adjust the width of your page to fit certain standard browser window sizes.

If this menu is not currently visible, click on the circled arrow in the upper-right corner to reveal a cascading menu that controls what you see in the status bar. Select Status Bar, Window Size Popup to make it appear. (Everything is visible by default, so you should only need to adjust this if working with a previously opened page where items have been deliberately hidden.)

The default window size for GoLive is 620, which means it measures 620 pixels wide, or about standard for a monitor set to 640×480. Other choices in the menu include 100, 200, 520, 580, and 780 (for monitors set to 800×600). If you have the screen space, it's wise to also make sure your pages look good at the higher resolutions.

You should also remember that in today's shifting Internet market, this list is by no means complete when considering all possible viewing options. As the cost of monitors drops, larger screens are becoming more and more popular on desktops, and it is not uncommon for users to set higher screen resolutions of 1600×1200 or even higher. At the same time, the shift toward mobile access has led to a number of smaller window options, including those on cellular phones and palm pilots, which is why the 100- and 200-pixel options appear on the list. Because of the wide range of width possibilities, GoLive allows you to customize your standard screen setting.

Follow these steps to choose a new default window size:

These window sizes only set the dimensions of the Page Window to assist you in making design choices that look good in a browser window set to that size. The actual page size viewed by the user is determined by whatever size they scale their browser window to. Use other tools such as Page Margins, the Layout Grid, Tables, or Cascading Style Sheets to more accurately establish your page dimensions and position elements precisely.

1. Drag your Page Window to the desired size using the lower-right corner. The current width will always display in the Window Size Menu.

2. From the Window Size Menu, choose Settings. The Window Settings box appears, as seen in Figure 8.4. Click OK to select the dimensions of your frontmost window as the new default window size. (Click Use Default Settings here to return to the original default.)

3. Create a New Page by choosing File, New Page or New Special, or pressing (Cmd-N) [Ctrl+N] on your keyboard. The new page will have identical dimensions—height as well as width—to the page used to create your new setting. This allows for efficient page layout when creating multiple pages for unusual window sizes.

Figure 8.4
Use the Window Settings screen to make your current settings the default.

There is no menu that limits the length of a page, because the width makes much more of an impact on how a page appears, and normally a page would simply scroll until it reached the end of its content. You can set the height with the same methods used to determine page width.

PAGE MARGINS

As noted earlier, setting a Window Size does not determine the actual size of your page, but Page Margins do influence page appearance directly. By default, your page begins about 6–8 pixels from the top and left edges of a browser, allowing sufficient space for it to be seen clearly without the content getting lost in the browser controls.

While intended to help the appearance of your page, sometimes this built-in space is unnecessary or problematic, and you may wish to eliminate it by setting your page margins to zero. Many pages have graphics that bleed all the way to the edge of the screen, and it's situations like this that require zero page margins.

To set page margins to zero

1. Place your cursor anywhere in the Page Window and Ctrl-click (Mac) or right-click (Windows) to open a helpful quick-editing menu, as shown in Figure 8.5.

2. Select Document, Set Margins to Zero. Instantly your Page Inspector reflects the change and your default margins vanish.

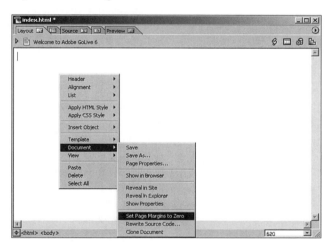

Figure 8.5
Right-clicking inside the Page Window is a fast way to set the page margins to zero.

If instead, you'd like to select a different size for your page margins, this is just as easy to do.

To set new page margins, place your cursor anywhere in the Page Window and Ctrl-click (Mac) or right-click (Windows) to open a helpful quick-editing menu. Select Document, Page Properties. Alternatively, you can click on the Page Properties icon in the upper-left corner of the Page Window. It looks like a single page next to the page title.

Either of these options opens the Page Inspector. Enter new numbers in the spaces provided for Margin Width and Height and press Enter/Return after each to make it so. Insert zero for each to remove the margin completely. Remember, Width sets the distance from the browser to the left edge of your page, and Height sets the distance from the browser to the top edge of your page. Figure 8.6 shows a page in a browser with margins that have been set to create a certain amount of blank space around the edges of the page content.

Figure 8.6
This page, viewed in a browser, shows what page margins look like.

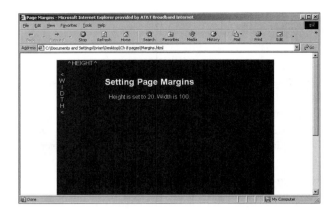

USING THE GRID

Now that you understand how your page appears in relation to the browser, let's concentrate on setting up the page itself. One of the aspects of GoLive that distinguished it from the competition early on was the presence of the Layout Grid. The grid creates an instant table, then within this table uses x and y coordinates to pinpoint the placement of each element for accurate WYSIWYG design.

Since objects adhere to the gridlines, and you can adjust the size of your grid squares, it makes layout a snap. The grid helps you align objects, and enables you to move selections using the arrow keys, even nudge them in small increments to ensure precision. It gives you the freedom to use placeholders. It allows you to move text in blocks and adjust the margins of a text box easily.

Although technically an object itself, contained as an item in the Objects palette and dragged into position on the page, the Grid serves as a map for all the other objects placed on top of it. It is by no means required on the page, but like a good map, it makes exploring new terrain so much easier that it seems indispensable. Furthermore, its identity as an object lends it extra flexibility: The Grid can be colored separately from the background. It can contain a distinct background image. It can be aligned to the page. It can be resized. It can be removed. It can co-exist on a page with multiple grids. A grid can be placed within any cell of a table. It can be copied and pasted, taking the contents with it. All in all, a pretty remarkable tool, the grid. Let's take a closer look.

Placing a Grid

To place a grid on your page, double-click (Mac) or right-click (Windows) on the Layout Grid icon in the Objects Palette. Alternatively, you could click and drag the icon into position. The first grid placed on a new page will automatically align itself to the top-left corner. Additional grids will align to the left side of the page, below existing grids. You may place a grid on the page itself or within the cell of a table.

Sizing a Grid

By default, the grid begins as a square about 200×200 pixels (actually 201). You can easily resize it by dragging on the selection handles along the sides. Hold down the Shift key while dragging the lower-right corner to maintain the even proportions of a perfect square. You can also indicate a precise pixel height and width in the spaces provided in the Layout Grid Inspector (see Figure 8.7). Simply select the grid, type the desired dimensions and press Enter/Return after each to make it so.

When you lay your page out on a single grid, the size of that grid is essentially the size of your page, since text and images adhere to those boundaries. Thus you should consider carefully when determining grid size.

Figure 8.7
Use the Inspector to set the basic properties of a layout grid.

Optimizing a Grid

Beside the width and height indicators in the Layout Grid Inspector is a button called Optimize. This function calculates the smallest size the grid can be, considering the elements you've placed upon it, and automatically reduces the grid to those dimensions. This is particularly useful for keeping your file sizes lean, allowing pages to load more quickly in the browser. This may also help you to determine the best page size to use.

Resizing Grid Squares

In addition to selecting the dimensions of the entire grid, you can also choose the size of the squares that comprise the grid. By default each measures 16 pixels square, but you can insert any value from 2 to 20,000 in the horizontal and vertical fields. The values need not even be identical for both, so your grid squares could be rectangles. Press Enter or Return and the grid adjusts automatically according to the values you've chosen. Since you can use your arrow keys to move objects one grid square at a time, larger squares would be beneficial for moving things great distances, whereas smaller squares would assist you in nudging items where precision was key. You might also choose a good incremental grid size, such as 10 or 25, to help measure your page in place of the Ruler. The choice is completely up to you.

Snap and Visibility

Other qualities you can apply to the Layout Grid include Snap and Visibility. Snap makes items "stick" to the lines of the grid, to assist in exact placement. Visibility determines whether you can see the grid

8

lines at all. You can control each of these attributes separately for the horizontal and vertical lines, and easily toggle them on and off using the check boxes in the Inspector.

Aligning the Grid

The Alignment menu in the Layout Grid Inspector refers to the grid's alignment to the page, and therefore to the browser. By default it begins with a left alignment, but you can also choose center or right. When using multiple grids on a page, each operates completely independently and can have its own alignment assigned.

Adding a Background Color

Choosing a background color for the grid is just as simple as selecting one for the page. By default the grid appears the same color as the page background, as if it were transparent, but in truth you can assign a unique color to each.

Follow these steps to select a background color:

1. Select the grid.

2. In the Layout Grid Inspector, click on the Color swatch to highlight it. This color will appear as a selected color in the Color Palette (white if no color previously selected).

3. Choose the color you'd prefer. The new color appears in the swatch of the Color Palette, replaces the color of the swatch selected in the Layout Grid Inspector, and becomes the new background color of your grid.

Optionally you can

- Drag a color from the Color Palette to an unselected swatch in the Grid Inspector to also change the color.

- Turn the background color off temporarily but keep it stored as a swatch by unchecking the Color checkbox.

Adding a Background Image

As with a page, you can also choose a background image for your grid. Images smaller than the size of the grid will repeat and wrap, thus you can achieve the same effects as with the background of a page. Remember that a background image will cover any background color you've selected.

To place a background image on your grid

1. In the Grid Inspector, check the Background Image box.

2. Connect to the appropriate image file by using Point and Shoot, typing the filename and path into the space, browsing your system until you find it, or selecting from recently used files in the inspector menu. The image appears instantly within the grid.

Using Multiple Grids

Because the layout grid is an object, you can design a page using more than one grid on the same page. Simply place each as you would a single grid.

To place a grid, double-click (Mac) or right-click (Windows) on the Layout Grid icon in the Objects Palette. Alternatively, you could click and drag the icon into position. The first grid placed on a new page will automatically align itself to the top-left corner. Additional grids will align to the left side of the page, below existing grids. You may place a grid on the page itself of within the cell of a table, creating a nested table.

Placing a Grid Within a Table

Since the layout grid actually creates a table within the source code, it is possible to place a grid inside the cell of another table, effectively creating nested tables. To do this, place your cursor within the table cell and double-click (Mac) or right-click (Windows) on the Layout Grid icon in the Objects Palette. If you prefer, you could instead click and drag the Grid icon to the proper table cell and release it when the cell was highlighted.

Copying a Grid

As with any object, you may copy and paste a grid. First click on the grid to select it. Then choose Edit, Copy from the menu or use keyboard shortcuts (Cmd-C) [Ctrl+C] to copy, and (Cmd-V) [Ctrl+V] to paste in a new location. Whatever objects have been placed on the grid will automatically come along for the ride, so you could effectively transfer large chunks of a page to another location this way.

LAYOUT RULERS

One option that seems to have strangely disappeared in this version of GoLive is the Ruler icon, which used to reside in the top-right corner of the Page Window. In truth, the Ruler hasn't really gone away. Choose View, Show Rulers or use the keyboard shortcut (Cmd-R) [Ctrl+R] to make it appear instantly, and you'll see the rulers shown in Figure 8.8. Do the same to Hide Rulers if you prefer.

Marked in pixels, the Layout Rulers help you ascertain correct sizes and distances for the objects on your page. When an object is selected, the rulers highlight in white the area taken by that object. For example, Figure 8.8 shows the rulers measuring a grid.

Rulers serve as guidelines when positioning items, increase the level of precision, and can help communicate placement decisions within a group to keep your site looking organized and consistent.

8

Figure 8.8
The Layout Rulers in action.

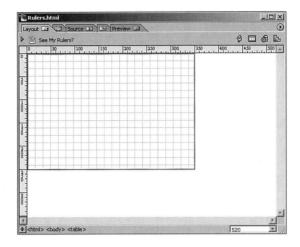

SELECTING PAGE COLORS

Click on the Page icon in the top left to display the Page Inspector. Here you can pick the colors for your page background, default text, and links.

First, notice the four color swatches labeled Text, Link, Active Link, and Visited Link. These correspond to color definitions set in the <body> code early in your document. Text refers to any non-linked text. Link specifies the color of an unclicked link. Active Link (or alink) refers to the color of a link as it's being clicked. Visited Link (or vlink) corresponds to the color of a link after it's been visited.

By default all four are unchecked, but you can check the boxes here to activate them and make your color selections. While you can still change the color of text for individual circumstances, these settings will determine the default colors when no other color is specified.

To select text and link colors, follow these steps:

1. In the Page Inspector, check the box next to the text or link you'd like to activate.

2. Click on the color swatch to highlight it. This color will appear as a selected color in the Color Palette.

3. Choose the color you'd prefer. The new color appears in the swatch of the Color Palette and replaces the color highlighted in the Page Inspector.

Optionally you can drag a color from the Color Palette to an unselected swatch in the Page Inspector will also change the color.

In the bottom of the Inspector, you'll see your options for background color and background image. By default, a GoLive page begins with a white background in most cases, but you can change the color of the background as easily as you choose text and link colors. Bear in mind that a background image, if selected, will cover the background color. Also remember that the layout grid may contain its own background color, which will lie on top of the background for the page.

To select a background color, follow these steps:

1. In the Page Inspector, check the background color box.

2. Click on the color swatch to highlight it. This color will appear as a selected color in the Color Palette.

3. Choose the color you'd prefer. The new color appears in the swatch of the Color Palette and replaces the color selected in the Page Inspector..

BACKGROUND IMAGES

Sometimes you'd rather use an image instead of a single color for your background. Since graphics smaller than the browser window automatically wrap and repeat, you can use relatively small images to create some impressive effects. Many backgrounds are available for use online, either for free or for sale, and the best ones create a pattern that repeats flawlessly, without a noticeable interruption at the edges of the graphic.

When creating your own background image, the most common formats are a 100×100 square (which will repeat across and down) or a wide horizontal strip (which will repeat vertically). When creating a strip, always remember to make it wider than you think you'll need it, to avoid unusual wrapping patterns in larger browser windows. With the horizontal strip, you can create the illusion of multiple frames or page sections by creating color columns in your background. While it's also possible to use a vertical strip in the same manner, it's difficult to anticipate the length of a page, so these are rarely used.

You may also place a large, non-repeating background on your page. Often the file size of such an image makes it impractical, but using a low-resolution or two-color image in a logo or simple graphic can sometimes create a nice touch. Simply create your image large enough to fill an entire browser window. Technically, it will repeat if the window expands far enough; the trick is to make it large enough that this will not happen.

Bear in mind that background image and background color are mutually exclusive settings. That is, if you've selected a background color, it will be covered up by the background image if you select one.

Placing a background image means merely linking to a file. Just tell GoLive which image you'd like to use as a background.

To place a background image, follow these steps:

1. In the Page Inspector, check the Background Image box.

2. Connect to the appropriate image file by using Point and Shoot, typing the filename and path into the space, browsing your system until you find it, or selecting from recently used files in the inspector menu.

8

Figure 8.9
If you've created a folder for your images, it's a snap to manage them all using the Site Window. Here everything resides in a folder called, cleverly enough, Images.

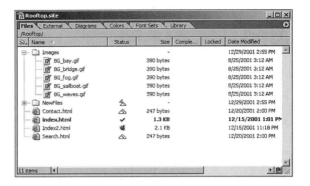

SAVING PAGES

To keep things simple, always create and open your pages from within the Site Window. This establishes the pages as part of the Site, and ensures that they will always be saved in the proper spot. It also allows you to save changes in a single step: Just select File, Save or press the keyboard shortcut (Cmd-S) [Ctrl+S] to re-save the page. See Figure 8.10.

If you create a page using the File, New command, you will need to take a few additional steps when saving it so that GoLive can acknowledge the page as part of your Site. First, select File, Save or press (Cmd-S) [Ctrl+S] on your keyboard to open the Save dialog box. Type a name for your page, then browse to select where to save the page. If your Site Window is open, a special pop-up menu appears to assist you. Select the Root Folder, and click Save to make it part of your Site. Without the Site Window open, you'll have to navigate to the Root Folder of your Site using the regular Save method of your machine.

Ideally, all of your Site images would be gathered and placed in one location, such as a folder called Images inside your Site folder (see Figure 8.9). This makes connecting to the necessary files much easier, and keeps all the necessary elements neatly organized. You may even wish to subdivide your image folder with creative naming techniques.

Figure 8.10
When saving a page in your site, the pop-up menu at the bottom gives quick access to the folders within your site.

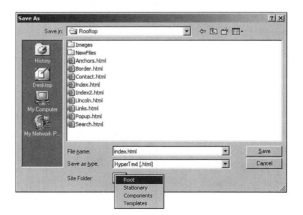

Saving a Page as a Template

A template page is a single page established as the default for every new page created in GoLive. Since only one page can be selected to act as a template, it should be very basic rather than Site-specific. If you prefer, you could simply change the template with each Site you work on. Creating a new template is easy.

Follow these steps to set a new template

1. From the menu choose Edit, Preferences, or press (Cmd-K) [Ctrl+K] to open your GoLive Preferences.

2. Select General, and then click the New Document checkbox.

3. Browse until you locate the page you'd like to use as your template. See Figure 8.11.

4. Click OK. The next time you create a new page, it will look like your template.

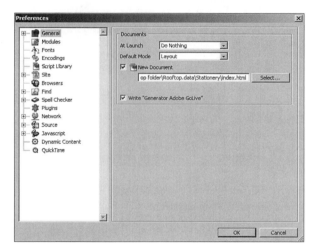

Figure 8.11
Use the General Preferences to define an existing page as the default template.

Saving a Page as Stationery

Because so many elements will be repeated on every page of your Site, it makes sense to create a Stationery template to use as the starting point for creating additional pages. A Stationery page gets stored with a particular Site, and is only available within that Site. However, you can create multiple Stationery pages for a Site, and even copy them easily between Sites. This grants you more flexibility than a template page, which must be applied to all Sites within GoLive.

You can save a page as Stationery at any point, either during the initial save or later in the development of the page. Any existing page can become a Stationery template.

When you save a page as Stationery, it gets stored in the Stationery folder within your Site's data folder, making it available for reuse. Thus one way to create a Stationery page is simply to drag a page into the Stationery folder.

Follow these steps to create a Stationery page by dragging:

1. Open the Site Window completely by clicking on the double-arrow in the lower-right corner.

2. In the left side of the Site Window, click the Files tab to bring it forward, and locate the page you wish to use as Stationery.

3. In the right side of the Site Window, click the Extras tab to bring it forward, and locate the Stationery folder.

4. Select the desired page in the left side and drag it into the Stationery folder on the right. See Figure 8.12.

Optionally you can create a copy of the page as you drag and leave the original in your Site files: Hold down the (Option) or [Ctrl] key while dragging.

Figure 8.12
In the Site Window, drag a file into the Stationery folder to make it available as Stationery.

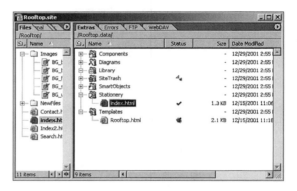

You may also create a Stationery page during the regular Save process.

Follow these steps to save a new, unsaved Page as Stationery:

1. With your Site Window open, choose File, Save, or press (Cmd-S) [Ctrl+S] on your keyboard to open the Save dialog box.

2. Type a name for your page.

3. From the Site folder pop-up menu, select Stationery as your destination folder.

4. Click Save or press Enter/Return to make it so.

The new page is now saved as a Stationery template. To save a copy as a regular page, you'll need to save it again in the root folder.

To save an existing page as Stationery, follow these steps:

1. With the Site Window and existing page open, choose File, Save As or press (Shift-Cmd-S) [Shift+Ctrl+S] to open the Save dialog box. See Figure 8.13.

2. Type a new name for your page, if desired, or keep the existing name.

3. From the Site folder popup menu, select Stationery as your destination folder.

4. Click Save or press Enter/Return to make it so.

This saves a copy of the page as Stationery, leaving the original untouched.

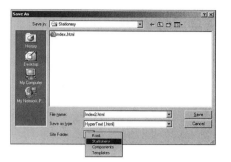

Figure 8.13
The normal Save As command can also be used to make Stationery out of a page you've created.

TROUBLESHOOTING

Forcing Changed Defaults to Take Effect

I've changed the default window size, but my new page still opens in the old dimensions.

Any adjustments to the default window size only take effect after you've quit and re-launched GoLive.

Setting a Grid Flush to the Left Margin

My page margins are set to zero, but there's still some extra room to the left of my grid. What gives?

Click on the grid to select it, and take a look at the Grid Inspector. Your alignment must be set to Default in order to press the grid flush against the side of the browser. Left alignment for some reason leaves a small gap.

GOING LIVE

To save time and avoid a multitude of hassles and complications, take advantage of the Open Recent Files option as often as possible. When you first open a page, do so correctly by opening the Site that contains it. Then each subsequent time you open that file, simply select File, Open Recent Files, and choose either the Site or the specific page you need. Apart from being speedy, this practice also ensures that you are updating the correct Site each time, and storing all relevant files

8

within that Site folder. Because GoLive keeps adding to this pull-down menu as you open files, this list can also be a handy tool for keeping track of which pages you've recently updated, where you left off in a project, or what pages another team member was working on.

9

WORKING WITH CODE

IN THIS CHAPTER

Breaking the Code   **140**

Source Editor   **140**

Using the Source Split View   **143**

Source Code Palette   **144**

Markup Tree   **145**

Outline Editor   **145**

Highlight Palette   **149**

HTML Element Find and Replace   **150**

Adding Head Tags and Scripts   **151**

Generating XHTML Code   **153**

Troubleshooting   **154**

Going Live   **155**

BREAKING THE CODE

Although Adobe GoLive initially impressed its users with the ability to create Web pages in a purely graphic format, without requiring prior knowledge of HTML, its custom coding techniques have continued to evolve, attracting an even wider audience. Even as HTML and scripting have grown more sophisticated, and Web programming has expanded to include a greater range of methods and languages, so GoLive has adapted to meet the needs of more tech-savvy users. By the same token, it has also developed ways to make coding simpler for users at any level.

In this chapter, we'll go behind the scenes and cover the coding essentials of the application. We'll introduce the features that go straight to the source, and show you how to use them to the best of your individual abilities.

Fact is, no matter how fancy the interface, any Web page you create is driven by code. Even those who don't consider themselves coders can see clear advantages in knowing what's under the hood. The better you understand the engine, the better luck you'll have in troubleshooting and tweaking your page, should the need arise. For visual thinkers, GoLive provides a range of tools that help bridge the gap between creative and technical, allowing you to master the markup language in your own style, at your own pace.

For hardcore programmers, new tools mean you now have more options, more control, and ultimately more power than ever before. The improvements in GoLive 6.0 enable you to do what you do best…even better.

SOURCE EDITOR

Just as GoLive enables you to lay out pages graphically using the Layout Editor, it also offers you the option to create pages by manually writing the code using the Source Code Editor. Click the Source tab in your Page Window to view the page in its full coded glory.

Remember that code here is treated just like text: You can select, cut, copy, and paste it just as you would in a word processing document. The color and style of the text in the source code editor is controlled by the settings in the preferences, so don't try to change these using the text formatting toolbar. (See the section "Setting Source Code Preferences" later in this chapter.)

By default, even a blank page includes the basic framework of a typical hypertext document: opening and closing HTML, Head, and Body tags. Contained within the Head are a few Meta tags to describe the type of page and the fact that it was created by GoLive, and a default Title, if you've specified these in your preferences. Within the Body, the page color is specified as white (or "#FFFFFF" in hexadecimal terms), and there's even a built-in paragraph, awaiting any text you might enter. Figure 9.1 shows the contents of the Source Code Editor window.

The Page Window itself displays buttons for additional tools that help you edit or change the appearance of the text you see. Here's a brief description of each, from left to right:

- **Syntax Check**. As shown in Figure 9.2, scans your code to see if its structure adheres to the syntactical rules of whatever boundary set you specify. Choices include various forms of HTML and XHTML, browser compatibility, DocType (if specified), and general well-formedness. In addition, you can allow for specific types of elements in your code, choose to display warnings or errors, and choose the result of your search. Show Alert brings up the dialog box that tells you if errors have been found. Show Highlight Palette opens the Highlight palette once the search is completed. From here, you can perform additional checks, or highlight certain elements for further troubleshooting. (See the section "Highlight Palette" later this chapter.)

Figure 9.1
The Source Code Editor Window is used to manually hand code or check your source code.

9

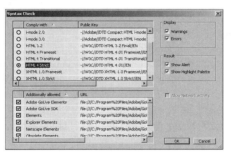

Figure 9.2
The Syntax Check window lets you specify the standards that your code's validity and compatibility should be judged by.

- **Colorize**. As shown in Figure 9.3, changes the color of certain types of tags for quick and easy visual identification. Colors are helpful for troubleshooting, or for simply keeping track of your place on the page. You can specify which colors to use in GoLive Preferences under Source, Colors, and even switch the color sets for each of the following colorization schemes:

  - **Nothing**. Leaves text all black.

  - **Detailed**. Colors all HTML tags. This is the default color setting.

  - **Elements**. Colors tags for any page elements.

  - **Media and Links**. Color media and link tags.

  - **URLs**. Colors any URLs contained on the page.

  - **Server Side Code**. Colors all server side code.

- **Word Wrap**. Keeps all your code in view, to avoid unnecessary horizontal scrolling. Any lines that extend beyond the width of the page window are wrapped, or sent to the next line as if you'd hit the Return key. Lines may appear to break in strange places, but wrapping does not actually affect the code itself, only how it appears to you.

- **Line Numbers**. Displays line numbers to the left of your code, for easy reference. This helps immensely when troubleshooting or communicating with others regarding source code for a page. Note that wrapped lines are still considered to be single lines. To make Line Numbers appear by default, check the box in GoLive Preferences under Source.

Figure 9.3
The Code Coloring pane in Preferences lets you set the colors and styles of the fonts as they appear in Source Code view.

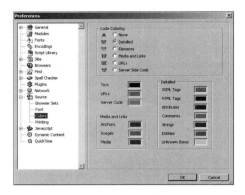

Line Breaks

Line Break characters can be of several different types: a simple line break, a line break that includes a line feed, or a line break that includes a carriage return. Your selection won't affect the validity of your code, but it can affect the way the source code is displayed if viewed on different text editors on different operating systems. The Return arrow in the lower right corner of the window enables you to select your Line Break mode from among different operating systems. The default is always the standard for the operating system currently in use.

Drag and Drop

Within the Source Code Editor, as with the Layout Editor, you can drag element icons from the Objects Palette and drop them into your HTML code. If you'd prefer not to drag and drop, simply position your cursor in the desired location within the code and double-click on the icon for the Object you wish to place. Using either method, the element tag will appear, ready for editing. You can fill in attributes and values, links, or whatever additional specifics are needed.

If color is a tag attribute, you can also drag and drop directly from the Color Palette. Just select your color, and then pull it from the preview pane and release it into your code. Additionally, you can drag pages and URLs straight from the Site Window in order to create a link. You can also highlight areas of code and drag the code itself to another location.

Drag and Drop eliminates excess typing and improves the accuracy of your code, since tags enter with correct syntax, almost like templates, reminding you which attributes should be used with that particular tag.

The number in the lower right corner of the Source Editor Window indicates which line your cursor rests on, whether line numbers are displayed or not. You may insert a number here, and the cursor will proceed automatically to that line, a handy trick for lengthy documents.

Source Editor Preferences

You can control many aspects of your source code by setting the appropriate preferences. To access these preferences, simply choose Edit, Preferences from the menu or press (Cmd-K) [Ctrl+K] on your keyboard, and then choose Source.

The Source Preferences contain a number of customization options for the viewing of source code, making it easier to read, share, dissect, and troubleshoot. You can check boxes to enable text dragging, set HTML tags in bold, auto-indent and set tab size, and use line numbers or word wrap.

Browser Sets

Since each browser is set up to interpret source code in a slightly different manner, you can choose from various browser sets in order to check compatibility. Select from a range of Netscape Navigator or Internet Explorer versions or create your own customized combination set. For example, if you know that your users are only using Netscape 4 or Internet Explorer 6, you could create a custom set including these two browsers. In this case, GoLive won't care if you write code that looks completely whacked on a different browser not specified.

Font

Here you can set the typeface, size, and style of the font used for your source code, and even view a sample of what it will look like onscreen. For example, the view shown in Figure 9.1 is Arial 12.

Colors

Select colors for the coding of regular text, plus links, media, and particular types of tags. This allows you to keep code more organized and troubleshoot it at a glance.

Printing

Since online and printed appearance can differ so greatly, GoLive allows you to create separate specifications for the printing of code. Here you can check printer-specific settings, plus set a font name, size, and style used only for printing.

USING THE SOURCE SPLIT VIEW

One handy new feature in GoLive 6 is the Source Split View, which allows you to examine your page in multiple views simultaneously (see Figure 9.4). You can see the source code while also viewing the page as a Layout, Frames Layout, Outline, or Preview. This is ideal for learning HTML, since you can instantly see the effects of your changes. It's also useful for troubleshooting, locating elements or errors, or simply for experimenting with a page layout.

You can access the Split View from any Editor (except Source) by clicking on the toggle switch in the lower-left corner. Alternatively, you could select View, Show Split Source from the menu, or press

9

(Cmd-Y) [Ctrl+Y] on the keyboard. Any of these methods reveals a panel of source code beneath the main Editor.

Select an element in the upper view and it becomes highlighted below in the Source view. Make a change within the top or bottom and the change is instantly reflected in the other view. You can use this feature to help you connect layout elements to their respective HTML tags, quickly select tags in the outline view and see the full code beneath, or see how code would be displayed in a browser.

By default, the Split View toggle should be visible. If it does not appear, click on the circled arrow in the upper-right corner to reveal a cascading menu filled with a variety of new options. This is where you control which elements appear in the lower status bar. Choose Status Bar, Source Split View to take advantage of this new combo.

Figure 9.4
The Source Split View lets you
see both views at once.

SOURCE CODE PALETTE

True to its name, the Source Code Palette (Figure 9.5) enables you to view the code behind your graphic document. Identical in purpose to the Source View or the Source Split View built in to the Page Window, the Source Code Palette has the distinct advantage of remaining mobile. As a separate window, it can be positioned anywhere on the user's desktop, even arranged for viewing on a second monitor, an option some Web professionals choose in order to expand their workspace.

One unique feature of the Source Code Palette is Local Mode. This zeroes in and displays only the particular line or section of code pertaining to what you've selected in the Layout or Source Editor. Local Mode lets you concentrate on one section of code at a time, without getting lost or distracted by the code around it, making it ideal for learning or troubleshooting. It can be very effective when used in conjunction with the Markup Tree or Outline Editor.

Other features of this palette keep it similar to the other Source views: Word Wrap places soft returns at the ends of lines to keep code in full view, Display Line Numbers provides line numbers along the left side of the code, and Dim When Inactive lets the palette fade slightly when not in use. These features can be checked or unchecked by clicking the arrow in the top-right corner of the palette and selecting each from the pull-down menu.

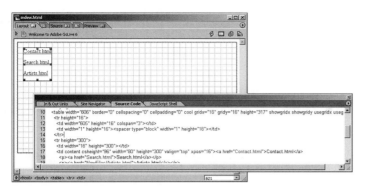

MARKUP TREE

The Markup Tree, formerly a separate palette but now part of the Page window status bar as shown in Figure 9.6, serves as a kind of bookmark for your HTML source code. It helps you quickly locate and select pieces that might otherwise get lost in the shuffle. When you click on a Markup Tree tag, it becomes simultaneously highlighted in the Layout Mode as well as the Source Code palette (if it's open). This speeds up your troubleshooting and updating efforts, particularly when trying to select items more difficult to grab in the Layout mode, such as an invisible GIF.

Figure 9.6
The Markup Tree is located in the Layout Editor Status Bar.

The Markup Tree

OUTLINE EDITOR

As the name suggests, the Outline Editor displays your source code in the form of an outline, with the main tags featured prominently, then sub-tags and attributes indented beneath them. It's a perfect way to break the code down to its fundamentals. Figure 9.7 shows a page broken down into this nested, collapsible view.

Here each tag becomes a kind of object, self-contained in its own box. Tags can be moved, edited, added or deleted, copied and pasted, expanded or collapsed, and some can even contain other tags. In a sense, the Outline Editor works like a hybrid of the Layout and Source Editors, dealing with code in a more graphic format. For this reason, it's a great place to start learning HTML, because the tags here don't seem as intimidating as the sight of an entire page of text. These tags also offer hints by displaying a menu of their attributes. Rather than remember all the specific traits for each tag, you can now simply select them from a menu.

Expanding and Collapsing Tags

Not only is this a neat, organized method of arranging the page, it's also extremely compact: The tags are collapsible, so you can see the whole page at a glance, or take a detailed look at a specific part. Each tag may be expanded in more than one way, depending on the situation. Let's take a look at the anatomy of an outline tag.

Figure 9.7
The Outline Editor provides a spiffy collapsible view of your code.

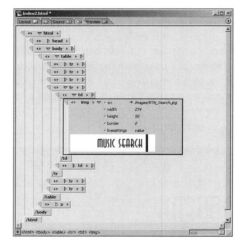

Each tag normally typed between brackets appears as a separate element in the Outline Editor. The tag name for each is featured in bold. The large gray arrow to the left of the name enables you to expand or collapse that tag within the outline. Collapse a tag and every sub-tag beneath it will be tucked up inside. Expand it and they're all displayed. Some tags, such as the body tag, contain many sub-tags. Others may contain none at all.

The image tag shown in Figure 9.7 has been popped open to display all its constituent sub-tags. Here you can click on each enclosed element to edit it individually. You could, as an example, click on the zero in the border element to change it to 1.

To the right of the tag name, a smaller dark arrow contains the menu of possible attributes for that tag. Click on the arrow and select from the list to add a new attribute. The large gray arrow to the right of this controls the expansion or collapse of the chosen tag attributes. When expanded, these are shown in a bulleted list with the values for each displayed in italics on the right. Color attributes, such as bgcolor for the body, also include a small swatch box to show you the chosen color.

Selecting Elements

Whenever an object is highlighted in the Layout or Source Editor, a black box surrounds it in the Outline Editor to show that it has been selected. Similarly, if you select a tag in the Outline Editor, the corresponding object or tag is automatically highlighted in the other Editors. This gives you many different perspectives when creating a page.

Adding and Modifying Elements

Since tags in the Outline Editor behave like individual objects, you can add elements to the Outline Editor simply by dragging object icons into position from the Objects Palette. Each object quickly transforms into the appropriate tag, with all the possible attributes at the ready.

Once placed in the Outline Editor, a tag can be dragged by its left side and moved to a new location within the outline, effectively changing its position on the page. Selected objects may also be cut, copied, and pasted with the same methods you would use on text or layout objects.

Each tag can also be edited as text. Click on the name of a tag to highlight it and type another tag in its place. Click on a value or attribute to edit these either as text or, in some cases, with a pull-down menu of options. Change color attributes by dragging a new color from the Color Palette and placing it in the swatch box beside the appropriate attribute.

Viewing Images

Not only can you view the links to your image tags, you can actually view the images themselves beside their appropriate tags in the Outline Editor. To take advantage of this option, simply check the Images box in the View Inspector, and your images will appear. This is ideal for locating images quickly within your source code or spotting an empty reference. Figure 9.7 shows this feature in action on the selected image.

Outline Editor Toolbar

The Toolbar for the Outline Editor (see Figure 9.8) provides additional options when planning your page in this view.

Figure 9.8
The Outline Editor Toolbar provides tools for quickly adding tags while in Outline mode.

Here's a brief description of the icons found here:

- **New Element**. Adds a placeholder tag (and end tag) where you can add any new element you please. This works effectively for nonstandard tags, or may be used in place of dragging objects from the palette. Simply type the name of the element in place of the word Element, and press Enter/Return to make it so. The end tag automatically takes the identical name, and if the tag is recognized, its full set of attributes will appear as a pop-up menu beside it.

- **New Attribute**. Adds a placeholder for a new attribute, which you can name and assign a value. Simply type the name of the attribute in place of the attr marker and press Enter/Return to make it so, then give the attribute a value.

- **New Text**. Allows you to place text on your page, contained within an outline tag so that it can be easily moved as a unit. The text is merely added as typed, without any formatting.

- **New Comment**. Adds a comment to the page. Comments in the Outline Editor are displayed in lighter gray to avoid confusion with visible tags.

- **New Generic Element**. Adds a placeholder for nonstandard HTML tags. A pull-down menu (see Figure 9.9) provides a list of possible tag types, including SGML, PHP, Lasso, Mercantec, and Web Siphon, and each selection gets independently formatted. SGML gets framed like a comment. PHP is surrounded by question marks. ASP and Mercantec use percent signs. Lasso gets square brackets. Web Siphon has double brackets. There's even a provision for generic Start and End HTML tags, which receive regular brackets. The generic element tag allows you to fully customize your page from here.

Figure 9.9
Special Elements allow you to work with tags unique to dynamic content sources (see the chapter on Dynamic Content for more information).

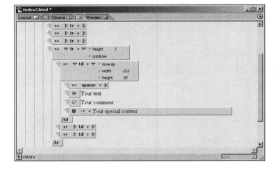

Figure 9.10 shows a page in Outline mode, and you can see that these items have just been added from the toolbar.

Figure 9.10
Here is the Outline Editor showing some of the tags that have just been inserted using the toolbar.

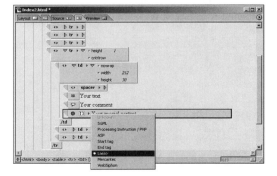

Ever since GoLive 5, you can use specially formatted tags, such as those used by PHP, JSP, ASP, and Lasso, without fear of GoLive altering the tags to make them conform to standard HTML. Older versions parsed your code whenever you switched from Source View to Layout, which caused problems for any code not recognized by the application. Now when GoLive encounters nonstandard code, it leaves the code as is. For this reason, you can feel secure introducing custom code elements to your pages.

HIGHLIGHT PALETTE

The Highlight Palette provides a quick and easy way to locate specific elements within your page. It serves the same function as applying a yellow highlighting marker to a book, drawing attention to an important passage. The Highlight Palette can be used in conjunction with the Layout, Source Code, and Outline Editors, and simply functions as a search.

From the palette menus in the Select tab, select an element or other item you wish to find. As the menu is released, the found items are highlighted in yellow in the page window, and the number of items found is listed beside it in the Highlight Palette. You may even select multiple items from the menus and search for several elements simultaneously. Best of all, since the element menu is taken directly from elements on your page, you can perform searches for custom elements and nonstandard tags you may have added.

From the Highlight Palette, you can also perform a Syntax Check (see the "Syntax Check" section earlier in this chapter), Rescan once updates have been made, or Return to the previously highlighted items.

Once a search is performed and the correct items are highlighted, you can save a Highlighting Set by clicking the small arrow in the upper-right corner of the palette and selecting this option, as shown in Figure 9.11. A dialog box asks you to name the set and choose a location. Later you can Load the Highlighting Set to examine it again.

Figure 9.11
Click the triangle button in the top right of the Highlight Palette to access the contextual menu for saving and loading Highlighting Sets.

Use the Color Tab (see Figure 9.12) to change your highlighting colors, increase or reduce the opacity of the color, or opt to outline the highlighted areas instead of covering them completely. Different types of items can be assigned different colors for quick reference.

Figure 9.12
Use the Colors tab of the Highlight palette to specify the coloration of your highlighting selections.

9

HTML ELEMENT FIND & REPLACE

When searching for HTML tags, take advantage of the web-savvy Element tab to perform a more accurate search than with a simple Find & Replace. Because a standard text search is programmed to look for literal strings, it can only find exact matches. A standard Find & Replace, for example, in searching for the tag `<body bgcolor="white">` would not find such a tag if it were missing quotation marks or had additional attributes such as `<body text="black" bgcolor="white">`. See how GoLive addresses this in Figure 9.13.

The Element tab, however, understands HTML structure and allows for variations within the tags. It also enables you to add, delete, or edit existing tags and attributes, making it a far superior search tool when working with HTML elements.

Figure 9.13
This Element tab of the Find & Replace window shows a search that's going to find everything with a bgcolor of white and change it to blue.

To perform a Find & Replace for HTML elements:

1. Open the Find window by choosing Edit, Find from the menu, or pressing (Cmd-F) or [Ctrl+F] on your keyboard.

2. Select the Element tab.

3. Choose your Search criteria in the top section. Dynamic pull-down menus offer extensive lists of HTML tags and their attributes. Make your selections and add any necessary values.

4. Set the Action in the middle section. Elements can be kept, deleted, renamed or replaced, or judged according to their content. Here you can enter a new name or create a new action to be performed on any elements and attributes found by the search.

5. Select the range of files to be searched in the lower Find In section. Choose to search a single file, several files, or a complete Site.

6. Click Start to initiate the search.

ADDING HEAD TAGS AND SCRIPTS

GoLive gives special attention to header tags, devoting an entire tab of the Objects Palette to them (see Figure 9.14) and providing a handy toggle switch in the Layout Editor for easy access to the Head section. The toggle appears as an arrow just to the left of the Page icon in the upper-left corner of the Layout window. As shown in Figure 9.15, click on the arrow to make the Head section appear, like a hidden sub-window in your document. To view tags as they're added, you may also wish to click the Source Split View.

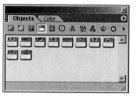

Figure 9.14
Grab icons from the Head tab of the Objects Palette to drag into the Head section of Layout View.

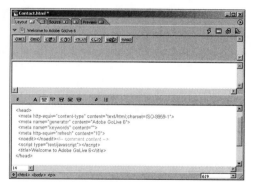

Figure 9.15
To add tags to the Head section, pop open the Head section of the Layout View window and drag tags in from the Objects palette.

Adding tags from the Objects Palette is easy: Simply drag the tag into place within the Head section, or position your cursor where you'd like the tag, and double-click on it. Then provide any necessary details in the Head Tag Inspector. There are ten tags available in the Head tab of the Objects Palette, and each is handled in a slightly different manner within the Inspector. Here is a brief description of each:

- **IsIndex**. Alerts browsers that they can use this page to perform a keyword search. This is an obsolete tag, not recommended for use.

- **Base**. Allows you to provide a base URL, an absolute place from which all relative links will originate. In case your Site is moved, the browser can still direct links to the correct location. This is an obsolete tag, not recommended for use.

- **Keywords**. Meta tag that allows you to list keywords to be used by search engines when indexing your Site. In the Inspector, type a keyword and press Enter/Return to add it to your list. Most search engines limit the number of keywords used, and set specific rules regarding the abuse of keywords. Visit individual search engine Sites to view the current regulations.

- **Link**. Helps you define relationships between linking pages within your Site or between your Site and other Internet Sites. Managing your Site with the GoLive Site Window eliminates the need for this tag.

- **Meta**. Provides information used to identify your page, such as the document type, creator, keywords, and so on. By default, you can instruct GoLive to place certain Meta tags in all your documents. This object allows you to use additional Meta tags in your page.

- **Refresh**. Meta tag that tells the browser to refresh your page after a specified interval of seconds. You can choose to refresh the same page or send viewers to another page. This can be helpful if a Site has moved, if your Site contains live up-to-the-minute content such as video, or if you wish to create a slideshow effect by sending viewers from one page to the next. In the Inspector, choose the number of seconds to wait before refreshing, and whether the Refresh will repeat the same page or send users to another. If another page is used, you must specify the URL here.

- **Tag**. Inserts start and end tags for unknown elements in your header to ensure compatibility with future browsers. In the Inspector, specify the tag name, attributes, and values you'd like to introduce.

- **Comment**. Places a hidden comment in your header. In the Inspector, write your comment and press Enter/Return to add it to the comments tag. Note that comments appear as a lighter gray in your source code to avoid confusion with visible elements.

- **Encode**. Specifies the character set encoding for the document. Default is Western (ISO-8859-1) but can be changed here.

- **Script**. Allows you to add scripts to the header of your page. See next section on Scripts for more details.

Adding Scripts to the Header

JavaScript can be added to the head or the body of your document, and many scripts contain code for both parts. Most commonly, head scripts are used to test for browser compatibility before proceeding to the rest of the script, or to pre-load images or other materials in preparation for a later script. To add a Head Script in GoLive, follow the instructions below. Figure 9.16 shows the Head Script Inspector. For Body scripts, see Chapter 18, "Using the JavaScript Editor and Inserting Java Applets."

Figure 9.16
When a script is placed in the head section, its properties are visible on the Head Script Inspector.

To place a Script in the Head Section of your page

1. Click the toggle switch in the upper-left corner of the page window to access the Head Section.

2. Choose the Head tab from the Objects Palette to view Head elements.

3. Click and drag the Script icon into place within the head section of your page window, or position your cursor where you'd like the script to appear, and double-click on the Scripts icon within the Objects Palette.

4. With the Script icon in place, provide additional details in the Script Inspector.

   - **Name**: Give your script a name for quick reference. The name does not affect the script at all, but makes it easier to recall later.

   - **Language**: From the menu, select the browser version your script will support to place the proper JavaScript language version in the field below it. This gives older browsers the option to ignore the script if it's too new for them to understand. To simply write "JavaScript" without specifying a version number, choose Navigator 2.x. You may also opt to leave the language blank.

   - **Source**: To paste in a script that's already written or to write your own script, click the Edit button to open the JavaScript Editor. To access an external script, check the Source button and select the appropriate .js file via Point-and-Shoot, browsing, or typing the location of the file. Before using an external script, you should place it within the Files tab of your Site Window. See Chapter 19 for more information about adding scripts to your pages.

GENERATING XHTML CODE

In an effort to increase compatibility and remain on the cutting edge of Internet technology, GoLive has broadened its range of acceptable source code. Now it's easier than ever before to expand beyond standard HTML and open your pages to new possibilities. XHTML in particular has grown to such a level in popularity that GoLive has introduced a new conversion tool for the express purpose of transforming HTML documents into acceptable XHTML pages.

Figure 9.17 shows how to convert an existing document to XHTML. Click the small menu arrow in the upper-right corner of the Page Window in Layout View, and select Markup, Convert to XHTML. Likewise, you may convert a document from XHTML back to straight HTML with the same menu.

Figure 9.17
Convert HTML to XHTML using the pop-up menus available on the Page Window.

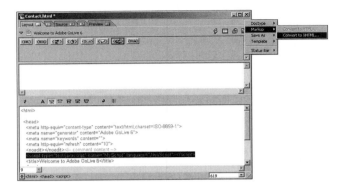

To create a brand new XHTML document, select File, New Special, and then choose between XHTML Page and XHTML Basic Page. Your new page will appear identical to a regular HTML page except for the DocType inserted in the header. As you build and test the page, however, it will adhere to different rules and standards.

For additional information on working with source code, see the appropriate chapters. Chapter 17, "Styles and Stationary," covers reusable components such as text macros. Chapter 19 contains more detail about scripting. See the table of contents or the index to locate the chapter you need.

TROUBLESHOOTING

Characters That Change Unexpectedly

Some of my characters keep changing into strange URL encoded things, and vice versa. What's up with that?

You need to pay special attention when typing your content directly in source code view. Some characters—such as < or " or & or many others—need to be URL encoded to properly display on a Web page. For example, if you want the < character to appear on your Web page, it must appear in the source code as <. If not, the browser may think that it's supposed to be part of some special tag and incorrectly interpret it, possibly blowing your whole page to kingdom come.

GoLive addresses this by automatically URL encoding anything you type in Layout view, and leaving alone anything you type in source code view. If you're creating an instructional Web page, and you want this to appear on screen

```
Use the <br> tag to indicate a line break.
```

Type that in layout view and the following code will be inserted into your page:

```
Use the &lt;br&gt; tag to indicate a line break.
```

This will render correctly. But, if you had typed the first example directly into source code, here is how your page would render:

```
Use the
tag to indicate a line break.
```

And that's not what you want. So remember a couple rules of thumb: Only type out HTML tags when in source code view, and only type special characters when in layout view.

GOING LIVE

Many advanced professional coders of Web pages don't use tools like GoLive at all, instead preferring to do all their work using the most awesome of high-end power tools: Notepad on the PC, and TextEdit on the Mac. (This is meant sarcastically. Those applications are bare-bones text editors.)

This is well and good for some people, but not often good for some of us who must view those Web pages. Because Notepad and TextEdit don't flag errors. And sometimes a browser will still render a page correctly even when some tags are improperly nested or not closed. This is where GoLive has a very real role in every developer's arsenal. Flagging errors, and pointing out browser incompatibilities, is essential to producing high-quality code.

Always use the syntax error-checking tools, and always specify a comprehensive browser set. Even if you only use GoLive's source code view and never even preview your page in layout view, please use those error-checking tools so everyone will be able to enjoy your pages error free.

9

STANDARD PAGE LAYOUT

IN THIS PART

10 Working with Text   **159**

11 Using Graphic Elements   **183**

12 Working with Links   **201**

13 Page Extras   **217**

WORKING WITH TEXT

IN THIS CHAPTER

Text on Your Pages   **160**

Jazzing Up Your Text   **166**

Putting It All Together   **172**

Troubleshooting   **180**

Going Live   **181**

TEXT ON YOUR PAGES

Early on, the Internet was nothing more than text, the exchange of ideas across distance via wires carrying the written word. And while we've made vast improvements in our formatting and graphics, done away with the wires, and evolved to a new state of grace, this basic exchange remains the same. We need to communicate effectively, and we still rely on our words to carry a message.

Given the influences of advertising and design, it's not surprising that the World Wide Web has lifted text to an exciting new level. With each new version of HTML came improvements in the treatment of type. We now wield more power over our wordplay than ever before, controlling every aspect of it nearly as precisely as our peers in print.

In this chapter we'll discuss the tricks of the trade in handling text on the Web. It may seem like a basic necessity, but the proper placement of words can enhance the appearance and effectiveness of any site.

Make no bones about it: The most important aspect of text is the content, the message that you're trying to convey. Appearance also says a great deal, and perhaps a picture is worth a thousand words, but you still need to choose your words with care.

Considering the amount of effort required to write all the text for a typical Web site, most people prefer to do their actual composing in another program of choice. This may afford you more flexibility, especially when non-Web professionals share writing roles, and GoLive certainly allows for this as a possibility. It's yet another benefit to the cooperation Adobe is trying to build between related applications.

Still, you always retain the option to write and edit your text entirely in GoLive, with all the modern conveniences of a typical word processing program. This high level of control also makes later changes and last-minute editing a piece of cake for anyone involved in the project. GoLive is set up to be simple and straightforward, to take the words right out of your mouth and carry your ideas out into the world.

Entering Text

Figure 10.1 shows four main options for the placement of text: You can type directly on the page layout, or insert your words within a text box, floating box, or any cell of a table. In every case, the text may be typed in directly or copied from an outside source and pasted onto the page. In most situations, you can also select and drag text from an outside program and drop it directly into its new location on the GoLive page.

Direct Typing

To enter text straight onto a page, simply create a new page or open an existing one, place your cursor on the layout, and begin typing. Whenever a new page is created, it actually begins much the same as any other word processing document, with a flashing cursor up in the left corner, waiting to take your dictation. Your text remains free to expand or contract, adjusting to the size of each user's browser window.

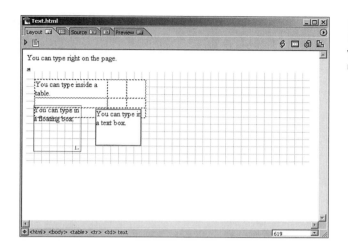

Figure 10.1
Here are some of the many ways you can enter text on a page using GoLive.

Typing into a Text Box

Since the text box was intended specifically to handle text, it too provides a great deal of control and flexibility. You determine the dimensions of the box, and the text adjusts by wrapping whenever necessary to fit within that width. A text box may only be used in conjunction with the layout grid.

Typing into a Floating Box

Floating Boxes operate much like text boxes, with the added advantage that they allow your words to have movement. Also, since they operate within a system of layers, objects may pass in front of or behind other objects, creating some impressive visual effects. A floating box may be used with or without the layout grid. For more about this, see Chapter 19, "Working with Layers and Floating Boxes."

Typing into a Table

To gain the most control over your writing, this is your best option. Once you've added a table to your page, you can place your cursor inside any cell and begin typing. With your words safely within the walls of the table, you can determine the size of each cell and choose more accurately where the line breaks will occur and how your words will appear in a browser. You can use a table with or without the layout grid. (See Chapter 15, "Working with Tables," for more specifics.)

Editing Text

To manipulate text within GoLive, you use standard methods common to word processing and other programs. Whenever the cursor is placed in the vicinity of text, the main toolbar automatically transforms into the Text Toolbar shown in Figure 10.2, containing a variety of buttons and pull-down menus you can use to facilitate the editing process. You may also use selections from the main menus or take advantage of keyboard shortcuts.

With the assistance of all these tools, you can add, select, cut, copy, and paste text. You can change the appearance of text by selecting a new font, size, style, structure, or color. You can also format the space around text, and control how it sits on the page by creating paragraphs or lists, setting indentation and line breaks, and adjusting the alignment.

Figure 10.2
The Text toolbar provides most common formatting functions.

Selecting Text

In order to edit any piece of text, you must first highlight it using one of the methods shown in Table 10.1.

Table 10.1   Text Selection Commands

To Select...	Do This
Any text, from a single character to a large block of text	Place your cursor where you'd like the selection to begin. Click and drag across the desired text, holding the mouse button down until you reach the end of the selection.
A word	Double-click on that word.
A line of text	Triple-click on the line (Note: A line of text is not the same as a sentence here).
A word, letter by letter	Hold down Shift as you press the arrow keys.
A line or phrase, word by word	Hold down Shift+Ctrl as you press the arrow keys.
A block of text, from the cursor to the end of the line (Mac only)	Hold down Cmd+Shift as you press the arrow keys. Up and down arrows select text line by line.
Any block of text (especially good for large sections)	Place the cursor in front of the first word of the desired selection. Hold down Shift and click at the end of the selection. Can also select from back to front.

Cutting and Copying Text

Once you've made your selection, text can be cut, copied, and pasted in the standard fashion, using an option from the Edit menu or the equivalent keyboard shortcut. Table 10.2 shows the keyboard shortcuts for copying and pasting.

Table 10.2   Copy and Paste Keyboard Shortcuts

Action	Mac	Windows
Select All	Cmd-A	Ctrl+A
Cut	Cmd-X	Ctrl+X
Copy	Cmd-C	Ctrl+C
Paste	Cmd-V	Ctrl+V

Dragging Text

You may also select and drag text to a new location, keeping these points in mind:

- If you drag to the grid, a new text box will be created around your text.

- You must create a floating box before you can add text to it.

- If you drag text to an empty text box or floating box, the text appears at the cursor.

- If you drag text to a box that already contains text, you can place the new text anywhere within the box.

Other Editing Options

To clear or delete text, select Edit, Clear (Mac) or Edit, Delete (Windows), or press the Delete (Backspace) key while text is selected. This removes the highlighted text entirely, without copying it to the clipboard.

To duplicate a text or floating box, select Edit, Duplicate or drag the box while holding the Option (Mac) or Alt (Windows) key. Remember that duplication only works if the selected object is on the grid.

10

Special Characters

We generally define special characters as those not readily visible on the keyboard, but which can be accessed by pressing particular key combinations. They consist mostly of symbols, some specific to math or science, some used in connection with finance, copyediting, or a foreign language. Some sets of special characters improve the appearance of a written piece, as in the case of curly quotes. Others are purely for amusement.

To view available special characters on your system, you can use Key Caps (Mac), or access the Windows Character Map by choosing Start, Programs, Accessories, System Tools, Character Map. To view GoLive's list of special characters, select Web Settings from the Edit menu and click the Characters tab. You can drag any character from this window and drop it into your document. If you view source, the URL encoded version will appear in your code.

Table 10.3 shows some commonly used special characters and their keyboard equivalents in GoLive.

Table 10.3 Special Characters

Character	Description	Encoded
&	Ampersand	&amp;
<	Less Than	&lt;
>	Greater Than	&gt;
™	Trademark	&#153;
©	Copyright	&copy;
®	Registered Trademark	&reg;

Table 10.3 Continued

Character	Description	Encoded
€	Euro	€
¢	Cent	¢
¶	Paragraph	¶
«	Left angle quote	«
»	Right angle quote	»
°	Degree	°
¥	Yen	¥

Checking Your Spelling

Just like other word processing programs, Adobe GoLive comes with its own built-in SpellCheck program to ease your mind and help you avoid potentially embarrassing orthographical errors. You can review a single page, multiple pages, or your entire Site, and add new words to your GoLive dictionary to render their usage acceptable in the future. Figure 10.3 shows the SpellCheck in action.

To perform a spelling check, follow these steps:

1. To check one page, open that page. To check multiple pages, start with all pages closed. GoLive will open individual pages that contain errors.

2. From the top menu, choose Edit, Check Spelling, or press (Cmd-Option-U) [Ctrl+Alt+U] on your keyboard. This opens the Check Spelling window.

3. Select a language and adjust your options in the window.

4. Add more pages to SpellCheck. (optional)

5. Click Start.

If any misspellings are located, you can select the intended word from a list of suggestions, choose to ignore the mistake, or add a new word to GoLive's dictionary by clicking Learn.

To add a new word to your dictionary, click Learn inside the Check Spelling window after a SpellCheck locates an unrecognized (supposedly misspelled) word. The word in question will automatically be added to your custom dictionary, shown in Figure 10.4. Alternatively, you can select Edit, Preferences, Spell Checker or press (Cmd-K) [Ctrl+K]. Click the Add icon to add a new word, and type this word in the blank provided. Click OK.

If you wish to delete a word from your dictionary instead, you may also do that here. Simply select the word and click on the trash icon. Click OK.

Finding and Replacing Text

Another problem-solving feature that GoLive offers to help you clean up files universally is Find & Replace, shown in Figure 10.5. Here you can search for a troublesome word and correct it in all instances throughout your Site. Among its many uses, it may serve to correct mistakes of spelling or grammar that wouldn't be caught doing a Spell Check (such as proper names or homonyms), update information (such as change of address), or simply maintain Site consistency (such as a search for fonts).

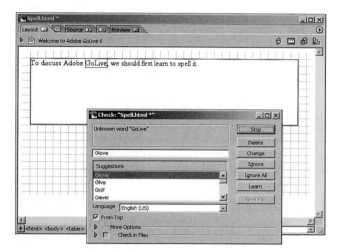

Figure 10.3
Use the SpellCheck feature to catch and correct any spelling errors.

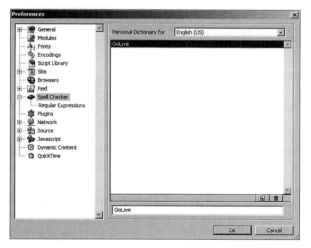

Figure 10.4
The list of custom dictionaries you have created is available inside Preferences.

Follow these steps to perform a Find and Replace:

1. Select Edit, Find or press (Cmd-F) [Ctrl+F] on your keyboard. This opens the Find & Replace window.

2. Enter a word to Find, specify details about capitalization requirements and other options, and click Find.

3. When the word is located, enter its new replacement in the space below and click Replace (or Replace All to correct the entire Site).

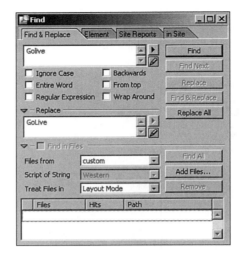

Figure 10.5
Use Find & Replace to quickly make universal changes to a particular word or phrase throughout a document.

JAZZING UP YOUR TEXT

Once you've mastered the techniques for managing the content of your Site, you're ready to fling a little zing into your words, and make them appealing to the eye as well as the mind. With all the formatting options available, it's easy to create a Site that reflects your own unique sense of style.

Keep in mind that words on the Web need not always be rendered as type. You may prefer to turn your words into graphics, as in the case of logos or navigational buttons. Animated type also has a dynamic effect, as you've probably seen in QuickTime videos and Flash or Shockwave-enhanced presentations. For these and other options, consult Part VII, "Movement, Multimedia, and Interactivity."

Formatting Text

The idea behind text formatting is to maintain control over the appearance of your pages online. Despite a multitude of variables, it's still possible to create a Site that looks fairly consistent from one viewer to the next. If you specify more details up front, you lower the likelihood that your Site's appearance will fall prey to individual preferences and settings.

Text formatting itself is fairly straightforward: Select the text, then ascribe traits to it in terms of font, size, style, structure, and color. The Type menu contains nearly all of the available type formatting options, clearly organized for easy access. Some formats may be selected using the Type Toolbar. For your convenience, many even have keyboard shortcuts.

Font Sets

Early in the history of the Web, the appearance of type on a page was limited by the fonts available on each user's machine. Since designers had no way of knowing which fonts each user had installed, they had little control over the way their type would be rendered.

Along came *font sets*. Introduced by Internet Explorer 3, they provided a means for controlling the look of type by assigning a list of possible fonts instead of just one. The fonts are listed in order of preference, and as soon as the user's browser encounters a font in the list that is installed on the user's computer, that font is used.

To create a new font set, follow these steps:

1. Select Type, Font, Edit Font Sets or press (Shift-Cmd-F) [Shift+Ctrl+F] to open the Font Set Editor.

2. Type the name of the new font set in the space provided. If you leave this space blank, your font set will be titled New Font Name by default, and you can choose a name for it later.

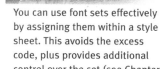

You can use font sets effectively by assigning them within a style sheet. This avoids the excess code, plus provides additional control over the set (see Chapter 17, "Styles," for more on style sheets). Considering this, you may wish to explore font sets as an option.

3. Click the icon to create a new font set. The first font will always take on the name of the font set.

4. Select fonts from the pull-down menu and click the icon to add the new font name. The fonts you add will become part of your new set.

5. Click OK. Your new set is added to your list of available fonts.

Optionally, you might choose to do one of the following:

- You may choose a font from the pull-down menu first, then click to make it the name of your font set.

- If an existing font set is similar to the one you'd like to create, you can select it above and click the plus sign icon to duplicate it, then edit it as you like.

- You may simply prefer to add more fonts to an existing font set. Do this by highlighting the name of the set above and clicking the icon to add a new font name.

- You may also delete fonts within a set or delete entire sets by highlighting them above and clicking the trash icon.

Font Size

Due to the huge number of variables, determining font sizes for the Web can be a terribly confusing endeavor. Each user can adjust the size that fonts appear in his or her browser, and each browser renders font sizes a bit differently. Some browser preferences adjust the font sizes using absolute numbers, as if they represent point sizes in a word processor. Others adjust sizes with relative terms such as Larger or Smaller. Fonts always appear a size or two larger on a Windows machine than on a Mac. And the supposed point sizes provided as size indicators have little relevance to the point sizes used in print.

In addition, there are even several different ways to select a font size. You can choose an absolute size (1 through 7) where 1 is smallest and 3 is the default or considered average size in a browser. Alternately, you can choose a relative size, which bases your fonts upon the defaults set in each user's browser preferences. These vary from -7, or seven sizes smaller than the user's default, up to

+7, or seven sizes larger than the default. Either way of specifying font size is acceptable. Figure 10.7 shows how many of these selections are rendered.

Figure 10.6
Create a new font set if you don't like any of the common ones provided with GoLive.

Figure 10.7
This shows how font sizes are rendered in one particular browser (Internet Explorer 5 on Windows).

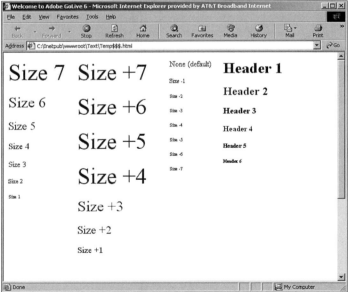

When you place text in GoLive, the default size is None, which means it adds no further size instructions and simply relies on the browser settings of each user. If you plan to use style sheets later, keep the size at None for now to avoid confusion. However, if you'd like to change font sizes individually, it's a simple two-step process:

1. Select the text to be changed

2. Choose Type, Size and pick a size, or use the Size menu in the Type Toolbar to do the same thing. The size update is reflected immediately.

Font Style

As with word processing applications, GoLive allows you to assign attributes to certain words to help them stand out, create an effect, or use in special situations. Three styles—Bold, Italic, and Teletype—are so commonly used that they've been placed as buttons on the Type Toolbar for easy access. All of the available styles can be accessed in the Type, Style or with a keyboard shortcut. Figure 10.8 shows how they look in a browser.

Figure 10.8
Here are the common font styles.

Here is a brief description of each style:

- **Plain Text** is exactly that, just plain and simple with no additional formatting. Remove a style from your text and return it to its pure, original state by selecting it and choosing Type, Style, Plain Text or pressing (Shift-Option-P) [Shift+Ctrl+P] .

- **Bold** makes the word appear darker and slightly fatter to draw attention. To make text bold, select it and choose Type, Style, Bold, or press (Cmd-B) [Ctrl+B].

  You could also click B in the Type Toolbar.

- **Italic** slants the word slightly to the right. It may be used to add emphasis, and is also commonly used to express a foreign word or new term. It often replaces quotation marks or underlines (when citing titles of books, films, articles, and so on) as a more elegant way of making a word appear distinct. To italicize text, select it and choose Type, Style, Italic, or press (Cmd-I) [Ctrl+I]. You could also click I in the Type Toolbar.

- **Underline** places a line beneath the word for emphasis. This is commonly done in print for titles and headings, but since links on the Web are usually distinguished by underlines, it's best to avoid using this style. But for now it's still an option. To underline your text, select it and choose Type, Style, Underline, or press (Shift-Cmd-U) [Shift+Ctrl+U].

> **Caution**
>
> Italic type can be difficult to read onscreen, particularly in smaller sizes. Be sure to check any italics you use in your pages to make sure that the type is large enough to be easily readable.

- **Strikeout** places a line through your text. This is rarely used except to produce an effect or show where editing has taken place. To strikeout your text, select it and choose Type, Style, Strikeout, or press (Shift-Cmd-A) [Shift+Ctrl+A].

- **Superscript** raises the baseline of the text. It is commonly used in mathematical expressions where a number is squared, cubed, or raised to the nth power in some way, but could be used for other effects. To superscript text, select it and choose Type, Style, Superscript, or press (Shift-Cmd-+). No shortcut exists in Windows.

- **Subscript** lowers the baseline of your text. It is commonly used in chemical equations, but could be used for other effects. To subscript text, select it and choose Type, Style, Subscript, or press (Shift-Opt--) (hyphen). No shortcut exists in Windows.

- **Teletype** is meant to imitate the old-fashioned type generated by teletypewriters when coded messages were transferred by telegraph. It produces a kind of no-nonsense effect, as if important facts are being transmitted. It may also remind some of Courier, as a generic typewritten monospaced font, and resemble the type seen in programming code or on non-GUI systems. In any case, it is available simply for effect. To teletype your text, select it and choose Type, Style, Teletype, or press (Shift-Cmd-T) [Shift+Ctrl+T].

  You may also click T in the Type Toolbar.

- **Blink** simply makes the text blink incessantly. It is used to draw attention, especially if something is new or updated in some way. To see the effect, you must preview your page in a browser. To make your text blink, select it and choose Type, Style, Blink. No shortcut exists.

Font Structure

Another option for spicing up your text is to apply a Font Structure. Like Styles, these assign certain attributes to change the appearance of the text. Yet structures are relative changes implemented by the browser, thus they have a less definite effect (see Figure 10.9). As the names reflect, these were implemented in the early days of the Internet, when it was used primarily for the exchange of scientific and technical knowledge. You can access any of the structures by choosing Type, Structure, and making your selection. There are no keyboard shortcuts assigned to these.

> **Caution**
>
> Because it is considered so distracting (read: annoying and tacky), the use of Blink is emphatically discouraged, and the effect is now totally ignored by Internet Explorer.

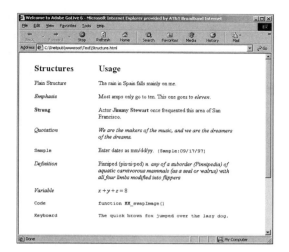

Figure 10.9
Here are several Font Structures rendered in a browser.

Here is a brief description of the available Font Structures:

- **Plain Structure** is just plain, unadulterated text. Use this to remove any structures and return text to its original state.

- **Emphasis** is meant to call attention to the text. It is similar in appearance to Italic.

- **Strong** makes the text appear Bold.

- **Quotation** denotes that you are quoting someone else. While it appears similar to Italic, it actually applies another HTML tag called `<cite>` which has growing uses on the Web. Thus it may be to your benefit to apply Quotation rather than simply italicizing your text.

- **Sample** is intended to show that you are displaying a sample from someone else's source. It appears as a monospaced font and is ideal for distinguishing examples.

- **Definition** tells the reader you are providing a definition.

- **Variable** is used for unknown entities normally represented by letters in mathematical equations, logic, and programming. It appears italicized.

- **Code** expresses that you are showing program code and appears in a monospaced font.

- **Keyboard** tells the reader that this text is to be typed. It also appears in a monospaced font, usually Courier.

Text Color

The color of text is an attribute handled neither in the Type menu nor in the Type Toolbar. Instead, all color decisions must be ratified by the Color Palette. This keeps color control centralized and easy to remember. A small swatch of color does exist on the Toolbar to display the chosen color of text, but clicking on it does nothing but open the Color Palette. You must actually make all your color choices with the Color Palette. That said, changing the color of text is quite simple.

To adjust the color of text, select the text to be changed, and then either click on the Type Color button in the Type Toolbar or open the Color Palette. Select a color. The new color is instantly applied to your text and appears immediately in the toolbar's text color swatch.

Optionally, you can also drag a selected color to unselected text to change the text color

Setting Text and Link Color for the Page

You can determine the color of overall page text and links by indicating these in the Page Inspector. In your layout window, click on the Page icon in the upper-left corner to open the Page Inspector.

Here you'll see four color swatches labeled Text, Link, Active Link, and Visited Link. These correspond the color definitions set in the <body> code early in your document. By default all four are unchecked, but you can check the boxes here to activate them and make your color selections. While you can still change the color of text for individual circumstances, these settings will determine the default colors when no other color is specified.

To change universal text and link colors, follow these steps:

1. In the Page Inspector, check the box next to the text or link you'd like to activate.

2. Click on the color swatch to highlight it. This color will appear as a selected color in the Color Palette.

3. Choose the color you'd prefer. The new color appears in the swatch of the Color Palette and replaces the color highlighted in the Page Inspector.

Optionally, you can also drag a color from the Color Palette to an unselected swatch in the Page Inspector to change the color.

PUTTING IT ALL TOGETHER

You now have the ability to enter and edit text, and to change its appearance to make it sparkle. But so far it's been all dressed up with no place to go.... Here's where it makes an entrance onto the page. Text needs to fit seamlessly into the overall design, and to achieve this, you'll need tools to group it and control the space around it. Let's take a look at some typical text formations.

Formatting Paragraphs

Placing text into paragraphs seems like an age-old convention, but it is especially important on the Web, where users must gulp information quickly in easy-to-swallow chunks. Proper formatting can boost your readers' retention rates as well as keeping your page looking organized. Figure 10.10 shows the following paragraph formatting options rendered in a browser.

Creating Paragraphs

Establishing paragraphs is so essential and widely used that it has its own HTML tag. The paragraph tag or <p> indicates that a block of text should be treated as a whole, and any alignments or other formatting should be applied to it as such. It also creates more vertical separation space than similar tags <div> and <br>.

To create a paragraph, select the text you wish to specify as a paragraph, and then choose Type, Paragraph Format, Paragraph. Alternatively, you can select Paragraph from the formatting menu on the Type Toolbar, or use its keyboard shortcut, (Shift-Option-Cmd-0) [Shift+Alt+Ctrl+0].

Block Quotes

When presenting a longer piece of quotation, it is commonly printed with indentations on both left and right margins in order to set it apart. This is known as a Block Quote, and it can be easily rendered in a similar fashion on the Web.

To create a Block Quote, follow these steps:

1. Select the quote. Because this format applies to the entire paragraph, it's not necessary to highlight everything; you need only place the cursor someplace within that paragraph. If you wish to quote multiple paragraphs, you should highlight at least a part of each one.

2. Select Type, Alignment, Increase block indent. You can increase the indent more by repeating this, or decrease an indent by selecting Decrease block indent instead.

The highlighted quote proudly displays its new format immediately, as seen in Figure 10.10.

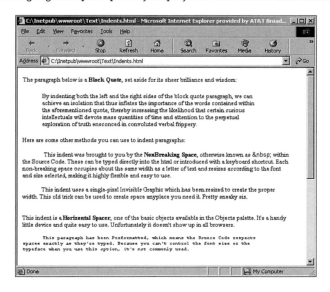

Figure 10.10
Here are some common paragraph formatting options rendered in a browser.

Indenting Paragraphs

One difference between a word processor and a Web page is that the Tab function doesn't exist in HTML. Browsers also don't recognize more than one space in succession. Therefore, indenting a paragraph requires that you manipulate the tools at hand to create the illusion of a tab. This may be accomplished in several ways. The most elegant solution, of course, is to use a Cascading Style Sheet (see Chapter 17 for details). Yet there may be instances when you'll want to create indents by hand. Here's how.

Non-Breaking Spaces   Short of a style sheet, this is the best indentation solution. The non-breaking space acts as a text element, which means it resizes with the rest of your text. If you change the font or the type size, your indent will adapt accordingly. Non-breaking spaces look just like regular spaces, but they place an indicator in your source code that looks like .

Each one of those represents a single space, so you'll need to add quite a few to create a sizable indent. Luckily this is easy to do.

To create a non-breaking space, place your cursor wherever you'd like the space to appear, and press Option-Spacebar (Mac) or Shift+Spacebar (Windows). Repeat as necessary. Optionally, you could instead simply type   directly into your source code, and then copy and paste more spaces as needed.

Using an Invisible Graphic   Another age-old method for tricking browsers into displaying more space is to create an invisible graphic, one-pixel by one-pixel so that it can be resized to fit any-where, and insert it where needed. In this case, we've resized our 1pixel.gif to be 40 pixels wide in order to imitate an indentation.

Invisible graphics like this can be used to create space between paragraphs, or anyplace else a little more white space is required.

Horizontal Spacer   Within the Basic tab of the Objects Palette lives a curious creature called the Horizontal Spacer. It looks like a Tab arrow pointing the way to a clever new method of indentation. Indeed the Spacer is devilishly easy to use.

To Insert a Horizontal Spacer, follow these steps:

1. Click and drag the Horizontal Spacer icon from the Objects Palette into proper position on your page.

2. With the Spacer still highlighted, adjust the width in the Inspector to meet your needs

Unfortunately, the Horizontal Spacer is not recognized at all by Internet Explorer, so IE users won't see the indent. For this reason, it's best to use the other options.

Preformatting

When you preformat text, it inserts the `<pre>` tag into your source code, telling the browser to rec-ognize everything that follows exactly as you type it. The advantage of this is that you can now type spaces and they'll be recognized as such. The downfall is that your text cannot be formatted with fonts, styles, and so forth because the browser is only reading the keystrokes, exactly as is. The resulting paragraph appears with a perfect indent, but in a monospaced font. Somehow the tradeoff doesn't seem worthwhile. Still it's one option.

Headers

Like titles and subtitles, headers indicate a certain hierarchy and help you keep longer pieces of text organized. They vary in size from Header 1 to Header 6, with 1 being largest, as shown in Figure 10.11. When applied to text, they also make the text bold and create extra space beneath them to separate them from the body of text they are intended to announce.

Follow these steps to create a Header:

1. Select the text you'd like to make a header. Because the header is applied to the entire paragraph, you need only place the cursor here instead of highlighting everything. This also means you cannot apply a header to a single word or phrase within a paragraph.

2. Choose Type, Paragraph Format, then your header size of choice, or select a header from menu in the Type Toolbar. You may also employ a keyboard shortcut for each, which consists of (Shift-Option-Command) or [Shift+Alt+Ctrl] plus the level of the header, 1 thru 6.

Figure 10.11 shows the relative sizes of headers. If you'd like to see how they compare to other text sizes, please refer to Figure 10.7. Because the size of headers is determined by the browser as a relative size, you do not have control over how your headers will actually appear.

Figure 10.11
Header sizes combine bold face, font size, and vertical spacing.

Alignment

Since we are accustomed to reading left to right, browser text carries a left alignment by default. Yet you also have the option to align text to the center or the right side of the page (see Figure 10.12). In all cases, the text shifts slightly according to the size of the browser window. This shift may simply be more noticeable with a center or right alignment.

To adjust the alignment of text, select the text you wish to re-align, and then choose Type, Alignment, and then finally choose Left, Center, or Right according to your alignment preference.

Alternatively, you can click on the proper alignment button in the Type Toolbar. Each alignment also has a keyboard shortcut, as shown in Table 10.3.

Table 10.3   Alignment Keyboard Shortcuts

Alignment	Mac	Windows
Align Left	(Shift-Cmd-L)	[Shift+Ctrl+L]
Align Center	(Shift-Cmd-C)	[Shift+Ctrl+C]
Align Right	(Shift-Cmd-R)	[Shift+Ctrl+R]

The new alignment takes effect immediately. Look at Figure 10.12 to see how each appears in a browser.

Figure 10.12
Text alignment defines your text's horizontal placement within its enclosing boundary.

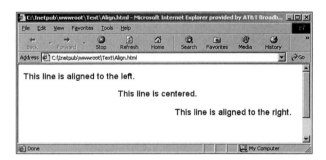

Line Breaks

Line breaks can be a tricky subject and a source of much frustration for designers, as browsers tend to interpret line breaks very differently from what was intended. For starters, a hard return creates an unusually large space that's not normally appropriate between lines of copy. Also, browsers don't recognize multiple returns, so additional space must be created another way. Furthermore, the way text lines wrap—when left to their own devices—is determined by the size of the browser window, which is different for each and every user. With such limited built-in control, designers must learn to keep a few aces up their sleeves. Here are a few methods for winning the line break game, shown in Figure 10.13.

Paragraph Return

When you type a Return (Enter), the code generated is <p> </p>, which actually denotes a fresh paragraph after what you've just typed. That's why the space it creates seems so unusually generous. There may be times when this space is preferred, such as between paragraphs, within poetry, or when listing single lines. If this is your desire, simply hit the Return/Enter key to end the line you're on and begin a new one. Can't get much simpler than that.

Figure 10.13
The different line break options determine how much vertical space is inserted between breaking lines of text.

Line Break Object

The Line Break provided in the Objects Palette is actually the best for creating breaks after single-spaced lines. It generates the code <br>, which is a simple line break, the equivalent to a typewriter return. In fact, it appears on your GoLive layout as a tiny return arrow to indicate a break on your page. You may use the Line Break Object several times in a row to create vertical space between lines, paragraphs, even other objects on the page, which makes it a handy tool indeed.

To create a line break using the Line Break Object, place your cursor where you would like the line break to occur, and then double-click on the Line Break icon in the Objects Palette. Repeat to create extra lines of space, if desired. Optionally, you may also drag the Line Break icon into position on the page.

Using Tables to Control Line Lengths

As Figure 10.13 demonstrates, text that's left to ramble unstructured will carry on to the edge of the browser window and appear very disorderly. A good way to control the width of your lines, while still maintaining the natural text flow, is to place your text within tables. In this way, you can set a definite width for the cell and the text will adhere to this limitation, forming orderly columns.

> **Caution**
>
> While using line breaks at the ends of paragraphs and at other clear stopping points is acceptable, this tag should not be overused as if it were a typewriter return. Because text still expands and contracts according to screen dimensions and browser window size, these forced line breaks can cause some unusual sentence interruptions for some users. It's best whenever possible to allow the text to flow and break naturally, in order to make allowances for these differences.

This is particularly effective when laying out pages with a newsletter style, where articles must align in rows and columns. We've kept the table borders in our example to show that it is indeed a table, but eliminating the borders creates a clean effect, and like an invisible fence, still performs the same function of keeping your text inside the yard.

NoBreak

While we're discussing breaks, we should mention that there are times when you want to ensure that no break occurs. When listing names, addresses, or phone numbers, for example, it is considered improper to split the information, and may even make the it more difficult to read. In these instances, you can use NoBreak to let the browser know that these items should remain together.

To specify a NoBreak:

1. Select the text that should not be broken up.

2. Choose Type, NoBreak. This checks the NoBreak option. If you wish to turn off this option, simply select it again to uncheck.

Lists

In addition to paragraphs, lists are an excellent way to organize and present information on your Site. Widely used throughout the Web, lists have evolved from the simple numbered or unnumbered lists of old into complex hierarchies with a whole variety of display options. In GoLive, they've become a Type sub-category in themselves, plus earned a significant place on the Type Toolbar. But never fear: The basics of list-making remain about the same.

On the Type Toolbar, you'll find four buttons pertaining to lists: two for creating lists (numbered and unnumbered) and two for level adjustment within a list (increase or decrease a level), as shown in Figure 10.14.

In the Type Menu, you'll also find a more complete set of list options, shown in Figure 10.15. These can be broken down into Numbered, Unnumbered, Term, Definition, and Level Adjustment.

The following are the options for numbered lists:

- Default Numbered List uses the numbered list option specified as the default. Generally this is Arabic.

- Arabic uses the numbers we use in everyday writing: 1, 2, 3...

- Upper Roman specifies uppercase Roman numerals: I, II, III...

- Lower Roman creates lowercase Roman numerals: I, ii, iii...

- Upper Alpha uses uppercase alphabet letters: A, B, C...

- Lower Alpha makes lowercase alphabet letters: a, b, c...

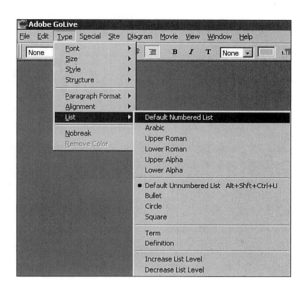

Figure 10.14
List buttons on the Type Toolbar let you quickly format a list.

Figure 10.15
List options in the Type Menu provide a more complete way to access list formatting.

10

The following are the options for unnumbered lists:

- Default Unnumbered List uses the unnumbered list option specified as the default. Generally this is Bullet.

- Bullet uses bullet points or solid circles.

- Circle uses a hollow circle.

- Square uses a hollow square.

- Term provides flush left alignment of the list items without any symbol whatsoever in front of the items.

- Definition indents the items for use as definitions. Terms and Definitions are made to be used in conjunction with one another.

The following are the options for level adjustment:

- Increase List Level indents your list one level deeper, changing the symbols accordingly. On a Mac, you can use the keyboard shortcut Cmd-+ to accomplish this.

- Decrease List Level removes one level of your list. Use keyboard shortcut Cmd–(hyphen) to do this on a Mac.

To create a list as you type, follow these steps:

1. Type the header or introduction for your list, and Enter/Return to begin your list on a new line.

2. Choose Type, List, or click a List button on the Type Toolbar to create a new list, and select a format. The symbol appears on your list line.

3. Type your first list item, then press Enter/Return to begin a new line.

4. Do one of the following:

   a. If the next list item is part of the top level, simply type it.

   b. If the next list item is a sub-category, choose Increase List Level on the toolbar.

   c. If you'd like to change the format, choose Type, List, or click the proper button on the toolbar, and then make you selection. You can mix and match as you like.

5. At the end of your list, press Enter/Return to start a new line, and then click Decrease List Level until you're back at the main level, plus once more to pull you out of list mode.

To create a list from existing text, follow these steps:

1. Highlight the first item from the text you wish to format as a list.

2. Choose Type, List and select the kind of list you would like to create, or select a list from the buttons on the Type Toolbar.

3. Highlight the next item from you wish to format as a list.

4. If this is an item on the top level of your list, repeat step 2. If it is a sub-category of the first item, choose Increase List Level instead.

5. Proceed in this way until all items are included in the list.

You've now mastered the all the essentials of laying out type for the Web in GoLive.

TROUBLESHOOTING

Achieving Standardization Across Platforms

I got my text to look nice, until I viewed it on both Macs and Windows, and on IE and Netscape. The difference was huge. What's up?

Mac font metrics have traditionally been based on 72dpi, while Windows chose 96dpi. For this reason, a standard size like 12 points looks too big on one platform, and too small on the other.

Recent versions of Mac browsers have tried to allow for this by letting the user specify 96dpi as the default baseline for determining font metrics, and it has helped, but not hugely. The best way to avoid this problem is to use style sheets (see Chapter 17) to define your fonts, because you can choose pixel size. Once a font size is specified in pixels, it looks pretty much the same across all recent browsers and platforms.

Choosing Fonts

I want to use this cool funky font. How do I do that?

If it's "funky" your users probably don't have it installed, and don't expect anyone to download it or install it just to view your Web page. There are two ways you can go.

First, if it's just for a headline or something brief, consider taking a screenshot and embedding it as a graphic. Photoshop, Illustrator, Freehand, and other graphics programs can help you with this too. Naturally, the graphic will look identical on all machines, at the expense of download time.

Second, you can specify that font for anyone who may happen to have it, and then specify some backups for those who don't. Choose a few standard system fonts that everyone will have: fonts like Times, Courier, Verdana, Arial, Helvetica. Then use a font set to make the "Funky" font the first choice, and one or two backups for everyone else: `<font face="Funky,Arial,Helvetica">Here's my text.</font>`.

GOING LIVE

Being aware of your users' browsers is important when laying out your text. Some people will have tiny little browser windows; others will have massive windows maximized to take up every pixel of their gigantic monitors.

For this reason, be sure to drag your browser window to all kinds of sizes and aspect ratios to make sure your text looks decent. If you have large blocks of text, don't let it expand horizontally to the point where single-spaced text lines are three feet wide in a large browser: It's too hard to read text that way.

Similarly, make sure you don't have big hefty fonts in a narrow column that will get squeezed to one (or less) words per line when the browser window is dragged tiny.

In both of these cases, you may need to take charge and enforce some formatting on your text. Put it into a table with defined width, to keep it easily readable for all users no matter what silly things they may do with their browser size.

11

USING GRAPHIC ELEMENTS

IN THIS CHAPTER

Easy on the Eyes **184**

Adding Images **184**

Horizontal Lines **186**

Manipulating Images **186**

Arranging Objects **190**

Using a Tracing Image **192**

Creating Image Maps **194**

Creating Rollovers **197**

Troubleshooting **199**

Going Live **199**

EASY ON THE EYES

What would a Web page be without the sparkle and color of eye candy, dazzling our minds and reaching inside us with images that linger longer than mere words? We're a visual society, so caught up in quick stimulation that without illustration a Web site would likely seem drab and fail to capture our interest at all. Images help to direct and instruct, create mood and setting, show us products and places, ping emotions, tell us more than a thousand words could ever say.

Now naturally, the same folks who brought you Photoshop and Illustrator share a passion for graphics, and GoLive carries this zeal with equal eloquence to the Web. In this chapter, we'll examine your optical options in the application, and see that you express your ideas with visual ease.

ADDING IMAGES

Since an image is simply considered an object, it's easy to add life to your page using images. Just drag the Image icon from the Basic tab of the Objects Palette and place it in your layout. Then, using the Image Inspector as shown in Figure 11.1, create a link to the graphic you'd like to use, and it appears automatically on your page. You can choose to lasso your image file using Point-and-Shoot, type the path and filename into the field provided, Browse to locate the image, or select from various menu options to obtain your image. (See Chapter 12, "Working with Links," for additional information.)

Figure 11.1
Use the Inspector to specify the pathname to your image.

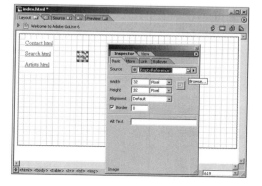

About Web Images

If you're new to using images online, there are a few basics you should bear in mind. First of all, to appear in a browser, your image must be saved in the format of a .jpeg (.jpg) or a .gif. Within these two file types, you still have some room to move.

Jpegs use algorithms to calculate the image compression. When saving files in this format, you can generally control the level of compression and determine how much picture quality you're willing to sacrifice for the sake of a smaller file size. Every image is essentially a balance of the two: Ideally you want to maximize the quality of your image while keeping file sizes as small as possible, so that your page will load quickly.

As a general rule, jpegs tend to work best with photographs and images with a wide range of colors or blended colors, since the compression system preserves this color variety much more accurately than a .gif would. This is a good way to avoid *dithering*, which is the process of combining two available colors that are close to the desired color in an alternating speckle pattern that tricks the eye into thinking it sees the desired color. Another advantage to using a jpeg might be the progressive option. That is, you can choose to save a jpeg image so that it appears on the page progressively, becoming clearer with each pass. This allows viewers to see something, albeit blurred, and know that an image is on its way, rather than stare at a broken image symbol until the real deal arrives. Some people prefer this; some don't.

One disadvantage with the jpeg is that you can't save it as a transparency, knocking out the background color so that it blends with the page. You also can't save animations as jpegs. These must be .gifs.

Gifs, on the other hand, try to break your image down into the smallest color palette possible, and assign a color to each of the pixels that compose your image. Of the 216 Web-safe colors, a gif seeks to re-create the image using only those it deems necessary, often shifting colors to their nearest cousins or by dithering. The way gifs are calculated makes them conducive to saving images with fewer colors and large blocks of the same color, such as cartoons, logos, and basic two-dimensional drawings or shapes. Gifs also tend to display right angles more accurately than curves, since pixels are square and must take the form of stair steps in an attempt to imitate an angle or rounded shape.

Gifs bring with them many advantages. Because gifs see images in color groups, images with fewer colors can be reduced to tiny files, making them easier to store and download. Gifs can be saved as transparent, so that the background color disappears and the image that remains may be used on a page with any color background. Animated gifs bring movement to your page without requiring any extra plug-ins or software.

Using Images in GoLive

When you place an image on your layout in GoLive, it need not be already saved as a jpeg or gif. The Adobe family of applications has become integrated so that you can now bring native Photoshop, Illustrator, LiveMotion, and other files directly into GoLive and manipulate them as you would a regular image file.

> For more information on integrating GoLive with other applications, **see** Part VIII, "Integrating GoLive with Other Programs" (Chapters 21-24).

One step you should take before linking your final image files, however, is to move all of your images into your Site Folder. This ensures that links will function properly, and that your graphics will be stored and uploaded with the rest of your Site files. Creating an Images folder within the Site Folder keeps everything neat and organized, so that no time is lost in a search for missing image files.

While it is not essential that you trim or resize images to their appropriate dimensions, since you have the option to resize images within GoLive, creating your graphics at the proper size allows them to load on your page more quickly than if left on a larger scale. Sizing graphics at the page level forces the browser to download the larger image from the server, then calculate the new size and transform the image, all behind the scenes. These extra steps waste time and memory that could be spent loading your page.

HORIZONTAL LINES

GoLive actually builds the most basic graphic right into its palette of Object options. The horizontal line has been used since the early Web days to separate paragraphs, partition a page, or simply add visual interest. To incorporate a horizontal line, choose the Line icon from the Basic tab of the Objects Palette and drag it into place on your page. With the line selected, you can then drag the blue handles to resize it, or manipulate it using the Line Inspector, shown in Figure 11.2. Choose from two styles: a solid, straightforward line, or a more three-dimensional engraved appearance. Set the width of your line in precise pixels. You can also set the alignment of your line in relation to the page.

Figure 11.2
The Line Inspector lets you set the basic properties of a horizontal rule.

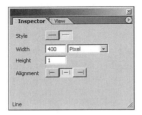

MANIPULATING IMAGES

Once your image is positioned on the page, the Image Inspector, shown in Figure 11.3, allows you to make additional adjustments to it. You can set the height and width, align the image to the page, add or eliminate a border, or include alternative text to describe the image. In addition, you can cut, copy, paste, duplicate, and delete images as you would with text or other objects. You can also size, position, and group images using the Transform Palette. Let's examine each of these options more closely.

Figure 11.3
The Image Inspector lets you force the dimensions of an image, set its alignment relative to other content on the page, and set whether it has a border. GoLive will set the dimensions for you automatically when you specify the pathname to your image.

Resizing an Image

Graphics can be resized in a variety of ways. With the image selected, you can drag the handles in any direction to size the image manually. Hold the Shift key down while dragging the right corner to keep the image proportional when enlarging or reducing it. Click the box-within-a-box icon in the Inspector to set an image back to its original size.

If your page demands precision, use the text fields in either the Image Inspector or the Objects Toolbar to specify an exact height and width for your image. You can indicate dimensions in pixels or as a percentage, or allow the natural height and width of the original image to serve as is.

Positioning an Image

Using the Objects Toolbar, shown in Figure 11.4, you can position a selected image precisely on the layout grid of your page. Simply enter the x and y coordinates for the upper left corner of your image, and press Enter/Return after each to confirm what you've entered. The image automatically repositions itself according to the specified coordinates.

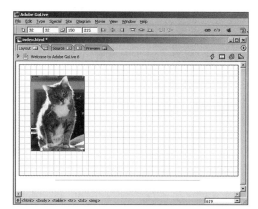

Figure 11.4
You can also use the Objects Toolbar to specify the position and dimensions of your image.

Aligning an Image

The Align pop-up menu within the Image Inspector, featured in Figure 11.5, allows you to establish an image's alignment to the page or within a text box, either vertically or horizontally. Simply select your choice and the image adjusts its position automatically.

Creating a Border

By default, GoLive gives images a border of zero, or no border at all. This enables you to create graphics that blend to the page and flow with one another, which is typically what designers desire. However, if you'd like to create a border around your image, simply type the pixel thickness you'd prefer in the space provided. Press Enter/Return to make it so, and your image will be automatically framed for a stunning gallery effect.

Since the border takes on the link color by default, you can change the color of your border by dragging a new color to the Link swatch of your Page Inspector, as shown in Figure 11.6 (see Chapter 5, "GoLive Interface Elements," for more on page basics), or set a new color directly in the HTML code.

Figure 11.5
A variety of alignment options are available within the Image Inspector.

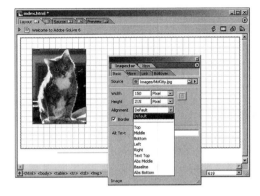

Figure 11.6
Use the Image Inspector to create a visible border around your image. The width of the border is specified in pixels.

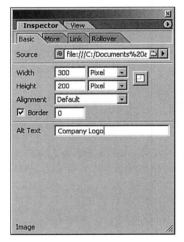

Including Alternative Text

While the use of alternative text remains...well, as an alternative, you should think seriously about taking advantage of this option. Text here can describe the image for visually impaired users or text-only browsers (including mobile devices). It also figures into some search engines that look for keywords in your page text.

If you've created graphics to use as your navigation labels, alternative text can be essential for helping to lead users through your Site when download times are slow, or if a graphic goes missing (see Figure 11.7). This small detail adds an extra level of courtesy and professionalism to your Site.

Figure 11.7
Here is the Inspector showing an Image with alternate text of "Company Logo." When the browser does not retrieve or display the actual image for any reason, this text will appear in its place.

Editing Images

Selected images can be cut, copied, and pasted in the standard fashion, using an option from the Edit menu or the equivalent keyboard shortcut.

Action	Mac	Windows
Select All	Cmd-A	Ctrl+A
Cut	Cmd-X	Ctrl+X
Copy	Cmd-C	Ctrl+C
Paste	Cmd-V	Ctrl+V

Other editing options available to you include

- To clear/delete an image, select it then choose Edit, Clear (Mac) or Edit, Delete (Windows), or press the Delete (Backspace) key. This removes the highlighted image entirely, without copying it to the clipboard.

- To duplicate an image, select Edit, Duplicate or drag the graphic while holding the Option (Mac) or Alt (Windows) key. Keep in mind that duplication only works if the selected object is on the grid.

Transform Palette

Adobe GoLive enables you to position objects precisely on your Web page and size them using a variety of methods. You can resize and reposition objects by dragging or employing the Image Inspector. The toolbar enables you to resize, reposition, and group objects. The Transform Palette, shown in Figure 11.8, provides all of these options. In addition, it also enables you to change the stacking order of items that overlap, such as hot spots on an image map or other layered elements.

Objects must first be placed on the layout grid before they can be repositioned or grouped. To reposition an object, enter new values for the x and y coordinates of the object's upper-left corner, and press Enter or Return after each to make it so. The object automatically migrates to its new home. Resizing works much the same way: Simply insert values for the height and width of the object in pixels, or enter one of these and check the box to constrain the ratio. When you press Enter or Return, the object transforms itself to fit the new dimensions.

Grouping enables you to move several elements as a single unit, so that you can maintain the proper spacing you've set up between them. To group elements, select one by clicking on it, then Shift-click to select the others. In the Transform Palette, under Grouping, click the icon on the left to group, or the icon on the right to ungroup. Similarly, to change the stacking order of overlapping objects, select an object, and then click the appropriate Bring to Front or Bring to Back icon under Z-Order. The objects should respond accordingly.

Figure 11.8
The Transform palette allows you to precisely position and scale your images.

ARRANGING OBJECTS

Not only can you manipulate and edit the images themselves; you can also easily arrange images on your page, alone or in groups, using the tools GoLive provides.

The Objects Toolbar

When you select an image or other object, the toolbar transforms itself into the Objects Toolbar, shown in Figure 11.9, providing options to help you position items on your page. Within the toolbar, you can set the size or position of an image, align it horizontally or vertically to the page, or group it with other items. You can also create a link, or unlink it if one is already created.

Creating Space

At times, you may wish to reserve extra space around an image to keep it from getting crowded by the elements around it. This is particularly true when images mingle with text. To ensure that your image gets enough breathing room, you can create a buffer zone around it by specifying values for the horizontal and vertical space.

Figure 11.9
The Objects Toolbar provides some of the same functions available on the Transform palette.

Click the More tab in the Image Inspector to view Hspace (horizontal) and Vspace, as you can see in Figure 11.10, then enter values for the distance of each in pixels and press Enter/Return to make it so. The items around your image will remain at bay.

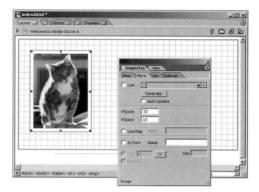

Figure 11.10
Use the Inspector to adjust the amount of blank space surrounding your image, both horizontally and vertically.

Align Palette

It's easy to arrange objects precisely on a Web page using the Align Palette, seen in Figure 11.11. To line up objects in relation to a parent, such as the document window or layout grid, first select the object or group of objects you wish to align. Then under Align to Parent, click a horizontal or vertical alignment button. The buttons in the Align Palette are identical to those on the toolbar, and enable you to align left, center, or right horizontally, and top, center, or bottom vertically.

You can also use the Align Palette to align and distribute objects in relation to each other.

First, select the objects by clicking on the first one and Shift-clicking on each additional object. Then under Align Objects, click a horizontal alignment button (left, center, right) or a vertical alignment button (top, center, bottom).

- Align Left aligns the objects along the left vertical axis of the object furthest left.
- Align Center aligns the objects along the vertical center axis between them.
- Align Right aligns the objects along the right vertical axis of the object farthest right.
- Align Top aligns the objects along the top horizontal axis of the highest object.
- Align Center aligns the objects along the horizontal center axis between them.
- Align Bottom aligns the objects along the bottom horizontal axis of the lowest object.

To distribute items in relation to each other using similar guidelines, first select the items to be distributed, then under Distribute Objects, click a horizontal distribution button or a vertical distribution button. The affected items will become more evenly spaced.

11

Figure 11.11
The Align palette allows positioning of one element relative to another.

USING A TRACING IMAGE

One exciting new development with this version of GoLive is known as the Tracing Image, and it comes complete with its own palette. Tracing Images allows you to import image files to place behind your layout as templates, so that you can design with perfect precision and consistency on top of them. What's more, you can actually cut out parts of the Tracing Image and use them as objects on your page, to avoid the redundant creation of images and thereby improve your workflow.

Formats that can be imported as Tracing Images include Illustrator native (ai), Photoshop 8-bit native (psd), gif, jpg, png, bmp, eps, pcx, pdf, pict (Mac), pixar, svg, targa, tiff, and Amiga iff.

To import a Tracing Image, follow these steps:

1. Select Window, Tracing Image. Within the Tracing Image Palette, check Source, and link to the desired image as you would link to any other image, by using Point and Shoot, Browse, or typing the image name and location into the Link Field.

2. Adjust the opacity of the tracing image as preferred as shown in Figure 11.12.

3. Enter values for the x and y position of the image, or select the Move Image Tool (the hand icon) which enables you to move the image freely using your cursor.

Figure 11.12
Adjust the opacity of a tracing image using the Tracing Image palette.

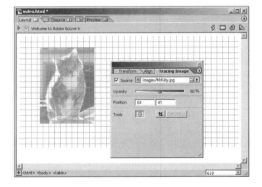

To cut out part of a Tracing Image, you would follow these steps:

1. Import and position a Tracing Image on your page, as directed above.

2. Select the Cut Out tool (looks like Photoshop's Crop tool) from the Tracing Image Palette.

3. Select a rectangular section of the image as shown in Figure 11.13.

Quickly resize your page to fit the dimensions of the Tracing Image by selecting Tracing Image from the Window Resolution pop-up menu on your page window.

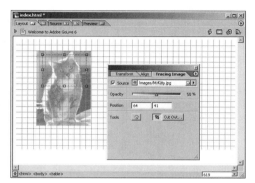

Figure 11.13
Use the cropping tool to cut out a Tracing Image.

4. Double-click the image selection, or click the Cut Out button to confirm your selection.

5. When the Save for Web dialog box opens (see Figure 11.14), select the image and adjust your optimization settings, and then click Save.

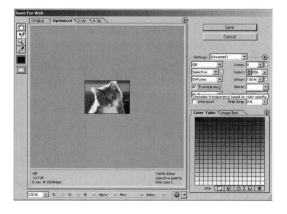

Figure 11.14
The Save for Web Dialog Box lets you save the current image as a Web-optimized gif or jpeg.

6. Choose a destination for your new file, and click Save again. The new image now appears as a floating box layer in your document window.

7. Reposition the original tracing image to 0/0 or align it with another selection on the page.

To remove a Tracing Image, you must deselect the source box in the Tracing Image Palette to make the Tracing Image disappear.

CREATING IMAGE MAPS

Often designers use images as navigational elements for their site. One way to achieve this is to make each individual rectangular image link to the correct page. Another means for achieving the same effect is to use an HTML image map. An image map is simply a set of coded instructions added to the HTML that specify linked areas (more commonly called *hot spots*) that each link to a separate destination.

For example, consider a map of the United States. When you click on a particular state, an HTML page with information on that state appears. This would be a particularly good implementation of an image map, simply because an image map can create oddly shaped links that would be appropriate for each of the states.

Keep in mind that an image map just specifies a hypertext reference (a link) for defined areas of an image. The link can lead to local files on your server, pages on other people's sites, and even to email addresses. For example, you can grab a picture of your family and link each person to their respective email address.

Image maps are often used for standard navigational bars: Rather than creating an navigation bar with eight separate linked images, the navigation bar could be one image with eight separate hot spots, each defining a link for the navigation bar.

There is a time and a place to implement an image map. For those purposes, the process for creating an image map is as follows.

Creating Image Maps in GoLive

Open an HTML page in the Document Window and drag an image from the Basic Tab of the Objects Palette. Do not forget to set the source of the image file via the Inspector.

To add an image map to an existing image in a document, select the image to which you would like to add the coded instructions and bring up the Inspector (Window, Inspector). The Inspector will display four tabs: Basic, More, Link, and Rollover. To apply an image map, select the More Tab, which provides access to a number of options, including the ability to add an image map. Check the Use Map checkbox to add an image map to the image, as shown in Figure 11.15. The Toolbar will change to provide hotspot drawing tools.

The most important of the Toolbar options include the Select Region Tool, and the Create Circle, Rectangle, and Polygon Hot Spot Drawing Tools.

Start by selecting the shape of the hot spot you want to draw from the Toolbar: rectangle, circle, or polygon. Then draw that shape over the desired area of the image. For rectangular- and circular-shaped hot spots, click and drag from the upper-left corner of the desired shape to the lower-right corner. For polygon hot spots, click at every point on the perimeter of the shape. Figure 11.16 shows several hot spots in an image.

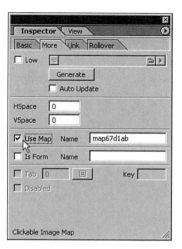

Figure 11.15
With the image selected, choose Use Map from the More Tab of the Inspector.

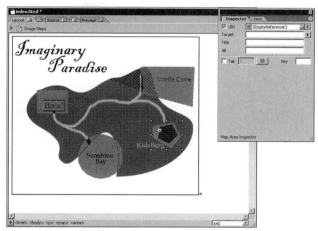

Figure 11.16
This image has four image map hot spots.

Notice that the Select Region Tool can be used to reposition and resize a hot spot. To reposition a hot spot, use the Select Region Tool to click and drag from the center of the shape. To resize a hot spot, use the Select Region Tool to first select the hot spot, then click and drag the handles of the hot spot, as shown in Figure 11.17.

As of yet, the hot spots have been created, but the pages to which the hot spots will be linked have not been defined. To define a link for an area, select the hot spot using the Select Region Tool and bring up the Inspector. For each hot spot, define the URL Reference (the link), the Target (the name of the frame in which to open, if applicable), and the Alternate Text (the text which will appear if the image is inaccessible to a user), as shown in Figure 11.18.

In addition, GoLive provides a means for setting the Tab order of the hot spots. As you may know, the tab key provides a means of selecting items on a Web page, including HTML form elements and links. To set the tab order for each hot spot, select the hot spot, check the Tab checkbox on the More tab of the Inspector, and set the number, as in Figure 11.18.

Figure 11.17
Use the Select Region Tool to move and resize hotspots.

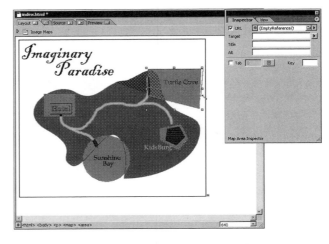

Figure 11.18
Use the Select Region Tool to select a hot spot. Then, using the Inspector, set the URL, target (if applicable), and Alternate text.

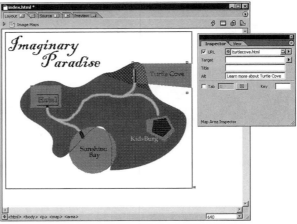

Figure 11.19
With the hot spot selected, set its placement in the Tab order of the page. This effect must be tested in a browser.

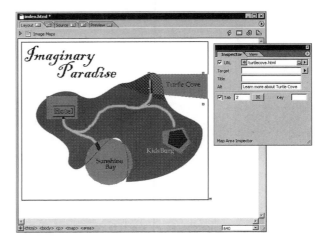

The tab order refers to the order the hot spots will be selected if the user chooses to navigate via the Tab key instead of the mouse. Notice that the tab order must be tested in the browser.

Applying Actions to a Hot Spot

Later, we will discuss GoLive's Actions (implementation of ready-made JavaScripts), particularly with regard to how to add an action to a link. Keep in mind that a hot spot is a link: That is to say, a hot spot may also have a set of GoLive actions associated with it. For more on Actions, see Chapter 20.

CREATING ROLLOVERS

The Rollover tab in the Image Inspector enables you to create mouseover and mousedown effects easily by specifying links to alternate image files and providing text messages. You can also check a box to preload these images.

To create a Rollover, you might follow these steps:

1. Add an Image to your page as usual.

2. With the image highlighted, select the Rollover tab in the Image Inspector, as shown in Figure 11.20.

3. Provide a name for your new rollover in the space provided, and press Enter/Return to make it so.

4. The name of the highlighted image appears as the original image. If this is accurate, leave it there. Otherwise select another original image.

5. Click the Over box to create a mouseOver effect, changing images whenever a mouse passes over the original image. Link to the appropriate mouseOver image using Point and Shoot, using Browse, selecting from the Popup Menu, or typing a file destination in the Link Field. The new image appears as a thumbnail in the Inspector. Indicate text to appear in the margin of the browser, if desired.

6. Click the Down box to create a mouseDown effect, changing images whenever a mouse button presses down on the original image. Link to the appropriate mouseDown image using Point and Shoot, using Browse, selecting from the Popup Menu, or typing a file destination in the Link Field. The new image appears as a thumbnail in the Inspector. Indicate text to appear in the margin of the browser, if desired.

7. Test your new rollover in a browser to view the changing effects.

11

Figure 11.20
The Rollover tab of the Image Inspector provides an easy way to turn a regular image into a rollover.

Rollover Options

Click the small circled arrow in the top-right corner of the Rollover tab to view additional options for creating rollovers. These options are

- **Detect Rollover Images**. Based on your Rollover Settings, GoLive takes the name of the file established as your original image file, and searches for appropriate images within that folder to serve as suitable mouseOver and mouseDown companions to that file. If it finds such companions, it automatically adds them to the Inspector, saving you multiple steps.

- **Clear Rollover**. Removes the rollover effects.

- **Rollover Settings**. This settings window, seen in Figure 11.20, allows you to create your own naming conventions for mouseOver and mouseDown image files, so that GoLive can automatically detect which files should be used together. For example, if you name your original file Button, then name the accompanying files Button_Over and Button_Down, GoLive will locate these images and load them automatically when you choose Detect Rollover Images from the menu.

Figure 11.21
Rollover Settings

TROUBLESHOOTING

Image Map Problems

When making image maps, I can't get my hot spot drawing tools to appear in the Toolbar.

Make sure you are selecting the image to which you want to add the image map. Also, make sure the Use Map checkbox is selected on the More tab of the Inspector.

When I test my links out in an image map, they don't work.

If you're testing a link to another Web site, make sure that you have included the external reference (the `http://`) as the start of the URL. For local links, make sure the path to the file is correct.

GOING LIVE

Take the time to think through your implementation of an image map. Although the consequences of applying an image map are few and far between (and minor at that), you will find there are always disadvantages and advantages of applying one means over the other.

The advantage of using an image map for the navigation bar is that only one image must be created, thereby easing your file management. Disadvantages exist as well. First, cutting the one image into smaller pieces will cause the page to download faster, despite the fact that the total data size of the images is equal in both cases. This is a result of the fact that browsers can download images in parallel, so one 40k image will take longer to load than four 10k images. Second, using an image map in place of separate linked items hinders the author's ability to create efficient and dynamic rollover effects. A rollover replaces one image for another, so to apply a rollover to a hot spot would result in the entire image swapping for another.

11

WORKING WITH LINKS

IN THIS CHAPTER

Linking Up with the World   202

Adding Navigational Links   202

Using Anchors   208

Creating URL Pop-up Menus   209

Managing Links   210

Troubleshooting   213

Going Live   214

LINKING UP WITH THE WORLD

Sure, it's great to create digital documents, design pages full of well-written text and eye-catching graphics. GoLive fluidly combines the editing capabilities of a word processing program with the design elements of a page layout application. Yet the distinguishing feature of a Web page lies in its links.

When you create pages to be placed online, you join a world that is, by its very nature, interactive. You establish connections between your own pages, venture to other Sites, and participate with users all over the globe. This connectivity—the ability to leap easily from place to place—is precisely what powers the Internet and makes it so unique.

In this chapter, we'll show you how to weave your way onto the Web by setting up links and using GoLive's tools to manage them.

ADDING NAVIGATIONAL LINKS

Links come in many forms. In effect, your page is composed of links even before it connects externally, since images and other elements are actually attached by linking to them within your Site folder. Links can originate from text or images. They can connect to anchor points on the same page, other pages within your Site, anchor points on other pages, external URLs, sound or multimedia files, .pdf documents, email addresses, and other files for opening or downloading. In this section, we'll discuss the ins and outs of establishing links through text, images, and other objects, for the purpose of navigating through your Site and referencing others.

It's important to note that in GoLive, you should make sure your page is saved into your Site before creating any links to or from it. Otherwise the link created will be saved as a link to the local directory on your hard drive rather than as a proper Site page, creating big problems when the page is moved or uploaded. For this reason, we highly recommend creating and opening pages from within your Site Window.

GoLive uses standard methods for establishing links, whether these are intended to connect page elements or to be used for the purpose of navigation. Within the Inspector, you have the option to use Point-and-Shoot (Fetch URL), type directly into the Link Field, Browse to locate the linking file, or select further options from the URL Menu. Let's examine each of these individually.

Point-and-Shoot (Fetch URL)

Beside the Link icons (or the URL checkbox, in the case of an image map) you'll find the *pick whip*, a small spiral that looks like a coiled-up rope lasso. This unique innovation lets you lasso your link just like a cowboy. Simply click using the pick whip and drag to extend the rope directly to the link destination file within your Site Window, as you can see in Figure 12.1. The name of the file appears instantly in the Inspector's link field, along with path information to that file.

Follow these steps to use the pick whip to make links:

- If your link destination is another point on the same page, drag to that location on the page and an anchor will automatically be created (see "Using Anchors" later in this chapter).

- If your link destination is another HTML page within your Site, a .pdf or .swf document, or a compressed file, drag to that item within the Files tab of your Site Window.

- If your link destination is a specific point on another HTML page within your Site, you can either open the page and drag directly to that point, or link to an existing anchor beneath that page in the Files tab of your Site Window.

- If your link destination is an external URL or an email address, and you've already collected the address, you can drag to it in the External tab of your Site Window.

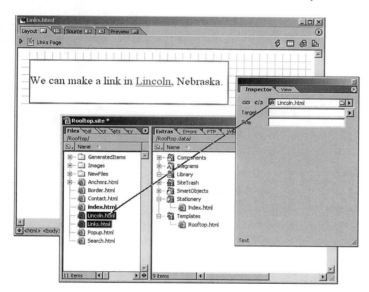

Figure 12.1
Use Point and Shoot to create links.

If your Site Window is not visible as you start to drag the lasso, simply pause your cursor over the Select Window button to pull the Site Window into view, as shown in Figure 12.2. If the necessary tab is not pulled forward as you begin to drag, rest your cursor on top of the tag until it moves to the front.

Link Field

If you know the name and location of the linking file, you can simply type the path and filename directly into the space provided, and press Enter/Return to confirm it. GoLive will find the file based on what you've typed. Be aware that the margin for human error widens whenever extra typing is involved. You might want to copy and paste filenames into the field, if this is the route you choose.

For email addresses, you need only type or paste the address itself. As you can see in Figure 12.3, GoLive adds the `mailto:` tag. For pages within your Site, you can simply type the page name with .html extension, since links are relative by default. For external URLs, you should type the entire URL as it would appear in a browser.

Figure 12.2
Pause over the Select Window to make the Site Window appear.

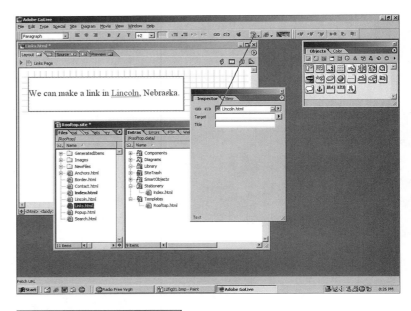

Figure 12.3
When you enter an email address, GoLive automatically adds the `mailto:` tag.

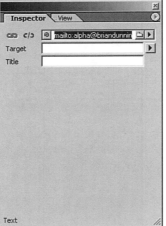

For all addresses, make sure you completely delete or select and type over the "(Empty Reference)" placeholder in this field.

To extend the field so that you can view a longer URL, click the arrow to the right of the field and select Edit, or on a Mac press (Cmd-E). This opens the Edit URL Window. Here you can view link addresses in their entirety, make changes to the URLs of previously established links, make a link absolute or relative, or set query parameters.

To open a page in its own browser window (recommended for external links so that users retain a connection with your Site), follow these steps:

1. Enter the URL of the destination you're linking to in the Link Field and press Enter/Return to confirm as usual.

2. Click the arrowed menu button to the right of the Target field, and select _blank from the list of options as seen in Figure 12.4.

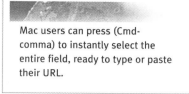

Mac users can press (Cmd-comma) to instantly select the entire field, ready to type or paste their URL.

Figure 12.4
Open a page in its own window.

To open a page in a new frame, complete the preceding steps, choosing the name of the target frame in place of _blank. GoLive assumes your link destination is a non-frames page, but you can also choose top, parent, self, and blank as constant options. Your custom names also appear in the menu if you've created your own frame names. Similarly, you can choose a Title for your frame pages here.

⇨ *For more detailed information about frames, **see** Chapter 14, "Working with Frames. "*

Browse

Click on the folder icon to the right of the link field to browse throughout your system and locate the files you need. Again, the name and path to the file you select appear in the link field. The Browse option may only be used for linking to local pages and downloadable files; you can't link to external URLs or to anchors within pages this way.

Keep in mind that pages you link to using the Browse option should already be contained within your Site Window. Otherwise, the link you establish will be saved as a link to the local directory on your hard drive rather than as a proper Site page, creating problems later.

12

Menu Options

Click on the small arrow to the right of the folder to view commonly used link options. Within this menu you can choose to make your links relative or absolute, edit the URL path, or choose from recently selected html files, images, miscellaneous URLs, or anchors in the list. This list is similar to the recently used files list found under your File menu, and changes continuously according to the files you've used.

Use the Edit option you see in Figure 12.5 to view link addresses in their entirety, make changes to the URLs of previously established links, make a link absolute or relative, or set query parameters.

Figure 12.5
Use the Edit URL Window to set various options for the links in your pages.

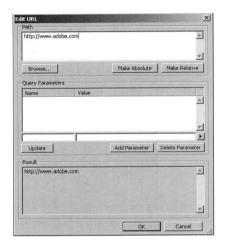

Creating Text Links

The most basic link uses text to connect. Standard text links appear blue and underlined, to indicate their status as links. You can set up a text link using a single character, a word, a phrase, or a whole paragraph. Links can stand alone or mingle within larger bodies of text. They can appear in any font, size, or style, and in other colors than the standard blue. Text that is linked can still be edited, moved, and manipulated as regular text.

To create a text link, you would follow these steps:

1. Highlight the text you wish to link.

2. Indicate to GoLive that you wish to create a link. You can do this in one of various ways:

   a. Click on the New Link icon in the Toolbar.

   b. Click on the New Link icon in the Inspector.

   c. Select Special, New Link from the menu.

   d. Press (Cmd-L) [Ctrl+L] on your keyboard.

   e. Ctrl-click (Mac) or right-click [Windows] on the highlighted text and select New Link from the contextual menu.

3. In the Inspector, specify the link's destination. You can do this using Point and Shoot (Fetch URL), typing the URL in the text field, browsing to locate the appropriate file, or choosing an option from the menu.

Creating Image Links

You can create links from images in their entirety or from parts of the image, in the form of image maps. (For more on image maps, see Chapter 11, "Using Graphic Elements.")

Follow these steps to create a link from an image:

1. Select the image you wish to link.

2. Indicate to GoLive that you wish to create a link. You can do this in one of various ways:

   a. Click on the New Link icon in the Toolbar.

   b. Click on the Link tab in the Inspector, then select the New Link icon.

   c. Select Special, New Link from the menu.

   d. Press (Cmd-L) [Ctrl+L] on your keyboard.

   e. Ctrl-click (Mac) or right-click [Windows] on the highlighted text and select New Link from the contextual menu.

3. In the Inspector, specify the link's destination. You can do this using Point and Shoot (Fetch URL), typing the URL in the text field, browsing to locate the appropriate file, or choosing an option from the menu..

4. Make sure the Border is indicated as zero in the Basic tab of the Image Inspector if you don't want your linked image to display a colored border around its edges (see Figure 12.6) .

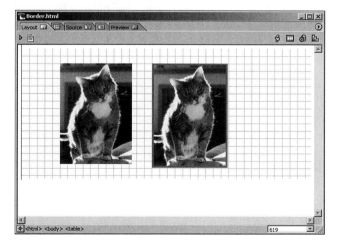

Figure 12.6
The same image appears both with and without a border.

USING ANCHORS

Standard links take the user to the top of the destination page, but in some instances, you may want to link to a point further down the page you're on, or to a particular spot on another page. An anchor's a way of creating a more specific link. Thus to set up an anchor link involves two parts: placing the anchor itself, and establishing a link to it.

Placing Anchors

When you place an anchor, you determine the exact destination of a link. Since the browser jumps to the vertical line where the anchor is positioned, not to a particular word or horizontal point within the line, this system works best when you place anchors at the beginnings of lines, making them easy to locate. Multiple anchors on the same line are redundant and can be consolidated to a single anchor. When referencing a table, you may wish to place the anchor before the table and allow viewers to see the entire thing. You may use anchors to pinpoint a specific word or subject, as in a definition or description, or you may simply divide your page into sections and let the anchor reference the start of each section. The uses for anchors are endless.

To place an anchor, do any one of the following:

- Drag the Anchor icon from the Objects Palette into place on your page. Choose a name for it in the Inspector, and use this name when creating later links to it.

- Position your cursor where you would like the anchor to be and double-click (Mac) or right-click on the Anchor icon. Choose a name for it in the Inspector, and use this name when creating later links to it.

- While creating a link, Point and Shoot directly to place the anchor on the page, and create an instant anchor. GoLive assigns a name to the anchor, using the page text that follows it plus a number, but you can replace this name by selecting the anchor itself and typing a more suitable name in the Inspector's text field.

Naming Anchors

Remember to follow normal Web protocol when naming anchors: Keep names brief, avoid spaces and unusual characters, and make each name unique. If you use the same name more than once on a page, the link won't know which anchor you mean.

It helps to use descriptive words so that you can easily determine which anchor you want when setting up links. In the Site Window, anchors are listed beneath the page on which they reside.

You should note that unlike most files in the Site Window, you cannot rename anchors by selecting them here and typing a new name. You must actually open the page that contains them, click on the anchor itself, and alter the name in the Inspector. Press Enter/Return to confirm the name, and refresh the Site Window to make the new name appear here.

When anchor links are created, the URL will include the page name followed by the number or pound sign (#) and then the anchor name, appearing something like this:

```
http://www.mypage.com/index.html#anchor1
```

Anchors referenced on the current page in view will appear as relative links, with only the pound sign and anchor name required.

Linking to Anchors

Setting up the link to an anchor involves similar procedures to those used when establishing a regular link. You can either place the anchors first and then create links to them, or create anchor links on-the-fly in a single step.

To link to an anchor, do any one of the following:

- Point and shoot to an existing anchor in the Site Window, as shown in Figure 12.7. Anchor links are listed below the page on which they appear.

- Point and shoot to an existing anchor on a page. (Naturally the destination page must be open in GoLive first.)

- Type or paste the destination URL into the Link Field, using a pound sign (#) plus the name of the anchor after the page name.

- Create an instant anchor link by Pointing and Shooting directly to the spot on an open destination page where the anchor should be. GoLive automatically assigns a name to the anchor, using the page text that follows it plus a number, but you can replace this name by selecting the anchor itself and typing another name in the Inspector's text field.

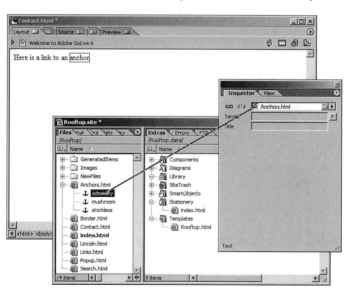

Figure 12.7
Link to anchors in the Site Window.

CREATING URL POP-UP MENUS

Sometimes, when creating a table of contents or complex Site navigation, you'd like a more elegant and compact solution than a mere list of links. You can conserve page space and still include all your links by using one of GoLive's built-in options, the URL Pop-up Menu. This object lets you quickly set up a list of links in handy pop-up format.

To create a URL pop-up menu, follow these steps:

1. From the Objects palette, select the Smart tab.

2. Click the URL Popup icon and drag it into place on your page window.

3. In the Inspector, click New Item (the page icon) to create a new menu item, or edit the existing menu by typing in the spaces provided. Label each menu item by entering a name for it in the Label text box, and provide a URL for each link in the menu. Links can be local (relative) or external (absolute).

4. Duplicate a menu item by selecting it in the Inspector and clicking the plus sign, or Duplicate button.

5. Delete a menu item by selecting it in the Inspector and clicking on the Trash can, or Delete button.

6. Reposition a menu item by selecting it and using the scroll arrows to move it up or down within the menu.

7. Preview your page using a Web browser, as shown in Figure 12.8, to see the pop-up menu in action and verify the links it contains.

Figure 12.8
A URL pop-up menu in action.

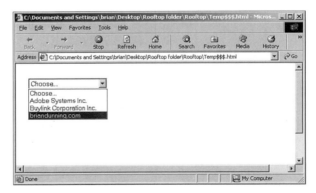

MANAGING LINKS

GoLive contains several tools and features to help you effectively manage the links used by your Site. When you store URL and email addresses in the External tab of your Site Window, you give yourself easy access to them for repeated use. You also enable GoLive to verify the URLs to avoid linking errors later.

There are many methods for assembling addresses. Because GoLive keeps track of what you've already gathered, there's no danger of duplication, so you can add new addresses as often as you like. In addition, GoLive enables you to edit, organize, and oversee the links for an entire Site just as easily as you would manage the contents of a folder. Let's take a look at some of your options.

Gathering Addresses From Your Pages

Using this collection method, GoLive automatically checks all the links in all of your pages, so you don't need to have any pages open. You can easily edit links that have been added this way as well, and GoLive will update all pages that link to that destination.

When the destinations are added, URLs get placed in a folder called New URLs, and email addresses are placed in one called New Addresses. These folders can be renamed, and you can move the contents out of these folders if you choose.

To gather addresses from your pages, you need to

1. Click on the Site Window to pull it forward and select the External tab.

2. Choose Site, Get References Used. The external links from this page are instantly added to your Site Window, as shown in Figure 12.9, where they can be linked to again and again.

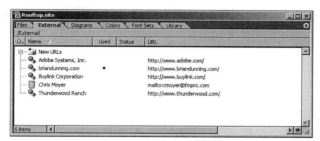

Figure 12.9
Collect addresses in the Site Window.

Adding Addresses Manually

If you choose, you may also add new destinations individually by following these steps.

Follow these steps to add an address manually:

1. From the Site tab of the Objects Palette, drag a URL icon (for URLs) or Address icon (for email addresses) to the External tab of the Site Window.

2. Click on the untitled address to select it, and then provide a Name and URL for it in the Reference Inspector, as you can see in Figure 12.10. Press Enter/Return after each to confirm it. Your new address is now added, and can be linked to as often as you like.

Gathering Addresses from a Browser

In most cases, you can add URLs directly from the browser window to your Site Window. This ensures that the address is correct, and makes gathering URLs a snap. You can also collect addresses from your bookmarks or favorites files as individual addresses or groups of addresses within folders.

To add an address directly from a browser window:

1. With your browser window open to the URL you wish to collect, position the Site Window so that you can see it, and click on the External tab to make it active.

12

Figure 12.10
Add addresses manually.

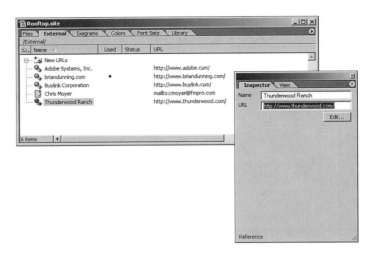

2. Drag the bookmark icon (Netscape) to the left of the location field or the @ sign in the location field (Explorer) to the External tab of the Site Window.

To add an address from Bookmarks/Favorites:

1. In Netscape Navigator, select Bookmarks, Edit Bookmarks. In Internet Explorer, select Favorites, Organize Favorites. This opens a window containing a list of your bookmarks/favorites.

2. Drag the desired address to the External tab of your Site Window, as shown in Figure 12.11.

Figure 12.11
Add an address from Favorites.

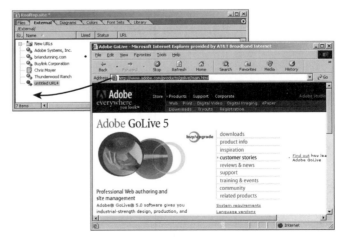

Organizing and Editing Links

To help keep your Site Window organized and make addresses easier to locate, you can add folders to group addresses at any point. Simply drag a Folder icon from the Site tab of your Objects Palette into the External tab of your Site Window, and place addresses within it. You may name your folders anything you like, and group your addresses in any way you choose.

You can also edit the addresses themselves at any point, and GoLive will update the addresses wherever it is used in your Site. Simply select the address to edit by clicking on it in the External tab of your Site Window. Once selected, you can make changes to the address in the Inspector. Then press Enter/Return to confirm the change. When GoLive asks if you would like to update links to this address, agree by clicking OK.

In & Out Links Palette

The In & Out Links Palette, seen in Figure 12.12, displays all links in and out of any selected page. This includes all the other elements on that page, plus all the other pages to which that page is linked. Links to the chosen page appear on the left, while links from it take their leave on the right.

What's truly remarkable about this palette is that it allows you to see all the links, both internal and external, even those embedded in PDF or multimedia files. And as if that weren't amazing enough, it even permits you to update these links. Any link you see can be edited and its destination switched by simply inspecting that page or address, then using Point and Shoot to attach a new address.

This feature proves extremely beneficial when troubleshooting or repairing broken links. When an empty reference appears, you know you've got a problem link, and you can correct the problem immediately, right inside the palette.

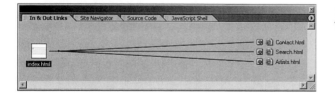

Figure 12.12
The In & Out Links Palette.

TROUBLESHOOTING

Avoiding the Absolute or Relative Problem

Sometimes when I link to a page, I get a 404 error or some other strange problem, even though I'm certain that the page exists.

What's probably happening is that your links may have been stored as absolute pathnames instead of relative. Sometimes when you view the source on your page, you'll find that the full pathname to a document on your hard drive somehow made it into the document, like `C:/Documents/Pages/MyPage.html`, which obviously won't work for someone across the Internet.

Absolute pathnames contain the full exact URL of the page, such as `http://www.briandunning.com/video.shtml`. A relative pathname contains only the path to the document relative to the current document's location. For example, `more/stuff.html` is going to look for a folder called "more" in the same directory as the current page, and then display the `stuff.html` document from there. Starting the address with a slash, like `/stuff.html`, will go all the way to the root level of the Web site and look for the page there. Other rules apply too, but you get the idea.

Normally GoLive does an excellent job of handling this for you. But stranger things have happened, so if your links are giving you a hard time, look at the source code of your page and see if the link is not formatted the way you expect it to be.

GOING LIVE

Linking to Special Windows

One cool trick that you see a lot these days involves browser windows that appear with no menu bars, scroll bars, or other stuff. This type of window can mimic an application screen, an alert box, or other interface element. You see these a lot these days in pop-up ads and other annoying things.

But there are other more benign uses for these windows. Sometimes you may want a form to pop up over the browser window, or a special alert. These specially modified windows are accomplished using JavaScript. Use the following JavaScript in your document; just substitute `page_address.html` with your actual link address. Notice the controls for the special window in the script. You can play with these to change the size and appearance of the window.

```
<head>
<script language="JavaScript">
<!-- Begin
function specialWindow(theURL) {
window.open(theURL,'','toolbar=no,menubar=no,location=no,width=500,
➥height=300');
}
// End -->
</script>
</head>
<body>
<a href="javascript:void(0);" onClick="specialWindow('page_address.html');">
➥Open Full Screen Window</a>
</body>
```

Here is another neat trick you've probably seen with links. When you click any link that takes you off of a page, presto, another little window pops up unexpectedly. This is also done with JavaScript, and here's the code that will accomplish it. Just replace the dummy URL `www.whatever.com/address.html` with the address of the page you want to appear.

```
<head>
<script language="JavaScript">
<!-- Begin
```

```
function popWhenExit() {
window.open('http://www.whatever.com/address.html','','toolbar=no,
➥menubar=no,location=no,width=500,height=500');
}
// End -->
</script>
</head>
<body onUnload="popWhenExit()">
<a href="http://www.briandunning.com">Click here to leave this page.</a>
</body>
```

PAGE EXTRAS

IN THIS CHAPTER

Adding Value with Extras   218

Adding Comments   218

Creating a Marquee   221

Date and Time Stamps   223

Viewing Document Statistics   224

Previewing Pages   225

Troubleshooting   226

Going Live   226

ADDING VALUE WITH EXTRAS

Once you feel comfortable laying out pages with text, images, and navigational links, you've got the basics of page creation covered. Now it's time to zero in on the extra details that help you better monitor your Site and make it shine. Promote teamwork and give yourself a break by including comments along the way. Create a scrolling marquee, or add date and time stamps to your pages. Check your document stats and learn how to preview your pages in all the latest devices. This chapter describes the little things that add up to a better, more professional, and manageable Site.

ADDING COMMENTS

Ever want you could write a little note to yourself in the margin of the page, detailing some feature or reminding yourself about future plans for the page? Ever want the programmer who started this Web page before you had left a set of instructions to explain what the heck he was thinking? Comment tags to the rescue!

Comments can help jog your own memory as you plan and assemble various parts of a large project, or allow those working on your team to see what was going on inside your noggin and better comprehend the mental process. Use these tags as you would sticky notes left on the monitors of your friends and colleagues, purely as reminders or as running commentary throughout the creation process. Comments can be creative, informative, demonstrative, silly, or simply provide an outlet for letting off steam in stressful situations. Let's explore some potential uses for the comment tag.

A wonderful use of the comment tag is to note where you left off at the end of the workday, so that you or others will know exactly where to pick things up when you begin again. This can be particularly handy if you're leaving for a weekend or holiday, where multiple days of downtime could potentially derail your train of thought. Not only do the comments help when you return; they allow you to leave your work at the office and enjoy time off without trying to keep project details fresh in your memory. Write it down and relax.

Comment tags can also be used to describe your ideas and visions. Been doing some brainstorming? Had an "aha!" breakthrough for solving a problem or a sudden epiphany concerning your Web site? Without skipping a beat, you can add a comment to immortalize your beloved bursts of creativity directly on the pages to which the ideas apply. Then when you're ready to fix the problem or lend expression to your ideas, your notes will already be safely in place.

Using comments to list problems you encounter along the way and the troubleshooting steps you've already taken or could take is a wonderful idea—and a great way to caution your comrades about any quicksand, rodents of unusual size, or other perils that have plagued you while traversing the fire swamp. By alerting others of known bugs, you help your teammates avoid the same pitfalls. Plus you improve the troubleshooting process tenfold by telling them what you've already tried, describing suspicious characters or clues to the mystery, and hypothesizing as to the final solution.

Some other great reasons to add comments when building your page include

■ **Explain how complex features work.** Comments can be invaluable for avoiding confusion when including scripts, layers, or any complicated elements that contain multiple moving parts. Add tags initially and you'll thank yourself later.

- **Give yourself some credit.** Plenty of Webmasters borrow and steal page pieces and parts from others online. If you've created something particularly cool or unusual, place a comment within the code to alert others that this script or feature is your very own handiwork. Conscientious collectors will include these lines of credit when they paste the piece into a new page. Likewise, if you take advantage of any free resources, Web ethics would suggest that you give credit where it's due and place a comment with the creator's name and URL within your page.

- **Rant.** That's right. Let it all out. Since comments are simply page elements, they can be changed or deleted long before the page becomes permanent. If a stressful situation's got you grasping for strands at your scalp, use comments to unleash your anger and frustration as fast as your typing fingers will fly. That way nobody gets hurt, friends and colleagues are spared from feeling your wrath, and the release will leave you calmer and better able to cope. Written rants can be incredible therapy—just remember to delete them before they reach the outside world.

- **Make suggestions for improvement.** Whether you're the project manager or working as part of a team, you may see reasons to add your two cents and help everybody build a better mousetrap. Managers can use comment tags as they review a work in progress, or after meeting with clients, to relay reactions and propose changes. You might even make suggestions to yourself, to note alternative directions to take or variations on a design theme.

- **Keep track of specifics.** If you need to keep an element at designated dimensions, note the size or position of the piece in a comment. Suppose a script only works in certain browsers, or the client likes a particular shade of background blue. Post a note to remember these details and keep all your specs together where they belong. This trick can pay off if you ever need to retrace your steps and defend a design decision.

- **Laugh.** Much like ranting, a laughter tag can lighten your load and make any project more fun. Including witty remarks, quotes, or bits of silliness helps everyone keep perspective and enjoy the job at hand. Remember, these can always be deleted before the Site is finalized.

- **Report your progress.** You may want to keep a kind of timeline or running log of what you've completed or updated on particular dates. Include keywords you can search for later, and these comments can be used for billing purposes, troubleshooting, or for maintaining Site consistency. It also gives you a written record of your accomplishments once raise-time rolls around.

One last thought on using comments…assume that you're going to be hit by a bus tomorrow, and someone else will need to decipher your muck and pick up where you left off.

Remember, comments cannot be seen when viewed in a browser, so your notes remain behind the scenes. That said, anyone who views the source code *can* see them, so avoid using profanity or other inappropriate remarks in the final versions of your pages. Some comments are meant to remain on the page for posterity while others exist only as temporary assembly notes while the crew is building your Site. Learn to use comments constructively, and the page creation process becomes a wee bit easier.

13

Adding comments to your page is as simple as following these steps:

1. Drag the Comment icon from the Basic tab of the Objects Palette and place it on your page. Comments placed on the Layout Editor appear as tiny cartoon dialog bubbles. In the source code, comments appear in a lighter color and are always contained within comment tags like this: `<! - - your comments here - - >`.

2. In the Comment Inspector, write or paste your text. It appears automatically in the source code as you see in Figure 13.1.

Figure 13.1
This is what a Comment looks like when viewed in the Inspector.

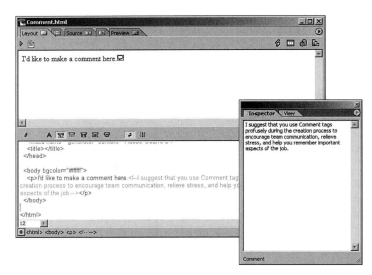

Or, you might follow these steps to add comments:

1. Drag the Comment icon from the Basic tab of the Objects Palette and place it inside the Outline Editor.

2. Type or paste your comment text to the right of the large arrow, as seen in Figure 13.2, where the comment will appear in full.

Figure 13.2
This is what a Comment looks like in the Outline Editor.

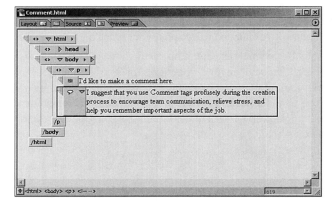

CREATING A MARQUEE

To make your comments boldly public and allow text to scroll on your page, you can make use of a marquee, as implied in Figure 13.3. Although lacking the same glamour or glitter, the marquee attempts to imitate the lighted signage of classic Hollywood, Broadway, and Times Square. Nowadays the scrolling marquee might be considered distracting or tacky in much the same way as the Blink attribute of text tends to annoy, and it should not be used except in rare circumstances. But if this is the kind of flair you want to impart on your page, scroll on.

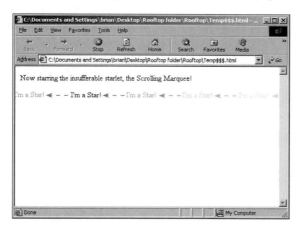

Figure 13.3
Hold this book at arm's length and move it rapidly side to side to simulate how this Scrolling Marquee, "I'm a Star!", looks in action.

If you want to create a scrolling marquee, follow these steps:

1. Drag the Marquee icon from the Basic tab of the Objects Palette and position it on your page.

2. In the Marquee Inspector, shown in Figure 13.4, type or paste the text you want to display. Keep the message as short as possible.

3. Select a Behavior from the pop-up menu and click Left or Right to determine the direction of the scrolling. Default and Scroll both scroll the message from one side to the other and the text disappears off the side of the screen. Slide scrolls as well, but keeps the message within sight when it's done scrolling. Alternate scrolls the message left and right, bouncing back and forth when it reaches the edges.

4. Indicate the number of loops for the scroll, or check the Forever box to create a continuous loop.

5. Type values for Amount and Delay to control the speed of the scrolling.

6. Save your page and open in a browser to see the effects.

Resizing a Marquee

You may change the size of your marquee manually by selecting it in your page window and dragging on the blue handles. You may also resize the marquee using the Inspector.

13

Figure 13.4
The properties of a Scrolling Marquee can be viewed and edited in the Inspector, Basic tab.

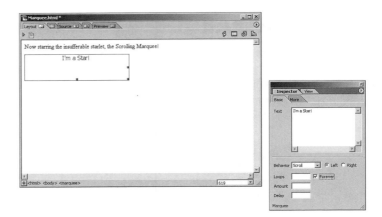

You would follow steps such as these to resize a marquee:

1. Select the marquee to be sized.

2. Click the More tab in the Marquee Inspector (see Figure 13.5).

3. Insert values for height and/or width, and select pixels or percent from the pop-up menus for each. The new sizes take effect immediately.

Figure 13.5
Additional properties are available on the More tab of the Inspector.

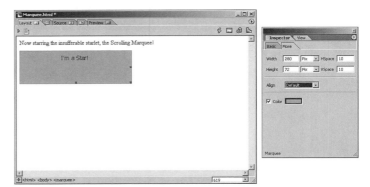

Other Marquee Options

The More tab of the Marquee Inspector contains additional options for controlling the appearance of your marquee. You can create a buffer of space between the marquee text and elements around it by indicating values for hspace (horizontal space) and vspace (vertical space). Align the marquee on the page using the Alignment menu. Drag a new color to the Color swatch to add a background hue.

CREATING DATE AND TIME STAMPS

Often affixing a date and time stamp to your pages proves to be highly informative for both creator and audience. It simply states the date and time of the page's last update, as recorded by the system clock on the computer housing the page.

This seemingly small addition can assist you in troubleshooting if future problems should arise, keep you abreast of regular Site maintenance, help with billing issues if work is billed by completion date, or simply jog your memory if any questions come to light concerning the Site. To your users, the stamp indicates the freshness of the Site content, and the level of commitment to Site upkeep.

Providing the date and time of updates serves to effectively communicate with the public. If your pages remain current, with up-to-the-minute accuracy, draw attention to their dynamic nature. If you post regular updates daily, weekly, or at any steady interval, the date stamp shown in Figure 13.6 tells return visitors that they're viewing brand new material.

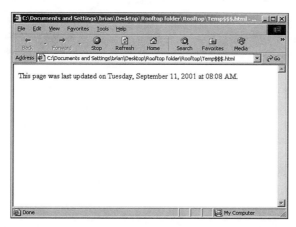

Figure 13.6
A Time and Date Stamp can show the current time and date on your Web page. It only shows the time and date as of when the page was loaded; it does not update dynamically.

One way to create a date or time stamp is as follows:

1. Type any descriptive text you'd like to add before the date or time stamp (Last revised, and so on) in your document window.

2. Click the Smart tab in the Objects palette.

3. Drag the Modified Date icon to your page, or double-click on it in the Objects palette.

4. In the Inspector, shown in Figure 13.7, select a country from the Format menu plus a format for your new date or time stamp.

5. Save your page. This sets the exact date or time to be displayed in the stamp.

Each stamp contains either the date or time format, not both. To include both the date and time, you will need to create two separate stamps, indicating a date format for one and a time format for the other.

13

Figure 13.7
Choose the format of your Time and Date Stamp in the Inspector.

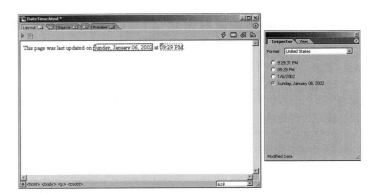

VIEWING DOCUMENT STATISTICS

When creating pages, you may find it helpful to see how long your page takes to download at various speeds, without having to perform all that testing yourself. Enter Document Statistics, GoLive's built-in gizmo for figuring just such estimates for you.

This window also provides instant word and character counts for your text plus byte counts for each element on the page and a grand total of all.

To view your Document Statistics, select Special, Document Statistics from the GoLive menu or press (Cmd-Opt-Shift-I) [Ctrl+Alt+Shift+I] on your keyboard. This pulls up a statistics window similar to that in Figure 13.8. Click OK or press Return to close the window again.

Figure 13.8
Your page's vital signs are available in the Document statistics window.

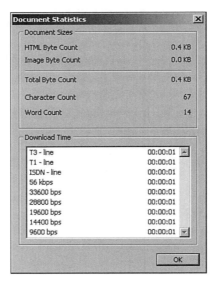

PREVIEWING PAGES

GoLive actually provides a wide variety of viewing options when it comes to pre-screening your pages. The document window allows you to look at framed or non-frame pages within the Layout Preview tab (and Frame Preview on Macs). Within these layouts, you can choose from different browsers and devices by simply making a new menu selection, enabling you to test your pages without even leaving the application.

Layout Preview

This window allows you to preview what your page would look like in a typical browser, and allows you to check the appearance of a page within several different browsers very quickly and easily. Just open your page and click the Layout Preview tab to see the results.

Use the pull-down menu in the View Window (click the View tab in the Inspector) to select from a range of viewing options, including an estimation of how your page would appear on a Web-enabled Nokia cell phone, as seen in Figure 13.9.

Figure 13.9
Here is how a basic Web page might look via a Nokia phone.

To learn more about developing for other platforms, **see** Chapter 25, "Developing for Wireless Devices."

Frame Preview

The Frame Preview functions identically to the Layout Preview but can only be viewed if frames are present on the page and if you are using GoLive on a Mac. In the Windows version, framed pages are viewed with the regular Layout Preview.

For more detailed information on frames, **see** Chapter 14, "Working with Frames."

13

TROUBLESHOOTING

I can't get my page to look the way I want in all different browsers. What do I do?

First, realize that this is common. Most pages won't look exactly alike in Netscape and Internet Explorer. A more realistic goal is to get it to look decent on both. Remember that if a Netscape user sees one version of your page, he's not necessarily going to realize that he's not seeing it the way you intended.

If worse comes to worst, you can always make different artistic choices that are more friendly to both browsers.

Marquee Compatibility

My scrolling marquee doesn't do anything. What's up?

The probable cause is that your browser does not support this tag. Netscape doesn't recognize the tag at all, and older versions of Internet Explorer won't do anything either. In these cases, the text will just appear static on the screen, and everything in the `<marquee>` tags will be ignored.

GOING LIVE

One other valuable way that comments can be employed is to "comment out" certain sections of code that you want to hide temporarily. Sometimes you may want to see how a page looks with or without a certain section, or you may have several sections that you activate and deactivate at will, and don't want to have to retype it all every time.

Commenting out code is simply a matter of adding comment tags before and after the code. At any time in the future, you can remove those tags and the whole block of code will be visible again. Let's take an example where you have a link to a page that is temporarily unavailable. Rather than allow the link to be broken, comment out the link temporarily. If your original code looks like this:

```
<a href="page.htm">Click here to see a cool page.</a>
```

You can comment it out quite easily by adding these tags:

```
<!--
<a href="page.htm">Click here to see a cool page.</a>
-->
```

Now that link will be invisible until you decide to remove the enclosing comment tags. It's a lot easier than cutting the code out and retyping it when the page becomes available again.

ADVANCED PAGE LAYOUT

IN THIS PART

14   Working with Frames   **229**

15   Working with Tables   **239**

16   Creating Forms   **255**

17   Styles   **279**

14

WORKING WITH FRAMES

IN THIS CHAPTER

Using Frames **230**

The Frame Editor **231**

Previewing Frames **234**

Using a Table of Contents Frame **234**

Displaying Two Frames from One Link **234**

Troubleshooting **236**

Going Live **236**

USING FRAMES

Hotly debated for years and still widely disputed, frames offer Web page designers a valid alternative for displaying certain types of pages. Since frames do have some disadvantages, they may not be suitable in most cases, and should only be used when dictated by circumstance. In this chapter, we'll discuss the pros and cons, and the proper usage of frames on the Web, so that you'll be comfortably equipped to handle them, should the situation arise.

When a typical page loads in a browser, users must wait for the entire page to download. Larger elements slow this load time and prolong the wait. Even if the same elements exist on multiple pages of the Site, they must be freshly downloaded each time the user calls a new page of the Site. With frames, this is not the case.

Frames essentially divide a larger page into several smaller pages, and join them together in a frameset. The frameset page combines the other pages in such a way that they appear unified as a single page—with one distinct difference. When the user calls a new page of the Site, the larger repeating elements remain in place, keeping load times speedy with less to download. Effectively used, frames offer an ideal solution and avoid unnecessary user frustration.

Frames may be the answer for any Site that contains large, repeating objects such as images, audio, or video. In some cases, the table of contents is kept in a separate frame while the individual pages load in the main part of the window. Some Sites contain streaming video or audio files that should not be interrupted as new pages are called. Others refer to large graphics in the form of charts, graphs, illustrations, or photos that would severely inhibit swift downloads. A video file playing in one frame can actually activate the content which appears in another frame via Web markers embedded in the movie. All of these make excellent candidates for framed pages.

On the other hand, frames do present some unique problems. For starters, framed pages cannot be bookmarked. Users can only bookmark the frameset page (typically the homepage), not the individual pages contained in the frames. Some Webmasters consider this advantageous, since it means visitors must enter through the front door of your Site each and every time. Yet it could also serve to confuse and frustrate users as well, since they must re-navigate to their favorite page each time they visit.

Framed pages cannot be externally linked. For the same reasons that individual pages can't be bookmarked, they can't serve as links from another Site. That means all links to your Site must go through the front gate and contain the full frameset. This presents additional problems if the Site linking to yours contains frames as well, and targets yours within one, creating the messy scenario of nested frames.

Framed pages cannot be refreshed. If a page fails to load properly and the user chooses to reset the page, the entire frameset page gets refreshed, meaning the user gets bumped back to square one and must wait for the larger elements to load anew and then find the desired page again.

Frames cannot be seen by all. True, frames have been supported by Internet Explorer and Netscape Navigator for several versions now, but certain older and text-only browsers still can't understand them. They also cause problems for certain hand-held devices (see Chapter 25, "Developing for Wireless Devices," for details) so you may be alienating a chunk of your audience simply by using frames.

14

Frames may create scrollbar problems. Since each frame of the frameset actually contains a separate page, each could contain a separate scrollbar as well, if your page were to appear in a smaller browser window than necessary. This could seriously compromise the flow and unity of your pages. On the other hand, if scrollbars were eliminated, a viewer's larger text settings could cause some of the text to be hidden and impossible to read. The scrollbar issue creates a double-edged dilemma for the conscientious designer.

Considering all the angles, only you can determine whether frames fit the needs of your Site. If, after weighing your options carefully, you decide to take advantage of frames for your design, GoLive's got you covered. Its easy-to-use frame editor makes them a breeze to create.

THE FRAME EDITOR

Within the Page Window, choose the Frame Editor tab to create a layout using frames. In this view, you're actually arranging the frameset—choosing the quantity, location, and size of the frames rather than laying out the pages contained within them. Once your pages are named and linked to the frameset page, you still need to open each in the Layout Editor in order to design it. In fact, it is preferable to design the individual pages before creating the overall frameset.

When you first click on the Frame Editor tab, it appears gray and announces No Frames to alert you that frames have not yet been selected. To create a new frameset, simply click on the Frame tab of the Objects Palette, shown in Figure 14.1, and drag the desired configuration icon onto the page window. GoLive offers 17 different frame templates, including a single variable frame that you can add to existing layouts create additional possibilities.

Figure 14.1
The Frames tab of the Object Palette offers a whole bunch of one-click predefined framesets.

Once the layout appears in the window, you must click on each frame and create a link to the page it will contain. In the Frame Inspector that you see in Figure 14.2, link to pages as you would create any other link, by using Point-and-Shoot, Browse, or Menu Options, or by typing a page name directly into the Link Field. If pages do not yet exist, create them first in the Layout Editor and save them to your Site Window. Naturally, pages need not be fully designed yet. You can create blank pages for now, simply to assist you in setting up your frames.

Within the Frame Inspector, you can control various aspects of each frame: You can create a link to the page it contains, name the frame itself, set the height and/or width of the frame, determine your scrollbar settings and resizing options, and click to preview the frame there within the frameset.

14

Figure 14.2
Click on a frame in the Page Window and you can edit its properties in the Frame Inspector.

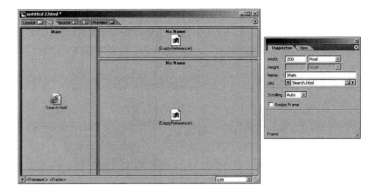

Set Versus Variable Frames

As you glance at the frame possibilities within the Objects Palette and hold your cursor over each icon, you'll notice that some frames are categorized as *variable*. These appear blue in the frame icons, while *set frames* appear pink. As you add frames to your page, set frames arrive with predetermined sizes for height or width, as seen in the frameset cols and rows of the source code in Figure 14.3. The asterisks here represent a kind of wildcard, which means the size will vary according to the size of the main page and the available space in the browser window. Variable frames like the Main one here have no set size by default, and will simply scale themselves as needed. By choosing Pixel from the height or width pop-up menus in the Inspector, you can change a variable frame into a set frame and determine at least one of its dimensions.

Figure 14.3
You can see both the visual representation of your frameset and the code that generates it using the Frame Editor, Split View.

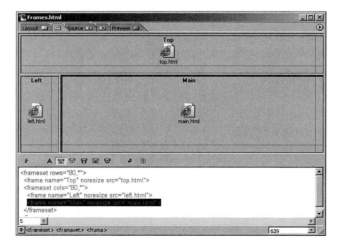

Resizing Frames

Frames may be resized in several ways: Drag on the bars between the frames to resize them manually, enter a new size in the height or width field of the Inspector and press Enter/Return to make it so, or type a new size directly into the source code. Sizes can be set in pixels or as percentages of the whole area. Variable frames (those whose size is set to scale) adjust according to the content of their pages, and cannot be reduced smaller than the content will allow.

The Resize Frame check box in the Inspector determines whether users will be allowed to resize the frames in their browsers. This can be helpful if users have unusually large or small screens and wish to customize the appearance of your page. Since the default is for no resize, however, you have ultimate control and must grant users permission to do this by checking the box.

Frame Names and Target Frames

Every frame in a frameset has its own name, which lets you specify by name which frame a linked page should appear in. Thus, the names you establish for each frame in your frameset become the target names for future frames. As such, they should be kept short, contain no spaces or unusual characters, and ideally be descriptive of the frame so that you can easily understand which frame each references. Typical names are "top," "bottom," "leftside," and so on. Names appear as part of the target list when creating links, to make it easy to select where you want the linked page to appear.

Here's a list of the standard target names and what they mean:

Default: removes any target previously set for the page

_top: page opens in a full browser window, replacing the entire current frameset

_parent: page opens in the next highest frameset in the hierarchy. If no parent exists, it defaults to the target _self

_self: page opens in whatever frame it's linked from, replacing the current page

_blank: page opens in a brand new, untitled browser window

Because these options already exist in the target list, creating new names is not always necessary. You could simply use the existing list of targets. However, naming the frames yourself may make your job easier and keep things more organized from a design viewpoint. The choice is yours.

Scrolling

Choose from Yes (scrollbars ever-present), No (scrollbars never present), or Auto (scrollbars appear as needed). By default, Auto is selected for every frame, but you can adjust your scrolling options as you desire. Beware that if you select No, there may be no possible way for a user to view content that is outside of the frame's dimension.

Preview

Click the arrow here to preview the frame within the frameset here. You may optionally double-click on any frame to open that page individually in the Layout Editor, or click the Frame Preview tab (Mac only) to view all frames as they would appear in a browser.

14

PREVIEWING FRAMES

The Frame Preview functions identically to the Layout Preview, but can only be viewed if frames are present on the page and if you are using GoLive on a Mac. In the Windows version, framed pages are viewed with the regular Layout Preview.

As previously stated, you may also view individual pages within the Frame Editor by selecting them and clicking the Preview button in the Frame Inspector. This provides a quick peek during the layout process, which can be handy for troubleshooting or just making sure you've linked to the correct page.

USING A TABLE OF CONTENTS FRAME

Since frames enable you to keep certain page elements visible at all times, you can place your Site's Table of Contents continuously at the fingertips of your visitors. Keep in mind that for each link in your contents list, you must specify the target frame in which the linked page will appear.

Follow these steps to create a table of contents frame:

1. Create a Table of Contents page.

2. Create a frameset as usual, and set your Table of Contents page to appear in one of the frames.

3. Open the Table of Contents page and link each listed item to a Web page.

4. For each link, specify a target frame by selecting an option from the Target pop-up menu in the Inspector. (Refer to the "Frame Names and Target Frames" section earlier in this chapter for more information.)

5. Re-save your Table of Contents page to include the new links.

DISPLAYING TWO FRAMES FROM ONE LINK

Target2Frames is an action that enables you to display two frames from a single link, creating dramatic effects and accessing the information on two separate pages at once.

Actions are events that occur when triggered by a mouse event. In this case, the mouse clicks on a link, which triggers the action of two frames displaying new pages. Within GoLive, you can easily set this up using the Actions palette.

To set the Target2Frames action, you might follow these steps:

1. Create a link as you normally would, except that instead of typing a URL in the Inspector, simply type a #. This creates an empty anchor and deactivates the link.

2. Open the Actions Palette and choose Mouse Click from the Events list.

3. For the Action, click the icon to create a New Action.

4. From the Actions menu shown in Figure 14.4, choose Link, Target2Frames.

5. You'll see the screen that appears in Figure 14.5. For Frame 1, enter the name of the frame where the first new page will appear when the link is clicked.

6. For Link, specify the page or URL to display in that frame.

7. For Frame 2, enter the name of the frame where the second new page will appear when the link is clicked.

8. For Link, specify the page or URL to display in that frame.

9. Re-save your page with the new link and actions in place, and test your page in a browser.

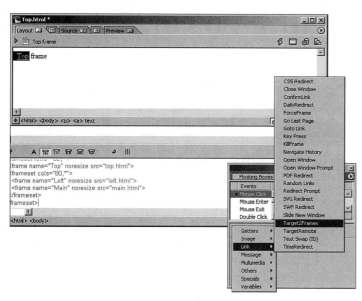

Figure 14.4
Select the Target2Frames Action to load two frames with two separate pages with a single click.

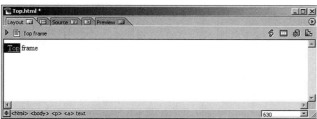

Figure 14.5
Specify the name of each frame and the pathname you wish to load it with in the Actions Palette.

14

TROUBLESHOOTING

Manually Adjusting Your Frame Size Controls

I can't get my stupid frames to space out correctly, no matter how much I mess with the size controls.

You may want to dive into source code view and adjust the height and width of your frames manually. Just remember that a number ("100") means an absolute number of pixels, a percentage ("10%") means the frame will take up that percentage of the available space, and a star ("*") means that it will fill the remaining space as needed.

You can certainly mix and match these. You could have three columns with widths "100", "*", and "10%". This should work, although you may get funky results in some cases. It's a lot like building tables, except that a table cell will expand to accommodate a large graphic, no matter how small you tell the cell to be. A frame, however, will chop off your content no matter how big it is.

Keeping Everything Visible Within Frames

I made frames and now I can't see some of my stuff.

If your page is too big for a frame, and you told that frame to never show scrollbars, then there is only one way the user can view the content, other than expanding their browser window as big as possible. This is to use anchor links. You can place anchors throughout the page, and as long as there are anchor links somewhere visible to click on, then the user will be able to navigate around a large page even without scrollbars.

GOING LIVE

Using Frames to Manage Dynamic Content

Another time when frames come in handy involves certain types of dynamic sites. One such example is an HTML chat application, where one portion of the screen must continually refresh to re-query and show the latest chat messages. If you did this full screen, it would be impossible for the user to type their new message, because the screen might suddenly refresh while they're in the middle of a sentence, wiping out whatever they had typed.

With a frames solution, the chat can refresh in one frame without disturbing other frames. This allows your user to spend as much time as he wants composing his message, then he can submit that form independently of the refreshing chat list.

Of course this is only one random example. Any situation where there are multiple forms onscreen that you need to be able to independently fill out and submit is a great usage for frames.

Preventing Framed Pages from Being Accessed Directly

One quick and dirty way to solve the problem of framed pages being accessed directly, which results in the user missing the rest of the framed content, is to use a simple JavaScript like this. Copy this script into the head of your document and it will not be possible to view this page directly. Instead, the browser will jump immediately to your main frameset page. Here the main frameset page is assumed to be named index.htm; just change it to whatever you name your frameset page.

```
<script language="JavaScript">
<!-- Begin
if (parent.location.href == self.location.href) {
window.location.href = 'index.htm';
}
// End -->
</script>
```

Linking to Other Pages While Retaining Your Site's Header

Here is another JavaScript that you've seen many times: You click on a link to view a different page on another site, but it loads within a frame that retains the original site's branding, no matter what you do. By now this is an old marketing trick.

First, put this script into the head section of your page. Where you see the number 150, that sets the height of the header frame to 150 pixels:

```
<script language="JavaScript">
<!-- Begin
function headerFrame(linkurl, headerurl) {
var framewin = window.open("","brandingframe");
with (framewin.document) {
write("<html><frameset rows=150,*>");
write("<frame src=" + headerurl + ">");
write(" <frame src=" + linkurl + ">");
write("</frameset></html>");
}
return false;
}
// End -->
</script>
```

And then format your links like this to go off the site, but retain a frame that shows your site's header. Assume that http://www.briandunning.com/ is the site you're linking to, but you want to retain a header located at http://www.mysite.com/myheader.htm:

```
<a target="_new" href="http://www.briandunning.com/" onClick="return
↪headerFrame('http://www.briandunning.com',
↪'http://www.mysite.com/myheader.htm');">Check out this cool site</a>
```

14

WORKING WITH TABLES

IN THIS CHAPTER

The Ubiquitous Table   240

Creating Tables   240

Table Palette   249

Creating Nested Tables   251

Converting a Table to a Grid   252

Troubleshooting   252

Going Live   253

THE UBIQUITOUS TABLE

With so many variables swirled in the mix—different operating systems, screen sizes, browser types and versions, just to name a few—the key to successful Web design lies in keeping control over your creation. The less you leave to chance, the more likely that your page will actually resemble the page you set out to create, once it reaches your target audience.

Tables grant you additional control, which is why they've become such a standard in Web design. Whether you use an invisible table simply to align elements and hold their positions, or express yourself through a unique table style, you can easily see why so many Web professionals rely on these multi-celled miracles.

Tables serve myriad uses online. Some merely store and arrange data. Some aid in organization, creating the framework that keeps the pieces in place. Tables make text behave, defining the size of paragraphs by the width of their cells. Tables can hold other objects, from QuickTime movies to still images to additional tables. Tables make forms easier to follow, keep news columns standing tall, align navigation buttons and headers, and help define the space on your page. Tables can be used in cooperation with a layout grid (actually a table in itself) for the ultimate in page layout precision.

In this chapter, we'll talk tables, and share some of the secrets you'll need to effectively make use of these marvelous tools.

CREATING TABLES

Tables consist of individual blocks (called *cells*) that form *rows* (horizontal groups of cells, like chairs in a concert hall) and *columns* (vertical stacks of cells, like classical pillars) in much the same configuration as a chessboard, a spreadsheet, or your average Brady family. You can set the number of cells per row and column, determine the size of borders and cell space, and choose background colors and alignment for individual cells. In addition, you can merge cells together, and add tables within other tables, performing complex feats of formatting.

GoLive makes table creation easy with the use of specialized controls such as the Table object, Table Inspector, Special Table menu, and Table Palette. Some commands even have keyboard shortcuts. Figure 15.1 shows a table's properties as you define them in the Inspector, including the number of rows and columns, and the dimensions of the whole table.

To create a table, follow these steps:

1. Drag the Table icon from the Basic tab of the Objects palette and position it on your page, or double-click the icon and it will appear naturally on the page.

2. In the Table Inspector, click the Table tab.

3. Enter values for the appropriate number of Rows or Columns.

4. Adjust the appearance of your table by setting the width, border size, cell padding and cell space, background color or image, and alignment.

Figure 15.1
The Table tab of the Table Inspector shows all the basic properties of the overall table.

Adding and Deleting Rows and Columns

Rows represent the horizontal planes of table cells, while Columns contain the vertical stacks of cells. By default, each table is created with 3 rows and 3 columns, but you can add or delete these at any time to create a table in any size you like.

To add more rows or columns to a table

1. Shift-click inside of a cell, right-click inside the cell and choose Select Cell, click on the border of the cell, or click on a cell in the Table palette to select it.

2. In the Cell tab of the Table Inspector, click the appropriate buttons to Add Row Above, Add Row Below, Add Column to the Left, or Add Column to the Right of the selected cell, as shown in Figure 15.2.

or

1. Shift-click inside of a cell, right-click inside the cell and choose Select Cell, click on the border of the cell, or click on a cell in the Table palette inside of a cell to select it.

2. Press * to add a new empty row above the cell, or press + to add a new empty column to the left of the cell.

or

1. Shift-click inside of a cell, right-click inside the cell and choose Select Cell, click on the border of the cell, or click on a cell in the Table palette inside of a cell to select it.

2. Select Special, Table from the GoLive menu, then choose Insert Column to the Left, Insert Column to the Right, Insert Row Above, or Insert Row Below.

3. Simply increase the values for the number of Rows or Columns in the Table tab of the Table Inspector. Press Enter/Return to make it so.

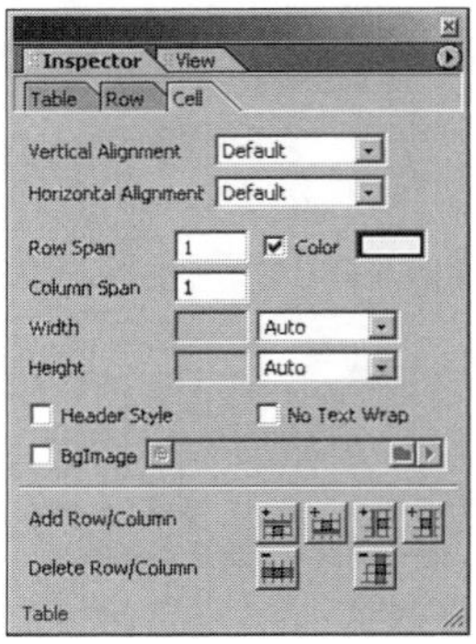

15

Figure 15.2
Use the buttons in the bottom of the Inspector to add or delete rows and columns, relative to the currently selected cell.

To delete rows or columns from a table

1. Select a cell.

2. In the Cell tab of the Table Inspector, click the Delete Row button to delete the row that contains the cell, or click the Delete Column button to delete the column that contains the cell.

or

1. Select a cell.

2. Press Shift-Delete to delete the row that contains the cell, or press Delete to delete the column that contains the cell.

or

1. Select a cell.

2. Select Special, Table from the GoLive menu, then choose either Delete Row or Delete Column, as shown in Figure 15.3.

Alternatively, you can simply decrease the values for the number of Rows or Columns in the Table tab of the Table Inspector. Press Enter/Return to make it so.

Merging Cells

Not only can you add or delete rows and columns, you can merge cells with adjoining cells both horizontally and vertically for full table customization.

To merge cells

1. Select a cell.

2. Select the Cell tab of the Table Inspector.

3. To merge a cell with those below it, enter a value in the rowspan field and press Enter/Return to make it so. To merge a cell with those to the right of it, enter a value in the colspan field and press Enter/Return to make it so.

Figure 15.3
Special, Table Menu options as an alternative way to insert or delete columns or rows.

The number indicates the number of cells the merged cell represents. That is, a cell with a rowspan of 2 takes the space of two rows. The default for a single cell is to have both a rowspan and colspan of 1.

Alternatively, follow these steps to merge a cell:

1. Shift-click inside of a cell to select it.

2. Select Special, Table from the GoLive menu, then choose Merge Cells Right or Merge Cells Down. Optionally, you can highlight multiple adjacent cells and select Merge Cells from the menu.

Yet one more way to merge cells:

1. Select the range of cells you want to merge.

2. Right-click in any selected cell and choose Merge Cells from the contextual menu.

To split (un-merge) cells

1. Select the merged cell you wish to split.

2. Select the Cell tab of the Table Inspector.

3. Enter a value of 1 in the Rowspan field to split from the cells below it and press Enter/Return to make it so. Enter a value or 1 in the Colspan field to split a cell from those to the right of it, and press Enter/Return to make it so.

The default for a single cell is to have both a rowspan and colspan of 1. Note that when merged cells split, the new cells return to default formatting and must be reset with color, alignment, and other attributes.

Alternatively, follow these steps to split a cell:

1. Select the merged cell.

2. Select Special, Table from the GoLive menu, then choose Reduce Merge Left or Reduce Merge Up. Optionally, you can simply select Split Cells from the menu.

or

1. Select the merged cell.

2. Right-click in the cell and choose Split Cell from the contextual menu.

Resizing Tables, Rows and Columns

As with most object adjustments, you have multiple options when resizing a table or its rows and columns. You may choose to resize the table or cells manually by dragging on the edges, or use the Table Inspector to indicate more exact dimensions.

To resize a table

1. Click on the top or left edge of the table or right-click the table and choose Select Table to select it.

2. In the Table tab of the Table Inspector, choose Pixel or Percent from the pop-up menu, and enter a value for the desired size for the Width and/or Height. Choose Auto to automatically adjust the Width or Height to accommodate the contents of the table.

or

1. (Option-click) or [Alt-click] on the right or bottom border of the table. This allows the table to be resized, by turning Auto sizing into pixels so that you can adjust the height and width.

2. Drag down to increase the table height, or drag to the right to increase the table width.

To resize a Table Row or Column

1. (Option-click) or [Alt-click] on the right or bottom border of a cell in the row or column you wish to resize.

2. Drag in the desired direction.

or

1. Select a cell, or select a row or column by clicking on its header in the Table palette.

2. In the Cell tab of the Table Inspector, choose Pixel or Percent for Width and/or Height, and enter the desired value. Press Enter/Return to make it so.

Creating Borders

A table's borders consist of the lines that frame the outer perimeter of the table and define the cell edges within. The outer edges of a table will continue to grow in thickness, forming a three-dimensional effect, while the inner cell edges remain relatively smaller. You can create a borderless or invisible table by setting the border value to zero, or set the borders to any desired thickness. Simply indicate the pixel value for your border in the appropriate field on the Table tab of the Table Inspector. Figure 15.4 shows a couple of tables, one with no borders, and another with fat borders.

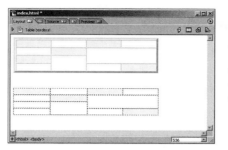

Figure 15.4
Here is a table with no borders, and a table with a 3-pixel border. Note how the outer border of the table is wider than the borders that divide its cells: we'll get to those next.

15

Cell Padding and Cell Spacing

Cell padding refers to the amount of space between the edge of a cell and its contents, whereas *cell spacing* refers to the amount of space placed between adjacent cells in a table and along the outer edges of a table. Figure 15.5 shows some tables with a variety of different settings. By default, a table's cell padding is one pixel and cell spacing is two pixels. You can combine these attributes with border size to produce many desired effects:

- Border=1, Cell spacing=0 creates the slimmest possible borders, just 2 pixels wide.
- Border=n (any number), Cell spacing=0 creates the slimmest possible interior border, with a slightly larger exterior border of (n+1) pixels wide.
- Border=1, Cell spacing=n (any number) creates a table with equal-width interior and exterior borders of (n+2) pixels wide with a 1-pixel chiseled edge on each.

Figure 15.5
These tables demonstrate the difference between cell padding (the amount of space surrounding each cell's contents) and cell spacing (the width of the borders between cells).

Setting Background Colors

Figure 15.6 shows a table with a variety of wacky, zany colors for the various cells. You may choose to set a single background color for the entire table, or choose colors for a row, a column, or an individual cell. As with most color schemes, you simply drag the desired color to its appropriate swatch in the Inspector. Your current table selection (whole table, row, column, or cell) and forward-most Inspector tab will determine how the color is assigned.

To set background color for a table

1. Select the table.

2. In the Table tab of the Table Inspector, check the color box or simply drag the desired color into the swatch next to it. Your table background instantly adopts the new color.

To set background color for a row or column

1. To color a column, click on the topmost border of the desired column. Your cursor changes to a downward arrow here, indicating that the column below it will be selected by clicking. To color a row, click on the leftmost border of the desired row. Your cursor changes to a right-pointing arrow, indicating that the row to the right of it will be selected by clicking.

2. With the appropriate row or column highlighted, select the Row tab of the Table Inspector and drag the desired color into the color swatch here. The Row or Column instantly adopts the new color.

To set background color for a single cell

1. Select a cell or range of cells.

2. With the cell highlighted, select the Cell tab of the Table Inspector and drag the desired color to the color swatch here. The selected cell instantly adopts the new color.

Figure 15.6
Select a cell and choose a color from the Color palette to change the background color of individual cells.

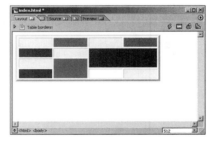

Setting a Background Image

Figure 15.7 shows how a table with a background image looks. For either an entire table or an individual cell, you may choose to display a background image, much as you would for a whole page. The process for setting this up is remarkably similar.

To set a background image for a table

1. Click on the top or left edge of the table to select it.

2. In the Table tab of the Table Inspector, check the bgimage box, or simply link to the desired image using the traditional means: Point and Shoot, browse, selecting a menu option, or by

typing the filename and path directly into the link field. Your table background instantly displays the new image.

To set a background image for a single cell

1. Shift-click inside a cell to select it.

2. With the cell highlighted, select the Cell tab of the Table Inspector and check the bgimage box, or simply link to the desired image using the traditional means: Point and Shoot, browse, selecting a menu option, or by typing the filename and path directly into the link field. Your cell background instantly displays the new image.

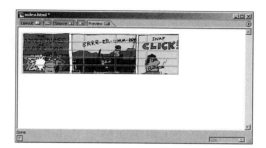

Figure 15.7
An example of a table with a background image. If the selected image is larger than the table, the image will be truncated.

Alignment

As with many elements, you have the option of aligning your table flush left, flush right, or centered on the page. In addition, you can establish an alignment for the contents of each cell individually, on both a horizontal and vertical axis. By default, all alignments are to the top and left.

To set the alignment for a table

1. Select the table.

2. In the Table tab of the Table Inspector, select Left, Right, or Center from the pop-up alignment menu. Your table adjusts accordingly.

To set the alignment for a row or column

1. To align a column, click on the topmost border of the desired column. Your cursor changes to a downward arrow here, indicating that the column below it will be selected by clicking. To align a row, click on the leftmost border of the desired row. Your cursor changes to a right-pointing arrow, indicating that the row to the right of it will be selected by clicking.

2. With the appropriate row or column highlighted, select the Row tab of the Table Inspector and select Top, Middle, or Bottom from the Vertical Alignment pop-up menu, and Left, Right, or Center from the Horizontal Alignment pop-up menu. The contents of your row or column adjust accordingly.

15

To set the alignment for a single cell

1. Select the cell

2. With the cell highlighted, select the Cell tab of the Table Inspector and select Top, Middle, or Bottom from the Vertical Alignment pop-up menu, and Left, Right, or Center from the Horizontal Alignment pop-up menu. The contents of your cell adjust accordingly.

Figure 15.8
When an entire row or column is selected, you can use the Inspector to set the alignment of every cell within that range.

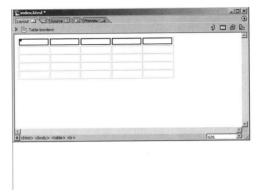

Creating Captions

Because tables fulfill so many uses as charts, spreadsheets, and other displays, GoLive provides an easy way to create a caption for your table. Captions are not often used, as the predefined formatting does not frequently happen to match the designer's creative choices. Figure 15.9 shows a caption in action.

To create a table caption

1. Select the table.

2. In the Table tab of the Table Inspector, check the Caption box and select Above or Below from the pop-up menu.

3. Type your caption directly on the page in the space created. Notice that the toolbar transforms into the Text Toolbar, allowing you to take full advantage of all the fonts, styles, and other formatting options you would normally have with text.

Figure 15.9
This table has a caption, which appears as text hovering above the table.

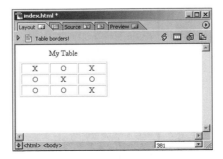

TABLE PALETTE

The Table Palette facilitates arranging data within your table, and helps you control the look and size of your table and its cells. The palette itself is broken down into two distinct parts: Select controls the cell content and provides a zippy way to select specific cells, rows, and columns, while Style controls cosmetic changes.

Setting Table Styles

Styles are built-in cosmetic schemes that you can apply to your tables, as an alternative to going through an existing table and applying each cosmetic attribute one at a time. The Styles mode makes it easy to change the color, cell size, and spacing of your tables. There are ten built-in styles to choose from, ranging in mood from Just the Facts to Seventies, plus you can import and export styles or create your own new styles to suit any page you can dream up. Figure 15.10 shows a table being formatted with one of GoLive's included styles, and Figure 15.11 illustrates how your own customized attributes can be saved as a new style for future reuse.

To suit your table in Style:

1. Select the table.

2. Select the Style tab of the Table Palette.

3. From the pop-up list of styles, choose one and click Apply to adorn your table in the selected style. Your table instantly adopts the new style.

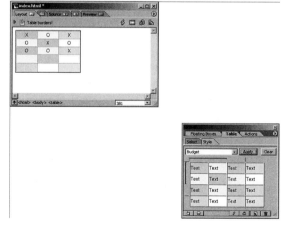

Figure 15.10
Choose a Style from the Style tab of the Table palette to automatically apply cosmetic formatting to your existing table.

To clear a Style

1. Click the top or left edge of the table to select it.

2. Select the Style tab of the Table Palette.

3. Click Clear to make the table plain and unstyled. Your table instantly drops the former style.

To add a new Style to the Style tab of the Table palette

1. Set up a table and customize its appearance.

2. Click the top or left edge of the table to select it.

3. Click the Style tab in the Table Palette.

4. Click New to create a new table style.

5. Enter a name for the new table style.

6. Click Capture to capture the style of the selected table and save it as a new table style.

Figure 15.11
Once you've customized your table and are satisfied with its appearance, use the Style tab of the Table palette to save that customization as a Style that you can then apply quickly to other tables.

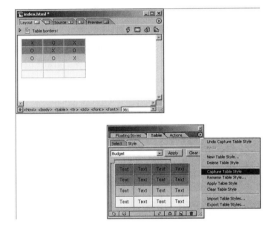

Sorting Table Content

Within Select mode, you can highlight individual cells, entire rows, or entire columns, and manipulate the data within them, as shown in Figure 15.12. The Sort feature shown in Figure 15.13 enables you to perform multi-level sorts on data, in ascending or descending order, by row or by column.

To sort the contents of a table

1. Select the table.

2. Click the Select tab in the Table palette.

3. Indicate which area of the table you want to sort by making a table selection either on your page or the Select tab of the Table Inspector. To sort the contents of the entire table, select the table. To apply the sort to specific rows, columns, or cells in the table, select that area of the table only.

4. Click the Sort button. When the Sort Table window appears, select the sorting order of the rows and columns by priority, and click OK to begin the Sort. The contents of the table adjust automatically.

Figure 15.12
To sort your table's contents, first select the range of cells that are to be re-ordered.

15

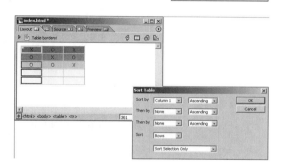

Figure 15.13
To complete the sorting of your table data, choose the parameters in the Sort Table window and then click OK.

CREATING NESTED TABLES

To place a table within the cell of an existing table (see Figure 15.14) requires the exact same process as creating a regular table. The only difference is the location.

To create a nested table

1. Click inside of the desired cell.

2. Drag the Table icon from the Basic tab of the Objects palette and position it on your page, or double-click the icon and it will appear naturally on the page.

3. In the Table Inspector, click the Table tab.

4. Enter values for the appropriate number of Rows or Columns.

5. Adjust the appearance of your table by setting the width, border size, cell padding and cell space, background color or image, and alignment.

15

Figure 15.14
Tables can be nested within other tables, as deep as you care to go, and every table can have its own set of unique attributes. Traits of nested tables are not inherited from enclosing tables.

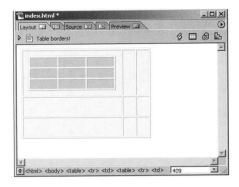

CONVERTING A TABLE TO A GRID

Since the GoLive layout grid is really nothing more than a table, you can easily convert an existing table into a layout grid (see Figure 15.15). Each table cell that contains text or another object becomes a layout text box that has the same content as the cell.

To convert a table to a layout grid with layout text boxes

1. Select the table.

2. Click the Table tab in the Table Inspector.

3. Click Convert to convert the table to a layout grid with layout text boxes.

Figure 15.15
This table has been converted into a layout grid.

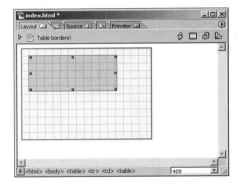

TROUBLESHOOTING

Fitting Content into Table Cells

My table cell is bigger than I told it to be. What do I do?

Table cells and tables will always expand to the content that you put into them. While a large background image will not cause a cell or table to grow past its defined dimensions, that same image placed inside a cell will. If you put a 100×100 pixel image inside a table cell, no power on earth can force that cell to be smaller than 100×100 pixels.

The same limitation applies with a lot of text. If the content of a cell requires more space than you've allotted with your definitions of the cell or table sizes, it will expand automatically. The best defense is to understand this behavior and make creative choices that accommodate it.

Dealing with Complex Dimensions

When I apply a change to one cell, it applies to all the other cells in that table or row, even though I don't want it to.

In some cases, this is going to happen whether you want it to or not, and that's actually correct. For example, let's say you set a cell to be 50 pixels wide. GoLive is going to automatically set all the other cells in that column to be 50 pixels wide. Logically, it has to be this way.

Other changes can be a little less predictable. Pretend that the top cell you set to be 50 pixels wide is actually two merged cells side by side, therefore there are two columns of cells beneath it. GoLive will set the first column's width to 50 pixels and ignore the second column. In this case, you will need to go into the source code view and fix this manually. Be sure to set widths for cells in both columns to add up to the width of the top merged cell.

Some tables can be quite complex, thus creating many options, and GoLive can't read your mind. If your table is really complex, with lots of merged cells in funky patterns, you may not be able to use GoLive's tools at all to make the settings you need. Go back to source code view and do it manually. Just be sure to add up all the dimensions on a piece of paper to make sure you're giving your cells valid parameters.

GOING LIVE

Tables are one of the Web designer's best friends. By modern convention, virtually every high-end site has a fundamental table structure to its layout. View the source on just about any professional Web site that you like, and you'll probably find it to be filled with table tags.

Many sites start with a basic enclosing table structure that's the same on every page, often leaving one big cell for the content of each page. And that cell often contains a nested table or two.

If you choose to follow this popular convention in coding your sites, one handy way to do it is to create header.ssi and footer.ssi include files. Header.ssi often has the site's header and everything up to and including the `<td>` tag that initiates the main page cell. Footer.ssi often includes the closing `</td>` tag for that main page cell, and everything that comes after it.

Using this trick, your pages will all look square and trim, be rich with consistent content, and all you need to code on each page is that page's unique content.

CREATING FORMS

IN THIS CHAPTER

About Forms	**256**
Form Elements	**257**
Form Navigation	**273**
Troubleshooting	**277**
Going Live	**278**

ABOUT FORMS

Online forms have become an extremely popular method of interaction between server and client, for several obvious reasons:

■ Because the Web never sleeps, online forms allow the flow of information to continue at any time of day or night. This means convenience for the sender as well as added efficiency for the receiver of the form.

■ Online forms provide instant feedback from anywhere in the world, freeing users from reliance on transportation and the time requirements of snail mail.

■ Online forms eliminate the extra staffing requirements, expenditures, and assorted hassles that accompany traditional customer service methods such as telemarketing or direct mailing.

■ Online forms cut costs and save valuable resources by reducing paper wastes.

■ Online forms mean increased accuracy in the data itself, since it's entered directly by the user and doesn't need to be transcribed or re-entered by a third party.

■ Online forms can feed information directly into electronic databases, where it can be efficiently stored, accessed, organized, and updated, searched and sorted, duplicated, and protected.

■ Online forms can be created dynamically, which means they can be customized and personalized for a particular user or purpose. This not only adds to the customer's satisfaction; it benefits the company by cutting costs plus providing valuable market research information.

■ Through careful wording and the use of properly planned menu selections, online forms can help edit and organize information, channeling it to the appropriate offices and serving as an excellent introduction or point of reference when follow-up service is required.

■ Online forms can take advantage of images, audio, video, animation, and virtually any type of multimedia available on the Web. Again this leads to higher customer satisfaction, can eliminate confusion, and can even save time since users can simply point and click on icons rather than type all the necessary information.

■ Online forms can provide customer service directly, by leading users to particular places within your Web site or elsewhere online.

Never before have forms been so simple to create. GoLive eases this often-tedious task by providing all the necessary form elements as drag-and-drop icons in a specialized tab of the Objects Palette. Simply place each element onto your Layout and arrange them as you would any other page elements, using the Inspector to supply the specifics of each.

See the following section, "Form Elements," for details on creating a form in GoLive.

Because the appearance of form elements can vary greatly between different browsers and different platforms, you should strongly consider setting up forms within the well-defined structure of tables.

This allows you to maintain better control over the placement of form elements, keeping your Site looking consistent and true to your design intentions.

Be aware that layout plays a particularly important role where forms are concerned, since an odd word wrap or misplaced element here not only leads to user confusion; it could in turn lead to countless errors in the gathering and processing of data. Invest a little extra time, and try to design a form that your users will find inviting and easy to use.

Suggestions for good forms include

- Make forms visually appealing by including colors and graphics, just as you would on any other Web page. This keeps the form connected to your Site stylistically, and also makes the exchange of information seem less intimidating. Remember that by placing a form online, you have in some way eliminated the human element. Since this form now represents your organization, it's your job to provide a kind of friendly face to the public.

- Keep any instructions brief, and keep all form language clear and concise. There's nothing worse than feeling confused and having no one to ask for help. To avoid placing your users in this awkward situation, use words they'll understand instead of complex terms or insider jargon. If you must use a technical term, offer a quick definition so that users won't feel so alienated. Many people are intimidated by forms, but you can put them more at ease by keeping things simple.

- Group like information with like. GoLive allows you to group form elements into sets, with visual cues such as bounding boxes to alert users that this information belongs together. You may even wish to break a longer form into multiple pages or sections to make it easier for users to digest.

- Pay attention to the tab order in your forms. Since this is most likely how users will move from one field to the next, the tabs should follow a logical progression and flow naturally. Again, if you group related information together, this shouldn't be a problem.

- Because som browsers may display form elements much larger than intended, be sure to include extra space in your layout, to compensate for any shifting that may occur. Be sure to test your forms often and thoroughly, on a variety of browsers and platforms, to make sure your layout is remaining intact.

FORM ELEMENTS

The Forms tab of the Objects palette, shown in Figure 16.1, contains all the elements you need to create a successful online form. Elements include buttons, labels, text and password fields, checkboxes, radio buttons, pop-up menus, list boxes, hidden elements, a file browser, key generator, and fieldset creator. Each form element is actually an HTML element, and will serve as a means of transmitting information that is input by your users.

Figure 16.1
The Forms tab of the Objects palette provides quick access to all the essential form elements.

16 Creating a New Form

To create a new form, follow these steps:

1. Select the Forms tab of the Objects Palette.

2. Select the Form element icon and drag it into place in your document window. The box that encloses this Form tag will house all the elements of your form, so it's essential that you place this icon first. Any elements not placed within this box will not function as part of the form.

3. Use the Form Inspector to name your form and provide essential information such as the Action, Target, Encoding, and Method.

4. If you wish to align form elements using a table (recommended), select the Basic tab of the Objects Palette and drag the Table icon into position within the Form tag box on your page. Specify the details of your table using the Inspector, and then return to the Forms tab of the Objects Palette to select the rest of your form elements.

5. Click the icon of any form element you want in the Objects Palette, and drag it into place within the box enclosing the Form tag (or within a cell of your table here). You may also position your cursor within the Form tag box and simply double-click on form element icons in the Objects Palette to place them.

6. For each element, use the Form Inspector to provide any necessary details.

7. Continue to add form elements until your form is complete (see Figure 16.2). For more information on how to set up a specific form element, see the detailed description of that element later this chapter.

8. Be sure to include a Submit button for users to send their information to you once they've completed the form online. You may also choose to include a Reset button as a courtesy to those who prefer to start over rather than send the form as it is.

9. Save your form document and test it thoroughly in various browser situations to ensure full functionality.

The Form Tag

The mother of all form elements, the one from which all others stem, is the Form tag itself. Like other elements, it actually corresponds to an HTML tag, in this case the dual tag `<FORM>  </FORM>`.

However, while browsers do allow for a certain margin of error and imprecision, and many end tags may be misplaced or even abandoned without any loss of meaning, Form tags must be positioned correctly to be understood.

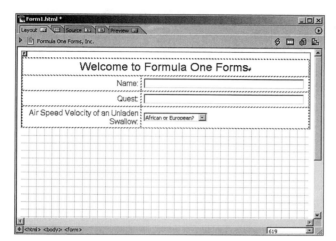

Figure 16.2
Here is a completed form with individual elements placed inside table cells.

Unlike standard Web pages, Forms are not simply created to appear in a browser; they must also perform a function. This function involves interaction with CGI scripts, which must transfer the form information input by the client over to the server, and typically into storage within a database. In order for this communication to occur, the opening Form tag announces the beginning of the form while the closing tag lets the CGI scripts know they've reached the end of the form.

Realizing the importance of the Form tags, GoLive now uses a convenient system that encapsulates all the form elements neatly within the proper area. The Form tag appears on the page surrounded by a bounding box. Simply set up all your form elements within this boxed area, and they become part of the form. Any elements left outside the box will not be considered part of the form. It's as simple as that.

Thus the Form tag, not coincidentally the first icon in the Forms tab of the Object Palette, will always be the first element you need to place when creating a form. Just click and drag the Form element icon into position on your page, and use the Inspector to set up the details of your form.

Through the Form Inspector (see Figure 16.3), you provide the values that allow your form to communicate with the CGI scripts and transfer your data where it needs to go.

The following are the settings for the Form Inspector:

- The form Name may be used for later reference. This is particularly important when using multiple forms simultaneously, but the default will suffice if it is your only form.

- The Action refers to the location of the script that will handle the data sent by the form. Type the filename and directory of this script, or link to it using point and shoot or browsing. A form cannot function without calling a proper Action, so be sure to talk to your Internet service provider or Server Administrator about what kinds of scripts are available for your use, and where they are located on the server.

16

Figure 16.3
The Form Inspector provides a place to edit the characteristics of a form.

- If using frames, specify a Target where the page returned by the Web server will appear.

- If you require special encoding, indicate it here.

- Choose a Form Method. Though both are correct, Get and Post function in slightly different manners, and you may find you prefer one over the other.

- The Inventory button leads you to a window that allows you to take a quick peek at what's included in your form so far (see Figure 16.4). This convenient feature helps you troubleshoot as you go, without sifting through lengthy lines of source code. In addition, you can export a list of the form elements you've used, or the action string as it stands, for use elsewhere. This comes in handy for duplicating forms, building databases, or troubleshooting your own form.

Figure 16.4
Here is the same form shown in the Form Inventory window.

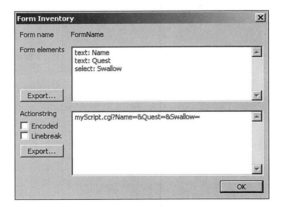

Creating Buttons

Three types of Button icons exist within the Forms tab, each with its own unique function:

- The Submit Button sends the data entered in the form to the CGI script to be processed.

- The Reset Button clears the form and returns it to the original default values.

■ The Custom Button, also known as a Universal Button, can be set up to behave exactly like a Submit, Reset, or Normal Button, but its appearance can be customized by adding an image, formatted text, or other content to make it more intuitive to the user (see Figure 16.5). Normal, or generic, buttons can also be attached to hrefs or JavaScript actions using the onClick command.

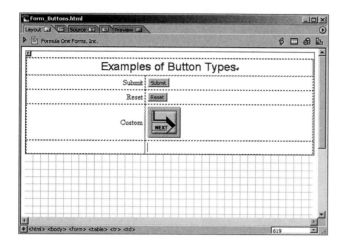

Figure 16.5
Here are some examples of button types.

16

To set up a Submit, Reset, or Custom Button:

1. Select the Forms tab of the Objects Palette.

2. Click and drag the desired Button icon into position within the Form tag box on your page.

3. Use the Button Inspector to specify details for your Button:

   ■ Select the button Type. Using the radio buttons in the Inspector, you can specify a button as Submit, Reset, or Normal. Custom buttons should always be set to Normal.

   ■ Provide a Name for each button. This is strictly for your use when referring to a button, and does not appear to the user on the form.

   ■ Label the button. This appears as text on the button itself. Submit buttons are by default labeled "Submit Query" and Reset buttons are labeled "Reset", but either label may be changed simply by checking the Label box and typing a new label into the field.

   ■ (Custom Button only) Highlight the text on the button itself to change the label. You may adjust the font, size, and style of the text just as you would in any regular text box, using GoLive's standard font tools.

   ■ (Custom Button only) Drag the Image icon from the Basic tab of the Objects Palette onto the top of the button to place an image here. Use the Inspector to select an image file and determine its dimensions just as you would with any image element.

   ■ (Custom Button only) Specify a Value for your button; that is, an action or value to be passed to the CGI script, as suits the purpose of your form.

Figure 16.6 shows a Submit button set up in the Button Inspector.

Figure 16.6
Here is a Submit button with its properties set in the Button Inspector.

16

Form Input Image

Another user-friendly option for sending information is the Input Image. Like a Custom Button, the Input Image allows you to place a clickable image on your page, which helps users navigate more easily through the form. Yet the Input Image actually uses the HTML tag `<Input>` just like a Submit or Reset button, whereas the Custom Button relies on the newer `<Button>` tag, which may not be accepted in all browsers.

To insert an Input Image, follow these steps:

1. Select the Forms tab of the Objects Palette.

2. Click and drag the Form Input Image icon into position within the Form tag box on your page.

3. In the Inspector, link to the desired graphic using the point and shoot lasso, browsing to the correct file, or typing the filename and path directly into the source field, as shown in Figure 16.7.

4. Specify details such as height and width, alignment, border size, and alternate text in the Inspector, as you would with any other image.

5. In the More tab of the Inspector, the Is Form option should be checked by default. Provide a unique name here to allow the CGI script to identify this Input Image and reference it later using x and y coordinates. This is particularly important when using multiple Input Images and triggering specific actions for each.

Labels and Text Fields

Although the Forms tab features multiple text elements, each performs a slightly different role. Labels serve as titles or indicators for other elements, but may also be used to activate or deactivate the associated element. Text Fields allow users to input single lines of text, such as individual words, numbers, or phrases. Password Fields resemble Text Fields except that the entered text string is not visible, providing protection to the user. Text Areas provide additional space for multi-line text entries, such as paragraphs. Let's take a moment to explore each of these options. Some examples are shown in Figure 16.8.

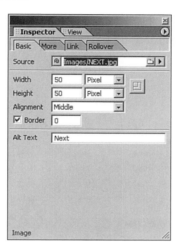

Figure 16.7
Images can also be used as buttons, shown here in the Form Input Image Inspector.

16

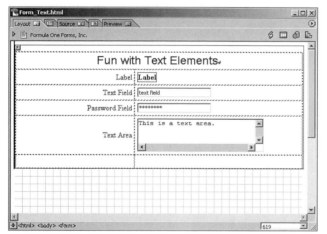

Figure 16.8
Here are several examples of Label and Text Fields.

Labels

The Label icon inserts a small text box, a kind of cue card that allows you to define the purpose of another element (check box, radio button, and so on) for your users. While the text of a Label may be edited and formatted much like a standard text box, the Label holds a distinct advantage over the text box in that the Label can also control the element it defines. By clicking on the Label, a user can activate or deactivate the associated object.

To insert a Label, follow these steps:

1. Select the Forms tab of the Objects Palette.

2. Click and drag the Label icon into position on your page, or simply double-click the icon in the Objects Palette.

3. Place your cursor in the content area of the Label and enter a Label name.

4. Select the name and format the text by adjusting the size, font, and/or style, as desired.

5. To link the Label with an element, first select the Label, and then do one of the following:

   ■ In the Form Label Inspector (see Figure 16.9), click the Point and Shoot lasso and drag it to the appropriate form element.

   ■ Alt-click (Windows) or Command-click (Mac) the border of the Label, and drag into the appropriate form element.

Notice the ID displayed in the Reference text box of the Form Label Inspector. This indicates a relationship between the Label and associated element. Click the Show button to check an association, a helpful tool on pages where multiple Label-element pairs occur.

Figure 16.9
Here a label is selected in the Form Label Inspector.

Text and Password Fields

Although created with two distinct element icons, the *Text Field* and the *Password Field* are nearly identical, save for the privacy feature of the Password Field. Both fields are intended for short, single lines of text, although the line length can be adjusted to suit longer strings of data.

To create a Text or Password Field, follow these steps:

1. Select the Forms tab of the Objects Palette.

2. Click and drag the Text Field or Password Field icon into position on your page, or simply double-click the proper icon in the Objects Palette.

3. Select the icon in your document window, and use the Inspector as shown in Figure 16.10 to set the desired specifications:

■ Enter a unique Name to identify your field.

■ For the Value (Windows) or Content (Mac OS), insert any default text for users to see, or leave this text box empty.

■ Visible refers to the number of characters that can be viewed in your new field. Enter the desired character length of your field here.

■ Max refers to the maximum number of characters your field will accept. Enter a character limit here, or leave this text box empty, and this limit will be determined by the Web browser used that views the form.

■ If your new field is indeed a Password Field, click the box to indicate so. If selected, the field will display bullets instead of displaying what's typed.

Figure 16.10
Here is a standard text field shown in the Form Text Field Inspector.

To create a Text Area

1. Select the Forms tab of the Objects Palette.

2. Click and drag the Text Area icon into position on your page, or simply double-click its icon in the Objects Palette.

3. Select the Text Area element in your document window, and use the Inspector as shown in Figure 16.11 to set the desired specifications:

■ Enter a unique Name to identify your field.

■ Rows refers to the maximum number of rows visible in your Text Area. Enter a number here to determine the height for your Text Area.

■ Columns refers to the maximum number of characters visible in your Text Area. Enter a number here to set the width of the Text Area.

- The Wrap pop-up menu allows you to control line breaks: Default uses the default settings of the browser. Off tells the browser to disregard the Columns limit and keeps text from wrapping on the right side of the box. Virtual and Physical both respect the Columns limit and wrap the text when it reaches the right margin.

- In the Content field, insert any default text for users to see, or leave this text box empty.

Figure 16.11
Here is a text area shown in the Form Text Area Inspector.

Checkboxes and Radio Buttons

When presenting multiple choice questions, from a simple Yes or No to those with many possible answers, checkboxes and radio buttons help you elicit quick, clear responses from your viewers. With one click of the mouse, the user can provide all the information you need, and move on to the next question. This keeps the form user-friendly.

Checkboxes and radio buttons (see Figure 16.12) also allow you, the Form Master, to maintain better control over the data produced by the form. Unlike text fields, where user responses may vary widely, you actually pre-determine the possible answers in a listed format. From here, you can sort the information into categories based on responses, set up scripts to flag certain criteria and perform designated functions according to the choices your users make, and calculate statistical data with greater accuracy. All of these benefits make checkboxes and radio buttons excellent choices for certain types of forms.

Modeled after the old push-button station changers once popular in AM car radios, the *radio button* only tunes in a single response to each question. Use it any time answers are mutually exclusive, as in the Yes or No scenario, or when you want to force users to choose the best answer.

Checkboxes, on the other hand, allow for multiple responses to a single question, as if the user were checking off a list of applicable replies. Use these anytime more than one answer may be equally valid.

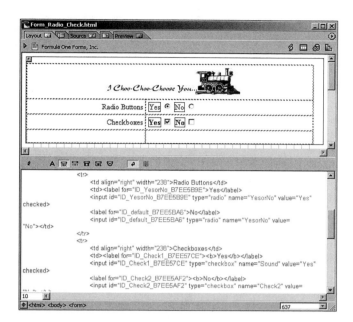

Figure 16.12
Here are some examples of radio buttons and checkboxes.

To create radio buttons, follow these steps:

1. Select the Forms tab of the Objects Palette.

2. Click and drag the Radio Button icon into position on your page, or simply double-click its icon in the Objects Palette.

3. Select the Radio Button element in your document window, and use the Inspector to set the desired specifications:

   ■ The Group name indicates which radio buttons belong together, such as all the buttons in response to a Question #8. In the likely event that several questions on your form make use of radio buttons, this ensures that only those from the same group will be compared with one another. Choose a descriptive name for each group and type it into the text field, or select an existing group name from the pop-up menu. (Note: Once a group name has been entered, it becomes available as a choice in the pop-up menu.)

   ■ The Value for the radio button is a unique response that serves to identify it within the group. A Value may be any Web-friendly alphanumeric character, or string of characters, without spaces. Values such as "A" (for lettered multiple choice questions), "1" (for numbered lists or for questions involving mathematical calculations), "Yes" (for Yes or No questions), and "Always" (for questions of preference or frequency) are common examples. When a viewer submits the form, this value gets passed to the CGI script, then sent back to you as usable data.

- In the Focus section, the Selected check box indicates that the radio button should appear selected by default, as shown in Figure 16.13.

4. (Optional but recommended) Drag a label icon from the Forms tab of the Objects palette and place it next to each button to indicate what it represents.

5. Repeat these steps for each button in the group.

Figure 16.13
Here is a selected radio button shown in the Form Radio Button Inspector.

To create checkboxes, follow these steps:

1. Select the Forms tab of the Objects Palette.

2. Click and drag the Checkbox icon into position on your page, or simply double-click its icon in the Objects Palette.

3. Select the Checkbox element in your document window, and use the Inspector to set the desired specifications:

   - Enter a unique Name to identify the checkbox.

   - Assign the checkbox a Value. A Value may be any Web-friendly alphanumeric character, or string of characters, without spaces. Values such as "A" (for lettered multiple choice questions), "1" (for numbered lists or for questions involving mathematical calculations), "Yes" (for Yes or No questions), and "Always" (for questions of preference or frequency) are common examples. When a viewer submits the form, this value gets passed to the CGI script, then sent back to you as usable data.

   - In the Focus section, the Selected check box indicates that the checkbox should appear selected by default, as shown in Figure 16.14.

4. (Optional but recommended) Drag a label icon from the Forms tab of the Objects palette and place it next to each checkbox to indicate what it represents.

5. Repeat these steps for each checkbox in the group.

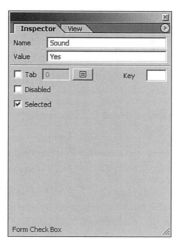

Figure 16.14
Here is a selected checkbox shown in the Form Check Box Inspector.

Pop-up Menus and List Boxes

Both the Pop-up Menu and List Box accomplish the same task, in that each displays a list with multiple items from which the user may choose, as shown in Figure 16.15. The only real difference lies in the appearance of the lists. In a *pop-up menu*, only one item appears by default. Users must click on the menu to view the full list, and the selected item becomes the one displayed. By contrast, the *list box* shows multiple items in a scrolling list. Users may use the scrollbars to view list items beyond the scope of the box, and any selections become highlighted. A List Box allows the user to select multiple items from the list as well, by holding the Shift key while clicking.

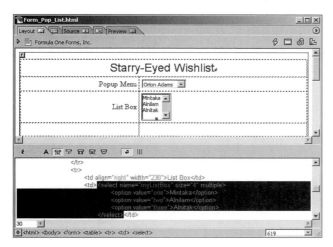

Figure 16.15
A Pop-up Menu and a List Box are shown here, along with the source code.

To create a Pop-up Menu or a List Box

1. Select the Forms tab of the Objects Palette.

2. Click and drag the Pop-up or List Box icon into position on your page, or simply double-click its icon in the Objects Palette.

3. Select the Pop-up or List Box element in your document window, and use the Inspector to set the desired specifications:

   - Enter a unique Name to identify the menu.

   - Rows refers to the number of rows you wish to be visible. In a pop-up menu, viewers see this number of rows when scrolling through the menu.

   - Check Multiple Selection to allow your users to select more than one item, if desired. If you select only one row to display and uncheck Multiple Selection, this will be a pop-up menu. Any other settings will revert it to a list box.

   - Select an item from the Label/Value list box, and edit these to your specifications. Editing options: Click Duplicate to make an additional copy of the currently selected item. Click New to add a brand new option.

   - Check the box here to display that option as the default selection.

Figure 16.16
A list box is shown here in the Form List Box Inspector.

Setting Up a File Browser

A *file browser* creates a handy way for users to search for files within the browser, in much the same way you'd browse for links on your own machine. The selected file can be uploaded to the Web server when the form is submitted (see Figure 16.17). For information on how to set this up, you will need to search your Web server documentation for "http file upload."

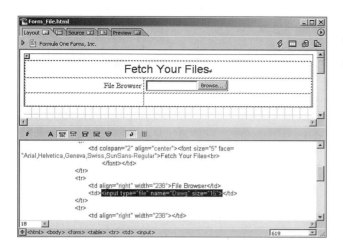

Figure 16.17
A File Browser can be used to permit a user to upload a file to the Web server.

To set up a file browser:

1. Select the Forms tab of the Objects Palette.

2. Click and drag the File Browser icon into position on your page, or simply double-click its icon in the Objects Palette.

3. Select the File Browser element in your document window, and use the Inspector to set the desired specifications, as shown in Figure 16.18.

   - Enter a unique Name to identify the file browser.

   - Visible refers to the number of characters that will be visible, much like a text field.

   - In the Focus section, indicate tab order, key access, or disable, if desired.

Figure 16.18
This is what the File Browser looks like in the Inspector.

Hidden and Disabled Form Elements

Sometimes there are elements of a form that you wish to keep hidden from view entirely or activate only when certain criteria are met, as shown in Figure 16.19. *Hidden elements* may include data or behind-the-scenes instructions not meant for the eyes of your users. Hidden elements are created using a special Hidden ico in the Objects Palette.

Disabled elements are regular elements that appear dimmed in the browser until a script activates them, based on a pre-designated event or when some condition is met. For instance, you could keep the Submit button dimmed until all required fields are filled. Legends, labels, text fields, password fields, text areas, Submit buttons, Reset buttons, check boxes, and radio buttons may be temporarily disabled in this way.

Figure 16.19
These form elements have been set to Hidden and disabled.

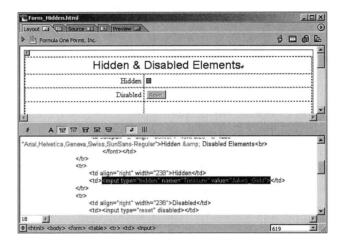

To create a hidden element:

1. Select the Forms tab of the Objects Palette.

2. Click and drag the Hidden icon into position on your page, or simply double-click its icon in the Objects Palette.

3. Select the Hidden element in your document window, and use the Inspector to set the desired specifications, as shown in Figure 16.20:

   ▪ Enter a unique Name to identify the hidden element.

   ▪ Assign a Value to this hidden element. This will be carried by the CGI script.

To disable an element:

1. Select the element you wish to deactivate in your document window.

2. Check Disabled in the Inspector as shown in Figure 16.21.

3. Write a script to enable the item based on logical conditions, and attach the script to the page or to another button.

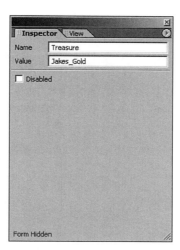

Figure 16.20
A hidden form element is shown here in the Form Hidden Inspector.

Figure 16.21
This reset button has been set to Disabled in the Input Button Inspector.

Read Only Form Elements

Any individual form element may be set to read-only status. Simply select the element in your document window, and check the Read-only box in the Inspector. These elements will not be transmitted when the form is sent, and cannot be edited or otherwise manipulated by the user.

FORM NAVIGATION

To make your forms easier to navigate, you can assign a particular tabbing order and even assign keyboard shortcuts. This feature allows users to select individual form elements by pressing Tab and/or a specific key combination. Not all browsers support form navigation control keys, but for those that do, it can be quite a time saver for your form users.

Tabbing Chains

You can define a tabbing chain for any set of form elements on the same page, as shown in Figure 16.22. The tabbing chain simply indicates in what order the form elements will be selected when users press the Tab key repeatedly. Labels, text fields, password fields, text areas, Submit buttons, Reset buttons, check boxes, radio buttons, pop-up menus, and list boxes all support tab indexing.

Figure 16.22
Set a tabbing chain to specify the order in which your fields will be selected when the user hits the Tab key.

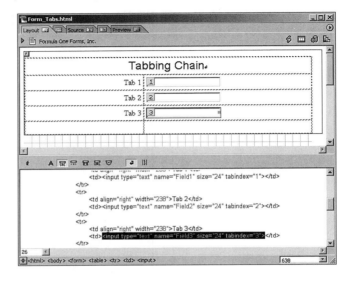

To create a tabbing chain automatically:

1. From the menu, choose Special, Start Tabulator Indexing. Or select the first element of your tabbing chain, and click the Start/Stop indexing button in the Inspector. (It looks like a number sign to the right of the Tab field.) A small yellow box will appear on top of each of the indexable elements on your form.

2. Click each element in the desired tabbing order, exactly in the order you wish them to be tabbed. Each will be assigned a number inside the yellow box on the element and in the tab index in the Inspector.

3. When you have finished creating the tabbing chain, choose Special, Stop Tabulator Indexing from the menu, or click the Start/Stop indexing button in the Inspector.

To create a tabbing chain manually, select each of the form elements in the desired tabbing order, and enter a number in the Tab text box of the Inspector.

To change an existing tabbing chain:

1. Select the element where you'd like to begin the tab change.

2. From the menu, choose Special, Start Tabulator Indexing, or click the Start/Stop Indexing button in the Inspector.

3. Click each element successively in the new tabbing order.

4. When you're finished, choose Special, Stop Tabulator Indexing from the menu, or click the Start/Stop Indexing button in the Inspector.

Figure 16.23
This field has been set to be the first in the tab order with a Tab Index Value of 1.

16

Defining Access Keys

You may define a unique access key for any form element on a page. This allows users to advance to a particular element by pressing a modifier key and a given alphanumeric key (Alt-S, for example, to activate the Submit button). Legends, labels, text fields, password fields, text areas, Submit buttons, Reset buttons, check boxes, and radio buttons all support access keys.

To define an access key:

1. Select the element you wish to have an access key.

2. In the Focus area of the Inspector, type any alphanumeric character into the Key text box, as shown in Figure 16.24.

3. Indicate the appropriate access key on your page by creating a label or text box, as indicated in Figure 16.25.

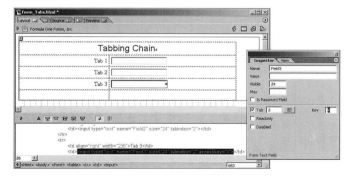

Figure 16.24
Use the Form Text Field Inspector to define a Tab Access Key.

Creating a Fieldset

The Fieldset icon creates a bounding box that visually groups form elements, making your forms more user-friendly, as shown in Figure 16.27. The legend may be used to indicate a title for the group of elements or give a reason why the elements are to be seen as a set.

Figure 16.25
This form field will be selected when the user types the defined access key of X.

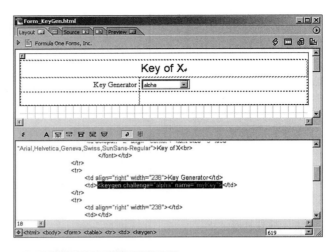

Figure 16.26
Here is the Form Key Generator Inspector.

To create a Fieldset

1. Select the Forms tab of the Objects Palette.

2. Click and drag the Fieldset icon into position on your page, or simply double-click its icon in the Objects Palette.

3. Select the Fieldset element in your document window, and use the Inspector to set the desired specifications, as shown in Figure 16.28:

   ■ Select Use Legend if you want a legend to appear in the field set bounding box.

   ■ Use the Alignment pop-up menu to align the Legend within your fieldset.

4. Highlight the legend in the field set, and enter in a name.

5. Drag an HTML or other form elements inside the fieldset, as desired.

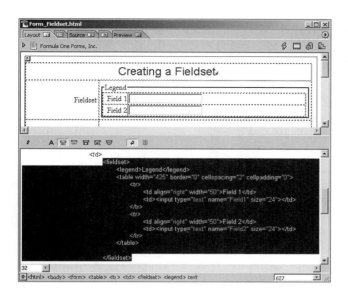

Figure 16.27
Here are several fields visually grouped within a Fieldset.

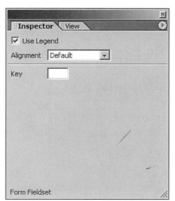

Figure 16.28
These are the options available in the Form Fieldset Inspector.

TROUBLESHOOTING

Making Your Forms Do Something

I've got this swell form, but what do I do with the data that is submitted?

This is the $64 question. A form won't do anything unless there's some sort of dynamic engine on the Web server that processes the form, perhaps takes some database actions, then returns the needed reply. When you're ready for this, go to Chapters 27 and 28, which discuss Dynamic Content and how to use GoLive to create a dynamic Web site with a database on the backend. You'll need a firm understanding of form construction.

Validating Form Data

How do I make sure that users input data into my forms that's formatted the way I want it?

This is called *forms validation*. It can be done on the server side, where an application running on your Web server checks the submitted data for validity and returns an error page if all is not well. But it's often easier to do it on the client side, using JavaScript forms validation.

When the Submit button is clicked, a JavaScript will first execute to check the contents of the form fields against criteria that you've specified for each. If any required fields are empty, or any fields contain data not formatted correctly, a friendly error dialog appears, and the form is not submitted. This ensures that any form that is submitted is full and correct. You can find a wealth of free validation JavaScripts on the Internet. My favorite source is `http://javascript.internet.com/`. You'll get short, simple blocks of code with full instructions on how to use them.

Another way to go is to make forms interface choices that don't allow freely entered text. For example, you've seen commerce sites that force you to select your credit card's expiration date by selecting from a pop-up list of months and years. This way, it's impossible to submit wrongly formatted information.

GOING LIVE

It's an established fact that forms are one of the main barriers to entry on a Web page. People want immediate information. They don't want to spend time filling out tedious forms, and in some cases, they may not want to tell you anything at all. Even if they want some information or a download that the form will lead them to, it's the action of filling out the form that's most likely to change their mind.

You can minimize the effect of this by following a few simple rules.

First, always keep your forms as short as possible. Collect only the information you really need. Make it quick and easy for your visitors.

Don't make very many of the fields required--only those that you absolutely can't do without.

Use fast selection tools like radio buttons, checkboxes, and pop-up menus, and prefill them with common selections. Again, make it fast.

Perhaps the most important rule of all is not to block entrance to your Web site with a form. Let the visitors in, let them poke around, and let them find something of value before you force them to go through a form.

Sometimes the best way to deploy forms on your site is to not use them at all.

17

STYLES

IN THIS CHAPTER

About Styles   **280**

Cascading Style Sheets   **280**

Implementing CSS in GoLive   **283**

Stationery and Templates   **294**

Troubleshooting   **298**

Going Live   **298**

ABOUT STYLES

One of the greatest challenges to Web design is ensuring that page information and design are consistent across an entire site. In fact, when hand coding, even minor edits can take a great deal of time to implement.

For example, consider a page footer containing copyright and location information across a large corporate site. With traditional coding, the developer would rewrite the code for the footer onto every page. When the footer's contents needed to change (perhaps the new year began or the company moved), the designer would have to edit every page that contained the footer. As a result, minor adjustments required a tremendous amount of time and resources simply because the edits necessitate changes on hundreds of pages.

As another example, consider a site designed with a particular color scheme and layout. After the entire site is developed, perhaps you decide to change the color scheme and add a few links to your main navigation bar. With hand-coded HTML, these changes would require intensive time: again, because every page in the entire site would need to be opened and edited.

One of the greatest powers of GoLive, therefore, is its capability to streamline these processes, both by implementing existing Web technologies as well as providing features specific to GoLive that aid in the development process. GoLive implements one Web technology developed specifically for streamlining these types of processes, Cascading Style Sheets, which provide a means for standardizing and centralizing font formatting across an entire site.

In addition, GoLive provides features inherent to the program that augment your ability to create and reuse content:

- Custom library objects and snippets —Allow the developer to store chunks of HTML code (snippets) in a library for easy access. Storing the code in a library means that you need not re-create the code for every page; instead, you can reuse the code stored in the library.

- Components—Allow the designer to store chunks of HTML code that can be inserted on multiple pages. Unlike library objects and snippets, modifications to the original component update every use of that component.

- Stationery and templates—Provide a foundation for creating page layout. HTML documents can then be created from these stationeries and templates. The difference between the two is simply that stationeries do not maintain a link to their child documents, and therefore changes to the stationery do not update the pages that it created. Templates, on the other hand, do maintain a link and will update the pages created from the template.

Each of these features proves to be a tremendous asset to the development process and will be discussed in detail in this chapter.

CASCADING STYLE SHEETS

Cascading Style Sheets (CSS) is a Web technology that extends HTML's formatting options and centralizes style specifications. You are no longer limited to font sizes ranging from 1 to 7 or background colors applied to simply the page and table elements. More importantly, CSS provides a means for formatting the text of a site in a central location. Changes to the page's formatting can then be made in one location, and all changes automatically update across all pages linked to that style.

For example, using CSS, you can specify that all text nested within a Header 1 (an <H1> tag) should render orange, a particular font size, and italic. Any text nested within an <H1> tag linked to that style definition would render as such. If you decide to change the style of Header 1, you need only change the code in one place, the style definition. All pages linked to that style definition would then update.

Browser Compatibility

Before delving directly into applying CSS to a site, it is important to have a fundamental understanding of the technology. CSS is partially supported by browser versions 4 and higher. Each evolution of the browser better supports a grander scope of all the CSS formatting options available, but keep in mind that no two browsers interpret the code exactly the same. As a result, it is important to test your pages on as many browsers and platforms as possible, particularly those that you expect your target users will be using. Although GoLive's View palette (choose Window, View) is handy in estimating how the different browsers (on different platforms) will display a site, actually testing the site on the different browsers and platforms is important.

Do not let browser differences hinder your desire to implement CSS. Using Cascading Style Sheets for even the most basic style formatting will provide an incredibly quick way to set style standards for your entire site.

Finally, know that CSS cannot add content to your pages; it can only format the existing content. Other features discussed in this chapter allow you to streamline content.

External and Internal Style Sheets

A *style definition* declares how a particular piece of text should be formatted. For example, a style definition may say that a piece of affected text should render orange, italic, with a normal font weight, and a background color of yellow. Perhaps the text should render in all capital letters, bold, and green. Regardless of the specifics of the style, the style can be defined in two distinct places: an external or an internal (embedded) style sheet.

An *external style sheet* is a separate text file with a .css extension in which style definitions can be stored. The advantage of storing styles in the external sheet is that more than one file can link to those styles—that is, more than one page can pick up the styles defined in the external style sheet.

An *internal style sheet*, on the other hand, embeds the CSS code in the HTML of an individual document. As such, the styles defined in an internal style sheet affect only a single page.

Keep in mind that an individual page might both have an embedded style sheet and be linked to an external style sheet. In fact, a single style sheet might also be linked to multiple external style sheets. Often, large corporate sites will take advantage of this feature. A set of generic styles will be created for the company in one external .css file. The department will then augment those definitions with a second external .css file, and an embedded style sheet will be used for specific purposes needed only for a single page.

GoLive can build both external and internal style sheets.

Element, Class, and ID Selectors

In addition to the different types of style sheets, CSS relies on different types of selectors. A *selector* simply refers to the item being formatted. The types of selectors include element selectors, class selectors, and ID selectors.

Element selectors format the appearance of existing HTML tags. To define a particular element, it is vital to know the HTML tag for that element. Don't worry if you are unfamiliar with HTML, GoLive provides a simple way for determining this information. Simply place the cursor in a block of text. In the lower-left corner of the Document window, a hierarchical structure (a markup tree, shown at the bottom left of Figure 17.1) of the tags affecting this text will appear, including the name of the element you might want to format.

Figure 17.1
Specify the HTML tags that you want to redefine via the Document window's markup tree.

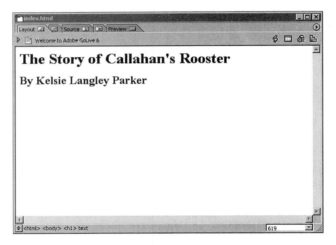

Class selectors, on the other hand, allow the author to create and store a style definition independent of the tag the text is nested within. When defining a class selector, the author provides a name for the class instead of relying on predefined tags in HTML.

Finally, ID selectors specifically apply to floating boxes as indicated by the floating box's name.

Whereas defining the appearance of an element (an HTML tag) automatically affects any text nested within the tag, the class and ID definitions affect only pieces of text and floating boxes defined to take on those styles.

Whether using element, class, ID selectors, or a combination thereof, the true power of CSS is that changes cascade throughout each linked document. That is to say, if you modify the style definition, any piece of text affected by that definition automatically picks up the changes.

Inheritance and Precedence

Suppose that you create two style definitions for an anchor tag (a link). The first defines that the anchor tag should render orange and bold; the second defines that the anchor tag should render yellow. How will the text inside the anchor tag appear?

The solution to this problem lies in the concepts of inheritance and precedence. *Inheritance* refers to the idea that a tag displays all the inherent properties of that tag in addition to any properties defined by a style. Suppose that the style definition indicates that the anchor tag should render orange. Any text nested within the anchor tag will actually render orange and underlined because links are inherently underlined.

Precedence, on the other hand, refers to the idea that a style definition takes precedence over the tag's inherent qualities when a conflict exists. So, if the style definition of an anchor tag indicates that the text should be orange and not underlined, the conflicting style definition takes precedence over the anchor tag's inherent appearance, and the link renders without an underline. In addition, the style specifications made most recently take precedence over style definitions earlier in the code.

Actually, a simple rule applies: The style definitions are additive unless there is a conflict. In the event that a conflict exists, the code last read by the browser takes precedence.

To answer to the previously posed question: Suppose that you create two style definitions for an anchor tag (a link or <a> tag). The first defines that the anchor tag should render orange and bold; the second defines that the anchor tag should render yellow. How will the text inside the anchor tag appear? The answer: Any linked text appears underlined by means of inheritance, bold as stated in the first style definition, and yellow as determined by the precedence of the second definition.

IMPLEMENTING CSS IN GOLIVE

To see how CSS works within GoLive, create a small sample site with duplicate pages that utilize the same HTML tags. Our example has two pages that use links, bold tags, Header 1, and Header 2 tags (see Figures 17.2 and 17.3). The pages are basic, and all text is black; CSS will add spark to the pages.

In addition, to demonstrate the ID tag selector, the page shown in Figure 17.2 has a floating box (note that this page also uses the Header 1, paragraphs, and bold text).

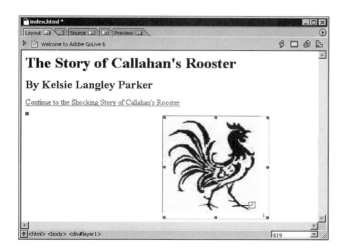

Figure 17.2
This page and the next are the starting ground for the site.

Figure 17.3
Currently, only basic HTML tags have been used on the page. Although currently bland, CSS can spice up the page's formatting.

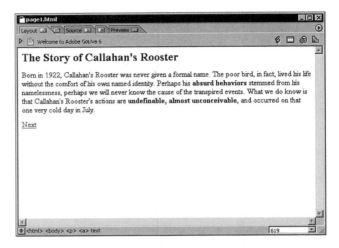

As the true power of CSS lies in its capability to define styles across an entire site, begin by creating an external style sheet. With the Site window open, create a new external style sheet by choosing New Special, Cascading Style Sheet from the File menu.

The CSS Definition Editor appears. Notice that the title bar indicates the filename that the styles will be stored in. The CSS Definitions panel uses four headings:

- Name—Provides the selector being defined.

- Status —Indicates whether a reference to an external style sheet is valid.

- Info —Provides pertinent information about an external style sheet's location.

- Source —Shows the source code for the selector.

In addition, notice the buttons at the bottom of the panel:

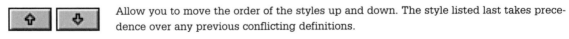

Allow you to move the order of the styles up and down. The style listed last takes precedence over any previous conflicting definitions.

Creates a New Element Style that defines the appearance of an HTML tag.

Creates a new Class style.

Creates a new ID style.

Adds a new link to an external style sheet.

Deletes the currently selected style.

Although three standard elements (HTML tags) have already been created, none of them include any CSS formatting. To add CSS formatting to an element, select one of the existing elements and bring up the Inspector.

When a style is selected in the CSS Editor, the Inspector displays all of CSS's formatting options, organized in eight sections:

- Basic—Shows the element's name and all source code.

- Font—Provides formatting options specific to text, including color, size, line height, style (italics), weight (bold), decoration (underline options), and font families.

- Text—Provides further formatting options for text, including text indentation, word spacing, letter spacing, vertical alignment (superscript, subscript, and so on), text transformation (uppercase, lowercase, capitalized), and alignment (left, center, justified).

- Block—Contains margin and padding options.

- Position—Used primarily for ID styles; sets positioning properties for floating boxes.

- Border—Contains options for adding borders to elements. Includes border colors, sizes, and styles.

- Background—Provides formatting options to add and set repeat properties of an element's background. Options include background color, background image, and how that background should tile.

- List & Others—Allows the author to define an image that appears in place of a bullet when used in conjunction with an <li> element. Also provides a means for adding other CSS properties that are not built into the GoLive interface.

To apply specific formatting to a selector, select the element in the CSS Definitions and choose the formatting options you want in the Inspector. The example shown in Figure 17.4 formats the body tag (all text within any linked page) to be Geneva font, gray in color, and 1 em (meaning 1 times the default font height) in height.

In addition to modifying the existing elements, you may also define a new element by selecting the New Element icon on the CSS Definitions palette. Immediately, an element is added to the CSS Definitions palette. Type the HTML tag you want to define in place of the word "element." For example, to redefine a Header 1, the element is H1. After the element has been declared, select that element from the CSS Editor and modify its formatting via the Inspector.

When finished defining the elements, save the external style sheet by choosing File, Save As and providing the file a name. Make sure that the appropriate Site window is open so that GoLive knows which site the style sheet is associated with, and note that a .css extension automatically is added to the file. The style sheet can be saved in any directory inside the root folder and must be uploaded to the server for the formatting to take place in the live site.

Before the formatting takes effect on the pages' text, the pages must be linked to the external style sheet. This can be accomplished in a number of ways. To link files to a style sheet without opening them, use the Site window in conjunction with the CSS palette, as shown in Figure 17.5. Start by selecting the file(s) you want to link to the style sheet and open the CSS palette. Click the arrow in the bottom-right corner of the CSS palette to see the list of external style sheets associated with this site. Select the external style sheet of choice and click the Add button.

Figure 17.4
In this example, the body tag's formatting is defined in an external style sheet. This style definition cascades through every page linked to the external style sheet.

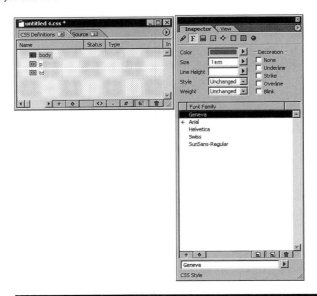

Figure 17.5
The CSS palette provides a means to link the external style sheet to the selected pages, without actually having to open each page.

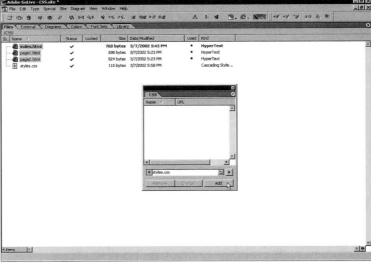

Each selected file should now take on the applicable formatting defined in the external style sheet. Notice that it is possible to add more than one external style sheet to an HTML page's Style palette. At any point in time, you may determine what external style sheets are linked to a file by selecting the file in the Site window and viewing the CSS palette.

To modify a style definition in an external style sheet, open the CSS Definition box by double-clicking on the CSS file from the Site window. The CSS Definition box opens, and modifications can be made by selecting the appropriate elements, making changes via the Inspector, and saving the external style sheet. All text affected by the changes automatically updates.

The previous example used an external style sheet and an element (or HTML tag) selector. Much of the process is similar regardless of whether you are defining the style in an external or internal (embedded) style sheet.

Recall that an internal style sheet affects only the individual page because the CSS code will actually be internal to the page's code.

To define a style in an internal style sheet, open the page in which you want to add the internal code. In the upper-right of the Document window, click the CSS icon to bring up the Cascading Style Sheets Definition Editor. Notice that the title bar of the CSS Editor indicates the page in which the style is being defined. In addition, any external style sheets the page is linked to will be listed in the External folder.

To add a style to the internal style sheet, create a new style while within the CSS Editor for the particular page, as shown in Figure 17.6. An Internal folder appears. This folder houses all styles defined in the embedded style sheet. Currently, an element (a specific tag) has not been selected, and the word "element" exists in its place.

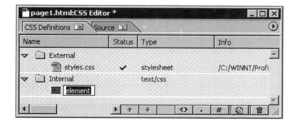

Figure 17.6
The CSS Editor displays the contents of any external style sheets, as well as any internal style definitions.

Use the Inspector to adjust the properties of the tag you want to modify. For example, you might want to redefine the bold tag using the Font section of the CSS Inspector, or set the text decoration (the underline option) for a link to none. When complete, the CSS Editor will update, listing the element and its source. Notice as you select the different formatting options that any text affected by the element you are defining changes in the Document window.

Whether creating an element, a class, or an ID style, the Inspector's formatting options remain the same.

You can modify the external style sheet's styles as well as create internal styles from the internal CSS Definitions Editor. To modify the external style sheet, double-click the style sheet from the page's CSS Definitions Editor, and a second CSS Definitions Editor, this one specific to the external style sheet, appears.

In fact, styles definitions can be copied from one location to another (from an external to an internal style sheet and vice versa). Open the CSS Definitions Editor for both the internal style sheet (by clicking on the CSS icon from the Document window) and for the external style sheet (by double-clicking on the external style sheet from the Site window, or by double-clicking on its reference in

17

the internal CSS Definitions Editor). With both windows open, you can click and drag style definitions from one style sheet to another. This does not move the style definition; rather, the style definition is copied.

It is possible to add a link to an external style sheet from within the CSS Definitions Editor for a specific page. With the CSS Definitions Editor open for a single page, Ctrl-click (right-click) and select New Link to External CSS from the resulting menu. An empty reference is added to the CSS Definitions Editor under the External directory. To define the style sheet's reference, select the empty reference, Ctrl-click (right-Click), and choose CSS File, Browse Link or Edit Link from the resulting menu. Browse Link allows you to browse to the file, whereas Edit Link provides a means for browsing to the file and setting whether the path to that file should be absolute or relative.

> **Caution**
>
> Not all properties affect the appearance of the page in the Document window because the Document window approximates what appears in a browser. In addition, keep in mind that not all CSS properties are supported by all browsers; the appearance of the formatting varies by both browser and platform. As a result, be sure to test the page in all target browsers to see the results of your CSS definitions. An all-encompassing guide to what style sheet elements work on which browsers is available at http://www.webreview.com/ style/css1/charts/ mastergrid.shtml.

Class and ID Styles

You should now be familiar with redefining the appearance of HTML tags by creating new element styles, as well as how this is accomplished whether it be in an internal or external style sheet. The process for creating a class or ID style is similar.

Recall that a class style provides a means of storing a style definition independent of a tag. That class can then be used to affect any text, regardless of what tags the text is nested within.

To create a custom class, start by opening the CSS Definitions Editor. Custom classes may be defined in either an external or internal style sheet, so open the CSS Definitions Editor appropriate for your purposes. Use an external style sheet if the class should exist across multiple pages; use an internal style sheet if the class need only exist for one page.

Create a custom class by clicking on the new class style icon. Provide a name for the class, as shown in Figure 17.7. Because class names always start with a period, GoLive automatically adds a period in the event that you provide an invalid name. The class created in this example is named .empha-sized.

Figure 17.7
A custom class definition does not require an existing HTML tag. Instead, provide the class a name. Browsers distinguish tags from classes by the period that must start a class name.

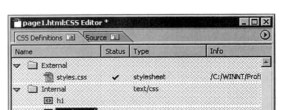

Just as you would define the formatting of an element style, define the formatting of the class by selecting the class name in the CSS Definitions Editor and modifying the format via the Inspector. The custom class in our example is set to be maroon, bold, and 2 em in size, and to have a gray background color.

When you have defined the class, close the CSS Editor. If you defined the class in an external style sheet, you are prompted to save your changes. For an internal style sheet, saving the HTML page also saves the style sheet.

Now that the class has been created, apply the class to any piece of text you want. Highlight the appropriate text in the page and open the CSS palette, shown in Figure 17.8, from the Window command. Any classes linked to the page (whether stored in an internal or external style sheet) are listed in the CSS palette.

Figure 17.8
The CSS palette lists any custom classes linked to the page, whether stored in an external or internal style sheet.

The class can be applied in three ways:

- Span—Refers to an inline HTML tag that can be applied to an individual character or set of characters. Use Span when only a word or piece of a paragraph should be formatted via the class.

- Par—Refers to applying the class to an entire paragraph.

- Div—Is best used when applying to multiple paragraphs.

ID Styles

ID styles are a special breed. They are specifically for setting the formatting of a floating box (or CSS layer). ID styles always start with a pound sign (#) which specifies that this is an ID style, and therefore applies to a floating box. Although floating boxes will be discussed in detail later, the application of CSS to floating boxes is simple.

When a floating box exists, a style definition is automatically associated with that floating box. A *floating box* is essentially a layer that can be moved around the page independently of all other page content. Any content within the floating box can be repositioned, perhaps even placed over other content, regardless of what else is on the page.

The example in Figure 17.9 shows the earlier created page, linked to the external style sheet. The styles still apply to text inside a floating box: The header styles and body styles created in the external style sheet render despite the fact that the text is nested within a floating box.

To see how an ID style works, select the floating box and open the internal style sheet by clicking on the CSS icon on the Document window. In this example, one ID style, called #rooster, is already defined for the floating box containing the image.

Figure 17.9
An ID selector is automatically created for each floating box and named after the layer.

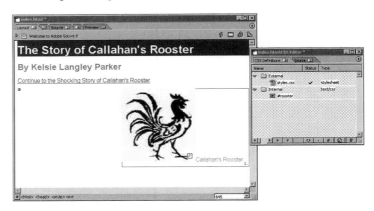

Any modifications you make to the floating box's position or properties via the Inspector automatically are defined as part of this ID style. Of course, the ID style can also be selected and modified further through the use of CSS (rather than the Inspector/Document window interface), just as a class or element can be defined in the CSS Definitions Editor.

Snippets

GoLive's Library Objects feature provides the developer a means for creating and reusing small portions of HTML. For example, consider a navigation bar. Rather than re-creating the navigation bar on every page, or copying and pasting the navigation elements over and over, you can store the page elements in GoLive's Library as an object or code snippet. As you maneuver through different pages of a site, the snippets can be inserted into the appropriate places. In short, storing the page elements once in the library enables you to easily insert that portion of code into multiple pages throughout the site.

There is no means to edit the contents of an object and have it update all places where the snippet has been used. GoLive does not track where a snippet has been used, and therefore does not automatically update changes. For this type of updating capability, consider using components, which are discussed in the following section.

GoLive allows the developer to store snippets in one of two libraries: a library specific to a site, or a library available while working with the GoLive application. Be sure to use the site library when collaborating with team members and working on a workgroup server. This ensures that the object is stored in the site project file shared across multiple computers.

To create a snippet, begin by creating the page elements in the Document window. The snippet can include links, images, table code, even head content such as meta keywords.

Select the page elements you want to store in the library. Keep in mind that this code will be inserted into another page. As a result, the object must include proper and complete HTML tags. The best way to ensure that the entire set of tags is selected is to use the markup tree bar in the bottom-left corner of the Document window to make the selection based on the tags that the code is nested within.

To store the snippet as part of the site (and therefore in the project site folder), select the Extras tab, of the Site window and from the drop-down, select Library. Drag the snippet into the Site window.

To store the object in the application's library to make it available to all sites, select the Library tab of the Objects palette. From the Document window, click and drag the appropriate page elements from the Document window to the Objects palette. An icon appears for the code, as shown in Figure 17.10.

GoLive provides default names for the objects in a library. However, the object can be custom named by Ctrl-clicking (right-clicking) the icon in the Objects palette, selecting Edit, and providing a new object name.

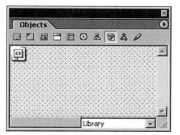

Figure 17.10
Library items can be stored in either the site's library (the Library section of the Site Extras tab) or GoLive's library (the Library panel of the Objects palette).

After the object has been stored in the library, inserting the object onto other pages is a simple feat. Open the page in which the item should be inserted and browse through the Objects palette to find the library item. Recall that it can be in one of two libraries: the library particularly for a site, or the library of the entire GoLive program. After the item is located, click and drag the icon from the Objects palette to the insertion point within the Document window.

Generally, it is best to store any object that contains a relative reference (such as a relative path to a file or image) in the site's library. GoLive tracks the paths inside a site's library item to ensure that the references are correct.

Components

Whereas CSS centralizes text formatting, components offer the capability to store content in a centralized location. Much like CSS, a change to a component automatically cascades to every instance of that component. GoLive's components actually insert the file's code as part of a greater page.

The advantage of a component is simple: you create the file once and have multiple pages refer to that file. Changes made to the external file (the component) automatically update the pages that use the component.

To create a component, open a blank page (choose File, New) and design the component as you normally would an HTML page.

Make sure that the correct Site window is open and open the Save As dialog box by choosing File, Save. GoLive, by default, saves pages in the root folder of the site; however, components need to be saved in the Components directory of a site project folder, as shown in Figure 17.11. To do this, select Components from the Site Folder menu in the Save As dialog box.

> Before relying heavily on components, consider that each component must exist on its own independent horizontal line unless nested within a table or layout grid. Without enclosing a component inside such an element, it will start and end with a line break, so you can't include other stuff on the same line.

Figure 17.11
To save the component, make sure that the correct Site window is open; then save the file (choose File, Save), being sure to indicate that the files should be saved in the Components folder.

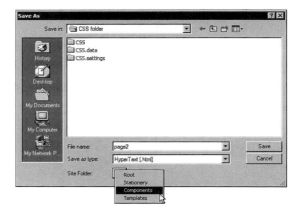

The Site Folder button does not appear if the Site window is not open within GoLive. Because you might be developing many sites at once, the open Site window is a means to communicate to which site the component belongs.

Provide the component a name, and click Save.

Figure 17.12 shows how the component has now been saved in the site's Project folder. In fact, from the Site window, you can navigate to all the contents of the Project folder, including the Components directory. The component you created is now listed as part of the site.

Now that the component has been created and stored as part of the site, the component can be inserted as many times as you want on your site's pages. To do this, open the page of choice, navigate to the Site Extras tab of the Objects palette, and select Components from the Site Extras drop-down menu, as shown in Figure 17.13.

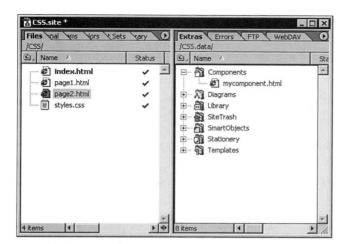

Figure 17.12
The components are saved in the Components directory of the site.

Figure 17.13
With the Site window open, browse to the Site Extras tab of the Objects palette and select Components. From this window, components can be clicked and dragged to the page.

Click and drag the Component from the Objects palette to the appropriate place in the page. Do not forget to save the page's modifications.

As you just saw, the benefit of a component is that the page elements need only be created once and then can be inserted onto your pages as many times as needed. As mentioned, other benefits of components exist as well. If any changes are made to the component, those changes automatically update in the pages that use that component.

To open a component for editing, either double-click on the listing for the component in the Site window, or double-click on the Object Panel's icon on the Site Extras tab.

A Document window with the component opens. Notice that the title bar displays the name of the component.

Make the desired modifications in the component's Document window. Save the page.

Close the component and check out the HTML pages in which that component was placed. GoLive tracked the component's use and automatically updates the HTML.

STATIONERY AND TEMPLATES

GoLive's Stationery and Templates features allow you to set up the grand scheme of your page layout and save that layout as a founding document. After the stationery or template is created, it can be used as the foundation for new documents in the site. Using these features saves time because you do not have to re-create the layout of your page. In addition, the process ensures better consistency in the look and feel across a site's pages.

The difference between templates and stationeries lies in their power to update the created pages. Stationeries are useful when you do not want your changes to update. For example, consider a site where the page layout is similar from section to section. Instead of creating duplicate stationeries that differ slightly, the designer can create a single stationery and develop one department's pages from that stationery. Then, only a few slight modifications will need to be made and saved to start creating the next section's pages. You need not fear that your changes will affect the pages already created.

On the other hand, at times the changes you make in the founding document should update the pages it created. In that case, look to templates as your solution. Whereas pages created from a stationery do not update when the stationery is changed, pages created from a template do maintain a link to the original template and therefore update as desired.

On occasion, developers find it helpful to break the link from the component's use to the original file. Perhaps on a particular page, the component needs to have an added page element that does not appear on the other pages. GoLive also provides a means for detaching a component from the link to its original file. Keep in mind, however, that breaking the link between the component's use and its original file means that changes to the component's original file will no longer update this particular instance.

To detach an instance of a component, open the page and select the Component. Ctrl-click (right-click) on the component, and select Detach Selected Component.

In addition to providing a starting point for a page's layout, the author can define which regions of a stationery or template can be edited when the page is created from that document. This feature is particularly helpful when working in teams: The lead developer can design the stationery or template for the content developers to work from, thereby controlling which areas of the page can be manipulated by setting editable regions.

When defining an editable region, the area is defined as one of three types of regions: inline selections, paragraphs, or object. When made editable, an inline selection allows characters to be modified, but additional paragraphs cannot be created. A paragraph, on the other hand, provides a means for editing and adding paragraphs as needed. The final type of region, objects, refers to images, table cells, floating boxes, and so on. When a new region is created, GoLive automatically defines the type of editable region based on the page elements selected.

Creating Templates and Stationeries in GoLive

To create a template or stationery, begin by creating a new page in the Document window. Lay out the page as you normally would keeping in mind which regions will be editable and which will not.

When finished with the main structure, define the editable regions. GoLive uses the Template Regions panel (choose Window, Template Regions) to create editable regions.

 Select an area that will be editable, and click the New Editable Region icon found in the Template Regions palette.

 GoLive automatically defines the region as inline, paragraph, or object based on the selection made. The HTML markup tree in the lower left of the Document window proves to be useful for selecting the right tags and creating the appropriate region.

Go throughout the page and make each editable region that you need. Each editable region is distinguished from other page elements by its color. In addition, the region will be provided a name and an icon indicating its type, as shown in Figure 17.14.

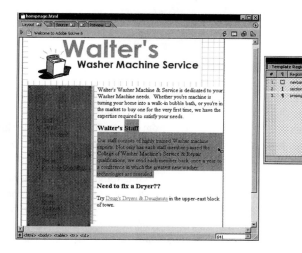

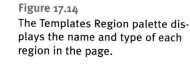

Figure 17.14
The Templates Region palette displays the name and type of each region in the page.

17

When finished adding in the editable regions, you have the option to lock the page. Locking the page applies only to inside the stationery or template itself; a locked page has no effect on any pages built from the page. Locking the page simply adjusts the appearance of the template or stationery by reversing the color of the editable and noneditable regions. In a locked page, the noneditable regions will appear in color, and the editable regions will be highlighted in white, as shown in Figure 17.15. Also, additional editable regions cannot be made. When finished building the stationery or template, lock the page to ensure that additional editable regions are not accidentally made.

To lock the template or stationery, Ctrl-click (right-click in Windows) and choose Template, Lock Page or Stationery, Lock Page. Likewise, a locked page can be unlocked in the event that more editable regions need to be defined by Ctrl-clicking (right-clicking) and selecting Template, UnLock or Stationery, UnLock.

When the template or stationery is complete, save the document. If creating a template, choose File, Save As and select Templates as the site directory. If creating stationery, choose File, Save As and select Stationery as the site directory. Remember that to have access to a site's directories, the Site window must be open.

Figure 17.15
The locked stationery indicates the editable regions in white and the noneditable regions in a dark color. In addition, the template cannot be modified when locked.

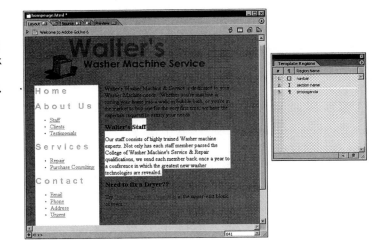

Creating Pages from a Template or Stationery

To create a new page based on the structure set forth in a stationery or template, choose New Special, Page from Template or New Special, Page from Stationery from the File menu and select the desired document. Remember that template modifications automatically update all pages created from that template, whereas pages built from stationeries do not automatically update.

Notice that only the editable regions can be changed. In fact, each editable region can be changed based on what type of editable region it is. Figure 17.16 shows a page with three editable regions. The navigation bar on the left is an object editable region, meaning that any of its contents can be altered. The text "Home" exists in an inline editable region. The content developer cannot begin a new paragraph when using an inline region. And finally, the "Welcome to Walter's Home Page" is in a paragraph editable region, which means that the paragraph can be changed and additional paragraphs can be made.

Make the modifications to the editable regions as desired and save the page. Be sure to save all pages in the site's root, not in the Templates or Stationery directories.

Modifying a Template or Stationery

To modify a template or stationery document, begin by opening the document. The most efficient means to open a template or stationery is to browse to the file in the Site window, and double-click the document's name to have it open in the Document window. Stationeries will be stored under the Stationery directory of a site. Likewise, templates will be stored under the Templates directory. To access the site data, click the icon in the lower-right corner of the Site window, shown in Figure 17.17. Site data directories will be revealed, including the Templates and Stationery directories.

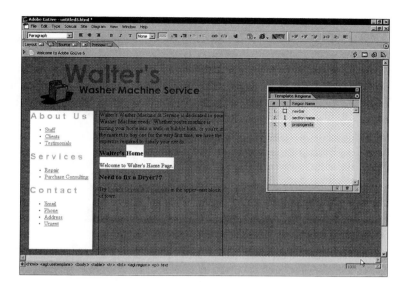

Figure 17.16
Perform your editing in a white editable region.

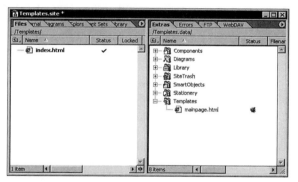

Figure 17.17
The templates and stationeries are stored as part of the Site window's site data.

When you attempt to open a template or stationery, GoLive pops up a dialog that asks you if you want to modify the existing document or create a new page. Select Modify.

After the template or stationery is opened, you may make edits as desired. Note that if the page is locked, you will first have to unlock the page by Ctrl-clicking (right-clicking) on the page and selecting Template, Unlock Page or Stationery, Unlock Page from the resulting menu.

While working with the original template or stationery, you can edit both the editable regions as well as the noneditable regions. New editable regions can also be created.

When you are finished with your modifications, lock the page for safekeeping by Ctrl-clicking (right-clicking) and selecting Template, Lock Page or Stationery, Lock Page. Additionally, be sure to save the changes by selecting File, Save. If the document is a template, you will be prompted to update pages built from that template.

If saving a modified stationery, you will not be prompted to update pages built from that stationery. Remember that changes made to a stationery do not update existing pages.

TROUBLESHOOTING

Making Your Styles Appear As Expected

I've applied CSS styles to my existing pages, but not all the styles are appearing as I expect.

Remember the rule of inheritance and precedence: the styles will all be additive unless there is a conflict. When a conflict exists, the style read last by the browser takes precedence.

This applies to both CSS styles, as well as to the order in which CSS is mixed in with HTML. Suppose that the Header 1 is defined to be orange. Then the following code exists in the page:

```
<h1> <font color="yellow"> My text </font> </h1>
```

The text appears yellow because the HTML deems so last, regardless of what the CSS style specifies.

For this reason, you might find it particularly helpful to strip your page of all HTML font formatting before applying CSS.

Saving Templates and Stationery

When I try to save the template or stationery, the Save As dialog box doesn't have the mentioned Site button.

Make sure that the appropriate Site window is open so that GoLive knows in which site to store the template/stationery. Then save the page. The button should appear.

Storing Objects in the Library

When I try to drag the snippet to the Objects palette, it doesn't allow me to store the snippet.

Remember to drag the snippet specifically to the Library tab of the Objects palette or to the Site Extras Tab of the Objects Palette (with the Library section selected) .

GOING LIVE

As you're already aware, Cascading Style Sheets truly refined the development process. Keep in mind that the power of the technology is not limited to the examples provided.

For example, even form fields can be formatted with CSS. The `<input>` tag is used for buttons, text fields, radio buttons, and check boxes. By defining the input element, therefore, you can add font formatting previously foreign to form elements. Likewise, the underline can be removed from links by defining that the `<a>` tag element should render without text decoration.

In addition, and perhaps even more powerfully, you can redefine a particular tag to have the appearance of standard text. For example, instead of defining a Header 1 to stand out from the surrounding text, you might define the Header 1 to have the exact same appearance as all surrounding text.

You're probably furrowing your eyebrows and asking why, but the answer is actually pretty simple. Search engines often crawl through the site looking for key information. Many search engines are programmed to assume that the contents of a Header 1 are most relevant to categorizing the site in its listings. In other words, search engines look to grab information from header tags to determine your site's rankings. So, nest the most important keywords in the text of your page inside header tags. Meanwhile, redefine the appearance of those header tags so that the flow of the text is not disrupted for your readers.

17

MOVEMENT, MULTIMEDIA, AND INTERACTIVITY

IN THIS PART

18 Using the JavaScript Editor and Inserting Java Applets   **201**

19 Working with Layers and Floating Boxes   **217**

20 Animation, Audio, and Video   **227**

18

USING THE JAVASCRIPT EDITOR AND INSERTING JAVA APPLETS

IN THIS CHAPTER

About Java and JavaScript   304

The JavaScript Editor   304

Inserting Java Applets   311

Troubleshooting   312

Going Live   313

ABOUT JAVA AND JAVASCRIPT

JavaScript and Java are both often used to enhance Web sites; however, the two languages actually have very little else in common. JavaScript is a scripting language that is executed within the user's browser and interacts with HTML and Cascading Style Sheets. In fact, without HTML, JavaScript has no purpose.

Java, on the other hand, is a compiled programming language that can be programmed to do just about anything to which you set your mind. A complicated and deep language, Java is often used to write applications and programs. Java Servlets are small programs that run on the application server and return formatted HTML to the browser.

JavaScript is usually included completely within the body of the HTML document, although it can also be a separately referenced file. JavaScript is rendered by the browser. A Java applet, however, is always a separate external application that can be "called in" to your page and can appear on the body of the Web page. Java programs run in the Java Runtime Engine, which must be installed on the user's computer. The latest version of the Java Runtime Engine (usually called JRE) is always available from `http://www.sun.com/`.

GoLive can integrate both JavaScript and Java applets into your Web site.

THE JAVASCRIPT EDITOR

18

Overview of JavaScript

JavaScript is a client-side technology that can interact with HTML. In fact, when you encounter features such as scrolling messages, jump menus, or interactive images, JavaScript is often the technology responsible.

Although GoLive includes ready-made JavaScripts (called Actions) that you can use to spice up your pages, the program also includes a great feature for your hand-coding efforts. GoLive's built-in JavaScript editor allows you to hand-code your JavaScript without leaving the application. In addition, instead of weeding through the HTML code in the Source View, GoLive's interface provides a means of adding JavaScripts to a page without leaving the Layout Preview. Like many text editors, the JavaScript editor can wrap the code and show line numbers. Unlike many text editors, however, the JavaScript editor can check the syntax of your code and highlight your errors.

JavaScript is an object-based scripting language meaning that the language is built around predefined *objects*, each which holds a set of *properties* (characteristics that describe the object) and *methods* (actions the object can execute). At a basic level, each JavaScript statement can set an object's property or invoke an object's method.

Although this concept may seem a little abstract, take the time to think of an everyday item to see how this works, as well as how JavaScript syntactically refers to objects, their properties, and their methods. As an example, consider your house.

Your house is an object, complete with properties and methods. Properties are characteristics that define the object. So for example, your house might have a color property. To access the color property in JavaScript, use dot-syntax notation. First you grab the object, then (following a period) you can grab the object's property. For example, the following code would return the value of the house's color.

```
house.color;
```

With JavaScript, you can actually do much more with a property than simply retrieve its value. The following code would assign a new color to the color property of the house object:

```
house.color = yellow;
```

Voilà! Your house is now yellow (the world of JavaScript can be pretty appealing). In addition to having properties, objects can also use methods to execute actions, also via dot-syntax notation. For example, imagine running the next line of code:

```
house.winterize();
```

Without lifting a finger, your house is ready for the upcoming winter. Or perhaps you invoke a different method:

```
house.clean('11am');
```

In our fictitious `house` object, the house would clean itself every day at 11 am. As you can see, methods are actions that the object can carry out, and typically follow with a set of parentheses. Often, to execute, the method will need additional information and this information goes within the parentheses.

In addition to methods and properties, objects also have associated event handlers. An event handler is what would tell the JavaScript to run. Unlike methods and properties, the event handlers are not accessed through dot syntax notation; rather, the event handler is treated as an attribute of the object's tag. For example, to have the house object clean on Mondays, you might code the following:

```
<house onMonday="house.clean('11am');">
```

Inside the HTML tag for the object itself, the event handler (in this case, `onMonday`) specifies when the house object should invoke the `clean` method. Meanwhile, the `clean` method needed additional information: what time to invoke. As mentioned, this additional information is required in the parentheses of the method.

In actuality, because the JavaScript is inside the `house` tag, the line of code above could also have been written as follows:

```
<house onMonday="this.clean('11am');">
```

Where the `this` keyword refers to the current tag in which the event handler is nested. Even further, any time you provide your objects (your tags) a unique identifier or name, JavaScript can access the objects via their names. For example, consider the following:

```
<house name="Bobshouse" onMonday="Bobshouse.clean('11am');">
```

Our introduction to JavaScript as it applies to the `house` object is almost complete. Before showing you a few of the objects that exist within JavaScript, there is one other very important factor to consider. Objects can be stored within other objects and are also accessed via dot-syntax n fact, there is a hierarchy with which the objects relate and are organized. For example, in the fictitious house object, consider the following code:

```
house.livingroom.vase.flower.bloom();
```

This line of code grabs the `flower` object through the object model. Starting with the topmost object (`house`) the dot syntax notation climbs from one object to the other until the appropriate object is accessed. At that point, the method for that object (the `bloom()` method for the `flower`) is invoked.

Now that you're familiar with objects, methods, properties, event handlers, and JavaScript's notation for each, let's examine objects within JavaScript in a little closer detail.

In JavaScript's Document Object Model (often coined the "DOM"), the window is considered an object, as is the document, the form, and the form fields. Each object carries intrinsic properties and many also have associated methods (actions) that the object can execute. Fortunately, you don't have to be a savvy JavaScript coder to write scripts with GoLive. GoLive incorporates a JavaScript editor in which you can write functions (stored sets of code). Also, when the JavaScript editor is open, the Inspector will provide access to all the objects, their methods, properties, and event handlers.

Creating a Simple JavaScript

Using the JavaScript Editor within GoLive, this example will demonstrate how to write a simple JavaScript function that calculates a total based on the user's selection of how many items she'd like to purchase. First, let's examine the JavaScript editor.

To open the JavaScript Editor, click the script editor icon in the upper-right of the Document Window. The JavaScript Editor is a small appearing window that allows you to create and edit existing JavaScripts. A number of editing features are provided on the top Toolbar of the Editor, including:

- Toggle Error Display: splits the editor into two, showing the script on the bottom and any errors or warnings in the top panel.

- Check Syntax: validates the syntax of the JavaScript.

- Display Errors: shows the total number of errors off to the right of the button, and toggles the display of the errors in the top half of the editor.

- Display Warnings: indicates the number of warnings off to the right of the button, and toggles the display of the warnings in the top half of the editor.

- Syntax Highlighting: toggles the syntax error highlighting on and off.

- Word Wrap: toggles the editor's wrap feature on and off. When off, text will continue beyond the right side of the window. When on, text will wrap to the next line.

- Numbers: shows line numbers and comes in particularly handy when editing.

- Create Script: provides a means for creating a new script. Notice the script is already named for you, but that you can change this name via the Inspector.

- Delete Script: deletes the currently selected script.

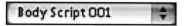

■ Script Name Drop-down list: provides access to all the different scripts you create via their predefined names. In this case, Head Script 001 is the name of the script.

When you first open the editor, a majority of the features will be inaccessible. Click the New Scripts button to start your first script.

Now that you have a new script started, start by declaring your function as follows:

```
function calc_total() {
}
```

All scripts that you want to store and call upon later (via an event handler) should be stored in a function. In this example, the `function` keyword declares a function, and `calc_total` is the name of the function that will be called. All statements that will be executed when this function is called will be stored between the opening and closing curly brackets.

Open the Inspector by choosing Window, Inspector. While working with the JavaScript editor, three tabs appear in the Inspector: Script, Objects, and Events. The Script tab stores a listing of all the scripts you have written and provides access to naming the script. The Objects tab stores a hierarchical representation of all the objects in the page, as well as provides access to their properties and methods. And finally, the Events tab provides access to object's event handlers.

As soon as a script is started, bring up the Script tab on the Inspector. Start by providing a name for the script rather than relying on GoLive's default names. As you add more and more scripts to the page, having each one intuitively named will save a great deal of your time. In this example, the script is named "calculate total of order form."

In addition, the Script tab of the Inspector allows you to define the browser for which you are coding, via the language version control. This adds the code that indicates to the browser which language and version of JavaScript is being written. One thing to know about JavaScript is that different browsers and browser versions support various renditions of the JavaScript language. The script in this example is fairly standard, and will be supported by a majority of browsers. Some of the more ornate JavaScripts you may encounter will work on just a subset of browsers—or better yet, will be coded to accommodate for these differences.

Finally, function names of a particular script will be stored inside the Script tab of the Inspector. In this case, the `calc_total` function already appears within the Inspector as part of this script.

Notice the other tabs on the Inspector, as shown in Figure 18.1: Objects and Events. The Objects tab, shown in Figure 18.2, provides a listing of all of the objects in a page, their properties, and associated methods. For example, if you wanted to add the code to the current script that accessed a particular form field's value, climb through the hierarchy to the form field, open its listing of properties and methods, select the value property, and then click and drag the value from the Inspector to the JavaScript editor. GoLive's JavaScript Editor writes the dot syntax notation for you. Climb through the hierarchy of the Document Object Model to grab the object you desire. Notice that the + beside an object opens a list to all of its child objects, and the − will collapse that list. Once you find the particular code you are looking for, click and drag from the Inspector into the current script in which you are working. GoLive will write the dot syntax notation for you that accesses the desired object, method, or property.

18

Figure 18.1
When the JavaScript Editor is open, the Inspector's Script tab provides a means for declaring the language version and a script name. In addition, any functions stored inside of the script will be listed.

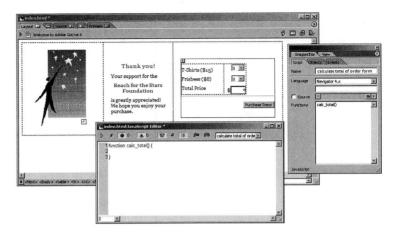

In this case, the two select lists in the form have been named `quan_tshirts` (for quantity of t-shirts) and `quan_frisbees` (for quantity of frisbees). Each of these fields has a value property that retrieves the value of the field. As this script requires a calculation based on those values, the two values are retrieved and stored into two variables, `num_tshirts` and `num_frisbees`. Using the Inspector's Object tab to find the value property of each object, click and drag from the Inspector to the Scripts editor.

18

Figure 18.2
The Objects tab of the Inspector provides a listing of all of the objects in a page, their properties, and associated methods.

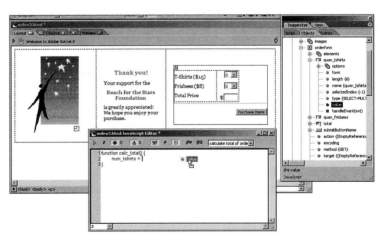

As you can see, some hand-coding is required. In this case, the Inspector is used to climb through the hierarchy to pull out the object and its property, but the rest is hand-coded. In the Inspector, green boxes indicate a property, and red bullets indicate a method.

Finish building the function, using both the Inspector and hand-coding. The final function should appear as follows:

```
function calc_total() {
    num_tshirts = document.orderform.quan_tshirts.value;
```

```
        num_frisbees = document.orderform.quan_frisbees.value;
        total = Number(num_tshirts) * 15 + Number(num_frisbees) * 8;
        document.orderform.total.value = total;
}
```

Let's examine each line of code. The first two lines of code grab the values of the two select lists and store them in the variables, num_tshirts and num_frisbees.

```
num_tshirts = document.orderform.quan_tshirts.value;
num_frisbees = document.orderform.quan_frisbees.value;
```

The third line of code calculates the total based on the price of t-shirts and frisbees, respectively, in addition to the quantity of t-shirts and frisbees selected.

```
total = Number(num_tshirts) * 15 + Number(num_frisbees) * 8;
```

Notice that the num_tshirts and num_frisbees variables are converted into numeric values. Form field values, by default, are not numeric in nature, rather they are strings (a string of characters). To do any type of mathematical calculation, the strings must be converted into numeric values. This is achieved via the Number() function incorporated in the JavaScript language.

Finally, the last line of code (built through a combination of hand-coding and using the Inspector) assigns the value of the total text field based on the previous demonstration.

The function is complete; however, the function has not been called via an event handler. The Events tab allows direct access to the objects in the page and their event handlers. In this example, shown in Figure 18.3, the code is specifying that the calc_total() function should be invoked onChange of the quan_tshirts' value. In other words, when the user changes the value of the select list, the calc_total() function will be called.

Using the Events tab, climb through the hierarchy to access a particular object and specify the JavaScript actions that will be invoked via that object's event. In essence, rather than having to weed through the HTML code to find a button and add the onClick event handler, you can simply use the Events tab to climb through the hierarchy, select the object, select the appropriate event, and add the code you desire.

In this example, the Events tab of the Inspector was used to find the onChange event handler of the select list (as accessed via their names). When the value of the select list is changed, the calc_total() function, previously written, will be called. That function, in turn, runs the statements, the last of which displays the total cost in the page's text field.

In this example, the Events tab was used to call a function previously stored in a script. The Events tab can also be used to add a single inline JavaScript statement to the code.

As you can see, GoLive truly enables you to write JavaScript in a quick and efficient manner via the JavaScript editor.

Although the object hierarchy in the Objects and Events tab is populated by the objects in the page, it is not populated by the particular language selected. That is to say, an object, property, or method not supported by Netscape 4.x may very well appear regardless of the fact that you have specified the JavaScript version language as Netscape 4.x.

18

Figure 18.3
The Events tab of the Inspector allows you to climb through the Document Object Model's Hierarchy, access an object, and code to a particular event handler for that object.

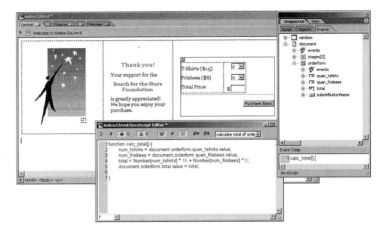

Checking for Syntax Errors

The JavaScript language requires a very specific syntax: As such, the JavaScript editor can search for syntax errors for you. As you write the script, click the Check syntax icon on the top of the JavaScript Editor Toolbar, as shown in Figure 18.4. If any errors or warnings exist, the JavaScript Editor will split into two, displaying both the error as well as the script that contained the error. Be sure that you have selected that the editor should display errors by clicking the Display errors icon. Likewise, if you want warnings to display, be sure the Display Warnings icon is toggled on. If you select the error in the top, the location of the error will be selected in the script at the bottom if you have the Error Highlighting feature turned on.

Figure 18.4
Click the check Syntax error to search for mistakes. The Editor will display errors in the top and the script in the bottom.

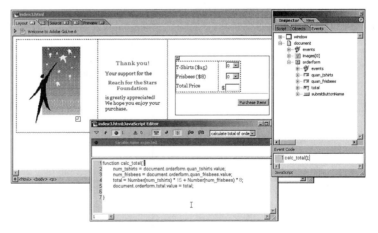

This particular example illustrated and explained a basic JavaScript function. JavaScript can do much more than retrieve and set the values of form fields; JavaScript can also open browser windows, animate layers, swap images, set cookies, and so on. For more examples of what JavaScript can accomplish, look into the section of Chapter 20 that describes the actions (prewritten JavaScripts) that ship with GoLive.

INSERTING JAVA APPLETS

Often, developers will embed Java applets into their page. An *applet* is simply a small program that is downloaded by and executed within the browser, as opposed to a Java application, which is a whole standalone program and doesn't require a browser. As soon as you start interacting with an applet, the computer does not need any other additional information to carry out the tasks at hand; the entire program is already accessible.

GoLive cannot write Java applets; it can only integrate an existing Java applet into the HTML page. If you don't have a Java applet at hand, but want to learn how to integrate an applet into your page, check out the Internet. There are a number of great resources where an applet can be downloaded and used for free. A good starting point is http://javaboutique.internet.com/.

To insert a Java applet onto your page, open the Basic Tab of the Objects palette, and click and drag the Java Applet icon to the correct location of your page. The Java applet can be placed inline with HTML, or directly onto a layout grid. Next, specify the Base (the source) of the Java applet via the Inspector. The Code for the applet will also appear in the Inspector. Finally, resize the Java applet (if desired) by clicking and dragging the handles in the Document Window, or by specifying the height and width of the object inside the Inspector. Each of these dimensions is specified in pixels.

Notice that the Inspector provides access to defining a few other attributes about the applet:

- alignment sets how the applet will align in relation to the text on that line.

- hspace adds horizontal space to the left and right side of the applet (specified in pixels).

- vspace will add space to the top and bottom of the applet (specified in pixels).

Some Java applets will require you to define specific parameters to execute correctly. The Inspector's Params tab will allow you to set both the name and the value of parameters needed. For each parameter, click the New button in the Params tab of the Inspector and provide both a name and a value in each of the fields.

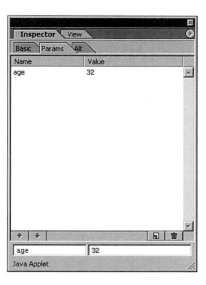

Figure 18.5
The Params tab of the Inspector allows you to define any parameters the Java applet needs to execute. For each parameter, specify both a name and a value.

18

Java Accessibility

As not all browsers and operating systems support Java, you may want to consider providing alternate text at the very least for your users. Likewise, GoLive allows you to provide alternate HTML that will display in the event that the Java applet cannot be viewed on the user's machine.

To set alternate text, select the applet in the Document Window, and set the text via the Alt Text field in the Inspector's Alt Tab. If you prefer alternate HTML to display in the applet's place, check the Show Alternative HTML checkbox in the Inspector. The applet's appearance in GoLive will change and you will now be able to type the contents of the alternate HTML in the applet's place.

TROUBLESHOOTING

I've tested the JavaScript in my browser, but users are complaining that it's not working.

Keep in mind there are dramatic differences in JavaScript, based on the browser and platform executing the code. Perhaps you used a part of the JavaScript Document Object Model specific to one browser while your user is testing the page on another.

In addition, JavaScript is a very nitpicky language when it comes to syntax and case sensitivity. Both Internet Explorer and Netscape Navigator offer consoles that can aid in locating the troublesome code. When Internet Explorer runs into invalid JavaScript, a small error icon displays in the lower-left of the browser window. Double-click that icon to bring up Internet Explorer's JavaScript error console.

Figure 18.6
To bring up Internet Explorer's JavaScript error console, double-click the error icon in the lower left of the browser window.

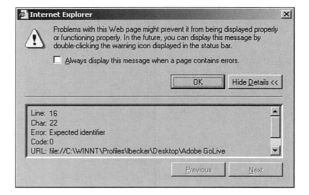

To bring up the error console in Netscape Navigator, type `javascript:` into the location bar of the previewed page. The error console appears, providing insight into the location of the error.

As you can see, the consoles are sometimes extremely helpful in providing descriptive leads to the error, and other times only point out that an error exists. You may very well have to do a little more intensive digging to find the error.

And finally, consider the fact that users can disable JavaScript through their browsers' options and preferences. It is possible that the user simply does not have JavaScript enabled.

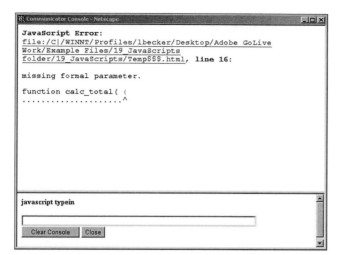

Figure 18.7
To bring up the error console in Netscape Navigator, type `javascript:` into the location bar.

GOING LIVE

Although knowing and understanding JavaScript and Java will be helpful to adding scripts and applets to your site, the Web is full of all kinds of free scripts that you can customize to your liking. For examples, try out `http://www.internet.com` and `http://www.dhtmlcentral.com`. In addition, online documentation and tutorials are also available. Check out `http://www.webmonkey.com` for tutorials, and `http://www.devguru.com` for an online JavaScript reference.

WORKING WITH LAYERS AND FLOATING BOXES

IN THIS CHAPTER

Layers, Floating Boxes, JavaScript, and DHTML   316

Using Floating Boxes (Layers) in GoLive   316

JavaScript and DHTML   321

Applying Actions in GoLive   321

Executing Actions Based on the Page's Events   326

Common JavaScript Applications (Uses of GoLive Actions)   328

Advanced Actions and DHTML   334

Troubleshooting   337

Going Live   338

LAYERS, FLOATING BOXES, JAVASCRIPT, AND DHTML

Initially, HTML was created purely for the purpose of disseminating information such as government and academic papers; aesthetically pleasing pages were less than imperative. As the Web progressed, however, designers demanded a means to make pages more appealing and user-friendly. Using tables for complex page layout became the solution to this problem. As a table data cell can hold any page element (including text, images, links, and other tables), HTML tables allow designers to develop sophisticated page design by nesting page elements in table cells.

However, developing a page layout with tables can be an excruciatingly taxing feat. In addition, modifying the page layout often requires the designer to start from scratch, as melding one table to another can prove very difficult. As a result, a simpler means of creating page layout has evolved: the use of layers.

Layers are like transparent sheets of paper, one stacked on top of the other, each holding a set of page elements. One layer can then be moved and manipulated without affecting the contents of the other layers. Furthermore, layers can be overlapped, thereby achieving a page layout effect previously foreign to the Web. GoLive's layers feature is referred to as "Floating Boxes".

Layers are actually a part of the Cascading Style Sheets Standard supported by the W3C. As a result, like CSS, layers are only supported by version 4.0 browsers and later. In addition, you may find slight differences between how the different browsers and platforms render the same code, so always be sure to test your pages on all the target browsers and platforms.

The most intriguing aspect of layers is that JavaScript (a client-side scripting technology) can interact with them, resulting in an interactive and dynamic interface. This integration of HTML, CSS Layers, and JavaScript is often referred to as DHTML (Dynamic HTML) and can be accomplished within GoLive via GoLive's Actions. An example of DHTML effects you have seen on the Web includes the ever-popular dynamic menu bar in which separate submenus appear and disappear based on the user's mouse movements. Even this effect can be achieved within GoLive.

To begin, this chapter will discuss the use of Floating Boxes (CSS Layers) for static page layout. Then, JavaScript and GoLive's Actions will be discussed, with special attention to the interaction of GoLive's Actions and a page's Floating Boxes. Finally, other JavaScript Actions built in to GoLive will be detailed.

In addition to the Floating-Box DHTML effects discussed in this chapter, you may want to explore how floating boxes can be animated within GoLive. This topic is covered in detail in the next chapter.

USING FLOATING BOXES (LAYERS) IN GOLIVE

As mentioned, GoLive refers to its implementation of CSS Layers as Floating Boxes. For all intents and purposes, the terms *floating boxes* and *layers* will be used interchangeably.

To reiterate, a floating box (or layer) is essentially a transparent sheet of paper that contains a set of objects. This layer (and all its contained objects) can then be moved throughout the page without affecting the layout of other page elements.

19

To create a Floating Box, open the Objects Palette's Basic Tab and drag the Floating Box Icon to the Document Window. A thin hairline box will appear, outlining the layer, and a yellow marker indicating the placement of the layer's code will appear (see Figure 19.1). The layer can be repositioned by approaching the floating box and clicking and dragging the box to the desired location.

A yellow marker indicates the floating box's position in the code. In addition, the floating box can be positioned by approaching, clicking, and dragging the appropriate layer's border to resize the box.

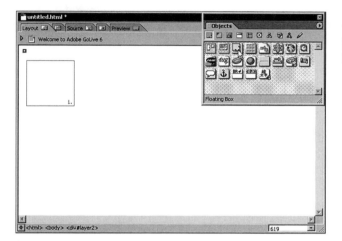

Figure 19.1
The thin hairline indicates the invisible outline of the floating box.

Figure 19.2 shows how the floating box can be resized by first selecting the floating box so that the handles appear, then clicking and dragging the handles to the desired size.

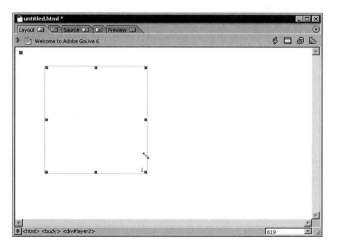

Figure 19.2
Click and drag the handles (the anchor boxes) to resize the floating box.

19

When a floating box is selected in the Document Window, the Inspector will provide all the properties for the floating box. Figure 19.3 shows a floating box's definition in the Inspector.

Figure 19.3
The Inspector provides the options for defining the parameters of a floating fox.

These properties include

- Name: used often for JavaScript purposes, provides an intuitive name that distinguishes each floating box on the page from others.

- Left: corresponds to how far from the left (in pixels) the floating box is positioned.

- Top: corresponds to how far from the top of the window the floating box is positioned.

- Z-index: determines the stacking order of the floating boxes relative to other layers on the page. The layer with the highest z-index will appear on top of the other floating boxes.

- Visible: sets the visibility of the floating boxes. Floating boxes are sometimes set to invisible upon the page's load by clicking off this check box. Later, some user event (such as moving the mouse over a link) will cause that layer to show using JavaScript and DHTML.

- Width: sets the width of the layer.

- Height: sets the height of the floating box.

- Color: sets the background color for the layer. Note that setting a background color overrides the floating box's inherent quality of being transparent.

- Bgimage: sets the background image for the floating box. Note that the background image will appear on top of any background color for the layer, and will also override the floating box's inherent quality of being transparent.

Designers often find the process of using floating boxes a bit cumbersome at first, particularly if they have never designed with layers. As a result, you may find it helpful to toggle the visibility of the different floating boxes on and off as you design the page, so that you may deal with one floating box at a time.

You also can set the left, top, height, and width properties for a floating box visually by selecting and moving/resizing the layer in the Document Window.

19

Each time a floating box is created, a marker (see Figure 19.4) indicates where that floating box lies in the code. If the layer is positioned from the upper-left corner of the Document Window (absolutely), the marker should appear stacked with others in the upper-left corner of the Document Window.

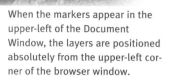

When the markers appear in the upper-left of the Document Window, the layers are positioned absolutely from the upper-left corner of the browser window.

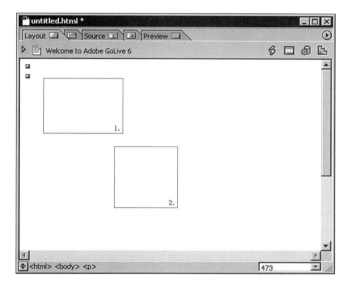

Figure 19.4
The yellow markers indicate the placement of the code for each floating box.

If the marker appears within the corner of another layer, the floating box is positioned relative to that layer (see Figure 19.5).

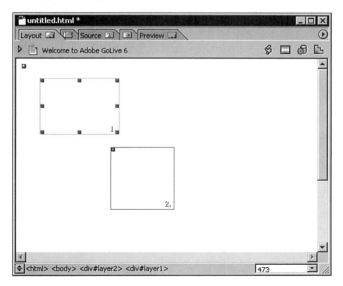

Figure 19.5
The marker appears within the corner of another layer, indicating that the floating box is positioned relative to that layer's upper-left corner.

19

You can drag the marker from one place in the Document Window to another; that is to say, by dragging the marker, you can change the floating box's position from absolute to relative and vice versa.

To put page elements inside a floating box, click the cursor inside the floating box's outline. Now you can type text, add links, and insert page elements as you desire. A floating box can hold any page element that the HTML document can contain.

Page elements can be dragged from one place on the page to another, including from one floating box to another, or from the page to a layer.

Managing Floating Boxes

GoLive provides a handy palette for managing floating boxes: the Floating Box palette (accessible by choosing Window, Floating Boxes). Figure 19.6 shows what the Floating Box palette looks like with a couple of floating boxes on the page.

Repositioning the floating box also repositions all of the objects internal to the layer, including other floating boxes (if applicable).

Figure 19.6
The Floating Box Palette allows the author to manage all of the existing layers in the document, as well as to add new layers.

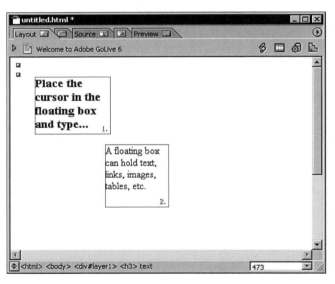

This palette lists all of the layers in the page. In addition, layers can be added and deleted via the palette's New Floating Box and Remove Selected Floating Box icons. Selecting a layer by its name in the Floating Box layer also selects that layer in the Document Window.

In addition to providing information and access to changing the layers' visibility, id (name), and z-index, the Floating Box palette provides one option not available in the Inspector. The Floating Box palette provides a means for locking a layer down so that it cannot be selected or edited in any way (see Figure 19.7). This is particularly useful as you design a page with multiple layers: Lock all the layers you are not working with so that accidental changes to the layers cannot be made.

Figure 19.7

To Lock a layer, click to the left of its name (under the lock icon in the Floating Boxes palette. The layer will not be editable unless you unlock it (by clicking again).

When you need to make modifications, simply unlock the layer via the Floating Box palette.

JAVASCRIPT AND DHTML

JavaScript is often responsible for making a page dynamic and interactive, and (when integrated with CSS layers) enhances your ability to create pages with Dynamic HTML. As JavaScript is a client-side technology, JavaScript will always react to something the user has done, whether the user has clicked a link, loaded the page, or hovered the mouse over an image. JavaScript will never invoke on its own, only in response to some user event.

In addition, because JavaScript is client-side, it will execute instantaneously. As the code is interwoven in the HTML and downloaded with the page, the JavaScript action can execute in the browser without utilizing further server resources. As a result, the JavaScript action will occur without hesitation, as no server-side interaction is required to carry out the actions.

To understand how to implement a JavaScript Action in GoLive, it is useful to understand the foundation of how JavaScript works. So, prepare for a short tutorial on JavaScript's structure, followed by a demonstration of how to implement GoLive's JavaScript actions within the Web editor.

JavaScript relies on a set of objects within a page. The document is an object, a form is an object, a link is an object, and so forth. Each of these objects can receive certain user events. For example, the document might be loaded or unloaded, the link could be clicked or hovered over, the form could be submitted or reset. Each of these are user events that the object can interpret. In conjunction with an object, the event can then invoke one or more JavaScript Actions. Perhaps the page's background color changes, a layer dynamically appears, or a form field is validated. Regardless of the specifics of the interaction, the process for adding an action to a page element is fundamentally the same. See Chapter 18 for more information on GoLive's implementation of JavaScript.

Consider using floating boxes for all of your page elements. Browsers position the layers from different points in the upper-left corner of the browser, causing the appearance of the layers to appear somewhat shifted depending on the browser in which the page is viewed. However, if every page element is in a floating box positioned from the same upper-left point of the document window, you need not fear this shifted effect.

APPLYING ACTIONS IN GOLIVE

The process for adding an action to a page element is three-fold: Start by selecting the object that will receive the event. For example, if moving the mouse over a link will invoke the

JavaScript, select the link within the Document Window. Then, bring up the Actions palette and select the desired user event. Finally, add and define a new action within the Actions palette. Regardless of the action being defined, this process remains the same.

The following demonstration details this process. In this example, the user will be able to drag the floating box and its contents by clicking and pressing down on a link.

The page has already been set up, and is shown in Figure 19.8. The page consists of one floating box named "yellowLayer" that contains a link.

Figure 19.8
The page has been set up: one layer (named "yellowLayer") which contains a link on the page. When complete, the user will be able to click and drag the layer around the page.

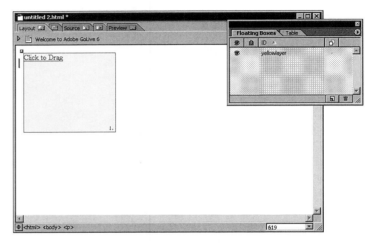

The text must be a link, as shown in Figure 19.9. Static text cannot interpret a user's click, but a link can. However, as the user should not actually be taken to another page, the link's source has been set to `javascript:void(0)`. This stops the browser from redirecting the page.

Figure 19.9
To receive a user's click, the text must be made a link.

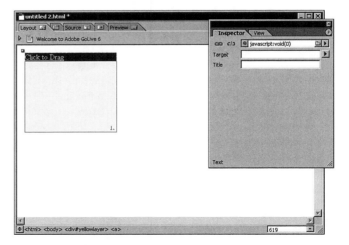

The first step to adding a JavaScript action is to select the object that will receive the event. You may find the markup tree in the lower-left corner of the Document Window a tremendous help in selecting the right object. In this case, the link will receive the user's event of a mouse press (called a Mouse Down in GoLive), so the linked text is selected and the Actions palette is opened by choosing Window, Actions as shown in Figure 19.10.

Figure 19.10
Select the object which will receive the user's event, and open the Actions palette. In this case, a link is going to receive the user's Mouse Down, and in turn run an Action.

The Actions Palette is comprised of three compartments: the event that will trigger the action to execute, the actions (listed on the right-side), and the actions definition panel at the bottom.

The next step is to select the user event. Note that the events will change based on the item being selected. For example, for a link, events such as Mouse Click, Mouse Enter, and Mouse Exit exist. When a form is selected, events such as a form submission or reset will appear as possibilities. For now, focus on the events associated with a link, many of which are fairly simple in nature:

- Mouse Click: when a user clicks the link.

- Mouse Enter: when the user's mouse moves over the link.

- Mouse Exit: when the user's mouse moves out of the link's area.

- Double Click: when the user double-clicks the link.

- Mouse Down: when the user's mouse presses down on the link. The mouse button does not need to be released for the actions to invoke.

- Mouse Up: when the user releases the mouse button after clicking a link.

- Key Down: when a keyboard key is pressed down. The key does not need to be released for the actions to take place.

- Key Press: when the user presses any key.

- Key Up: when the user releases a key.

For this particular problem, the Mouse Down is the appropriate user event, so be sure to select Mouse Down.

Next, add an action to the event. To do this, with the correct event selected, click the New Item button in the Actions palette, as shown in Figure 19.11.

Action

Initially the new action will be defined as None. To define the action, select the action currently listed as None and click the Action button in the lower left of the palette. A list of all possible actions will appear (see Figure 19.12) .

Figure 19.11

Once the correct object is selected in the Document Window (in this case a link), select the desired user event (such as Mouse Down) and add a new Action.

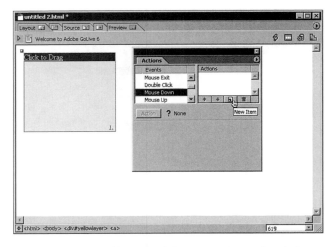

Figure 19.12

With the user event and the undefined action selected, choose the desired action from the list. For actions dealing most prominently with floating boxes, select an option from the Multimedia list.

19

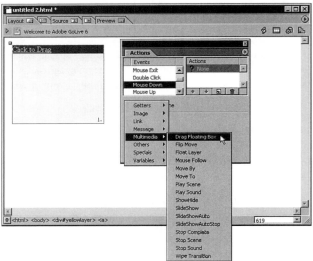

You will find the majority of the actions associated with floating boxes listed under the Multimedia option. In particular, the following options that apply to floating boxes are as follows:

- Multimedia, Drag Floating Box: allows the floating box to be dragged.

- Multimedia, Flip Move: moves the floating box back and forth between two sets of horizontal/vertical (x,y) coordinates each time the event is invoked.

- Multimedia, Float Layer: causes the layer to float in place as the page is scrolled.

- Multimedia, Mouse Follow: causes the layer to follow the mouse.

- Multimedia, Move By: moves the layer by horizontal (x) and vertical (y) dimensions each time the event occurs.

- Multimedia, Move To: moves the floating box to a specified x,y coordinate. Similar to Flip Move, except that the animation occurs in one direction only.

- Multimedia, ShowHide: allows the developer to show and hide floating boxes in a page.

- Multimedia, Wipe Transition: animates a floating box to fade in or out via various animation techniques.

As described previously, this particular example allows the user to drag the layer whenever the link is clicked. As a result, Multimedia, Drag Floating Box is the appropriate choice.

Most JavaScript actions will not execute within GoLive; the page will have to be tested with a browser to see the final result. Once an action has been chosen, its particular parameters need to be set. In this case, the only information GoLive needs to execute the Drag Floating Box action is which Floating Box should be dragged. Use the drop-down menu in the Actions palette to select the floating box via its name (as provided via the Inspector) .

Reading the Actions Palette

Once actions have been defined for a particular object, the Actions palette provides a number of clues indicating how the actions are set up. First and foremost, notice that selecting the object that receives the event dynamically populates the Actions panel with the possible events. Make sure the correct object is selected when trying to view existing events.

Second, take note of any events that have a small dot off to the left side, as shown in Figure 19.13. The dot indicates that the event does have an associated action.

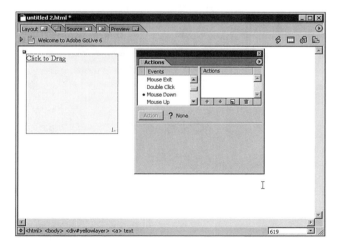

Figure 19.13
The dot to the side of the event indicates that the event has an action associated with the object.

Finally, select the event to browse through the listings of actions associated that event. Notice that more than one action can be associated with a particular event. In this case, shown in Figure 19.14, the Mouse Down triggers two actions: both a Drag Floating Box and a Set BackColor (background color of a page). JavaScript does execute in order from top to bottom through the actions listed for a particular event. In addition, the Actions palette provides a means for reordering the actions.

Figure 19.14
One event can have multiple actions associated with it.

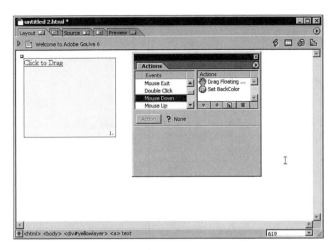

EXECUTING ACTIONS BASED ON THE PAGE'S EVENTS

As mentioned, a JavaScript action always invokes based on a user event. In addition, the process for applying a JavaScript action in GoLive is to start by selecting the object that receives the user event, and specifying the event and action in the Actions palette. What page element would you select to create an action that executed when the page loaded?

To accommodate this, GoLive has created what is referred to as a *Head Action*. A Head Action is simply JavaScript that executes based on some page event, such as loading or unloading a page. The process for defining such an action is slightly different than the previous example, so take the time to follow through with this next demonstration to learn what differences exist.

To insert a Head Action, start by opening the head content of the page. Recall that this can be achieved by clicking the **Head icon** in the upper-left of the Document Window's Layout View. Open the Smart Tab of the Objects Panel, and drag the Head Action icon to the head of the page, as shown in Figure 19.15.

Figure 19.15
Drag actions in the head of a document to add an action that invokes when a page loads or unloads, or to store code that can be called upon later.

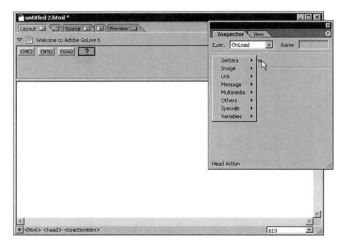

With the Head Action selected, bring up the Inspector. Unlike actions that execute based on an event of a page element, the Inspector (*not* the Actions palette) defines the actions associated with an entire page (with a head action).

Begin by selecting the event that should execute the action. The options for a head action include

- OnLoad: executes when the browser has finished loading the page.

- OnUnload: executes when the user exits the page.

- OnParse: executes when the page is parsed.

- OnCall: executes when called upon by another event in the page. Use this action to store JavaScript actions that will be executed later.

In the following demonstration, a layer will be animated upon the page's load. As a result, OnLoad is the selected event.

Action   Once the event has been declared, define the action by clicking the Action button and selecting the desired action from the resulting menu, as shown in Figure 19.16. As this particular demonstration relies on the animation of a Floating Box, you should select Multimedia, Wipe Transition as the action of choice, as shown in Figure 19.16.

Figure 19.16
Select the action you would like to have executed for this particular head action.

19

Do not forget to fill out the Inspector's parameters for the particular event: This is usually much-needed information that will make or break the interaction you desire.

Another slight difference between applying head actions versus actions to page elements is the means by which more than one action can be added. When specifying the action of a page element, more than one action can be added to each event in the Actions panel. In addition, the order of the events can be reordered.

Each head action can only invoke one JavaScript action. However, you can insert multiple head actions into the page with the same specified event. In addition, you can reorder the events by clicking and dragging the order of the head actions in the head of the Document Window. Head actions with the same specified event will execute in order from left to right.

COMMON JAVASCRIPT APPLICATIONS (USES OF GOLIVE ACTIONS)

As you may have noticed, there are many actions available. This chapter does not exhaust all possible actions, but instead provides a foundation for applying actions in general, as well as insight into how to implement common JavaScript effects. This section will delineate the processes for a few of the more common actions: particularly the processes for using GoLive to open pop-up windows when a link is clicked, validate form fields when the cursor exits the field's focus, and detect whether a user has been to a site before.

Generating Pop-Up Windows

GoLive can create the code necessary to generate pop-up windows. Widely used on the Web for advertising, these windows allow the user to view a different page in a separate window. The page can be either a page within your own site or a page of another person's site.

Start by determining what event will trigger the pop-up window to appear. Many sites will open a pop-up window with an advertisement when a user first loads a page; others will often generate a pop-up window based on the click of a link.

If you want the window created when the page loads, add a Head Action from the Smart Tab of the Object's panel. Note that the specifics of a Head Action are defined within the Inspector, and the specified event is onLoad, which invokes when the page completes loading.

If you want the window to generate upon the click of a link, create the link within the Document Window, select the linked text, and open the Actions panel. Select the user event (often an onClick) and add a new action.

From this point, regardless of whether you are defining a Head Action or an object action associated with a link, the process for defining a pop-up window is the same.

Click the Action button and select Link, Open Window from the resulting menu. The panel will display the parameters that JavaScript can set for the pop-up window. These parameters include

- Link: the page that will be viewed in the pop-up window.

- Target: the name of the pop-up window. For pages to load in the same pop-up window instead of creating multiple windows, set the name of the target equal to each other across all instances where a pop-up window is called.

- Size: the dimensions (height and width) of the pop-up window.

- Resize: a true/false value for whether the user can resize the pop-up window.

- Scroll: a true/false value for whether the user can scroll the content of the pop-up.

- Toolbar: a true/false value that determines whether the browser should display the browser's toolbar.

- Menu: a true/false value for whether the menu bar should appear as a part of the pop-up window.

- Dir: a true/false value that specifies whether the directory should exist.

- Status: a true/false value determining the existence of the status bar at the bottom of the pop-up window.

- Tools: a true/false value specifying whether the toolbar functions are available regardless of the toolbar's presence, such as by right-clicking, and so on.

- Loc: a true/false value that determines whether the location (the address bar) should appear within the pop-up window.

Define the parameters as desired. An example defining a 400 × 400 sized, scrollable and resizable pop-up window displaying the home page for Adobe is shown in Figure 19.17.

Figure 19.17
Associated with an onClick of a link, the action opens a pop-up window in which the window's features have been controlled, and Adobe's site appears as the window's content.

You also have the ability to specify a target name. The target name is a temporary name that refers to the pop-up window. Any call to a pop-up window that targets that name will load in the window. If that window does not already exist, have no fear. The browser will create and name the window automatically.

Form Validation

Because JavaScript is a client-side technology, it has a powerful ability to check form fields for validity. The beauty of using JavaScript for this form validation lies in the fact that the code executes instantaneously and does not require any server resources: The form's fields can all be checked before the user actually submits the information to the server.

> Targeting a _blank window via a link can achieve a similar effect that is cross-browser compatible for the older browsers. However, JavaScript's ability to generate a pop-up window provides you with much greater control over the window's features.

The following demonstration illustrates how to add form validation to an existing form. If you are in search of detailed information about form elements in particular, check out Chapter 16, "Creating Forms."

Create a page with a basic form, such as that shown in Figure 19.18. This form consists of two text fields, one named fullname, the other named email. In addition, a set of radio buttons named Gender capture additional information. Note that these radio buttons are between the validated text fields.

Figure 19.18

In this example, the two text fields will be validated through GoLive's actions.

JavaScript relies heavily on naming particular objects. In addition to naming the fields, be sure to name the form as well via the Inspector. To do this, select the form, bring up the Inspector (Window, Inspector) and provide a name.

Once the form has been set up and named, select a text field and open the Actions panel. The user event associated with a form validation is most commonly Submit; however, the JavaScript generated by GoLive is best implemented when the user blurs his cursor from a text field (that is, forces the cursor to leave a text field either by clicking somewhere else on the page or tabbing to the next form field). With the form field selected, choose Key Blur (see Figure 19.19) as the user event. Add a new action, and click the Action button to define this action as Getters, Field Validator.

Figure 19.19

The Key Blur means that the actions will invoke when the user's cursor leaves the text field. In this case, when the cursor leaves the field, the text field will be validated.

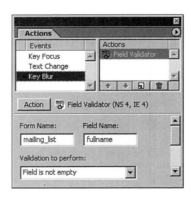

Finally, define the necessary parameters. Start by filling in the form name and field name. Note that in JavaScript, names are case sensitive. Then choose the type of validation you desire for this particular form field. Options include

- Field is not empty: checks to see if any value has been entered into the form field.

- Field contains numbers only: checks for numeric values. Note that numeric values do accept decimal points.

- Field contains letters only: determines whether the field contains anything other than letters.

- Field has this many characters: ensures that the length of a value is an exact number. Good for phone numbers, social security numbers, and any string where the possible number of characters is fixed.

- Field = exact test string: tests the value to see if it exactly matches the string you provide.

- Field is proper email format: searches for basic email structure. In other words, the field must include an '@' sign, a '.', and at least two characters thereafter.

- Field is proper Credit Card format: tests to see if the entered data matches the pattern of the typical credit card number.

In addition, specify the text you would like alerted in the event that the above condition is not met.

A Caution When Implementing Form Validation in GoLive

The means by which GoLive's JavaScript form validation is carried out contain one possible usability flaw. The code is written so that upon exiting the text field, the field is validated. In addition, the JavaScript refocuses the cursor back into the unsatisfied text field.

Imagine that two form fields exist in the page, one directly following the other. When the user exits the first field without appropriately filling in the necessary information, an alert appears. Meanwhile, if the user used the tab key to navigate the form, her cursor has now entered into the second field which also has an associated validation. As soon as the user clicks the OK button on the alert box, the cursor is placed again in the first field, thereby blurring the second field and causing a second alert. This process continuously cycles, blurring one text field then the other, causing alert box after alert box in which the user cannot escape without completely ending the browser session.

The fix to this problem is to add form labels and to set the tab order of those labels. In other words, following each form field that is validated, add a label that contains nothing more than a space that serves as an item in the tab order of the page. The labels serve as a buffer between two validated form elements so the continuous alert cycle does not invoke.

For example, the form shown in Figure 19.20 has two validated form fields with labels between them that escape such an infinite loop of alert boxes.

Those familiar with hand-coding JavaScript may question why the validation is not associated with a form's submission. Although hand-written JavaScript would serve perfectly well for this purpose, GoLive's JavaScript does not return a value of true or false to the browser. As a result, applying GoLive's form validation code to the onSubmit event handler of a form will check each specified form element for validity, but would not stop the form from being submitted to the server, thereby defeating the purpose.

Figure 19.20
Use labels to separate validated text fields. Each label should also be given a tab order.

Detecting a Loyal User with a JavaScript Cookie

Adobe GoLive can also implement JavaScript cookies. A cookie is a text file temporarily created on the user's computer that the Web server can use to store variables without utilizing server resources. Cookies are often useful for customizing the delivery of content based on the user's preferences or identity.

As a developer, do keep in mind that some users are suspicious of cookies, and have their browser preferences set to block them. For this reason, you cannot always rely on being able to set and read cookies as you can other types of variables. And, since a cookie is a simple text file that anyone can sit down and read, don't store data in a cookie that might be useful to an unauthorized person, such as a user's password or credit card number.

The example shown in Figures 19.21 and 19.22 shows you how to set a cookie that determines whether a user has been to the site before. In actuality, two pages will exist: the "Welcome new user" page which will be responsible for setting the cookie, and the "Welcome back!" page which will appear in the event that the cookie already exists.

To begin, create a page for your new user. View the Head Content by clicking the arrow in the upper-left corner of the Document Window, and drag a Head Action from the Smart Tab of the Objects Palette to the head content. This particular test should be conducted onLoad, so that the user is immediately redirected to the second page if returning to the site.

Figure 19.21
Here is a page testing for the presence of a cookie, not finding one, and displaying one set of content that assumes the user is new.

Figure 19.22
Here is the same page after finding a cookie and recognizing the return user.

Select the head action and bring up the Inspector to define the user event and actions. Define the user event as onLoad, and the action as Variables, Visitor Cookie.

Finally, fill in the requested information in the Inspector, as in Figure 19.23. Two pieces of information are particularly crucial to the implementation of the cookie: a cookie name (in this case `recent_user`) and the page which the user will be redirected to in the event he is a loyal customer (in this case, `home.html`). The appropriate action can be found under Variables, VisitorCookie and requires two pieces of information, the name for the cookie and the page to which the user should be redirected.

Note that like most JavaScripts, this cookie action must be tested in the browser.

19

Figure 19.23
Define the Head Action via the Inspector.

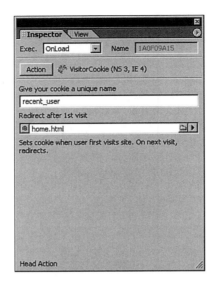

ADVANCED ACTIONS AND DHTML

No Web designer will argue that they have too much space to put their information in: Managing the screen's real estate has become a challenge in and of itself. Especially when a page needs to link to many different pages, many Web sites have developed DHTML submenus.

If you have spent any time on the Web, you have seen a drop-down submenu in action. You roll your mouse over a link, and *Voilà!* More options pertinent to that link appear, without forcing you to download an intermediary page.

Submenus actually rely on DHTML (the integration of HTML, CSS, and JavaScript). Although the user sees a menu, what actually occurs is that a floating box appears and disappears based on the user's action. Initially, the submenus (the layers containing the more extensive options) are set to be invisible. Then, upon rolling over the main link, the floating boxes appear, revealing the items in the submenu.

Simple? Not quite. Only half of the problem is described—rolling over the link shows the menu. But what makes the menu then disappear when the user is done?

The trick is that a floating box exists below all of the menu options. This floating box contains one image that is linked, but to a voided JavaScript action rather than to another page. The image is transparent, so although you might notice your cursor change to a hand (indicating the link), you won't see the image itself. Actions added to this linked image indicate that when you roll over the image (thereby rolling off of the menu options), an action changes the visibility of any submenus, thereby making them disappear again.

The following demonstration will show you how to implement the submenu effect step-by-step, including the solution to the previously posed question. Before embarking on this particular problem, make sure you are comfortable with how JavaScript is implemented in GoLive: the process of choosing an object, selecting a user event, and adding and specifying an action for that user event. Having that as a foundation for this demonstration will prove a tremendous asset.

Start by creating a page of floating boxes. Each main heading should be a link contained in its own floating box, with separating space from one to the next. In addition, each submenu should appear below its respective headings, without any space between the floating boxes. It should look like the page shown in Figure 19.24.

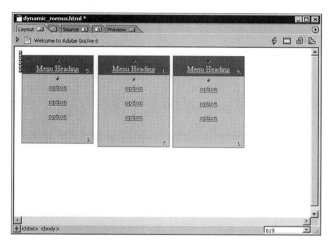

Figure 19.24
The headings and submenus are set up and ready for action. Note the necessary space between each set of menus.

For each floating box, indicate the z-index (submenus should have the highest z-index, headers should follow just below those) and take the time to provide an intuitive name for the layer. Finally, check off the visibility for each of the submenus, thereby forcing them to initially be hidden. All of these tasks can be completed via the Inspector.

Add one additional floating box to the page, this one big enough to cover all the edges of the headings and submenus. Make sure that you name this floating box intuitively as well, and that you provide this floating box the lowest z-index of the bunch. Finally, insert into this floating box one big transparent image, and set its link to `javascript:void(0)`. This will enable you to add an action without actually having the image link to another page.

Once the page has been set up, check the Floating Boxes palette in Figure 19.25 to make sure all is in order. Make sure the z-index for the big layer in the background (in this case called "hidelayers") has the lowest z-index of the bunch. Also, make sure the visibility of the submenus is off. Now you're ready for action.

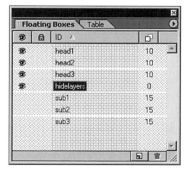

Figure 19.25
The Floating box palette indicates the z-indexes and visibility of all the floating boxes in the page.

19

Now that the page structure has been created, the links are ready for action. Keep in mind that static text cannot determine when a user's mouse has moved over it; linked text (or a linked image, for that matter) can.

Select the link in the first header. Bring up the Actions panel and add an action to the Mouse Enter event as in Figure 19.26. Define the action for this event as Multimedia, ShowHide. Finally, fill in the two pieces of information the action needs to execute: the name of the layer you would like to appear, and the Mode for that floating box.

Figure 19.26

The action is set. When you mouse over the link, the action will execute, showing the floating box called "sub1".

Repeat this step for each heading link, each one revealing its associated submenu.

Although not necessary, it is a good idea to go ahead and test out the progress of your page so far. Load it into the browser and check it out: Each time the mouse hovers over a link, a submenu should appear below. Note that thus far, we have not specified how those menus will close. Adding the actions that close the menus comes next.

Once the first half of the page is working, lock the floating boxes down via the Floating Boxes palette. This is just to ensure that modifications are not accidentally made to your finished floating boxes.

Now, for the final action. When you roll the mouse off of any one of the floating box head-submenu sets, you want the menus to hide. So, select the linked image in the secret floating box in the back of the page. Note that because its z-index is the lowest of all of the floating boxes in the page, the Mouse Enter action essentially triggers when you roll the mouse off of the headers or submenus.

Grab the secret linked image and open the Actions palette. Add an action to the Mouse Enter event, and define that action as Multimedia, ShowHide. Select one of the submenus by name from the Actions panel drop-down and specify its mode as Hide. Add and define a Multimedia, Action to the same Mouse Enter event for each submenu that will disappear. The Inspector should indicate all of these, as in Figure 19.27.

Figure 19.27
The transparent image in the background floating box has three ShowHide actions applied, each one instructing the browser to hide the submenus.

TROUBLESHOOTING

Fixing Problems with Actions

I have added my actions to my link, but when I hover over the link, nothing happens.

Most often this problem is caused by adding the action to the wrong event. Remember that an event dictates when an action should invoke. In the previous example, events such as Click, Double-click, Mouseover, Mouseout, and onLoad were all discussed. Go back to the link that is not working correctly, and bring up the Actions palette. Make sure the dot indicating an action is next to the correct event. If it is not, you will need to delete the existing action (which is currently attached to the wrong event), and then add that action back to the correct event.

Identifying Browser Problems

When I test out my pages initially, it works fine. But if I resize the window I lose all the information about my floating boxes (CSS layers) and my DHTML animations no longer work correctly.

Chances are you are using Netscape's browser. Netscape (specifically versions 4.x) encapsulates a bug that causes the browser to lose all of the CSS information when the browser is resized. This includes any Cascading Style Sheets you may have attached to the page, as well as information about floating boxes, their positions, and so forth.

In short, the error is not yours, not GoLive's, but rather internal to the browser (nobody, not even Netscape, is perfect after all). Fortunately, GoLive offers a fix for the problem regardless. GoLive's Netscape CSS Fix forces the browser to reload the information about the page when the window is resized. To add this fix to your page, add a Head Action. Then, using the Inspector, specify the onLoad event for this head action, and add the Netscape CSS Fix action (Action, Others, Netscape CSS Fix). In fact, as some of your users may be using Netscape to view your pages, it is a good idea to always add this action into the page when using CSS layers (GoLive's Floating Boxes) .

GOING LIVE

When you add Actions to your pages, GoLive writes the JavaScript code in one of two places: either internal to each page or in a separate (external) file that is loaded by each page. Which option GoLive chooses is determined by the Site's preferences. You can tell GoLive how you where you want the JavaScripts written in three ways: so that it affects all newly created pages, all pages within a Site, or for a single page.

To set where the JavaScripts should be written for all new pages, select Edit, Preferences and select Script Library in the left pane.

To set where the JavaScripts should be written for all pages within a Site, open the appropriate Site Window and click the Site Settings button on the Toolbar. Then, choose Script Library in the left pane followed by Site Specific Settings in the right pane.

To set where the JavaScripts should be written for an individual HTML file, select the HTML page in the Site Window and open the Inspector.

Be sure the right Site Window is open. Regardless of which files you are setting this option for, you will have the opportunity to write the code into the page or import GoLive's script library. The bene-fit of importing the script library is that all of the pages in a Site can share the same JavaScript code, meaning that the code is downloaded once (in the external file) and then reused from page to page.

Note that the JavaScript file is put into a folder named GeneratedItems by default. This folder and all of its contents must be uploaded to the server for the files to work correctly.

Finally, the last thing you want to consider with regard to saving your users download time is the amount of content that resides inside the JavaScript Script Library. The script library does not con-tain purely the JavaScripts used by the Site, but rather all JavaScripts that GoLive can write. As a result, you will want to flatten this script: That is to say you will want to weed this script of any code that is not used by the pages in your particular Site. This will save a tremendous amount of download time for your users, as your users will not be downloading unnecessary code.

To manually flatten the JavaScript Library, open the Site Window and select Site, Flatten Script Library from the menu.

Also, you can flatten the library upon upload of the Site by modifying the Site's preferences. Select Edit, Preferences and expand the Site option. Then, select Upload/Sync Times and select the option to Flatten Script Library and click OK.

As you can see, adding JavaScript can add both user-friendly functionality as well as intriguing spunk to your pages. Although GoLive has many other actions available for you to explore, the most common and universally useful actions, as well as the logical structure for implementing an action, have been described and detailed. With the foundation for how GoLive Actions are implemented, you'll have pages brimming with JavaScript in no time.

As mentioned, DHTML can animate your floating boxes even further. For detailed instructions, check out the next chapter explicitly covering DHTML animation.

Like most Web technologies, however, JavaScript also works differently in each of the browsers. The first iteration of JavaScript is supported by browser versions 4.0 and later. To its credit, Adobe has done a considerable job of writing code that will work in many of the browsers, but it will always be in your benefit to test the pages in as many target browsers and platforms as possible.

ANIMATION, AUDIO, AND VIDEO

IN THIS CHAPTER

Pizzazz on Your Pages **342**

Animation with DHTML **342**

SWF and SVG **350**

Audio and Video Clips **351**

Editing QuickTime Movies **354**

Troubleshooting **364**

Going Live **365**

PIZZAZZ ON YOUR PAGES

Animation and audio can really jazz up an otherwise boring page, but this can lead to a trap that many Web surfers have fallen into: unwanted music that suddenly blares from the computer's speakers, long load times to bring up an intro movie that you'd rather just skip, and things floating across the page when all you want to do is read the content.

Properly used, these tools can add to the experience, rather than detract from it. Most types of animations and sound files are imported from other sources, and can be displayed on a Web page using just a link to download the external file, which is then handled by the user's browser. But many of these files can also be displayed directly in the browser, and controlled by the Web developer. This section shows you how to take control over your user's audiovisual experience. Putting these tools in the hands of the wrong developer can be compared to giving a hyperactive child a drum set for his birthday, so please use good sense in deploying these features.

ANIMATION WITH DHTML

DHTML (Dynamic HTML) can be used to create layered floating objects. When used with the Timeline Editor, these objects can fly around on your screen, with all kinds of actions triggering them. Buttons can fly into the screen, and fly away again once they're clicked. Designers can create art element layers that slide across the screen. You can even make annoying little advertisements that fly around in front of your Web page.

Objects can be defined to move along predetermined paths. You can draw curves, zigzags, or linear paths. You can even set them to appear and disappear.

These objects can contain graphics, text, or both. They can also have transparent backgrounds or solid backgrounds. If you use a transparent GIF as the content of your floating box, there will be no square background and it will look like you have a cool shaped object flying around.

You can, in fact, go as crazy as you like with the contents of a floating box. You can put tables, layout grids, other animations, or just about anything inside one. The limiting factor usually turns out to be browser bugs. If you're going to make an elaborate floating object, test it thoroughly on lots of different browsers.

Creating a Floating Object

To begin, grab the Floating Box icon from the Basic tab of the Objects palette and drag it into your document, as shown in Figure 20.1. You can move it around later, so don't worry about exactly where you put it now.

In the Inspector, name your floating box, as shown in Figure 20.2. You can see that the dimensions of the box are specified here in pixels, in a percent of its current size, or as Auto, which will size the box to the contents. Also, the starting x, y, and z coordinates are defined here. The Z-Index is only relevant if you're going to have multiple layers on top of each

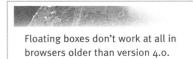

Floating boxes don't work at all in browsers older than version 4.0.

other, in which case the lowest box has an index of 1, the next highest has an index of 2, and so on. A background color or image can be applied here as well.

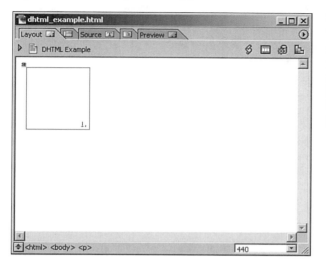

Figure 20.1

This is an empty floating box, freshly dropped into your document. The little yellow marker defines the original point of insertion on your page. If your floating box moves around, the yellow thing won't.

You'll also notice that there's a pop-up menu to select the shape of animation. This applies once multiple keyframe locations are defined for this box, so at this stage it won't do anything. More on this shortly.

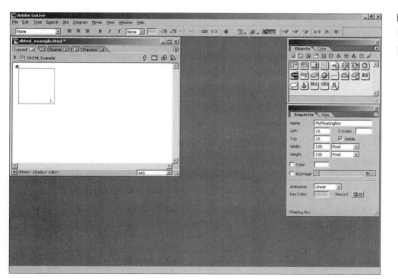

Figure 20.2

Use the Inspector to adjust the properties of your floating box.

Animating a Floating Object with the Timeline Editor

Animating floating boxes is all about the Timeline Editor. You use the Timeline Editor to specify keyframe locations at desired locations on the screen and points in time. The user's browser will do the rest, filling in all the intermediate locations and completing the animation. You can also specify the shape of the path the box takes as it moves from one keyframe to the next: choose from straight, curved, or random.

Let's start with a simple transparent GIF that we want to float around over our page. Click the Image icon in the Objects palette and drag it into our floating box. Then select your image file.

Now that we have a simple floating box defined, let's animate it. Be sure that it's selected: You can do this by clicking on the edge of its box, on its little yellow icon, or by selecting it from the Floating Boxes list.

Then click the Timeline Editor icon from the top of the page window. This brings up your new friend, the Timeline Editor, detailed in Figure 20.3.

Don't drag image files directly into a floating box. Instead drag in the Image icon from the Objects palette, and then define the image file. Dragging the image file directly can cause a problem with Netscape browsers and cause your floating box to be invisible. Netscape will also ignore the specified width of your box, instead using the width of your contents.

Figure 20.3
The Timeline Editor. A. Time cursor B. Autoplay button C. Scenes menu D. Actions track E. Time tracks F. Track selection indicator G. Loop button H. Palindrome button I. Playback controls J. Keyframe indicator K. Frames per second menu

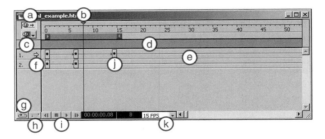

When you first bring up this window, you'll see only a single keyframe shown. This is the current (only) location of your floating box. The next thing to do is to create one more keyframe, and you do that by Ctrl-clicking (Windows) or Command-clicking (Mac) further to the right along the time track. Alternately, you can Alt-drag (Windows) or Option-drag (Mac) an existing keyframe to create a new one.

Create as many keyframes as you like. Typically, keyframes represent each corner along a zigzagged path, or each major turn along a curved path.

Once you have two or more keyframes defined, clicking on one will update the contents of the Inspector. Here is where you can precisely specify the position of each keyframe, and also whether the path leaves this point along a straight, curved (shown in Figure 20.4), or random path.

Use the Play button in the Timeline Editor to preview your animation. You can also drag the vertical time cursor bar back and forth manually to see in detail exactly how your floating box will move.

When creating curved paths, you can't manually adjust the curve like you can in Adobe Illustrator or other popular vector graphics programs. All you can do is position the keyframes, and the curve will be automatically defined.

You can also move each keyframe around manually. Select the keyframe in the Timeline and place your cursor over the top left corner of your floating box. The cursor changes into a hand, and now you can drag that keyframe into a new position on the screen.

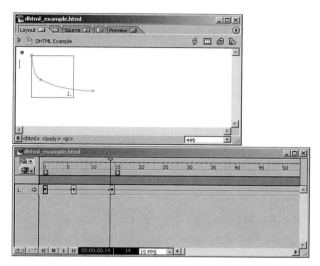

Figure 20.4
Here you can see a curving animation path and its corresponding timeline.

Delete unwanted keyframes by selecting them in the Timeline editor and hitting your Backspace or Delete key.

Click the Loop button to cause your animation to repeat by starting over at the beginning once it gets to the end. To cause your animation to bounce back and forth between the beginning and the end, select both the Loop and Palindrome buttons.

The Random animation type on the Inspector will cause your floating box to zigzag all over the place from one keyframe to the next.

The None animation type will cause your floating box to stay right there on that keyframe until the time index hits the next keyframe, at which point it will suddenly reappear at the next keyframe and proceed as defined from there.

To speed up or slow down your animation, drag your keyframes back and forth along the time index. You may have to play with your keyframe positioning considerably to achieve the desired effect.

By default, animations are set to play at 15 frames per second, and you can change this if you want on the Frames per Second pop-up menu in the Timeline editor. However, 15 represents a good balance between animation quality and the ability of most computers to display the motion.

There is one other cool way to record your floating box's movement. Select any keyframe, then click the Record button in the Inspector. Then position your cursor over the top left corner of your floating box. When the cursor changes into a hand, drag the floating box along the path you want it to follow. GoLive will automatically insert keyframes at significant points along the path you define. Click the Record button again to stop recording. You can now go back and edit the automatically created keyframes if you need to.

20

Showing and Hiding a Floating Box

To make an object appear or disappear, use the Visible checkbox on the Inspector. Leaving this box unchecked will cause your floating box to remain invisible until the next keyframe is reached.

For example, to make your object start invisible, appear after a few frames, move around, and then disappear, just make your first and last keyframes invisible. An example of this is shown in Figure 20.5.

Figure 20.5

This floating box has been set to become invisible at the third keyframe, and to reappear at the fourth.

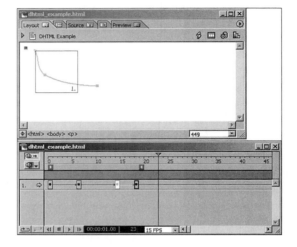

Triggering Your Animations with Actions

 By default, your animation will begin as soon as the page loads. To turn this off, deselect the Autoplay button in the top left corner of the Timeline Editor.

You can use a mouse action attached to an image, rollover button, hyperlink text, or form element to trigger the script. You can also initiate an animation from a keyboard event.

Select the image, rollover button, hyperlink text, or form element and select the type of event from the Actions palette. Then, from the Action pop-up menu, select Play Scene from the Multimedia sub-menu. Then select the name of your scene from the Scene pop-up menu.

You can also stop a scene in the same way. This capability enables you, for example, to create Play and Stop buttons on the page to let your user control the animations (see Figure 20.6). You could also use the Mouse Enter event to make the button animate when the user hovers his mouse over it, then return to normal when the mouse goes away with the Mouse Exit event.

Managing Multiple Floating Boxes

You can create as many floating boxes as you like, though keep in mind that each animation will incrementally tax the user's browser. Their animation paths can cross each other onscreen, which is where you will need to manage the stacking order.

Figure 20.6
Here the Action palette shows a mouse event to trigger an animation to begin.

Objects with a high stacking order, or Z-Index, will appear to be above those objects with lower numbers. Just as you can select a keyframe in the Inspector and adjust its position and other properties at that keyframe, so you can also adjust its Z-Index.

Let's take an example of two objects that will pass in front of one another as they move around: a black hole and a red giant star orbiting each other, a precedent for galactic catastrophe.

We'll create an object with an oval path, with its beginning and ending keyframes at the same point along the long side of an ellipse.

Create the second floating box, and give it five keyframes, but starting and ending on the opposite side of the ellipse. Run the animation now, and one object will always appear to be closer to the viewer than the other. Stellar bodies do not exhibit this behavior in reality, so it's now necessary to go into the Z-Indexes of each path and cause them to trade positions at the right time.

Figures 20.7 through 20.11 show the process to create the illusion that the two objects are orbiting each other. In Figure 20.7, the beginning and end point of object 1 are in the same place as the middle point of object 2, and vice versa. Figure 20.8 shows their timelines in the editor, with the keyframes all aligned between the two tracks. This is not absolutely necessary, but makes it easier to manager and produces more predictable results.

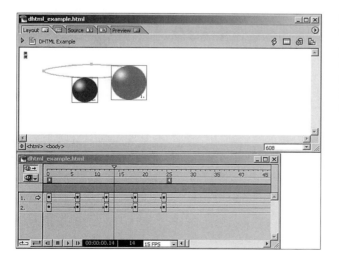

Figure 20.7
These two objects have their paths aligned so that they will orbit each other. The screen coordinates for the keyframes are in the same places, but not at the same time.

20

Figure 20.8
Both tracks are shown here in the Timeline Editor. Note how all the keyframes are aligned between the two tracks.

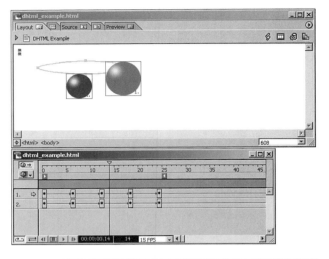

Figure 20.9
The small black object, with a Z-Index of 2, appears to be in front of the large red object, with its Z-Index of 1.

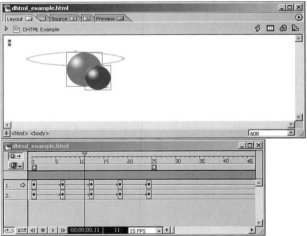

Figures 20.9 and 20.10 show the initial default overlap of the black dwarf in front of the red giant. Switch positions when they are separated. Then, as shown in Figure 20.11, the red giant will appear to be in front the next time they orbit past. It's important to position the keyframes where the Z-Indexes trade places at a location on the screen where the objects are not currently overlapping, or else the animation will not look right.

By choosing a keyframe at a time index when the objects do not overlap each other, we can create the illusion of smooth motion in three dimensions. This is why it's important to choose appropriate time indexes and screen locations for your critical keyframes.

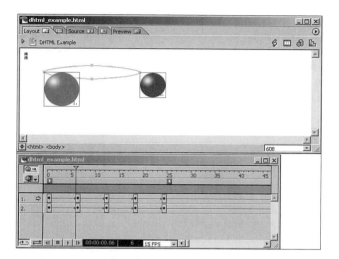

Figure 20.10
Now that the objects have orbited away from each other and are not overlapping, this is a good time to reverse their Z-Index positions on the current keyframe.

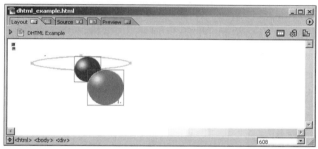

Figure 20.11
Now the large red object, with its new Z-Index of 2, appears to be in front of the small black object with its new Z-Index of 1.

Using Scenes

Everything we've just created can be defined as a *scene*. Two celestial bodies orbiting one another may seem extraordinary enough, but one may wish to add even more players to this interstellar drama.

This can be accomplished in two ways. More floating boxes and paths can be added to the list of two already present in our Timeline Editor. This is simple to manage, but it imposes a restriction that all items listed in the same timeline will happen at the same time. This may not be a problem. But in some cases, you may have several things that you want to happen asynchronously. If this is the case, you'll need to create a scene for each independent timeline you want to create.

 To create a new scene, go to the Scenes menu in the Timeline Editor. From here you can delete, rename, or create new scenes. Once you have multiple scenes defined, you also use this menu to select the one you want to work with.

When you select a new scene, the time tracks for the elements in your other scene still appear. The keyframes disappear, though; keyframes are specific to the scene they appear in.

You can now create new floating boxes, new keyframes, and everything that makes up a fully independent animation. You can even use floating boxes from another scene. However, if you do this, be careful not to try to make the same object appear in two different places at once. It won't work.

By default, all scenes are set to Autoplay, which means that they all start playing at once as soon as the browser loads the page. If you turn this off by deselecting the Autoplay button in the Timeline Editor for one or more tracks, they won't play at all until you trigger them. You can have one scene trigger another. One way to do this is to go to the Actions track in the Timeline Editor and Ctrl-click (Windows) or Command-click (Mac) a new Action wherever you'd like the current scene to trigger another scene. In the Action Inspector, choose the Play Scene action and specify the scene you would like to trigger. Similarly, you can insert a Stop Scene action in any scene and specify which scene you'd like stopped (including the current scene) .

SWF AND SVG

Flash and SVG graphics enjoy tremendous popularity on the Web, mainly for their ability to convey a lot of graphic detail in a minimum of bandwidth. Unlike bitmapped graphic formats, Flash and SVG artwork and animations are encoded only with vector data, which requires much less data to describe than each individual pixel in a bitmap animation.

Both of these formats require browser plug-ins, but both plug-ins are universal and are already installed on most browsers. Inserting a Flash or SVG animation into your page is as simple as dragging in an icon from the Basic tab of the Objects palette and setting a parameter or two.

Shockwave Flash (SWF)

Flash movies have become about as ubiquitous on the Web as browsers themselves. They can range from small graphic buttons all the way to rich full-screen animated movies with sound and music.

Flash movies can be created with a variety of applications, such as Adobe LiveMotion, Adobe After Effects, or of course, Macromedia Flash. You can create your own animation to play with, you can use a sample SWF file that ships with GoLive, or you can browse the Web to find one you like, and download it.

 Drag the SWF plug-in icon from the Basic tab of the Objects palette into your page, then select an SWF to work with. Four tabs appear in the inspector: Basic, More, Attribs, and SWF.

On the Basic tab, you can adjust the height, width, and alignment of the animation. You probably will not need to adjust the other settings. You can probably leave More and Attribs alone also. But under the SWF tab are a few items that you'll want to double-check, as shown in Figure 20.12.

- Select **Autoplay** to make the Flash movie play automatically as soon as the page is loaded.

- Select **Loop** to make the Flash movie play endlessly. As soon as it ends, it will start over again.

- The **Quality** menu lets you select options that define the two primary quality factors in a Flash movie: frame rate and rendering quality. Default uses the player's settings, overriding your settings. Best sends maximum quality and frame rate, which gives the best possible results but may cause users on slower connections to drop frames. High produces the best possible appearance, and sends all the frames. Autohigh produces maximum appearance but sends only as many frames as bandwidth permits. Autolow is just the opposite, sending a high frame rate but only the best quality permitted by bandwidth. Low quality always sends the lower quality appearance and all frames at a lower frame rate.

Figure 20.12
Use the SWF Inspector to adjust the quality of a SWF animation.

- The **Scale** menu lets you define the appearance of the movie within the boundaries you set on the Basic tab. Default displays the full animation within the defined boundaries, with its original aspect ratio. No Border completely fills your boundaries and maintains the original aspect ratio, so some portions may be cropped. Exact Fit scales the animation to completely fill the boundaries.

Scalable Vector Graphics (SVG)

SVG graphics are treated similarly to Flash movies. To embed an SVG file into your page, grab the SVG icon from the Basic tab of the Objects palette and drag it into your document, then select an SVG or SVGZ (compressed) file. Just like with a SWF file, the Inspector will show four tabs: Basic, More, Attribs, and SVG. Really, the only options worth playing with on these four tabs are the dimensions and alignment on the Basic tab. The SVG file will always appear in its original aspect ratio, and it will fill the boundaries you set on the Basic tab as much as possible without cropping. This is similar to the Default setting on the SWF tab, but without the No Borders and Exact Fit options.

AUDIO AND VIDEO CLIPS

GoLive ships with support for two popular audio and video plug-ins: Real and QuickTime. Both are nearly ubiquitous on users' browsers, and between them, they can handle just about any type of media file anyone's ever designed.

RealMedia Files

If you want to serve Real audio or video files (.rm, .ram) on your page, drag in the Real icon from the Basic tab of the Objects palette. You'll get a big 100×100 Real icon on your page by default. Use the Basic tab to select your RealMedia file on your computer, or on the Web.

One unique feature of the Real plug-in is that you will need to add additional Real icons onto your page for each control (Play, Pause, and so on). This allows you to separate your image window and your controls. In fact, you can have multiple images and controls scattered throughout your Web page.

For each Real icon on your page, there are two important items to set on the Real tab of the Inspector: Controls and Console. The first, Controls, determines which function the current Real icon will perform, and the list of selections is available in a pop-up menu (see Figure 20.13).

Figure 20.13

On the Real tab of the Real Inspector, the pop-up menu lists all of the Control choices.

- **Image Window** is where your movie will play (this is only for Real Video clips).

- **Control Panel** provides default controls for your media clip, including Play, Pause, Stop, Fast Forward, and Rewind buttons, Position and Volume sliders, and Mute.

- **Play Button** gives a Play/Pause button.

- **Play Only Button** provides a Play button (no pause).

- **Mute Control** gives a Mute button.

- **Mute Volume** gives a Mute button and a Volume slider.

- **Position Slider** gives a clip position slider that lets you scroll back and forth through the media clip.

- **Clip Information** gives a little info window that tells about the clip.

- **Home Control** gives a Real logo (Whoopee!).

- **Info Volume** gives a combination of the Clip Information and the Mute Volume controls.

- **Info Panel** gives a little info window that tells about the presentation of the clip.

- **Status Bar** gives a combination of the position slider and a network congestion LED, plus any network information messages.

- **Status Field** gives a little window in which errors and other messages display.

- **Position Field** gives a combination of the Position Slider and the total clip length.

It's necessary to use the Console field when you have multiple Real clips on the page. The Console field is used to link all the controls of each clip together, so it knows which clip to start when you click the Play button, for example. Type the name for your group in each clip control's Console text box. Be sure to use the same name for every control in each group. Alternately, you can select one of the choices from the pop-up menu. _Master links the current control to all other controls on the page (use one Play button to start all clips playing, for example). _Unique unlinks the current control from all other controls (for example, an Image Window set to Autostart that will ignore all controls on the page).

If you only have one clip on the page, it's not necessary to put anything in the Console field.

QuickTime Movies

It's easy to put a QuickTime movie (.mov) on your site. From the Basic tab, just drag the QuickTime movie icon onto your page. In the Inspector, the Basic tab lets you specify the movie's location on your computer (or its URL). Open it, and it will fill in the rest of the information about your movie's dimensions and type. Changing the dimensions here will crop the movie.

On the QuickTime tab of the Inspector (see Figure 20.14), select from a variety of options. Check Show Controller to display the standard QuickTime controller bar along the bottom of the movie. Setting the Cache checkbox will allow the browser's cache to improve quality during playback. Autoplay will set the movie to play as soon as it's loaded. Loop will set the movie to play over and over again, and Palindrome will set it to play backward back to the beginning as soon as it gets to the end. Play Every Frame will override a slow connection and force each frame to load completely before going to the next one; this results in the smoothest playback of video, but the audio will drop out whenever the playback has to wait for a frame to load. Color sets a background color that will be visible if the QuickTime movie has any transparent elements. Volume and Scale can be set with an integer from 0 to 100 to set the volume level and scale of the movie.

For information about streaming servers, see the last section in this chapter.

20

Figure 20.14
Adjust the advanced properties of your QuickTime movie using the QuickTime tab of the QuickTime movie Inspector.

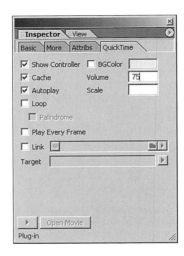

EDITING QUICKTIME MOVIES

Adobe GoLive includes one of the most powerful QuickTime movie-editing utilities around; in fact, it's practically an entire application in itself, and it seems a shame to devote only a portion of one chapter to it. The QuickTime movie editor can be used to tweak and modify existing QuickTime movies, but where it really shines is in its capacity to build a movie from scratch using audio and visual elements.

When you open a QuickTime movie in GoLive, it opens in its own little window with a Preview tab and a Layout tab, as shown in Figure 20.15. The Layout tab includes rulers that measure in pixels. The Preview tab is selected by default, and it allows you to view the movie.

Figure 20.15
The movie window in GoLive has a Preview tab to let you watch the movie, and a Layout tab that shows a ruler to help you position new elements on the screen.

Perhaps the most important tool for editing movies is the Timeline Editor, available from the Movie menu.

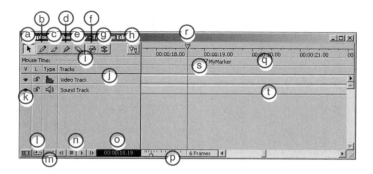

Figure 20.16

The Timeline Editor. A. Standard selection and editing tool B. Create sample C. Divide sample D. Glue samples E. Delete sample F. Swap samples G. Move samples H. Marker popup I. Current mouse time J. Track list K. Show/hide track info L. Loop M. Palindrome N. Playback controls O. Current movie time P. Timeline resolution Q. Time ruler R. Time cursor S. Marker T. Track

This may be a good time to discuss some new terms used in the QuickTime Editor.

- **Background**: If you're creating a QuickTime movie from scratch, it automatically has dimension of 0×0. Using a background track gives you a placeholder that keeps the dimensions as big as you define. You can also specify a background color. Once you have content in your movie, the background track can be deleted, and the movie will shrink to the dimensions of the next largest video element.

- **Chapter**: Chapters are a way to provide the viewer with navigation points within a movie. These can be selected from a pop-up window in the movie controls when viewing a QuickTime movie. Chapters are defined by adding a Chapter Track.

- **Filter**: Add a filter track to create a transition between two video tracks (a two-source filter track), to apply special video effects to a single video track (a one-source video track), to create a funky graphic track to overlay on your others (a generic filter track), or to create a blend between two video tracks with a specified luma mask (a three-source filter track).

- **Flatten**: When you choose Save As, your movie will be flattened in order to be presentable on the Web. Flattening doesn't mean that all the tracks are wiped out and everything is compressed into one finished product, the way flattening behaves in Photoshop. Your tracks will still be preserved and you can edit them. Flattening a QuickTime movie just means that the original media items that make up your tracks will all be retrieved and included in the file, making it fully self-contained. Until your movie is flattened, all these media items are stored in your movie only as references to the original item. You can also flatten your movie at any time by selecting Flatten Movie from the Movie menu.

- **Marker**: A handy little way to bookmark points along your Timeline to assist you in your work. Markers do not have any effect on the finished movie; they just make it easier for you to navigate around inside your movie as you work.

- **Sample**: A sample is a constituent of a track. For example, you have one chapter track, but many chapters within it. Each of those chapters is a sample in GoLive lingo, and they all appear on the samples track right below the main chapter track. The tools in the Timeline Editor (Create Sample tool, Delete Sample tool, and so on) all function on samples.

20

- **Sprite**: A sprite is a little graphic that you can insert into your movie and use as a button. You can assign any of a whole variety of actions to a sprite, controlling the movie itself or doing other things like opening URLs. You can also add a number of graphics into an individual sprite, so it can have different contents depending on the mouse state. Basically, it gives you rollover buttons within your movie.

- **Track**: A track is any major component of your movie. Video, sound, text, chapters, filters, and others are all tracks.

Another area to become familiar with is the toolbar, which changes when you're working with a QuickTime movie.

Figure 20.17
The movie toolbar. A. Show Movie Window B. Show Timeline Window C. Export Movie D. Export Track E. Export as Streaming Movie F. Position/Resize Track G. Skew Track H. Rotate Track I. Lock Track J. Lock Track K. Unlock Track L. Bring to Front M. Send to Back

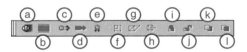

Now let's take a look at the types of tracks available on the QuickTime tab of the Objects palette, and learn how each is used:

- Drag in a **Movie Track** to include an existing QuickTime, AVI, MPEG, or other type of movie within the one you're editing. If this movie is elsewhere on the Internet, you can specify its URL, or just select it locally on your disk. Use the Inspector to set a wide range of options for how this movie behaves within yours. You can even apply an action to it: All the same actions that can be applied to sprites (see later in this list) can also be applied to an embedded movie, and the actions are triggered when the embedded movie is completely loaded.

- A **Video Track** is an image or image sequence, and provides the visual component of your movie. If you have an animated GIF or other sequence that you'd like to include in your movie, drag this icon in and select the file. A wide range of file types can be imported. You can adjust its properties in the Inspector, including its dimensions, start time and duration, and mode (see "Setting the Mode for a Video Track," later in this chapter).

- Use a **Color Track** to create a solid background color, or an overlay, for your movie. In the Inspector, you can define its position and size, the color to be used, and also its mode. Combine multiple colored panels, with various transparency modes, with other tracks to create some cool effects. It's not uncommon to start building a new QuickTime movie with a solid background of specified dimensions to assist with the layout and presentation of a movie comprised of smaller elements.

- A **Picture Track** is a really cool way to display images in a slide show format. Drag the track into the Timeline Editor and set its properties. The Inspector has an Images tab that lets you select your images, and a Slideshow tab with some cool options to let you specify the duration of each slide, whether to use any of a multitude of transition effects between slides (Alpha Compositor, Chroma Key, Cross Fade, Explode, Gradient Wipe, Implode, Iris, Matrix Wipe, Push, Radial, Slide, Wipe, and Zoom), and how many times to loop each image. When you click the triangle in the Timeline Editor to display the samples track, each image appears along the track. Select each to view its individual properties in the Inspector. Figure 20.18 shows a Picture Track in the Timeline Editor. Note the transitions between the slides. Click on any picture sample to edit its properties, or even change its image, in the Inspector.

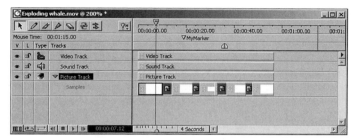

Figure 20.18
A Picture Track in the Timeline Editor can be sliced and diced using the sample tools.

- A **Generic Filter Track** will create a video track of a cloud effect, a fire effect, or a ripple effect. Drag this filter into your movie, and then select its parameters from the Inspector. You can define its dimensions here if you don't want it to fill your entire movie window. Click the triangle beside the track in the Timeline Editor to display the sample track. Select the sample track, then go to the Inspector and choose the type of effect desired, and select the effect's parameters.

- Add a **One Source Filter Track** to apply a video effect to one specific video track. Drag it in and select the desired video track in the Inspector. You can also specify other parameters here, just like the Generic Filter Track. When you click the triangle in the Timeline Editor to display and select the sample track, you'll find that you have quite a large list of filters to select from. They're all pretty cool, so enjoy playing with them. You can choose Alpha Gain, Blur, Brightness & Contrast, Color Style, Color Tint, Edge Detection, Emboss, Film Noise, General Convolution, HSL Balance, Lens Flare, RGB Balance, and Sharpen. To combine effects, just drag an additional one-source filter track into the Timeline Editor, and set the parameters the same as for your first filter, but choose a different effect.

- The **Two Source Filter Track** lets you create transitions between two video tracks. Drag the track into the Timeline Editor, and in the Inspector, specify which two tracks you want to perform the transition on (you will need to have at least two video tracks in your movie for this to work). Click the triangle to open the sample track, select the track, and go back to the Inspector to choose the type of transition. Most have a few parameters you can tweak, and a little preview window shows you exactly what each transition is. Your choices include Alpha Compositor, Chroma Key, Cross Fade, Explode, Gradient Wipe, Implode, Iris, Matrix Wipe, Push, Radial, Slide, Wipe, and Zoom. Check them all out.

- A **Three Source Filter Track** lets you apply one video track as a luma mask to two other video tracks. When you drag this track into the Timeline Editor, you can choose all three of these

20

tracks, the dimensions, and the mode under which the mask is applied. Click open the sample track and go to the Inspector to define whether to apply the mask Normal, Inverted, or Gradient.

 ▪ Inserting an **MPEG Track** is just like adding any video track to your movie. The MPEG will appear in your movie according to the properties you set in the Inspector.

 ▪ To add a **Sprite Track** and create interactive controls to your QuickTime movie, drag it into your Timeline Editor, and set the properties to include its size, position, start time, and duration. On the Images tab of the Inspector, define all the images you want to use in your sprites, including different images for different mouse states, if desired. This creates the "Image Pool" for this sprite track. Choose images from the pool on the Basic tab of the Inspector (see Figure 20.19). In the Timeline Editor, click the triangle to open up your sprite track. Use the Create Sample tool to add multiple sprites within your sprite track. When a sprite is selected, the Inspector lets you choose images from the Image Pool for each sprite, set its visibility, and define its action from a long list of choices. The sprite persists for the entire duration of the sprite track, but adding multiple sprites within the track allows you to change the sprite's state over the duration, for example, to make it appear and disappear, or to change the URL it would open if clicked on. Sprite actions (Figure 20.20) let you do things like control the playback of the movie, set its volume, turn tracks on and off (a neat way to select from multiple languages!), open other movies, or, if your QuickTime movie is a QuickTime VR panorama, control the zoom and viewing angle.

Figure 20.19

The Basic tab of the Sprite Inspector shows some images selected from the Image Pool for a couple of different mouse states for this particular sprite.

 ▪ Insert a **SWF Track** by dragging the icon into the Timeline Editor. It behaves just like any other visible element in your movie, and has the same options on the Basic tab of the Inspector. The Inspector also has two additional tabs for button actions and labels within your SWF animation. The SWF movie will inherit the frame rate of your QuickTime movie, and will retain its original duration.

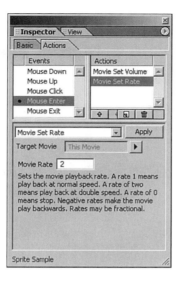

Figure 20.20
The Actions tab of the Sprite Inspector shows that this sprite will mute the volume and double the playback speed whenever the mouse is hovered over it.

■ The **3D Track** icon lets you insert a QuickDraw 3D element into your QuickTime movie, if you are one of the four people in the world who do this. The Inspector properties are the same as for other visible elements.

■ An **HREF Track** turns your QuickTime movie into one giant button for opening a URL. Drag the track into the Timeline Editor. It's invisible by default (notice that the little eye icon is grayed out at the left end of the track). To make the URL appear in the movie, click the eye icon to make it visible. Adjust the mode and dimensions in the Inspector. To add your URLs, just click the triangle on the track to open up the samples track. Use the sample tools to create and delete sample bars. Click on a sample to edit the URL and its properties in the Inspector. Autoload will cause the URL to be opened automatically when the movie gets to that point. If this is not selected, the URL will be opened when the user clicks on the movie window. A frame can also be specified here. This lets you display your movie in one frame and have relevant URLs appear in an adjacent frame. Talk about multimedia possibilities. A movie can only have one HREF track. It's worth noting that Adobe Premiere and Adobe After Effects are also capable of producing QuickTime movies with HREF tracks that can be edited using GoLive.

■ A **Chapter Track** lets you define chapters within your movie that the viewer can select via a pop-up menu in the QuickTime player. Add one chapter track to your movie, and then you can specify as many chapters within that track as you like. Chapters cannot overlap one another. Drag a chapter track into the Timeline Editor, and click its triangle to open it up and display the constituent chapters, which all appear on their own track line called the sample track. You can shrink it by dragging the end of it back and forth, or by typing its start and end times in the Inspector. Use the Create Track tool to draw additional chapters (the Master Chapter Track will expand or condense depending on the chapters you create below it), and type the name of each in the Inspector.

- A **Text Track** allows the display of text in your movie, and it can even be linked to a URL (see Figure 20.21). This is similar to the HREF track, but it's more flexible because you can display any text you want, rather than just show the URL. You can also attach other actions besides just opening a URL, and you can also use other mouse triggers besides just a mouse click. Drag the track icon into the Timeline Editor, adjust its properties in the Inspector, and click its triangle to open up its sample track. Use the sample tools to create new text samples. Select each and edit its properties in the Inspector. Text can even be scrolled using the Properties tab of the Inspector (see Figure 20.22), and some advanced formatting can be applied on the Layout tab (see Figure 20.23).

Figure 20.21
The Text tab of the Text Inspector shows that this text will open a URL when it is clicked.

Figure 20.22
The Properties tab of the Text Inspector can be used to scroll the text, among other things.

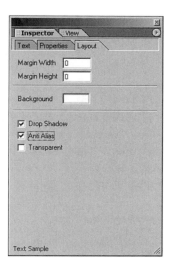

Figure 20.23
The Layout tab of the Text Inspector shows that this text has a drop shadow and is anti-aliased.

- A **Sound Track** allows pre-recorded sound files (AIFF/AIFC, System 7 Sound, WAV, MP3 files, Sound Designer II) to be added to your movie. The only property you can edit in the Inspector is the start time and duration of your clip. Changing the duration of the clip will increase or decrease the playback speed of the sound file, making it sound like either Mickey Mouse or James Earl Jones. You can't adjust the volume of a sound track.

- Adding a **MIDI Track** puts a standard MIDI file into your movie. Drag it into the Timeline Editor and adjust its start time and duration, using either the Inspector or dragging it in the Timeline. Increasing or decreasing the duration will play it back faster or slower, but unlike sound files, the pitch will not change, just the tempo. You can't adjust the volume or other parameters of a MIDI track. You will need to add instruments to your MIDI file for it to play back correctly, once it's flattened.

- The **Instrument Track** provides instruments for your MIDI file to play back with. Before your movie is flattened, your MIDI file will play back correctly even before you've added an instrument track, but beware: You will need to add instruments before you select Save As or Flatten Movie to make your movie self-contained. To do this, just drag the Instrument Track icon into your Timeline Editor. It doesn't really matter where you put it in your movie; the start time and duration don't seem to make any difference. On the Instruments tab of the Inspector, you can add as many instruments as your MIDI file requires. Be sure to add one of the required instruments. The instruments available here depend on the QuickTime synthesizers you have installed using your system's QuickTime control panel. This can include external devices. See your synthesizer's documentation for adding them to your QuickTime control panel.

- A **Streaming Track** is necessary when you are creating a link to other streaming content. For more on streaming, see the streaming section below.

- The **Folder Track** is going to come in really handy now that you have dozens of random tracks in your movie. Drag one of these bad boys into your Timeline Editor, and you'll find that you can organize your mess of tracks by dragging some of them into folders. You can even drag folders into other folders. There is no restriction on what types of tracks can be stored or grouped into folders; it's strictly up to you to manage and organize your stuff the way you like.

Setting the Mode for a Video Track

If you've gotten this far, you've certainly noticed that the Basic tab of the Inspector for virtually every visible track or sample in a QuickTime movie has a setting called Mode. The mode affects the way this sample will combine with any visual elements beneath it. Here are what the various choices mean:

- **Dither Copy** makes the current element opaque, and simply lays it on top of any elements below it. Dithering is used to improve the appearance on systems with a low number of display colors, like 256. This is the default selection.

- **Copy** is also opaque and works the same as dither copy, but there is no dithering. This requires a higher number of display colors to look good.

- **Blend** makes the current element partially transparent so you can see whatever's below it. The degree of transparency is defined by the color you select. Choose a darker color to make it more opaque; choose a lighter color to make it more transparent.

- **Transparent** is like a transparent GIF image: specify one color to be transparent. The rest of the element will be opaque, but all pixels of the specified color will be invisible.

- **Straight alpha** will use your alpha channel in the most basic way: The transparency of each pixel is based on the alpha channel.

- **Premul white alpha** is best if your image has a premultiplied alpha channel and was designed to look good on a white background.

- **Premul black alpha** is best if your image has a premultiplied alpha channel and was designed to look good on a black background.

- **Straight alpha blend** is just like Straight alpha, but it adds the functionality of Blend. You can choose a color to set the level of transparency for the most opaque parts of your image, as defined by the alpha channel.

- **Composition (Dither Copy)** works like Dither Copy, but is optimized for the display of animated GIFs. Choose this mode if the element you're using is an animated GIF.

> Some visual elements have *alpha channels*. An alpha channel is an extra, invisible color layer that defines which parts of a graphic should be invisible, or "masked," so that the background shows through. It's sort of like the transparent color in a transparent GIF image, except that each pixel of an alpha channel has its own value, not simply on or off.

Creating Streaming Movies

A *streaming movie* is one that plays while it's still downloading. This is useful whenever your movie is anything longer than a tiny download, and is necessary when the content is a live broadcast, in which case there is no file to download.

Streaming can be accomplished in several ways. The most basic is to use HTTP (Hypertext Transfer Protocol, in case you didn't know) streaming. To do this, save your movie as a normal self-contained QuickTime (.mov) file, drag the QuickTime icon from the Basic tab of the Objects palette into your document, and set the properties in the Inspector.

The upside to this method is that the complete movie downloads to your user's browser, where it can be viewed again and again, with all the data intact. The downside is that the movie's playback rate may exceed the download speed, which will cause it to pause, and result in an unsatisfactory viewing experience.

The other way to serve streaming content is via RTSP (Real Time Streaming Protocol). In this method, no file is actually downloaded to the user's computer. The upside is that the stream will compensate for any slowing of the transfer rate; for example, the picture might get really bad or the sound may even drop if the connection goes completely to seed, but there is no total interruption of the stream. The downside is that the user does not get the complete file for offline viewing (in some cases, this may be a business requirement and not necessarily a downside).

To serve an RTSP stream, you need a streaming server (available at `http://www.apple.com/quicktime/products/qtss/`). Export your movie by choosing the Export icon from the toolbar. Then add a link on your Web page pointing to its location on the streaming server, using the following format:

```
<a href="rtsp://100.100.100.100/mycoolmovie.mov">
Click here to see my cool movie.
</a>
```

And presto, your movie will be streamed out to thousands of users.

Streaming movies cannot contain sprites or SWF animations. If the movie you want to stream includes these components, there is a solution. You need to create two movies. First, build your movie with everything in it. Click the eye icon to make your sprite and SWF tracks invisible. Export the movie as a streaming movie, and put this version on the RTSP server. Then turn those tracks back on, delete everything else, and add a streaming track that references the RTSP version (see Figure 20.24). You've just created what's called the client movie, and it will initiate the streaming content and insert the sprites and SWF animations at the appropriate places.

20

Figure 20.24

The RTSP tab in the streaming track Inspector, showing the reference to the RTSP server containing the content to be streamed in.

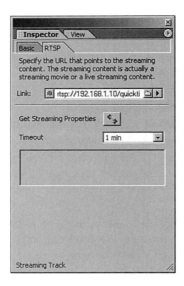

TROUBLESHOOTING

Achieving a Professional Look

I found some neat stuff with Flash on a Web page, but I can't get my movie to behave the same way. What do I do?

The controls in GoLive are sufficient to do anything that current technology permits. Nevertheless, this doesn't mean that it's easily done. If you find a page that has functionality you want to duplicate, the best first step is always to pull its source and see how it's being done. If you're using GoLive's tools to try to duplicate its behavior, check your own source and compare.

What's important to remember is that only so much of the behavior of the animation is controlled by the page controls inserted by GoLive. Much of it is, of course, contained in the animation file itself. So if you're using the exact same page source code but still not getting the right behavior, chances are the difference is in the SVG, SWF, Real, or QuickTime file itself. And if that's the case, you'll need to go back to the authoring tool you used to create it.

Creating Animation Files

So what do I use to create all these cool animations?

There are a variety of tools available to create just about any of these animation and movie formats. It's not possible to try to list them without offending some software publisher by omitting mention of their product, so without attempting to list them all, here goes a list of the tools personally preferred by this author.

For SVGs, use Adobe Illustrator or Macromedia Freehand.

For SWF movies, use Macromedia Flash or Adobe LiveMotion.

For RealMedia files, use Discreet Cleaner.

For QuickTime movies, use Discreet Cleaner, Adobe Premiere, or Apple Final Cut Pro.

More About Streaming

I can't figure out all this streaming video stuff. Where can I get more information?

If you're going to get into streaming movies at all, then by all means download the Adobe Streaming Media Primer at `http://www.adobe.com/smprimer`. This provides a wealth of fog-clearing information.

GOING LIVE

Probably the biggest issue you'll face when creating QuickTime movies for Web delivery is file size, and this is something that GoLive doesn't really help you out with. The trick is to get the smallest possible file size that still looks and sounds acceptable. Often sites will provide two or three different versions from which viewers can choose based on their connection speed. So the big question really becomes "How do I do this?"

If you buy a Pro license for Apple's QuickTime Player, you can use it to save condensed versions of your movies. Most editing programs, such as Apple's iMovie, Final Cut Pro, or Adobe Premiere, offer such options. There are also dedicated applications such as Sorenson Squeeze, or the market leader, Discreet Cleaner. Use your editing program to save Digital Video or Full Quality QuickTime, and then use a product such as Cleaner to compress it with the best possible quality.

The novice will be disappointed to learn how many different cryptic options there are: literally dozens for audio and for video. However, most compression programs provide preset settings and wizards to walk you through the process. But you're likely to find that you're not completely pleased with the results of any of these presets. You may also find that presets that produce good results also produce unacceptably large file sizes. The reason for this is that every movie has different properties: different sound tracks, different lighting in the video, different amounts of movement, and so on. Use the presets and wizards to find the setting you're happiest with, and then start tweaking from there.

It may save a lot of useless experimenting to explain that the biggest drivers of file size and quality are frames per second and data rate. Start with a decent preset. Choose the slowest frame rate that still looks decent. And then play with the data rate. A slow data rate will make your picture look like big horrible digitized squares that don't update very often, while a fast data rate produces crystal-clear video with great resolution.

20

Once you've found the settings you like, programs such as Cleaner allow you to save the settings for easy future reuse. But don't expect to depend too much on these. As stated before, settings that look great on one movie may not necessarily work well for another.

And another word to the wise: Compressing the video can take a long time. For experimentation purposes, edit out a couple seconds of your movie. Include a few seconds of big action and move-ment, and a couple seconds of a more still segment. Use this short clip to experiment with, and once you've found your ideal settings, run the same compression on your full size movie. This tip alone will save you hours. Happy editing!

VIII

INTEGRATING GOLIVE WITH OTHER PROGRAMS

IN THIS PART

21 Smart Objects   **229**

22 Integrating with Photoshop, Illustrator, and LiveMotion   **239**

23 GoLive Plug-Ins   **255**

24 Lasso Studio for Adobe GoLive   **279**

21

SMART OBJECTS

IN THIS CHAPTER

About Smart Objects   **370**

Inserting a Smart Object   **371**

Troubleshooting   **380**

Going Live   **381**

ABOUT SMART OBJECTS

As you already know, GoLive features extend far beyond writing basic HTML pages, as the program incorporates powerful site management features. *Smart Objects* are one such feature.

GoLive's Smart Objects refer to a powerful image management feature. To the end user, the image will look no different than if the image had been created and inserted using a basic image. However, the difference to you as the developer is drastic. By using Smart Objects, you can create multiple optimized versions of an original image, export and optimize an image without leaving GoLive, and ensure that any changes made to the original file automatically translate to the optimized version as well.

To begin, let's review how images are traditionally incorporated into a page. The image is created in an image-editing program (such as Adobe Photoshop) and saved as in the original file format (such as a `.psd` file). The original file format maintains all of the information about fonts, font sizes, vector graphics, and layers. In essence, in exchange for the flexibility of modifying the original file, the file maintains a large file size.

Another version of the image is then also created from within the image-editing program, this one compatible with the Web. By converting the image into a `.gif`, `.jpeg`, or `.png`, the image's data size decreases dramatically, making the image suitable for delivery over the Web. Keep in mind that as the data size decreases, the image also loses some of its clarity. The challenge of balancing a reasonable file size with a professional-looking image is referred to as image optimization.

The `.gif`, `.jpeg`, or `.png` version of the image is then inserted into a Web page via HTML or a Web editor such as GoLive. Traditionally, all changes to the image—whether they are changes in the optimization settings or changes in the form of the picture—must be made within the image-editing program. Every time a change is made, the original file must be resaved and the optimized version must be exported again.

Smart Objects streamline this process. Instead of juggling the two programs, Smart Objects enable you to use the image-editing program simply for changing the form of the picture. All optimization and exporting of that image to a Web-suitable format can be done in Adobe GoLive. Once the image is created and saved in its original form, all you need to do is drag that image (in its non–Web-compatible format) to the page. Within GoLive, you can adjust the image's file size by toying with the file's dimensions and providing the optimization settings. Hence, the exported version is created from within GoLive.

A few added features arise from optimizing the file within GoLive. First, you can tamper with the image's settings without opening another program. Second, each time you drag the original file to the Document Window, a separate Smart Object is created. This means that you can reuse the same original file to create multiple exported versions without fear of accidentally overriding the settings of another optimized instance. And, finally, GoLive's Smart Objects includes one additional feature: The exported version stores all of the optimization settings and maintains a link to the original file. If the original file changes, the optimized version automatically updates as well, given the designated compression settings.

21

INSERTING A SMART OBJECT

Now that you're familiar with what Smart Objects have to offer, let's see how they are implemented. The following demonstration illustrates how to use an existing file created by an image-editing program as a Smart Object; it does not teach you how to build the image itself. For more information about integrating with other programs, see Chapter 23, "GoLive Plug-Ins."

Although not required, the best place to save the original image file is part of GoLive's site. In fact, you will find that for every site declared, a folder called SmartObjects is created for this exact purpose. Each site contains a folder with all of the elements that are uploaded to the Web Server, a data directory, and a settings folder. The SmartObjects folder resides in the data directory, and is the ideal location to store all of the original image files for a particular site. This way, if the site is moved to another location on your hard drive, the relative path between the original image and the exported version remain constant.

GoLive's Smart Objects are categorized into Photoshop, Illustrator, LiveMotion, and Generic Smart Objects. The Smart Tab of the Objects panel stores an icon for each, shown in Figure 21.1.

PhotoShop
Illustrator
LiveMotion
Generic

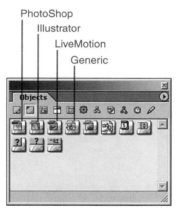

Figure 21.1
The Smart Tab of the Objects panel contains icons organizing the GoLive Smart Objects into four categories.

Although you can click and drag the appropriate icon to your page and use the Inspector to provide information about the location of the original file, you'll find it will be more efficient to use the Site Window to implement your Smart Objects. Make sure both the Site Window and page are simultaneously accessible, and view the Site Extras Tab in the Site Window. More specifically, open the contents of the SmartObjects directory. Click and drag the appropriate file in its original format (in this case a .psd file) from the Site Window to the Document Window, as shown in Figure 21.2. Note that if the Site Window is not showing the Site Extras Tab, you can toggle it open via the double-arrow in the bottom-right corner of the Site Window. Likewise, you can toggle open and close the contents of the SmartObjects folder by clicking the SmartObject icon.

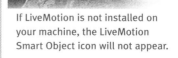

If LiveMotion is not installed on your machine, the LiveMotion Smart Object icon will not appear.

21

Figure 21.2
Click and drag the original file from the SmartObjects directory to the Document Window.

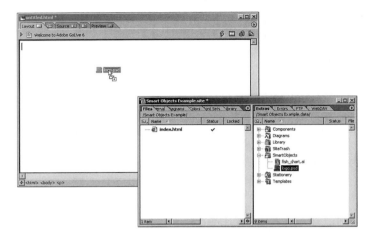

A placeholder for the image will appear in the Document Window temporarily, and GoLive will prompt you to complete the process based on the type of image you inserted onto the Document Window. Table 21.1 shows the type of Smart Object that will be inserted onto the page, based on the file type you inserted.

Table 21.1   Smart Object File Types

File Type	Type of Smart Object	Types of Target Files That Can Be Created
PSD, BMP, PICT (for Mac OS), PCX, Pixar, Amiga IFF, Tiff, and Targa	Photoshop	Bitmap (.gif, .jpeg, .png)
AI, SVG	Illustrator	Bitmap (.gif, .jpeg, .png), SVG, and SWF
LIV	LiveMotion	SWF

As of this writing, bitmapped graphics formats (GIFs, JPEGs, and PNGs) are most commonly used on the Web. As such, this example will walk you through the process of inserting a Photoshop .psd file and creating a bitmap. Later, creating SVG and SWFs from Illustrator and LiveMotion files will be detailed.

As Photoshop can only create bitmaps, the Save for Web dialog box will automatically open with your original file inside when you drag the file to the Document Window. Likewise, when inserting an Illustrator file, the option to export the optimized version of the file as a bitmap will appear, as well as the options to save the file as a SVG or SWF. Finally, when inserting a LiveMotion file, the Save as Macromedia SWF file will automatically open.

Creating a Bitmap

When creating a bitmap, the Save for Web dialog box will open. The Save for Web dialog box, shown in Figure 21.3, provides an opportunity to optimize the image: to create a target file (a Web version) with a smaller data size from the original. Notice the setup of the Save for Web dialog.

Figure 21.3
The Save for Web dialog box
allows you to change and view
the optimization settings for the
exported bitmap.

A toolbar on the left side allows you to adjust the view and select different components of the image. Here is an explanation of each of the tools available in the top-left corner of the Save for Web dialog:

- Hand Tool provides a means to span an image (to drag it to a different section) so that you may view all areas of the image.

- Slice Select Tool selects individual slices so that each may be optimized independently of the others. In this example, the image only contains one slice. For more information on slicing, check out the following chapters, "Linking to Photoshop Files" and "Linking to Illustrator Files."

- Eyedropper selects a color in the page. That color will then populate the Eyedropper Swatch.

- Eyedropper Swatch displays the last color selected by the Eyedropper tool.

- Toggle Slices Visibility toggles the visibility of slices on and off.

In addition, four tabs appear at the top-left of the Save for Web Dialog Box, each with a distinct purpose. Here is what each tab does:

- Original shows the image in its original form, exactly as it appears in the authoring program.

- Optimized provides a preview of the image given the current optimization settings (to be discussed shortly).

- 2-Up provides a side-by-side comparison of the original file and the compressed (target) version.

- 4-Up provides views of the file in its original format with side-by-side comparisons of three target versions. This will be discussed in more detail in just a moment.

21

Finally, the right side of the dialog box includes options for saving, canceling, modifying the optimization settings, and resizing the image.

For example, in the following demonstration, a .psd file (Photoshop file) is inserted from the SmartObjects folder in the Document Window. The temporary placeholder appears, and the Save for Web Dialog box automatically opens.

Using the Settings panel off to the right of the dialog box, you can select what type of image you would like created. GIFs tend to be better for art with solid bands of color or black and white photographs, and JPEGs are more suitable for color photographs. PNGs, the final type of bitmap supported by the Web, are a special breed of their own and will be discussed in more detail later in this chapter. In this case, the JPEG format is selected from the drop-down menu, as you can see in Figure 21.4.

Figure 21.4
The different file formats are all available from the Type drop-down menu in the Settings panel.

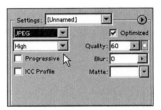

The other options in the Settings panel populate based on the type of image you opt to create. The most important are described here.

For the GIF image, the number of colors that the final image should support is an important option. The fewer colors the image is set to support, the smaller the file size will be. Figure 21.5 shows a setting with 256 colors selected.

Figure 21.5
The GIF settings panel includes an option to adjust the number of colors supported by the image. Lowering the number of colors an image supports consequently reduces the data size of the image.

To compress the data size of a JPEG, lower the quality of the image. The lower the quality setting, the smaller the data size of the final image. The panel shown in Figure 21.6 shows a High quality setting selected.

PNG-8 and PNG-24 are two different versions of Portable Networks Graphic. The Portable Networks Graphic is a more recent addition to bitmaps supported by the Web, and includes not only information about the image itself, but also information about the platform on which the image was authored. This means that the image should appear the same regardless of what platform authored the program and which platform is being used to view the image.

PNG-8 supports 8-bit (and lower) color, and PNG-24 supports 24-bit color.

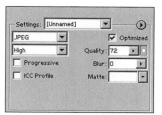

Figure 21.6
JPEG's data sizes adjust based on the quality setting. To lower the data size of an image, decrease the quality setting of the JPEG.

Although well supported by more recent browsers, the PNG format, shown selected in Figure 21.7, does not necessarily decrease the file size any better than GIF and JPEG, but it is lossless compression. This means that the compression algorithm does not result in any ugly artifacting like you can experience with JPEGs.

Figure 21.7
The PNG-24 supports 24-bit color, but generates quite a large file size in the process. The advantage, however, is that the image would appear the same in color and form as you intended.

Make sure that as you adjust the optimization settings, you are viewing at least the Optimized Tab of the dialog: You will not see any differences in the quality of the image if you are viewing the Original Tab. Consider using the 2-Up Tab (see Figure 21.8) and 4-Up Tab (see Figure 21.9) for side-by-side comparisons of the original and the target version.

Notice that for each iteration, there is information about the image's data size, as well as a calculation estimating how long the image will take to download.

In addition to modifying the optimization settings, GoLive also provides a means for changing the dimensions of the target file without altering the dimensions of the original file. Notice the two tabs on the right side of the dialog box: The Color Table shows swatches of the colors in a given image, and the Image Size Tab allows you to adjust the image's dimensions. Simply click the Image Size Tab (see Figure 21.10), make the modifications in the different fields for the height and width of the image, and click Apply. Note that this does not change the dimensions of the original image, only the target version.

Figure 21.8
The 2-Up Tab provides a side-by-side comparison of the original and the optimized (target) version.

Figure 21.9
The 4-Up version allows you to compare the original against three iterations of the same image, each with different compression settings.

Figure 21.10
The Image Size Tab can be used to reduce the dimensions of the target version without altering the height and width of the original image.

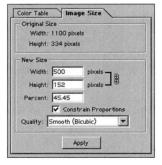

When complete making the adjustments to the file, click the Save button in the upper-right corner. You will be prompted to save the file. Be sure to save it in your GoLive site.

Notice that you can use the same original file for multiple target files. If you make modifications to the original file (perhaps you modified the text or altered the graphic), the compressed version will automatically update. The optimization settings are stored with the target version of the file that maintains a link back to the original.

When a Smart Object is selected in the Document Window, the Inspector shows many of the same options as for a normal image, including fields to link, align, and set alternate text for the image. In addition, two additional buttons appear: Settings and Variables. The Settings button reopens the Save for Web dialog box so that changes can be made to the optimization settings of an image. The Variables button enables you to set and/or change any variables associated with the file.

Creating a SVG File via an Illustrator Smart Object

The process for inserting an Illustrator Smart Object is very similar. Simply drag and drop the original file from the Site Extras Tab of the Site Window to the Document Window. Because Illustrator can create files other than bitmaps, you will be prompted to choose which type of file you would like to create, as shown in Figure 21.11.

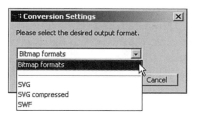

Figure 21.11
Select the type of file you would like to generate from the drop-down menu.

Choosing Bitmap files from the drop-down box will open the Save For Web Dialog box as discussed in the previous version. The other three versions, SVG, SVG Compressed, and SWF work a bit differently.

SVGs and SVG Compressed

SVG refers to Scalar Vector Graphics, and is an open-source XML language that can generate images. Although this chapter will walk you through the details of creating an SVG from an Illustrator file, check out Chapter 22 for more details on the technology behind SVGs.

Selecting either SVG or Compressed SVG yields the following dialog box in which you can specify how the fonts and images should be incorporated into the SVG, as shown in the dialog in Figure 21.12.

For both fonts and images, you have the opportunity to either set that the file should be embedded or linked. *Embedded* means the font or image will be directly tied into the individual file, whereas *linked* stores the data in an external file that can be referenced from multiple SVG documents. Notice that if you select None (Use System Fonts), no options exist for embedding or linking the fonts. If, on the other hand, you choose Glyphs only, you will only have the option to embed the data in the page. *Glyphs* refer to outlines of the font rather than the font itself, and decrease the total file size. Consider using the other options (Common English, Common English + Glyphs Used, Common Roman, Common Roman + Glyphs) for any dynamically generated text.

Figure 21.12
When an Illustrator Smart Object is inserted into the page, GoLive will prompt you to select which type of file you would like to create. Select SVG and this dialog will appear.

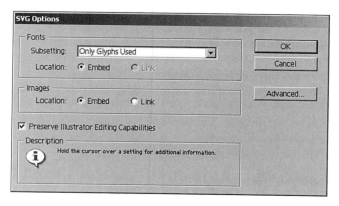

Click OK, and Illustrator (in conjunction with GoLive) will process the SVG. Upon finishing with the creation of the file, you will be prompted to save the file in your Site. A SVG file will have a .svg extension, and a Compressed SVG will be provided a .svgz extension. The Compressed SVG can dramatically decrease file size, but cannot be opened with a basic text editor.

The difference between SVGs and Compressed SVGs is discussed in detail in Chapter 22. Know that, however, for a Compressed SVG, both the SVG and the compressed version must be loaded in the same directory on the server.

SWFs

In addition to creating bitmaps and SVGs, Illustrator files can also generate SWFs (Macromedia Flash) files. Notice that this is also the only option supported by LiveMotion files, so when you insert a LiveMotion file into the page, the Macromedia Flash dialog box will automatically open.

SWF files are vector-based images that rely on the Macromedia Flash plug-in to render correctly. Unlike SVGs, SWFs are not open-source—that is to say you cannot open the source code in a text editor and make modifications. Because the images are vector-based, they maintain quality at varying resolutions, and simple graphics often render with a smaller file size as compared to the equivalent bitmap. Used particularly for animations, SWF files have helped integrate animation into the Web without sacrificing file size and download time.

The last option provided when inserting an Adobe Illustrator Smart Object is to generate an SWF (Macromedia Flash) file. When this option is selected, Illustrator will open with options in the Macromedia Flash SWF File Format Options dialog box, shown in Figure 21.13.

The "Export As" option in the dialog defines how the artwork will convert to an SWF file:

- AI File to SWF File converts the Illustrator file to a single, static SWF Vector image.

- AI File to SWF Frames converts each layer to an individual frame in one SFW file. Each layer thereby serves as a piece of the final animation.

- AI Layers to SWF Files converts each layer to an individual .SWF file.

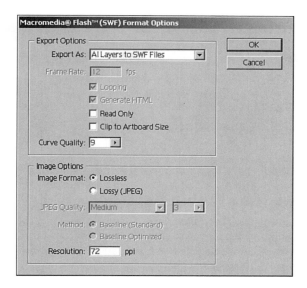

Figure 21.13
The Macromedia Flash (SWF) Format Options dialog box provides a way to customize the file.

Set the additional options as desired. The options are as follows:

- Frame Rate. Available when AI Layers to SWF Frames is selected; determines how fast the frames will play. Standard frame rate is 12 fps (frames per second).

- Looping. Available when AI Layers to SWF Frames is selected; determines how many times the animation should repeat.

- Read-Only. When checked, protects the source of the file from doing anything but viewing the file in its final format.

- Clip to Artboard Size. Exports any artwork inside the artboard, shedding the .SWF file of any artwork in the perimeters (outside the artboard).

- Curve Quality. Specifies the accuracy of any curves (specifically any bezier curves). The more accurate the curves, the greater the file size will be.

- Image Format. Determines the format of the image. Lossy converts images to JPEGs, thereby providing access to the JPEG quality option below. Lossy compression acheives a smaller file size by losing data and reducing the quality of the image. Lossless compression maintains the greatest quality of the image, but sacrifices download time.

- JPEG Quality. When the Image Format is set to lossless, the JPEG Quality setting allows you to alter the range of compression. The lower the quality, the smaller the file size will render.

- Method. When the Image Format is set to lossless, specifies the method for the lossless compression. Options include Baseline (standard) and Baseline Optimized (which further optimizes the image).

- Resolution. Determines the final resolution setting for bitmaps in the .SWF file from 72 pixels per inch (ppi) to 2,400ppi. Keep in mind that as you increase the pixels per inch, the file size (and download time) will increase as well.

21

Changing the Export Settings

For any Smart Object, the Inspector will provide access to all of the options for that image. For example, the Inspector will provide a means for adjusting the height and width parameters in the HTML, creating an image map, linking an image, and defining alternate text.

Because image editing programs and GoLive can be memory-intensive, be sure to save your files as you go along.

In addition, the Inspector houses a Settings button that, when clicked, opens the Optimization dialog box for the Smart Object for you to adjust.

Opening the Original File from Within GoLive

To open the original file, simply double-click on the Smart Object in the Document Window. The file will open in its native authoring program for you to edit. When the changes have been saved to the file, check out any Smart Object that had been created from that file. Voilà! The modifications have updated the target version while maintaining the desired optimization settings.

TROUBLESHOOTING

Ensuring Your Changes Update

I keep making changes to the original file, but when I view the compressed versions the changes do not update.

A number of possible reasons exist for as to why this is occurring. Perhaps you moved the original file (or the Site, for that matter) and so the path is no longer correct between the Smart Object and its original source file. Regardless, select the Smart Object within GoLive, and on the Inspector's Basic Tab (Window, Inspector) make sure that the source is correct. The best way to fix this is to delete the currently existing source and browse to the file to refresh the system's memory.

When Users Can't See Your Content

I compressed the file as an SVG or an SWF, but my users are complaining that they can't see the file.

As of this writing, SVGs and SWFs still require a plug-in. Either your users will need to download that SVG plug-in from Adobe's site (`http://www.adobe.com`) or Macromedia's SWF plug-in from `http://www.macromedia.com`, or you'll need to pick a more standard file format such as a GIF or a JPEG.

Optimizing Download Times

My users are complaining that my images take too long to download.

Consider whether you're using the right file formats for these images. Remember that GIFs typically fare well either for logos and images with solid bands of color, as well as black-and-white photographs. JPEGs, on the other hand, are the format of choice for color photographs. You may need to simply sacrifice a little more quality and/or color to achieve the necessary data size.

Your last option is to consider slicing the image. Look to the chapter regarding integration with other Adobe programs for information on how to slice an image (ImageReady is the slicing program of choice). Slicing means taking one big image and slicing it into smaller pieces. In essence, you might end up downloading four 10k images instead of one 40k image. Despite the total file size, the four 10k images will download faster because the computer can (and does) download images in parallel, meaning that it can download more than one image at a time, thereby saving on your users waiting time.

GOING LIVE

As you can see, GoLive's Smart Objects are incredibly powerful. First, you have the ability to optimize the image within GoLive. Second, those optimization settings are maintained and the target file(s) are automatically updated as you make changes to the original. Streamlining your image management through the use of Smart Objects no doubt decreases the time you'll spend fumbling to locate images on your directory.

There will be times, however, that you do not wish the target file to update based on the changes made in the original file. GoLive provides a way for you to break the Object's smart feature, thereby breaking its link to the original file and protecting it from unwanted updates. To do this, select the Smart Object in the Document Window, Ctrl-click (on a Mac) or right-click (in Windows) and select Convert to Regular from the contextual menu that appears.

22

INTEGRATING WITH PHOTOSHOP, ILLUSTRATOR, AND LIVEMOTION

IN THIS CHAPTER

About Inter-Application Integration   **384**

Building Mockups   **384**

Slicing a Photoshop Mockup   **386**

Using a Photoshop or Illustrator File as a Tracing Image   **409**

Adobe Support for Scalar Vector Graphics   **410**

Troubleshooting   **413**

Going Live   **415**

ABOUT INTER-APPLICATION INTEGRATION

One of the greatest benefits to choosing GoLive over competing Web editors is its tight integration with other Adobe products. Particularly as Adobe's software tools have become the industry standard in graphic design, the simplistic and powerful integration of Adobe GoLive with Adobe Photoshop, ImageReady, Illustrator, and LiveMotion has proven a valuable asset for Web designers.

Smart Objects are one such integration feature and are discussed in the previous chapter. On its most simplistic level, Smart Objects allow you to create optimized Web versions of a Photoshop, Illustrator, or LiveMotion file without ever leaving GoLive. The other programs offer powerful features that work remarkably well with GoLive as well. That is to say, each can do a tremendous amount of work toward the finished HTML page before you ever open Adobe GoLive.

Not intended to provide a thorough introduction to Photoshop, Illustrator, or LiveMotion, this chapter is dedicated to exploring the features available in each that are particularly useful for forward integration with Adobe GoLive. Specifically, the concepts of creating mockups to generate tracing images, sliced images, and HTML code reassembling sliced images via HTML and CSS will be discussed.

Although this chapter assumes a basic understanding of creating images in Adobe Photoshop and HTML pages in Adobe GoLive, even beginners will find it handy. Understanding what a program can do can help you gauge whether learning the basics are worth accessing some of the advanced features.

BUILDING MOCKUPS

The term *mockup* refers to any static image that can be used as a staging ground for a site's design. Often designers create any number of mockups to present to the client for decision-making purposes. Without ever getting into the technicalities of coding, the possible designs can be evaluated, allowing decisions to be made before the expensive development process begins.

Adobe Photoshop, Illustrator and LiveMotion are all often used for creating mockups. But each program can do much more with that mockup than meets the eye. In addition to providing a staging ground for decisions, the mockup can be used as a backdrop for a page's development as a tracing image. Furthermore, and perhaps even more handy, the mockup can be used to create the small individual images that will be incorporated into a page. In addition, each program can actually generate the HTML code that reassembles the individual images into a cohesive page.

In short, this means that all you have to do to start out is create a graphical rendition of how the page will look in your program of preference: Adobe Photoshop, Illustrator, or LiveMotion. Then, slice the page into smaller pieces, and export the HTML for the page. Rather than relying on GoLive to create the foundation HTML for the page, the HTML is generated based upon the manner in which you sliced the mockup. This means you don't have to worry about laying out table cells exactly right or making sure you create a table that's big enough to fit all of the content. This feature can easily cut your production time in half.

Which to Choose: Photoshop, Illustrator, or LiveMotion?

Although many developers probably choose whichever program they are most comfortable with, there is a better means to selecting which program to use to generate your mockup. Each program has its strengths, weaknesses, and most importantly, file versions that it can export. In selecting your program of choice, consider the following information about each package.

Photoshop and ImageReady

Adobe Photoshop & ImageReady is a package pair of programs that ship together as of this writing. Although Photoshop was originally created simply for editing bitmaps and ImageReady was created to export that bitmap for Web display, the two programs increasingly overlap in duty and function. Don't be surprised if, in a few years, the two programs are completely merged into one.

Photoshop works exceptionally well with raster graphics (bitmaps) and increasingly better with vector objects. To review, *raster graphics* (bitmaps) are a compilation of pixels, their addresses, and their colors. Clumping these pixels together creates the appearance of a shape or picture. *Vector objects*, on the other hand, are mathematical objects—visual representations of formulae stored inside the file. This difference means that as you zoom into or resize a raster graphic, you'll see distortion—the pixels can't grow. On the other hand, your vector objects can. The program simply multiplies the formula by two, redraws, and Voila! In short, you'll find that vector objects are far more flexible and easier to edit than a raster graphic. On the other hand, a raster graphic does a far better job of capturing soft variations in light and color, particularly as it applies to a photograph.

Therein lies the true strength of Photoshop: Initially designed as purely a raster graphic editing tool, Photoshop deals extremely well with photographs. If you expect to have a page that is very photo-heavy, Photoshop is most likely your best bet: you will find far more options for editing and tweaking that photo in Photoshop than you will in any other Adobe program.

Also, consider Photoshop's and ImageReady's exporting capabilities. The two programs, designed as bitmap editors, can export GIFGIFs, JPEGJPEGs, and PNGs for Web display.

Illustrator

Illustrator, on the other hand, is Adobe's program that works exceptionally well with vector shapes and objects. Each object is its own entity, negating the need for layers to separate one object from another. You'll find, once you know the two programs equally well, your production time in Illustrator will be somewhat less than the production time required to create the same effect in Photoshop. Notice, however, that Illustrator's bitmap editing capabilities are quite limited. Special effects such as brightening a photograph, distorting someone's head, or drawing attention to a particular area of the photograph is far easier to complete in Adobe Photoshop.

Also consider the file types that Illustrator is capable of exporting: In addition to the standard GIF., JPEG., and PNG, Adobe Illustrator can also create SVGs (Scalar Vector Graphics) and SWF (Macromedia ShockWave-Flash) files. SVG is an emerging XML language that empowers the developer with the ability to create data-driven images. This file format is explained in detail at the end of this chapter. The latter, SWF, is a more conventional substitute for SVG: vector-based images displayed on the Web via a plug-in. The advantage of SVG over SWF is simply its proprietary nature: SVGs rely on an open-source technology purported by the W3C, and SWFs are proprietary, not open source.

LiveMotion

LiveMotion, the third and final option, was designed specifically to create SWF files, proprietary vector-based images. Typically, an SWF is used in lieu of the traditional GIF.gif or JPEG.jpeg for the purpose of incorporating an animation into the page. LiveMotion is more an animation program than a vector-based drawing program: you'll find Illustrator is far superior in its drawing capabilities.

Finally, LiveMotion as well has certain file formats that it can export for Web display. Although LiveMotion can generate Macromedia SWF files, when using LiveMotion's AutoLayout (slicing feature), GIFs, JPEGs, and PNGs can be created from an individual image.

SLICING A PHOTOSHOP MOCKUP

In the following examples, a mockup has been created. First, we will use a mockup for the contact page of a fictitious site to demonstrate Photoshop's capabilities and ImageReady's ability to build a rollover. Then, we'll focus on Illustrator's slicing capabilities. Finally, slicing as it pertains to LiveMotion will be detailed.

Second, the mockup can be used to create smaller sliced images. *Slicing* refers to cutting the one image into smaller pieces. Each slice (or piece) can be custom optimized, so that one piece may be exported as a GIF, whereas its neighbor can be exported as a JPEG. Typically, the slices are then reassembled into a cohesive page via HTML code—either using floating boxes (CSS layers) or layout grids (HTML tables).

Photoshop's Integration Features

In the example shown in Figure 22.1, a mockup page is completely drawn as one large image in Adobe Photoshop and saved as a PSD (Photoshop file). The page does not have any functionality, HTML, or Web-compatible images.

Once approved, this mockup can be used for a number of purposes. First and foremost, the Photoshop file can be used as a tracing image in GoLive. A *tracing image* simply serves as a backdrop for the design of a page. Transparent to the user and only viewed by the Document Window in Adobe GoLive, the tracing image provides a framework for you to line all your page elements against.

Although you can create the HTML code purely in GoLive, you can also have Photoshop export the HTML page. This HTML page provides a starting ground for you to work with as you refine the page layout and design in GoLive, thereby dramatically cutting down the work you have to re-create.

The following demonstration walks you through all the advanced integration features that Photoshop offers. Starting with the mockup, the PSD file will be sliced and custom optimization will be detailed. Then, the steps to export the sliced images and the HTML code will be discussed. Finally, you'll learn how to use the original .psd as a tracing image.

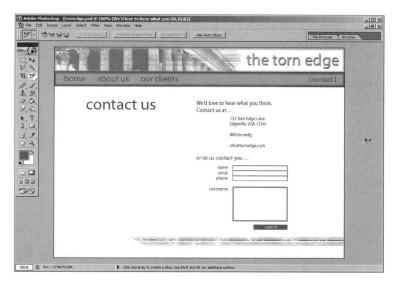

Figure 22.1
An example of a mockup created in Photoshop. As of yet, this mockup is nothing more than a single static image.

Slicing a Page in Photoshop

Once the PSD file has been created, Photoshop offers a slice tool that allows you to cut the large image into smaller chunks. Notice that the slice tool also offers a companion tool, the slice select tool, which is used for selecting an existing slice. Start by selecting the Slice Tool.

To create a slice, select the slice tool and click and drag from the upper-left corner of the slice to the lower-right corner, as shown in Figure 22.2. A slice will be created and the outline for the table cells will appear.

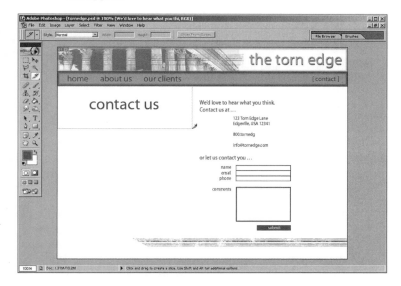

Figure 22.2
Use the slice tool to define each piece. Click in the upper-left of the slice and drag to the bottom-right corner of the piece.

Each slice that you create will generate an HTML table data cell. There are a few simple rules you should follow:

- Because table data cells cannot overlap, your slices should not overlap.

- Try to keep the slices as simple as possible. Although Photoshop will create the HTML table code for you, having to deal with a complex layout will prove tedious in the long run.

- Don't worry if you accidentally create a slice of the wrong size or misplace the borders of the piece. Just use the slice select tool to click and select the slice. Then, use the anchor points to resize or adjust the placement of the piece. When a slice is selected, you can use your arrow keys for repositioning.

Slice every relevant piece in the page (see Figure 22.3), being careful to create as simple a table as possible.

Figure 22.3
Every page element should belong to a slice (to an HTML table data cell). In addition, slices cannot overlap.

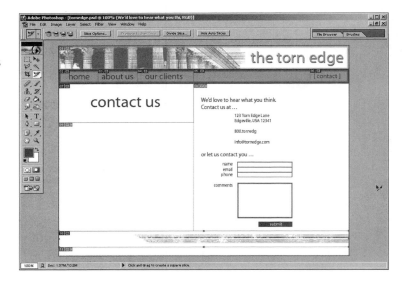

In this example, each slice was drawn manually. Photoshop also offers a few shortcuts that provide greater control via the dynamically populated Toolbar at the top of the program. These options include:

- Style. These include Normal, which allows any size slice; Fixed Aspect Ratio, which allows unlimited scaling at the same aspect ration; and Fixed Ratio, which constrains the slice size to a specified ration.

- Slice from Guides. Particularly useful when the slices of the table will have a checkerboard-look, Slice from Guides allow you to use the file's Guides to define the separate pieces of the page. Guides are straight horizontal and vertical lines that can be dragged from the page's rulers.

In addition to the slices you manually create, Photoshop will automatically generate Auto slices. Auto slices are simply pieces required to capture the other page elements and to assemble a full

HTML table. Although you cannot manually adjust an Auto slice's height, width, or location, you can promote the slice to a User Slice and then make the adjustments.

Notice that the toolbar at the top of the window offers a few unique features when the Slice Select Tool is chosen:

- Bring to Front Bring Forward, Send Backward, and Send to Back are the four buttons to the left of Slice Options in Figure 22.3. These manage the stacking order of the slices when overlaps do occur. Moving the slices one on top of the other via the Slice Select Tool can overlap slices, which results in the creation of CSS floating boxes as opposed to a basic HTML table.

- Slice Options. When clicked, toggles open a Slice Options dialog box that contains HTML customization, shown in Figure 22.4. For each slice you can define the Type of data for the cell (image or no image). If an image, other options exist, including the name for the sliced image, the URL to which the image should be linked, the Target (frame or window name), the message and alternate text for accessibility purposes. If you select no image, a blank box will appear in which you can enter HTML text (and tags) for the cell's contents. In either case, specific dimensions of the image can be adjusted, and a background (both image and color) can be set for the table data cell.

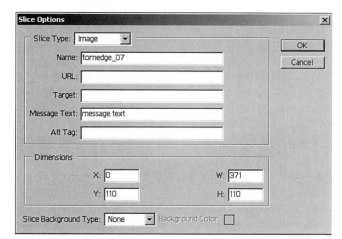

Figure 22.4
The Slice Options dialog box provides specific control over the slice. In addition, a number of HTML attributes can be set for the cell, including the linked URL, alternate text, and background characteristics (color or image) can be set.

- Promote to User Slice promotes an Auto slice to a slice that the user created, thereby providing access to controlling the piece's height, width, and location. Although not necessary, you may find it helpful to promote every Auto Slice to a User Slice. GoLive forbids you from making edits to an Auto Slice in Adobe GoLive or Photoshop, so ensuring you have control later in the process will prove useful.

- Divide Slice provides a quick way to divide a slice horizontally, vertically, or both with very specific control over the generated pieces' heights and widths.

- Hide/Show Auto Slices (toggle) changes the display of the Auto Slices (the slices you did not create).

You definitely will want to take the time to name each slice. Photoshop will automatically name the slices based on the name of the file and the cell number it associates with that slice. However, as a developer, you'll find it quite difficult to remember what slice number 1 contained as opposed to slice number 3 when reassembling the page or managing your files. Take the time to provide intuitive and descriptive names for each piece to save the hassle of renaming them (and changing the references to them in the HTML code) .

Exporting the Slices as Individual Images

When exporting the image, you have a few options. If you're working within Photoshop, select File, Save for Web from the menu and the dialog box will open. If you're in GoLive or have already saved and closed your sliced PSD, you can import and optimize your graphics as a Photoshop Smart Object. A Photoshop Smart Object will maintain a link back to the original file. So, if the contents of a particular slice in the file change, saving those modifications to the original will automatically update the compressed version. Notice when you set the source of an image using Adobe GoLive's Photoshop Smart Object feature, the Save for Web dialog box opens.

In either case, once inside the Save for Web dialog box, use the Slice Select Tool to select each piece. By holding down the Shift key, you can select and optimize more than one slice at a time. Then, using the Settings panel in the right side, define the optimization settings for that slice as desired, and be sure to keep a watchful eye over the download time and data size associated with that slice. Repeat until each slice has been given compression instructions.

Make sure you select each piece in the page using the dialog box's slice select tool, and optimize each one accordingly. The Optimized, 2-up, and 4-up tabs work the same as previously discussed.

Finally, click Save to go to the next step.

Now, instead of saving a single image, you are saving multiple images. In addition, you have the option to save HTML table code reassembling each of the pieces to a cohesive page. Begin by providing a File Name. In addition, modify the other options as desired.

Start by defining whether you would like to export images and the HTML, the images only, or the HTML only. Typically the first time you export the page you'll opt to export both the images and the HTML. The exception to this rule is when you plan on reassembling the images into a cohesive page manually either using floating boxes (CSS layers) or a layout grid (HTML Table). Exporting the file after you have already previously done so will show the value of the other two options: export HTML only and images only. Use HTML only if you've made a modification to a cell that affects only the HTML, not the images. For example, perhaps you've changed the background color on a specific cell, modified the alternate text, or fixed a broken link. On the other hand, use Images only when you've made modifications to an image without making any changes to the generated HTML. When in doubt, export both, ensuring that the code and the images' contents are updated accordingly.

Next, specify the settings using the dialog shown in Figure 22.5. Although default settings will work fine for most purposes, you will find the ability to adjust the coding of the HTML quite useful. Change the settings from default settings to other. Once inside the settings dialog box (accessed by selecting Other from the Settings drop-down menu), use the drop-down to access and alter the available settings for the HTML code, the slices, the background image (if any), and saving files.

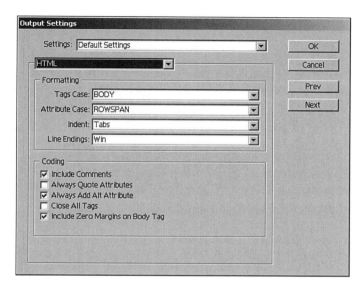

Figure 22.5
The Settings dialog box allows you to customize the code, slices, background image of the page, and method for saving and naming files without leaving Adobe Photoshop.

HTML options provide a means for accessing and controlling the layout and design of the code. Although HTML has traditionally been relatively forgiving of loose formatting, the next evolution of HTML (XHTML) is quite exacting and enforces well-formedness. Options for controlling HTML include

- Tags case. Refers to the case with which the tags will be written. Options include all capitals, first-letter only capitalized, and all lowercase. For XHTML compliance, choose all lower case.

- Attributes Case. An attribute is an element that modifies an existing tag. Choices are also all capitals, first-letter only capitalized, and all lowercase. For XHTML compliance, choose all lower case.

- Indent. Sets the indentation of the code. Options range from none (no spaces) to 8 spaces.

- Line Endings specifies the line endings that should be written into the code (the hard returns). Options include Win, Mac, and Unix.

- Include Comments adds in HTML comments mapping out the code.

- Always Quote Attributes. Traditionally, only certain circumstances required that attribute values be nested within double quotes. For XHTML-compliance, quote all attributes.

- Always add Alt text adds in alternate text for all images for 508 compliance.

- Close all tags adds a corresponding closing tag to every instance of an HTML tag. Check this option as well for XHTML-compliance.

- Include Zero margins in body tag. By default, Netscape Navigator and Internet Explorer have slightly different margins from the upper-left corner of the browser window. Check this option if you want neither browser to add in any padding from the upper-left of the browser window. This simply adds margin attributes to the HTML body tag.

In addition to determining the setup of the HTML code, the Slices menu choice provides further options. Here, you will find options for generating Floating Boxes (CSS Layers) over HTML tables, as well as options for determining how Photoshop should treat empty table cells.

The first choice to make is whether you would like the code generated to rely on an HTML table or CSS Layers (GoLive's Floating boxes). If you select HTML table, the following options will enable.

- Empty Cells determines the behavior for empty table cells. Options include inserting a GIF with a specified width and height into the table cell, inserting a GIF into a sized (width and height) table cell, or leaving the table data cell empty but fixed in height and width with the nowrap feature turned on. All three of these options will work fine. Just know that Netscape collapses empty table cells. To accommodate for this quirk, if you choose the latter be sure to add in spacer cells (to be discussed shortly).

- TD W&H specifies how the table data cell's widths and heights should be added in: automatically as needed, always, and never.

- Spacer Cells. Options include Auto, Auto (Bottom), Always, Always (Bottom), and Never. *Spacer cells* refer to added in cells that hold a fixed height and width as well as a blank image that maintains that cell's size. The reason for added cells is so that, when a table is viewed in Netscape, table data cells without content do not collapse. Auto puts small spacer images in automatically as needed, whereas Auto (Bottom) adds an additional row at the bottom of the table (transparent to the user) that houses nothing but table data cells with spacers inside. Likewise, Always follows suit, and Never leaves empty table data cells empty without the spacer image. Really, this option depends on your preference. Your best bet is to choose one of the first four, just to make sure Netscape does not collapse your empty table cells and ruin your fantastic page layout.

If you choose to generate CSS (Floating boxes) , the option to choose your layer's reference will appear. Referenced by ID creates the references to the floating boxes via ID names in the CSS Style Sheet. Referenced by class, on the other hand, creates a separate custom class for each floating box and references the class name. Finally, inline writes the positioning code directly in the `<div>` tag (the CSS layer) tag itself. This option also relies on the preference of the developer and does not make a substantial difference unless you plan to hand-edit some of the code.

Regardless of whether you're creating HTML tables or CSS Floating Boxes, Photoshop gives you complete control over the names of your slices, allowing you to concatenate (string together) a variety of naming conventions for each slice.

The Background drop-down menu incorporates additional options for setting the relative path to a background image, as well as a background color (if any) for the page.

Finally, the last customizable menu, Saving Files allows you to control the naming convention of your files with which platforms the filenames should be compatible, whether images should be put in a subfolder named images, whether the background image should be copied when saved, and whether a copyright should be included in the code.

When you have finished altering the settings as you desire, click OK. The final option is whether you would like to export all slices or simply the selected slices.

Browse to the location where you would like to save the file and click Save. *Voila!* Based on the preferences you set in the Save Optimized As dialog box and the optimization settings you specified for each slice, your images have been exported and your HTML page has been created.

Using ImageReady to Generate Rollovers Images

As discussed, Photoshop can do quite a bit of the work for you in piecing together an HTML page. Photoshop, however, is still truly a program designed for editing photos and creating interesting graphics. As the Web became popular and Photoshop's capabilities remained focused on print design, Adobe built a companion program (called ImageReady) responsible for translating the print design to a Web compatible format. Although, as you have seen, Photoshop has since taken on many of the Web-focused capabilities (such as slicing, custom optimization, and generating HTML page code), a few ImageReady-specific features still exist that make ImageReady a handy tool.

Photoshop's Tools panel houses a shortcut that opens the current PSD file in ImageReady. Once the file is open in ImageReady, take a little time to notice the differences between the two programs.

Many of the tools and panels will look quite similar to Photoshop, but upon close inspection you'll notice that the drawing tools in ImageReady are not nearly as powerful as the drawing tools in Photoshop.

Notice that ImageReady also has Slice and Slice Select Tools. In ImageReady, the slices can be optimized without opening a separate dialog. Simply select a slice, and use the Optimize panel (Window, Optimize) to adjust the compression settings.

In addition to the Optimize panel, another additional panel exists, shown in Figure 22.6. This one houses features unavailable in Photoshop. The Rollovers panel (Window, Rollovers), for creating rollovers images which are temporarily swapped out with an alternate image whenever the user's mouse passes over. This panel provides access to creating images not only for the initial state, but also for varying states of the user's interaction. For example, perhaps you want the text to start dark but lighten when your user rolls her mouse over the image. The Rollovers panel provides access to creating multiple states of an image.

By default, every slice contains a single state (the normal state) that is displayed when the user first loads the page. However, by clicking the [ic:2304] icon in the bottom-right of the Rollovers panel, you can create additional states.

Possible options include

- Over invokes the image swap when the image is hovered over.

- Down changes the image when the image is pressed down.

- Click changes the image when the image is pressed down and released.

- Custom changes the image based on a custom built event. Advanced JavaScript knowledge is required for creating such an effect.

- Selected changes the image based on when the image is selected.

- Out swaps the image when the user takes her mouse away from over-top the image.

- Up invokes the image change when the user releases the mouse.

- None creates an additional slice but does not export it as an interactive state.

Figure 22.6
ImageReady's Rollovers panel provides access to a unique feature not available in Photoshop: the ability to create a rollover effect visually rather than by hand.

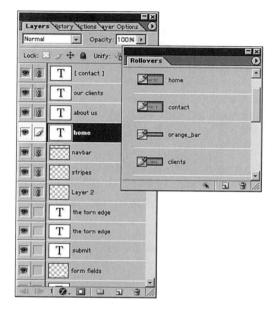

Creating a rollover effect for a particular site requires you to juggle both states and layers. For any specific state, you are going to build what that state will look like via the available layers. Typically, you should start out designing your page first, then add in the bells and whistles via the varying states as the final step. This will keep your page organized and coherent, and minimize the need to make time-consuming changes. So, first design your page. Once you are comfortable with the page layout, you can start adding and defining the states of the various slices.

Select the slice to which you would like to add a state. In this example, an over state in which the text highlights is going to be applied to the home button.

Once the slice has been selected, choose Window, Rollovers to open the Rollovers palette, and then locate and select the appropriate slice (see Figure 22.7). Click the new state icon button. By default, the over state will appear. Clicking the new state icon button a second time will yield a down state, and so forth. However, at any point in time you can change the designated state by double-clicking the slice listing in the Rollovers panel and specifying the correct state via the Rollovers State options dialog box.

With the Over State selected in the Rollovers panel, create the look and feel of the page. Specifically, change the components of the page by adding layers and hiding layers so that the page appears differently for the over state than for the normal state.

In this example, an additional layer titled "home - highlighted" was added. That layer is only visible via the over state of the home slice. Figures 22.8 and 22.9 show this process.

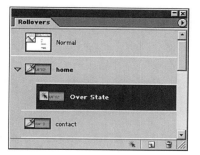

Figure 22.7
In this example, an over state is added to the slice containing the link to the home page.

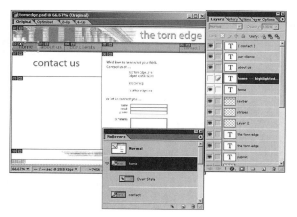

Figure 22.8
Create the additional layer called "home - highlighted."

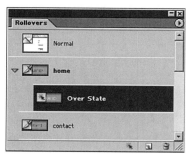

Figures 22.9
Click the Over State in the Rollovers palette to specify the new layer's visibility.

Making changes can be tricky, so ImageReady provides a means for you to tell the program whether layer additions should apply to all states or simply to the state with which you are currently working. By opening the context menu of the Rollovers dialog as shown in Figure 22.10, a menu will appear with the option "New Layers Visible in all States/Frames". If you want the additional layer to be visible in all states, check this item. If not, make sure that it is not selected by default.

To see the results of your changes, preview the page in a browser (File, Preview in Browser).

All export settings for a particular slice also apply to each state for that slice. When you export the HTML page (File, Save Optimized) and its corresponding pieces, ImageReady will create all of the individual slices that will be swapped one for the other. In addition, the html page will incorporate the JavaScript that swaps these slices based on the user's interaction with the page.

Figure 22.10
New Layers Visible in all States/Frames provides a way for you to specify whether the additional layers you are creating should apply to all states of the slice, or to simply the state with which you are working.

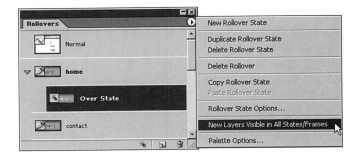

Using Illustrator to Slice a Pages

Many of the integration features Adobe Photoshop offers GoLive are paralleled by features supported by Adobe Illustrator. For example, GoLive's capabilities include Photoshop and Illustrator-specific Smart Objects, and both Photoshop and Illustrator provide slicing and optimization features. This section intends to illustrate the Web-specific features incorporated in Adobe Illustrator, including both slicing and applying an image map within Illustrator.

Although ImageReady is adding JavaScript to the HTML page, that JavaScript is not picked up by Adobe GoLive's Actions palette. If you foresee needing to make many changes to the source of the rollover image, you might consider using ImageReady to simply create the slices, and GoLive to reassemble them via a Rollovers.

If you're already familiar with slicing in Adobe Photoshop, you're encouraged to skim this section quickly as many of the concepts are the same. Keep in mind the major differences: first, the implementation is dramatically different. Second, whereas Photoshop slices can only generate bitmaps (GIFGIFs, JPEGJPEGs, and PNGs), Illustrator slices can additionally create SVGs and Flash files.

Slicing in Illustrator

Much like Adobe Photoshop, Illustrator can be used to slice a mockup: that is, to cut a large image of the entire page into smaller pieces. In addition to creating and exporting the smaller pieces of the image, Illustrator can, upon exporting the page, reassemble all of the smaller pieces into an HTML table so that it provides the illusion of a coherent page. Notice that in addition to exporting the slices as a GIFGIF, JPEGJPEG, or PNG, Adobe Illustrator can also export each piece as a SWF (Macromedia Flash) or SVG (scalar vector graphic).

Although ImageReady's slicing is a great foundation for getting the page layout started, you are encouraged to use the slicing mechanism as a starting ground, not as the end-all solution to developing your page's layout. Although Illustrator's slicing is a handy feature, GoLive is by far a superior product for developing HTML and editing HTML.

Remember, when slicing you are generally creating HTML table cells. As a result, as HTML table cells cannot overlap, make sure your slices do not overlap either.

To slice a mockup, you will use both the Slice Tool and the Slice Select Tool, as contained by the Toolbar, shown in Figure 22.11.

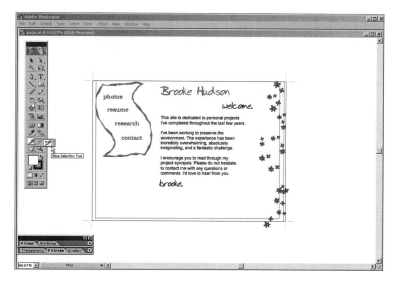

Figure 22.11
The Toolbar contains both the Slice Tool and the Slice Select Tool.

Select the Slice Tool, and click and drag a rectangle around the area you would like to define as a slice. Alternatively, for precise slices that closely fit a particular object's space, you may select the object and add a slice from the menu by choosing Object, Slice, Make. Regardless, once the slice is created, use the Slice Select Tool to grab a hold of a slice. Using the Slice Select Tool, you can resize and move a slice. In addition, once the slice is selected, you can specify the options for that piece.

Illustrator stores Slice Options in a dialog, shown in Figure 22.12, that you can call up by selecting Object, Slice, Slice Options from the main menu once the slice has been selected. The dialog immediately requests you to specify the slice type, with the options of No Image, Image, or HTML text. Depending on which of these you select, the rest of the dialog box will populate with available options.

Notice that the Slice Tool and Slice Select Tool are both in the same area of the Toolbar. To access both, click and hold down on the small arrow in the bottom-right corner of icon to reveal all the possible tools in that set.

No image empties the cell of the image and provides room for you to write in HTML that should be included in the cell. In addition the dialog provides a means for you to align the cell's contents both horizontally and vertically, as well as to specify a background color (if you desire one) for the table cell.

Image records the image and will insert that image as the contents of the cell. Later (when saving the page for the Web) you will have the opportunity to optimize each piece, to specify the image format and compression settings.

When you deem that the slice will hold an image, a number of options will appear for you to specify, not including the type of image file to which the selected slice should export. Modifying the file format is achieved later upon exporting the page.

Figure 22.12
When No image is selected, you have the opportunity to fill in the HTML text, set the cell's alignment (both vertically and horizontally) and set a background color.

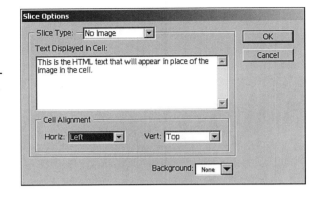

Figure 22.13
Slice Options has different selections when the slice contains an image.

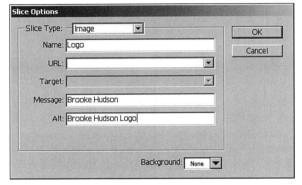

The options of the Slice Option dialog are as follows:

- Name details the filename with which the image should be saved.

- URL specifies a single URL to which the image should link. Do not use the URL if you plan on also incorporating an image map in that area.

- Target determines which frame or window the new page will load when the linked image is clicked. Notice this option is only enabled when you have specified a URL.

- Message displays a customized message in the bottom-left corner of the browser's document window, specifically in the status bar of the browser.

- Alt provides alternate text for those relying on screen readers to read off the information.

- Background sets the background color (if any) for the table data cell.

Finally, the last option, HTML text, only applies when the slice was created via the menu bar over top of a text object. The HTML text automatically populates the dialog with HTML code that most likely mirrors the image's contents (if possible), as shown in Figure 22.14. In other words, the text's appearance in Illustrator is described as best as possible using HTML.

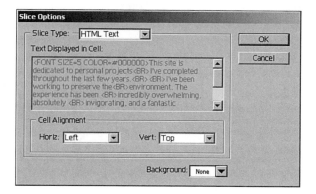

Figure 22.14
The HTML text option automatically populates the cell's contents with an HTML version of the text typed into that cell within Illustrator.

Keep in mind that images provide much greater control over font sizes, font types, etc. Therefore, do not be surprised if selecting HTML text results in the text display being far different than you originally intended, because in many cases, HTML does not have the capability to mimic such specific and ornate font formatting. Of course, by giving up such formatting, you simultaneously save on download time.

In addition, the dialog provides a means for aligning the cell's contents both horizontally and vertically, as well as for setting the background color of the table data cell if desired.

Set the options for each slice as desired by selecting each slice with the Slice Select Tool, bringing up the Slice Options dialog (Object, Slice, Slice Options...) and completing the dialog as pertinent to each piece.

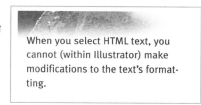

When you select HTML text, you cannot (within Illustrator) make modifications to the text's formatting.

Once you are finished setting the options for each slice, export the page by selecting File, Save for Web from the main menu. You will first be prompted to optimize each slice within the Export dialog box, then to save the images and the HTML page.

To do this, use the Slice Select Tool internal to the Save for Web dialog box to select each slice. Then, in the settings panel, provide the optimization settings for the piece (specify if the piece should be exported as a GIF, JPEG, PNG, SWF, or SVG and the parameters for each). If you're unsure as to the various options, consider looking back to the Smart Objects chapter for detailed explanations of the most important parameters available in the Save for Web settings section. See Figure 22.15.

As you optimize each slice, be sure to keep a watchful eye on the download time. Remember, your goal is to produce professional looking graphics with as small a data size as possible.

Illustrator's Save for Web dialog box also allows you to view a preview version of the page in a Browser. In the bottom-right corner, the icon for a browser will appear. Click the icon and the page will open in a browser.

As you modify the optimization settings for each slice, be sure to check out how those optimization settings will actually render by checking out the Preview tab. The original tab will give you the appearance of the image as it appears in Illustrator, but the Preview tab illustrates how the image will actually appear upon exporting it.

Figure 22.15
Select the slice using the Slice Select Tool internal to the dialog box, then use the settings to adjust the file type and optimization settings as you desire.

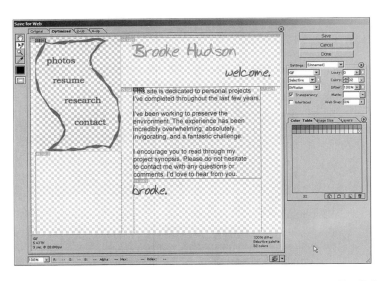

In addition, the Save for Web dialog box allows you to control the image size via the Image Size Tab, as shown in Figure 22.16. Simply type in the new dimensions. If you would like Illustrator to do the proportional calculations for you, be sure to have the Constrain Proportions checkbox checked. Changing the dimensions here will not permanently change the dimensions of the original image: it will only change the dimensions of the exported version of the file.

Figure 22.16
Use the Save for Web's Image Size Tab to control the dimensions of the final output.

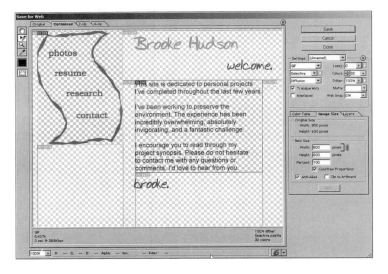

Finally, the last option provided to you in the Save for Web dialog, shown in Figure 22.17, is the option to export the file as CSS layers (GoLive's floating boxes). This translates each layer in the Illustrator file into one CSS layer in the HTML page. Exporting the page as CSS layers means that each layer in the Illustrator file will be exported as an individual CSS layer, or an individual floating box.

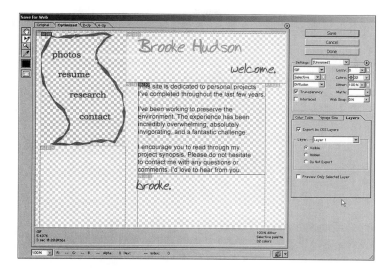

Although exporting the page via CSS Layers is a handy feature, the integration with Adobe GoLive and the generated code is less than ideal. First, you must be sure to go into the output settings box and choose to export the CSS via Layers ID, and even then you'll find the preview in Adobe GoLive will not pick up the location of the layers (although browsers will render the code fine). The reason for this is simply because there are numerous ways to write the code that positions a CSS layer (a floating box) on the page, and Adobe GoLive has been written to code one (the most common) of these methods—meaning not only does GoLive not code the other methods, the program also does not understand and render them. For these reasons, you are encouraged to stick with table slices, particularly when you are unfamiliar with the code at hand.

Although this is a limitation of the program, you are encouraged to use tables anyway to ensure accessibility to your page both by screen readers and by older browser versions.

If you still prefer to use CSS layers, consider using Illustrator to create each individual image, then reassemble them into a cohesive page via GoLive's interface and its floating boxes.

Once you have optimized the page and each of its corresponding slices, select Save You will finally be prompted to save the HTML page. Specify the name of the HTML file and directory in which you want the files saved. Illustrator will simultaneously export each individual slice and reassemble them via an HTML page.

Illustrator does provide some control over the HTML code that will be generated, as shown in Figure 22.18 through 22.20. By clicking the HTML options button, you can define whether you want the code to be uppercase or lower case, and so on. Use the Next and Prev buttons to navigate through all of the options Illustrator provides for formatting the HTML.

Figure 22.18
Specify the attributes of the HTML table.

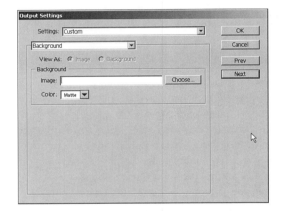

Figure 22.19
Select a background image or color.

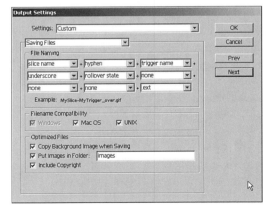

Figure 22.20
Select the filename formatting and the location to save the files.

Do not be afraid to stick with the default settings, particularly if you don't plan on delving into and editing the code by hand yourself. Although XHTML (HTML with stricter rules and specifications with regards to the coding) requires lowercase tags, all attributes enclosed in quotes, etc., browsers have in the past and will probably continue to support all renditions of HTML—those compliant with the rules of XML and those that are not.

Finally, click Save. Illustrator will export the HTML page and all associated images to the location you specify, an example of which is shown in Figure 22.21. Notice that the code will render based on your specifications (use of CSS layers or not), and each of the table cells will contain the content you specified, whether it be HTML text or images.

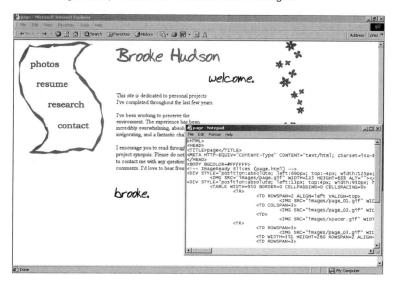

Figure 22.21
Illustrator outputs an HTML page that contains all your slices and other elements.

Applying Image Maps in Illustrator

Chapter 11 discusses image maps in great detail. In this section, we explore the use of Illustrator to generate them. Remember, an image map is simply an additional set of HTML instructions that provide information about different hotspots in the image: Each hotspot specifies a link. As a result, one image can actually be linked to multiple destinations.

Be careful not to apply a URL to a slice that contains hotspots as certain browsers will react differently to the resulting improper code. If a slice contains hotspots, make sure that that slice does not have a URL specified for it.

To create a hotspot, select the vector object in Illustrator to which you would like to add the link. In this example, the navigation bar will continue to be one slice (one image). So, to make each piece of text linked, a hotspot will be added.

Begin by selecting the vector object (in this case, the text) which will be linked. Then, bring up the Attributes palette via Window, Attributes from the menu command. Each time you bring up a palette in Illustrator, it displays any number of options. If the options you are looking for do not appear, click the tiny arrow in the bottom-right of the palette's tab to toggle the different options on and off. In this case, you are looking for the image map options on the Attributes palette, which resides in the second tier of the palette.

22

To add a hotspot, with the appropriate object selected in the page, select the hotspot shape you would like to add as shown in Figure 22.22. Options include

- None (the default) which indicates the area will not be linked.

- Rectangle creates a rectangular shaped hotspot around the vector object.

- Polygon creates a polygon shaped hotspot based on the perimeter of the vector object.

After selecting the shape of the hotspot, the URL field will populate, allowing you to type in the page to which you would like the hotspot to link. Remember, if referencing a local file (a file on the same server), the path must account for any changes in the directories. If referencing an external link (a file on another server or another site), the path must be prefaced with the http:// protocol reference. And finally, if creating an email link (one that opens an email dialog box if their computer is configured to support that feature), the link must be prefaced with mailto: and followed by the email address.

Figure 22.22
Use the Attributes panel to select a vector object, then designate its hotspot type (rectangular), and the path to the correct file.

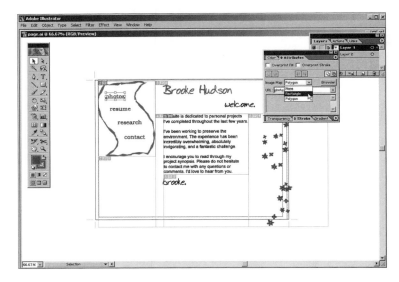

The appearance of the object will not change within Illustrator, and the HTML page must be exported (File, Save for Web) for the Image map HTML instructions to be generated. In addition, you may have noticed that alternative text is not an available option within the Illustrator interface. This simply lends to the fact that Illustrator is intended to produce graphics and integrate with GoLive—it is not intended to write hearty HTML. You will definitely want to edit the HTML via GoLive's interface for full control over the image map's options.

You cannot adequately test out local links (links to relative files) via the preview generated from Illustrator's Save for the Web dialog box. Simply stated, the preview generates a temporary file and the local path from that temporary file to the file to which it is linking will not be correct, as the temporary file is stored in a different directory on your machine.

Slicing in LiveMotion

Of all the programs discussed in this chapter, LiveMotion is by far the least used with regards to creating a mockup. Recall that LiveMotion's primary strength is to create animations. Although the program is capable of exporting and creating animated GIFs, the program is more often used to create Macromedia Flash files (SWF). Websites incorporating vector-based images usually consist of mostly HTML text with small partial snippets of SWF files. The alternative would be to have an entire site built in the Macromedia Flash (SWF) file—including references to other pages, other sections of the site, and so on. Rarely, however, will you find a site's mockup created in LiveMotion. Instead, perhaps a small snippet of the page is created in LiveMotion and then incorporated into the greater HTML page.

For all intents and purposes, since incorporating a small portion of the LiveMotion file into a greater HTML page is commonly used, the technique for completing this will be demonstrated here. Although not recommended, you could create the entire mockup in LiveMotion using the same process.

Start by creating the portion of the page you want to export for inclusion in your greater HTML file. Going into the details of how to create the animation and the objects is well beyond the scope of this book, however you'll find the Help files as well as other published resources on Adobe LiveMotion very useful.

In this example, a small navigation bar has been created in Adobe LiveMotion. As LiveMotion's greatest strength is its animation capabilities, the navigation bar does encapsulate a simple animation, shown in Figure 22.23 through 22.25.

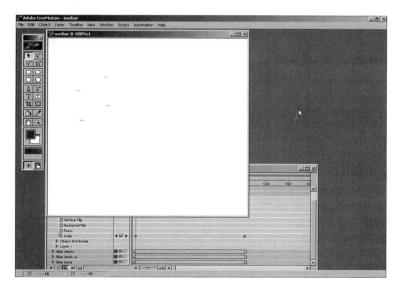

Figure 22.23
This animation starts with very small text...

Figure 22.24
...which grows...

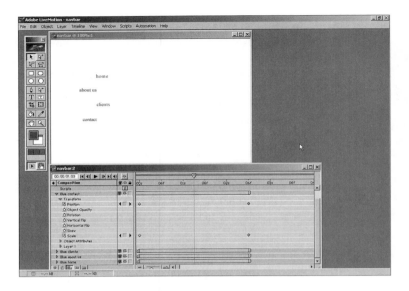

Figure 22.25
...and grows to become a navigation bar.

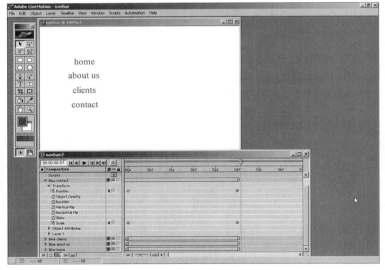

Once the graphic is complete, bring up the Export settings. You can accomplish this in one of two ways: by selecting File > Export Settings from or by choosing Window, Export from the command menu.

LiveMotion's slicing capability does not allow you to define the specific slices as Photoshop and Illustrator. Instead, LiveMotion automatically slices the components based on the structure of the objects in the page. This option is called AutoLayout and is available in the drop-down listings of the Export palette, shown in Figure 22.26.

Figure 22.26
Select AutoLayout from the drop-down listing in the Export Settings palette.

The AutoLayout feature will automatically slice the object into smaller pieces. You can select a blanket optimization setting for each of the objects in the piece (create one optimization setting that will automatically be applied to every slice) via Document settings. For pieces requiring custom optimization, you can specify object export settings.

To begin, the animation will be exported with one blanket optimization setting. In the AutoLayout section, simply define the settings with which you would like the piece optimized. In this case, the slices are optimized as a GIF of 12 colors. LiveMotion will automatically export every slice it generates with these settings. Take the time to explore the other options in the Export settings palette. The options, from left to right, include:

- Export HTML page toggles whether the HTML reassembling the slices should be generated.

- Export HTML report toggles the option to generate an HTML report along with the HTML page.

- Trim composition upon Export. When clicked, trims the composition as necessary.

- Preview Export Compression shows a preview version of what the images will look like while within LiveMotion when pressed. So, as you alter the compression settings, you'll see differences in the appearance of the slices.

- File Type: options include GIF, JPEG, PNG, and so on. Based on the selected file type, the next section of the palette will automatically be populated. For example, if GIF is selected, you'll have the option to reduce the number of colors, if JPEG is selected, the option to reduce the quality of the image will appear, and so on.

- Folder name provides a field in which you specify a directory name for the exported slices. Default is images.

In this case, the images are all going to be exported as a single animated GIF. LiveMotion will automatically make these animated GIFs for the slices that contain animations. In this case, transparency will be preserved (notice the pressed transparency option) and the images will be interlaced (as indicated by the progressive option)—that is to say that when loading, they will start out blurry and fade into focus as opposed to loading in pixel row by pixel row. Figure 22.27 shows that each slice will be a GIF of 12 colors, transparent, and interlaced.

Figure 22.27
The Document Settings specifies the default optimization settings for the page.

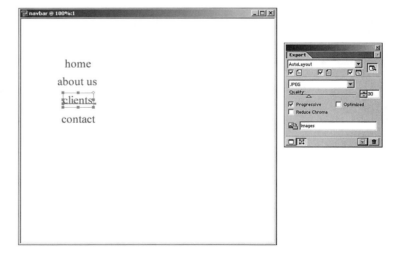

For any piece that you want to specify alternative optimization settings, select the object in the page, and click the Create new Object setting icon in the Export settings palette. When you press the new Object Setting icon, LiveMotion will automatically toggle you to setting the object's export settings rather than the Document's. You can tell by the icons in the lower-left corner of the Export palette. When clicked, the option on the left indicates that you are setting the optimization settings for the document and any object that has not been optimized otherwise. When the icon on the right is clicked, you are setting the currently selected object's optimization settings. Note that you will not be able to select the option to the right if you have not created a new Object Setting for each object you want to custom optimize. In Figure 22.28, the Clients item in the navigation bar is going to be exported as a JPEG. Keep in mind, as JPEGs do not support animation, the "Clients" text will lose any of the animation created within LiveMotion.

Figure 22.28
In this example, the object settings are being specified for an individual piece of the page.

When you are finished setting the Document (default) optimization settings as well as the settings for any particular objects, you can export the page by selecting File, Export or File, Export as. LiveMotion will generate all the necessary table code reassembling the slices into a cohesive unit, and export each individual image according to its optimization settings as set by the Export palette.

USING A PHOTOSHOP OR ILLUSTRATOR FILE AS A TRACING IMAGE

Whether you have created your mockup in Photoshop or Illustrator, you can use either of these programs' native file formats (PSD, AI, and AVI) as a tracing image within GoLive. A tracing image simply serves as a backdrop with which you can line all your page elements against, and is particularly useful for manually assembling pieces of the page together.

To specify a tracing image for a page, select Window, Tracing image from GoLive's command menu at the top of the interface. This palette houses all of the possible options for a tracing image, starting with its source. Simply browse to the location of the Photoshop or Illustrator file that will serve as the tracing image. Second, specify its opacity. Although you can adjust the opacity at any point in time, you may find it handy to select an opacity that is light enough that it is not distracting from what actually exists on the page.

In addition to indicating the source and opacity of the tracing image, the Tracing Image Palette provides a means for indicating where the tracing image should be positioned based on the upper-left corner. Likewise, the hand icon (when pressed) lets you click and drag the tracing image to the area of the page you desire.

Finally, the last option actually has to do with slicing. As you know, you actually have numerous options for how the reassembled slices are created. You could export the slices either from Photoshop or Illustrator as discussed throughout this chapter. Likewise, you could insert the page as a Smart Object and generate the custom optimized images within the GoLive interface as discussed in the previous chapter. The third and final option is to slice directly from the tracing image.

To slice directly from the tracing image, use the press the crop tool in the Tracing Image palette and click and drag a box around the area you would like to slice. Then, click the "Cut out" button on the Tracing Image palette. The Save for Web dialog box will open, with the cropped area available for you to optimize and export.

Scalable Vector Graphics (SVG) is a W3C XML-based language for rendering Vector graphics on the Web. The advantage of utilizing SVGs in place of the more traditional GIFs and JPEGs include the following:

- SVGs are comprised of nothing more than code, and therefore typically require smaller data size than an equivalent GIF or JPEG.

- SVGs are vector-based images, whereas the more traditional image formats are raster based (bitmaps). A bitmap is simply comprised of pixels and information about those pixels. If you zoom into the picture, you are in essence zooming into the pixels and the image loses its clarity. Likewise, an animated bitmap is truly a number of bitmaps played one after the other to give the illusion of animation. Vector-based images, on the other hand, are simply composed of paths based on mathematical formulas. As a result, zooming into a vector-based image does not compromise the image's quality, as the mathematical formula is redrawn at a bigger dimension.

- SVGs are actually written in an emerging XML language, an open source technology. Although proprietary programs can (and are often) used to produce SVGs, you could actually create one with a simple text editor. Likewise, you can edit the code without a proprietary program.

22

- SVG is based on XML source code that can be generated by a program or script on the server. This means that the vector graphics can actually be dynamically generated by a database. In addition, client-side technologies such as JavaScript can dynamically interact with the graphics based on the user's behaviors or actions.

Adobe has made quite a commitment to SVG, and has integrated support for the technology both in GoLive as well as in Illustrator.

> SVG is an emerging technology and the current generation of browsers does not support it without the assistance of an SVG viewer. At the time of this writing, Adobe has created an SVG viewer (a plug-in) that can be downloaded and installed on the user's computer to overcome this shortfall.

ADOBE SUPPORT FOR SCALAR VECTOR GRAPHICS

Adobe GoLive supports SVG in two ways: First, using the Basic Tab of the Objects Palette, you can click and drag an SVG object and embed that object into your page. Second, GoLive will open an SVG document in Layout, Source, and OutLine editor modes, letting you make any code modifications you deem necessary.

Embedding an SVG Element in an HTML Page

As mentioned, Adobe GoLive supports embedding an SVG element into an HTML page. Simply drag the SVG object from the Basics tab of the Inspector to the place in the page where you would like the SVG to appear.

The SVG object will appear in the HTML document, very much like the standard image placeholder appears after inserting an image into the document. Use the Inspector to set the File (the source of the SVG file), as shown in Figure 22.29. In addition, the Basic Tab of the Inspector provides a means for you to specify the height, width, and alignment of the object.

Figure 22.29
Once the SVG has been added to the page, use the Inspector to modify the source file for the SVG, as well as its height and width.

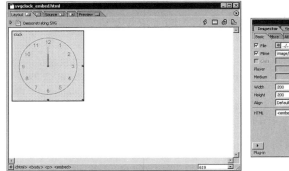

The default height and width is 100 pixels, regardless of what the SVG specifies. Open the code and locate the height and width attributes of the `<svg>` tag to determine the intended dimensions of the SVG.

The Inspector houses a few other tabs when the SVG is selected: the More, Attributes, and SVG tabs.

- The More tab allows you to provide the SVG a name and specify that the SVG should be hidden. Both of these features are specifically for dynamic JavaScript interactions you might add into the page.

- The Attribute tab provides access to the changing the SVG elements' attributes. Use this only if you are comfortable with the XML based SVG language.

- The SVG tab contains one option, the option to use a compressed SVGZ in place of this file. An SVGZ is a compressed version of the SVG that can be created with Adobe Illustrator 10. Although SVGZ is not endorsed by the W3C, you may find the smaller data size a worthy effect. In addition, SVGZ are unzipped (decompressed) automatically by the SVG Viewer. Note that both the SVG and the SVGZ files must be uploaded into the same directory of the Web Server.

After specifying the plug-in attributes, your SVG element is ready to go and is embedded into your page.

Opening an SVG in Adobe GoLive

When Adobe GoLive opens an SVG document, only three of the typical five tabs are available for viewing that SVG. The Document Window's Layout Tab, Source Editor, and Outline Editor can all be used to view and modify the SVG.

When in Layout View, the SVG's code is displayed and the various elements of the code can be selected in the Document Window and modified via the Inspector. The Inspector serves as an XML item Inspector, and provides a method for selecting the various tags in the XML document and exploring (as well as editing) each of those tags' attributes.

Click the triangle beside each element to access the nested elements. Each time an element is selected, the Inspector shows the attributes of that tag, and allows you to modify them, as demonstrated in Figures 22.30 and 22.31.

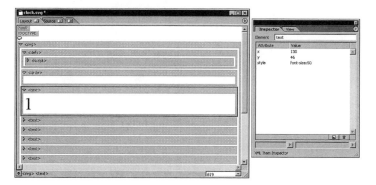

Figure 22.30
In this example, the font size of the number 1 has been changed to 50 via the Inspector and Layout View.

Figure 22.31

The numeral 1 now appears in the larger font size.

The Source View and Outline Editor behave as they normally would if just viewing a typical HTML page. The code can be accessed and modified in either of these views as well.

GoLive does support basic syntax checking of the SVG file. To check the syntax, open the file and view its contents in the Source Editor. Right-Click (Windows) or Ctrl-Click (Mac) and select Check Syntax from the resulting menu.

Errors will be generated and tracked in the Highlight Palette. Notice that if you select an error from the Highlight Palette, GoLive will also highlight the error in the source code, as shown in Figure 22.32.

Figure 22.32

GoLive can check the basic syntax of an SVG from the Source Editor. All errors will be displayed in the Highlight Palette.

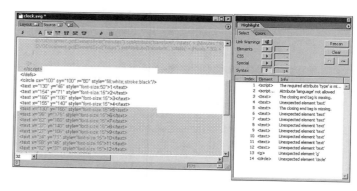

Creating SVGs

As hand-coding an SVG object can be very difficult, Adobe has also incorporated creating SVGs through Adobe Illustrator 10, easing the pressure on designers to become programmers.

Adobe Illustrator even has the power to slice SVGs, making the integration between GoLive, Illustrator, and their support of SVGs even more powerful.

Keep in mind that other features discussed (such as slicing an Illustrator file and maintaining a link to that Illustrator file via GoLive's Smart Objects) still hold.

In addition, if you plan on modifying your SVG by hand, you may find storing an SVG element as a snippet particularly helpful to avoid having to reinvent the code every time you want to add another path or piece of text.

TROUBLESHOOTING

Making the HTML Match the Mockup

When I look at my sliced and reassembled page via the browser, it does not render as I expect (see Figure 22.33). For example, although my page looked fine in Illustrator, when I opened it in a browser the layout didn't quite fit together.

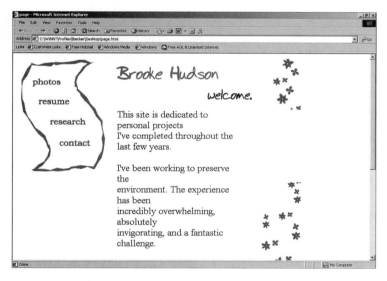

Figure 22.33
This HTML page didn't quite turn out the way it was meant to: notice the flowers are split in half.

Keep in mind that in HTML, there are a number of variables to contend with. In this example, the browser allows for user's to control the font-size of the text, making the page disjointed. Viewing the page with medium text renders the correct appearance, as shown in Figure 22.34.

You will most likely not have control over how your users will view the page. Will they be using Internet Explorer, Netscape Navigator, or some other browser? Are they equipped with PCs or Macs? Will they be viewing the page on a high or low resolution? Will they have adjusted the default font-sizes, tampered with the JavaScript settings for the browser, or view the page over a monitor that only supports 256 colors? The (hopefully!) large audience your site will cater to will each view the site differently as a result of these variables.

Figure 22.34
The broken image has been fixed by manually adjusting the rest of the HTML.

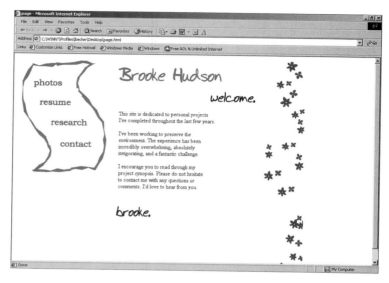

Your best bet is to try to make your page as fluid as possible and cater to one of the lower common denominators. For example, in this case the hard returns (the breaks) at the end of each line should be foregone for free-flowing text that fills the table data cell.

Other ways to manage the variables include creating images at 72dpi since most monitors are set to display at this resolution and doing so manages the data size that your users will have to download. In every case, be sure to always have contact information available to your users so that they may tell you of any shortcomings they find.

Maximizing Your Image Quality

My graphics aren't as clean and sharp in the exported version as when I view them in Illustrator.

Adobe Illustrator primarily works with Vector objects. When viewed, vector objects are sharp and clean because they are based on mathematical formulas. When you optimize an image for the Web—perhaps you create a GIF or a PNG—you are creating a version that is no longer vector, but is instead a bitmap. Bitmaps consist of information about pixels, their addresses, and their colors and rely on tiny squares of colors to display the image. These tiny squares can occasionally be not as clear as a vector image. However, most users will not notice a dramatic difference if the image is optimized well.

For more information, check out the Going Live section of this chapter.

Finding Elusive Options

I've opened the Attributes panel in Illustrator, but I can't find anything about a hotspot.

Any palette in Illustrator (or Photoshop, for that matter) can display any number of its options in a set of tiers. In Illustrator's Attributes palette, the image map information is stored in the second tier. So, click the small arrow in the bottom right corner of the Attributes tab to toggle through the different tiers until the image map options appear.

Dealing with Problematic Slices

I can't get my sliced table code to be clean. No matter how careful I am with the Slice Tool, extra tiny cells are created, making the page hard to manage and update.

This is a common result of using the Slice tool and its automatically generated HTML. Remember that utilizing the automatically generated HTML is a matter of choice. Although an incredibly handy feature, it is not an end-all solution. In fact, many developers instead use the slice tool and custom optimization to create the individual images quickly and easily, but rely on GoLive's interface to build the HTML finding that they have greater control over the page's layout. If you continuously have trouble with the table code generated by the slice tool, consider the benefits of recreating the page yourself in GoLive. Although this will increase your production time initially, you may find the time investment worth the resulting greater control and flexibility afforded to you in the long run.

Errors in SVG Files

When I try to open the SVG file in Adobe GoLive, I get errors about illegal characters, and the file opens with encoded text.

Illegal character encoding is often the result of authoring the code on one platform, then trying to open the file within Adobe GoLive while on another platform. However, this can be quickly solved. As an SVG file is simply code, open the graphic in a browser and View the Source of the file. Then, copy and paste the code into a new SVG file and save it. Open the new file in Adobe GoLive. The page should be free of illegal encoding.

GOING LIVE

When you save an Illustrator graphic as a GIF or JPEG, Illustrator rasterizes the graphic. That is to say that Illustrator converts the graphic to a bitmap, particularly at a resolution of 72dpi. So you will see differences between the vector version as it appears in Adobe Illustrator and the exported bitmap.

Illustrator also provides a means of previewing the bitmap version before you get to the exporting stage via its Pixel Preview mode. The advantages to checking out the image as it would appear as a bitmap are twofold: First, you'll have a better estimation of how the graphic will appear on the Web. Second, you'll actually be able to control the quality of the pixelation to some degree. This will be demonstrated shortly.

To view a graphic in pixel mode as shown in Figure 22.35, open the graphic and select View, Pixel Preview from the command menu. The image will automatically be rendered as it would appear as a bitmap. Although the differences may not be very obvious when the graphic is viewed at one-hundred percent, zooming into the image will make the differences apparent.

Figure 22.35
Viewing the graphic with Pixel Preview turned on (View Pixel Preview) provides a means for determining what the image would look like once converted to a bitmap such as a GIF or JPEG.

Vector graphics tend to appear much cleaner than raster (bitmapped) graphics, but how you align the image with the pixel grid can also modify the appearance of the lines once converted to a bitmap. Automatically, when you selected to preview the image in Pixel Preview, the object was snapped to an imaginary pixel grid of 72dpi. Snapping the object to the pixel grid generally will have cleaner effects. If you toggle the snap to pixel grid off (Select View, Snap to Pixel so that the checkmark indicating its selection disappears), you can click and drag an object so that it does not align with the pixel grid. The effects of anti-aliasing (the fading of pixels from one color to another) react differently when the object is snapped to a pixel versus when it is not. In the example shown in Figure 22.36, the object on the left is snapped to the pixel grid resulting an anti-aliasing edge that is more gradual, and will provide a smoother edge when viewed from a distance. The object on the right, on the other hand, will appear to have harsher edges as a result of not being snapped to the pixel grid.

As you can see, even where the object aligns with regards to the imaginary pixel grid can alter its appearance. In any case, be sure to test your images in bitmap mode to make sure the quality of your images doesn't suffer dramatically by converting it to a raster graphic.

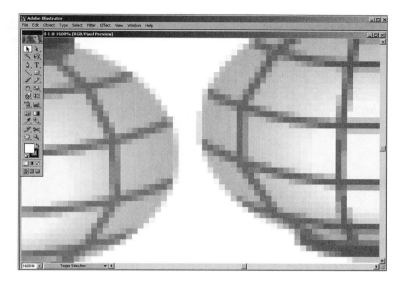

Figure 22.36
Here are two examples of anti-aliasing quality.

GOLIVE PLUG-INS

IN THIS CHAPTER

Extending GoLive with Plug-Ins   420

Downloading and Installing Existing Extensions   420

Creating Your Own Menu Items   423

Troubleshooting   429

Going Live   430

EXTENDING GOLIVE WITH PLUG-INS

While using GoLive's tools, have you ever found yourself wishing for more? Perhaps there's a particular command you commonly utilize that you wish was more accessible. Or what if there were an additional menu on the Objects palette that housed your most commonly used objects? Wouldn't it be nice to be able to customize GoLive to your specific needs?

If you ask, Adobe answers. Perhaps the greatest strength of Adobe's Web editor lies not in what the package provides for you at first launch, but the customizable flexibility the program lends to you as a developer. Right out of the box, Adobe GoLive provides the majority of the common tools that developers commonly need: inserting images, building tables, creating table styles, working with frames, FTP access, generating data-driven content, and so on. You name a conventional Web development task, and Adobe GoLive has served it to you on a silver platter. But surprisingly enough, you aren't limited to the tasks you see before you. Truth be told, Adobe GoLive is an exceptional software program that allows you to add in menu options and tasks particular to your team's development, all through GoLive's Extend Script SDK (Software Development Kit).

The GoLive Extend Script SDK provides a means for building additional floating palettes, initiating modal dialogs (those that halt the processing of the program until dealt with), incorporating more extensive menu options, and creating additional HTML elements that can be modified via the Inspector. Using JavaScript as the backbone scripting language for customizing GoLive, developers can use languages they're already familiar with to further augment GoLive's interface.

GoLive 6.0 in particular offers great support for the SDK, providing all the tools necessary to building your own extensions within the GoLive interface. Unlike previous versions of the program, when you install GoLive 6.0, the Extend Script SDK module is already installed. You should have little (if any) need to install additional components into the program. In the event that you find you do, updates to the SDK and documentation are available at www.adobe.com.

If you're biting your fingernails in horror, have no fear. Although you may not become a sophisticated developer overnight, you can benefit both by having a basic understanding of how the SDK works, as well as the extensions that have already been created and are accessible to you. Adobe's Developer Network and Xchange contain an online repository of extensions built by other developers, many of which are free. Perhaps the very extension you need has already been developed.

This chapter will begin by showing you where to download and how to install an existing extension. Then, the chapter will delve a bit deeper, showing you the very basics of creating an additional menu item, a palette, and so on. Once you've got the basics down, you can explore Adobe's extensive online documentation on creating customized pieces. With a little bit of work and effort, your version of GoLive will provide all the features you're wishing for.

DOWNLOADING AND INSTALLING EXISTING EXTENSIONS

At the most basic level, an extension is an HTML file stored appropriately within Adobe GoLive's directories. Of course there is a little more to it than that: specific tags and functions exist that you'll have to utilize to really extend GoLive's capabilities. But as more and more extensions are developed, you'll find it is generally best to see if someone has already done the work for you and so generously provided access to that work.

This is where Adobe's Xchange comes in, which you can access at `http://xchange.studio.adobe.com/`. For nominal user information, Adobe's Xchange provides an online repository of free modules and extensions that you can download and install. In fact, in addition to finding extensions, you'll find Integration Templates, JavaScript Actions, Site Templates, and Tutorials available for download.

For this example, Tomohiro Ueki's Insert Index Extension (listed under the Extensions category of "Other") will be demonstrated. Any extension found on Adobe's Xchange can be downloaded and installed in this manner, so if you like to follow along, go ahead and download one now. This particular extension was designed to parse the HTML page for header tags (Header One, Two, Three, Four, Five, and Six) and build a linked index based on those Headers.

Download an extension you're interested in from Adobe's Xchange. You'll need an Internet connection, as well as a username and password (which are free for providing some basic user information). If need be, unzip any compressed files.

In this demonstration, the file has been downloaded and extracted to the user's desktop. A folder named TMInsertIndex appears, with a single file, main.html, inside.

Don't be surprised if you open `main.html` in a browser and see nothing. The HTML page contains special tags for the purpose of the extension, tags that are interpreted and understood by GoLive, not by your typical browser.

To install the extension, the directory and its child file(s) must be put into the correct directory on your machine. Navigate to the program's files (to the directory entitled GoLive 6.0). Inside that directory you'll find a Modules folder, and inside that folder you should find a directory entitled Extend Scripts. The default contents of this folder are shown in Figure 23.1. This is the directory in which all active extensions should be stored. Each folder must be uniquely named and must contain at least one page named `main.html`. So, providing that the folder you've just downloaded does have a unique name in comparison to all other folders in the Extend Script directory, drag in the folder you downloaded and extracted from Adobe's Xchange.

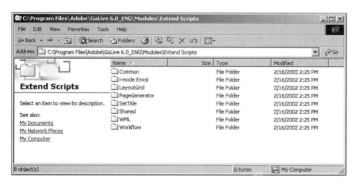

Figure 23.1
Inside the program files for Adobe GoLive, you'll find a set of directories with the path Adobe GoLive 6.0/Modules/Extend Scripts/. To install an extension, simply move the extension's folder to this directory.

Keep in mind GoLive loads the extensions every time it loads your program. This means that there are two different points you'll want to consider. First, when installing the extension, make sure the Adobe GoLive program is not running. If you don't, you will have to shut down and reopen GoLive to see the installed extension. Second, the more extensions you run, the more processing memory you'll use on your computer. If you find yourself not using an extension very often, consider uninstalling it (essentially removing it from the directory) to save your resources and speed GoLive's efficiency.

Now, open GoLive. The extension is installed and ready for use.

In the example shown in Figure 23.2, the extension added an "Insert Index" option under the Special menu. An extension could add menu items, floating palettes, modal dialogs, or objects to the Objects Palette. If you are testing the same extension, make sure that you have a page with headers—as mentioned, this particular extension parses the page for the headers and generates a linked index (or table of contents) based on the application of the header tags in the HTML.

Figure 23.2
This particular extension added an "Insert Index" option under the Special menu.

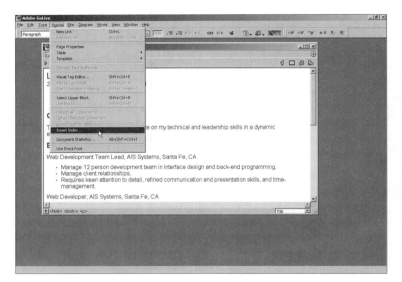

Based on how the extension is set up, you may need to answer some basic questions. In the example shown in Figure 23.3, questions that must be answered are with regard to which headers to use, where to put the generated results, and which results should be linked.

The result is displayed in Figure 23.4. Thanks to the hard work of a GoLive Xchange member, you don't have to hard-code each of those links! Using the extension not only saves on production time, but also the process for implementing the extension for other pages is quick and easy.

As you can see, an extension isn't really that fancy. Simply stated, an extension is a file named main.html that sits in the Adobe GoLive 6.0/Modules/Extend Scripts directory. The file itself holds code that interacts with GoLive and can alter the behavior of the program. Now that you're familiar with how to install the extension, explore how to create a basic extension within GoLive.

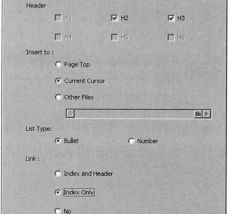

Figure 23.3
You may need to answer some basic questions for the extension to execute.

23

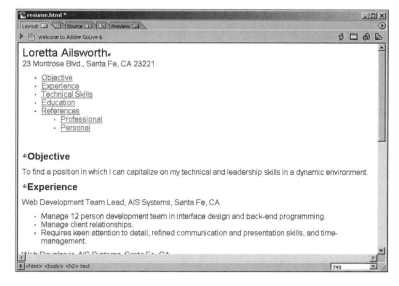

Figure 23.4
With a click of the added menu item, the extension generated a linked index to all of the headers within a page.

CREATING YOUR OWN MENU ITEMS

As mentioned, Adobe's SDK affords you the ability to create customized tool options, palettes, dialogs, and so forth. Although an extensive look into all of the possible options is well beyond the scope of this book, a few simple demonstrations might spark some interest and some excitement into the process. For that reason, the following provides a simple illustration of creating a customized GoLive extension.

This example will use GoLive to create an extension that adds to the existing menu items. In particular, a menu item named "Support" will be added that contains a few options: GoLive Interface, Technical, and Sanity (see Figure 23.5). Upon selecting any of these options, instructions will be provided as to where to find that support in an alert box, shown in Figure 23.6.

Figure 23.5
In this example, a Support menu will be added to the menu bar consisting of three options: GoLive Interface, Technical, and Sanity.

Figure 23.6
Take that, O overworked Web designer.

Although fairly simple in design, this demonstration will show you how easy it is to customize GoLive's interface. Prepare to be surprised by your own capability.

Start by opening a new page in GoLive. An extension is just an HTML page saved as `main.html`. The page contains JavaScript code and tags set up particularly for the purpose of extending GoLive's interface. And finally, the page will be saved in a uniquely named folder in GoLive's program files. But one step at a time. Start with the code.

Now that you have the new page open, leave the Layout Preview. You'll need to have direct access to the code, so click on the Source tab. Although not necessary, you may want to strip out the paragraph tags GoLive automatically inserts. In short, delete the opening (<p>) and closing (</p>) paragraph tags so the body tag is empty.

Now to start coding. Although you'll find a strong foundation in HTML and JavaScript helpful as you walk through this tutorial, it is not necessary. At the very least, you can follow through the code step-by-step to its final product, even if you're not the most savvy of programmers.

Every extension should be nested within a set of <jsxmodule> tags, and each module should be given a unique name. In this case, the code to start out with is as follows:

```
<jsxmodule name="customized_menu_example">

</jsxmodule>
```

The name is just a unique identifier, but must be unique as compared to all other module names. These module tags will hold all of the information necessary to carry out the action: both the JavaScripts that will be executed and the menu items that will be added. All of the executed scripts will be nested in a set of <script> tags, and all of the menu items will be nested in a set of <jsxmenubar> tags. Go ahead and add these tags now. You'll fill in the scripts and the menu items in just a moment:

```
<jsxmodule name="customized_menu_example">
    <script>
```

```
    </script>

    <jsxmenubar>
    </jsxmenubar>

</jsxmodule>
```

First, you'll see how to format the menu itself, so you'll fill in the needed information between the `<jsxmenubar>` tags. Then, using JavaScript, functionality will be added to the menu items by working between the `<script>` tags.

Adding a menu is simple. Between the `<jsxmenubar>` tags, add in a set of `<jsxmenu>` tags. Provide both a name and a title for this particular menu. The name is for JavaScript purposes, and must be unique as compared to all other names. The title attribute determines the text that will appear on the menu bar itself. In this case, the word "Support" will show up on the menu bar, so Support is the value of the title attribute. This portion of the code now should look like the following:

```
<jsxmenubar>
    <jsxmenu name="support_menu" title="Support">
    </jsxmenu>
</jsxmenubar>
```

For each item you want to add, simply add in a `<jsxmenuitem>` tag. In this case, three options will be available, so three `<jsxmenuitem>` tags have been added between the `<jsxmenu>` tags. For each item, both a unique name (for JavaScript purposes) and a title (how it will display to the user) are provided:

```
<jsxmenubar>
    <jsxmenu name="support_menu" title="Support">
        <jsxitem name="sup_golive" title="GoLive Interface">
        <jsxitem name="sup_tech" title="Technical">
        <jsxitem name="sup_sanity" title="Sanity">
    </jsxmenu>
</jsxmenubar>
```

This code generates the additional menu item on the menubar, titled Support. When Support is selected, three menu options will appear, the first titled "GoLive Interface," the second titled "Technical," and the third titled "Sanity." The menu option has now been configured, but functionality has not been added. To add in functionality, put your cursor between the `<script></script>` tags you added in earlier. Just like you walked through the configuration of the menu, you'll walk through the JavaScript that selecting one of these menu items will execute step-by-step.

When a menu item is selected, GoLive automatically calls a menuSignal event. So, if you want to write code that executes when the menu item is selected, store that code in a function called menuSignal.

```
<script>
    function menuSignal(menuItem) {
    }
</script>
```

Notice the opening and closing curly brackets that indicate the start and end of the executed code. Also, note the menuItem between the parentheses. When the menuItem is selected, a reference to the `<jsxmenuItem>` tag will be passed to the function and stored inside a variable named menuItem. For now, think of it as passing information. When the user selects the second menu item, information about that second menu item's tag will be passed to the function and stored inside a container referred to as menuItem. This will be used in the next step to extract the name of the selected menu item, as you'll see by the added code:

```
<script>
    function menuSignal(menuItem) {
        switch (menuItem.name) {
        }
    }
</script>
```

The added code initiates a switch, which will in turn provide alternative actions based on the selected menu item. Notice that the switch captures the reference to the menuItem selected, and specifically extracts the name of that menuItem. So, if the first item in the menu is selected, then the string `sup_golive` will be used to determine which alternative to take. If the second item is selected, then the string `sup_tech` will be used to determine the appropriate method of action. And finally, if the third menu item is selected, then the string `sup_sanity` will be used to determine what code should be executed.

Finally, add in the actions you want to be executed based on the menuItem selected. In this scenario, there are three alternatives, requiring a total of three cases. Based on the name of the menuItem selected, a different alert will be displayed:

```
<script>
function menuSignal(menuItem) {
  switch (menuItem.name) {
    case "sup_golive": alert("Please call Karen for GoLive Questions at
    ➥XXX.XXX.XXXX");
    break;
    case "sup_tech": alert("Please call Tanya for Technical Questions at
    ➥YYY.YYY.YYYY");
    break;
    case "sup_sanity": alert("You need a break. Go grab some coffee and we'll
      ➥see you in ten.");
  break;
  }
}
</script>
```

Notice the second command for each case: The break stops the JavaScript from continuing to the next line of code.

The code for the module, in its entirety, should appear as follows. Check for syntax mistakes, misspellings, missing curly brackets and semicolons, and so forth before continuing on.

```
<jsxmodule name="customized_menu_example">
  <script>
```

```
    function menuSignal(menuItem) {
      switch (menuItem.name) {
        case "sup_golive": alert("Please call Karen for GoLive
          ➥Questions at XXX.XXX.XXXX");
        break;
        case "sup_tech": alert("Please call Tanya for Technical
          ➥Questions at YYY.YYY.YYYY");
        break;
        case "sup_sanity": alert("You need a break. Go grab some
          ➥coffee and we'll see you in ten.");
        break;
        }
      }
  </script>

  <jsxmenubar>
    <jsxmenu name="support_menu" title="Support"">
      <jsxitem name="sup_golive" title="GoLive Interface">
      <jsxitem name="sup_tech" title="Technical">
      <jsxitem name="sup_sanity" title="Sanity">
    </jsxmenu>
  </jsxmenubar>
```

The code is complete; now the code simply has to be saved and stored appropriately within GoLive's program files.

Choose File, Save As from GoLive's menu. When saving this file, there are a few simple points you want to consider. First, the page must be saved as main.html. Second, the file must be saved in its own uniquely named subfolder and stored inside the appropriate place inside GoLive's program files. So, start by navigating to GoLive's program files. Once you find the GoLive 6.0 directory, you need to dig a bit deeper. In specific, go inside Modules/Extend Scripts. The complete path is GoLive 6.0/Modules/Extend Scripts/.

The Extend Scripts folder stores all extensions and plug-ins you want to add into GoLive. To add in the file you've just created, create an additional folder with a unique name. In this example, the new directory is called Support Menu, although its name is solely for file management purposes and will have no influence on how the program will treat the extension.

Go inside the newly created file folder, and save the page as main.html.

Close the page and close out of GoLive. Every time GoLive loads, it runs through the folders looking for the extensions and their behaviors. To see the results of your hard work, you'll need to exit out and reload GoLive.

When you reopen GoLive, you should see an additional command on the menu bar titled "Support". Select that option and test out the three menu items. Based on the menu item you selected, you should get a different alert informing you of who to contact with questions.

If you can't contain your excitement, consider modifying the code in main.html. You actually have much more extensive control over a menu: You can code for submenus, toggle a checkmark for those submenus, enable and disable menu items, and even add in items to the existing File, Special, Edit,

Type, and Help menus. Working from the previous demonstration, slight modifications have been made to incorporate some of these capabilities. Now, instead of being a part of its own Support menu, the item is listed under the previously existing Help menu. In addition, the three options (for GoLive Interface, Technical, and Sanity Support) are listed in a submenu titled "In House Support" under the Help menu, as shown in Figure 23.7.

Figure 23.7
The code for this extension was changed so that the added menu options are stored as a submenu under Help, In House Support.

Once the user has taken his sanity break, he can't take that break again. A checkmark and a candid message inform you of your mistake the second time you try to select Sanity, shown in Figure 23.8. Try a third time, and now the Sanity option is gone completely, as shown in Figure 23.9.

Figure 23.8
The code for the scripts were also modified to dynamically check the menu item and display a different alert once the Sanity option had already been checked.

Figure 23.9
By the third round, the Sanity option is completely disabled.

The only thing that has changed in this demonstration is the code, which has been modified slightly in both the `<scripts>` section and the `<jsxmenu>` section.

The differences in the menu's configuration are minor. Now, the `jsxmenu`'s `name` attribute references `help`, an existing menu in the GoLive interface. In addition, to get the three options to appear in a submenu, an additional set of `<jsxmenu>` tags have been added. The `<jsxitem>` tags are all nested directly between the additional opening and closing `<jsxmenu>` tag. Changes to the code are shown in bold:

```
<jsxmenubar>
    <jsxmenu name="help">
        <jsxmenu name="support_menu" title="In House Support">
            <jsxitem name="sup_golive" title="GoLive Interface">
            <jsxitem name="sup_tech" title="Technical">
```

```
            <jsxitem name="sup_sanity" title="Sanity">
        </jsxmenu>
    </jsxmenu>
</jsxmenubar>
```

The JavaScript has changed as well, but only in terms of the third case. First, an `if` conditional has been added, testing to see if the `sup_sanity` menu item within the `support_menu` has not been checked. If not, the alert runs, telling the user to take a break, and an additional line of code runs that dynamically checks the Sanity menu item.

```
case "sup_sanity":
if (!support_menu.sup_sanity.checked) {
    alert("You need a break. Go grab some coffee and we'll see you in ten.");
    support_menu.sup_sanity.checked = true;
} else {
    alert("Nice try. You already took your break. Get back to work.");
    menuItem.enabled = false;
}
break;
```

In the event that Sanity is checked, the statements between the else brackets run, alerting the user to his error and disabling the menu item.

```
case "sup_sanity":
if (!support_menu.sup_sanity.checked) {
    alert("You need a break. Go grab some coffee and we'll see you in ten.");
    support_menu.sup_sanity.checked = true;
} else {
    alert("Nice try. You already took your break. Get back to work.");
    menuItem.enabled = false;
}
break;
```

As you can see, once you get through the basics of working with GoLive's SDK, extending that capability is simply an issue of digging a little deeper into the options. As you go forward, you'll find a strong foundation in HTML, JavaScript, and perhaps a little insight into XML will prove a fantastic starting ground, but is hardly required, for building customized extensions.

TROUBLESHOOTING

Finding an Installed Extension

I've downloaded and installed an extension, but I can't find it.

First, make sure that you've shut down and restarted GoLive. Your operating system need not shut down, but the program itself must reboot in order to pick up all extensions.

If that doesn't do the trick, keep digging. Unfortunately, many of the extensions leave little description as to what would install access to that extension. Your options are to keep digging or, if you're feeling extra savvy, you might open the main.html page for that extension and take a look at the code.

If the extension is written in the form purported by Adobe, the code in which you're most interested is most likely the code directly beneath the closing `</script>` tag. For example, in the installed extension described in the first part of this chapter, the information was provided within the first three lines of code following the `</script>` tag:

```
</script>
<jsxmenubar>
<jsxmenu name="special" title="none">
    <jsxitem name="TM_InsertIndex" title="Insert Index..." dynamic>
```

All GoLive's extension tags are prefixed with `jsx`. More important to solving the mystery were the tags used. `<jsxmenubar>` indicated that it would be added to the menu. `<jsxmenu>` provided a little more detail, showing that it would be inserted on the Special menu. And finally, the `<jsxitem>` tag provided the text label for the extension, "Insert Index".

Other tags you might run across include the following: `<jsxdialog>` for modal dialog boxes, `<jsxpalette>` for additional floating palettes, and `<jsxinspector>` for adding capabilities to GoLive's existing Inspector. As you can see, many are fairly intuitive.

Finally, if you've downloaded a fairly new extension, consider looking on Adobe's site for information about the latest and greatest SDK. Although as of this writing, GoLive 6.0 ships with all of the installed SDK support necessary, technology is ever-changing. Perhaps the extension you desire needs additional SDK information installed. Instructions on how to do this are available on Adobe's site, along with documentation and instructions on Adobe GoLive 6.0's SDK.

GOING LIVE

If you're itching for more examples on how to code and implement other extensions, look to Adobe's online SDK documentation. The documentation and reference push close to 300 pages, but offer a great resource (even for beginners) for developing extensions.

To get more comfortable with the variables you can toy with as an SDK developer, consider downloading, installing, and experimenting with many of the existing extensions. Chances are many of them are pretty complex, but familiarizing yourself with how an extension is set up will definitely help in the process.

LASSO STUDIO FOR ADOBE GOLIVE

IN THIS CHAPTER

About Lasso Studio   **432**

Installing the Lasso Suite   **432**

Scoping Out the Functionality   **439**

Creating Your Databases   **439**

Troubleshooting   **462**

Going Live   **463**

ABOUT LASSO STUDIO

One of the most complete and useful GoLive extensions is Lasso Studio for GoLive, a visual development environment for the Lasso Web Data Engine. Lasso Studio takes advantage of the rich Web editing capability of GoLive and extends it with wizards and additional tag support for building Lasso-powered Web sites.

Lasso, from Blue World Communications of Bellevue, WA, is a popular application server for database-driven Web applications. Lasso is *middleware*, a term that describes a piece of software that sits between the Web server and the database, converting user requests from the Web server into database requests, and formatting the database results into meaningful Web pages that are transmitted back to the user by the Web server.

Lasso works by adding markup tags to HTML pages that contain database commands and other dynamic tags processed by the Lasso Web Data Engine (WDE). This markup language is called LDML, or Lasso Dynamic Markup Language. Lasso Studio for GoLive adds support for these tags to GoLive. It also provides a number of *builders*, or wizards, for creating individual Lasso-compliant forms, and even entire database-driven Web sites.

When a Web server receives a form submitted by a Web user that contains Lasso tags, or receives a request for a page with a filetype extension defined as a Lasso page, the Web server passes the request off to the Lasso WDE. Lasso then does its business: performs any needed communication with a database, sets or retrieves cookies, makes any mathematical calculations or conditional checks, and then uses a specified *format file* (a page created by Lasso Studio for GoLive containing LDML tags) to generate a page of finished HTML containing the requested data that is then returned to the user by the Web server.

Lasso Studio works with your database by referring to a "snapshot" file. This little text file contains all the information about your databases and the fields in them. Thus you can work with your Site even when a live connection to the databases is not available. One of the first things you'll do when working in Lasso Studio is create the snapshot file.

Trial versions of Lasso Studio for GoLive and the Lasso Web Data Engine can be downloaded from Blue World Communications, `http://www.blueworld.com`.

INSTALLING THE LASSO SUITE

When you install Lasso Studio, it's going to install the Web Data Engine along with its accompanying bells and whistles, and it's also going to install Lasso Studio for GoLive into your existing Adobe GoLive installation. So it's important that you have already installed GoLive first.

It's also critical that you have already installed your Web server. For the purposes of this book, it's assumed that you are running Microsoft Internet Information Services (IIS) on Windows, or Apache on Mac OS X. Your Web server should be fully installed, but switched off.

Let's dive right in and install Lasso Studio. Adobe GoLive will never be the same again.

> Lasso Studio can be uninstalled at any time, leaving your GoLive installation as fresh and pristine as the day it came off the CD-ROM.

Installing Lasso Studio on Windows

The Windows installer is pretty straightforward. In fact, the installation of all the extra stuff into GoLive will happen without you even knowing it.

The installer will pause when it puts the Lasso resources into your Web server folder, and here it helps to have a standard installation of IIS on your machine, using IIS' default folders and directory locations.

You'll be asked to select your data source (see Figure 24.1), and here you'll want to check the FileMaker radio button, since that's the database we're using in this exercise.

> To turn IIS off to permit this installation, it's not enough to simply choose "stop" from the Personal Web Manager system tray icon. You actually have to go into Services (in Administrative Tools) and turn the World Wide Web Server service off.

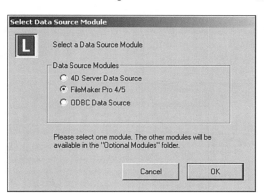

Figure 24.1
Select the data source you want to use.

24

Next you'll be asked to specify the IIS directory, as shown in Figure 24.2. This is not the Web site's root directory, but rather one level up from that: the directory that contains the root directory. Usually this is C:\InetPub, and Lasso pre-selects this by default. Hopefully you won't have to change it.

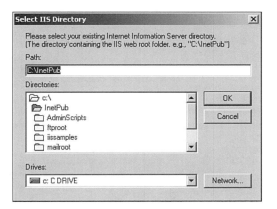

Figure 24.2
Select the IIS directory.

Next you will need to specify the Scripts directory as shown in Figure 24.3, and by default, this has been set to C:\InetPub\scripts. Once again, you probably should not have to change this.

Figure 24.3
Select the IIS scripts directory.

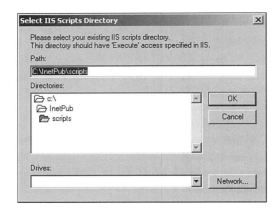

Last, you need to specify the root directory of the server as shown in Figure 24.4. In a standard IIS installation this is C:\InetPub\wwwroot, and that's what the Lasso installer has selected by default. Click OK unless you need to change this.

Figure 24.4
Select the Web root.

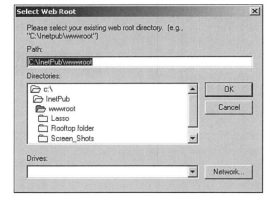

Around this time, Lasso will ask you for your serial number. Evaluation serial numbers, which make Lasso fully functional for 30 days, are available at no charge from Blue World at http://www.blueworld.com.

The installer should now finish up, and it will go ahead and put all the Lasso Studio stuff in with your GoLive installation.

You can now switch the World Wide Web Server service back on to reactivate IIS. Once that's done, the Personal Web Manager should reappear in the system tray, and then we can select it to make one final setting. Right-click on the Personal Web Manager and select Properties.

When the Main screen appears, click on Advanced. You'll notice that the <Home> directory is highlighted by default. Click the Edit Properties button, and you should see the screen shown in Figure 24.5.

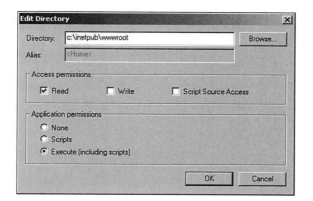

Figure 24.5
Edit Directory inside the Personal Web Manager.

You'll need to click the Execute (including scripts) radio button in the Application Permissions section. This will allow Lasso to operate within this Web site.

Once that's done, click OK to finish. If you haven't already, start the Web services back up again. You're officially up and running.

Installing Lasso Studio on Mac OS X

The installation of Lasso into Apache on Mac OS X requires less configuration checking than the Windows install. Verify that Web Sharing is turned off in your Sharing system preferences panel, as shown in Figure 24.6. Then you can launch the Lasso Studio installer

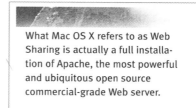

What Mac OS X refers to as Web Sharing is actually a full installation of Apache, the most powerful and ubiquitous open source commercial-grade Web server.

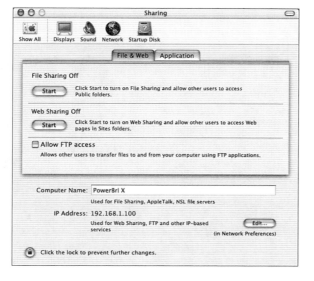

Figure 24.6
The Web Sharing system preferences panel in OS X. Notice that Web Sharing is turned off.

The installer will put all the Lasso stuff where it belongs in the Apache folders, and also install all the GoLive extensions to create the complete Lasso Studio for GoLive plug-in.

The installer will also ask you for your serial number. Evaluation serial numbers, which make Lasso fully functional for 30 days, are available at no charge from Blue World at `http://www.blueworld.com`.

When the installation has completed, go back to the Sharing system preference panel and activate Web Sharing. It takes a moment or two to start up, and once it does, Lasso and Apache are both up and running.

Installing FileMaker Pro

FileMaker Pro is quite simple to install, with little configuration needed. The installer CD, or the downloadable demo installer from FileMaker's Web site, will do almost everything necessary.

It's important at this point to understand the Web Companion, a component of FileMaker that is installed by default. Web Companion is in fact a lightweight Web server designed to make FileMaker data available over the Web, or in this case, available to the Lasso Web Data Engine. This means that we're going to be running two Web servers in tandem on the same machine. This is okay for our little development environment, but would not be recommended for a production environment. In production, each component should ideally be placed on a separate machine, for maximum performance, stability, and scalability.

Running two servers on the same machine also produces a conflict. Both servers are trying to use the same resources to do the same thing, which doesn't work. Specifically, they're both trying to serve data over port 80, the standard port for HTTP servers. We'll fix this by going into FileMaker's configuration and setting Web Companion to serve on port 591, which is an alternate port reserved by FileMaker Inc. for Web Companion. This is only necessary because we're running both Web servers on the same machine for development purposes, and is not something you would do if FileMaker's Web Companion is the only server running on the machine.

Figure 24.7
Web Companion's configuration screen, showing the Web server set to port 591. Your IP Guest Limit will either show 10 or Unlimited, depending on whether you're using FileMaker Pro or FileMaker Pro Unlimited.

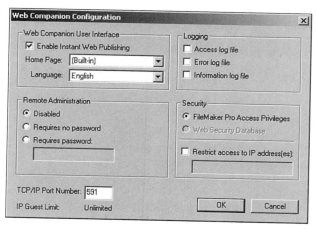

To do this, go into FileMaker's Edit menu and under Preferences, select Application. Click the Plugins tab, select Web Companion (make sure it's checked), and click Configure. Set the TCP/IP port number to 591, as shown in Figure 24.7. Click through all the OK's to get out of there, and you're done.

Later, when we create the FileMaker databases, we'll share them over port 591, and Lasso will be able to access them.

Configuring Lasso

Now let's tell Lasso where to find these databases. Lasso is running now, so open your Web browser to http://(your IP address)/lasso. In most cases, it should also work if you user localhost or 127.0.0.1 in place of a valid IP address. See Figure 24.8.

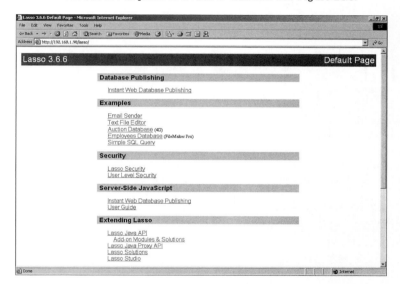

Figure 24.8
Lasso's default page provides access to administrative functions.

To get to the database configuration screen, click the link called Lasso Security.

If this is your first time administering Lasso on this computer, Lasso will require you to select an Administrator password. Choose whatever you like (something you'll remember), and Lasso will guide you through this process.

At the bottom of the Lasso Security screen is a section called Global Administration. Click the link in that section called FileMaker Remote, shown in Figure 24.9.

Here is where we're going to tell the Lasso Web Data Engine where it can find the FileMaker databases. In our case, that's right here on the same machine, running on port 591. So in that top field under Add a New FileMaker Host, type in your machine's IP address followed by a :591. In most cases, you can also type localhost:591 or 127.0.0.1:591. If your FileMaker databases reside on a different machine, type that machine's IP address in instead, and you have installed FileMaker separately, you probably did not need to switch Web Companion to port 591, so you can omit the :591.

Figure 24.9
Lasso's FileMaker Remote configuration screen is used to specify
the location of your FileMaker
databases.

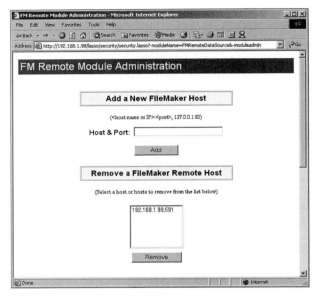

The only other thing to do is to enable whatever database actions we anticipate Web visitors needing. Our Site's users will need to initiate actions that result in database records being searched,
added, updated, and deleted. So go to the bottom of the Lasso Security screen again and click on All
Users Settings. Check the boxes for Search, Add, Update, and Delete, as shown in Figure 24.10, and
click the Update button. Now Lasso will allow Web visitors to perform these actions.

Figure 24.10
All Users security settings.

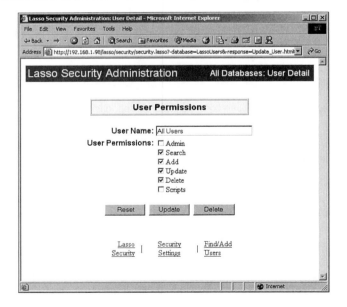

Once this has been done, the complete Lasso configuration should be up and running. All that's missing is a developed Web application to run in this wonderful new environment. So let's keep moving.

SCOPING OUT THE FUNCTIONALITY

We've arrived at the point in our database-driven Web site where we need to know exactly what the site is going to do. This is necessary to create the databases and the Lasso format files. Let's start with a set of business requirements that will detail the site's functionality from a layman's perspective. Once the business requirements are in place, technical requirements can be created that translate the business requirements into the nitty gritty specifics of what needs to be accomplished.

Table 24.1 lists some very simplified business requirements and the related technical requirements. The site we'll build will permit fans of Rooftop Records to create membership accounts, specify their own music tastes, and then search for other members with similar tastes.

Table 24.1   Lasso Site Requirements

Business Requirements	Technical Requirements
Allow a Web user to become a club member by creating an account containing his personal information.	Database: a Members database that stores information about each member. Application: a form that users can fill out to create a new member record in the Members database.
Maintain a list of musical genres that can be used to classify songs and club members' tastes.	Database: a Genres database containing a list of musical genres. Application: in some places throughout the site it will be necessary to list all the genres in the database. No Web interface to edit or modify this database.
Allow club members to specify which musical genres they like.	Database: a join file, Likes, will link each member with each genre. For example, if a member likes three genres, three Likes records will be created. Application: in a member profile area, a member should be able to view all of the genres he already likes, select new genres, and deselect his existing choices. This will create or delete records in the Likes table.
Allow club members to search for other club members based on similar musical interests.	Application: a member should be able to search the Likes database to retrieve information about members who share those Likes.

CREATING YOUR DATABASES

For this example we'll use FileMaker Pro databases. FileMaker is a user-friendly workgroup database program, and has quite a large following among the Lasso community. Databases can be easily constructed in a point-and-click interface without knowledge of SQL, yet the data can be accessed by industrial-strength application servers, or reside comfortably within an enterprise. A trial version of FileMaker Pro can be downloaded from http://www.filemaker.com.

The first thing to do is to construct the three database tables our system needs, and set them to be available to the Lasso Web Data Engine.

Select New Database from FileMaker's File menu. Name it *Members* and save it in a convenient place. The Define Fields screen will appear.

Create the fields shown in Figure 24.11. This is the basic information we're going to collect about each member in our club: their name, email address, age, and gender. The member_id field will be used as a relational key to uniquely identify each record, and match it to related records in the Likes database. The screen_name will allow users to choose fun online names, to allow them to participate in chats and forums without the need to be identified by their actual names.

Figure 24.11
This is the Define Fields screen for the Members database, listing all the fields to be created.

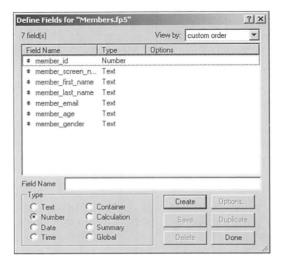

Next we'll create the Genres database. Choose New Database from the File menu again, and follow the same steps, this time creating the fields shown in Figure 24.12.

Figure 24.12
This is the Define Fields screen for the Genres database, listing all the fields to be created.

The genre_id field will be the unique identifier. genre_name will be the type of music, and genre_description will provide a place for Rooftop Records' site editors to give lively descriptions of all the new types of music out there.

Last, we'll create the Likes database. This join file, as you database aficionados will know, provides back-end data structure rather than storing any actual data. The Likes records link members to genres. If a member likes three kinds of music, then we'll create three Likes records, each one containing the member's ID and each genre's ID. This type of structure allows unlimited flexibility, as members can specify as many genres as each likes, without the need to modify the database structure to accommodate different members. See Figure 24.13.

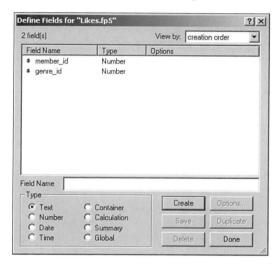

Figure 24.13
This is the Define Fields screen for the Likes database, listing all the fields to be created.

Making the Databases Accessible to Lasso

Before we can continue, it's very important to take a couple of extra steps with our FileMaker databases to make them visible to Lasso, and a little bit easier to work with. The first and most important thing to do is to make certain that FileMaker's Web Companion is sharing each database, so Lasso can see it.

To do this, go to FileMaker's File menu and select Sharing (see Figure 24.14). In the Companion Sharing section of this screen, check Web Companion. You will need to do this once for each of the three database files we've just created. Now FileMaker's Web Companion is sharing them and making their data available over the network to Web browsers or other applications, such as Lasso, that use TCP/IP.

One additional step is not absolutely necessary, but it makes things a bit simpler and makes your FileMaker data sources conform to standard naming conventions a little bit better. Lasso and other application servers see FileMaker database files each as a separate data source, and the layouts within FileMaker as database tables. Each database action that we initiate with Lasso will need to specify the table being operated on, and thus it's useful to have a simple and compliant name for each. By default, FileMaker names its first layout *Layout #1*, which contains a space and a pound sign. These characters need to be URL encoded, and so to avoid this mess, we're going to rename each layout *web*.

Figure 24.14
Use FileMaker's Sharing screen to share each FileMaker database with Web Companion, making it accessible to Lasso.

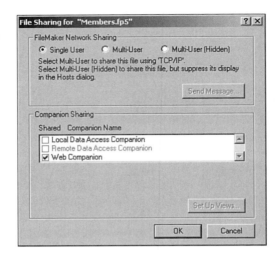

From FileMaker's View menu, select Layout Mode. Then select Layout Setup from the Layouts menu, as shown in Figure 24.15. Name the layout web. Do this for each of our three database files.

Figure 24.15
Use the Layout Setup screen in FileMaker to change the name of each layout to web.

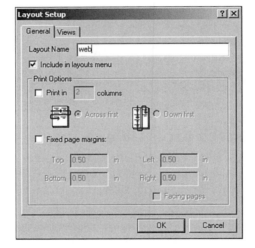

When you're done, your Members database should look something like Figure 24.16. Note the layout name in the top of the status bar on the left side of the FileMaker window.

That's it. Your databases are all set; in fact, you shouldn't ever need to touch them again. You might want to minimize FileMaker at this point to get it out of the way. You must leave it running, though; otherwise Lasso will not be able to access the databases.

The name "web" is a convention among Lasso developers, particularly those accustomed to working in FileMaker. You can name the layouts whatever you like, but if you want to be hip with the in crowd, web is the only way to go.

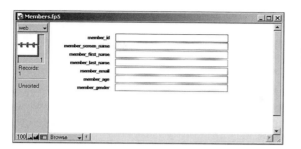

Figure 24.16
Here is what the completed Members database should look like (sans data).

Lasso Studio for GoLive

The first new thing you'll notice in GoLive is a new menu: Lasso Studio. We'll use most of these menu items later in this chapter. Before all of the features in this menu become available, you'll need to enter your serial number one more time using the Register Lasso menu item at the bottom of the Lasso Studio menu.

There are also three new tabs on the Objects palette: Lasso Form, Lasso Data Access, and Lasso Programming. Figures 24.17 through 24.19 show what's on these new tabs.

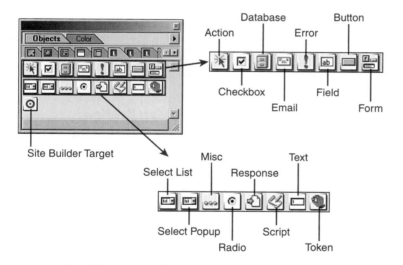

Figure 24.17
The Lasso Form tab.

The following are the objects on the Lasso Form type, going from left to right and top to bottom:

- Action Input: A hidden tag telling Lasso what type of action to perform in the current form.

- Checkbox Input: A checkbox input field.

- Database Input: A hidden tag telling Lasso what database table to act upon with the current form.

- Email Input: A hidden tag instructing Lasso to send an email.

- Error Input: A hidden tag telling what response file to use in the event of an error.

- Field Display: A tag that will be replaced by a field's current contents.

- Button: A tag to place a Lasso connected button on the layout.

- Form: A tag to create a Lasso connected form.

- Select List: A multiple selection menu input field.

- Select Popup: A single selection pop-up menu input field.

- Misc Input: A generic input field.

- Radio Input: A radio button input field.

- Response Input: A hidden tag telling Lasso response file to use.

- Script Input: A hidden tag telling Lasso to run a FileMaker Pro script.

- Text Input: A text entry field.

- Token Input: A tag recalling the value of a token set on the previous page.

- Site Builder Target: A tag specifying the location of the Form Builder's output in a template file.

Figure 24.18
Lasso Data Access tab.

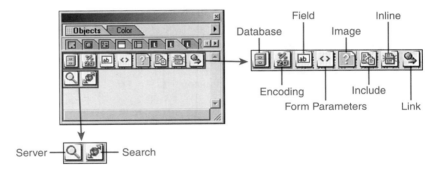

The following are the objects on the Lasso Data Access tab, going from left to right and top to bottom:

- Database Object: A tag telling Lasso what database to act upon.

- Encoding Object: A tag telling Lasso what type of encoding to use.

- Field Object: The contents of a field from the database.

- Form Param Object: A tag to specify the parameters used in the previous form.

- Image Object: An image from the database.

- Include Object: A tag to specify a server-side include file.

- Inline Object: A tag to insert a Lasso inline action.

- Link Object: A tag to insert a link.

- Search Object: A tag to specify a search action.

- Server Object: A tag to specify the server to be used.

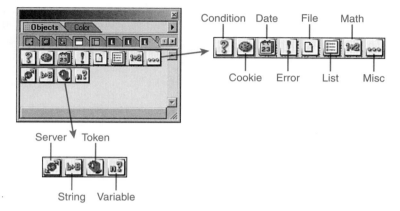

Figure 24.19
Lasso Programming tab.

The following are the objects on the Lasso Programming tab, going from left to right and top to bottom:

- Condition Object: Inserts a conditional branch, such as an If statement.

- Cookie Object: : Inserts a tag to read or write a cookie.

- Date Object: : Inserts a date.

- Error Object: : A tag that will be replaced by the current error.

- File Object: : Specifies a file action, such as reading or writing to a text file.

- List Object: : Specifies a list or array.

- Math Object: : A tag to perform any of various math functions.

- Misc Object: : A generic programming tag that you can customize.

- Server Object: : A tag to specify the server to be used.

- String Object: : Used to perform string operations.

- Token Object: : Used to set and read token variables passed from page to page.

- Variable Object: : Used to set and read variables used within a single page.

As discussed earlier, the very first thing GoLive is going to need is a snapshot file, containing all the information about the databases we're going to work with. The snapshot file is created using the Lasso Configuration Wizard, which is shown in Figure 24.20. Select it now.

Figure 24.20
The Lasso Configuration Wizard helps you set up and configure Lasso Studio.

Enter your IP address as shown, and click Create Snapshot File. This file will scan your FileMaker databases, and store all the information about the available fields.

Creating the Membership Registration Screens

Referring back to our requirements document, our starting point will be an interface for a user to create a membership record for himself. Boiled down to its raw elements, this will be a simple function of adding a record to a database.

One of Lasso Studio's builders will help us create the format files necessary to add a record, but first we want to create a template page for Lasso to base each of the format files on. The Site Builder Target tool on the Lasso Form tab of the Objects palette provides a way to do this. We'll start with a basic Rooftop Records page, and then drag in the target where we'd like Lasso to insert the form object on each page (see Figure 24.21). Save this file somewhere convenient.

Figure 24.21
This basic Rooftop Records page is to be used as a template, with the Site Builder Target dragged in.

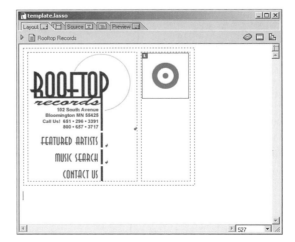

Now go to the Lasso Studio menu and launch the Lasso Site Builder. Figure 24.22 shows the Lasso Site Builder screen, where you can select your destination folder for the Lasso format files to be created, and also specify the template page you just created. Then, in Figure 24.23, tell the Builder what type of site you'd like to create: a site to permit the searching of records, or a site designed to add records.

Figure 24.22
Start with the Lasso Site Builder Screen.

Figure 24.23
Choose a Site Action.

On the next screen, shown in Figure 24.24, the Lasso Database Selector allows you to choose the database the current action will be performed upon. For our exercise, choose the Members database.

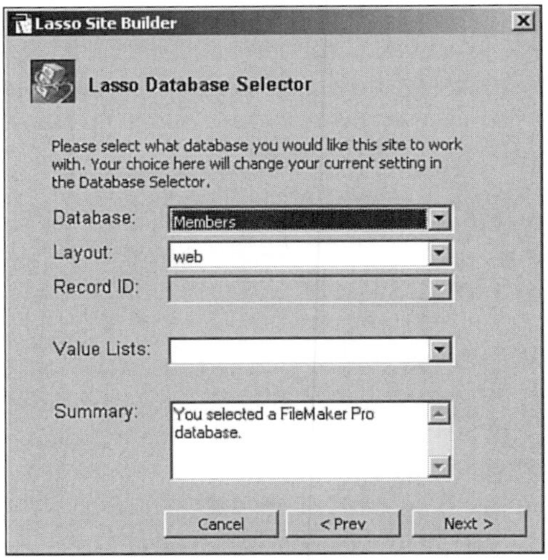

Figure 24.24
Specify a database using the
Lasso Database Selector.

Figure 24.25 shows the Create Add Page screen. On this screen, specify what you'd like the page title to be, what you'd like the file name to be (I changed it from add.lasso to add_member.lasso to differentiate it from other add pages we're likely to create for our site), the fields you'd like to appear on the form, and whether the response page will be for display only (field contents you just added appear hard coded on the screen) or for update (field contents you just added will appear in editable fields, allowing the user to make changes to the record just created).

Figure 24.25
Select your database fields to add
with the Create Add Page.

Figure 24.26 shows the Create Display Page screen. This defines the response page we'll see after creating the record. Specify the page title, a name for the format file, and the fields you'll want to appear on that screen.

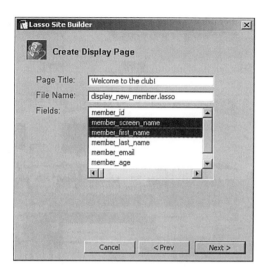

Figure 24.26
Specify the response page on the Create Display Page screen.

After a final review screen, the Lasso Site Builder will create all the format files necessary to allow a new member to add their own record to the Members database. This is the simplest type of form, so only three LDML pages are required: the add form, the response page seen after a successful add, and an error page, shown if the add fails for any reason.

Figure 24.27 shows how the pages will look with Lasso's default form inserted where the target had been in the template page.

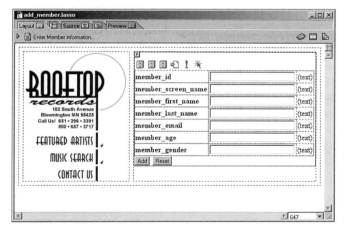

Figure 24.27
The completed site, as built by the Lasso Site Builder.

Before we try it out, we're going to make a few changes. Change the member_id field from a text field to a hidden field, and insert [RandomNumber:Min='111111111111',Max='999999999999'] for the value. Lasso will replace this LDML tag with a 12-digit random number, which is an easy way of generating unique identifiers for new records. Change the member_gender field to radio button selections for M or F, and make whatever other aesthetic improvements you want to the form. You can also take this chance to make any improvements you want to the display_new_member.lasso response page.

It's actually fully functional now. Open your browser and go to `http://(your IP address)/rooftop/add_member.lasso` and you'll see it in action (see Figure 24.28). Fill in the form and submit it, and you'll see the reply in Figure 24.29, showing the two fields, member_last_name and member_screen_name, that we selected in the Site Builder in Figure 24.26. Then you can check the FileMaker database (see Figure 24.30) and see that the record has been created!

Figure 24.28
The tweaked Add form in action.

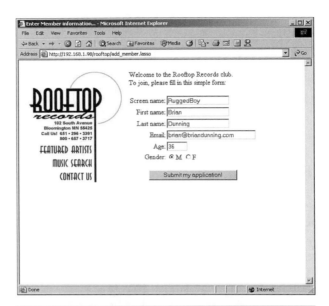

Figure 24.29
Presto! The response page shows the two fields specified in the Site Builder.

Figure 24.30
The newly created record appears in FileMaker.

Before we move on, we're going to take one additional step. We want the site to be able to easily identify each user. So we're going to set a cookie with the `member_id` that was just created. Lasso allows us to do this with a single piece of code. Pull up the `display_new_member.lasso` page. Go to the Lasso Programming tab on the Objects palette and drag the Cookie object anywhere onto the page. You can use the Inspector to set the parameters, but some Lasso programmers will find it faster to just type it into the source. We'll name the cookie `member_id` and fill it with the contents of the field that was just created. The finished LDML will read
`[Cookie_Set:'member_id'=(Field:'member_id')]` and it can go anywhere on the page.

Creating the Genres Page

Now let's take a look at the genres. I typed in sixteen musical genres, assigned them `genre_id` values by using FileMaker's Replace feature to put serial numbers in, and made up some descriptions for each genre.

Visualize a page that lists all the available genres, with a link be each to select or deselect. The most obvious element here is the list of all the genres, so we'll start with that.

Rather than using one of Lasso's Builders, we're going to create this one from scratch. Start with your template page and save it as `genres.lasso`. We'll use what's called an Inline search to retrieve the sixteen genres. An inline search contains all the code to specify the search parameters, execute the search, and display the results all on the same page. Multiple inlines can be executed on any page. This allows a great deal of functionality to be built into a small number of pages.

First, let's tell Lasso that we're going to work with a different database now. Grab the Lasso Database Selector from the Lasso Studio menu and change the database selection to Genres, as shown in Figure 24.31. This little tool will become your best friend as you work with Lasso Studio.

Figure 24.31
Use the Lasso Database Selector to work with a different database.

Go to the Lasso Data Access tab in the Objects palette and drag the Inline object into your genres.lasso page. Select the first of the four little icons that appears in your document, and you'll see all the default parameters appear in the Lasso Tag Inspector, as shown in Figure 24.32.

Figure 24.32
The Lasso Tag Inspector shows the Inline search action high-lighted in the Page window.

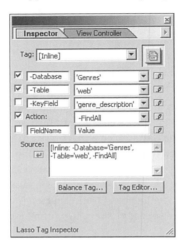

Check the three name/value pairs that we're going to need: -Database = Genres, -Table = web, and Action = -FindAll. Then click the little red return arrow icon, and the code for this inline will be inserted into your page.

The two icons in the middle are the [Records] and [/Records] blocks. Whatever appears between these tags will be repeated once for each record returned by the inline search.

Use GoLive's tool to create a four column, single row table, and move the opening and closing inline tags before and after it. Then go into source and move the [Records] blocks to outside of the <TR> and </TR> tags, but *inside* the <TABLE> and </TABLE>. This will put your [Records] blocks in no-man's land (see Figure 24.33); they will no longer appear in layout view, so you'll just have to remember that they're there. What this will accomplish is to display sixteen rows, one for each record returned by the search, and all inside a single table. Make sense? Figure 24.33 shows how the source might look.

Figure 24.33
This is the source code for the table rows inside the [Records] blocks.

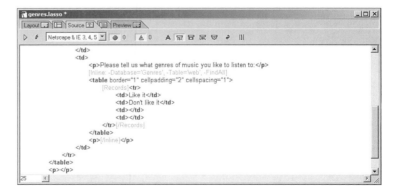

Drag the `genre_name` and `genre_description` fields in from the Lasso Data Access palette, and for each one, select the field from the Inspector.

Run it by pointing your Web browser to `genres.lasso`, and you should see all your genres listed for you.

The next step is to create the real guts: the creation and deletion of Likes records. There are a variety of user interfaces that could be used here. The one we'll choose will say "Like it" and "Don't like it" on every genre. The chosen one will be bold; the other will be linked. In other words, if a Likes record exists for the current user for the current genre, "Like it" will be bold and "Don't like it" will be linked to an action that deletes the Likes record. If the Likes record does not exist, "Like it" will be linked to an action that creates the Likes record and "Don't like it" will be bold. Whatever action is used, the same page will be reloaded as the response page, giving the impression of a single interactive form.

We're going to work with the Likes database now, so grab our new friend the Lasso Database Selector from the Lasso Studio menu and choose Likes.

Now drag in another Inline, this time putting it around the "Like it" and "Don't like it" (see Figure 24.34).

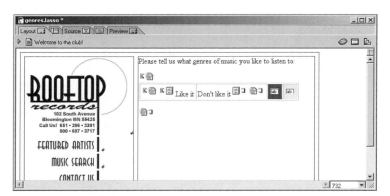

Figure 24.34
Here are the two nested inlines: one is used inside each row of the table, and the outer inline generates all the table rows.

Click on the leading inline tag, and this time click on the Tag Editor button inside the Inspector palette. This brings up Lasso's Tag Editor, and here you can see all the name/value pairs of this inline. We specify the database, table, and the type of search action. There are also two additional pairs: the two fields we're searching on, `member_id` and `genre_id`. As discussed, `member_id` needs to match the cookie of the same name, and `genre_id` needs to match the genre row that we're currently on. Figure 24.35 shows the Inline search in the Tag Editor.

When nesting inlines, references to existing fields will always be pulled from the enclosing inline. Field values from farther away than that will not be available to the current Inline.

Figure 24.35
Here is the Lasso Tag Editor showing the inline search for Likes.

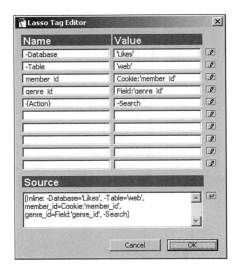

We know that we're going to want to link the Like it/Don't like it text to actions that either create or delete Likes records, and to do that we'll need to have the `member_id` and `genre_id` available. The `member_id` will come from the cookie, so that's always available. However, these links will be inside an inline search of the Likes database, and if no record is found for the current genre, the `genre_id` from the current row will not be available. So right before we run this inline, we're going to set a variable called `genre_id` from the enclosing inline that generates this row. You can do this by dragging the variable tag from the Lasso Programming palette into your document, and place it just before the inline. Name it `genre_id` and set it to the value of the current `genre_id` field retrieved by the enclosing inline. See Figure 24.35 to see what this should look like in the Inspector.

In Lasso, variables can be set anywhere in a format file, and they are valid throughout the rest of that format file during processing. They do not persist, however. If you need a variable to be valid across more than one format file, you must use either a cookie or a token.

Now let's create our conditional. This will test whether the inline found a valid Likes record. If it did, it will display one set of links; if it did not, it will display another. Grab the Condition object from the Lasso Programming palette and drag it into your row. It will create an If, an Else, and an End If. These three statements do exactly what their names imply. If the "If" statement is true, the subsequent block of HTML will be displayed; "Else" the next block of HTML will be displayed, up until the "End If." You'll want to move your Like it/Don't like it text in between two of these, then duplicate it and put it in between the other two. You should end up with If, Like it/Don't like, Else, Like it/Don't like it, End If. Move the records blocks inside the first pair; the second pair will only be shown if no record was found.

Define the If statement by selecting it and setting the values in the Inspector, as shown in Figure 24.36. Compare the Lasso tag `Found_Count` to see whether it's greater than zero.

If you run it now from your browser, you should see a full column of bolded Don't Like Its, since there are no records at all in the Links database. The only thing that remains is to define the links that let the user create and delete records.

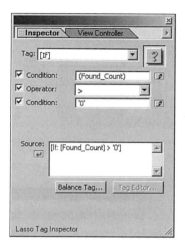

Figure 24.36
Define your conditional statement using the Inspector.

To delete the record in Lasso, the link on the "Don't like it" text in the first block will read as follows:

```
Action.Lasso?-Database=Likes&-Table=web&-RecordID=[RecordID_Value]&
➡-AnyResponse=genres.lasso&-Delete
```

Action.Lasso is the form action to take for all Lasso actions, and the tags following it define what the action will be. -Database and -Table specify the Likes database and the Web layout in FileMaker. -AnyResponse tells it to load this same form again as the response. -Delete tells it that the action to be performed is to delete a record, and -RecordID tells it which record to perform that action upon. [RecordID_Value] is a replacement tag that Lasso will replace with its internal record identifier for each record when this page is generated.

To create the new record on the "Like it" text on the second block, the link should read as follows:

```
Action.Lasso&-Database=Likes&-Table=web&genre_id=[Variable:'genre_id']&
➡member_id=[Cookie:'member_id']&-AnyResponse=genres.lasso&-Add
```

The differences here are the -Add action instead of -Delete, and the two fields that are going to be inserted, genre_id and member_id, derived from the genre_id variable and the member_id cookie.

Figure 24.37 shows how the finished query will look in the Page window. Starting from left to right in the table row, the line reads: Variable set for genre_id | Inline search for matching Likes records | If a record was found | Begin records | Like it /next cell/ Don't like it | End records | Else if no records were found | Like it /next cell/ Don't like it | End if | End inline. Figure 24.38 shows the source code.

Figure 24.37
Here is the finished query.

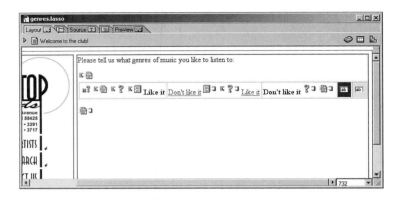

Figure 24.38
Here is the same screen shown in source view.

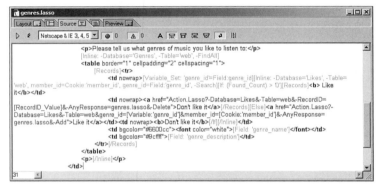

This completes the genres.lasso page. Check it out in your browser and play with it: It's fun to make the records appear and disappear.

Building the Member Search

This function allows the user to select a musical genre, and find a list of all the members who like that genre.

At first glance, building a member search interface would seem to be a quick and dirty breeze through the Site Builder. But the problem is that we're not searching for fields that reside in the Members database. We're searching for Likes records, and retrieving fields from the Members database. And when we search for Likes records, we're going to display genre names from the Genres database. So this seemingly simple function is going to require working with all three of our databases. Figure 24.39 shows the finished product, the eventual fruit of our efforts.

To start, we'll make the form that's going to find all the Likes records. Figure 24.39 shows what we ultimately want it to look like. Let's start with a new page from our template, and call it `search_genres.lasso`. Put your cursor on the page where you want to insert the new search form. Now we're going to use the Lasso Form Builder. Grab it from the Lasso Studio menu and you'll be presented with the window shown in Figure 24.40.

Figure 24.39
Here is the finished search screen viewed in the browser.

Figure 24.40
Choose the type of form you want to create in the Lasso Form Builder.

The first two options on this screen are for creating forms. A "Pre-Lasso" page does not contain any LDML tags that Lasso needs to process, so it can be served directly to the user by the Web server without the need for Lasso to process it. A "Post-Lasso" page does contain LDML tags, and this is the choice we're going to select. We'll get to those tags a bit later. Choose Search Database from the action pop-up menu.

The next screen is the familiar Lasso Database Selector. Choose the Likes database.

Figure 24.41
Choose response pages and
fields to appear on them.

The next screen, shown in Figure 24.41, lets us specify which fields we want to appear on the results page, and also the name of the –Error and –Response pages to use. Choose member_list.lasso for the –Response page, and we'll stick with the error.lasso page created earlier.

Finish the Builder. Lasso Studio will create the requested form, with all the tags properly formatted, and insert the form wherever you placed the cursor in the current page.

This form gives us a decent start, but we're going to do a lot to it. Our users don't want to search on the genre_id and member_id fields, so we're going to take those off the form. We're also going to run an inline search of the genres database, retrieve the name of each genre, and create a Select List item for each one. That way we'll end up with a single text pop-up list built on the contents of the Genres database. The form we just created will search the Likes database for any records matching the genre_id we select from the pop-up list.

So drag an inline into the form and set it to search the Genres database with an action of –FindAll. Retrieve the genre_name and genre_id, and build a select list using the [Records] blocks to create on option for each record returned.

Figure 24.42
Your source code for the finished
search screen should look like
this.

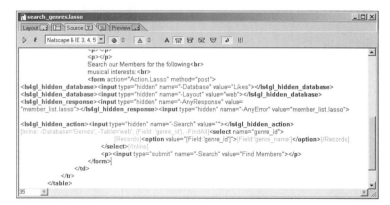

When you're done, the code should match Figure 24.42, and Figure 24.43 shows how all the little Lasso icons should line up in layout view.

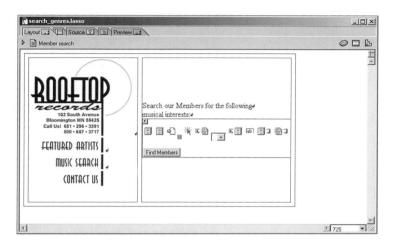

Figure 24.43
If the planets are properly aligned, here is how the finished search screen should appear in GoLive.

At this point it's okay to load the page in your browser. The inline search should populate the pop-up list correctly, and if you view source, you should see that the numerical genre_id values have been generated as well. But don't submit the form, because it's looking for a –Response page that we haven't built yet, but that's shown in Figure 24.44.

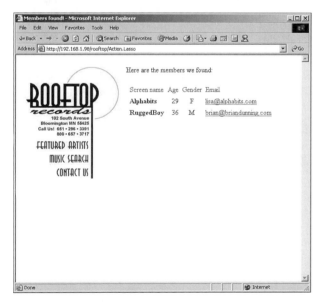

Figure 24.44
This is what we want the final result of the member search to look like.

So let's build it. Open up your template document again and save it as `member_list.lasso`. Create a table to view the results in. Enclose a row within `[Records]` blocks to repeat the row once for each record found by the search executed by the form that called this page.

This gives you a table full of Likes records, which is not what the user wants to see. The user wants information on the member related to each Likes record that was found. So rather than display any information from the Likes record on each row, we're going to use the `member_id` retrieved in each record to execute an inline search of the Members database, and retrieve all there is to know about that member.

Figure 24.45
Here is what the finished member list screen should look like in GoLive.

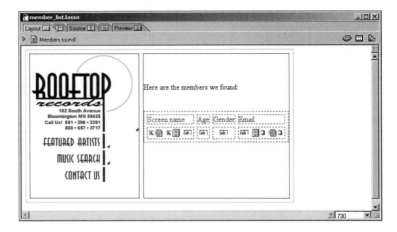

Referring to Figure 24.45, you can see that contents in each row of the table are enclosed in an inline search and its accompanying [`Records`] blocks. Keep in mind that this is distinct from the enclosing [`Records`] blocks that include this entire row.

The inline search should refer to the Members database with an action of –`Search`, and pull the record matching the current `member_id`. Refer to the source code in Figure 24.46.

Figure 24.46
For reference, here is the source code for the finished `member_list` screen.

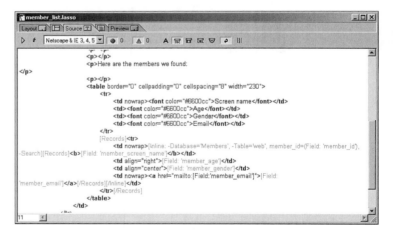

At this point the site is finished. You can run the member search and should see correct results. Let's add one more thing: an easy way to navigate around the site.

Creating Navigation

The simplest way to do this is to make an include file that we can insert onto each of our pages. Then if we ever want to change or add to our navigation, we only have to change one file and the whole site gets updated.

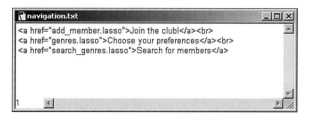

Figure 24.47
To create reusable code, create an include file like this that can be called into the site in many places.

Create a text file called `navigation.txt`, like that shown in Figure 24.47, and put in it just the HTML needed to make your navigation. Then go to each page you want to include this on and add the following code:

```
[Include:'navigation.txt']
```

It's as simple as that. Lasso will replace the tag with the contents of the specified file, and your results will look like Figure 24.48.

Include files can include other LDML tags, and even include other include files. You can go crazy even thinking about it.

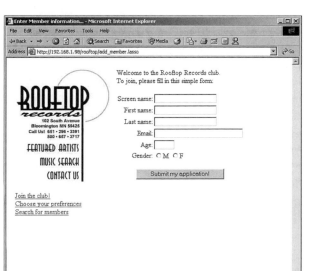

Figure 24.48
Here is a page on our site showing the navigation include in the lower left of the browser window.

Obviously, there is a lot more we could do with this site, but the purpose of this chapter is to provide an overview and an introduction to the general capabilities of Lasso Studio for GoLive.

Lasso Studio Wrap Up

We've touched on only a few of Lasso Studio's capabilities, and barely scratched the surface of the Lasso Web Data Engine itself. What we have done is illustrate in brief how quickly virtually any user, even without great knowledge of Web programming, can add a powerful dynamic capability to a GoLive Web site. The Lasso Studio plug-in to GoLive makes a skilled programmer out of almost anyone.

More information about Lasso, including searchable support archives, mailing lists, and additional downloads, is available at http://www.blueworld.com.

TROUBLESHOOTING

24

Customizing Your Queries

I want to build a page that's nothing like what the Lasso Form Builder and Site Builder provide. Can I do that?

Absolutely. You can even hand-code all of your Lasso pages, which is what many professional Lasso developers do. But the tools in Lasso Studio are still very useful.

For example, using the wizards to build a query, even though it's not exactly the right one, is a great way to get all the syntax perfect and give you a head start on development. It's a lot easier and more reliable to edit a wizard-built page than it is to type a new one from scratch.

Even if you don't use the wizards at all, use the Objects palette to drag and drop Lasso tags into your page. You can then edit them using the Inspector, or even manually in Source Code view. But at least this way the syntax, including punctuation, commas, quotes, brackets, and other things that are easy to get wrong, are always right.

Making Your Site Secure

What's the best way to make my Lasso site secure?

Often, the output of a wizard tool produces a page or a site that is fairly basic in structure, and not necessarily optimized using modern development conventions and architectures. Powerful as it is, Lasso Studio is no exception.

The biggest security risk in many Lasso sites is its simplicity. Look at the URL after clicking on a hitlist item to view a detail page, and it's easy to see how you could manually edit the URL in the browser's address window and view a different record, or possibly even delete one.

Advanced architectures avoid that problem by using code design that hides the logic and critical identifiers from the user. Lasso developers have a pet name for modern site architecture as it is applied to the Lasso technology, and this is the "Corral Method." Essentially the same concept used by advanced PHP and JSP programmers, the Corral Method involves the use of inline actions, variables, and extensive use of include files to not only provide stronger security, but also to create more separation between logic and design. Anyone interested in getting deeper into Lasso development is advised to check out `http://www.corralmethod.com/` to learn more.

GOING LIVE

Lasso is a growing technology, and as such, it has a growing community. There is an annual Lasso Summit for Lasso developers, and several active mailing lists and code archives.

As a starting point, join the Lasso Talk mailing list at `http://www.blueworld.com/blueworld/lists/lasso.html`. When you're ready for Lasso Summit, go to `http://www.lassosummit.com/`.

A variety of trainers teach courses around the country, and you can find a list of them at Blue World's site. For books and tutorial, the author's own Lasso Master Class provides a deep dive into Lasso 3.6 and is available at `http://www.briandunning.com/`. The new version, Lasso Professional 5, is represented by some new commercially available books that should be out by the time you read this.

24

IX

WIRELESS AND COLLABORATION

IN THIS PART

25 Developing for Wireless Devices   **467**

26 The WorkGroup Server   **481**

25

DEVELOPING FOR WIRELESS DEVICES

IN THIS CHAPTER

Wireless: A Growing Market **468**

WML, XHTML-Basic, and CHTML **468**

Developing in WML **470**

Developing in XHTML-Basic and CHTML **477**

Troubleshooting **480**

Going Live **480**

WIRELESS: A GROWING MARKET

An increasingly useful weapon in the arsenal of today's professional Web developer is fluency in wireless languages. As more and more services become available over mobile phones and other wireless devices, and as airtime charges come down, these devices will become increasingly ubiquitous.

Pages created for wireless devices are viewed on microbrowsers. Microbrowsers include those built in to many mobile telephones, pagers, and PDAs, and also include a large array of devices just hitting the market over the next few years.

As of this writing, about half the mobile phones out there have microbrowser capabilities. Of those, only a small fraction of owners ever actually use the microbrowser capabilities. Look for these numbers to change dramatically over the coming years, especially as wireless devices become less limited to mobile phones, PDAs, and pagers, and start to appear in automobiles and home appliances.

WML, XHTML-BASIC, AND CHTML

It may be helpful to take a moment and examine the way wireless Web pages work with phones, using WML (Wireless Markup Language) as an example. WML pages can be created and output by virtually any Web server or application server. There is no black magic involved there; however, there is some black magic in the process of how your phone accesses that server. First of all, a microbrowser-equipped phone does not directly access the Web server that creates the WML pages. Instead, the phone makes a call back to the mobile service provider. They maintain a special set of servers called WAP (Wireless Access Protocol) gateways. The WAP gateway acts as a sort of proxy Web browser, and it is what accesses the Web server with the request generated by the phone. The WAP gateway takes the resulting WML page that the Web server provides, translates it into something that the phone understands, and transmits it back to the user over the mobile phone network.

GoLive supports the three leading technologies in wireless Web development. They are

- **WML** is the current standard for most wireless Web sites in North America and Europe. Since telephone bandwidth is currently at a premium, and since wireless Web charges are still up there, WML employs a neat trick to combine several pages into a single transmission from the server. This trick involves calling your pages *cards* and calling a collection of pages a *deck* of cards. A whole deck is transmitted to your phone with each WAP request, speeding subsequent navigation and minimizing the number of calls that must be made to the server.

- **XHTML-Basic** (Extensible Hypertext Markup Language, Basic) is a W3C defined standard that all future browsers (micro and otherwise) will support, no matter what kind of device they're installed in. Many devices in development for future release, such as automobile and home appliance applications, are designed around support for XHTML-Basic.

- **CHTML** (Compact Hypertext Markup Language) is the official name for the format so popular in Japan and commonly known by its trademarked name, *i-mode.* Folks in Japan sure love to use their mobile phones, and thus CHTML is undoubtedly the format that gets the most use worldwide for the time being.

Why are there three competing standards? Would that there was an easy answer to that. No matter which—if any—ends up prevailing, GoLive 6 has you covered.

Planning Your Development

The first thing to keep in mind is to think in minimalist terms. For the time being, most micro-browsers exist within the confines of a one-square-inch grayscale liquid crystal display. Please, curtail your use of massive Flash animations, huge imagemapped graphics, scrolling advertisements, and streaming multimedia content. They don't play here.

Without a doubt, better display devices are available already, and even more tomorrow. But until the majority of users have color screens and larger displays, your best bet will be to appeal to the lowest common denominator. Make design and navigation choices that will look great even if your users have the lamest phone from last year. For example, stick with a minimalist style. Use short text and grayscale images that look great in black and white, and avoid cosmetic or decorative graphics unless you're absolutely certain there will be enough room to display them without scrolling.

Palettes and Preferences

XHTML-Basic and CHTML are subsets of regular HTML, so you can use GoLive's normal page editing functions to develop them. More accurately, you can use *some* of those functions. An easy way to manage this is to limit the functions available in the Objects palette to just those that your markup language of choice permits. To do this, select the Objects palette menu, choose Configure, and select your language from the pop-up list, as shown in Figure 25.1. For example, when you choose XHTML-Basic 1.0 from this list, you'll notice that the number of icons on many of the Objects palette tabs suddenly shrinks. No, you haven't reverted back to GoLive 2.0, you've just made it a bit easier to avoid using features that microbrowsers may not support.

Figure 25.1
The Configure submenu on the Objects palette menu shows the markup specification choices to limit the Objects palette contents to permissible tags only.

WML is an XML format, so you need to use the special WML palette to author in it. The WML palette does not appear by default, but you can go into Preferences, select Modules, look in the

Extend Scripts folder, and check the box next to the WML module. When you restart GoLive, you'll see a new tab on the Objects palette, as shown in Figure 25.2.

Figure 25.2

The spiffy new WML Elements tab on the Objects palette magically appears after you activate the WML module in Preferences.

Previewing with an Emulator

There's a really good reason not to use your phone or other wireless device for the bulk of your testing while developing a wireless site: cost. You're incurring airtime charges the whole time, and many service providers don't include wireless Web time in your plan's monthly minutes.

For this reason, and also convenience, Adobe provides a CHTML device emulator called the Access Compact Viewer (Windows only, apologies to everyone else). Once you've installed this option from the GoLive CD, you use this to preview your work just like any other browser. Go to your Preferences, choose the Browsers tab, and navigate to `Simulator.exe`. Now, when you preview your CHTML work, you can select to view it through the eyes of an actual i-mode phone.

DEVELOPING IN WML

There are two main differences between WML and most of the HTML-based languages that you'll develop with using GoLive. First, it's an XML-based language, so the DocType is going to be XML instead of HTML, the XML is absolutely required to be well-formed, and very few of the familiar HTML tags you use are supported. Second, it uses the "deck of cards" metaphor as previously discussed, so you'll need to rethink your notions about navigation and site structure. For this reason, even beginning developers need to play with a full deck.

Since WML is XML-based, you'll need to restrict your usage of the Objects palette to just the tags available in the WML Elements section. If you don't have this section, go to the Modules section in Preferences, enable it, and then restart GoLive.

Building a Basic Deck

To start creating a simple WML deck, select New Special from the File menu and choose WML Deck. You'll get a new document. Figure 25.3 shows what a completely empty WML deck looks like, and just so you have an idea of where we're

> WML must be well-formed XML. The practical implication of this is that you can't use sloppy HTML the way you can with Web pages, which let you get away with tags that are not closed, such as `<BR>` and even using a `<P>` without a `</P>`. In WML you will need to use that `</P>` tag, and for tags that are solitary and not usually followed by a closing tag, you would write them as `<BR/>`, or `<INPUT NAME="MyField"/>`. The slash before the closing bracket means that this lone tag opens and closes all by itself. The term "well-formed" carries other restrictions with it as well, but this is the main one you'll need to stay on top of. For more information on these restrictions, refer to the XML specifications at `http://www.w3.org/TR/xmlp-reqs/`.

going with this, compare it with Figure 25.4, which shows two cards in the deck. This should help you to understand what portion of the code comprises the required WML wrapper, and what portion is your domain to play in.

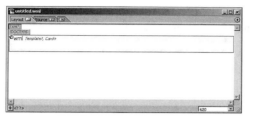

Figure 25.3
Here are the bare bones of a new blank WML deck.

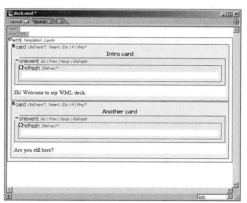

Figure 25.4
This WML deck has two Cards in it.

25

 This is the raw container for your WML site; there's not much you can do with it here. You have to add at least one Card: A Card is the metaphor for a single screen on the wireless device. Grab the Card icon from the Objects palette and drag it into the WML deck.

Figure 25.5
The Card Inspector shows the basic properties of the overall card.

As soon as you do this, you'll see the Inspector lit up with all kinds of new attributes, as shown in Figure 25.5. Let's look at what each one of these mean:

- **id**: The ID that will be used to identify this Card in your deck navigation, and so on. GoLive makes up a unique ID number for any element that requires one, and you'll usually want to change this to something a little easier to work with, like a short one-word description.

- **class**: If you want to group this Card with other Cards or elements, put a class name here. If a Card or element belongs to more than one class, then separate the class names with spaces.

- **title**: This is how the Card will be titled in the microbrowser. Limit your title to 15 characters or less to make sure it doesn't get cut off in some browsers.

- **newcontext**: True if you want the microbrowser to clear its history and variables when this page loads; False if not. You will probably usually want to leave this on False.

- **ordered**: This refers to any input fields that appear on the Card. True means they need to be entered in a specific order; False means they can be entered in any order.

- **onenterforward**: Specify the event that you want to trigger when the user arrives at this Card via forward navigation.

- **onenterbackward**: Specify the event that you want to trigger when the user arrives at this Card via backward navigation.

- **ontimer**: Specify the event that you want to be triggered by a Timer. Each Card can have one Timer included.

- **xml:lang**: Use this if you want to specify a particular XML language for this Card. You can usually leave this alone.

If all the Cards in your deck share the same onenterforward, onenterbackward, and Ontimer actions, you may want to start your deck off with a *Template*. A Template is like a Card (it must always be the first one in the deck), but it doesn't do anything by itself. All other Cards in the deck will inherit their actions from it.

To start your deck off with a Template, grab the Template icon from the Objects palette and drag it into your deck. Be sure that you place it above any Cards. Then go to the Inspector and edit the action properties. Then you won't have to edit the action properties on your Cards. Figure 25.6 shows a deck with a template.

One-inch square screens are not that exciting, so consequently, there are not a lot of exciting options in WML. Your screens will consist basically of text, images, anchors, and form elements.

Entering Text

Click your cursor in the white area of a Card and type. You can use the Return key to start a new paragraph, or shift-Return to start a new line. That's about it. Notice that the formatting options on the Type menu or in the toolbar are not available in WML.

You can also define a preformatted type area. Drag in the Preformatted text icon from the Objects palette, click inside its white area, and type your preformatted text.

Any time you attempt to do something not allowed, like place your Preformatted text area someplace other than inside a Card, GoLive will alert you. It's hard to do anything wrong and get away with it.

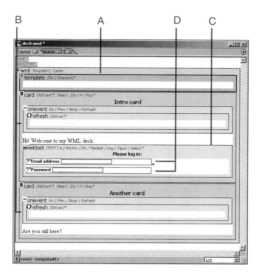

Figure 25.6
This deck starts with a Template (A). All the subsequent Cards in the deck (B) will use this Template's actions. This figure also shows a Fieldset (C) and some text input fields (D).

Using Images

WML does support images, but only one kind: WBMP (Wireless Bitmap). Use the Img icon from the Objects palette to insert an image. On the Inspector, specify the image's location. Also on the Inspector, many of the familiar HTML properties are available: alt text, vspace, hspace, align, height, and width. Height and width will be set for you automatically when you specify the image's location. localsrc is used to specify the location of an image saved on the wireless device itself.

Anchor Navigation in WML

Use anchors to navigate through your deck, to other decks, or to other Web sites. Drag either an <A> icon or an Anchor icon from the Objects palette and drop it into your Card. You can put text, images, or both inside anchors.

<A> is used to specify a URL to navigate to, and an Anchor is used to trigger a navigation event. Events are discussed later in this chapter.

For each, you'll need to go into the Inspector and enter the accesskey, if desired. The accesskey specifies what key on the mobile phone will trigger the Anchor if pressed. On most phones, keys 1 through 9 and the pound key (#) are available to be used as accesskeys. An example might be "Hit 5 to visit our home page."

For an <A> tag, you also enter the URL on the Inspector. This determines where the microbrowser will go next if this Anchor is triggered.

The Anchor tag serves as a container for an event, discussed later in this chapter. The event that you drag into the Anchor tag will determine what action is taken.

Form Elements

The available form elements boil down to text input fields and selection lists. Drag an Input icon from the Objects palette to create a basic text entry field. On the Inspector there are a whole variety of properties you can set for a text Input field. Here are the choices, not including some previously discussed:

Figure 25.7
The Inspector shows a WML text input field.

- **name**: As you might guess, the name for this text field.
- **type**: Text will show readable characters as the user types; Password will show unreadable bullets.
- **emptyok**: True to allow a null value; False to require the user to input something.
- **size**: Just like in HTML, the number of characters wide the Input field should be.
- **maxlength**: Just like in HTML, the maximum number of characters that can be entered into the field.
- **tabindex**: The tab order of this field, relative to any other elements on the page that also have a **tabindex**.
- **value**: If you want to specify the value that will be used instead of whatever is entered into the field, type it here.
- **format**: If you want to restrict the contents of the field to only certain characters, enter those characters here (for example, "0123456789").
- **title**: The field title that appears on the screen next to the field.
- **accesskey**: Use this to specify a key on the wireless device that the user can press to activate this field with the contents of the value attribute.

Text Input fields can be visually grouped by using the Fieldset command. Drag the Fieldset icon from the Objects palette and drop it into a Card. Place Input fields inside this Fieldset area, and they will be visually grouped onscreen. In the Inspector, set the title that you wish to display with the visual grouping onscreen.

Select lists consist of a Select tag with one or more Option tags inside. Within a Select list, Options can be further subdivided into Option groups, which function similarly to Fieldsets above.

Drag a Select list icon from the Objects palette and drop it inside a Card, or inside a Fieldset. Go to the Inspector and set the following attributes:

- `name`: The name of the field.

- `multiple`: True if multiple selections from the list of enclosed Options are allowed; False if only a single selection is permitted.

- `tabindex`: The tab order of this field, relative to any other elements on the page that also have a tabindex.

- `title`: The field title that appears on the screen next to the field.

- `value`: The default value of this attribute.

- `iname`: This is interesting. Say you have three options in your Select list called "Color", and they are Red, Blue, and Purple. `iname` lets you define an additional field that will be set with the index value of whatever is selected for Color. So if you enter "ColorNumber" in `iname`, then not only will Color be set with whatever color is selected, but also ColorNumber will be set with 1 if Red is chosen, 2 if Blue is chosen, or 3 if Purple is chosen. If nothing is chosen, then ColorNumber will be set to 0.

- `ivalue`: Lets you specify a default value for the field you define in iname.

Now that you have defined your Select list, it's time to add the enclosed Options. Drag in any number of Option icons from the Objects palette, and make sure you place them inside the Select list. You can also place them inside an Option group, and we'll talk about that in a moment. In the Inspector

- `title`: The text that will be displayed onscreen for this Option.

- `value`: The actual contents that will be submitted if this Option is selected.

Several Options within a Select list can be grouped visually into an Option group. You can have multiple Option groups within a Select list. An Option group cannot be within another Option group. Some Options can be inside an Option group, and others can be outside, all within the same Select. To create an Option group, drag the Optgroup icon from the Objects palette and drop it inside a Select list. Select the title, which will be displayed onscreen, in the Inspector.

Events in WML

If you want something to happen when the user enters a Card, exits a Card, selects a given Option in a Select list, or the Timer expires, use Onevent. Onevent covers actions that happen as a result of an element in a Card.

Drag an Onevent icon from the Objects palette and put it in a Card, a Template, or an Option. Select the type of event in the Inspector:

- **ontimer**: The event will be executed when the Card's Timer expires.

- **onenterforward**: The event will be executed when the user arrives on the Card.

- **onenterbackward**: The event will be executed when the user leaves the Card.

- **onpick**: The event will be executed when the Option is selected. Only choose this type when the Onevent is inside an Option.

Next, you'll need to specify what the event is. Do this by dragging an event (Go, Prev, Refresh, Noop) inside the Onevent box. These events are all discussed below.

A Do event can be triggered by a user action, such as pressing a key on the phone. Create a Do event by dragging the Do icon from the Objects palette and dropping it inside a Card, a Fieldset, a text paragraph area, or a Template. Set the following attributes in the Inspector:

- **type**: Choose the type of event you want to attach this Do element to.

- **label**: Some browsers might display Do elements as little icons, some might display them as whatever text you put in here. It's limited to six characters.

- **name**: As with any element, you can choose a name for the event binding.

- **optional**: True will allow a browser to ignore this element; False will not allow it to be ignored. Unless you're big on having your code ignored by browsers, most of the time you'll probably leave this at the default of False.

The Go tag will go to an URL that you specify, along with form field contents and variables. Drag a Go tag icon inside an Anchor tag, then go to the Inspector and specify the URL of the next Card to be shown. On the Inspector, set the following attributes:

- **method**: If you're submitting form information to a server, enter either Get or Post, depending which method your server requires.

- **accept-charset**: If your server requires you to enter the list of data encoding formats that it accepts, list them here, separated by commas. This is never needed if your method is Get.

- **sendreferer**: True will send the URL of the current along with the request; False will not.

Prev will simply go backward to the previous Card. Drag a Prev icon from the Objects palette and drop it inside a Do element, an Onevent, or an Anchor. This one's simple; there isn't really anything you need to set in the Inspector.

Refresh is similar to Prev except that instead of going back one Card, it will reload the current Card.

Timers in WML

Each Card in a WML deck can have a Timer associated with it. Often, such Timers are used to trigger an event. When the Card is loaded, the value of the Timer is 0. It counts up in 1/10th second increments until the user leaves the Card.

To use a Timer in your Card, drag in the Timer icon. It must be the first element in the Card. In the Inspector, change the value to the desired time period, in tenths of a second. For example, enter 5 if you want a half second, or 100 if you want ten seconds. The event that will happen is specified in the Card's `ontimer` attribute.

Variables in WML

Variables allow you to pass data between cards, and also to submit data to servers. They allow the creation of simple name/value pairs which are preserved from card to card.

 `Setvar` is used to store a variable that can be retrieved on another card. Drag the Setvar icon from the Objects palette and drop it into a Go, Prev, or Refresh element.

 `Postfield` is used to submit an additional name/value pair along with a form submission. Drag the Postfield icon from the Objects palette and drop it into a Go element. Postfields are only useful when submitted along with a Go event.

DEVELOPING IN XHTML-BASIC AND CHTML

There's a lot to learn from scratch when creating your first WML site. Fortunately, your first XHTML-Basic and CHTML sites are somewhat easier: almost nothing new to learn, and only a few things to forget. It's like rolling off a log, and not even having to do a very good job.

The main difference between developing for these formats and developing in standard HTML is the restrictions. Physical size is restricted, the number of legal tags is restricted, and you should try to restrict the download size of each page. The good news is that once you configure GoLive to enforce these restrictions, you can let your creative juices flow and use GoLive's tools to their fullest.

25

Planning Your Site

Since you can use the full suite of GoLive features to develop in XHTML-Basic and CHTML, you'll probably want to create a site. When you do this, you'll get an `index.html` page. The first thing you'll want to do is rename that page (`index.xhtml` or `index.chtml`), then open it and make the tweaks necessary for it be a valid wireless page.

For XHTML-Basic, open the page and go to the document window menu, that little pop-up menu near the top right of the document window. Select Convert to XHTML from the Markup menu. Click OK. You now have a valid XHTML-Basic page. Basically the only thing that was changed at this stage was the `!DOCTYPE` tag at the beginning of the page.

Then, go to the document window menu again and select XHTML-Basic 1.0 from the Doctype menu.

For CHTML, open your renamed `index.chtml`. All you need to do here is go to the document window menu and choose i-mode 1.0 from the Doctype menu.

Save your document.

Now you have a site set up with an index page properly formatted for your wireless document type. There are two more things that you might find helpful to do, but are not absolutely necessary.

You can also create a new XHTML-Basic page from the New Special menu item in the File menu.

First, you may prefer to view your work in a mockup of its intended delivery platform. Bring up the View window, by either selecting it from the Windows menu or clicking the View tab on the Inspector. By default, Profile is set to Adobe GoLive.

Figure 25.8
Check your work in the Nokia XHTML Phone view.

If you're developing in XHTML-Basic, choose the Nokia XHTML Phone, as shown in Figure 25.8. For CHTML, choose one of the i-mode phones like the DoCoMo D503i. As you can see, the viewable area on your screen just shrank dramatically. This is a realistic view of your new world.

This is not the same as using a proper software phone emulator to test your site, but it serves most of the same purposes and will really help you to see how your site looks within the defined physical limitations of the format.

Second, you may wish to save your new index page as a stationery file. A quick way to do this is to go to the document window menu and select Save as Stationery from the Save As menu. By default it will store this document in the Stationery folder of your site. From now on, when you add a page to your site, just go to the File menu and select Page from Stationery from the New Special menu. Choose the stationery page you've just created, and you're on your way.

Customizing GoLive's Environment

Here's the main thing you need to do when developing for one of these alternate formats, and it couldn't be any easier. Just go to the Objects palette, choose Configure from the little pop-up menu, and select either XHTML-Basic 1.0 or i-mode 1.0, depending which one you're developing for. Suddenly all the features not supported in your format will disappear from the Objects palette tabs, and many of the menu options and toolbar items will gray out. This is GoLive's way of preventing you from hurting yourself. Now, unless you go into the source code and start typing wacky esoteric HTML tags, you can't do anything you're not supposed to do.

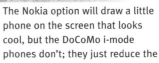

The Nokia option will draw a little phone on the screen that looks cool, but the DoCoMo i-mode phones don't; they just reduce the available space on screen. So don't be alarmed when no phone appears.

If you're creating a CHTML site intended to display in Japanese, you'll have to do a quick thing or two to get the Japanese Emoji characters to display properly on screen. If your pages are going to contain the Emoji characters, your page needs to have a particular content attribute in the `meta` tags. The Encodings module needs to be activated to do this. Also, the iModeEmoji module needs to be activated to view the Emoji characters.

Figure 25.9
Choose the format you want from the Objects palette pop-up menu.

Go into Preferences and select the Module item. On the right, make sure that both Encodings and iModeEmoji are checked. If they weren't, you'll need to quit and re-launch GoLive before anything will happen.

Once you've done that, go to the File menu and from Document Encoding, select Japanese (Shift_JIS). This will insert the proper `meta` tag that will allow the i-mode servers to deal with your Emoji characters.

Emoji is a font—if someone were to view your CHTML site with a Web browser, they would need to have the font installed or they would see only gibberish. When you drag an Emoji character from the Objects palette and into your page, you need to use the Inspector to choose which of the 196 Emoji characters will appear. Emoji characters are represented in the HTML code as a five digit number like this: *〹*.

Finishing Your Site

When you finish a page, or during editing if you're ever in doubt about the legality of your code, just select Check Syntax from the Edit menu and choose either i-mode 1.0 or XHTML-Basic 1.0. When you click OK and start the check, anything you need to fix will be listed in the Highlight window.

Figure 25.10
Check your syntax for compliance with i-mode 1.0 CHTML format.

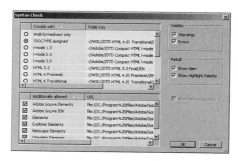

TROUBLESHOOTING

Getting a Connection with Your Phone

When I try to test my wireless site with my phone, it just returns some error. What am I doing wrong?

This is far and away the most common problem that wireless developers have. Usually the problem is that your test Web server is not set up to handle the WML MIME type. How you set this depends entirely upon what Web server you're using. However, here's a brief description of the norm.

Most Web servers will have a configuration text file called mime.types, and in that file, you'll need to add a line of text like this:

```
text/vnd wap wml
text/vnd wap wmlscript wmls
```

Restart your server and the problem should go away. If it doesn't, research the way your server maintains its MIME types; you may need to enter something formatted slightly differently, or the text file may have a different name.

GOING LIVE

Whatever you do, test your site on as many different wireless devices as you can. Not only mobile phones, but also Palm and PocketPC devices. And even those new snazzy ones that combine both into a single box. The only problem with doing this is that many developers do not have a wide variety of devices available to them for extensive testing.

One author has solved this problem by going into the local mobile phone store, where all the phones are connected, and tested his site on each by pretending that he's going to buy a phone.

There are also a variety of freeware and shareware emulators appearing on the Internet. Check the Web sites of phone manufacturers, and also keep an eye on wireless developer portal sites like `http://www.internet.com/sections/wireless.html`. But don't forget: An emulator is not a substitute for testing with the actual device.

THE WORKGROUP SERVER

IN THIS CHAPTER

Playing Nicely with Others   **482**

Web Workgroup Server Administration   **482**

Interacting with the Workgroup's Site Window   **486**

Publishing Workgroup Sites   **490**

Troubleshooting   **490**

Going Live   **490**

PLAYING NICELY WITH OTHERS

The process of designing, developing, and maintaining even the smallest of Web sites can quickly supersede the time constraints of one individual. More often than not, you'll be one of an onslaught of developers working together to complete a site. Adobe GoLive's Workgroup Server is new to version 6.0, and greatly enhances your ability to manage the development process by streamlining your team's work in one central location. With the Workgroup Server, your team can simultaneously work on pieces of the site without interfering with each other's progress.

GoLive's Workgroup Server is simply a central repository for a Site's files. There's no need to fear the Workgroup Server; all of the conveniences of the single user's Site are still available. In fact, the Site Window still serves as your access to the site: components, libraries, templates, stationeries, and all. The difference is that other team members will have the same access to the Site's files. In addition, very powerful collaboration features will be integrated into your development.

The Workgroup Server provides added features to the development process that streamline a team's work: files are stored in one central location, developers can check-out and check-in files, team members can track what other developers are working on, and version tracking is controlled.

WEB WORKGROUP SERVER ADMINISTRATION

The Web Workgroup Server supports a default server administrator, and provides access to all administrator functions through Web access. The system administrator has the highest level of privileges while working within the server, and can set up user accounts, passwords, and entire Workgroup Web sites.

When you first enter the Workgroup Server Administration Web Access, you'll be prompted to run through the Setup Wizard. The Setup Wizard is just a shortcut to accessing the six major sections of the Server Administration, each of which is listed in the left navigation bar of the page. These six sections (and the Setup Wizard) are all available each time you log onto the Server Administration site.

The Users section provides access to creating new users and modifying existing users' accounts. The first page will list the various users and their basic account information.

- To edit a user's profile and access, click the to the left of his name.

- To delete the account, click the to the right of the user's name.

- To add a new user, click the New User link.

Note that users can be granted administrative privileges, have their log access disabled, and can be provided access to specific sites. In addition, information such as the user's name, phone number, and email can all be stored within the server.

Next, the Sites section, shown in Figures 26.1 and 26.2. The Sites section provides the administrator access to creating new sites, as well as editing, duplicating, cleaning up, backing up, and deleting existing sites.

Figure 26.1
Editing a Site allows you to define which users have access to the Site, as well as create new users.

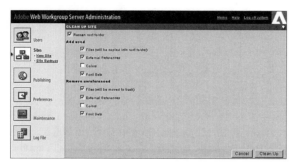

Figure 26.2
Cleaning up a Site forces the Workgroup server to look for references, colors, and files listed in the Site that are not listed in the Site Window. In addition, the Site can be stripped of any unused elements.

The Publishing Section (Figures 26.3 and 26.4) is where you define the publication settings for each site, whether the publishing be through the network or through FTP (file transfer protocol). Note that settings can also be made in the Site Settings while in GoLive, as well as accessed via the Sites Section of the Server Administration Web Access.

Figure 26.3
The Publishing Section allows you to define the location of the server to which the Site will be published.

26

Provide each server an intuitive and descriptive name. As any team member can publish the Site, it will be important to make sure that other users know which server they are publishing to. In this case, a staging server is being referenced. In addition, once the publishing server has been defined, the Workgroup Server provides access to setting a Site's specific publication settings.

These options include

- Publish Conditions: sets whether "Publish" states of directories and files should be honored. By default, if a file is referenced, it will be published. If a directory is not empty, it is by default published. Here, the Server Administrator can force the server to publish only referenced files, as well as files not part of a Site. Any publication setting set forth by the administrator will override an individual user's setting made via GoLive.

Figure 26.4
The Publishing section provides access to publishing a Site, as well as defining how it will be published. Note that this option will actually publish the Site.

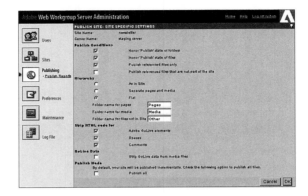

26

- Hierarchy: determines how the files should be structured on the server. As in Site uploads the Site's files to the server as-is. The Separate pages and media option creates two folders in the root directory, one which stores all HTML pages, the other which will store all media. The final option, Flat, strips any directory structure from the Site and places all content into the one root folder on the server.

- Strip HTML code for: provides access for cutting unnecessary code from the live version of the site. This includes GoLive elements (proprietary code GoLive uses to track GoLive features such as layout grids, and so on), spaces, and HTML comments.

- GoLive Data: provides access for stripping the uploaded media files of any GoLive data that was generated on account of being imported as a Smart Object.

- Publish Mode: specifies whether the files should be uploaded incrementally, or whether the entire site will be uploaded.

Notice that clicking OK from the Publish Site: Site Specific Settings screen actually does publish the site to the server as you've specified. In addition, Publish Reports will be generated, indicating any errors incurred.

To edit an already defined server (the username, password, publication directories, and so on), go through the Sites Menu. Select the site whose publishing server you want to modify. Then, click the edit icon beside the server you want to change. That will bring you back to the server definition dialog in which you can make the necessary changes, as shown in Figure 26.5.

The Preferences Section provides access to setting a number of Workgroup Server settings, including the server's ports and log records. Notice that if you change the port for the server, all team members must also change their port settings when logging on to the site. Also, note the options for the server's log. The options include errors (the least resource-intensive), warnings (which tracks both errors and warnings), and info (the most resource-intensive, tracking errors, warnings, and all actions that the server is making).

Figure 26.5
Changes can be made to server settings through the Sites section of the Server Administration. Simply select the site whose publication server you want to edit, then select the specific server.

The Maintenance Section of the Server Administration provides access to basic maintenance functions that you can perform on a site.

- Synchronize Site syncs the files on the Workgroup Server with the files in the Workgroup Admin. If GoLive is used to modify files, you will rarely (if ever) need to synchronize a site. However, if a user deletes, moves, or renames a Site manually rather than through the GoLive interface, differences will result. Synchronizing the Site will therefore alleviate any mismatches.

- Clean Up Revisions clears the revision list for a particular site. As will be discussed, each time a user modifies a file, the older revision is saved on the Workgroup Server as a precaution. Having tons of revisions stored on the server can clog up the server and cause it to process slower. As a result, cleaning up the revisions is a process you should invoke every once in a while. The Clean Up Revisions command allows you to specify how many revisions should be stored, as well as give a date that determines whether a revision should be deleted.

- Reset User Locks unlocks all of the files that a particular user currently has invoked on the system. Notice that this does not allow you to specify a file or even a Site in which you want this action invoked. Typically this feature will be used when a team member has moved on to other projects.

The final section is the Log File, which tracks and displays the errors, warnings, and information (invoked processes) of the server.

Creating a Workgroup Site

Once the Workgroup Server has been installed and started, any site can be stored in the central repository. To create a new Workgroup Site, open GoLive and choose File, New Site to open the Site Wizard. Instead of creating a Site for a single user, create a Site for your team. This Site will be stored on the Workgroup server. Notice that only users with Administrative privileges (as set by the user account) have the power to create a Site.

When you opt to create a Workgroup Site, the wizard prompts you to choose one of four options:

- Blank Site: creates a new blank Site stored on the Workgroup server. Includes a home page (`index.html`) and Site data. Essentially, this option matches the option of creating a blank Site for the single user, except that the files are stored in a central location as opposed to your local drive.

26

- Mount a Site: creates a local copy of an existing workgroup Site, thereby allowing you to collaborate with your team on an already existing Site. Use this option if you are simply trying to connect to an existing workgroup Site.

- Import from GoLive: creates a workgroup Site based on an existing local Site on your hard drive that has previously not been managed by GoLive. Use this option when a directory with Site files exists that has never been integrated with GoLive's Site management features.

- Import from GoLive Site: creates a workgroup Site based on a GoLive Site or GoLive templates.

Regardless of which selection you make, you will be requested to enter a username and password. All user accounts are created and managed by the site administrator. In addition, each user will be prompted for the server and port. The site administrator also configures each of these.

When mounting a Site, you will be prompted to select the Site on which you would like to collaborate. Each user who wants to collaborate on a particular project will need to mount the Site.

When creating a Site, you will be prompted for a Site name, and asked whether a project folder should package the Site shortcut, main directory, and Site data.

When importing a Site, you will be prompted to browse to the Site folders you would like to import.

When the wizard has completed, interacting with the Site will seem not much different than when you interacted with a single user's Site. The Site Window will open, displaying all of the files and directories associated with a Site. As discussed, however, you are now collaborating on a Site with all of your team members. As a result, a few very powerful team collaboration features are accessible.

Converting an Existing Single User Site to a Workgroup Site

To convert an existing single user Site to a workgroup Site, open the Site window for the existing local Site, and choose Site, Workgroup, Convert to Workgroup. The Site's files will be copied onto the Workgroup server, and your local Site will serve as a copy of the server's files.

Notice that there is no option to directly FTP an existing Site from a server into a Workgroup server. Simply download the Site to your local computer first, and then import those files into a new Workgroup Site.

INTERACTING WITH THE WORKGROUP'S SITE WINDOW

Your interaction with the Site Window of a Workgroup Site will not differ dramatically from the interaction with the Site Window of a single user's Site. All of the powerful site management features to which you have become accustomed still exist, including naming files, renaming files, checking links, and so on. However, a few added features do exist.

Notice the title bar of the Site window not only displays the name of the Site, but also the IP address (or Server name) for the server as well.

An added toolbar exists at the top of the application when viewing the Site Window. This toolbar is specific to working with a Workgroup, and can be toggled on or off via the Window, Workgroup Toolbar command. A number of added collaboration features are easily accessible via this toolbar, including

- Check Out: allows you to check out the currently selected file and lock the file from editing by your team members. Other team members will still be able to open the file, however only in a read-only form. The fact that you have checked the file out will be indicated by a pencil beside the file name and under the Locked category. Likewise, the padlock icon indicates to other team members that the file has been checked out (and locked).

- Check In: allows you to check a file back in once your changes have been made and saved. Overwrites the previous version of the file with your new, edited version. In addition, once a file is checked back into the system, other team members can access the files and modify them.

- Undo Check Out: checks in an unmodified version of the file. Use this if you prefer to revert back to the file in its original form upon checking it out; in other words, to not save the changes you made.

- Compare to Server: shown in Figure 26.6, compares the file stored locally with the file on the server for differences. The code for each file will be opened in a dialog, and you can browse to each difference and compare the HTML code side by side.

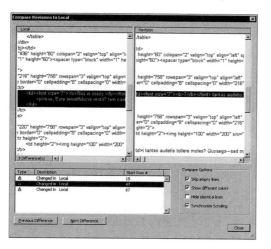

Figure 26.6
The Compare to Server option compares the local version of a checked out file with the file located on the remote server.

26

- Revision List: shown in Figure 26.7, displays a list of revisions made to a particular file, with access to open and/or revert back to a version that has since been saved over. Notice the options to view which team member made the changes to the page at each iteration, as well as the option to revert back to a file by selecting a previous version and clicking the Make Current button. In addition, you can compare side by side the HTML code of two iterations of the file by Shift-clicking on a Mac (Ctrl-click on a PC) and selecting Compare Revisions.

488 | Chapter 26: The Workgroup Server

Figure 26.7
The Revision List tracks all revisions of a file, including who made the changes to the file. The revision list will come in particularly handy for accessing an older version of the file in case a mistake was made or the file was accidentally lost.

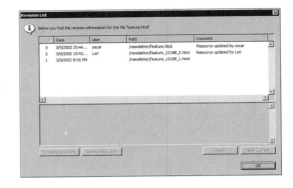

- User Activity: shown in Figure 26.8, toggles open the User Activity Tab, an additional tab in the Site Window. This tab simply lists all team members who have access to this Workgroup Site and lists all files that each person has checked out.

Figure 26.8
The User Activity Tab tracks all users who have access to a Workgroup Site, as well as which files have been checked out and by whom. Use the + and - to toggle the listings of checked out files for each person open and closed.

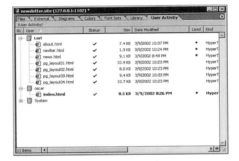

Notice that if you simply open a file by double-clicking it from the Site Window, you have opened that file in a read-only state. Until you make a change and try to save that change, the file is not explicitly checked out.

Each time a team member checks out a file, a copy of that file is stored in that team member's local copy of the project site folder. Rather than saturating each person's machines with copies of every file in the system, GoLive simply stores a temporary copy of the files that the individual has checked out for editing. Checking the file back in does not delete the temporary version, but you may force GoLive to remove local copies of checked-in files by right-clicking anywhere within the Site Window and selecting Site, Remove all local files from the resulting context menu.

You may come across a situation in which you would like to edit files while not connected to the Workgroup Server. For example, perhaps you'd like to take a few files with you via your laptop on a business trip. GoLive's Workgroup Server accommodates this as well. Simply check out the files you would like to work with. To avoid garnering errors with regard to broken links that will result from working offline, you can download a copy of the remaining files as read-only, thereby creating a temporary local Site with which you can work. To download the files, select the files of interest and choose Site, Download from the menu.

Notice that when you try to edit a file offline, GoLive will alert you that you are not connected to the Workgroup Server. Don't fear the alert; just select OK to bypass the message and open the Site regardless. Later, when you are connected to the server, you can check-in the files as usual.

The Site Window does not refresh in real-time; that is to say there is a delay with regard to the Site Window showing the most recent, up-to-date status of the files. You can force the Site Window to Refresh (to load the current data) by right-clicking (Ctrl-clicking on a Mac) and selecting Refresh View.

The Files Tab of the Site Window also has a couple added categories to the right of the Status Category: To be Edited and Completed. These two categories provide a means for tracking the completion of a particular page, as well as globally indicating who is responsible for the page's progress. To modify the values of the To Be Edited and Completed fields for a particular file, select the file and open the Workflow palette (see Figure 26.9) from the Window command on the menu (Window, Workflow). The Workflow palette provides access to specifying the person responsible for working on the file next, as well as an estimated percentage of completion.

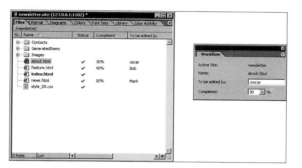

Figure 26.9
The Workflow palette provides a means for indicating how far along the page is toward its final completion, as well as which team member should next work with the file.

When working with a Workgroup Server, an additional tab, User Activity, exists in the Site Window. This tab provides access to a listing of all users who have access to the Site, as well as information about which files your team members are working with.

GoLive's site management tools for the Workgroup Server are incredibly powerful. Suppose your team member checks out a group of files, all which link to a file that you then rename. Not only will GoLive track the changes within the currently checked-in files, GoLive will also keep track of the necessary changes to the pages that are currently checked out. When your team member checks the group of pages back in, its links also get updated to reference the new name of the file.

Changing the User and Passwords

As mentioned, the Server Administrator defines the users and their passwords. Each team member will want to take the time to change her password for logging on to the

Caution

There is a potential pitfall to avoid when modifying a Component or Template. Suppose you check out a component, make modifications, and save the page. Then, you try to check the file back in. By default, GoLive will go through and try to check out all the files that use that component. Although that works wonderfully for the files that are currently available, those that are not available cannot be checked out, and errors will occur. As a precaution, check out all files that use the component first, then make and save the changes, and check the files back in.

26

server's files. To change a password, open a Workgroup Site in GoLive and select Site, Workgroup, Change Password from the menu. You will be prompted to enter your old password, as well as to enter your new password twice. Fill in the appropriate information and click OK.

Notice that the Workgroup option from the Site Menu houses two other options you may find handy: Change User and Open Workgroup Administration. The first, Change User, enables another team member to log on to the Workgroup server and work with a Site from the same GoLive application. The second, Open Workgroup Administration, is a shortcut to opening the Web-based Server Administration tool previously discussed.

PUBLISHING WORKGROUP SITES

In addition to providing a central repository for a Site's files and a collaborative environment for your team, GoLive also incorporates the ability to publish from the Workgroup Server to a live server. In most cases, it will be to your benefit to publish not only to the server where the Site is live, but also to an intermediary staging server where you can test a Site before making it public.

A Workgroup Site can be published by a Site's administrator within the Workgroup Administration, or by a Site's developer from within GoLive. To publish a Site from within the Web Workgroup Server Administration, log on as a user with administrative privileges and use the Publishing section as detailed previously in this chapter.

Users can also publish the Site without leaving GoLive. There are three fundamental steps to this process, but this process is not much different than if you were publishing a single user's Site. To learn more about publishing a Site, check out Chapter 31. Any differences between publishing a single user's Site and a Workgroup Site are detailed in that chapter.

TROUBLESHOOTING

Accessing the Web Administration

I can't get into the Web Administration interface to do anything. What's the deal?

The Workgroup Server operates just like a Web server, only it's running on port 1102 by default, rather than the port 80 that most Web servers use. This means that you should always be able to access it at `http://(machine address):1102`.

However, it is worthy of note that this port can be changed on the Preferences tab of the Web interface. If someone changes this port to something else, say 1234, then the next time the server is started it will only be accessible at `http://(machine address)):1234`.

GOING LIVE

As with all software products, technology can only provide one half of the solution. The human element plays a large part in the effectiveness of the Workgroup Server.

Inevitably, in any workgroup of any size, there are people who prefer to do things the old fashioned way, or who want to take a local copy of the document to work on it from home later. Even you yourself may get lazy once or twice and circumvent this system "Just to do something really quick, just this one time." This is well and good, but as soon as you have multiple unsynchronized copies of your pages floating around, trouble will brew. Don't blame GoLive's Workgroup Server.

Use it smartly, use it effectively, and always remember that half of the burden of maintaining clean code is on your own shoulders. The Workgroup Server will pull its end of the work, but you have to pull yours too.

26

X

USING DYNAMIC CONTENT

IN THIS PART

27 About Dynamic Content   **495**

28 Using Dynamic Content   **505**

29 Custom Merchant   **539**

ABOUT DYNAMIC CONTENT

IN THIS CHAPTER

The Dynamic Web   **496**

How Dynamic Web Sites Work   **496**

Using GoLive to Build a Dynamic Web Site   **497**

What GoLive Provides   **498**

Troubleshooting   **503**

Going Live   **504**

THE DYNAMIC WEB

These days, surfing a static Web site is about as much fun as watching a broken TV. Nearly every site in the real world is dynamic: Everything from a popular search engine, to a news site, to an online retailer, are all dynamic sites.

A dynamic site is generally defined as a site that draws a portion of its content from a changing data source, such as a database of news stories, or a database of shopping cart items and products. Every time you click to view a page, a database has to churn in the background somewhere to retrieve your content, and then an HTML page is automatically built especially for you.

Sometimes that changing data doesn't come from a database, but from a directory of static content that is frequently updated, or sometimes it comes from you and your own actions. Whatever the source, dynamic content provides the real value of the World Wide Web: access to information that is current and immediately available, no matter how far away.

HOW DYNAMIC WEB SITES WORK

No matter what type of site they are, all dynamic sites basically work the same way. The user clicks a link or a button in his browser, initiating an HTTP request. Often this may include information like a search term the user typed in a search box. The Web server receives the request, and the filename extension in the URL is a tip-off that this is a dynamic content request. For example, let's say the server receives a request for this page:

```
http://www.myserver.com/search.jsp
```

The Web server is going to pick out that .jsp and it will say "Ah, this isn't a request for static content. It's not for me, it's for the application server." In this case, the application server is a JavaServer Pages server.

Figure 27.1 shows the process flow. The application server receives the request, looks at search.jsp, and reads from it the instructions that the database should be searched for records containing the search term that was submitted along with the request. The database results are retrieved, and a page is built using instructions contained in search.jsp. Then the application server provides a complete, clean HTML page (suitable for display in a browser) that is then served back to the user via the Web server.

An application server differs a bit from a Web server. *Web servers* deliver content that is already pre-pared, but an *application server* builds and delivers dynamic content. Application servers and Web servers are both pieces of software. Sometimes they run on the same machine; sometimes they don't.

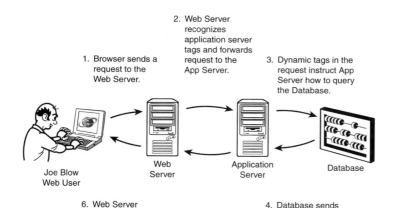

2. Web Server recognizes application server tags and forwards request to the App Server.

1. Browser sends a request to the Web Server.

3. Dynamic tags in the request instruct App Server how to query the Database.

Joe Blow
Web User

Web Server

Application Server

Database

6. Web Server sends HTML back to Joe Blow.

5. App Server uses Database results to create an HTML document.

4. Database sends the results back to App Server.

Figure 27.1
These are the adventures of a request for a dynamic page on its thrilling journey through the server.

USING GOLIVE TO BUILD A DYNAMIC WEB SITE

The Web server, the application server, and the database know how to do their jobs: It's up to you to provide the code to instruct them what to do.

GoLive comes with support for three popular technologies: ASP, JSP, and PHP. This means that out of the box, GoLive is able to generate all the valid code needed to make dynamic sites using any of those three technologies. GoLive can also be used to create pages for any other application server technology, but you will have to do the typing in source code view, and GoLive will probably flag any unrecognized tags as errors.

To use GoLive, you're going to need to create a development environment. This means that you'll need access to a real application server and database. In some cases, this might be your actual production server—in which case you probably don't want to provide public access to the areas you're working on until they're finished and functioning correctly. In other cases, you may have a second set of development servers to use, or in yet other cases, you may choose to just install everything on the machine you do your work on. Whatever the configuration, you will need to have a fully functional server to use GoLive's Dynamic Content tools.

Adobe has been kind enough to load your CD with installers that will create everything you need to build JSP or PHP servers on your Windows or Mac OS X system. See the section on these near the end of this chapter.

The following several sections present a criminally brief overview of each of the three supported technologies.

27

ASP

Microsoft's Active Server Pages is as popular as Microsoft Web servers...which basically means that it's already on most computers in the world. This runs on Microsoft IIS (Internet Information Server), and requires that your Web server is running Microsoft Windows. The components are commercially available from Microsoft and cannot be downloaded for free anywhere. Recommended ASP usage with GoLive is for Windows 98 or later running Personal Web Server or IIS, and a Microsoft Access, SQL Server, or Oracle database. For more information, go to `http://msdn.microsoft.com/asp/`.

JSP

JavaServer Pages is a technology developed by Sun Microsystems. XML-like tags, written in the Java language and embedded in your page, talk to server-side components called servlets. Servlets are like small application servers that run alongside a Web server. Since they're written in Java, servlets are platform-independent. Recommended JSP usage with GoLive is for a Mac OS X, Linux, Solaris, or Windows server running a JSP server such as Tomcat, and any JDBC-compliant database such as MySQL, PostgreSQL, Oracle... the list goes on. Tomcat is free and you can download it from `http://jakarta.apache.org/`. MySQL is also free and can be downloaded from `http://www.mysql.org/`, or it can be installed from your GoLive CD. For more information about JSP, go to `http://java.sun.com/products/jsp/`.

PHP

PHP stands for PHP: Hypertext Preprocessor. This doesn't really make any sense, but that's what it stands for nevertheless. PHP is a free technology; it's not a commercial product that anybody owns. It was developed by the Apache Software Foundation (`http://www.apache.org/`), the same folks who brought us the popular Apache Web server. You can get all kinds of information and download PHP from `http://www.php.net/`. Recommended PHP usage with GoLive is for Mac OS X, Linux, or Windows 95 or later servers with a MySQL database and an Apache Web server.

These chapters are not intended as a guide to learning these programming languages, so we're not going to go into the code generated by GoLive. Instead we're going to focus on the tools that GoLive uses to create that code. GoLive has been designed to allow you to create dynamic sites using these technologies without having to learn the code.

If there is enough of a programmer in you to want to get deeper into the technologies, plenty of additional resources are available. You may want to begin your search at the following official sites:

- For ASP, `http://msdn.microsoft.com/asp/`
- For JSP, `http://java.sun.com/products/jsp/`
- For PHP, `http://www.php.net/`

WHAT GOLIVE PROVIDES

GoLive provides an exciting set of tools and resources to help you create your dynamic site. These range from the tools built into the software to included installers, sample sites, and even partnerships with service providers. It is truly an end-to-end solution.

27

Dynamic Content Module

The tools included in the GoLive application to assist you with creating a dynamic site are jointly called the Dynamic Content module. There are four basic elements: the Dynamic Bindings Palette, the Dynamic Content Toolbar, the Content Source Editor, and the Content Source Inspector.

Dynamic Bindings Palette

This palette, shown in Figure 27.2, enables you to specify the data source binding for any dynamic element on a page. For example, if your page contains a text field for a person's name, this palette lets you specify the database where contacts are stored, and also the field within that database where the name is stored.

Figure 27.2
When a dynamic element is selected in a page, the Dynamic Bindings palette allows you to select the data source and field name that it is bound to.

Dynamic Content Toolbar

The Dynamic Content Toolbar is available from the Window menu, and is shown in Figure 27.3. Its three icons allow you to work online or offline, toggle highlighting of any dynamic elements within your page, and open the Dynamic Content page of the Site Settings window.

Dynamic Site Wizard

This wizard is used to convert a static site into a dynamic one. From the Site Settings window, click on the Dynamic Site Wizard button to launch the wizard. See Figure 27.4.

Your data source needs to already be set up, and your server as well. The wizard will ask you where everything is located; you'll select the server technology you wish to use, and the wizard will do everything else, turning your site into a dynamic one and enabling all the rest of the Dynamic Content module tools.

Content Source Editor

A content source is one step more specific than a data source. A data source is a complete database, whereas a content source is the specific query of the database. For example, a data source might be a Contacts database, and a content source might be the first name of a desired contact.

27

Dynamic Content Site Settings
Go Online/Offline
Toggle Dynamic Highlighting

Figure 27.3
The Dynamic Content Toolbar gives quick access to three features that you'll probably hit a lot when developing a dynamic site.

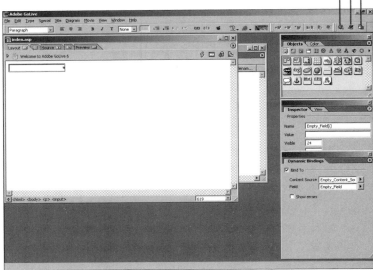

Figure 27.4
Select a server technology on the Dynamic Site Wizard.

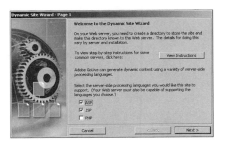

Figure 27.5
The Content Source Editor shows a few sample sources.

The Content Source Editor, shown in Figure 27.5, is accessed by clicking the icon of the same name near the top right corner of the page window. This editor lets you create, edit, or delete any content sources for the current page. Highlight any source in this list to view its attributes in the Inspector.

Content Source Inspector

The Inspector enables you to set the attributes of a content source selected in the Content Source Editor (see Figure 27.6). This is where you specifically define what data source is used for each content source.

Figure 27.6
The Content Source Inspector shows the data source used by this particular content source.

The different types of content sources are

- **Database Query**: Depending on the server technology you're using, this will be ADO (ASP), JDBC (JSP), or MySQL (PHP). This is the most common type of content source.

- **XML Data Source**: Supplies elements and attributes from XML. Depending on how the XML data source is configured, this source can return one record or many records.

- **Navigation Block View**: Returns a list of records describing blocks of records returned by another content source. This is usually used for building page navigation in result record sets.

- **Custom Merchant Shopping Cart**: Manages the contents of a Custom Merchant shopping cart.

- **Custom Merchant Order Form**: Manages a Custom Merchant order form.

Custom Merchant

Now that we've just cryptically mentioned Custom Merchant in passing as if it's something you should know, let's take a look and find out exactly what it really is.

Custom Merchant is the result of a partnership between Adobe, Evocative Software (http://www.evocative.com/), and Plug 'n Pay (http://www.plugnpay.com/). Evocative makes an online shopping cart system called ProCart, and Plug 'n Pay provides a transaction clearing service. This partnership lets you create your own nifty commerce site in GoLive, then use the Dynamic Bindings to link your pages to the power of the services provided by these two vendors. In short, it gives you a huge head start on an e-commerce site.

To learn more about Custom Merchant, see the GoLive CD.

27

EasyHost

EasyHost is another partnering solution, brought to you by Adobe and AdHost (http://www.adhost.com/). AdHost has set up their servers specifically to work with GoLive's Dynamic Content module to make it easy for you to develop and host your site without needing to configure your own servers. They've already done it for you.

To learn more about the EasyHost service, visit http://golive.adhost.com/.

Preconfigured Servers

If you're using JSP or PHP, Adobe has taken the additional step of providing installers on the CD to create complete JSP or PHP server environments on your Windows or Mac OS X computer. These installers will load you up with MySQL, PHP, or (if you're using JSP) Tomcat, and the Apache Web server. Best of all, the installers will then configure everything just the way GoLive wants to see it. This step will likely spare you some amount of grief.

PageGenerator

GoLive also provides support for one other way to serve dynamic content, and that is to convert it all to static pages. This method works well if your data doesn't change very often. Another good example would be to create a product catalog from a company whose products are best browsed by category, rather than found by parameter searches. Static sites have the added benefit of being extremely friendly to high server load. Since there is no application server or database needed to serve such a site, the efficiency goes way up and your site will have a much higher tolerance to heavy traffic.

You will still need to go through the process of setting up one of the dynamic technologies on your server, because GoLive will need to access that server to perform the actual generation of the static site.

The other thing you'll need to provide is an HTML file with a big table listing all the static files you want to create, and the parameters necessary to create those documents. This page is best generated by your dynamic site as well.

PageGenerator (see Figure 27.7) will go through your HTML table line by line, as if it's reading instructions, and on each line, it will query the server, retrieve the finished page, and save it as a static file with the filename you've provided in the HTML table.

The \modules\PageGenerator folder inside your Adobe GoLive application folder has some advanced examples of this.

Figure 27.7
The PageGenerator screen. PageGenerator will go line by line through the file specified in the first field, then output the resulting Web pages to the location specified in the second field.

Essentially, you're creating a big macro list for GoLive to follow. Your table file will need to look like this:

Template	sku	Tax	Output File
http://www.mysite.com/search.asp	11	yes	sku11.html
http://www.mysite.com/search.asp	12	yes	sku12.html
http://www.mysite.com/search.asp	13	yes	sku13.html

GoLive will then hit your server with the following three requests:

```
http://www.mysite.com/search.asp?sku=11&tax=yes
```

```
http://www.mysite.com/search.asp?sku=12&tax=yes
```

```
http://www.mysite.com/search.asp?sku=13&tax=yes
```

And store the resulting pages as static files with the filenames in the rightmost column.

TROUBLESHOOTING

Getting the Preconfigured Servers to Run

I've installed Adobe's Preconfigured Servers, but they're not working.

You may have a conflict with an existing server already on your computer, or there may have been a configuration problem or error during the install. Uninstall them, and check to make sure you don't have any other Web sharing enabled on your computer. Reinstall them again. The servers should work, so if they still don't, even after following this process, something is screwy. Contact Adobe's technical support, or for free and fast support, search the archives at Adobe's user forum for GoLive (`http://www.adobe.com/support/forums/main.html`).

Broadening Your Horizons

I can't do what I want to do using GoLive's tools. Am I stuck with this?

Not at all. The tools we'll be using in the next chapter provide fast access to common functions, but they don't prevent other functions from being handcoded. If you are a PHP guru, for example, and can't accomplish what you want using GoLive's wizards, you can still code your PHP tags directly into source code view and everything will work. GoLive is completely friendly to dynamic server code, even if it didn't generate it.

The downside to this is that you'll need to learn the programming code at a fundamental level. Refer back in this chapter to the home pages for each of the supported programming languages, and you'll find good starting points for whatever tutorials you'll need.

27

GOING LIVE

Another great way to learn is to pick up bits and pieces of open source code that are widely available. The home pages mentioned before all lead to great sources, but also check out the larger general interest portals like `http://www.webreference.com`, `http://webmonkey.com`, and `http://www.webdeveloper.com`.

27

USING DYNAMIC CONTENT

IN THIS CHAPTER

Overview of Dynamic Content   **506**

About Web Applications   **506**

About Data Sources   **508**

The Dynamic Content Tools   **509**

Building the Dynamic Site   **514**

Security   **536**

Troubleshooting   **536**

Going Live   **537**

OVERVIEW OF DYNAMIC CONTENT

Dynamic content, as opposed to static content, is content on your Web pages that changes. Surf any page of Yahoo!, eBay, or Amazon, and you will find more dynamic content than static content. The information on those pages changes based on information from that company's database (an item's current price, or a list of today's headlines); information sent by you the user (results from that search you just did, or the items in your shopping cart); or from other sources (today's date and time, the number of hits a page has received, or the type of browser you're using).

There really aren't any popular Web sites that are completely static, and the reason is simple: When you've seen it, you've seen it; there's no reason to return. So if you plan a successful career as a Web developer, you're almost certainly going to need at least a fundamental understanding of how dynamic sites work. At a minimum, even a designer needs enough knowledge to work with the application developer if the site is going to be a good one.

This chapter is *not* intended to be a tutorial for PHP, JSP, or ASP. That's well beyond the scope of this book and not necessary to use the tools provided by GoLive. It certainly helps to know French when reading the menu, but this chapter is intended to be the English translation below each entrée. In other words, it's just enough to put snails on your plate.

A lot of good information is available in the GoLive manual regarding installing and configuring various databases on different servers. That information will not be duplicated here; rather consider this a practical guide to using these tools after they're installed and configured.

ABOUT WEB APPLICATIONS

A *Web application* is a software program that you access via a Web browser. It can be the shopping cart application on Amazon, your company's intranet where you find the date of the next company picnic, a powerful accounting program, a Web search engine, or even the signup form to receive a newsletter from some corporate Web site.

Most Web applications have no client-side code. All the important code and data reside on the server. Your computer could explode suddenly, and none of your work would be lost. Web applications also have the benefit of being accessible to users wherever they are, allowing the user to, among other things, collaborate with co-workers on the other side of the ocean, or place an order with a company and not care where it's located.

Web applications consist of an application server and the code. The application server may or may not be separate from the Web server. Often it is just a Web server plug-in or an applet running on the same (or a different) machine. The server processes the instructions in the code and then returns the results to the user.

The code also resides server side. In some technologies, the code is embedded in HTML pages used by the server to build the pages sent to the users. In other technologies, the code can be compiled into the application itself, and it builds pages as needed.

Adobe GoLive provides a development environment for creating applications using three popular technologies that use the paradigm of embedding all the instruction codes within HTML pages. These technologies are ASP, JSP, and PHP. Certainly other technologies work this way (see Chapter

24, "Lasso Studio for Adobe GoLive," for one example), but these are the three natively supported by GoLive out of the box.

An important thing to note about all three of these technologies is that fundamentally, they're similar. To power and control the logic of the dynamic Web site, all these rely exclusively on code embedded within the HTML. And though the syntax and commands differ, the overall logic and the general idea behind each are the same. This similarity allows GoLive to shield you from the actual code, if that's what you want. The development methodology is the same for each of these three technologies, and you'll notice that there is a single set of icons on the Dynamic Content tab of the Objects palette. Those little icons, take the text field as an example, insert dynamic text fields into your page; and you don't even have to know whether it was done in ASP, JSP, or PHP.

The following sections look at each technology in detail.

About ASP

Active Server Pages (ASP) is the Microsoft technology built into IIS (Internet Information Server, the powerful commercial Web server that comes with the high-end versions of Windows). ASP is notorious for working with all things Microsoft, and only things Microsoft. Ever shop for a Web hosting facility, and notice that many of them offer "FrontPage extensions"? If you use Microsoft FrontPage to build a dynamic Web site, it creates ASP pages without even telling you that's what it did. You'll need to choose such a host if this is what you've done.

Choose ASP if

- You run Microsoft servers and databases, and you know for a fact that you will never change.

- You require hardware and software that is supported by a manufacturer.

Obviously, ASP is not an option if you're on Macs or any other non-Windows operating system.

As of this writing, ASP is fading away, to be replaced with ASP.NET, which is a newer, snappier version based on the C# (pronounced C Sharp) language.

About JSP

Java Server Pages (JSP) were originally created by Sun as an alternative to the Microsoft-centric world of ASP. This is nice because your pages can run on virtually any Web server or platform, without being limited to Microsoft. Java scripting is embedded within the HTML page to define the processing logic.

It's worthwhile to note the difference between JSP and Java servlets. *Servlets* are Java applets that sit on the server and receive HTTP requests along with certain parameters and then build a page according to instructions within the servlet and send it back out to the user. In contrast, a JSP is a page of code directly requested by the user, often with certain arguments or other parameters, and then the Java code within that page executes inside the server's JVM (Java Virtual Machine) and is replaced with the appropriate HTML. Then the finished page is sent back to the user. JSP and servlets are often combined, but they don't need to be. GoLive provides an environment to create Java Server Pages, not servlets, so this is where we will concentrate.

28

Choose JSP if

- You're not absolutely tied to Microsoft hardware and software.

- You want to be able to easily change server hardware or software.

- You want to use free, open-source server software.

- You prefer the ease and popularity of Java.

About PHP

PHP is another free and popular Web application technology. It was originally created by some guy named Rasmus Lerdorf (for real) to track visitors to his home page, and he called it "Personal Home Page tools." Since then it's been taken over by the Apache Software Foundation. PHP relies exclusively on code embedded within the HTML page. The primary difference between PHP and Java code is that PHP is more similar to PERL or C. A nice thing about PHP is its compatibility with just about every kind of database and network, including IMAP, SNMP, NNTP, POP3, or HTTP. PHP is available for all major platforms.

Choose PHP if

- You're not absolutely tied to Microsoft hardware and software.

- You want to use free, open-source server software.

- Your programming background is more Perl or C than Java.

ABOUT DATA SOURCES

There's a difference between your database, where your data resides, and GoLive's term *Data Source*. When GoLive refers to a Data Source, it's actually talking about a little file that it's going to create for your site containing information about a particular database. The Data Source includes everything such as where the database is on the network, what type of connection is needed to reach it, and what username and password to use. Data Source files are stored inside the *datasources* folder, which is inside the *config* folder that GoLive creates for every dynamic site.

GoLive does all the work to create the Data Source; you typically never need to know about it or worry about it. Later, when we build our dynamic site, we'll go through the steps to tell GoLive what it needs to know to define its Data Sources.

For the purpose of reading and understanding the GoLive documentation, it's important to note specifically what a Data Source is in GoLive terminology.

The following list outlines the more popular databases supported by GoLive, listed by the Web application language you've chosen, and showing the type of Data Source GoLive creates for it.

- .mdb—A Microsoft Access database file can be placed directly within the config folder and serves as its own Data Source. This Data Source is not supported by JSP or PHP.

- `.udl`—Connects to any ADO- or ODBC-compliant database defined in Windows's ODBC Data Sources administrative tool, such as Oracle, SQL Server, FileMaker Pro, Microsoft Excel, or Microsoft Access. This Data Source is not supported by JSP or PHP.

- `.sbs`—For JSP, this Data Source connects to a JDBC-compliant database, such as MySQL or FileMaker Pro. Check with the database vendor to obtain a driver, and then place it inside your site's WEB-INF/lib folder. For PHP, this Data Source connects to a MySQL database. The Dynamic Server installer that ships with GoLive installs and configures everything you need to use it. This Data Source is not supported by ASP.

- `.xds` — This Data Source connects to an XML or XSLT database. This can be as simple as a big XML text file. The Data Source also has to describe where all the data resides within the XML schema.

- `.ecp`—This Data Source contains all the information needed to connect to the Custom Merchant database, which is not resident on your server at all, but instead is located at the Custom Merchant service provider's location.

The databases themselves are the real meat. GoLive does not create your database for you, or even help you create it. That's the responsibility of the database you choose and whatever tools are available for it.

THE DYNAMIC CONTENT TOOLS

Tom Sawyer would have described GoLive's Dynamic Content offering as "a whole slather of tools." Before you dive into building a dynamic site, you should know what these tools are, why you need them, where to find them, and what to do with them.

Before you can do anything, you need to make sure that the Dynamic Content module is turned on. Go into Preferences, click the Modules pane, and make sure that there's a check next to Dynamic Content. If there isn't, check it and then restart the application.

Adobe GoLive's Dynamic Content module is comprised of eight basic elements: the Dynamic Bindings tab of the Objects palette, the Dynamic Bindings palette, the Dynamic Content toolbar, Dynamic Site Wizard, Content Source Editor, Content Source Inspector, the Dynamic Content Preferences pane, and the Dynamic Content site settings pane.

Figure 28.1 shows the Dynamic Content tab of the Objects palette, and all of its various tools. You'll be using many of these icons as you build your site.

Figure 28.1
The Dynamic Content tab of the Objects palette. See the next section for an explanation of each icon.

28

When your page shows a customer name from the database, placeholder text on your page is "bound" to the Content Source that contains the customer name from the database, and all that is defined on the Dynamic Bindings palette shown in Figure 28.2.

Figure 28.2
Use the Dynamic Bindings palette to define the content of every dynamic element on your page.

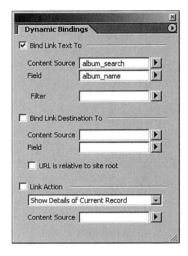

While working with dynamic content, the toolbar provides some options for managing your environment, detailed in Figure 28.3. Here you can go online or offline (make your connection to the data source live or not), to toggle highlighting of dynamic page elements, and to bring up the Dynamic Content site settings pane.

Figure 28.3
The Dynamic Content toolbar contains icons to let you manage the Dynamic Content editing environment.

The Dynamic Site Wizard, shown in the Figure 28.4, takes your static site and asks you easy questions to guide you through the process of converting it to a fully dynamic site. This wizard does most of the work for you, and once its done all of the Dynamic Content tools are live and available for working with your site.

Figure 28.4
The Dynamic Site Wizard adds everything to your site needed to convert it from static to dynamic, and allows you to specify all your data sources.

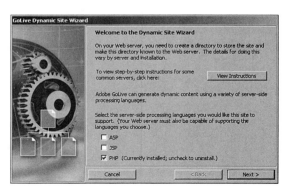

28

Every piece of dynamic content on a page requires what GoLive calls a Content Source, which is a stored query like "find the price of an apple," allowing you to use that price on the page. Figure 28.5 shows a Content Source's definition in the Content Source Editor. The Content Source's properties can then be edited in the Inspector, shown in Figure 28.6.

Figure 28.5
The Content Source Editor specifies the query that defines each dynamic element on your page. This window enables you to manage all your Content Sources on a page.

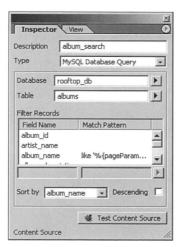

Figure 28.6
The Content Source Inspector. The Inspector lets you edit the properties of each content source.

The Dynamic Content tools also have their own sections in Preferences (see Figure 28.7) and Site Settings (see Figure 28.8), which store the most basic and crucial information about your dynamic site: the language(s) used, your data sources, a place to launch the wizard, and information about where your site is stored and how it's accessed.

Dynamic Content on the Objects Palette

The Dynamic Content tab on the Objects palette contains most all the elements you need to build a dynamic page. The first few items contain the required items, such as the content source. Most of the rest of the icons represent dynamic elements within the page, such as an image or text field, that are filled with results from your database. Simply drag these items onto your page, choose the content source for each, and you've got a true dynamic element.

28

Figure 28.7

The Dynamic Content Preferences pane. This lets you manage the cache GoLive uses to cache information from your data sources when online or offline.

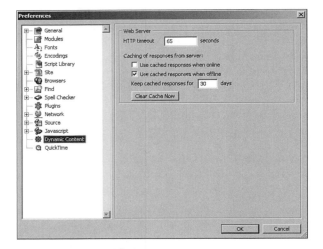

Figure 28.8

The Dynamic Content site settings pane provides an overview of your entire dynamic site.

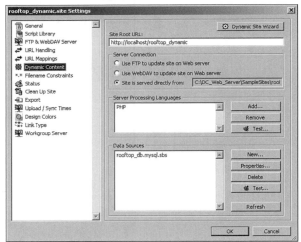

Let's look at each of the icons on the Objects palette tab:

- **Content Source**—A content source is a specific query of a data source. For example, your data source might be the customer database, and the content source might be a list of those customers with overdue invoices. This is the specific query you want to display on your Web page. Drag a Content Source icon into the head section of the Layout window and edit its parameters using the Inspector. You need to have one content source for each specific query returned on your Web page.

- **Container**—Drag this into your page to define the boundaries of data from your content source that is either conditional (may or may not appear, depending on something) or repetitive (multiple records retrieved). Data from the content source that do not have these requirements do not need to be inside a container.

- **Hide Content**—Drag this into your page to create a container that either displays or not, depending on the outcome of a condition you define in Dynamic Bindings. This is just the Container object with a few options preset.

- **Repeat Content**—Drag this into your page to create a container that repeats its contents once for each record returned by a search. Say that you're Google, and you found 10 Web sites. Drag one Repeat Content onto the page, fill it with the right code to display a single Web site's information, and when it's run you'll have 10 exact duplicates of whatever you put in there. This is just the Container object with a few options preset.

- **Replace Rows**—Drag this into your page to create a table where each found record appears in its own row. Rows repeat top to bottom for as many records as needed. The properties of the table can be adjusted as for a normal static table.

- **Repeat Cells**—Drag this into your page to create a table where each found record appears in its own cell. Cells repeat left to right, top to bottom, for as many records as needed. The properties of the table can be adjusted as for a normal static table.

- **Show Previous Record**—Creates a link to refresh the current detail page with the previous found record.

- **Show Next Record**—Creates a link to refresh the current detail page with the next found record.

- **Show Details of Current Record**—Insert this on a list of found records, and it creates a link to a detail page for each found record. The detail page needs to have the same content source name as this one.

- **Bound Image**—Creates an image tag for an image whose source comes from the content source.

- **Submit Action**—A submit button for a form.

- **Button Action**—A button that can be used to trigger an action.

- **Image Action**—An image that can be used to trigger an action, often used as a submit button for a form.

- **Bound Label**—A label containing data from the content source.

- **Bound Text Field**—A text field filled with data from the content source.

- **Bound Password**—A password field (bullets) filled with data from the content source.

- **Bound Text Area**—A text area filled with data from the content source.

- **Bound Checkbox**—A check box set with data from the content source.

- **Bound Radio Button**—A radio button set with data from the content source.

- **Bound Popup**—A pop-up menu populated with data from the content source. By default, this creates a static list that you can populate yourself, but if you want it populated dynamically, click the Construct Dynamically check box in the Dynamic Bindings palette.

- **Bound List Box**—A selection list populated with data from the content source. By default, this creates a static list that you can populate yourself, but if you want it populated dynamically, click the Construct Dynamically check box in the Dynamic Bindings palette.

- **Bound Hidden**—A hidden form field containing data from the content source.

Most of these elements can be created another way: by selecting a static element in your page and then clicking the Bind To check box in the Dynamic Bindings palette. This converts any static element, such as a selection of text, into a dynamic element that comes from your database.

BUILDING THE DYNAMIC SITE

The actual process of building a dynamic site in GoLive need not be as daunting as you might fear.

There is more than one way to go about it. You could go into Source Code view and just start typing raw PHP code. Before you laugh, know that most advanced developers will do just that. The tools in GoLive are great, but they're not entirely comprehensive. Because they are designed to support a variety of technologies, they are therefore rather generic, and for an advanced developer to take advantage of a Java-specific trick, he would need to get in there and type out his code.

Another way to go is to build one page at a time. Start at the beginning of the site—for example, the search page on Google—and create the look of the page and all the code necessary to a search form. Then move onto the second page, which is the list of results, and so on.

Yet another way is to build the logic of the whole site first: don't pay any attention to what the site looks like, just write the raw ugly code and get the site working. When it works, make it look nice.

But the methodology presented herein (and in the GoLive documentation) is more designer centric. Most of your work will be what you do best: designing an attractive and ergonomic site that looks good and is easy and elegant to use.

Some Web application development environments, such as Lasso Studio for GoLive presented in Chapter 24, provide a wizard to walk you through the process of defining the logic of your site and creating the required pages. For example, the wizard may ask you what you want the site to do, such as perform a search of a database, list the results, click on a result to see details, and perhaps edit those details or add a new record. There is no such wizard in the Dynamic Content module. You are on your own to determine what you want the site to do, and how the pages should flow.

The process presented in these pages will help you to plan your site flow, translate that into a succession of physical pages that your users will go through, then turn you loose with GoLive's design tools to make a sharp-looking prototype, and finally, convert that static prototype into a dynamic dynamo of a Web site.

The first step is to get your ducks in a row and make sure that the test servers are working.

Preparing the Servers

One of the coolest things about GoLive is that it includes installers for preconfigured servers: everything you need to run JSP or PHP on Mac OS X or Windows (ASP users can find all they need already on most Windows 2000 or XP machines). The preconfigured servers give you full Apache, PHP, and Tomcat installations, and the installers are swell enough to configure everything properly for you. Not only does this make it easy to create a test server on the same computer you do your GoLive work on, but you can even use these installers to build your live production servers. The installers also install a variety of sample sites that are good resources.

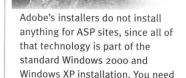

Adobe's installers do not install anything for ASP sites, since all of that technology is part of the standard Windows 2000 and Windows XP installation. You need one of those operating systems anyway to develop in ASP.

If you have your own servers already installed and running, you can skip this section. The following items are installed:

- Apache (`http://httpd.apache.org/`) is the world's most popular Web server for a couple of good reasons: no server is faster or more powerful, and it's free. It runs in Windows and virtually any flavor of Unix, including Mac OS X.

- Tomcat (`http://jakarta.apache.org/tomcat/index.html`) is a servlet container, often run in conjunction with Apache. Tomcat handles JSP pages, processing them with its servlets, and then lets Apache serve the results back to the user.

- PHP (`http://www.php.net/`) installs the CGI binaries to provide full PHP support for Microsoft IIS and Apache. It comes preconfigured with support for MySQL. Many hosted servers, and most Web servers in general, already have PHP support built in.

Run the installer provided on the GoLive CD to configure your server for JSP and PHP. At one point, it asks you what port you want to install everything on, and the default is 82. Unless you are running a different Web server on port 80 of your machine and you don't want to interrupt that, change 82 to 80, which is the default port for Web serving.

After the installation is finished, verifying that it works is simple because GoLive graciously provides a bunch of sample sites. These also come in handy later on when you're trying to do something and can't figure it out; you can pop open one of the sample sites and see how they did it.

Starting and Stopping the Servers

After the servers are installed, you need to start them. In Windows, GoLive puts a handful of scripts into the *Dynamic Content Server* folder, usually located in the *Adobe* folder in the Programs menu.

In Mac OS X, these scripts will also be located in the install directory. You can create desktop shortcuts, you can launch them directly from the install directory by double-clicking on them, or you can run them from a terminal window if you're so inclined.

To access the sample sites as shown in Figure 28.9, just point your browser at `http://localhost/`.

Before you can play with the sample sites, you'll need to create the databases they require. Fortunately, there are scripts that do this, and you can run those scripts by clicking the big Create

28

Sample Site Databases button in the middle of the page. While you're at it, click the next one down as well, which creates a test database for building a Custom Merchant site.

Figure 28.9
The sample sites home page provides accessed to the several sites installed by the preconfigured server installer.

Now you can go ahead and play with the sample sites listed down the left side of the page. They give a pretty good idea of some of the capabilities of GoLive's dynamic content tools.

Preparing the Databases

To build our dynamic site, we're going to need a database for Rooftop Records' lists of albums and artists.

You can build this database using whatever database you want. I used the preconfigured MySQL installation to build the example database used in this chapter. Also installed is a GUI interface called `WinMySQLadmin`, which has an interface that I wasn't too thrilled with, so I downloaded a shareware admin tool called SQLion from `http://www.exxatools.com/` that I found easier to use to define my tables and fields and enter sample data. Of course if you're handy with SQL, you can do all of this from a terminal window, but that's not my style.

If you're doing all of this from Mac OS X, it may be more difficult to find a decent GUI tool for MySQL. If you have a Windows box on the network, you can install SQLion onto that and remotely administer your Mac's MySQL database. Or more likely, you may choose to use FileMaker Pro as a JDBC source. The FileMaker Pro manual provides details about how to set this up.

The Rooftop Records database is simple as far as relational databases go. There are many artists. Each artist has many albums, and each album has many tracks. To make this structure work, it's necessary to store only the related `album_id` in each track record, and the related `artist_id` in each album record. Here are the tables I set up:

Field	Type	Setting
albums		
album_id	int(10)	auto increment
artist_id	int(10)	
artist_name	char(50)	
album_name	char(50)	
album_description	char(255)	
album_image_filename	char(50)	
artists		
artist_id	int(10)	auto increment
artist_name	char(50)	
artist_image_filename	char(50)	
artist_description	char(255)	
tracks		
track_id	int(10)	auto increment
album_id	int(10)	
track_number	int(10)	
track_name	char(50)	
track_time	char(10)	

Build these databases and then put in some sample data—just enough to test with. Make yourself a rock star if you want. Just remember to correctly link each track to an album record, and correctly link each album to an artist record.

Building the Prototype Site

The first step in building a dynamic site is simple, and you don't have to know a thing about databases or Web applications. But you will have to spend a lot of time. You're about to build the whole site as a static prototype.

It won't remain a prototype forever. When it's finished, you'll go through it and replace all the static content with dynamic content, one page at a time, gradually converting your functional static site into a functional dynamic site.

The most important step is planning. The best tool for this is a flowchart. You're going to diagram out your entire site (or at least the dynamic portion of it), and when you're finished building it, the Navigation window should pretty much match the flowchart you've drawn.

Depending on the size and importance of your site, you can use the Design Diagram function in GoLive to create a flowchart, or you can just whip it up quickly with pen and paper, as shown in Figure 28.10. Figure 28.11 shows the final version in Navigation.

28

Figure 28.10
This is an example of a flowchart drawn to plan a dynamic site.

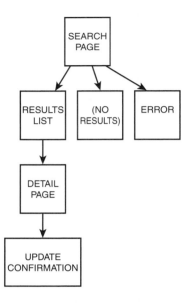

Figure 28.11
The finished site seen in Navigation; note how it matches the flowchart in Figure 28.10.

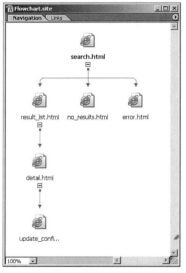

This process is not to be taken lightly. Mistakes at this early stage can mushroom into big headaches down the road. There is no wizard to assist you with this process; it's up to you to imagine every possible page that your users might see. A search page might lead to a list of successfully found records, but what page do you want your users to see when no records are found? Or too many? Or what if there's a server error?

When your user adds an item to his shopping cart, do you want to take him directly to the cart, to an acknowledgement screen, or leave him right where he is?

Even something as simple as a login screen can have an unexpectedly large number of permutations. Your user may already have an account, or he may need to create one. Maybe the username he chooses is already taken. Maybe he input the wrong password. He may choose to view a hint or have it mailed to him. The list goes on and on, and only by going through the laborious process of flowcharting can you truly be sure that you're catching everything up front. Pages in a dynamic site are usually navigationally dependent on one another, so it's not always a simple matter to insert an acknowledgement page that you overlooked before.

We're going to build a system to search the Rooftop Records site for albums (see Figure 28.12). A search page contains a box to input a keyword (`search.html`). A list of matching albums appears (`album_list.html`), followed by a detail screen (`album_detail.html`) that tells all about the album, tells about the artist, and lists the tracks. We'll end up with a site full of three static pages, shown in Figure 28.13.

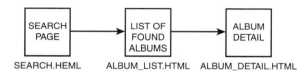

Figure 28.12
This flowchart is for a basic Dynamic Content example site.

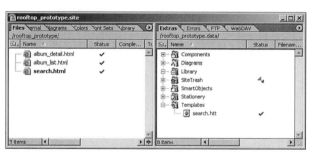

Figure 28.13
The Site window of our prototype site, showing the three pages, also the template. Notice that all pages here are just plain HTML pages, not PHP or JSP or ASP or any such funky thing yet.

Start by creating a page with all the elements common to the whole site to save as a template. In this case, we want the search field to appear on every page, so we're going to create the full `search.html` and save it as a template in the site, as `search.htt`, shown in Figure 28.14. Figure 28.15 shows what it looks like in a browser.

You do not need to do anything to prepare for the dynamic content at this stage. As long as your flowchart diagram is solid, and you have a firm logic for the flow through your site, only worry about the design and the user friendliness at this point.

The form with the text field and submit button should be given an action of `album_list.html`, which is the name of the results page.

Next we'll build a prototype of `album_list.html`, shown in Figure 28.16, starting with the template and adding a sample list of found results. Enter whatever you want here for sample data, just so that you have something as a placeholder for the actual dynamic data down the road. Link each of the albums to `album_detail.html` for now: Remember, the idea here is to get the whole site working as a prototype.

28

Figure 28.14
The search page, also saved as search.htt, is shaded because the whole thing is taken from the template, except for the one blank cell on the right where the additional content will go on the subsequent pages.

Figure 28.15
The search.html page as seen in a browser.

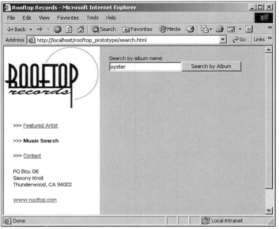

Figure 28.16
The album_list.html page is seen here in a browser.

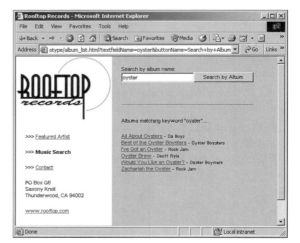

Finally, build `album_detail.html` to show everything about this particular album. In Figure 28.17, there are three types of data on the page: data about the album, data about the artist, and data about the tracks on the album. It's going to take three separate queries to build this page.

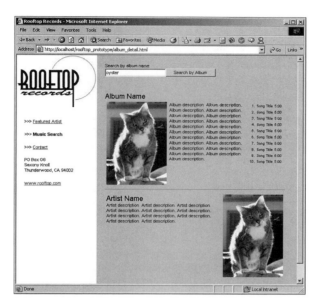

Figure 28.17
The `album_detail.html` page is seen here in a browser.

Not all album covers have a cat on them, and not all artists look like cats, so even those images are placeholders for dynamic data.

Thoroughly test your prototype site for broken or missing links, make sure that you have placeholders for all conceivable dynamic data, and then you're ready for the next step.

Converting the Static Site to Dynamic

Three basic steps are needed to change a static GoLive site to a dynamic one.

The first is to make the site dynamic. This copies needed resources into your site folder, defines your application technology and data sources, and prepares the site to function dynamically.

The second step is to make each page dynamic. When GoLive recognizes a page as being dynamic, the Dynamic Content module functions can then be applied to it.

The third step is to replace (or "bind") all your placeholder data with dynamic data. After page content is bound to dynamic data sources, you'll still see your placeholder data when you work on the page in GoLive, but you'll see the live dynamic data when you run the site from a server.

Let's begin by making the site dynamic.

Making the Site Dynamic

When the Site window is open, choose Settings from the Site menu and click on the Dynamic Content icon (see Figure 28.18).

28

Figure 28.18
Here is what the Dynamic Content section of Site Settings looks like when your site is still static.

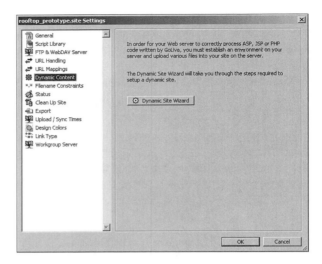

Click the Dynamic Site Wizard button to get things started. This wizard walks you through the process of defining your data sources and properly configuring your test server to work with GoLive (see Figure 28.19).

Figure 28.19
On the first screen of the wizard, choose the language(s) you want your dynamic site to support.

The first thing you'll need to do is choose the language, or the application technology, that you want to use. The choices are ASP, JSP, or PHP. If you want to use something else, such as Perl scripts or WebLogic, then you're using the wrong tool; but you also probably haven't bought this book and are not even reading this.

GoLive doesn't particularly care which you choose. Your choice will be decided by the issues discussed earlier in this chapter. GoLive's tools are designed to shield you from having to deal with the actual code, and the tools provided are intended to be generic enough to work the same across all three languages.

Tell GoLive where your site is being served, as shown in Figure 28.20. It's going to make life easier to do all your development and testing on the same machine, to avoid the need to transfer files each time you test a newly developed feature. Usually this single machine is going to be the one you're using, but it can also be a remote machine if you're accessing the site over a network or using

WebDAV. In either case, try to set things up so that you can test the server on the same files that you have open in GoLive. Then tell GoLive the URL to access your site. If your site is served from the same location where you're developing, you can probably just enter something similar to what's shown in Figure 28.21.

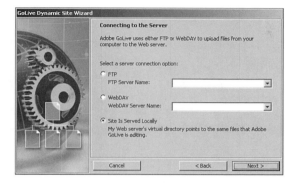

Figure 28.20
On the second screen of the wizard, choose where your site is being served relative to where your GoLive site is saved.

Figure 28.21
On the third screen of the wizard, enter the URL of your site. This is what you'd type into your browser to view the files you're working on now.

By now you'll need to have your test server up and running, or the wizard won't be able to complete. If you haven't done this yet, go back and do it now.

The fourth screen of the wizard, shown in Figure 28.22, explains how you'll manage the security of your site, because the same features that allow GoLive to manage it could become a potential security breach that others could exploit. We'll talk more about this in the "Security" section later.

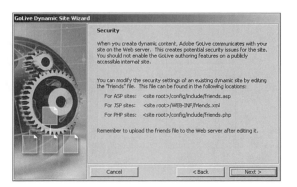

Figure 28.22
This screen provides some information about security.

28

If your server was installed and configured properly, you should see Figure 28.23 next. Click the Test button to make sure that everything is hunky dory.

Figure 28.23
Test your site's connection from this screen.

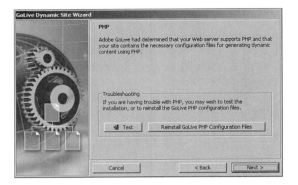

Among other things, the wizard creates a Config folder in your site, full of various items, depending on the chosen language. It uploads some other files to this directory to test the server with. If you've installed GoLive's servers from the Adobe CD and not made any strange manual changes, everything should check out fine when the wizard tests your site (see Figure 28.24). If the test doesn't succeed, the most likely cause is that you haven't properly entered the locations of your server folder and your site. If this is the case, GoLive should alert you here.

Figure 28.24
If everything is working properly, clicking the wizard's Test button brings up a browser with contents something like this, showing that all tests passed.

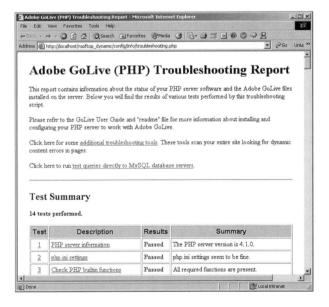

You also need to have your databases set up and running now, shown in Figure 28.25. If you haven't done this yet, exit the wizard now and get your databases set up. It also can't hurt to have a little bit of sample data in them. Make sure that the database you choose is supported by GoLive and by the language you've chosen.

Figure 28.25
The sixth screen of the wizard shows a list of your data sources. If you haven't defined one yet, click the New button.

The Add Data Source window shown in Figure 28.26 gives you a chance to specify the type of data source you're about to create. Only types supported by GoLive's implementation of your selected application technology are listed. In the case of this example, PHP was the selected language, so XML, CustomMerchant, and MySQL are the only choices listed in this picture.

Figure 28.26
Select the type of Data Source using the Add Data Source window.

If everything has been set up correctly, defining a new data source here should be simple. If the Test feature fails, take the time to troubleshoot it now. As stated before, if you use the servers that ship with GoLive and run those installers without changing anything, it's unlikely that the test will fail.

The Data Source window shown in Figure 28.27 is used to define a new data source, and it also appears when you click the Properties button of an existing data source. Name it whatever you want. The host name is the machine name (or IP address) of the computer hosting the database. Database refers to the database's name on the host machine.

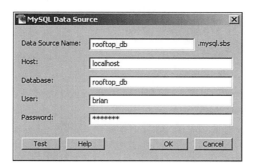

Figure 28.27
The Data Source window shows the connection information for your database.

28

You may notice that in this example PHP was selected for the application language and MySQL was used as the data source. The flow of the wizard is the same no matter what choices you make, so don't worry if what you see listed onscreen as choices doesn't match what you see in the figures in this chapter.

After you successfully complete the wizard, Figure 28.28 shows what the Dynamic Content section of Site Settings looks like. When you see this, it's a snap to change anything you selected in the wizard. You can change the application language; add, delete, and test data sources; and fiddle with stuff until everything is just the way you want it.

Figure 28.28
Here is what the Dynamic Content section of Site Settings looks like when your site is dynamic. Everything selected when running the wizard can be set and changed here as well.

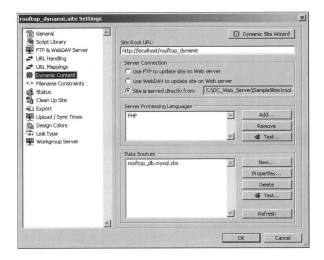

The next step is to go through each page of the completed prototype site and convert the pages to be dynamic.

Making a Page Dynamic

After a site has been made dynamic, opening any HTML page in your site causes the Dynamic Bindings palette to look like it does in Figure 28.29.

Really all this does is rename the page from `.htm` or `.html` to `.php`, `.jsp`, or `.asp`. You can do this yourself by renaming the page in the Site window. After the page has a dynamic file type extension, then GoLive permits the use of dynamic elements in the page. Click the Convert Page button shown in Figure 28.29 to make it a dynamic page and able to accept dynamic elements.

Be aware that when a page is renamed with this feature, other pages that reference it need to be updated. GoLive does this for you automatically, but it pops up a confirmation window showing a list of the pages that need to be updated.

Adding the Dynamic Elements

At this point, you have a working server, working databases, a fully dynamic site, and dynamic pages with (drum roll please) totally static content.

28

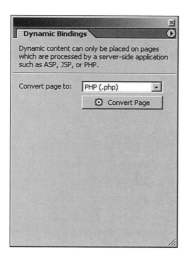

Figure 28.29
The Dynamic Bindings palette looks like this whenever you have a static page open in a dynamic site.

Imagine a kitchen. The previous steps have been analogous to stocking the pantry, and now we have arrived at a state where we can simply grab whatever pieces we want to build our smorgasbord.

So let's take it from the top, page by page, and go through the site, beginning with the first page.

Making the Search Page Dynamic

The first page is easy. It has no dynamic elements on it, and so there's nothing to change. In fact, we don't even need to make this page dynamic: it works equally well if we just leave it as an HTML page.

No elements on the search page get replaced with dynamic data. But, who knows: In the future we may decide to add some dynamic stuff to this page. There's no harm in renaming it now. So, if for no better reason than to get our feet wet, open it up, look at the Dynamic Bindings palette, and convert the page (refer to Figure 28.29).

Test the page by viewing it in a browser. If your test server is working correctly, the server processes the page, and the browser displays the page properly, even with its new file type extension.

Just make sure that the text search field is named *keyword* and the form action is `album_list.php` (or `.asp` or `.jsp`).

So onto the next page…

Making the Results List Page Dynamic

Open up `album_list.html` and make it dynamic using the Dynamic Bindings palette.

This page has one area of dynamic content: the list of found albums. It's a simple type of data because it all comes from a single query of the albums database.

This is where content sources come into play. Remember, for each query of a data source, we need a content source. In other words, to show a list of matching albums, we need a content source that is equal to "a query of the Albums database for albums matching the search term." Once that content source exists, we can bind elements on our page to it, and those elements will be replaced by the results of that query whenever the page is run.

To create our first content source, drag the Content Source icon from the Objects palette into the head area of the page, as shown in Figure 28.30.

Figure 28.30
A content source has just been dragged into the head area of the page. Now its properties can be set in the Inspector.

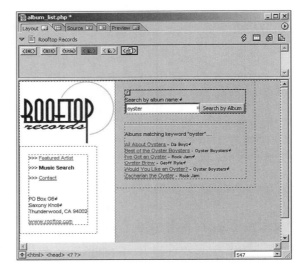

Now to name and define that content source, follow these steps:

1. In the Inspector, set its name to `album_search`.

2. From the Type pop-up, set it to MySQL Database Query (unless you're using something else for your data source, obviously).

3. From the Database pop-up, select your database. This one was named `rooftop_db` in MySQL.

4. From the Table pop-up, select the `albums` table because this is a search of the Albums database.

5. In the list of field names, we need to select the field that is being searched. Not the field(s) being retrieved; but the field that our query is operating on. Our keyword search was intended to scan through the album names, so click on the `album_name` field to highlight it.

6. Now click on the little pop-up menu below the list of fields to see the list of available operators. There are four different types of variables that we can try to match: a request parameter, which is an argument submitted along with the form such as the text field where the user typed his keyword; a cookie name, of which we have not set any; a session variable; and an application variable, both of which are not what we want. We want a request parameter. But—and here is where you're going to jump and scream—we don't want to *match* it. We want a list of all

albums *containing* our search term in the name, not *matching* it exactly. Unfortunately, MATCH is the only operator that GoLive gives us. So, right out of the gate, we are going to need to type in some manual code instead of using the GoLive tools. Instead of selecting something from that menu, put your cursor into that field where the = is and type the following code:

For PHP: `like '%{pageParameter("keyword","")}%'`

For ASP: `like '%" & Request("keyword") & "%'`

For JSP: `like '%{request.getParameter("keyword")}%'`

7. In the Sort By pop-up, select `album_name` to sort the found albums alphabetically by name.

8. Click the Test Content Source button shown in Figure 28.31. If there's any problem, most likely you made a typo. Try again. Usually the result for testing a query like this will be nothing found, which can sometimes generate an odd error message.

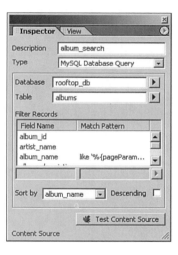

Figure 28.31
The `album_search` Content Source is defined here in the Inspector.

Now let's take our results and make them dynamic. We'll start by replacing our placeholder text for the list of albums. Grab the Repeat Content container icon from the Objects palette and drag it into the page right before our sample album list. Then take the first result and drag it inside the container (being sure to include the <br>). Now select the container by clicking on the yellow icon in the top corner of the container box and set the properties in the Inspector, as shown in Figure 28.32. Figure 28.33 shows the defined container on the page.

Now let's bind that placeholder text to the content source so that when the page runs, each found record will be replaced by the actual data from the database. First select the sample album name. Then, in the Dynamic Bindings palette, click the Bind Link To check box, select the `album_search` content source, and select the `album_name` field, as shown in Figure 28.34. This text is linked to the detail page, so also go to the bottom of the Dynamic Bindings palette and click the Link Action check box to Show Details of Current Record.

28

Figure 28.32
These settings will repeat everything inside the container once for each record found by the query.

Figure 28.33
The Repeat Content container has been dragged into the page and one row of sample data placed inside of it.

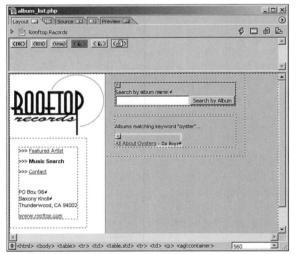

The green highlighting of bound elements on your page can be turned on and off by clicking the middle icon on the Dynamic Content toolbar (see Figure 28.36). This makes it easy to identify objects that you don't want to delete or screw up if you're just making design changes to the page.

Also, notice that content on the page, even though it's been bound to a content source, still shows your sample data in Layout mode. If you look at the source code, scroll all the way to the bottom and you'll see that GoLive has inserted some tags to maintain this placeholder content. This makes it possible to edit the pages, and still see what they'll look like when run, even when your computer is offline or otherwise disconnected from the data source.

Now let's do the same thing with the artist name. Select the placeholder text in the Layout window. In Dynamic Bindings, click the Bind To check box, choose the `album_search` content source, and the `artist_name` field (see Figure 28.35).

28

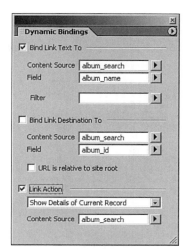

Figure 28.34
The album_name field has been bound in Dynamic Bindings to the content source and linked to the detail page.

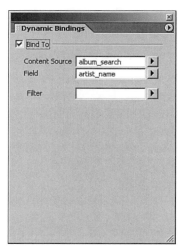

Figure 28.35
The artist_name field has been bound to the content source in Dynamic Bindings.

Figure 28.36
Highlighting of dynamic elements has been selected in the Dynamic Content toolbar.

One more thing. Notice on our album_list page that we threw the keyword used onto the results page to show you what list you're looking at. Again, this is a custom tag that must be hand-coded into the source. So, where we wrote "Albums matching keyword 'oyster,'" go into the source code, select the word "oyster," and replace it with

- For PHP: `<?php echo pageParameter("keyword","") ?>`
- For ASP: `<%= Request("keyword") %>`
- For JSP: `<%= gl.pageParameter("keyword","") %>`

Now the page should be done, as shown in Figure 28.37.

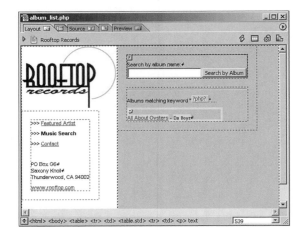

You can now test the site, and you'll see that you're able to search and find any of the records you entered into the database.

So now let's move on to the third and final page, the album detail page.

Making the Detail Page Dynamic

Open up `album_detail.html` and make it dynamic using the Dynamic Bindings palette.

This page is more complex because it has three different content sources, but the good news is that there's no hand-coding of custom tags needed. Let's start with those content sources.

Drag the first one in and call it `album_search`, as shown in Figure 28.38. This will be used to retrieve the details of the album specified by Show Details of Current Record from the `album_list` page.

The next content source is `artist_search`, shown in Figure 28.39, used to pull the details of the artist specified by Show Details of Current Record from the `album_list` page.

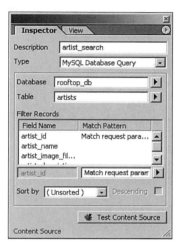

Figure 28.39
The `artist_search` content source is shown here in the Inspector.

The next content source is `track_search`, shown in Figure 28.40, used to list the tracks of the album specified by Show Details of Current Record from the `album_list` page. This one is sorted by `track_number`.

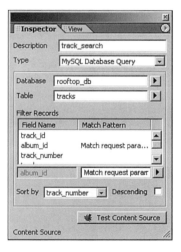

Figure 28.40
The `track_search` content source is shown here in the Inspector.

Now that the content sources have been defined, it's possible to select each placeholder element on the page and bind it to the appropriate content source. Start by selecting the big "Album Name" and use the Dynamic Bindings palette to bind it to the `album_name` field in the `album_search` content source.

Bind the long album description to the `album_description` field in the `album_search` content source.

28

Select the album cover photograph and bind it to the `album_image_filename` field in the `album_search` content source. This updates the `img src` pathname to whatever you have in the database. If your images are stored in a directory, you may need to check the code and manually add the directory name into the image tag. If you want, you can also specify the alt text in the Dynamic Bindings palette, and you may want to set that to `album_name`.

Now let's attack the track list. The first thing to do is to select the entire track list placeholder table (do this by selecting the table normally—for example, by right-clicking inside it and choosing Select Table)—and then in Dynamic Binding, click the Replace Rows check box as shown in Figure 28.41. This causes a row to be created for each record found by the query. Specify the `track_search` content source.

> The tools provided by GoLive's Dynamic Content module do not directly support the retrieval of images from databases—for example, when images are stored as BLOBs (binary large objects). Instead, GoLive lets you pull the filename or even full pathname from a database field. You can use BLOBs for images, but you will need to learn the code and type it into your pages manually.

Figure 28.41
The track list table with Replace Rows turned on in Dynamic Bindings.

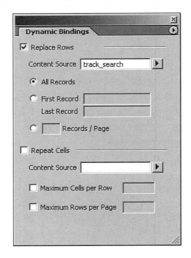

Now, one at a time, select each placeholder element in the first row and bind it appropriately. Using the `track_search` content source in each case, select the track number placeholder and bind it to the `track_number` field; select the song title placeholder and bind it to the `track_name` field; and select the track time placeholder and bind it the `track_time` field.

Now let's move to the lower half of the page and bind all the artist elements.

Select the "Artist Name" placeholder text and bind it to the `artist_name` field in the `artist_search` content source.

Select the long artist description placeholder text and bind it to the `artist_description` field in the `artist_search` content source.

Select the placeholder artist image and bind it to the `artist_image_filename` field in the `artist_search` content source. Also click Bind Alt Text To and select the `artist_name` field in the `artist_search` content source. Now your page should be complete, as shown in Figure 28.42.

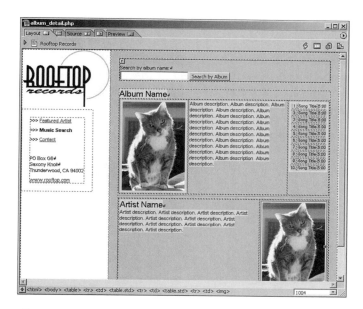

Figure 28.42
In the finished `album_detail` page, all the placeholder data is still visible to allow easy editing, but it's all bound to the dynamic elements.

You can now test the site. If you've followed all the instructions to the letter, it should run perfectly (see Figure 28.43). And you should have a good enough understanding of GoLive's dynamic content module tools to make an unlimited range of modifications and additions to our little Rooftop Records site.

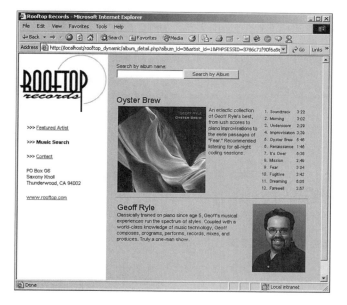

Figure 28.43
The finished `album_detail` page seen in a browser, with all the dynamic elements drawn from the database. Yowza!

28

SECURITY

The Adobe GoLive 6 manual includes important security information about your dynamic site. It is suggested that you read and understand the section "Making a Dynamic Site Secure."

GoLive Dynamic Site Security

The config folder that GoLive creates inside your dynamic site folder contains some documents that, if downloaded by an unscrupulous user, could compromise your site's security by providing that user with site and database passwords and configuration information. Note that appropriate steps have been taken to give this folder reasonable protection from any but serious hackers. Nevertheless, you should take any, or all, of the following steps to protect your site:

1. Render that information useless by running the database on a separate machine not accessible from outside your firewall.

2. Configure your Web server so that it will not serve anything from that folder.

3. Block all ports to your server except 80. If you don't know what this means, consult your systems administrator. If you don't have a systems administrator, thank your lucky stars (just kidding, systems administrators), and consult with your service provider. Web servers serve pages out over port 80, and all other services, such as FTP or database connections, use different ports.

4. Allow only specific IP addresses (namely your own) access to this folder. To do this, open the friends file inside the config folder (it's inside the /include/ folder for PHP or ASP, and the /WEB-INF/ folder for JSP). Use a text editor to open it. This document contains detailed instructions for adding IP addresses, but it's pretty simple: you basically just type them in at the bottom of the document. Normally, any user whose IP address is not listed in this document can't access anything in the config folder.

5. For your production server, disable write privileges for the config folder. (Write privileges are needed for development.)

6. Move that folder outside the server folder entirely. You need to edit some documents to do this, and that process is explained in the GoLive manual.

TROUBLESHOOTING

Making a Database Connection

When I try to test my Data Source, it always fails. What can I do?

This process should be fairly bulletproof. Most likely you've made a typographical error setting up the Data Source. If this is not the case, and it still fails, try reinstalling the Adobe Dynamic Content Server.

Run the sample sites. If they work, then you know for certain that the problem lies with the information you've entered. Load one of the sample sites and see how the Data Sources are defined.

If this still doesn't clear up the problem, there may be a problem unique to your machine's configuration. Try contacting Adobe's technical support. You can reach them at `http://www.adobe.com/support/`.

Abstract Queries

I need to define a Content Source that's more complicated than the examples in this chapter. How do I do that?

Most likely you just need to define a more complex SQL query. SQL is easy to learn, and extremely powerful. A great place to start is a free online tutorial such as the one found at `http://www.sqlcourse.com/`.

GOING LIVE

Here are some additional security issues that are not necessarily specific to dynamic sites created by GoLive, but are good rules of thumb to follow for any site. These are the author's personal suggestions, and are not endorsed by the CIA, KGB, or any other international espionage agency:

- You might not expect to see this listed as the first security tip, but it's one that I think is pretty important. Know your realistic security concerns and don't go overboard. Security overkill costs money, imposes restrictions and inconveniences, and in 999 out of 1,000 cases, isn't necessary. What's the worst that can happen? What are the realistic chances that someone has any interest in your site? Have you done something foolish like put unencrypted bank or credit card account numbers in a document or database accessible to that server? Do your customers have any real interest in hiring the needed talent to illegally hack in and view your other customers' records, and even if they did, would that harm anyone? Know the answers to these kinds of questions before you spend money on security.

- You might notice on the Rooftop Records site that some of the links to detail pages and so on end with something like this: `detail.php?album_id=3`. You could go to that URL and see album number 3; then you could put your cursor into the address field, backspace over the 3, type in a 4, and then you could view album number 4. You can see how it's possible that one customer could easily view another customer's record this way, or one salesperson could view another salesperson's accounts. Solve this by using server-side variables, session variables, or cookies rather than URL arguments whenever possible. These cannot be edited by the user. If access to some of your records requires a user to be logged in (I can't change my credit card on Amazon unless I'm logged in), set a cookie or a session variable for that user, embed that value in all his authorized database records, and be sure to include that parameter in all queries.

- Most developers never think of this, but statistically, it's far more likely that someone will walk into your office and carry your server away than it is that you will ever be hacked. Take physical security precautions, and you will remove most of the threat right then and there.

28

- Hacking is much easier from inside your office over the LAN than from outside via the Internet. Take appropriate network security measures as well as server security measures. And lock the door where the server lives.

- Usually the sensitive information is not on your Web server at all but rather on a database server or file server. Take care that these machines receive the bulk of your physical and electronic security before you worry about the Web server. Professional thieves know that there are a hundred ways to steal your data without having to learn Unix.

- Don't put anything inside your server folder that doesn't have to be there. ASP works with a Microsoft Access database residing inside the config folder. Don't do that.

- Use unguessable passwords and change them at frequent, irregular intervals. Don't write them down. Don't type them in a document and put it on a computer that's on your network.

Be thorough with your security where it makes sense, and don't stress it where it doesn't. Not following these procedures is like a knight wearing armor on half his body: It doesn't matter how thick that armor is.

29

CUSTOM MERCHANT

IN THIS CHAPTER

About Custom Merchant   **540**

Implementing Custom Merchant   **541**

Troubleshooting   **556**

Going Live   **557**

ABOUT CUSTOM MERCHANT

29

Custom Merchant is Adobe's name for a program where they offer supplementary merchant services to users building e-commerce Web sites. These services, basically credit-card processing and related services, are provided by companies who have done some work to integrate well with GoLive's authoring environment. In practice, this means that you still get to design and host your own site and maintain 100% control over it. But the most problematic links in the shopping cart and credit card processing chain are handled by someone else, and they're handled transparently.

Credit-card processing is a crucial part of most commerce Web sites. Charging your customers is obviously critical to your business, but it also introduces a whole host of technical headaches that you'd rather do without. Custom Merchant can take those headaches away.

This arrangement brings what I consider the key benefit: It relieves you of adding one more hat to the many you probably already wear—that of Full Time Credit Card Exceptions Processing Clerk.

In the real world, a lot of credit card transactions don't go through on the first try. And of those, a lot don't go through on any subsequent tries. Cards are expired. Numbers are entered wrong. Cardholders are deadbeats. The bank's modem is temporarily unavailable because the FBI shut the power down in mid-winter to freeze a mad streaking fanatic out of his basement hiding place. When you set out to process credit cards on your own Web site, you must prepare to handle every imaginable error; and if you want to recover those sales, you need to manually do something about each of them. Chances are you don't have time for this. In many cases, the tiny fees charged by commerce partners to handle this for you is well, well worth it.

But credit card processing is by no means the only benefit of using Custom Merchant. There are other services, such as calculating shipping amounts, verification that an address is correct, and verifying that an address is a legal shipping destination for your chosen shipper. Many shippers such as UPS provide Web-based tools to facilitate such functions, but a Custom Merchant service provider has already done all of that work for you.

The way this works is simple. You design your Web site the way you like, and you add your own "Add to Cart" buttons and so forth. Design your own cart view and checkout screens. Design your own "Thank You for Ordering" screen. But use the Custom Merchant service provider's data source (see Chapter 28, "Using Dynamic Content" to learn about data sources). The service provider will worry about the database, shopping cart records, and processing the charge at checkout. All you have to worry about is shipping the orders that were successfully charged, and watching the money appear magically in your bank account. Then sit back, pop open a cold one, and click on the TV to watch how the streaker crisis winds up. This is way things are supposed to work in life.

Downsides to using such a system include an extra link or two in the chain, which affects performance and can affect uptime. When your user makes a call to your Web site, your server must then make another call to the service provider, which then makes an additional call to authorize the credit card transaction. This involves lots of servers and Internet hops. Rarely is there ever a problem, but when you double the number of servers that must be contacted, you double the response time and you double the likelihood of a connection failure. This is not to alarm you: It's rather like two needles in the haystack rather than just one, but it's worthwhile to be aware of.

IMPLEMENTING CUSTOM MERCHANT

The ideal guinea pig for our Custom Merchant site is to add online commerce to the record album search we built in Chapter 28. Let's take it step by step.

Add the Custom Merchant Data Source

Before we can do anything like add buttons or functions or stuff, we need to have a Custom Merchant data source. As stated above, this is a data source that is maintained by a service provider, as opposed to a data source that comes from a local database you maintain. This means that your Web server will make calls across the Internet to read and write records to the service provider's database. In test mode, which we'll do here, this is not encrypted. But in practice, if you actually set up a live account with a service provider, it will be encrypted. This protects any credit card numbers entered onto your site as your server transmits them to the service provider for settlement.

Open up the Site Settings window (see Figure 29.1) and click the New button in the Data Sources section. This brings up the Add Data Source window (see Figure 29.2), and here you can select Custom Merchant Provider. Click the Add Data Source button.

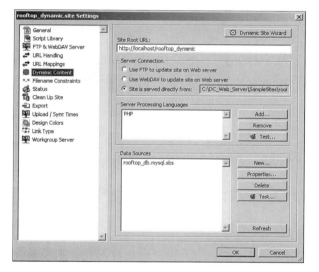

Figure 29.1
The Site Settings screen. Click the New button in the Data Sources section to add a Custom Merchant data source.

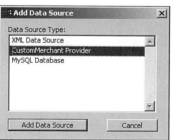

Figure 29.2
Select CustomMerchant Provider in the Add Data Source window.

Next, you'll need to define the Custom Merchant Provider. Theoretically, this can be anyone who is set up to work with you. Check your Adobe GoLive documentation to find out what service providers are listed currently. For the purposes of this demonstration, we're going to use the test server of ProCart Live, a service of Evocative, Incorporated. As of this writing, Evocative is one of the companies from which you may choose to set up an actual Custom Merchant account. You may certainly complete the example in this chapter using a different provider.

Figure 29.3 shows the window that pops up next. Under Data Source Name, enter **procartlive** to identify this data source (you can name it whatever you like). The Provider URL is the address that your server is going to contact across the Internet to reach Evocative's actual database. Enter **http://demo.procartlive.com:8080/CustomMerchant/dispatch.cfm** in this field. Note that the .CFM extension means that this service provider is using a different programming language on their site to provide their service than the JSP, PHP, or ASP that you are using. Their server is completely separate from yours, and is doing its own thing, so there is no need for that filetype extension to match yours. Finally, the Merchant ID tells the service provider who you are. If you buy a real account, they'll give you a real number. But for Evocative's test server, just enter **1**. Click Test, and if the planets are aligned, you'll see something like Figure 29.4 to indicate that the test server is running and you have access to some real fake data. Click OK to get back to the Site Settings window and it should now look like Figure 29.5, showing the new data source in place and available throughout your site.

Figure 29.3
This screen allows you to specify the location and name of your Custom Merchant service provider's server.

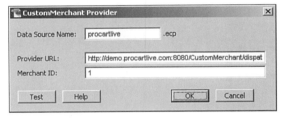

Figure 29.4
Here are the results of a successful test of Evocative's test Custom Merchant server.

Building an Add to Cart Button

Now that the data source exists, it's possible to take elements on pages and bind them to the data source. The first step we'll take with this newfound freedom is to add an "Add to Cart" button on our album_detail.php page.

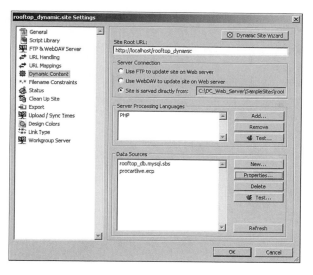

Figure 29.5
The Site Settings window now shows that you have two data sources: the one previously set up to search the albums database, and the new Custom Merchant data source for creating online orders.

To do this, we first need a Content Source in the page. Open that page and drag a Content Source icon from the Dynamic Content section of the Objects palette into the header section of the page (see Figure 29.6). In the Inspector, give it an obvious description like `shopping_cart` and select Custom Merchant Shopping Cart from the Type pop-up menu. Select procartlive, or whatever you named the Custom Merchant data source, from the Cart Provider pop-up list. This content source will be used for all shopping cart–related activities while using Custom Merchant.

Now let's add the "Add to Cart" button. Since it's going to be a Submit button, the first thing we'll need is an enclosing form. Drag in a form from the Forms section of the Objects palette and drop it into a convenient place on the layout. In the Inspector, set the form's action to `config/actions/custommerchant.action6.php` (or jsp or asp).

Drag a bound Submit button into the form from the Dynamic Content section of the Objects palette (see Figure 29.7). On the Inspector, click the Label checkbox and type **Add to Cart**, or whatever you'd like the button to say.

Next, we'll use the Dynamic Bindings window (see Figure 29.8) to bind this button to the Content Source we just created. The fields that appear in this window are defined by the Custom Merchant service provider. In other words, you'll see that an SKU, Description, and Unit Price are all required. The Customer Merchant service provider has defined these and requires you to fill them in. To bind the button and include all the right information, follow these steps:

1. From the Action pop-up menu, select Custom Merchant, and then, from the submenu, select Add to Cart. This is one of the predefined actions defined by your Custom Merchant service provider.

> **Caution**
>
> Some early versions of GoLive 6 had a bug that inserted an extra question mark into the code directly after the previous form action. If you follow this exercise and nothing is being added to your cart, go into source code view mode and, if there is an extra question mark immediately following the form action listed above, delete it.

Figure 29.6
A new Content Source has been dragged into the header and named shopping_cart, and defined as a Custom Merchant Shopping Cart bound to the pro-cartlive data source.

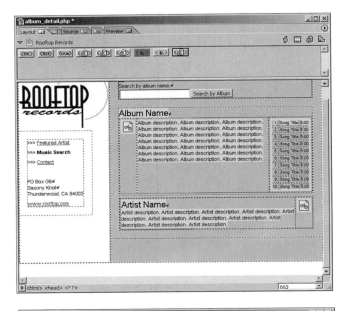

Figure 29.7
A Submit button has been dragged into the page from the Objects palette and named "Add to Cart." It's red because it hasn't yet been bound to a valid content source.

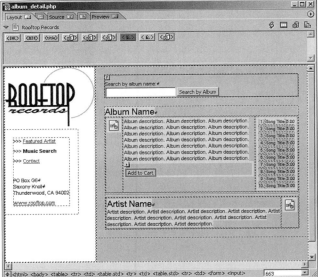

2. Select procartlive from the Cart Provider pop-up menu. This is the data source you defined earlier.

3. Next, choose the SKU by selecting album_search (the content source that retrieved this album) from the pop-up menu. Choose album_id from the submenu.

4. Under Description, select album_search from the pop-up menu, and choose album_name from the submenu.

5. Next we need to tell it the price. We chose not to include a price in our Rooftop Records database, but we might as well have; in which case it would be one of the fields in the `album_search` content source. Since it's not, we'll be generous and offer all Rooftop Records albums at the bargain price of $10. Enter **"10"** in quotes. Quotes mean that it's a literal value, rather than a database field named 10.

6. Click the "On success" checkbox and tell it to redirect to a new page we haven't made yet, `view_cart.php` (or jsp or asp), to view the shopping cart.

Viewing the Cart

Before we can test the process of adding items into a shopping cart, we need a page that displays the cart contents so we can verify that an item was added.

Let's go back to our original template for the Rooftop Records site and create a new page called `view_cart.php` (or `.jsp` or `.asp`). Add the same `shopping_cart` content source used above, and your page should look like the one shown in Figure 29.9.

Drag a form into the page to enclose the shopping cart display and Update Cart button. Go to the Dynamic Content section of the Objects palette and drag a Replace Rows table into the form. Then use GoLive's other tools to make the shopping cart look however you like. When you're done, you'll have something that looks like Figure 29.10, and includes all the shopping cart standards like an editable quantity field, the product name, and a unit price and extended price. You could also add other fields that your Custom Merchant service provider supports as well. Also, add an Update Cart button, used to save changes to the quantities of each line item. Enter zero for the quantity to remove an item from the cart.

The Check Out button can be a simple link to a checkout screen; it does not need to be within the form. If your Custom Merchant service provider already knows enough to display the current cart, then they know enough to begin the checkout process. So we can proceed to that screen without the need to pass any further parameters.

To make this cart display live information, we need to bind the objects. First we need to define the form. Select the form and go to the Inspector. Like all of our Custom Merchant forms, it needs to be set to `config/action/custommerchant.actions6.php`, and the method should be `post`.

Select the Update Cart button. In Dynamic Bindings, check Action and choose Custom Merchant, Update Cart Totals from the pop-up menu. Then select the `shopping_cart` content source, as shown in Figure 29.11. Leave the redirect field blank so that we see the updated cart right here on the same screen after the action is processed.

> **Caution**
>
> Using the actual values from your database for the SKU is the way this works in practice. Custom Merchant service providers such as Evocative require that your product database be on file with them. They provide a test database of products for test usage, which differs from the Rooftop Records product database we've created. Therefore, trying to add our Rooftop Records albums to Evocative's test shopping cart will not work. If you are using a test account, you can work around this limitation by using Evocative's test SKU numbers, which are TEST1 and TEST2 (as of this writing). To do this, go into your album database and use these values for the `album_id`. Or, for now, just enter **TEST1** into the SKU field in the Dynamic Bindings example above. Every time you add any album to the shopping cart, the same strange test product will appear in your cart instead. Don't worry; that means everything is working.

Figure 29.8
The Add to Cart button is bound to the `shopping_cart` Content Source using the Dynamic Bindings window.

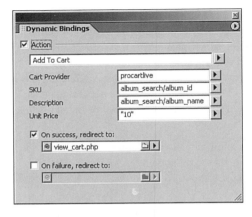

Figure 29.9
Use the original Rooftop Records template to create a `view_cart` page, and add the `shopping_cart` content source.

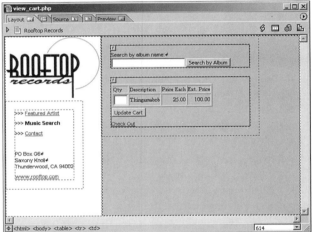

Figure 29.10
Design your own shopping cart view screen using dummy data. Make it as elaborate and funky as you like. Then use the Dynamic Content tools to bind your dummy to the Custom Merchant content source to make it live.

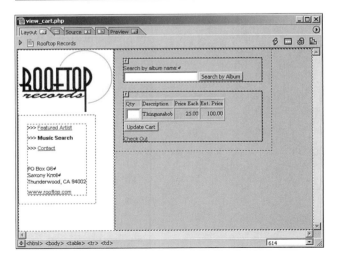

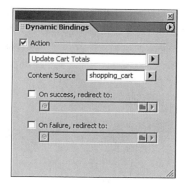

Figure 29.11
Define the Update Cart button's bindings in the Dynamic Bindings palette.

Figure 29.12 shows the Update Cart button in the Inspector. It's a Submit button with a custom label of Update Cart, and you'll find that GoLive has named it _UpdateTotals.

Figure 29.12
Define the Update Cart button's appearance and function in the Inspector.

Next we'll deal with the Quantity field. Select it and go to Dynamic Bindings as shown in Figure 29.13. Bind it to the shopping_cart/Item List content source, and select the Quantity field. Then, if you look at it in the Inspector, you'll see that it's been named qty[i]. Once you run this page in a browser and view source, you'll see that one of the things Custom Merchant does is number each line item in the cart qty[1], qty[2], and so on. This is how it achieves unique field names for every row in the cart.

Figure 29.13
Define the Quantity field in Dynamic Bindings.

Select the placeholder text for the product description, use Dynamic Bindings to bind it to the shopping_cart/Item List content source, and select the Description field. Do the same for the Price and Extended Price fields.

Notice that for these price fields, there are some additional formatting options in Dynamic Bindings (see Figure 29.14). You can choose to format it as currency, and specify the number of decimal points, thousands separator, and the character to be used for the decimal.

Figure 29.14
Number fields can be given extra formatting in Dynamic Bindings.

There is another trick that can be employed on this page. What if the cart is empty? Rather than displaying an empty table, it's nicer to show a message that the cart is empty instead. This can be achieved easily using the Hide Content tool [icon:3301] on the Objects palette. When you drag a Hide Content box onto your page, it creates a boundary into which you can insert content that may or may not display based on certain criteria. For example, you can hide the cart if no records were found. And you can create a second Hide Content area into which you can put a friendly message, and set that area to display if no records are found.

To do this, drag the Hide Content tool from the Dynamic Content frame of the Objects palette and drag it into your page. Then grab the form we just designed, and drag it inside the Hide Content area. Select the Hide Content area, go to Dynamic Bindings (see Figure 29.15), and set it to hide if no records are found.

Figure 29.15
Use a Hide Content area to display content that may or may not appear based on the criteria you define.

Next, using the same technique, create a second Hide Content area and put a friendly "empty cart" message inside it. Go to Dynamic Bindings and choose the opposite setting: to show if no records are found. When you're done, your cart screen might look something like Figure 29.16.

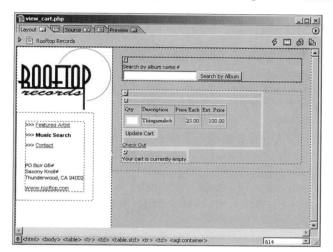

Figure 29.16
When you have multiple Hide Content areas within your dynamic page, you can have certain areas that appear and certain areas that do not, thereby achieving significant dynamics on a single page.

The last thing to do is link the Check Out text to the name of the page we'll use next, which will be checkout.php (or .asp or .jsp). You can do this using the Inspector normally; there's no Dynamic Content involved here.

The Check Out Screen

This brings us to the checkout screen. Here the user will provide Custom Merchant with the customer and billing information, including the billing address and credit card. Design a screen to collect all these fields inside a form. Start with your site template if you like; it should look something like Figure 29.17.

When you drag the Content Source into this page's header, beware: We're going to use a different one this time. Up until now we've always used the Custom Merchant Shopping Cart. This time, drag in the Custom Merchant Order Form. Set it to the procartlive provider as before. And this time, name it order_form instead of shopping_cart. The reason for this change is that we're no longer dealing with a cart full of stuff; we're now dealing with a single order that has customer data associated with it and checkout actions instead of shopping cart actions. So the other Content Source provides a different feature set.

Now to make this page dynamic. Start by setting the form action, as with all Custom Merchant forms, to config/actions/custommerchant.actions6.php (or .asp or .jsp).

Using the Dynamic Bindings palette, bind each of the fields to the order_form content source, and select the field name from the Field pop-up menu, as shown in Figure 29.18. Each time you do this, it automatically sets the right properties in the Inspector, so you don't need to worry about that. You'll find that there are many more fields available in this content source than you were planning to use. Use the ones you want to. And in some cases, your Custom Merchant service provider may tell you that some are required.

Figure 29.17
To make the checkout screen, start with a mockup of a screen to collect billing and credit card information.

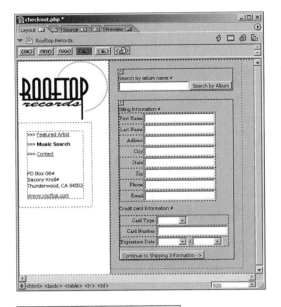

Figure 29.18
Use Dynamic Bindings to bind each field on the checkout screen to the matching field in the `order_form` content source.

When you get to the credit card fields, there is a new trick that Custom Merchant has for us. Not only do you select the content source and field name, but you can also request Custom Merchant to automatically build the list of accepted credit cards, based on your account with the service provider. Figure 29.19 shows how you first select the `order_form/available-creditcardbrand` content source, and then specify that the pop-up menu uses Credit Card Brand ID for the field value that gets submitted, and the Credit Card Brand Name for the label that is displayed on the Web page. Very cool. The pop-ups for the month and year need to be built manually (see Chapter 16, "Creating Forms," for more information) .

Next bind the Submit button to the `order_form` content source and select Update Order Form as the action. As shown in Figure 29.20, set `shipto.php` as the redirect page (which we'll build next) for a successful edit of these cart fields. In the event of an error, leave the On Failure field blank, which will cause this same page to be reloaded if any error was returned. This could be any number of things: a required field omitted, a bad credit card number, what have you.

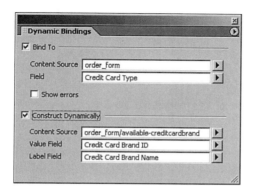

Figure 29.19
Custom Merchant will automatically build the list of credit card types that are available to your buyers.

29

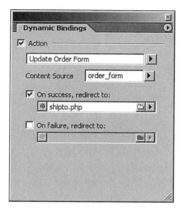

Figure 29.20
The checkout submit button should stay on the current page if there's an error, or proceed to the shipto page if all is well.

To notify the user of such an error, let's create some red placeholder text (see Figure 29.21) at the top of the page, and bind it to the order_form/Validation Errors content source, and select Error Message as the field (see Figure 29.22). All this will have the effect that, in the event of invalid form data being entered, the page will refresh itself with a bold red error message telling the user exactly what needs to be fixed.

The Ship To Page

Your `shipto.php` page allows the user to specify a shipping address. Custom Merchant provides a checkbox field that can be clicked to simply use the billing address, already entered, for the shipping address. Otherwise, everything on this page is the same as the last page. It uses the same form action, the same Content Source (`order_form`), and the exact same error message text and bindings. You can see a sample screen in Figure 29.23.

When you bind the fields, bind them to the Shipping fields, not the Billing fields. And the Submit button should link (upon success) to the next screen, `shipvia.php`, where we'll choose a shipping method.

Figure 29.21
Put some placeholder error message text where you'd like any errors to appear on the page.

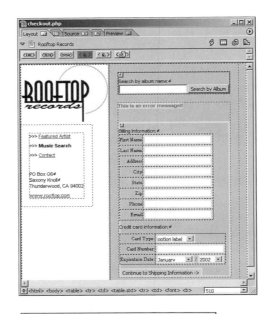

Figure 29.22
Bind the placeholder error message text using the Dynamic Binding palette.

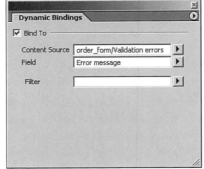

The Ship Via Page

Now that the Custom Merchant server knows the shipping address, it can provide a list of available shipping methods along with the cost for each. Figure 29.24 shows how you might design your shipping screen. All the elements of this page should be familiar to you by now.

In this case, I threw on some placeholder text to show the currently selected shipping address. Each term is bound to the appropriate field in the `order_form` content source. If the user thinks all the shipping options are too expensive, he can click the link to change the address. This text is simply hyperlinked straight back to `shipto.php`.

The tool provided by Custom Merchant to select a shipping method is really snazzy. Figure 29.25 shows the pop-up menu's bindings in the Dynamic Bindings palette. It is set to submit the Shipping

Method ID from the `order_form` content source. And, notice that it's also defined to be constructed automatically. Depending on the destination address and what shippers your Custom Merchant service provider has deals with, all available shippers are shown, and the price has already been calculated. If you look at the available choices under the Label Field pop-up, you'll see that you can choose to display the shipper's name, the amount, or a couple of combinations.

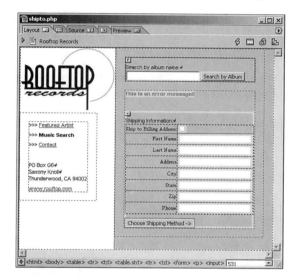

Figure 29.23
The shipto screen provides nearly the same function as the checkout screen. In fact, it's certainly possible to combine both of these onto a single screen.

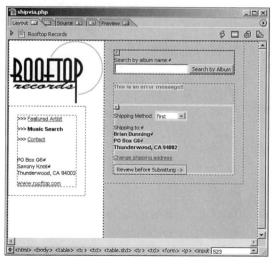

Figure 29.24
Create a page like this for your users to choose their preferred shipping method.

The Submit button is bound to redirect, upon success, to `review.php`.

Figure 29.25
Custom Merchant can dynamically build a pop-up menu with all available shipping methods, and even the cost already calculated.

The Review Page

We're almost at the end. The review page gives the shopper a final opportunity to make sure everything is okay: view his total, the cart contents, and the billing and shipping addresses. If all is well, he can submit the order. See Figure 29.26 for an example of how this page might look.

Figure 29.26
The review page shows all the information collected into the cart and the order so far.

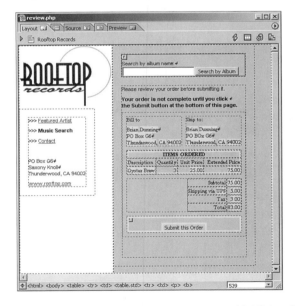

Everything is the same on this page, except the Submit button (Figure 29.27) is a Submit Order Form button instead of an Update Order Form button. Also, upon success, this page goes to the receipt page.

Notice that in the center of the review page, we list the cart contents. This is still done with the `order_form` content source: There is no need to add the `shopping_cart` content source to this page as well. Figure 29.28 shows how the cart fields are bound to the order_form/Item List content source.

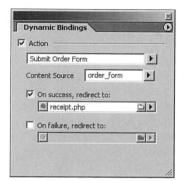

Figure 29.27
Bind the final Submit button to the Submit Order Form action instead of the Update Order Form action.

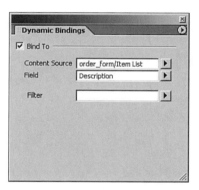

Figure 29.28
Even on an `order_form` content source, you can display dynamic data from the shopping cart.

The Receipt Page

Figure 29.29 shows the receipt page, which is almost identical to the review page. In fact, you can probably create this in about 90 seconds if you just start with a copy of the review page, delete the Submit button, and change some of the text.

Thus concludes our whirlwind tour of Custom Merchant. As you've seen from making selections in the menus and submenus on the Dynamic Bindings palette, we've touched lightly on most parts of Custom Merchant, but by no means have we used all its capabilities. With a little curiosity and creativity, you can explore further and come up with more ideas for your online store.

And the best part of all is that somebody else is dealing with all the headaches and grief. You are free to concentrate on what you do best: Web design.

Figure 29.29
The receipt page shares most of the same content as the review page. This is a good place to invite your users to continue shopping.

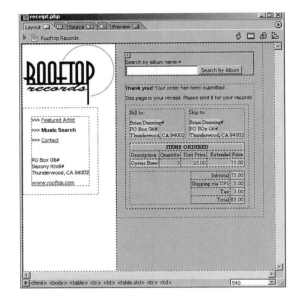

TROUBLESHOOTING

Fixing a Content Source That Fails

When I create a Custom Merchant data source, it fails the test. What do I do?

Seven times out of ten, the cause of a failed data source test is a typo in the URL. If you've used the test source listed here in the book, it's possible that the service provider may have changed their test address since this book went to print. The eighth time out of ten, you may be using an invalid merchant ID. In either of these cases, you're going to need to telephone the service provider and check your information. They'll be glad to help: They want you as a customer.

The ninth of any ten failures may be the odd Internet kink that temporarily denies your server access to the service provider. Be patient. If you're absolutely certain that your settings are right, this may indeed be the cause.

And, the rare one in ten failures may be caused by some esoteric bizarreness that neither you nor I can predict. Call the service provider and let their support personnel work it out for you: They are motivated to help.

Using Test Data

I've done everything exactly right, but clicking Add to Cart still doesn't add anything to my shopping cart.

Refer to the caution on page 545. Custom Merchant service providers have a test product database that probably doesn't match the product SKUs in your local product database. You'll need to temporarily use "TEST1" for the SKU of every product you add to the shopping cart while using Evocative's test server. (If you're using a different service provider's test server, they may have different test SKUs.)

Using SSL for the Custom Merchant Connection

My service provider requires me to use SSL and I don't have a certificate or don't want to use it. Do I have to?

There are two halves to this equation: the calls that your server makes to the service provider for each Custom Merchant action, and the calls that your Web visitors make to your server.

In the first case (calls that your server makes to the service provider), no SSL hardware or software is required on your end. That is handled on their end. For testing, most service providers do not require it, but they all will for production with a live account and real credit card numbers.

In the second case (calls that your Web visitors make to your server), there is no technical reason why this needs to be encrypted. However, most service providers will require you to use it to add a layer of protection for themselves from liability. Even though Internet transactions are far more secure than telephone or swiped credit card transactions, there are always consumers who file complaints. Your service provider has a real concern to protect themselves against such filings, so be prepared to bite the bullet, buy an SSL certificate, and use encryption for the commerce parts of your site if you expect to work with a Custom Merchant service provider.

GOING LIVE

Probably the first stumbling block you'll encounter while using Custom Merchant is the limitation imposed by the finite number of provided functions.

When you look at it that way, you're only considering the functions available on the service provider's data source. Remember that you can still use your own data sources on the same pages, so you're really not limited at all. Unless you expect your cart provider to calculate totals in Tibetan currency, or require some other unusual abstraction that's closely tied to the shopping cart function, you can still add whatever functionality you can create using GoLive's Dynamic Content module.

But in truth, it doesn't even stop there. The tools that GoLive provides easy shortcuts to are only a tiny subset of the capabilities of PHP, JSP, or ASP. If there's something you want to do on your Web page, and you just can't find a way to do it using Custom Merchant or Dynamic Content, relax. It can still be done, but you might need to go out and buy a book on PHP, JSP, or ASP. GoLive fully allows native code to exist within pages, even if it wasn't created using GoLive's tools.

Good starting points for learning more about each language's capabilities are the home pages for each technology. Refer to Chapter 27, "About Dynamic Content," to find out where to start.

XI

VIEWING AND MANAGING WEB SITES

IN THIS PART

30 Streamlining Site Construction   **561**

31 Publishing Your Site   **571**

30

STREAMLINING SITE CONSTRUCTION

IN THIS CHAPTER

Optimizing and Troubleshooting   **562**

The Site Window   **562**

Keeping Files Clean   **568**

Troubleshooting   **569**

Going Live   **570**

OPTIMIZING AND TROUBLESHOOTING

You have worked with your development team to define the site's purpose, goals, and audience. You have built the site, designed the page layouts, linked each of the pages, inserted the images, and integrated dynamic content. Now what?

Some designers immediately load the site to a server, cross their fingers, and hope they caught any and all of the mistakes made along the way. Others comb through each of the pages, gather a group of beta testers, and scrutinize the site's setup. Of course, the latter takes time and resources, perhaps time and resources you do not have to meet the deadline of your site's launch. Consider using Adobe GoLive's site management features to cut down on the testing time. GoLive's built-in site management features allow you to test out the site, check for used and broken links, visualize site colors and font-families, manage files, and more.

Using GoLive's site management features to manage your site and its corresponding files will usually avoid generating errors. For example, if you link a page via GoLive's point and shoot feature, GoLive tracks the link for you. If you rename a file midway through development via the Site Window, GoLive changes all links that reference that file. When errors do occur, they'll typically result from using other venues to manage a file. For example, perhaps you rename a file or move an image from one folder to another within Windows or Mac OS. When those changes do not occur via the Site Window, GoLive cannot automatically track the changes.

This chapter is devoted to demonstrating how to use GoLive's Site Window to manage the site. Many of the Site Window's features have been discussed throughout different chapters of the book, so this chapter will revisit the Site Window and its available features in its entirety. In addition, as errors will occasionally occur, this chapter will discuss what the different types of errors mean, how to read them, and better yet, how to fix them. Finally, different aspects of the site that should be considered before the site's launch will be detailed, as well as the features GoLive offers to help you streamline the final stages of the development process.

THE SITE WINDOW

As you know, GoLive's Site Window serves as the repository for managing all of your site's files. Whether you begin with a blank site consisting of only an individual home page (`index.html`), or mount an existing site on the Workgroup server, the Site Window's available functions stay the same.

The Site Window is broken up into two sides, each of which houses a number of tabs delineating the various sections. Figure 30.1 shows the Site Window open to both halves.

The first half of the Site Window includes tabs called Files, External, Diagrams, Colors, Font Sets, and Library, each of which is detailed later in this section. The second half of the Site Window, on the other hand, is not always visible. To open the second half of the site window, click the in the lower right corner of the Site Window to toggle it open.

The Files Tab stores all files, images, and code that will be uploaded the to the server upon completion of the site. This section also allows you to manage your files (rename, move, and so on), and automatically updates any links that need to be changed when you make a change.

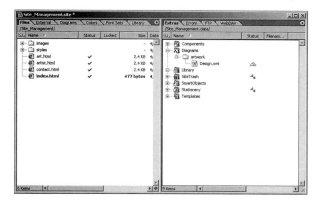

Figure 30.1
The Site Window provides an interface to manage all the documents that reside within your site folder.

For example, to move a file, click and drag that file from one directory in the Site Window to another. To rename a file, select the file in the Site Window by simply clicking on it once and pausing. The name field will open and you can type the new name as you desire. Notice that in either case, once a change has been made, GoLive prompts you with regard to which files contain links that need to be updated, and will actually update them for you, as shown in Figure 30.2.

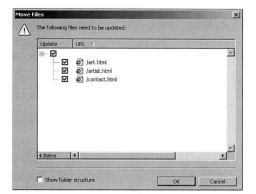

Figure 30.2
When you make a change to a file name or a file's location, GoLive will automatically track the necessary changes that need to be made to all links within the site.

Click OK to make the changes take place, or Cancel if you have other intentions.

The Files Tab of the Site Window can be very helpful in providing information about each piece of your Site. Notice that when a file is selected in the Site Window's Files tab, information about that file appears in the File tab of the Inspector. This information includes the file name (which can also be changed here), its status (if any), when it should be published, when it was created and last modified, and its total size. In addition, the Inspector includes other tabs dependent on the type of file with pertinent information. These tabs include

- Name specifies whether the file meets the file naming requirements set forth for the site.
- Page appears only when HTML pages are selected; provides access to the encoding information as well as to the page title.
- Content provides an illustration of the file's contents.

By right-clicking (Win) or Ctrl-Clicking (Mac), a contextual menu will appear providing access to creating new files. Likewise, you can drag a file from one folder to another and rename a file by selecting a file with a single click and pausing, then entering in the new name.

Notice that the Site Window's view can be customized (see Figure 30.3). The View palette provides access to controlling which information should be displayed and which should not. Likewise, by right-clicking on the bar at the top of the Site Window, a contextual menu appears, providing the same type of customizable control.

Figure 30.3

Customize what information you want to see within the Site Window by bringing up the contextual menu of the bar with either a right-click (Win) or a Ctrl-click (Mac).

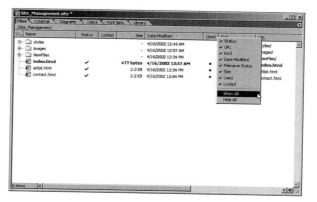

Clicking each title sorts the information by that parameter. For example, click the Size option on the top bar of the Site Window to sort the data by size—by clicking again, you can toggle whether it displays that information in ascending order or descending order.

Notice that one of the options, Status, displays a small icon beside the file name (see Figure 30.4). A checkmark indicates that all relative links are working within the page and all image source files are set appropriately—in other words, the file is ready to go. A warning icon indicates an empty page: one that has been created through the Site Window but not modified. A green bug icon demonstrates that the file has a broken link or an image file's source is not set appropriately. The folder-bug icon illustrates directories that contain a file with a bug (a broken link or image). Another icon that might occur is a stop sign, indicating a missing file.

Figure 30.4

The Status column of the Files Tab in the Site Window indicates any link errors that might occur as you're developing the page.

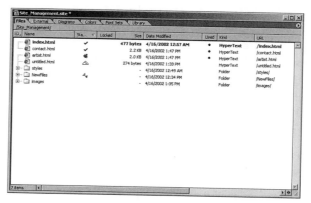

If you find that your site has errors, double-click the bug icon to open the page with the Link Warnings turned on. This can also be achieved by opening the page, and then selecting Edit, Show Link Warnings. In either case, the page will display with any possible errors highlighted by GoLive, as in the example shown in Figure 30.5.

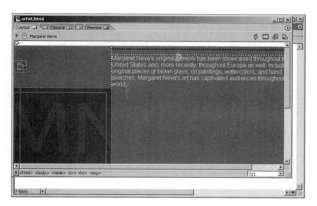

Figure 30.5
Turn the Link Warnings and GoLive will highlight the known errors throughout the page. Note the missing image highlighted near the upper left of this page.

30

In addition, look for broken image source icons. For each error, use the Inspector to change the link or image source. In some cases, GoLive may perceive an error where one does not actually exist. For safe keeping, go ahead and delete the link or source file and re-create it, ensuring that not only does the page function correctly, but GoLive also understands and can manage its files correctly.

While checking over your Site, you may find the In & Out Links palette handy in checking through the structure of how your Site links together, as well as for finding any broken links. Simply select a page in the Site Window (without necessarily opening it), and open the In & Out Links palette (Window, In & Out Links). The palette will appear, showing the relationships for how this page links (and is linked) to all others, as shown in Figure 30.6. In addition, notice that any errors in the linking of the page are indicated in the In & Out Links.

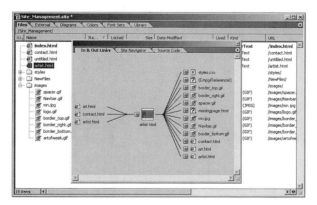

Figure 30.6
The In & Out Links palette provides a visual representation of how this page links to and is linked by other pages in the Site. Notice that broken links and source files are also indicated.

The In & Out Links palette can even be used to navigate through the site—double-click a file name and the file will open. Also, without opening the page, broken links can be fixed using the point and shoot method. Simply click on the target icon next to the listed link and drag to the file to which it should reference, as indicated in Figure 30.7.

Figure 30.7
Use the In & Out Links palette to fix broken references. Click and drag the target to the appropriate file.

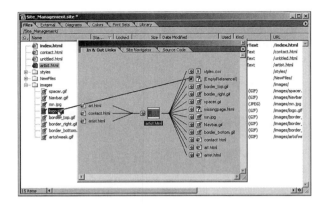

Notice that this means for locating and fixing broken links does not check external references; that is to say, the Files tab does not track the links that go to other sites, nor email links. Email links, unfortunately, cannot be checked through any site management feature. However, external links (those that reference pages of other Web sites) can. The next tab in the first section of the Site Window, the External tab, allows you to do just this.

The External tab maintains a list of all external links including those that refer to other Web servers as well as those that link to an email program. As the Site Window does not automatically pull in this information, you may need to right-click (Ctrl-click on the Mac) and choose Get References Used from the resulting contextual menu. GoLive will search all the pages for external references and list them within this tab.

The next tab in the first section of the Site Window stores all of the Site's diagrams. Diagrams stores any site diagrams and hierarchies which you created throughout the development process. After completing the site diagram, each can be anchored into the existing Site, allowing you to design the big picture of the Site's structure first before tinkering with the details of each page. For more information, look to Chapter 4, "Working with Sites." Diagrams are discussed in detail.

The next two tabs are also particularly helpful during pre-launch. As a developer, you want to make sure that your Site is consistent in look, feel, and design. In addition, making sure that you didn't use obscure colors and fonts ensures that users will see a consistent site independent of what computer platform or browser they are using. The Colors Tab (see Figure 30.8) and the Font Sets Tab (see Figure 30.9) provide access to the colors and font-families used within the Site. View each tab and look for any obscure fonts (such as Beezwax) or non–Web-safe colors. Replace them with more popular fonts and standard colors, to ensure compatibility across the widest audience.

For both the Colors Tab and the Font Sets Tab, you can organize the items via the Inspector. The Inspector enables you to select an item (whether it be a color in the Colors Tab or a font-family in the Font Sets Tab), provide the item a name, and change its specifications.

Finally, the last tab (Library) within the first half of the Site window houses all items stored inside your Site's Library.

The contextual menu also offers an option to check External Links. You must have an Internet connection to run this safety check. Also, although it may lead you to errors in the link, it is not foolproof—you will want to test the external links for yourself as well.

Figure 30.8
The Colors tab displays all the color sets used throughout the site. Used for consistency in design from page to page, this tab enables you to check for non–Web-safe colors.

30

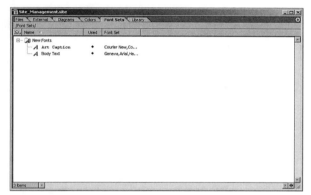

Figure 30.9
The Font Sets Tab centralizes a listing of all of the fonts used throughout a Site.

The second section contains tabs called Extras, Errors, FTP, and WebDAV. The FTP and WebDAV tabs will be discussed in detail in the next chapter. For now, let's focus on the first two tabs.

The Extras Tab contains folders for GoLive's site management features such as Templates, Smart Objects, Components, Diagrams, and so on. Basically, this tab provides access to all of the data stored in the Site's project folder, but not in the root folder of the Site.

You'll find the Errors tab (see Figure 30.10) very helpful, particularly at the final stages of your site development. The Errors tab contains a list of errors (missing files) found within the site.

Use the In & Out Links palette to determine what pages link to the missing file. You will want to consider searching for the file in case it has been accidentally moved, re-creating the file, or deleting all references to the file.

GoLive encapsulates a search system, shown in Figure 30.11, that can look for files if you think you have a decent idea of its name. Select Edit, Find from the command menu and select the Site Tab. Then, using the available fields and drop-down menu, fill in the parameters for your search. In this case, GoLive will look for all files that end in .html:

After you set up the search via its parameters, click Find. GoLive will highlight any files that meet the specified criteria in the Site Window. If that file is not the one for which you were looking, click Find Next and the next file meeting the set criteria will be highlighted in the Site Window.

Figure 30.10
The Errors tab lists any pages that may be missing in the Site by checking links for broken references.

Figure 30.11
Using GoLive's search feature can cut down on the time you devote to troubleshooting. In this case, the Find feature is going to seek out each page that ends in .html.

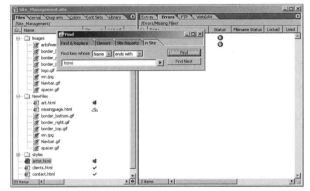

If you find the correct file, use the In & Out Links palette to replace the incorrect reference. Simply point and shoot from the missing file icon in the In & Out Links palette to the correct file within the Site Window to correct the error.

You might also consider looking in the Site Trash. The Site Trash is stored in the Extras tab of the second half of the Site Window, and stores all files deleted from the Site. In the event that you do locate the file in the Site Trash and want to restore it to the Site's current files, simply click and drag the correct file from its location in the Site Trash to the Files Tab of the Site Window.

KEEPING FILES CLEAN

As you develop a Site, you will end up with a number of references, colors, and links that are obsolete or not used at all. You can use GoLive's Clean Up Site (see Figure 30.12) to search through your Site and strip it of unused files, link references, colors, and font-families.

To use the Clean Site command, select Site, Clean Up Site from the command menu. You can actually set what the Clean Up Site Command should and should not do when executed. The Clean Up Site command can

- Refresh the views of the Files, External, Colors, Font, and Library tabs.

- Remove unused files (for example, an image file that is never referenced by a Site).

- Search for and add in colors, fonts, and references that are not currently listed within the Site Window.

- Remove unused colors, references, and font sets.

To specify what actions the Clean Up Site command should take, choose Edit, Preferences from the menu. Then, under the Site heading, select Clean Up Site. (Note that you may need to toggle the menu open by clicking on the plus to the left of the Site option).

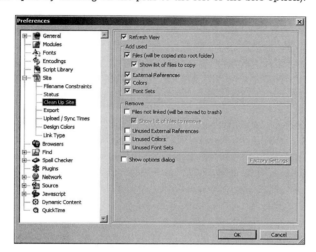

Figure 30.12
Specify what actions the Clean Up Site command should take via the preferences dialog. To run the Site cleaning, select Site, Clean Up Site from the command menu.

When complete setting your preferences, click OK.

Occasionally, after running the Clean Up Site command, you may realize that you did not intend to rid the Site of unused files, or perhaps there is a reference you were storing for later use. You can undo a Site Clean Up by selecting Undo, Undo Cleanup Site. Note that the Undo menu tracks the last action taken, so this can only be done immediately following a Site Clean Up.

TROUBLESHOOTING

When I try to do a search for a file, the Find button is disabled.

Remember, when searching for a specific Site, GoLive returns the results in the Site Window. Make sure your Site Window is already open. This ensures the program knows which Site to look through for the file, and provides a means for returning the appropriate files.

Bugs are appearing in the Status of a number of my pages. In each of them, though, I've opened them up and tested them out. They seem to work fine. What should I do?

You are more intelligent than your machine, so if testing the pages yields that they're fine, they probably are. The one exception is if the link refers to a file on your hard drive that is not inside your Site. First check that. If that is not the case, the link or file reference is fine.

You may want to consider reasserting the reference again regardless. Obviously, GoLive (like any Web editor) ships with a lot of power and a few quirks, this being one of them. Fixing the error in GoLive, however, means that you can rely on GoLive's error finding features in the future. The time required to fix the problem will probably be worth the time you'll save weeding through errors in the future.

GOING LIVE

30

The next chapter will finally show you how to take the fantastic Site you've completed and put it up on the server for live presentation. Before jumping the gun, however, consider setting up a limited-access section of the site for beta testers. Or, better yet, consider building a staging server.

A staging server is just a repository where files can be stored before the Site goes live. The purpose is so that once a Site has been tentatively completed, a select group of users (often referred to as *beta testers*) can run through the Site looking for errors, improvements, and so forth. You'll be surprised how much feedback you can get when you solicit it from your users, and you'll find this feedback invaluable in preventing large, overbearing errors.

If at all possible, do not consider yourself an adequate substitute for a beta tester. Particularly at this stage in the development process, your eyes are probably glossing over every error left behind in the Site. Make sure you request a pair of fresh eyes to check out the site for you.

31

PUBLISHING YOUR SITE

IN THIS CHAPTER

Publishing Overview   **572**

Setting Up FTP and Internet Access   **572**

Connecting to an FTP Server   **574**

Transferring Files   **575**

WebDAV Server   **578**

Publishing Workgroup Sites   **580**

Troubleshooting   **580**

Going Live   **581**

PUBLISHING OVERVIEW

You probably have a good idea as to the final step of this process. Although you've built a fantastic Web site full of useful and pertinent information, the site is still stored only on your local machine (or on Adobe's Web workgroup server) and is therefore available only to you and your team. You still have to publish the site to make it live and accessible to the public.

Publishing a site not only means placing the original files up on the Web for public access but also updating the site. Bear in mind that every time you make a change to the local site, you'll want to publish that change to the server as well.

There are a number of ways to load the files to a Web server. Traditional means include copying files through the network to the appropriate directory on your server and using FTP (File Transfer Protocol) to log in to the remote server and transfer the files, the latter of which requires a software program. Traditionally, third-party FTP software clients would have to be launched to transfer the local files to the server; however, Adobe GoLive includes an internal FTP client negating that need for a third-party program.

Adobe GoLive actually includes two built-in FTP clients: the FTP browser and the FTP tab of the Site window. In addition, Adobe GoLive offers a built-in WebDAV (Web-based Distributed Authoring and Versioning) client for connecting to WebDav servers. All these topics, including setting up your FTP access, will be detailed in this chapter. In addition, publishing a site via the workgroup server will also be discussed.

SETTING UP FTP AND INTERNET ACCESS

Your Internet Service Provider (ISP) may specify how you can connect to its server for security purposes. In particular, your ISP may require you to work in passive mode to avoid complications when working with a server behind a firewall, or your ISP may be using a proxy server. Your ISP (or Server Administrator) will be able to tell you whether it requires the use of passive mode or a proxy server. You, in turn, then specify how GoLive connects to the Internet.

To set up and customize your Internet Access, open Adobe GoLive and choose Edit, Preferences from the menu. Click the heading for Network to access the following options, shown in Figure 31.1:

- If your ISP requires the use of an FTP or HTTP proxy, select the appropriate choice and fill in the server's address and port number. Your ISP should be able to provide all details with regards to the proxy server if it does indeed require one.

- The Keep Connections Alive option forces GoLive to maintain a connection with the server. This option is particularly useful for slow connections and large uploads, in which the connection may time out because of perceived idleness. Select this option in the event that you run into recurring timeout errors.

- Select Resolve Links to upload the originals of all files referenced by shortcuts or aliases. If you choose not to Resolve Links, such files will not be transferred.

- In addition, Macintosh users have the option to use the Internet control's panel settings by clicking the Import Now button and selecting Use Always, and to use Macintosh's Keychain security system for storing and managing passwords.

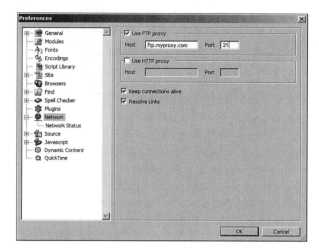

Figure 31.1
Use the Network panel in Preferences to set up your options for FTP transfers.

After the Internet access has been defined, you can begin the process for uploading your site. The first step is to set up your FTP access. Specifically, you need to tell GoLive the FTP server to which you are going to connect and provide some basic information. Note that setting up access to a WebDAV server is similar.

To set up your FTP access, choose Edit, Servers from the menu. The dialog box shown in Figure 31.2 appears, providing direct access to setting up the servers to which you want to connect. Note that you can set up more than one server.

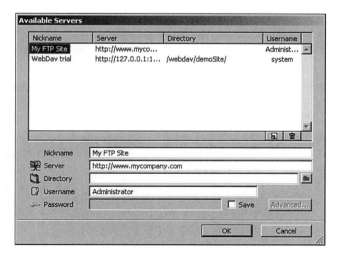

Figure 31.2
The Available Servers dialog box provides a forum for dedicating and storing information about which servers (either FTP or WebDAV) you plan to use.

To add a server to the listing, click the New Item button. Notice the icon for the that allows you to delete an existing server. For each server, specify the following:

- Nickname—An intuitive name that you can use to distinguish the server from others.

- Server —The server address or domain name, such as www.mycompany.com.

- Directory —The directory to which the FTP window will point you. Note that many user accounts are set up so that you do not need to specify the directory because logging on to the system via your username automatically directs you into the correct folder.

- Username —Your unique username, as provided by your server administrator.

- Password —Your password for logging on to the system.

When you are finished setting up the server's specifications, click OK. Notice that you can list more than one server's information in this dialog box.

Setting up the servers simply stores the connection information in Adobe GoLive. In addition to setting up the server's connection, you will want to tell the site which server (if any) should serve as the site's default FTP client, and which server (if any) should serve as the site's default Web Server.

To select a server for a specific site, choose Site, Settings from the menu. Click on FTP & WebDAV Server, and two menu items appear. Using the drop-down list, select the server of choice from the drop-down menus, one for FTP and one for WebDAV.

CONNECTING TO AN FTP SERVER

GoLive offers two FTP clients that connect to an FTP server. The first, and far more powerful, is incorporated into your Site window as the FTP tab. The second replaces the need for a third-party FTP client and is the FTP browser. Begin by looking to the FTP tab of the Site window.

After the server's information has been stored, you are ready to transfer the files between your local machine and the server. First, you must actually connect to the server. Open the Site window for the site that you want to publish and click on the FTP tab of the Site window. The local files appear in the left, and the pane on the right remains empty until you connect to the server.

Start by ensuring that you are connected to the Internet. Then, to connect to the server, first select the server to which you want to connect by choosing Site, FTP Server, Server Nickname where Server Nickname is the name of the server you provided when first setting up the server. Then, to connect to that server, choose Site, FTP Server, Connect. Alternatively, click the connect icon on the program's toolbar.

After you are connected to the FTP server, the FTP tab's pane displays all the files stored on the server, as shown in Figure 31.3. If this is your first time loading the files, this pane may very well be empty. After you have selected and connected to the server, the Files tab illustrates the local version of the site (the files as they are stored on your machine), and the FTP tab depicts the files as they exist on the server.

> If the FTP tab is not already activated, connecting to the FTP server by choosing Site, FTP Server, Connect brings that tab forward.

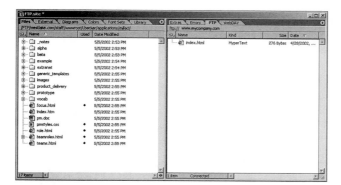

Figure 31.3
The Site window (and its corresponding FTP pane) provides FTP access to the server. In this example, only the index page (the home page) currently resides on the server.

TRANSFERRING FILES

You can transfer files from your local machine to the server and vice versa via the Site window in a number of ways. The first time you upload your site, you will want to copy the entire site over the server. Thereafter, updates will typically be synchronized—that is, instead of updating every page, only those that have changed will be uploaded to the site.

The toolbar at the top of the program gives you direct access to the four major uploading commands. Simply click and hold down on the Upload button to access the following four options:

- Incremental Uploads rely on the dates of modification for both the files on the local machine as well as those on the server. Essentially, GoLive compares the two modification dates. If the file on the local machine is newer than the file on the server, the file will be uploaded to the server. In addition, if the page does not exist on the server, it will be uploaded to the server as well. If both the dates of the server's file and the local machines have changed, but the server's file is newer than that of the local machine, the file will not update via an Incremental Upload.

- Modified-item Uploads rely on the dates of the local files but compare the dates of the local files to the date of the previous upload instead of comparing them to the modification dates of the mirrored files on the server. In this case, imagine that the local file's modification date was older than the server's modification date. If the local file had been modified since the last update, the local file would be uploaded to and replace the server's version.

- Selection Uploads rely on a selection in the Site window of which files you want to update. Using the Ctrl key, you can select more than one item. Then, when you choose to invoke a Selection Upload, only those items that were selected (or were contained in a selected directory) will be uploaded to the server. Note that this update will occur regardless of the modification dates of either the local or the remote files.

- Update All uploads every file to the server.

Select the type of update you want; then click the Upload button to execute the action.

For either Incremental or Modified-Item uploads to occur, the server's files must be synchronized against the local machine's. Synchronization of the time stamps for the various files can be broken a number of ways, including using a different FTP client. For example, suppose that you modify a file on your local machine and upload this folder to the server via an external (non-GoLive) FTP client. The next time you visit the Site window, the time stamp on the local file will be wrong, and GoLive will count the local file as the older of the two, regardless of the fact that the files are exactly the same. This is simply because GoLive's time stamps for local files refer to the last date and time the file was uploaded. As a result, the program will download the server version to the local machine despite the fact the files are exactly the same, thereby using unnecessary time and resources.

GoLive, therefore, provides a way for you to manually synchronize the time stamps for your files without actually transferring any data. In fact, two choices exist: You may synchronize all the files in the site, or simply those selected within the Site window. To synchronize files' time stamps manually, activate the Site window's File tab with a click. Then choose Site, FTP Server, Sync Modification Times All (to synchronize the entire site) or Site, FTP Server, Sync Modification Times Selection (to synchronize any files currently selected within the Site window). This can also be achieved by right-clicking (Windows) or Ctrl-clicking (Mac) the File tab of the Site window and choosing FTP Server, Sync Modification Times All or Sync Modification Times Selection. In either case, fill out the Sync Times Option Box as appropriate. The options are as follows:

- Honor Publish States of Group/Pages—When checked, GoLive loads the files based on the publication settings specified via the file's Inspector.

- Sync Referenced Files Only— When checked, will only sync files that you have marked with a publish state, using the File tab of the Inspector when the file is selected in the Site window.

- Show List of Files to Sync— When checked, shows a list of all the files whose time stamps will be altered via the Synchronize command.

Be wary of the option to synchronize all files manually. This option equalizes the time stamps for the local machine and the server for all files within the site, including those whose changes have yet to be updated to the server. As a result, the next time you choose to upload the files via an Incremental or Modified-Item upload, the edited versions of the file will not upload to the server.

In addition to uploading the files to the server via the Site window, the Download button provides access to the two similar options for downloading a file to the local machine:

- Incremental downloads only the files whose modification dates on the server are newer than those on the local machine.

- Selection downloads the files you have currently selected from the server to your machine.

First, select the type of download you want to execute by clicking and holding down the Download button to select the type of download. Then, to invoke that action, click the Download button.

In addition, you can click and drag files from one pane to the other. To download a single file or directory from the server, click and drag that file from the FTP tab over to the Site window's Files tab. Likewise, to upload a single file or directory, click and drag the appropriate file from the Files tab to the FTP tab.

By holding down the Ctrl key, you can select more than one file in either pane. When selected, you can transfer the files simply by clicking and dragging the selected items from one pane to the other.

When you are finished with the transfer, be sure to disconnect from the server by right-clicking (Windows) or Ctrl-clicking (Mac) within the FTP pane and selecting Disconnect from the contextual menu.

GoLive's FTP Browser

The beauty of the Site window's File and FTP tabs is that you have side-by-side comparison of the local files against those on the server. As a result, the previously described option for managing, uploading, and downloading your files is robust. GoLive also offers another option for transferring files via FTP: the FTP browser.

The major difference between the FTP browser and the FTP tab of the Site window is that the FTP tab is particularly useful for transferring files from a Site window. However, perhaps you completed a single page without building the accompanying GoLive site files. The FTP browser allows you then to upload files via FTP—from the Site window as well as from your computer's directories.

To open the FTP browser, choose File, FTP Browser from GoLive's menu. The FTP browser is a separate window that provides FTP access. Files can be uploaded and downloaded from your local machine to the server, but GoLive's handier site management features (such as incremental and modified item uploads) are accessible only in the FTP tab of the Site window.

After you have opened the FTP browser, you must select the server to which you want to connect from the drop-down list. Servers will be listed by the nickname you provided during the setup process. After you have selected the appropriate server, click the Connect button. If needed, you are prompted for your username and password. The FTP browser connects to the server, and a directory of the files available to you as they exist on the server appears in the FTP browser.

Using the FTP browser, you can upload and download files by clicking and dragging the desired files from one location to another (see Figure 31.4). If you click and drag files from your local machine, you are uploading files. If you click and drag from the FTP browser, you are downloading files. Note that in addition to clicking and dragging from the Site window, you can also click and drag files from any directory on your local machine by restoring GoLive's window so that it does not take up the entire screen.

As you transfer files from your local machine to the server and vice versa, the Network Status window, shown in Figure 31.5, keeps track and records any errors that occurred in the process. Watch the Network Status window for helpful clues as to what went awry through the FTP process.

Notice that the errors are listed in the top pane. Selecting an error in the top pane displays any possible remedies to the problem in the lower half of the Network Status window.

Figure 31.4
Use the FTP Browser to upload individual files not part of a site to the server. Note that the FTP browser can be used for any FTP purpose, not just transferring Web files.

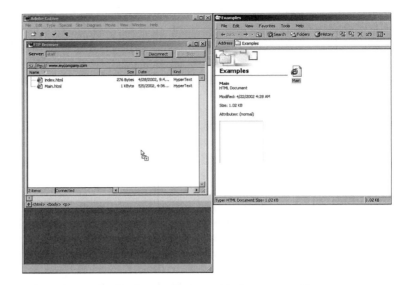

Figure 31.5
The Network Status window keeps track and records any errors that occur during file transfers.

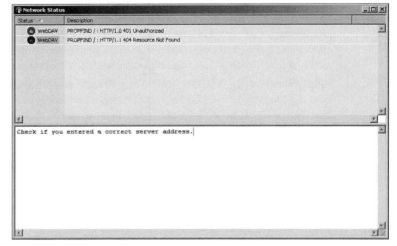

WEBDAV SERVER

WebDAV is a fancy term for a set of extensions to the HTTP protocol that empower the server so that users can manage and edit files within a collaborative server environment, regardless of what application is being used.

Consider, for example, a site being developed in conjunction with a number of different companies. One company might simply hand-code, another might use Macromedia Dreamweaver or Microsoft FrontPage, and you are using Adobe GoLive. Traditionally, integrating these different methods of developing hindered the site management capabilities of a team: Features available in one program might not be available in another, and tracking which team member was working with a particular file often proved to be a project management challenge. WebDAV overcomes some of these challenges, allowing developers with different means of developing to work in a collaborative environment. In short, think of WebDav as an Adobe Web Workgroup Server on steroids, one that extends beyond the blinders of just working with Adobe's programs.

WebDAV is supported by Microsoft IIS 5 (included with Windows 2000), Apache (with the mod_dav module installed), and Novell NetWare 6.0. Other servers do not support WebDAV. The live server does not need to have WebDAV support because developers can build on a WebDav Web server internally and then FTP that site to the live site.

Working with a WebDav server does not dramatically change the way that you interact with the server, nor the way you'll interact with that server via GoLive. You'll encounter a few additional features, but you are still using GoLive as the intermediary between your local files and the Web server.

WebDav's major advantages include the capability to lock files, as well as the capability to access properties that describe the file.

To connect to a WebDav server, start by selecting the server to which you want to connect for the site. To select the server, choose Site, WebDav Server, Server Nickname, where Server Nickname is the name you provided the server when setting up its information. To connect, right-click (Ctrl-click on a Mac) within the WebDAV tab of the Site window and choose Connect. GoLive connects you to the WebDAV server in much the same way it connects to an FTP server. Notice that the files stored on the server appear on the right under the WebDAV pane, and the files on the left illustrate the site as it exists on your directory.

Much of the functionality available to you via the FTP pane is also available to you via the WebDAV pane. Notice that the WebDav toolbar highlights, allowing access to uploading modified files, downloading all files, synchronizing the files, and disconnecting from the server. In addition, files can be selectively clicked and dragged from one pane to the other. To upload, click and drag the file from the local pane to the WebDAV pane. To download, click and drag from the WebDav pane to the local pane.

In addition, a few features specific to the WebDAV server exist, specifically the capability to lock a file. Locking a file simply means that you have locked the files from editing by other people. In addition to locking the file, the WebDAV server provides visual cues as to what files other members are of your team are working with.

To lock a file, select the file in the WebDAV pane and bring up the contextual menu with either a right-click (Win) or a Ctrl-click (Mac). From the contextual menu, two options appear:

- Lock—Indicates to others that the file has been secured by an individual for editing. Files that you have locked for editing are indicated by a pencil, whereas files exclusively locked by another individual are indicated by a lock.

- Shared Lock—A shared lock does not actually lock the file from use, but instead indicates that a team is participating in the editing process. Two faces illustrates file locked by a group to which you do not belong, whereas two faces with a pencil illustrates a shared lock in which you can participate. Note that all servers (including Adobe's Workgroup Server) do not necessarily support the Shared Lock feature of WebDAV.

Likewise, to unlock a file, select that file from its listing in the WebDAV pane, right-click (Win) or Ctrl-click (Mac) and select Unlock from the resulting menu.

When working in WebDAV, the Inspector provides file information disbursed among three tabs:

- The File Tab provides the file's name, URL, modification date, and size.

- The Special Tab provides the file's document type information.

- The Lock Tab indicates the user (if any) who has locked the file, as well as properties of that lock (such as its expiration, whether the lock is exclusively scoped, and so on).

As always, after you complete the work with the server (uploading and downloading pages, locking and unlocking files, and so on), be sure to disconnect from the server both to save on your server's resources and to avoid unwanted mishaps from occurring.

PUBLISHING WORKGROUP SITES

Publishing workgroup sites does not differ dramatically from publishing files via FTP or via WebDav. The one difference to consider is that the user publishing the files must have administrative access. If you do not have administrative access, you will not be allowed to publish the files to the live Web server.

In addition to publishing the files through GoLive's interface, you can also publish the files through the workgroup's Web-based administrator. Open the administration system and log on via your username and password. You will see a section entitled Publishing. Click on that section, and you are prompted to select the site you want to publish, followed by the server to which you want to publish the site. If the server of choice is not listed, you will have to create a reference to a new server and provide the server's information (including domain name, username, password, port, and so on). Although the interface is different, the information required is the same as required when setting up an FTP or WebDAV server. Fill in the information as required and continue to define how the Web site should be published. These options mimic those available when exporting a site and are discussed in this chapter's "Going Live" section.

After you specify all the options, click OK. From the server's Web-based administration tool, you can upload and publish your Web files.

TROUBLESHOOTING

I am connected to the live server, but my changes (uploads and so forth) are not appearing in the pane that shows the server files.

You might need to refresh the view of the server's files. Refreshing the view forces the connection to request the latest and greatest iteration of the files. Particularly if you are publishing and editing files simultaneous to another developer, you will find that refreshing the view ensures that you are dealing with the most recent file hierarchy.

To refresh the view, activate the pane for the server with a click (either the FTP pane or the WebDAV pane). Within the appropriate pane, right-click (Windows) or Ctrl-click (Mac) and select Refresh from the resulting menu.

I uploaded the files, but when I view the live site, the changes that I've made don't appear. I've checked the files time and time again by downloading them through GoLive and making sure that my changes are there, but still when I request the page through a browser I get the old file.

More likely than not, your browser is possibly viewing the cached version of the file. The cache refers to short-term memory of the computer. Instead of fetching the file from the server, the browser views a page it previously downloaded to save on resources. To view the most recent page and override this client-side caching, hold down the Shift key as you refresh/reload the page. Doing so forces the browser to request the latest version of the file from the server.

Going Live

Typically, the best way to set up your site and your server is so that they mirror each other: file for file, directory for directory. On occasion, you might come across a situation where the local site's architecture does not match the server's. GoLive therefore offers an intermediary step: exporting a site. Exporting a site allows you to adapt the folder structure specific to a particular FTP server's needs. In other words, instead of reworking the original site or the final site's file structure, you create an exported version on your local machine from the original that mirrors the server. And yes, as you'd expect, GoLive aids this process.

As mentioned, note that few Web servers require that you first export the site and adapt its folder structures. Before exporting a site, take the time to contact your server administrator to determine whether the export is necessary.

To export a site, start by setting up the export settings. With the site open, click the Site Settings button on the toolbar and click Export. The dialog shown in Figure 31.6 appears in which you specify the export settings. Although you rarely need to export a site, the more common server requirements are listed as options so that you don't have to re-create your site hierarchy and organization scheme based on clunky server requirements.

Export Conditions allows you to incorporate some of the features of the site into the export. For example, you can honor the publication states of the directories and files that you set via the Inspector, as well as determine what to do with orphan files by clicking the option to Export Files That Are Not Part of the Site.

The Hierarchy option defines how the files should be organized into the separate directories. As In Site mirrors the exported version of the site with that of the files in the Site Window Separate Pages and Media creates two directories, one for all HTML pages and one that holds all media items, and the Flat option strips the site of all hierarchies and places all the site's assets in one root folder. In addition, the dialog provides access to naming the directories.

Figure 31.6
The Export pane of the Site Settings window provides access to determine how the exported version of the site is organized.

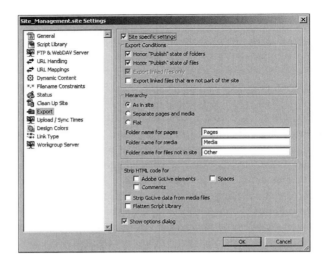

The next section, Strip HTML Code For, provides control over what codes should be stripped from the exported version, with the option to strip all whitespace, HTML comments, and GoLive elements. GoLive elements are proprietary codes added into the pages for site management purposes that are ignored by the browser. In addition, the option to Strip GoLive Data from Media Files strips the Smart Objects of their powers by removing the GoLive data responsible for tracking a Smart Object to its original file. Stripping data of course reduces your file size, but the appearance of the site does not change. Finally, Flatten Script Library put all GoLive generated JavaScripts into one page referenced by the appropriate pages. The last option, Show Options Dialog, allows you to modify the site's export settings when you actually execute the export.

When you are finished setting the export options for the site, you can invoke the export by closing all HTML files, activating the correct Site window with a click, and choosing File, Export from the menu. If you requested the Options dialog to show, you have the opportunity to modify the export settings you previously declared. Otherwise, the Export Options dialog is skipped, and you are prompted to store the exported version of the site onto your local drive. Choose a location and click Save.

When you are finished creating the exported version of the site, GoLive asks whether you want to see a short recorded report of the export. Generated in HTML, this file automatically opens and details which pages were exported appropriately, as well as what options were set for the export.

Note that exporting a site does not make that site live: The site now has two versions—the local site that you created and edit, and the exported version that meets your server requirements. To make the site live, you must then upload the exported version via GoLive's FTP browser. Make sure that when uploading via the FTP browser that you drag the contents of the root directory you created, not the directory in its entirety. The latter adds an extra folder layer to the site, and it does not display correctly.

XII

APPENDIXES

IN THIS PART

A What's on the Companion CD   585

B Palette Definitions   589

WHAT'S ON THE COMPANION CD

IN THIS CHAPTER

The Companion CD   **586**

Lasso Professional 5 Evaluation Edition   **586**

Lasso Studio for Adobe GoLive   **586**

Evocative's ProCart Live   **586**

CatalogIntegrator Cart from eCatalogBuilders   **587**

digital.forest Coupon   **587**

THE COMPANION CD

We've thrown in a few items of exceptional value to enhance your GoLive experience. Check out the items on this book's companion CD. Some items are required to complete the examples in this book; others are just there for your benefit should you choose to try them. Following are descriptions of each of the items on the CD. Enjoy!

LASSO PROFESSIONAL 5 EVALUATION EDITION

Included on the CD is a complete installer for Lasso Professional 5, the powerful and fast-growing application server from Blue World Communications. Lasso and its visual authoring environment, Lasso Studio, are required to build the online commerce example site in Chapter 24, "Lasso Studio for Adobe GoLive."

Lasso Professional 5 includes an integrated version of MySQL called LassoMySQL, complete with a Web-based visual management environment. Lasso Professional 5 also works with many other popular databases including FileMaker Pro.

A 30-day evaluation serial number is required to try Lasso Professional 5, and they are freely available at `http://www.blueworld.com/`.

LASSO STUDIO FOR ADOBE GOLIVE

Lasso Studio is the visual authoring environment for data-driven Web sites powered by Lasso. Using Lasso Studio, even a novice can build complex and powerful sites, yet no functionality is sacrificed for power builders. Lasso Studio is required to build the online commerce example site in Chapter 24.

Lasso Studio is an extension to Adobe GoLive that adds a wealth of features and capabilities, including a number of wizards to assist you in designing and building the pages for your dynamic site, news frames for the Objects Palette, and new functions in the Inspector to permit detailed editing of complex Lasso tags within the HTML of your page.

A 30-day evaluation serial number is required to try Lasso Studio, and they are freely available at `http://www.blueworld.com/`.

EVOCATIVE'S PROCART LIVE

Chapter 29 discusses GoLive's CustomMerchant feature using one of Adobe's partner companies, Evocative. Included on this CD is a finished, fully functional shopping-cart site to use with Adobe GoLive 6 that demonstrates nearly all the features available with the content source provided by Evocative. Using this functional example site as a starting point, you can quickly and easily get up to full speed building your Evocative powered commerce site. See Chapter 29 for more details.

Also included is an exclusive coupon only for those of you special enough to buy this book. This coupon entitles you to a discount of $150 off the initial fees to set up a ProCart Live account with Evocative. Use it, and you've more than paid for this book!

CATALOGINTEGRATOR CART FROM ECATALOGBUILDERS

CatalogIntegrator Cart Lite, is a freeware ASP-based shopping cart built around GoLive 6 that runs on any Windows 2000 or NT server. It is based on the full commercial version of CatalogIntegrator Cart, and GoLive BuyObjects Palette contains all the objects available in the full commercial version but omits some of the bells and whistles. There is no limit on the number of products you can sell with it. It incorporates a built-in browser Admin Module, which allows you to view and print out orders, which you can process through an existing Merchant Account, such as one intended for a "brick and mortar store."

DIGITAL.FOREST COUPON

You'll also find a coupon on the CD for Web hosting for that awesome solution you've built in GoLive. Founded in 1994, digital.forest is the premier database- and application-hosting company serving small and medium-sized businesses and corporate workgroups around the globe. Find out more at `http://www.forest.net/`.

digital.forest offers both shared- and dedicated-server solutions for Web-enabled databases and applications on Macintosh, Unix, and Windows systems. digital.forest is known as a pioneer in FileMaker Pro hosting. And its expertise extends to MS SQL Server 7.0, QuickTime, WebObjects, and the Lasso Web Data Engine.

PALETTE DEFINITIONS

In this appendix, you'll find quick reference to some of the most frequently used—and almost always visible—buttons and widgets in GoLive's most popular screens. The Color and Objects Palettes are open nearly all the time, and the Objects Palette has an awful lot of little icons, and it's not always so clear what each one does.

In addition, the Page Window, which is where you do almost all of your work, is peppered with little buttons. Let this section serve as a cheat sheet so you never get stuck looking for something that's probably right in front of you.

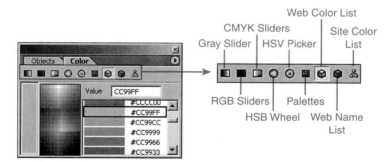

Figure B.1
The Color Palette icons.

Appendix B

Figure B.2
GoLive's Objects Palette, Basic
tab icons.

Table B.1   Objects Palette Basic Icons

Icon	Name
	Layout Grid
	Layout Text Box
	Floating Box
	Table
	Image
	Plugin
	SWF
	QuickTime
	Real
	SVG
	Java Applet
	Object
	Line
	Horizontal Spacer
	JavaScript
	Marquee

Table B.1 Continued

Icon	Name
	Comment
	Anchor
	Line Break
	Tag
	i-mode Emoji

Figure B.3
GoLive's Objects Palette, Smart tab icons.

Table B.2 Objects Palette, Smart Tab Icons

Icon	Name
	Smart Photoshop
	Smart Illustrator
	Smart Generic
	Component
	Rollover
	Modified Date
	URL Popup
	Body Action

Table B.2 Continued

Icon	Name
	Head Action
	Browser Switch

Figure B.4
GoLive's Objects Palette, Forms tab icons.

Table B.3 Objects Palette Forms Tab Icons

Icon	Name
	Form
	Submit Button
	Reset Button
	Button
	Form Input Image
	Label
	Text Field
	Password
	Text Area
	Check Box
	Radio Button
	Popup

Table B.3   Continued

Icon	Name
	List Box
	File Browser
	Hidden
	Key Generator]
	Fieldset

Figure B.5
GoLive's Objects Palette, Head tab icons.

Table B.4   Objects Palette Head Tab Icons

Icon	Name
	IsIndex
	Base
	Keywords
	Link
	Meta
	Refresh
	Element]
	Comment

Appendix B

Table B.4 Continued

Icon	Name
	Encode
	Script

Figure B.6
GoLive's Objects Palette, Frames tab icons.

Table B.5 Objects Palette Frames Tab Icons

Icon	Name
	Frame
	Frame Set: two columns, variable right
	Frame Set: two rows, variable bottom
	Frame Set: two columns, variable left
	Frame Set: two rows, variable top
	Frame Set: fixed left, variable bottom right
	Frame Set: fixed left, variable top right
	Frame Set: fixed right, variable bottom left
	Frame Set: fixed right, variable top left
	Frame Set: fixed top, variable bottom right
	Frame Set: fixed bottom, variable top right
	Frame Set: fixed top, variable bottom left

Table B.5   Continued

Icon	Name
	Frame Set: fixed bottom, variable top left
	Frame Set: three columns, variable middle
	Frame Set: three rows, variable middle
	Frame Set: three columns, variable left and right
	Frame Set: three rows, variable top and bottom

Figure B.7
GoLive's Objects Palette, Dynamic Content tab icons.

Table B.6   Objects Palette Dynamic Content Icons

Icon	Name
	Content Source
	Container
	Hide Content
	Repeat Content
	Replace Rows
	Repeat Cells
	Show Next Record
	Show Previous Record

Table B.6   Continued

Icon	Name
	Show Details of Current Record
	Bound Image
	Submit Action
	Button Action
	Image Action
	Bound Label
	Bound Text Field
	Bound Password
	Bound Text Area
	Bound Checkbox
	Bound Radio Button
	Bound Popup
	Bound List Box
	Bound Hidden

Figure B.8
GoLive's Objects Palette, Site tab
icons.

Table B.7   Objects Palette Site Tab Icons

Icon	Name
	Generic Page
	URL
	Address
	Color
	Font Set
	Folder
	URL Group
	Address Group
	Color Group
	Font Set Group

Figure B.9
GoLive's Objects Palette, Diagram tab icons.

Table B.8   Objects Palette Diagram Tab Icons

Icon	Name
	Page
	Section
	Group
	Annotation

Table B.8 Continued

Icon	Name
	Box
	Level
	ASP Element
	Atmosphere Element
	CGI Script
	Database
	DIR
	Form
	iTV
	Java Applet
	JSP Element
	Multiple Pages
	PDA
	PDF
	PHP Element
	Secure
	SMIL
	Static Page
	SVG
	SWF
	Video
	Wireless CHTML

Table B.8 Continued

Icon	Name
	Wireless WML
	Wireless XHTML-Basic

Figure B.10
GoLive's Objects Palette, WML Elements tab icons.

Table B.9 Objects Palette WML Elements Tab Icons

Icon	Name
	Card [OnEvent*, Timer?, (Do I P Pre)*]
	Template [Do I OnEvent]
	Do [Go I Prev I Noop I Refresh]
	OnEvent [Go I Prev I Noop I Refresh]
	Postfield []
	Go [(Postfield I Setvar)*]
	Prev [(Setvar)*]
	Refresh [(Setvar)*]
	Noop
	Setvar []
	Input []
	Select [(Option Group I Option)+]

Appendix B

Table B.9 Continued

Icon	Name
	Option [(Text | OnEvent)*]
	Optgroup [(Option Group | Option)+]
	A [(Text | Img)*]
	Fieldset [(TEXT | a | Anchor | Do | Fieldset | Img | Input | Select)*]
	Anchor [(TEXT | Go | Img | Prev | Refresh)*]
	Img []
	Timer []
	Pre [TEXT	a	Anchor	Do	Input	Select)*]

Figure B.11
GoLive's Objects Palette,
QuickTime tab icons.

Table B.10 Objects Palette QuickTime Tab Icons

Icon	Name
	Movie Track
	Video Track

Table B.10 Continued

Icon	Name
	Color Track
	Picture Track
	Generic Filter Track
	One Source Filter Track
	Two Source Filter Track
	Three Source Filter Track
	MPEG Track
	Sprite Track
	SWF Track
	3D Track
	HREF Track
	Chapter Track
	Text Track
	Sound Track
	MIDI Track
	Instrument Track
	Streaming Track
	Folder Track

Appendix B

Figure B.12
The Page Window as seen within GoLive.

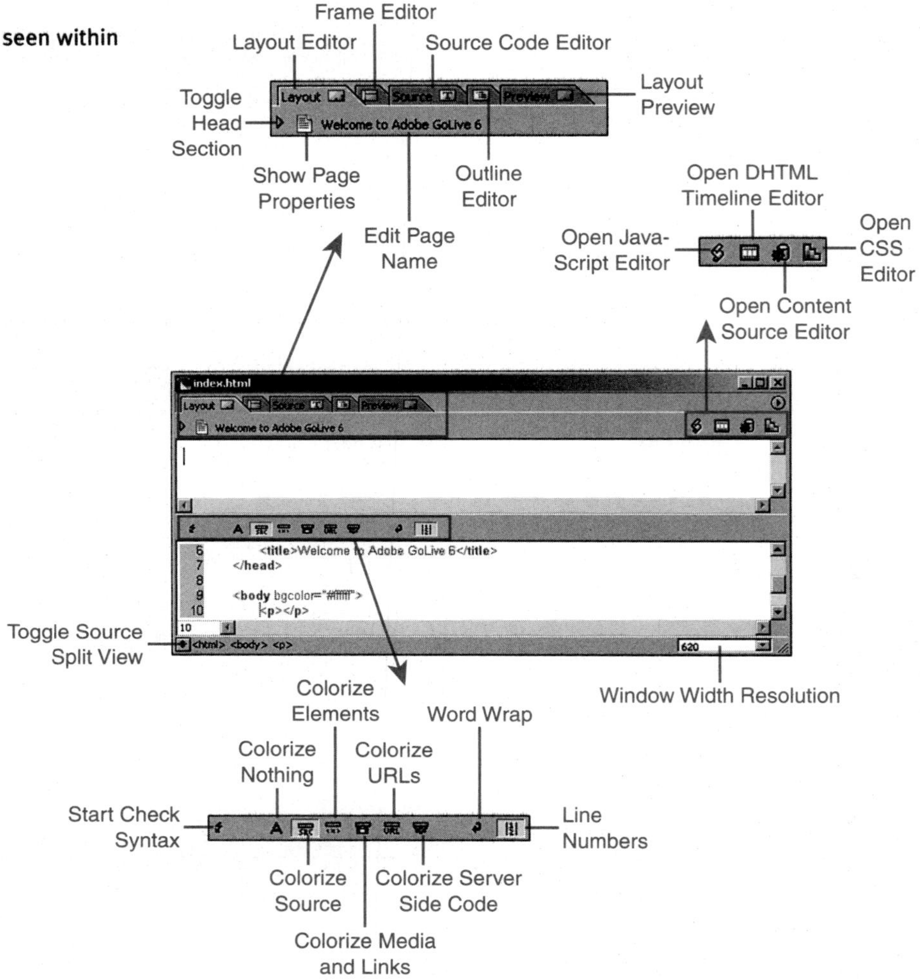

Frame Editor

Layout Editor

Source Code Editor

Toggle Head Section

Layout Preview

Show Page Properties

Outline Editor

Open DHTML Timeline Editor

Edit Page Name

Open Java-Script Editor

Open CSS Editor

Open Content Source Editor

Toggle Source Split View

Colorize Elements

Word Wrap

Window Width Resolution

Colorize Nothing

Colorize URLs

Start Check Syntax

Line Numbers

Colorize Source

Colorize Server Side Code

Colorize Media and Links

INDEX

Symbols

 # (pound sign), 208-209, 234, 289, 473

%HH escaping (URL Handling preference), 94

** indicator, 174**

* (asterisk), 232, 241

? (question mark), 543

+ (plus sign), 307

Numbers

2-up tab, 373, 390

4-up tab, 373, 390

8-bit images, 374

24-bit images, 374

A

absolute pathnames, links (troubleshooting), 213

absolute positioning, floating boxes, 320

absolute size, fonts, 167

accept-charset property (Go tag event), 476

access, 572-574

Access Compact Viewer, 470

access keys, 275-276

Accessibility Reporter, 16

accessing
code, 424
databases (Lasso Suite), 441-442
file properties (WebDAV), 579
images (Dynamic Content module), 534
Java applets, 312
objects (JavaScript), 309
palettes, 28, 82, 113
preferences, 92
rulers, 79
servers (wireless devices), 468
Web applications, 506
Xchange, 421

accesskey, 473-474

accounts, user accounts, 482-486

Action button, 323, 328-330

Action Input object (Lasso Form), 443

Action pop-up menu commands
Custom Merchant, Add to Cart, 543
Custom Merchant, Update Cart Totals, 545
Multimedia, Play Scene, 346

Action setting (Form Inspector), 259

actions
defining, 323
DHTML, 334-336
executing (JavaScript), 326-328
floating objects, triggering, 346
frames, 234
Head Action, 326
image maps, 197
JavaScript, 321-325, 421
Lasso Studio, 455
menu items, 426
options, floating boxes, 324-325
parameters, 325
recorded actions, 30, 86
Target2Frames, 234
troubleshooting, 337
user events, adding, 323
viewing, 325

Actions command (Window menu), 323

Actions menu commands, Link, Target2Frames, 234

Actions palette, 234, 323-325

Actions panel, 322, 336

Active Link color swatch, 132, 172

Active Server Pages (ASP), 497, 506-507

Add check box, 438

Add Data Source, 525, 541

Add to Cart button, Custom Merchant, 542

Add Used (Clean Up Site preferences), 101

Address icon, 211

addresses
  adding manually, 211
  Bookmarks/Favorites, adding, 212
  browsers, adding, 211
  email addresses, 95, 203
  IP addresses, dynamic content security, 536
  Web pages, adding, 211

AdHost Web site, 502

administrators, site administrator, 486

Adobe
  folder, 515
  Web site, 21

Align Bottom, 33, 86, 191

Align Center, 33, 85, 191

Align Left, 33, 85, 191

Align Middle (Align palette), 86

Align palette, 33, 85-86, 191

Align pop-up menu, 187

Align Right, 33, 85, 191

Align to Parent (Align palette), 85, 191

Align Top, 33, 86, 191

aligning
  forms, 258
  grids, 130
  horizontal lines, 186
  images, 187, 190
  Java applets, 311
  marquees, 222
  objects, 33, 85

options, Align palette, 85-86
  tables, 247-248
  text, 175-176

Alignment pop-up menu (Fieldset icon), 276

Alignment, Center command (Type menu), 175

Alignment, Increase Block Indent command (Type menu), 173

Alignment, Left command (Type menu), 175

Alignment, Right command (Type menu), 175

alpha channels, 362

Alt
  option (Slice Options dialog box), 398
  tab, 312

Alt Text field, 312

alternate text, 188, 312, 377

Always Add Alt Text, HTML option (exporting slices), 391

Always Quote Attributes, HTML option (exporting slices), 391

anchor icon, 52, 208

Anchor Pages group, 52

anchors, 208-209, 473

animations
  DHTML (Dynamic HTML), 342-350
  floating objects, 342
  gifs, 185
  LiveMotion, 386, 405
  looping, 345
  SVG (Scalable Vector Graphics), 351
  SWF (ShockWave Flash), 350
  troubleshooting, 364

Annotation Inspector, 57

Annotation tab, 51, 57-58

annotations, site design, 57-58

Apache, 498, 508, 515

applets, Java, 311-312

application servers, 20, 496-497, 506

applications
  integration, 384-386
  JavaScript, 328-333
  Web applications, 506-508

applying
  classes, 289
  JavaScript actions, 321-325

Arabic (numbered list), 178

Ask User (Images preferences), 95

ASP (Active Server Pages), 497, 506-507

asterisk (*), 232, 241

At Launch
  General preference, 93
  menu commands, 25, 93

Attribs tab, 350-351

Attribute tab, 411

attributes. *See* properties

Attributes Case, HTML option (exporting slices), 391

audio, 351, 353

Auto slices, 388-389

AutoLayout, 386, 406-407

Autoplay, 346, 350, 353

Available Servers dialog box, 573

avoiding errors, 562

B

Back icon, 190

Background (QuickTime Editor), 355

background color, 130, 133, 245

Background Image check box, 130, 133

background images
grids, 130
slices, 392
tables, 246
Web pages, 133-134

Background option (Slice Options dialog box), 398

bars
Markup Tree Bar, 88
navigation bar, LiveMotion, 405
scrollbars, frames, 231
status bar, Page window, 78
Status Bar (RealMedia Control), 353

Base, Java applets, 311

base filenames, child pages (site design), 54

Base tag (Head tab), 152

base URLs, 152

Basic option (CSS formatting), 285

Basic tab, 83, 184-186

benefits
forms, 256
SVG (Scalable Vector Graphics), 409-410

Bgimage
box, 246
property (floating boxes), 318

Bind Link To check box, 529

Bind To check box, 514, 530

bindings, 449, 550-552

bitmaps
alternate text, 377
colors, 373-374

managing (Smart Objets), 373
optimizing, 373-375
Photoshop, 385
PNG (Portable Networks Graphic), 374
saving, 377
sizing, 374
slices, 373
Smart Objects, 372-377
spanning (Smart Objets), 373
target files, 375

_blank, target names (frames), 233

Blank Site (Site Wizard), 38-39, 485

blank Web pages, creating, 122

blank Web sites, creating (Site Wizard), 38-40

Blend (QuickTime mode), 362

Blink style (text), 170

Block Quote, paragraphs, 173

Blue World Communications, 432

Bold style (text), 169

bookmark icon, 212

bookmarks
addresses, adding, 212
frames, 230
Markup Tree, 145

Bookmarks menu commands, Edit Bookmarks, 212

borders
cell padding/cell spacing, 245
creating (tables), 244
images, 187-188, 207

bounding boxes
fieldsets, 275
Form tags, 259

box-within-a-box icon, 187

boxes. *See also* check boxes; dialog boxes; floating boxes; text boxes
Bgimage, 246
bounding boxes
fieldsets, 275
Form tags, 259
Caption, 248
CSS Definition box, 287
Images, 147
List Box, forms, 269-270
Sync Times Option, 576
Window Settings, 126

Bring Backward button, 389

Bring Forward button, 389

Bring to Back icon, 85

Bring to Front
button, 389
icon, 85

broken image source icons, 565

broken links, files (Site window), 564-565

Browse (Link Inspector), 81

Browse Link command (CSS File menu), 288

Browser preferences, 103

browser sets, Source Code Editor, 143

Browser Sets preference, 105-106

browsers
addresses, adding, 211
compatibility, CSS, 281
file browsers, 270-271
floating boxes, 321, 337-338
Form tag, 259
forms, 256-257
frames, 230
FTP browser, 574, 577
JavaScript, 304, 307

microbrowsers, Web pages, 468

slices, previewing (Illustrator), 399

SVG (Scalable Vector Graphics), 410

Web pages, troubleshooting, 226

windows, opening Web pages, 205

Browsers tab, 470

browsing navigational links, 205

builders, Lasso Studio, 432

building
dynamic content
converting static sites, 521-526
database preparation, 516-517
dynamic elements, 526-535
logic, 514
prototype sites, 517-519
servers, 515-516
Source Code view, 514
dynamic Web sites, 497-498
mockups (integration), 384-386
prototype sites (dynamic sites), 517-519

Bullet (unnumbered list), 179

Button
icon, 260-261
object (Lasso Form), 444

Button Inspector, 261

buttons
Action, 323, 328-330
Add Data Source, 541
Add to Cart, Custom Merchant, 542
Align Bottom, 33, 191
Align Center, 33, 191
Align Left, 33, 191

Align palette, 33, 191
Align Right, 33, 191
Align Top, 33, 191
Autoplay, 346, 350
Bring Backward, 389
Bring Forward, 389
Bring to Front, 389
Check Out, 545
Colorize, 141
Connect, 577
Convert Page, 526
Create Sample Site Databases, 516
CSS Definitions panel, 284
Custom, 261
Cut Out, 193, 409
Delete Column, 242
Delete Row, 242
Delete Selected Item, 63
Downloading, 576
Duplicate, 210
Dynamic Site Wizard, 499
Edit Properties, 434
forms, creating, 260-261
Import Now, 573
Inventory, 260
labels, 261
Line Number, 141
List, 180
Make Current, 487
naming, 261
New, 541
New Item, 323
New Next Page, 62
New Parent Page, 62
New Previous Page, 62
New Scripts, 307
Optimize, 129
Page Window, 140
Palindrome, 345
Play (RealMedia Control), 352
Play Only (RealMedia Control), 352
Preview, 234

radio buttons
Execute, 435
FileMaker, 433
forms, 266-267, 269
Gender, 330
Recall Design, 58
Reset, 258-260
Select Window, 203
Send to Back, 389
Settings, 377
Site Folder, 292
Site Settings, 60
Sort, 87, 250
Start/Stop Indexing, 274
Submit, 258-260, 543, 547, 550, 554
Submit Design, 58
Submit Order Form, 554
Syntax Check, 140
Tag Editor, 453
Test Content Source, 529
Toggle Orientation, 69
Type Color, 172
types, 261
Universal, 261
Update, 438
Update Cart, 545-547
Upload, 575
Variable, 377
Word Wrap, 141

byte counts, 224

C

C, PHP, 508

Cache
check box (QuickTime), 353
preferences, 96

cached responses, Web servers, 108

calc total() function, 309

calling functions (JavaScript), 309

Caption box, 248

captions, tables, 248

Card Inspector, 471

cards, WML decks, 471-472

Cascading Style Sheets (CSS). *See* CSS

Case Sensitivity Checking (Site Wizard), 41

cell padding, tables, 245

cell spacing, tables, 245

Cell tab, 241-244, 247-248

cells
alignment (tables), 247
background images (tables), 247
HTML table data cells, image slices, 388
merging (tables), 242-244
tables, troubleshooting, 252

central panes, site views, 69

CGI scripts, Form tags, 259

changes, tracking (Workgroup Server), 489

channels, alpha channels, 362

Chapter (QuickTime Editor), 355

character counts, 224

characters
Japanese Emoji, 479
special characters, 163-164
troubleshooting (code), 154

Characters tab, 163

check boxes
Add, 438
background color, 133
Background Image, 130, 133
Bind Link To, 529
Bind To, 514, 530
Cache (QuickTime), 353
Color, 130
Create Project Folder, 40

Delete, 438
Don't Show Again, 25
Hierarchy, 65
Honor Publish States of Group/Pages (Sync Times Option box), 576
Label, 261, 543
Line Numbers, 142
Link Action, 529
Links, 65
Make New Link Absolute, 95
New Document, 135
"On success", 545
Replace Rows, 534
Resize Frame, 233
Search, 438
Show Alternative HTML, 312
Show List of Files to Sync (Sync Times Option box), 576
Show Options Dialog, 101
Site Specific Settings, 56, 60
Sync Referenced Files Only (Sync Times Option box), 576
Tab, 195
Update, 438
URL, 202
Use Always, 105
Use Map, 194
Visible, 346
Web Companion, 441

Check In (Workgroup toolbar), 487

Check Out, 487, 545

Check Spelling, command or window, 164

Check Syntax command, 412, 479

Check URLs case-sensitive (URL Handling preference), 94

Checkbox icon, 268

Checkbox Input object (Lasso Form), 443

checkboxes, forms, 266-269

checking in files (Site Window), 488

checking out files (Site Window), 488

checkout screen, 549-551

child, Web page hierarchy, 53

Child link, pending link, 55

child pages, 54, 62

CHTML (Compact Hypertext Markup Language), 468-470

Circle (unnumbered list), 179

class card attribute (WML deck), 472

class selectors, 282

class style icon, 288

classes, 288-289

Clean Up (Site preferences), 101

Clean Up Revisions, Maintenance Section (Server Administration Web Access), 485

Clean Up Site, 569
command (Site menu), 568
panel, 100

Clear command (Edit menu), 63, 163, 189

Clear Rollover (Rollover tab), 198

clearing
images, 189
styles (tables), 249
text, 163

Click state, slices (rollover images), 393

Clip Information (RealMedia Control), 353

Clip to Artboard Size (Macromedia Flash SWF File Format dialog box), 379

Close all Tags, HTML option (exporting slices), 391

CMYK color, 84

code. *See also* Source Code
accessing, 424
browser sets, 143
color, 141-143
colorization schemes, 141
dot-syntax notation, 305
Drag and Drop, 142
errors (JavaScript), 310
Find and Replace (HTML elements), 150-151
fonts, 143
GUIs (graphical user interfaces), 14
head tags, 151-153
headers, adding scripts, 152-153
Highlight palette, 149
JavaScript shells, 14
line breaks, 142
line numbers, 141
managing (Source Code Editor), 140
Markup Tree, 145
Outline Editor, 145-149
scripts, 151-153
Source Split View, 143
Split View feature, 13
SVG code, 411-412
Syntax Checker, 14
tags, 140
troubleshooting, 154
verifying, 14
viewing, 12
Web applications, 506
wrapping, 141
XHTML code, generating, 153
XML, 14

Code (Font Structures), 171

collection spotlights, Web pages, 68

color
background color, 130, 245
bitmaps, 373-374
borders, 188
CMYK, 84
code, 141
custom colors, creating, 114
dithering, 185
file organization (Status preference), 100
gifs, 185
Grayscale, 84
Highlight palette, 149
HSB color, 84
link color, setting, 172
marquees, 222
RGB, 84
sites, 102
source code, 106-107
Source Code Editor, 143
swatches, 172
text, 171-172
Web color, 84
Web pages, 29, 84, 132-133

Color (QuickTime), 353

Color check box, 130

Color palette, 29, 84, 130-132, 142, 171

Color Picker (Design Colors preference), 102

Color property (floating boxes), 318

Color swatch, 130-132

Color tab, 114, 149

colorization schemes (code), 141

Colorize button, 141

Colors command (Source menu), 141

Colors preference, 106-107

Colors tab, 46, 562, 566

ColorSync preference, 98

columns
Filename Status (Error tab), 46
Locked (Error tab), 46
resizing (tables), 244
Status (Error tab), 46
tables, 241-242
Used (Error tab), 46

commands
Action pop-up menu
Add to Cart, 543
Custom Merchant, Update Cart Totals, 545
Link, Target2Frames, 234
Multimedia, Play Scene, 346
At Launch menu
Create New Page, 93
Do Nothing, 93
Show Intro Screen, 25, 93
Bookmarks menu, Edit Bookmarks, 212
Check Syntax, 412
CSS File menu, 288
Default Mode menu, 94
Design menu, 54, 58
Diagram menu
Move to Scratch, 64
New, Child Page, 62
New, Next Page, 62
New, Parent Page, 62
New, Previous Page, 62
New Design Diagram, 50
New Pages, 62
Site Design, 53
Solve Hierarchy, 65
Doctype menu, 477
Document menu, 127
Edit menu
Check Spelling, 164
Check Syntax, 479

Clear, 63, 163, 189
Copy, 131, 162, 189
Cut, 162, 189
Delete, 163, 189
Duplicate, 163, 189
Find, 70, 150, 165, 567
Group, 59
Keyboard Shortcuts, 115
Paste, 162, 189
Preferences, 25, 92, 135,
    143, 569, 572
Preferences, Application,
    437
Preferences, Spell
    Checker, 164
Select All, 162, 189
Servers, 573
Show Link Warnings,
    565
Ungroup, 59
Web Settings, 163
Favorites menu, Organize
Favorites, 212
File menu
    Document Encoding,
        Japanese (Shift_JIS),
        479
    Export, 408
    Export As, 408
    Export Settings, 406
    FTP Browser, 577
    Mount Workgroup Site,
        122
    New, 134, 292
    New Database, 440
    New Page, 76, 122, 126
    New Site, 25, 39, 41-44,
        485
    New Special, 14, 122,
        126, 284, 477
    New Special, Basic Page,
        154
    New Special, Page from
        Stationery, 124, 296,
        478
    New Special, Page from
        Template, 124, 296

New Special, WML Deck,
    470
New Special, XHTML
    Page, 154
Open, 26, 76
Open Recent Files, 122
Preview in Browser, 395
Save, 134, 136, 292, 297
Save As, 136, 285, 427
Save As, Stationery, 295
Save As, Template, 295
Save for Web, 390, 399,
    404
Save Optimized, 395
Sharing, 441
GoLive menu
    Special, Document
        Statistics, 224
    Special, Table, 241-243
Incremental Uploads (Site
window), 575
Lasso Studio menu
    Lasso Database Selector,
        451-453
    Lasso Form Builder, 456
    Lasso Site Builder, 447
Layouts menu, Layout
Setup, 442
Link menu, Open Window,
328
Markup menu, Convert to
XHTML, 477
Modified-item Uploads (Site
window), 575
Multimedia menu
    Drag Floating Box, 324
    Mouse Follow, 324
    Move By, 324
    Move To, 325
    ShowHide, 325
    Wipe Transition, 325-327
Navigation tab menu, 68
Object menu, 397-399
Objects palette menu,
    Configure, 469
Pane menu, 45

Preferences menu, Modules,
509
Selected Constraints menu,
100
Selection Uploads (Site win-
dow), 575
Site Extras menu,
Components, 292
Site Folder menu,
Components, 292
Site menu
    Clean Up Site, 568
    FTP Server, Connect, 574
    FTP Server, Server
        Nickname, 574
    FTP Server, Sync
        Modification Times All,
        576
    FTP Server, Sync
        Modification Times
        Selection, 576
    Get References Used,
        211
    Settings, 60, 521, 574
    Settings, Link Types, 56
    Site Report, 70
    View, Navigation or Site,
        45
    WebDAV Server, Server
        Nickname, 579
    Workgroup, Change
        Password, 490
    Workgroup, Change
        User, 490
    Workgroup, Convert to
        Workgroup, 486
    Workgroup, Open
        Workgroup
        Administration, 490
Slices menu, 392
Source menu, Colors, 141
Special menu
    Insert Index, 422
    New Link, 206-207
    Start Tabulator Indexing,
        274
    Stop Tabulator Indexing,
        274

Stationery menu, 297
Template menu, 295-297
Type menu
  Alignment, Center, 175
  Alignment, Increase
    Block Indent, 173
  Alignment, Left, 175
  Alignment, Right, 175
  Font, Edit Font Sets, 167
  List, 180
  MySQL Database Query,
    528
  NoBreak, 178
  Paragraph Format, 175
  Paragraph Format,
    Paragraph, 173
  Size, 169
  Structure, 170
  Style, 169
  Style, Blink, 170
  Style, Bold, 169
  Style, Italic, 169
  Style, Plain Text, 169
  Style, Strikeout, 170
  Style, Subscript, 170
  Style, Superscript, 170
  Style, Teletype, 170
  Style, Underline, 170
Type pop-up menu, Custom
  Merchant Shopping Cart,
  543
Undo menu, Undo Cleanup
  Site, 569
Update All (Site window),
  575
View menu
  Hide Rulers, 131
  Layout Mode, 442
  Show Rulers, 131
  Show Split Source, 143
Window menu
  Actions, 323
  Export, 406
  Floating Boxes, 320
  In & Out Links, 565
  Inspector, 194, 307, 330

  Optimize, 393
  Rollovers, 393-394
  Save as, Save as
    Stationery, 478
  Site Navigator, 67
  Template Regions, 295
  Tracing Image, 192, 409
  View, 281, 478
  Workgroup toolbar, 487
  Workspace, Default
    Workspace, 29, 82
  Workspace, Manage
    Workspace, 114
  Workspace, Save
    Workspace, 114
Window Size menu,
  Settings, 126

Comment icon, 220

Comment Inspector, 220

Comment tag (Head tab), 152

comments, 218-220

commerce sites, creating, 501

**Compact Hypertext Markup
  Language (CHTML), 468-470**

Companion Sharing, 441

**Compare to Server
  (Workgroup toolbar), 487**

compatibility
  browsers, CSS, 281
  PHP, 508
  WebDAV, 579

Completed (Files tab), 489

components
  Actions palette, 323
  benefits, 293
  creating, 292
  CSS implementation,
    291-294
  inserting, 292
  instances, 294
  links, 294
  opening, 293
  saving, 292

  Site Window, 45
  styles, 280

Components command, 292

**Composition (QuickTime
  mode), 362**

Compressed SVGs, 377-378

compression
  images, 184
  lossless compression, PNG
    (Portable Networks
    Graphic) bitmaps, 375
  lossy compression, SWFs,
    379
  SVGZ, 411

concatenating slices, 392

Condition object, 445, 454

conditionals, genres, 454

Config folder, 508, 524, 536

**Configure command (Objects
  palette menu), 469**

Connect button, 577

connections
  database connections, trou-
    bleshooting, 536
  FTP servers, 574-575
  WebDAV servers, 579

Console, RealMedia, 353

constraints, filenames, 59-61

**Container icon (Object
  palette), 513**

**content, Web page content
  (CSS), 281.** *See also* Dynamic
  Content

content sources
  checkout screen, 549
  creating, 528
  Custom Merchant,
    troubleshooting, 543, 556
  defining, 528-529
  dynamic detail pages, 532
  dynamic results list pages,
    creating, 528

editor, 78, 499, 509-511
icon, 528, 543
Inspector, 501, 509
managing (Content Source
Editor), 500
naming, 528-529
troubleshooting, 537
variables, 528

contextual menus, 15

**Control Panel (RealMedia
Control), 352**

Controls, RealMedia, 352

Convert Page button, 526

**Convert to XHTML command
(Markup menu), 477**

converting
images (SWF files), 378
single user sites, 486
static sites, 499, 521-526
tables (grids), 252

Cookie object, 445, 451

cookies, 332-333, 451

Copy
command (Edit menu), 131,
162, 189
QuickTime mode, 362

**Copy from Template option
(Site Wizard), 44**

copying
annotations, site design, 57
grids, 131
images, 189
style definitions, 287
text, 162

**correcting errors (History
palette), 30**

**Create a New Page (At
Launch General preference),
93**

**Create a New Site (At Launch
General preference), 93**

Create Add Page screen, 448

Create Circle tool, 194

**Create Display Page screen,
448**

**Create New Page command
(At Launch menu), 93**

**Create Project Folder check
box, 40**

**Create Sample Site Databases
button, 516**

Create Sample tool, 358

credit card processing, 540

**CSS (Cascading Style Sheets),
280**
browser compatibility, 281
editor, 78
external style sheets, 281,
284-285
formatting, 285
icon, 287, 290
implementing, 283-287
classes, 288-289
components, 291-294
ID styles, 289-290
snippets, 290-291
indenting paragraphs, 174
inheritance, 283
internal style sheets, 281
layers, 316, 400
option, New Page, 123
palette, 289
precedence, 283
properties, 288
selectors, 282
Web page content, 281

**CSS (Floating Boxes) com-
mand (Slices menu), 392**

CSS Definition
box, 287
editor, 284, 287-289, 588
palette, 285
panel, 284

CSS File menu commands, 288

**cursors, Source Editor
Window, 142**

**Curve Quality (Macromedia
Flash SWF File Format dialog box), 379**

Custom button, 261

**custom classes, CSS
implementation, 288**

Custom Color palette, 84, 114

**custom library objects, styles,
280**

**custom library snippets,
styles, 280**

Custom Merchant, 20, 501
Content Sources, 543
credit card processing, 540
data sources, 540
enclosing forms, 543
functions, 540
implementing
Add to Cart button, 542
checkout screen, 549-551
data sources, 541-542
receipt page, 555
review page, 554-555
shipping methods, 552
shipto screen, 551
shopping cart, 545-549
limitations, 540
providers, 542
troubleshooting, 556

**Custom Merchant, Add to
Cart command (Action pop-
up menu), 543**

**Custom Merchant, Update
Cart Totals command
(Action pop-up menu), 545**

**Custom Merchant Order Form,
501, 549**

**Custom Merchant Shopping
Cart, content source, 501**

**Custom Merchant Shopping
Cart command (Type pop-up
menu), 543**

custom objects, storing, 115

Custom Objects palette, 115

custom palettes, 114-115

Custom state, slices (rollover images), 393

customizations
browsers sets, 105
CHTML development, 478
desktops, 113-116
interfaces, 424
planning, 112-113
workspaces, 82
XHTML-Basic development, 478

Cut command (Edit menu), 162, 189

Cut Out, 193, 409

cutting
text, 162
Tracing Images, 193

D

data, sorting, 87, 250-251, 564, 567

Data folders, files (Extras tab), 46

Data Sources, 509
bindings, 499
Custom Merchant, 540-542
databases, 508
dynamic content, creating, 525
encrypting, 541
window, 525
Windows, Lasso Suite installations, 433

Database Input object (Lasso Form), 443

Database Object (Lasso Data Access), 444

Database Query, content source, 501

databases
accessing (Lasso Suite), 441-442
actions (Lasso Suite), 438
configuration screens, Lasso Suite, 437
connections, troubleshooting, 536
content sources, 499
creating, Lasso Suite, 439-445, 462
genres, 451-455
member searches, 456-460
membership registration screens, 446-451
navigation, 461
Data Sources, 508
dynamic content, 524, 536
dynamic Web sites, building, 497
Lasso Studio, 447
placeholder text, 510
preparing (building dynamic content), 516-517
records, adding (Lasso Studio), 449
tables, creating (Lasso Suite), 440

datasources folder, 508

Date Object (Lasso Programming), 445

date stamps, creating, 223

decks, WML decks, 470-473

Decrease List Level (level adjustment list), 179

Default, target names (frames), 233

Default menu commands, 94

Default Mode (General preference), 94

Default RGB (ColorSync preferences), 98

defining
actions, 323
content sources, 528-529
design groups (site design), 59
HTML, 285
pop-up windows, 328

Definition
Font Structures, 171
unnumbered list, 179

Delete
check box, 438
command, 100, 163, 189

Delete Column button, 242

Delete Row button, 242

Delete Selected Item button, 63

deleted files, Site window, 568

deleting
annotations, site design, 58
columns (tables), 242
floating boxes, 320
images, 189
keyframes, 345
records (Lasso Studio), 455
rows (tables), 242
text, 163
Tracing Images, 194

Description field, 548

design. *See* site design

Design Annotation icon, 57

Design Colors (Site preferences), 102

Design Diagram, prototype site design, 517

Design folder, 50

Design Group icon, 59

design groups, site design, 59

Design menu commands, 54, 58

Design Pages group, 58

Design Section, 50, 53

Design Staging, Recall Design command (Design menu), 58

Design Staging, Submit Design command (Design menu), 58

Design tab, 51-53, 58

Design view, 18, 51-52

desktops, customizing, 113-116

detail pages, dynamic results list pages (creating), 532-535

Detect Rollover Image (Rollover tab), 198

developing
    CHTML, 477-479
    WML, 470-477
    XHTML-Basic, 477-479

devices. *See* wireless devices

DHTML (Dynamic HTML), 316
    actions, 334-336
    animations, 342-350
    floating boxes, 316, 321-325
    floating objects, 346-349
    submenus, 334-336

DHTML Timeline Editor, 78

Diagram
    pane, 53
    tab, 50-51, 84, 562, 566
    view, 58

Diagram menu commands
    Move to Scratch, 64
    New, Child Page, 62
    New, Next Page, 62
    New, Parent Page, 62
    New, Previous Page, 62
    New Design Diagram, 50
    New Pages, 62
    Site Design, 53
    Solve Hierarchy, 65

diagramming sites, 61-65

diagrams, storing, 566

dialog boxes
    Available Servers, 573
    Export, 399
    Find, 70
    Macromedia Flash, 378
    Macromedia Flash SWF File Format, 378
    Manage Workspaces, 114
    Optimization, 380
    Preferences, 92
    Rollovers State Options, 394
    Save, 134-136
    Save As, 292
    Save for Web, 193, 372, 377, 390, 399-400, 409
    Save Optimized As, 393
    Save Workspace, 114
    Settings, 390
    Slice Options, 389, 398-399
    Sort Table, 87

dictionaries, managing, 104

Dim When Inactive, Source Code, 32, 89, 144

dimensions, Web pages, 125-126

Dir parameter (pop-up windows), 329

directories
    Extend Scripts directory, 421
    IIS, Windows (Lasso Suite installations), 433
    Windows (Lasso Suite installations), 434
    Scripts, Windows (Lasso Suite installations), 433
    site data directory, 296
    SmartObjects, 371
    Stationery, 296
    Templates, 296
    Xchange directory, 421

Directory setting (Available Servers dialog box), 574

disabled elements, forms, 272

Display Line Numbers, Source Code, 32, 89, 144

Display Warnings icon, 310

displaying
    forms, browsers, 256
    frames, 234-235
    source code (line breaks), 142
    Web pages, 52

Distribute Objects (Align palette), 86, 191

distributing
    images, 191
    objects, 86

Dither Copy (QuickTime mode), 362

dithering, 185

Div, classes (applying), 289

Divide Slice option, 389

Do event, 476

Do Nothing command (At Launch menu), 93

docking palettes, 82, 113

Doctype menu commands, 477

DocType option, 78

Document Encoding, Japanese (Shift_JIS) command (File menu), 479

Document menu commands, 127

Document Object Model (DOM), JavaScript, 306

Document Statistics, 224

Document Type Definition (DTD), 14

Document window, 294-296, 312, 372

documents. *See* files

DOM (Document Object Model), JavaScript, 306

Don't Show Again check box, 25

dot-syntax notation, object storage, 305

Double Click user event (links), 323

Down state, slices (rollover images), 393

downloading
extensions, 420-422
files, 488, 576-579
Java applets, 311
MySQL, 498
Tomcat, 498

Downloading button, 576

downloads, Incremental or Selection, 576

Drag and Drop, code, 142

Drag Floating Box command (Multimedia menu), 324

dragging
events, 476
text, 163

drawing tools (ImageReady), 393

DTD (Document Type Definition), 14

Duplicate
button, 210
command, 100, 163, 189

Dynamic Bindings, 548
palette, 499, 509-510,
526-529, 549
tab, 509
window, 543

Dynamic Content
application servers, 20
building
converting static sites,
521-526
database preparation,
516-517
dynamic elements,
526-535
logic, 514
prototype sites, 517-519
server preparations,
515-516
Source Code view, 514
creating, 521, 526
Custom Merchant, 20, 501
Data Sources, 508-509
EasyHost, 502
Hide Content tool, 548
icon, 521
modifying, 526
module, 500-501, 509
Content Source Editor,
499
Content Source
Inspector, 501
Dynamic Bindings
palette, 499
Dynamic Content tool-
bar, 499
Dynamic site Wizard, 499
PageGenerator, 502-503
preconfigured servers, 502
preference, 108
previewing, 526
security, 536
tab, 83, 507, 511
troubleshooting, 536
Web applications, 506-508
Web sites, building, 496-498

Dynamic Content Preferences pane, 509

Dynamic Content Server folder, 515

Dynamic Content Site Settings pane, 509-510

Dynamic Content toolbar, 499, 509

Dynamic Content Tools, 509-514

dynamic detail pages, creating, 532-535

dynamic elements, 526
adding, 529
dynamic detail pages,
creating, 532-535
dynamic results list pages,
creating, 527-532
dynamic search pages,
creating, 527

Dynamic HTML. *See* DHTML

dynamic pages, creating or renaming, 526

dynamic results list pages, creating, 527-532

dynamic search pages, creating, 527

Dynamic Site Wizard, 499, 509-510, 522

E

EasyHost, 502

.ecp, Data Source database, 509

Edit Bookmarks command (Bookmarks menu), 212

Edit Link command (CSS File menu), 288

Edit menu commands
Check Spelling, 164
Check Syntax, 479
Clear, 63, 163, 189
Copy, 131, 162, 189
Cut, 162, 189
Delete, 163, 189
Duplicate, 163, 189
Find, 70, 150, 165, 567
Group, 59
Keyboard Shortcuts, 115
Paste, 162, 189
Preferences, 25, 92, 135,
143, 569, 572

Preferences, Application, 437
Preferences, Spell Checker, 164
Select All, 162, 189
Servers, 573
Show Link Warnings, 565
Ungroup, 59
Web Settings, 163

Edit Properties button, 434

Edit URL window, 204

editable regions, 294-296

editors
Content Source editor, 78, 499, 509-511
CSS Definitions Editor, 294, 287-289
CSS Editor, 78
DHTML Timeline Editor, 78
Frame Editor, 231-233
JavaScript Editor, 77, 304-306
Layout Editor, 12, 151, 220, 233
Outline Editor, 12, 145-149, 220
QuickTime Editor, 354-356
Source Code Editor, 140-143
Source Editor, viewing code, 12
Tag Editor, 453
Timeline Editor, 343-345, 354

effects, mouseDown or mouseOver, 197

element selectors, CSS, 282

Element tab, 150

elements
adding (Outline Editor), 147
disabled elements, forms, 272
dynamic elements, 526, *adding, 529*
dynamic detail pages (creating), 532-535
dynamic results list pages (creating), 527-532
dynamic search pages (creating), 527
form elements, WML development, 474-475
hidden elements, forms, 272
HTML elements, Find and Replace, 150-151
modifying (Outline Editor), 147
nested elements, SVG, 411
page elements, floating boxes, 320
read only elements, forms, 273
selecting (Outline Editor), 147

email addresses
mailto:, 95
navigational links, 203

Email Input object (Lasso Form), 443

embedded fonts, SVG files, 377

embedded images, SVG files, 377

embedding
JavaScript, 98
SVG, HTML pages, 410

Emoji characters, 479

Empty Cells option (HTML Tables), 392

empty child pages, pending links, 62

empty next sibling pages, pending links, 62

empty parent pages, pending links, 62

empty previous sibling pages, pending links, 62

emulators, 470

enclosing forms, 543

Encode tag (Head tab), 152

Encoding Object (Lasso Data Access), 444

Encodings preference, 98

entering text, 160-161

Error Highlighting, 310

Error Input object (Lasso Form), 443

Error Object (Lasso Programming), 445

errors
avoiding, 562
code errors (JavaScript), 310
correcting (History palette), 30
file transfers, 577
files (Errors tab), 46
SVG, 412
Web sites, 565

Errors (Network Status preference), 105

Errors tab, 47, 567

event handlers, JavaScript, 305-307

events
Do, 476
dragging, 476
Go tag, 476
menuSignal event, 425
objects, JavaScript, 321
ordering, 327
parameters, 327
pop-up windows, 328
Prev, 476
user events, 323, 330
WML development, 475-476

Events list, 234

Events tab, 307-309

Evocative Software Web site, 501

Execute radio button, 435

Export (Site preferences), 101

Export As (Macromedia Flash SWF File Format dialog box), 378

Export As command (File menu), 408

Export command, 406-408

Export Conditions (Export preferences), 101

Export dialog box, 399

Export icon, 363

Export Settings
command (File menu), 406
palette, 407-408
Smart Objects, 380

exporting
files (Illustrator), 399
HTML, Photoshop mockups, 386
images, 385-386
site files, 101
slices, 390-393, 400

expressions, managing, 104

Extend Script SDK, 420

Extend Scripts
directory, 421
folder, 427
Module preference, 97

Extended Price field, 548

extending Link field, 204

eXtensible Hypertext Markup Language, Basic. *See* XHTML-Basic

eXtensible Hypertext Markup Language (XHTML), 153-154

eXtensible Markup Language (XML), 20

extensions
file extensions, .site, 26
installing/downloading, 420-422
loading, 421

nesting, 424
storing, 421, 427
SVG files, 378
troubleshooting, 429-430

external links, 566

external references, 566

external style sheets, 281, 284-287

External tab, 46, 203, 211-213, 562, 566

Extras tab, 46, 50, 136, 291, 567

eye icon, 363

Eyedropper Swatch tool, 373

Eyedropper tool, 373

F

Factory Settings (Design Colors preference), 102

family spotlights, Web pages, 68

Favorites, addresses (adding), 212

Favorites menu commands, Organize Favorites, 212

features, Photoshop, 386-396

Field = exact test string parameter (Javascript forms), 331

Field contains letters only parameter (Javascript forms), 331

Field contains numbers only parameter (Javascript forms), 331

Field Display object (Lasso Form), 444

Field has this many characters parameter (Javascript forms), 331

Field is not empty parameter (Javascript forms), 331

Field is proper email format parameter (Javascript forms), 331

Field Object (Lasso Data Access), 444

Field proper Credit Card format parameter (Javascript forms), 331

fields
Alt Text, 312
content sources, checkout screen, 549
database tables (creating), 440
Description field, 548
Dynamic Bindings window, 543
Extended Price field, 548
Link field, 81, 203-205
Password Fields, forms, 263-266
Position Field (RealMedia Control), 353
Price field, 548
Shipping fields, shipto screen, 551
Status Field (RealMedia Control), 353
text fields, 263-266, 331
text input fields, 474

Fieldset icon, 275-276

fieldsets, access keys, 275-276

File Browser icon, 271

file browsers, 270-271

file extensions, .site, 26

file formats, Tracing Images, 192

File Inspector, 59

File menu commands
Document Encoding, Japanese (Shift_JIS), 479
Export, 408

Export As, 408
Export Settings, 406
FTP Browser, 577
Mount Workgroup Site, 122
New, 134, 292
New Database, 440
New Page, 76, 122, 126
New Site, 25, 39-44, 485
New Special, 14, 122, 126, 284, 477
New Special, Basic Page, 154
New Special, Page from Stationery, 124, 296, 478
New Special, Page from Template, 124, 296
New Special, WML Deck, 470
New Special, XHTML Page, 154
Open, 26, 76
Open Recent Files, 122
Preview in Browser, 395
Save, 134-136, 285, 292, 297
Save As, 136, 427
Save As, Stationery, 295
Save As, Template, 295
Save for Web, 390, 399, 404
Save Optimized, 395
Sharing, 441

File Object (Lasso Programming), 445

file structure, Server Administration Web Access, 484

File tab, 580

File Transfer Protocol. *See* FTP

File Type option (Export Settings palette), 407

FileMaker
database, 439-442
radio button, 433

FileMaker Pro, 436-437, 516

Filemaker Remote link, 437

Filename Constraints (Site preferences), 99-100

Filename Status column (Error tab), 46

filenames
constraints, 59-61
site design, 54
rules (Filename Constraints), 99

files
broken links (Site window), 564-565
checking in (Site Window), 488
checking out (Site Window), 488
Compressed SVGs, 377-378
creating (Site window), 564
Data folder (Extras tab), 46
deleted files, Site window, 568
downloading, 488, 576-579
errors (Errors tab), 46
exporting (Illustrator), 399
format files, Lasso Studio, 432, 447
include files, LDML tags, 461
locking (WebDAV), 579
managing (Files tab), 46
media files, 70, 484
modifying (Site Window), 489
moving (Site window), 563
opening (ImageReady), 393
organizing, 100
original files, opening (Smart Objects), 380
properties, accessing (WebDAV), 579
referenced files, Server Administration Web Access, 484
refreshing (Site window), 489

renaming (Site window), 563
revisions (Workgroup Server), 485
searching, Site window (troubleshooting), 569-570
Site Document, managing, 26
site files, 99-102
snapshot files, 432, 445
space files, 16
stationery files, index pages, 478
status (Errors tab), 46
SVG (Scalable Vector Graphics), 377-379, 411-412
SWFs, 378, 386, 405
synchronizing (Workgroup Server), 485
target files, bitmaps, 375
time stamps, 575
transferring, 575-577
unlocking, 485, 580
uploading, 577-579
XHTML files, creating, 154

Files tab, 46, 52, 71, 122, 136

Filmstrip icon, 78

Filter (QuickTime Editor), 355

Find
command (Edit menu), 70, 150, 165, 567
dialog box, 70
preferences, 103-104
window, 150

Find & Replace, 164

Find All (Browsers preference), 103

Find and Replace, code (HTML elements), 150-151

Flatten (QuickTime Editor), 355

flexibility, SDK (Software Development Kit), 21

Floating Box icon, 317, 342

floating boxes, 316. *See also* floating objects

   action options, 324-325
   adding, 320
   browsers, 321
   creating, 317
   defined, 289
   deleting, 320
   DHTML, 321-325, 334-336
   entering text, 161
   formatting, 289
   ID selectors, 282
   JavaScript, 321-333
   links, 322
   locking, 320
   managing, 320
   markers, 319
   page elements, 320
   positioning, 320
   properties, 318
   selecting, 320
   sizing, 317
   tables, 161
   text, 322
   troubleshooting, 337-338

Floating Boxes command (Window menu), 320

Floating Boxes list, 344

Floating Boxes palette, 320, 335

floating objects, 342
   multiple floating objects, 346-348
   paths (keyframes), 344
   previewing, 344
   recording movement, 345
   scenes, 349
   showing/hiding, 346
   speed, 345
   Timeline Editor, 343-345
   triggering, 346
   zig zagging, 345

Focus setting
   Checkbox icon, 268
   File Browser icon, 271
   Radio Button icon, 268

Folder icon, 212

folders
   Adobe, 515
   Config folder, 508, 524, 536
   Data folder, files (Extras tab), 46
   datasources, 508
   Design folder, 50
   Dynamic Content Server folder, 515
   Extend Scripts folder, 427
   Images, 185
   Internal, 287
   local folders, imported Web sites, 41-42
   Modules, 421
   New Addresses, 211
   New URLs, 211
   Root Folder, 134
   root folders, imported Web sites, 40
   site design, 54
   Site folder, 65, 185
   SmartObjects folder, 371
   spring-loaded, 99
   Stationery, 135

Font, Edit Font Sets command (Type menu), 167

Font preference, 106-107

Font Set Editor, 167

font sets, 166-167

Font Sets tab, 47, 562, 566

Font Structure, 170-171

fonts
   Emoji, 479
   formatting, slicing (Illustrator), 399
   size, 167
   source code, 106-107
   Source Code Editor, 143
   styles, 169-170
   SVG files, 377
   troubleshooting, 181

Fonts preference, 97

Form element icon, 258

form elements, WML development, 474-475

Form Input Image icon, 262

Form Inspector, 258-260

Form Label Inspector, 264

form labels, text fields (form validation), 331

Form Method setting (Form Inspector), 260

Form object (Lasso Form), 444

Form Param Object (Lasso Data Access), 444

Form tags, 258-260

form validation, JavaScript applications, 329-332

format files, Lasso Studio, 432, 447

format property (text input field), 474

formats, file formats (Tracing Images), 192

formatting
   classes, CSS implementation, 289
   CSS formatting (HTML), 285
   floating boxes, 289
   fonts, slicing (Illustrator), 399
   options, CSS, 285
   paragraphs, 172-174
   preformatting, paragraphs, 174
   text, 166

forms, 256-257
   alignments, 258
   benefits, 256
   browsers, 256-257

buttons, creating, 260-261
check boxes, 266-269
creating, 256-258
disabled elements, 272
enclosing forms, 543
file browsers, 270-271
Form tag, 258-260
hidden elements, 272
Input Image, 262
labels, 262-264
layout, 257
List Box, 269-270
naming (JavaScript), 330
navigating, 273-276
parameters (JavaScript), 331
Password Fields, 263-266
Pop-up menus, 269-270
radio buttons, 266-269
read only elements, 273
tabs, 257
text, 257, 266
Text Areas, 265-266
Text Fields, 263-266
troubleshooting, 277

Forms tab, 83, 257, 261-264

forms validation, 278

Frame Editor, 231-233

Frame Inspector, frames (managing), 231

Frame Preview, 80, 225, 233-234

Frame Rate (Macromedia Flash SWF File Format dialog box), 379

Frame tab, 231

Frame view, 79

frames
actions, 234
bookmarks, 230
browsers, 230
displaying, 234-235
Frame Editor, 231-233
limitations, 230

links, 230-231
managing (Frame Inspector), 231
naming, 233
opening Web pages, 205
previewing, 233-234
refreshing, 230
repeating objects, 230
resizing, 232
scrollbars, 231
scrolling, 233
set frames, 232
Table of Contents, 234
target frames, 81, 233, 329
troubleshooting, 236
variable frames, 232

Frames command (Default Mode menu), 94

Frames Preview command (Default Mode menu), 94

Frames tab (Objects palette), 83

framesets, 230-231

FTP (File Transfer Protocol)
access, 573
browser, 574, 577
publishing, 572-574
servers, 573-574, 577
Site window, 572
tab, 47, 574
Web sites, importing, 42

FTP Browser command (File menu), 577

FTP Server, Connect command (Site menu), 574

FTP Server, Server Nickname command (Site menu), 574

FTP Server, Sync Modification Times All command (Site menu), 576

FTP Server, Sync Modification Times Selection command (Site menu), 576

functionality
Lasso Suite, 439
menu items, 425

functions
calc total(), 309
calling (JavaScript), 309
Custom Merchant, 540
names (JavaScript), 307
Number(), 309
storing JavaScript, 307

G

Gender radio buttons, 330

General preferences, 93-94

generating
HTML (mockups), 384
XHTML code, 153

Generator tag, 94

Generic Smart Objects, 371

Generic XML Document option (New Page), 123

genres, 451-456

Get References Used command (Site menu), 211

gifs, 185, 407

glyphs, fonts (SVG files), 377

Go tag event, 476

Gold Star Cookie Jar icon, 78

GoLive Data, Publishing Section (Server Administration Web Access), 484

GoLive menu commands
Special, Document Statistics, 224
Special, Table, 241-243

grab handles, 95

graphical user interfaces (GUIs), 14-15

graphics. *See* images

Grayscale color, 84

green bug icon, 564

Grid Inspector, 130

grids
    aligning, 130
    background color, 130
    background image, 130
    converted tables, 252
    copying, 131
    Layout Grid, 15, 128
    layout grids, Java applets,
      311
    multiple grids, 131
    navigating, 129
    optimizing, 129
    placing, 128
    sizing, 128
    Snap, 129
    square size, 129
    tables, placing, 131
    troubleshooting, 137
    Visibility, 129

group child pages, pending
    links, 62

Group command (Edit menu),
    59

Group Inspector, 59

Group setting (Radio Button
    icon), 267

grouping
    Design Pages group, 58-59
    images, 190
    Live Pages, 58
    objects, 32, 85
    Options, creating, 475
    text input fields, 474
    Web pages, spotlighting
      (Navigation view), 67

GUIs (graphical user inter-
    faces), 14-15

H

Hand
    icon, 192, 409
    tool, 373

handles, grab handles, 95

Head Actions, 326-328

Head Scripts, 152-153

Head tab, 83, 151-153

Head Tag Inspector, 151

head tags, adding, 151-153

headers
    scripts, adding, 152-153
    text, 175

headings, CSS Definitions
    panel, 284

Height property (floating
    boxes), 318

help, 21

hidden elements, forms, 272

Hidden icon, 272

Hide Content tool, 548

Hide Rulers command (View
    menu), 131

Hide/Show Auto Slices, 389

hiding
    floating objects, 346
    shopping carts, 548
    submenus, 335

hierarchies
    site hierarchies, solving,
      64-65
    Web pages, 52-53

Hierarchy, Publishing Section
    (Server Administration Web
    Access), 484

Hierarchy (Export prefer-
    ences), 101

Hierarchy check box, 65

Highlight
    palette, 141, 149, 412
    window, 479

highlighting text, 162

Highlighting Sets, 149

Hints palette, 16

History palette, 30, 86

Home Control (RealMedia
    Control), 353

Honor Publish States of
    Group/Pages check box
    (Sync Times Option box), 576

horizontal lines, 186

horizontal space, Java
    applets, 311

Horizontal Spacer, 174

horizontal strips, background
    images, 133

hotspots. *See* image maps

HP, Web applications, 506-508

HSB color, 84

Hspace
    image space, 191
    marquees, 222

HTML (Hypertext Markup
    Language)
    CSS formatting, 285
    defining, 285
    elements, Find and Replace,
      150-151
    exporting, Photoshop mock-
      ups, 386
    generating, mockups, 384
    images, exporting
      (Photoshop), 390
    integration, troubleshoot-
      ing, 413
    Java, 304, 311
    Lasso Studio, 432

options (exporting slices), 391
pages, 69, 203, 410
snippets, 291
source code, translating, 88
tables, 388, 396, 401
tags. *See* tags

HTML Page option (New Page), 123

HTML Styles, 17

HTML Tables command (Slices menu), 392

HTML Text option (Slice Options dialog box), 398

HTTP (Hypertext Transfer Protocol)
streaming movies, 363
Web sites, importing, 43

Hyperlink, pending link, 55

hyperlinks, 64-66

Hypertext Markup Language. *See* HTML

Hypertext Transfer Protocol. *See* HTTP

I

I-mode. *See* CHTML (Compact Hypertext Markup Language)

icons
Address, 211
Anchor, 208
anchor icon, 52
Back, 190
bookmark, 212
box-within-a-box, 187
Bring to Back, 85
Bring to Front, 85
broken image source, 565
Button, 260-261
Checkbox, 268
class style, 288

Comment, 220
Container (Object palette), 513
Content Source, 528, 543
Content Source Editor, 500
CSS, 287, 290
Design Annotation, 57
Design Group, 59
Design Section, 53
Display Warnings, 310
Dynamic Content, 521
Dynamic Content toolbar, 499
Export, 363
eye icon, 363
Fieldset, 275-276
File Browser, 271
Filmstrip, 78
Floating Box, 317, 320, 342
Folder, 212
Form element, 258
Form Input Image, 262
Gold Start Cookie Jar, 78
green bug, 564
hand, 192, 409
Head Action, 326
Hidden, 272
Horizontal Spacer, 174
Image, 83, 184, 261, 344
Label, 263-264
Layout Grid, 128, 131
Line, 186
Line Break, 177
Link, 202
List Box, 270
Marquee, 221
Modified Date, 223
Navigation View, 62
New Attribute, 148
New Comment, 148
New Element, 147, 285
New Generic Element, 148
New Link, 206-207
New Text, 148
Objects palette, 512-514
Open, 122

Optgroup, 475
Options, 475
Outline Editor toolbar, 147
padlock, 487
Page, 27, 76, 80, 132
Page Properties, 127
Password Field, 264
Pop-up, 270
QuickTime, 363
Radio Button, 267
Ruler, 79, 131
Script, 153
Scrolling Script, 77
Stair Step, 78
SVG, 351
Table, 87, 240, 251, 258
Text Area, 265
Text Field, 264
Timeline Editor, 344
Trash, 574
URL, 211
URL Popup, 210

id card attribute (WML deck), 472

ID styles, CSS implementation, 289-290

identifiers, records (database), 449

IIS (Internet Information Server)
ASP (Active Server Pages), 497, 507
turning off, 433

Illustrator
image maps, 403-404
mockups, 385, 396-404
palette options, 403
Smart Objects, 371
SVG files, 377-379, 411-412
tracing images, 409-410

Image Format (Macromedia Flash SWF File Format dialog box), 379

Image icon, 83, 184, 261, 344

Image Inspector, 81, 184-189, 197

image links, 207

image maps
Actions, 197
creating, 194, 197
hotspots, 403-404
Illustrator, 403-404
links, 195
positioning, 195
sizing, 195
tab order, 195-197
troubleshooting, 199

Image Object (Lasso Data Access), 444

Image Size tab, 375, 400

Image Window (RealMedia Control), 352

ImageReady
drawing tools, 393
files, opening, 393
JavaScript, 396
mockups, 385
Optimize panel, 393
rollover images, 393-396
Rollovers panel, 393
Slice Select tools, 393
Slice tools, 393

images. *See also* animations;
slices; SVG (Scalable Vector
Graphics)
accessing (Dynamic Content
module), 534
adding, 184
aligning, 187, 190
alternative text, 188
arranging, 190-191
Auto slices, 388-389
background images, 130,
133-136, 246, 392
borders, 187
color, dithering, 185
compression, 184

converting (SWF files), 378
copying, 189
creating, 370
distributing, 191
exporting, 385-386
gifs, 185
grouping, 190
horizontal lines, 186
Input Image, forms, 262
integration, troubleshooting, 414
jpegs, 184
lassoing, 184
linking, 190
links, 82
Low Source images (Image
preferences), 95
managing. *See also* Smart
Objects
modifying, 189
mousedown, 82
mouseovers, 82
navigation labels, 188
placeholders, 372
positioning, 187, 190
raster images, Photoshop,
385
rollovers, 197-198, 393-396
saving, 371
sizing, 185-187, 190
stacking order, 190
storing, 185
Tracing Images, 192-194,
384-386
Transform palette, 189
User Slices, 389
viewing (Outline Editor),
147
WBMP (Wireless Bitmap),
473
Web images, 184-185
WML development, 473

Images box, 147

Images folder, 185

Images preferences, 95

Images tab, 356

Images window, 95

implementing
CSS (Cascading Style
Sheets), 283-287
classes, 288-289
components, 291-294
ID styles, 289-290
snippets, 290-291
Custom Merchant
Add to Cart button, 542
checkout screen, 549-551
data sources, 541-542
receipt page, 555
review page, 554-555
shipping methods, 552
shipto screen, 551
shopping cart, 545-549

**Import from Folder option
(Site Wizard), 41**

**Import from GoLive Site (Site
Wizard), 486**

**Import From Server option
(Site Wizard), 42**

Import Now button, 573

importing
Tracing Images, 192
Web sites, 40-43
Workgroup Sites, 486

**Importing a Site option (Site
Wizard), 38**

In & Out Links
command (Window menu),
565
palette, 213, 565
window, 89

In & Out palette, 567

**iname attribute (Select list),
475**

**Include Comments, HTML
option (exporting slices), 391**

include files, LDML tags, 461

Include Object (Lasso Data Access), 444

Include Zero Margins in Body Tag, HTML option (exporting slices), 391

incoming spotlights, Web pages, 68

Increase List Level (level adjustment list), 179

Incremental downloads, 576

Incremental Uploads command (Site window), 575

Indent, HTML option (exporting slices), 391

indenting paragraphs, 174

index pages, 477-478

index.chtml page, XHTML-Basic development, 477

index.html page, XHTML-Basic development, 477

indicators, , 174

Info heading (CSS Definitions panel), 284

Info Panel (RealMedia Control), 353

Info Volume (RealMedia Control), 353

information
  live information, shopping cart, 545
  obtaining, Inspector, 28

inheritance, CSS, 283

Inline Object (Lasso Data Access), 444

inlines
  genres, 451
  nesting, 453
  searches, member searches, 460
  selections, 294

Input Image, forms, 262

Insert Index command (Special menu), 422

inserting
  columns, tables, 241
  comments, 220
  components, 292
  Head Actions, 326
  Java applets, 311-312
  rows (tables), 241
  Smart Objects, 371
    bitmaps, 372-377
    Export settings, 380
    opening original files, 380
    SVG (Scalar Vector Graphics) files, 377-379
  snippets, 291

Inspector, 27, 82
  Annotation Inspector, 57
  Button Inspector, 261
  Card Inspector, 471
  command (Window menu), 194, 307, 330
  Content Source Inspector, 501, 509
  File Inspector, 59
  Form Inspector, 258-260
  Form Label Inspector, 264
  Grid Inspector, 130
  Group Inspector, 59
  Head Tag Inspector, 151
  Image Inspector, 81
  Java applets, 311
  Lasso Tag Inspector, 452
  Layout Grid Inspector, 129-130
  Link Inspector, 56, 80
  Objects palette, 83
  Page Inspector, 80, 127, 132-133, 172
  QuickTime, 353
  Script Inspector, 153
  Section Inspector, 54
  tabs, 307

installers, server preparations (building dynamic content), 515

installing
  extensions, 420, 422
  Lasso Suite, 432, 439
    FileMaker Pro, 436-437
    Mac OS X, 435-436
    Windows, 433-435
  MySQL installations, building databases (dynamic content), 516
  WDE (Web Data Engine), 432

instances, components, 294

integration
  applications, 384-386
  Illustrator
    slicing mockups, 396-404
    tracing images, 409-410
  mockups, 385-386
  Photoshop
    slicing mockups, 386-408
    tracing images, 409-410
  programs, 17
  Smart Objects, 17
  SVG (Scalable Vector Graphics), 410-413
  troubleshooting, 413-415
  variables, 17

Integration Templates, 421

interfaces
  customizing, 424
  Inspector, 80-82
  Page window, 76-80
  palettes, 82-89
  toolbar, 76

Internal folder, 287

internal style sheets, 281, 287-288

Internet
  access, 572-574
  Xchange, 421

Internet Control Panel, 105

Internet Information Server (IIS), 507

Internet Server Providers (ISP), 572

Inventory button, 260

Invisible Elements preferences, 96

invisible images, indenting paragraphs, 174

invisible tables, creating, 244

IP addresses, dynamic content security, 536

IsIndex tag (Head tab), 151

ISP (Internet Service Provider), 572

ISS directory, Windows (Lasso Suite installations), 433

Italic style (text), 169

ivalue attribute (Select list), 475

J

Jakarata Web site, 515

Japanese Emoji characters, 479

Java, 304, 311-312, 507

Java Runtime Engine (JRE), 304

Java Script option (New Page), 123

Java Server Pages (JSP), 498, 506-508

Java Virtual Machine (JVM), 507

JavaScript, 17, 304-310
  actions
    applying, 321-325
    defining, 323
    executing, 326-328
    options, floating boxes, 324
    parameters, 325
    user events, 323
  Actions palette, reading, 325
  applications, 328-333
  browsers, 307
  code errors, 310
  coding, 304
  creating, 306-309
  DOM (Document Object Model), 306
  dot-syntax notation, 305
  editor, 304
  embedding, 98
  event handlers, 305-307
  floating boxes, 316, 321-325
  function names, 307
  Head Action, 326
  ImageReady, 396
  methods, 304
  naming, 307
  objects, 304, 321
  preferences, 107
  properties, 304
  shells, 14
  storing, 307
  troubleshooting, 312

JavaScript Actions, 421

JavaScript Editor, 77, 306

JavaServer Pages (JSP), 498

JPEG Quality (Macromedia Flash SWF File Format dialog box), 379

jpegs, 184-185, 408

JRE (Java Runtime Engine), 304

JSP (Java Server Pages), 498, 506-508

<jsxitem> tag, 428

<jsxmenu> tag, 425, 428

<jsxmenubar> tag, 425

<jsxmenuitem> tag, 425

JVM (Java Virtual Machine), 507

K

Key Blur user event, 330

Key Down user event (links), 323

Key Press user event (links), 323

Key text box, 275

Key Up user event (links), 323

Keyboard (Font Structures), 171

keyboard shortcuts
  Alt+Ctrl+N, 25, 39-44
  Alt+Ctrl+Y, 60
  Cmd+K, 92
  Cmd+N, 76
  Cmd+Y, 93
  Cmd-A, 162, 189
  Cmd-B, 169
  Cmd-C, 131, 162, 189
  Cmd-comma, 205
  Cmd-E, 204
  Cmd-F, 150, 165
  Cmd-I, 169
  Cmd-K, 92, 135, 143, 164
  Cmd-L, 206-207
  Cmd-N, 76, 122, 126
  Cmd-Option-U, 164
  Cmd-Q, 109
  Cmd-R, 131
  Cmd-S, 134-136
  Cmd-V, 131, 162, 189
  Cmd-X, 162, 189
  Cmd-Y, 93, 144
  Ctrl+A, 162, 189
  Ctrl+Alt+U, 164
  Ctrl+B, 169
  Ctrl+C, 131, 162, 189
  Ctrl+F, 150, 165
  Ctrl+I, 169

Ctrl+K, 135, 143, 164
Ctrl+L, 206-207
Ctrl+N, 122, 126
Ctrl+R, 131
Ctrl+S, 134-136
Ctrl+V, 131, 162, 189
Ctrl+X, 162, 189
Ctrl+Y, 144
Ctrl-Q, 109
Opt-Cmd-N, 39-44
Opt-Cmd-Y, 60
Option-Cmd-N, 25
setting, 115
Shift+Alt+Ctrl, 175
Shift+Alt+Ctrl+0, 173
Shift+Alt+Ctrl+K, 115
Shift+Ctrl+A, 170
Shift+Ctrl+C, 176
Shift+Ctrl+F, 167
Shift+Ctrl+L, 176
Shift+Ctrl+R, 176
Shift+Ctrl+S, 136
Shift+Ctrl+T, 170
Shift+Ctrl+U, 170
Shift+Shift+P, 169
Shift-Opt—, 170
Shift-Cmd-+, 170
Shift-Cmd-A, 170
Shift-Cmd-C, 176
Shift-Cmd-E, 176
Shift-Cmd-F, 167
Shift-Cmd-L, 176
Shift-Cmd-S, 136
Shift-Cmd-T, 170
Shift-Cmd-U, 170
Shift-Option-0, 173
Shift-Option-Cmd-K, 115
Shift-Option-Command, 175
Shift-Option-P, 169
troubleshooting, 116

Keyboard Shortcuts command (Edit menu), 115

keyframes, 343-345

keys, access keys, 275-276

keyword searches, 151-152

Keywords tag (Head tab), 152

L

Label
check box, 261, 543
icon, 263-264

label property (Do event), 476

Label/Value setting, 270

labels
buttons, 261
form validation, 331
forms, 262-264
navigation labels, images, 188
text boxes, 263

languages
dynamic content, creating, 522
Java, 304
JavaScript, 304

Lasso Configuration Wizard, 445

Lasso Data Access, 443-444, 452

Lasso Database Selector, 447, 451-453

Lasso Dynamic Markup Language (LDML), 432, 461

Lasso Form, objects, 443-446

Lasso Form Builder command (Lasso Studio menu), 456

Lasso Programming
objects, 445
palette, 454
tab, 443, 451

Lasso Security, 437

Lasso Site Builder command (Lasso Studio menu), 447

Lasso Studio
actions, 455
builders, 432

Create Add Page screen, 448
Create Display Page screen, 448
databases, 447-449
format files, 432, 447
genres, creating, 456
HTML, 432
Lasso Web Data Engine, 432
menu commands
Lasso Database Selector, 451-453
Lasso Form Builder, 456
Lasso Site Builder, 447
records, deleting, 455
snap files, 432
troubleshooting, 462-463
users, idenitfying, 451
variables, 454

Lasso Suite
configuring, 437-439
databases, 439-462
functionality, 439
genres, 451-455
installing, 432, 439
FileMakerPro, 436-437
Mac OS X, 435-436
Windows, 433-435
member searches, 456-460
membership registration screens, 446-451
navigation, 461
security, 462

Lasso Tag Inspector, 452

layer references, exported images, 392

layers. *See also* floating boxes
CSS (Cascading Style Sheets), 316, 400
rollover images, 394-395

Layout command (Default Mode menu), 94

Layout Editor, 220, 233
   head tags, 151
   viewing code, 12

Layout Grid, 15, 109, 128-131

layout grids, Java applets, 311

Layout mode, 26, 76, 442

Layout Preview, 79, 225, 424

Layout Rulers, 131

Layout Setup (Layouts menu), 442

Layout tab, 354, 411

Layout view, 76-79, 153

layouts
   creating (frames), 231
   forms, 257
   site design, 51

Layouts menu commands, Layout Setup, 442

LDML (Lasso Dynamic Markup Language), 432, 461

Left property (floating boxes), 318

level adjustment lists, 179

libraries, snippet storage, 290

Library tab, 84, 291, 562, 566

Likes records, genres, 453-454

limitations, Custom Merchant, 540

line breaks, 78, 142, 176-178

Line Endings, HTML option (exporting slices), 391

Line icon, 186

Line Inspector, 186

Line Number, 141-142

lines
   horizontal lines, 186
   link lines, Web pages, 56

Link
   color swatch, 132, 172
   field, 203-205
   icons, 202
   menu commands, Open Window, 328
   parameter (pop-up windows), 328
   swatch, 188
   tab, 82, 194, 207
   tag (Head tab), 152

Link Action check box, 529

link color
   setting, 172
   Web pages, 132

Link Field (Link Inspector), 81

Link Inspector, 56, 80

link lines, Web pages, 56

Link Object (Lasso Data Access), 444

Link Type (Site preferences), 102

Link, Target2Frames command (Actions menu), 234

linked fonts, SVG files, 377

linking
   anchors, 209
   frames, 231
   images, 190
   Web pages (external style sheets), 285

links
   anchors, 208-209
   broken links, files (Site window), 564-565
   components, 294
   Console (RealMedia), 353
   creating, 80
   external links, 566
   external style sheets, 288
   FileMaker Remote, 437
   floating boxes, 322
   frames, 230, 234-235
   hotspots, 404
   image links, 207
   image maps, 194-195
   images, 82
   Likes records, 454
   local links, hotspots (image maps), 404
   managing, 81, 210-213
   modifying, 212
   navigational links, 202-207
   New User, 482
   organizing, 212
   pending links, 55-56, 61-64
   Photoshop Smart Objects, 390
   pop-up windows, 328
   submenus, 336
   text links, 206-207
   to child and back, 62
   troubleshooting, 89, 213
   URL pop-up menus, 209
   user events, 323
   viewing, 89, 213
   virtual links, 17
   Web pages, site design, 52

Links check box, 65

links view, 52, 66

Links View command (Pane menu), 45

List, button or command, 180

List Box, 269-270

List Object (Lasso Programming), 445

listing objects (JavaScript), 307, 309

lists
   creating, 180
   Events, 234
   Floating boxes, 344
   level adjustment, 179

numbered lists, 178
Recent Files list, 122
Select lists, form elements (WML), 475
text, 178-180
unnumbered, 179

live information, shopping cart, 545

Live Pages group, 58

LiveMotion
animations, 405
AutoLayout, 386, 406-407
mockups, 386
navigation bar, 405
slicing, 405-408
Smart Objects, 371
SWF files, 405

loading extensions, 421

Loc parameter (pop-up windows), 329

local folders, imported Web sites, 41-42

local links, hotspots, 404

Local Mode, Source Code, 32, 89, 144

Lock Page command (Stationery menu), 297

Lock Page or Stationery, Lock Page command (Template menu), 295

Lock tab, 580

Locked column (Error tab), 46

locking
files (WebDAV), 579
floating boxes, 320
Web pages, 78, 295

Log File Section, Server Administration Web Access, 485

logic, dynamic content (building), 514

Loop
QuickTime, 353
SWF tab, 350

looping animations, 345

Looping option (Macromedia Flash SWF File Format dialog box), 379

lossless compression, PNG (Portable Networks Graphic) bitmaps, 375

lossy compression, SWFs, 379

Low Source images (Images preferences), 95

Lower Alpha (numbered list), 178

Lower Roman (numbered list), 178

M

Mac OS X
databases, building (dynamic content), 516
Lasso Suite installation, 435-436

Macromedia Flash dialog box, 378

Macromedia Flash SWF File Format dialog box, 378

mailto:, email addresses, 95

Maintenance Section, Server Administration Web Access, 485

Make Current button, 487

Make New Links Absolute check box, 95

Manage Workspaces dialog box, 114

managing
annotations, site design, 57-58
bitmaps (Smart Objects), 373

code (Source Code Editor), 140
content sources (Content Source Editor), 500
design groups (site design), 59
dictionaries, 104
expressions, 104
filename constraints, 60-61
files (Files tab), 46
floating boxes, 320
frames (Frame Inspector), 231
images. *See* Smart Objects
links, 81, 210-213
multiple floating objects, 346-348
objects, 29, 32
palettes, 28
plug-ins, 104
Site Document, 26
site files (Site preferences), 99
sites, 65-69, 482. *See also* Site window
source code, 31, 143
tables, 31, 240-249
tags, 146, 150
user accounts (Workgroup Sites), 486
Web pages, 27, 45-47
Web sites, 18-19
workspaces, 114

manual help, 21

maps. *See* image maps

margins, Web pages, 127

Marker (QuickTime Editor), 355

markers, floating boxes, 319

Markup menu commands, Convert to XHTML, 477

Markup option, 78

Markup Tree, 78, 88, 145, 323

Marquee Inspector, 221-222

marquees, 221-222, 226

Master tab, 51

Math Object (Lasso Programming), 445

Maximum History States, History palette, 86

maxlength property (text input field), 474

.mdb, Data Source database, 508

media, viewing (plug-ins), 104

media files
Scratch pane, 70
stripping, 484

member searches, 456-460

membership registration screens, databases, 446-451

memory, extensions (running), 422

menu, Quality menu (SWF tab), 350

menu items, 425-426

Menu Options (Link Inspector), 81

Menu parameter (pop-up windows), 329

menus. *See also* submenus
contextual menus, 15
items, creating, 423-429
navigational links, 206
pop-up menus
Align, 187
forms, 269-270
Page window, 78
Scale menu (SWF tab), 351
Type menu, formatting text, 166
URL pop-up menus, 209
Window Size Popup, 79

menuSignal event, 425

merging cells (tables), 242-244

Message option (Slice Options dialog box), 398

Meta tag (Head tab), 152

Method (Macromedia Flash SWF File Format dialog box), 379

method property (Go tag event), 476

methods, JavaScript, 304

microbrowsers, Web pages (viewing), 468

Microsoft, ASP (Active Server Pages), 498, 507

middleware software, Lasso Studio, 432

Misc Input object (Lasso Form), 444

Misc Object (Lasso Programming), 445

mockups
building (integration), 384-386
HTML generation, 384
Illustrator, 385, 396-404
ImageReady, 385
LiveMotion, 386
Photoshop mockups, 385
HTML exports, 386
slicing, 386-408
tracking images, 386
tracing images, 384

modes
Layout mode, 26, 76
Line Break Mode, 78
Local Mode, 89, 144
passive modes, ISPs, 572
Select mode, tables (managing), 31
Styles mode, tables (managing), 31
video tracks (QuickTime), 362

Modified Date icon, 223

Modified-item Uploads command (Site window), 575

modifying
dynamic content, 526
elements, Outline Editor, 147
external style sheets, 287
files (Site Window), 489
images, 189
links, 212
orientations, views, 69
pages, Site Reports, 71
QuickTime movies, 354-359, 362-363
servers, 484
stationeries, 294-296
SVG code, 411
tabbing chains, 274
templates, 294-296
text, 161

modules
command (Preferences menu), 509
Dynamic Content module, 499-501, 509
Extend Script SDK module, 420
folder, 421
naming, 424
preference, 97

More tab, 82, 191, 194, 222, 262, 350-351, 411

Mount a Site (Site Wizard), 486

Mount Workgroup Site command (File menu), 122

Mouse Click user event (links), 323

Mouse Down user event (links), 323

Mouse Enter user event (links), 323

Mouse Exit user event (links), 323

Mouse Follow command (Multimedia menu), 324

Mouse Up user event (links), 323

mousedown, images, 82

mouseDown effects, creating, 197

mouseOver effects, creating, 197

mouseovers, images, 82

Move By command (Multimedia menu), 324

Move Image tool, 192

Move To command (Multimedia menu), 325

Move to Scratch command (Diagram menu), 64

movie clips, troubleshooting, 364

movies, streaming movies
    sprites, 363
    SWF (Shockwave Flash), 363
    troubleshooting, 365

moving
    annotations, site design, 57
    files (Site window), 563
    keyframes, 345
    pending links, 64
    slices (Illustrator), 397
    Web pages, site design, 56

Multimedia, Play Scene command (Action pop-up menu), 346

Multimedia menu commands
    Drag Floating Box, 324
    Mouse Follow, 324
    Move By, 324
    Move To, 325
    ShowHide, 325
    Wipe Transition, 325-327

multiple floating objects, 346-348

multiple grids, 131

multiple inlines, genres, 451

multiple properties (Select list), 475

Multiple Selection setting, 270

multiple servers, Web Companion, 436

Mute Control (RealMedia Control), 352

Mute Volume (RealMedia Control), 352

MySQL
    downloading, 498
    installations, databases, building (dynamic content), 516

MySQL Database Query command (Type menu), 528

N

Name heading (CSS Definitions panel), 284

Name option (Slice Options dialog box), 398

name property
    Do event, 476
    floating boxes, 318
    Select list, 475
    text input field, 474

Name setting, 259, 268-271

names. *See also* filenames
    function names (JavaScript), 307
    menu items, extracting, 426

naming. *See also* renaming
    anchors, 208-209
    buttons, 261
    content sources, 528-529
    forms (JavaScript), 330
    frames, 233

JavaScript, 307
menu items, 425
modules, 424
site design, 53
slices, 390

navigating
    bars, LiveMotion, 405
    databases, 461
    forms, 273-276
    grids, 129
    HTML tables (Illustrator), 401
    labels, images, 188
    Web sites (In & Out palette), 565
    WML decks, 473

Navigation Block View, content source, 501

Navigation tab, 71

Navigation tab menu commands, 68

Navigation View, 52, 58, 61, 65
    command (Pane menu), 45
    icon, 62
    page groupings, spotlighting, 67
    site views, 66

navigational links, 202-207

nested elements, SVG, 411

nesting
    extensions, 424
    inlines, 453
    menu items, 424
    tables, 131, 251

Network preferences, Network Status, 105

Network Status
    preference, 105
    window, 577

New Addresses folder, 211

New Attribute icon, 148

New button, 541

New command (File menu), 134, 292

New Comment icon, 148

New Database command (File menu), 440

New Design Diagram command (Diagram menu), 50

New Document
check box, 135
General preference, 94

New Element icon, 147, 285

New Floating Box icon, 320

New Generic Element icon, 148

New Item button, 323

New Link, command or icon, 206-207

New Next Page button, 62

New Page
command, 54, 62, 76, 122, 126
options, 122-123

New Page From Stationery option (New Page), 123

New Page From Template option (New Page), 123

New Parent Page button, 62

New Previous Page button, 62

New Scripts button, 307

New Site command (File menu), 25, 39-44, 485

New Special, Basic Page command (File menu), 154

New Special, Page from Stationery command (File menu), 124, 296, 478

New Special, Page from Template command (File menu), 124, 296

New Special, WML Deck command (File menu), 470

New Special, XHTML Page command (File menu), 154

New Special command (File menu), 14, 122, 126, 284, 477

New, Child Page command (Diagram menu), 62

New, Next Page command (Diagram menu), 62

New, Parent Page command (Diagram menu), 62

New, Previous Page command (Diagram menu), 62

New Text icon, 148

New URLs folder, 211

new User link, 482

newcontext card attribute (WML deck), 472

Next link, pending link, 55

next sibling, Web page hierarchy, 53

Nickname setting (Available Servers dialog box), 574

NoBreak, 178

non-breaking spaces, indenting paragraphs, 174

None option (hotspots), 404

None state, slices (rollover images), 394

Number() function, 309

numbered lists, 178

O

Object menu commands
Slice, Make, 397
Slice, Slice Options, 397-399

Object palette, head tags, 151

Object tab, 53

objects. *See also* images; Smart Objects

accessing (JavaScript), 309
aligning, 33, 85
Condition object, 454
Cookie, 451
custom library objects, 280
custom library snippets, 280
custom objects, storing, 115
distributing, 86
floating objects, 342-346, 349
grouping, 32, 85
JavaScript, 304, 321
Lasso Data Access, 444
Lasso Form, 443-444
Lasso Programming, 445
Line Break object, 177
listing (JavaScript), 307-309
managing, 29, 32
multiple floating objects, 346-348
positioning, 32, 85
repeating objects, frames, 230
selecting (markup trees), 323
sizing, 85
stacking objects, 85
stationeries, 294
storing, 305
templates, 294
transforming, 84
vector objects, 385
Web pages, 82

Objects palette, 29, 59, 82
Diagram pane, 53
Drag and Drop (code), 142
forms, creating, 256
icons, 512-514
Inspector, 83
Layout Grid, 128
menu commands, Configure, 469
panes, 83-84
wireless devices, 469

Objects panel, 371

Objects tab, 307

Objects toolbar, 187, 190

obtaining information (Inspector), 28

"On success" check box, 545

OnCall option (Head Action), 327

onenterbackward
  card attribute (WML deck), 472
  property (Onevent), 476

onenterforward
  card attribute (WML deck), 472
  property (Onevent), 476

Onevent, WML cards, 475

online forms. *See* forms

online help, 21

OnLoad option (Head Action), 327

OnParse option (Head Action), 327

onpick property (Onevent), 476

Ontimer
  card attribute (WML deck), 472
  property (Onevent), 476

OnUnload option (Head Action), 327

opacity Tracing Images, 192, 409

Open an Existing File (At Launch General preference), 93

Open command (File menu), 26, 76

Open icon, 122

Open Recent Files command (File menu), 122

Open Window command (Link menu), 328

opening
  components, 293
  files (ImageReady), 393
  original files (Smart Objects), 380
  stationery, 296
  SVG (Scalable Vector Graphics) files, 411-412
  templates, 296
  Web pages, 122, 205

Optgroup icon, 475

Optimization dialog box, 380

Optimize
  command (Window menu), 393
  panel (ImageReady), 393
  tab, 373, 390

Optimize button, 129

optimizing, 562
  bitmaps, 373-375
  grids, 129
  LiveMotion slicing, 407-408
  slices, 390, 399

optional property (Do event), 476

options
  action options, floating boxes, 324-325
  alignment options, Align palette, 85-86
  Divide Slice, 389
  Export Settings palette, 407
  form elements (WML), 475
  formatting options, CSS, 285
  groups, creating, 475
  Head Actions, 327
  HTML, 391-392
  image slices, 388
  integration, troubleshooting, 415
  New Page, 122-123
  palettes (Illustrator), 403

Promote to User Slice, 389
  properties, 475
  Slice Options, 389, 398

Options icon, 475

order, stacking order
  objects, 85
  slices, 389

ordered card attribute (WML deck), 472

ordering events, 327

Organize Favorites command (Favorites menu), 212

organizing
  files, 100
  images, 134
  links, 212
  palettes, 15

orientations
  pending links, moving, 64
  site management, 68
  views, modifying, 69

original files, opening (Smart Objects), 380

Original tab (Save for Web dialog box), 373

Out state, slices (rollover images), 393

outgoing spotlights, Web pages, 68

Outline command (Default Mode menu), 94

Outline Editor, 145, 220
  elements, 147
  images (viewing), 147
  tab, 411
  tags, managing, 146
  toolbar, 147, 149
  viewing code, 12

Outline view, 79

Over state, slices (rollover images), 393-394

overlapping multiple floating objects, 347-348

P

<p> tag, 173

padlock icon, 487

page elements, floating boxes, 320

Page icon, 27, 76, 80, 132

Page Inspector, 80, 127, 132-133, 172

Page Margins, Web pages, 127

Page Properties, 76, 80, 127

Page window, 26, 153
  buttons, 140
  Frame Preview, 80
  Frame view, 79
  Layout mode, 76
  Layout Preview, 79
  Layout view, 76-79
  Markup Tree, 145
  Outline view, 79
  pop-up menus, 78
  Source Code view, 79
  splitting, 93
  status bar, 78
  toggles, 78
  types, 94

PageGenerator, 502-503

pages. *See also* Web pages
  child pages, 54
  dynamic pages, 526
    detail pages, creating, 532-535
    results list pages, creating, 527-532
    search pages, creating, 527
  empty child pages, pending links, 62
  empty next sibling pages, pending links, 62
  empty parent pages, pending links, 62
  empty previous sibling pages, pending links, 62
  group child pages, pending links, 62
  HTML pages, 69, 203, 410
  index pages, 477-478
  Post-Lasso page, Lasso Form Builder, 457
  Pre-Lasso page, Lasso Form Builder, 457
  receipt page, Custom Merchant, 555
  review page, Custom Merchant, 554-555
  scratch pages, 61
  section pages (site design), 53

palettes. *See also* Inspector
  accessing, 28, 113
  Actions palette, 234, 322-325
  Align palette, 33, 85-86, 191
  arranging, 113
  CHTML (Compact Hypertext Markup Language), 469-470
  Color palette, 29, 84, 130-132, 142, 171
  combining, 113
  CSS Definitions, 285
  CSS palette, 289
  Custom Color palette, 84
  custom palettes, 114-115
  desktops, planning, 113
  docking, 113
  Dynamic Bindings palette, 499, 509-510, 526-529, 549
  Export Settings palette, 407-408
  Floating Boxes palette, 320, 335
  Highlight palette, 141, 149, 412
  Hint palette, 16
  History palette, 30, 86
  In & Out Links palette, 213, 565
  In & Out Links window, 89
  In & Out palette, 567
  Inspector, 27
  Lasso Programming, 454
  managing, 28
  Markup Tree, 78, 88
  Objects palette, 29, 59, 82, 261-262
    Diagram pane, 53
    Drag and Drop (code), 142
    head tags, 151
    icons, 512, 514
    Inspector, 83
    Layout Grid, 128
    panes, 83-84
    wireless devices, 469
  options (Illustrator), 403
  organizing, 15
  Rollovers, 394
  Source Code palette, 31-32, 144
  Source Code window, 88-89
  Table, 241
  Table palette, 30-31, 87, 249-251
  Template Regions palette, 295
  Tracing Image palette, 192, 409
  Transform palette, 32, 84, 186, 189
  troubleshooting, 34, 90
  View palette, 281, 564
  windows, 82
  WML palette, 469-470
  Workflow, 489
  XHTML-Basic (Extensible Hypertext Markup Language), 469-470

Palindrome, 345, 353

Pane menu commands, 45

panels
Actions panel, 336
Clean Up Site panel, 100
Control Panel (RealMedia Control), 352
CSS Definitions panel, 284
Hints panel, 16
Info Panel (RealMedia Control), 353
Internet Control Panel, 105
Network Status, 105
Objects panel, 371
Optimize (ImageReady), 393
Preferences panel, 92
Rollovers (ImageReady), 393
Settings panel, 374, 390
Sharing System Preferences panel, 435
Template Regions panel, 295
Tools panel (Photoshop), 393

panes
Diagram pane, 53
Dynamic Content Preference pane, 509
Dynamic Content Site Settings pane, 509-510
FTP tab, 574
Objects palette, 83-84
Panorama pane, 69
peripheral panes, site views, 67
Reference pane, 70
Scratch pane, 64, 69
site views, 69-70
WebDAV, 579

Panorama pane, 69

par, classes (applying), 289

Paragraph Format, Paragraph command (Type menu), 173

Paragraph Format command (Type menu), 175

paragraphs, 172-174, 294

parameters
actions, 325
events, 327
forms (JavaScript), 331
Java applets, 311
pop-up windows, 328

Params tab, 311

_parent, target names (frames), 233

parent, Web page hierarchy, 53

Parent link, pending link, 55

parent pages, empty parent pages (pending links), 62

passive modes, ISPs, 572

Password Fields, 263-266

Password setting (Available Servers dialog box), 574

passwords
Lasso Security, 437
Site Window, 489
Workgroup sites, 486
Xchange, 421

Paste command (Edit menu), 162, 189

Pastel Settings (Design Colors preference), 102

pasting text, 162

pathnames, links (troubleshooting), 213

paths, floating objects, 344

pending links, 55-56, 61-62

Pending pane, 67-69

pending spotlights, Web pages, 68

peripheral panes, site views, 67-69

PERL, PHP, 508

Perl Script option (New Page), 123

Personal Web Manager, Lasso Suite installations, 434

Photoshop
images, slicing, 387-390
mockups, 385
  HTML exports, 386
  slicing, 386-408
  tracing images, 386
slices, 390-393
Smart Objects, 371
Tools panel, 393
tracing images, 409-410

Photoshop Smart Object, 390

PHP (PHP: Hypertext Processor), 498, 515

pick whip, 202

pixels
cell padding/cell spacing, 245
grids, 129

placeholder text
checkout screen, 551
databases, 510
dynamic detail pages, 533
dynamic results list page, 529
shipping methods, 552
shopping cart, 548

placeholders, images, 372

placing
anchors, 208
grids, 128

Plain Structure (Font Structures), 171

Plain Text style (text), 169

planning
CHTML development, 469
customizations, 112-113
prototype sites, 517-519
site planning, 477-478
Web sites, 25
WML development, 469
XHTML-Basic development, 469

platforms, text (troubleshooting), 180

Play button (RealMedia Control), 352

Play Every Frame (QuickTime), 353

Play Only button (RealMedia Control), 352

Plug 'n Play Web site, 501

plug-ins, 420
  extensions, installing/ downloading, 420-422
  managing, 104
  menu items, creating, 423-429
  RealMedia, 351-353
  storing, 427
  troubleshooting, 429-430

Plug-ins tab, 437

Plugins preference, 104

plus sign (+), 307

PNG (Portable Networks Graphic), bitmaps, 374

Point and Shoot, 246, 264
  Fetch URL, 202-203, 208-209
  images, lassoing, 184
  Link Inspector, 81

Polygon Hot Spot Drawing tool, 194

Polygon option (hotspots), 404

Pop-up icon, 270

pop-up menus
  Align, 187
  Alignment (Fieldset icon), 276
  forms, 269-270
  Page window, 78
  Switch Line Break Mode popup menu, 78

pop-up windows, 328-329

port 80, installer (server preparations), 515

port 82, installer (server preparations), 515

Portable Networks Graphic (PNG), bitmaps, 374

ports, dynamic content security, 536

Position Field (RealMedia Control), 353

Position Slider (RealMedia Control), 352

positioning
  floating boxes, 317, 320
  Form tags, 259
  image maps, 195
  images, 187, 190
  objects, 32, 85
  tracing images, 409

Post-Lasso page, Lasso Form Builder, 457

Postfield variable (WML), 477

pound sign (#), 208-209, 234, 289, 473

<pre> tag, 174

precedence, CSS, 283

preconfigured servers, 502-503

Preferences
  accessing, 92
  Browsers preferences, 103
  Cache preference, 96
  CHTML (Compact Hypertext Markup Language), 469-470
  ColorSync preference, 98
  command (Edit menu), 25, 92, 135, 143, 569, 572
  dialog box, 92
  Dynamic Content, 108, 511
  Encodings preference, 98
  Find preferences, 103-104
  Fonts preference, 97

General preferences, 93-94
Images preference, 95
Invisible Elements preference, 96
JavaScript preferences, 107
menu commands, Modules, 509
Modules preference, 97
Network preference, Network Status, 105
panel, 92
QuickTime, 108-109
Script Library preference, 98
Site Filename Constraints, 59
Site preference, 99-102
Source, 105-107
Source Code Editor, 143
Spell Checker preferences, 104
troubleshooting, 109
updates, 92
URL Handling preference, 94
User Interface preference, 95
window, 92
WML (Wireless Markup Language), 469-470
XHTML-Basic (Extensible Hypertext Markup Language), 469-470

Pre-Lasso page, Lasso Form Builder, 457

Preferences Section, Server Administration Web Access, 484

Preferences, Application command (Edit menu), 437

Preferences, Spell Checker command (Edit menu), 164

preformatting paragraphs, 174

Premul black alpha (QuickTime mode), 362

Premul white alpha (QuickTime mode), 362

preparations, building dynamic content, 515-517

Prev event, 476

Preview
button, 234
command (Default Mode menu), 94
tab, 26, 76, 354, 399

Preview in Browser command (File menu), 395

previewing
dynamic content, 526
floating objects, 344
frames, 233-234
slices, browsers (Illustrator), 399
Web pages, 225

Previous link, pending link, 55

Price field, 548

Primary Site Window (Site Window), 45

Printing preference, 107

printing source code, 107

ProCart, Evocative Software, 501

processing credit card processing, 540

productivity, 15-17

programming languages, JavaScript, 304

programs, integration, 17

Promote to User Slice option, 389

properties
cards, WML decks, 471
CSS properties, 288
Do events, 476
files, accessing (WebDAV), 579
floating boxes, 318

Go tag event, 476
JavaScript, 304
Page Properties, 76, 80
Select list, 475
text input fields, 474

prototype sites, building (dynamic content), 517-519

providers, Custom Merchant, 542

proxy servers, ISPs, 572

Publish Conditions, Publishing Section (Server Administration Web Access), 483

Publish Mode, Publishing Section (Server Administration Web Access), 484

Publish Reports, Server Administration Web Access, 484

publishing
file transfer, 575-577
FTP (File Transfer Protocol), 572-575
Internet access, 572-574
troubleshooting, 580
WebDAV server, 578-580
Workgroup sites, 490, 580

Publishing Section, Server Administration Web Access, 483

Q

Quality menu (SWF tab), 350

question mark (?), 543

QuickTime, 353
icon, 363
modifying, 354-359, 362-363
objects, managing (Objects palette), 29
preference, 108-109

streaming movies, 363
tab, 84, 356-361
video tracks (mode), 362

QuickTime Editor, 354-356

QuickTime Movie option (New Page), 123

Quotation (Font Structures), 171

R

Radio Button icon, 267

radio buttons
Execute, 435
FileMaker, 433
forms, 266-269
Gender, 330

Radio Input object (Lasso Form), 444

raster images, Photoshop, 385

read only elements, forms, 273

Read-Only (Macromedia Flash SWF File Format dialog box), 379

Real Time Streaming Protocol (RTSP), streaming movie, 363

RealMedia, 351-353

Recall Design button, 58

recalls, 58-59

receipt page, Custom Merchant, 555

recording actions, 30, 86

records
databases, adding (Lasso Studio), 449
deleting (Lasso Studio), 455
Likes records, genres, 453-454

Rectangle option (hotspots), 404

Rectangle tool, 194

Reference
  peripheral pane (site view), 67
  pane, 70
  text box, 264

referenced files, Server Administration Web Access, 484

references
  external references, 566
  layer references, exported images, 392

Refresh tag (Head tab), 152

refreshing
  files (Site Window), 489
  frames, 230
  Web pages, 152

Regular Expression preferences, 104

relative pathnames, links (troubleshooting), 213

relative positioning, floating boxes, 320

relative size, fonts, 167

remote servers, imported Web sites, 40-43

Remove (Clean Up Site preferences), 101

renaming
  dynamic pages, 526-527
  files (Site window), 563

repeating objects, frames, 230

Replace Rows
  check box, 534
  table, 545

Report tab, 71

reports, Site Reports, 70-71

Reset button, 258-260

Reset User Locks, Maintenance Section (Server Administration Web Access), 485

Resize Frame check box, 233

Resize parameter (pop-up windows), 328

resizing
  columns (tables), 244
  frames, 232
  marquees, 221-222
  rows (tables), 244
  tables, 244

Resolution (Macromedia Flash SWF File Format dialog box), 379

resolutions, Web pages, 125

Response Input object (Lasso Form), 444

responses, cached responses (Web servers), 108

restrictions, CHTML or XHTML, 477

results list pages, dynamic results list pages, 527-532

review page, Custom Merchant, 554-555

Revision List (Workgroup toolbar), 487

revisions, files (Workgroup Server), 485

RGB color, 84

rollover images, 394-396

Rollover Settings (Rollover tab), 198

Rollover tab, 82, 194, 197

rollovers, 197-198

Rollovers command (Window menu), 393-394

Rollovers palette, 394

Rollovers panel (ImageReady), 393

Rollovers State Options dialog box, 394

root directory, servers (Windows), 434

Root Folder, 134

root folders, imported Web sites, 40

Row setting (List Box icon), 270

Row tab, 246-247

rows, tables, 241-244, 247

Rows setting (Pop-up icon), 270

RTSP (Real Time Streaming Protocol), streaming movie, 363

Ruler icon, 79, 131

rulers, accessing, 79

rules, filenaming rules (Filename Constraints), 99

S

Sample
  Font Structures, 171
  QuickTime Editor, 355

sample sites, building dynamic content, 515

Save
  command (File menu), 134-136, 292, 297
  dialog box, 134-136

Save As
  command (File menu), 136, 285, 427
  dialog box, 292

Save As, Save as Stationery command (Window menu), 478

Save As, Stationery command (File menu), 295

Save As, Template command (File menu), 295

Save for Web
command (File menu), 390, 399, 404
dialog box, 193, 372, 377, 390, 399-400, 409

Save Optimized As dialog box, 393

Save Optimized command (File menu), 395

Save Workspace dialog box, 114

saving
bitmaps, 377
components, 292
external style sheets, 285
Highlighting Sets, 149
images, 371
slices (Illustrator), 401
Web pages, 134-137
workspaces, 114

.sbs, Data Source database, 509

Scalable Vector Graphics. *See* SVG

Scale (QuickTime), 353

Scale menu (SWF tab), 351

scenes, 349-350

schemes, colorization schemes (code), 141

scratch pages, 52, 61

Scratch pane, 64, 69

Scratch peripheral pane (site view), 67

scratch volumes, 108

screens
checkout screen, 549-551
Create Add Page, 448
Create Display Page screen, 448
membership registration screens, databases, 446-451
shipto, 551

Script
icon, 153
tab, 307
tag (Head tab), 152

Script Input object (Lasso Form), 444

Script Inspector, 153

Script Library preference, 98

scripts
adding, 151-153
CGI scripts, Form tags, 259
extend scripts (Module preference), 97
sample sites, building dynamic content, 515
servers, starting/stopping (building dynamic content), 515

Scripts directory, Windows (Lasso Suite installations), 433

scripting languages, Java, 304

Scroll parameter (pop-up windows), 328

scrollbars, frames, 231

scrolling frames, 233

scrolling marquees, 221, 226

Scrolling Script icon, 77

SDK (Software Development Kit), 15, 21, 420

Search check box, 438

search engines, keywords, 152

Search Object (Lasso Data Access), 445

search pages, dynamic search pages (creating), 527

searches
inline searches, member searches, 460
member searches, tables, 459
Site window, 567

searching files, Site window (troubleshooting), 569-570

Secondary Site Window, 45

Section Inspector, 54

section pages (site design), 53

Section tab, 54

sections, site design, 53-54

security
dynamic content, 523, 536
Lasso Security, 437
Lasso Suite, 462

Select (Table palette), 87

Select All command (Edit menu), 162, 189

Select List object (Lasso Form), 444

Select lists, form elements (WML), 475

Select mode, tables (managing), 31

Select Popup object (Lasso Form), 444

Select Region tool, 194

Select tab, 250

Select Window button, 203

Selected Constraints
menu commands, 100
text box, 61

Selected state, slices (rollover images), 393

Selection downloads, 576

Selection Uploads command (Site window), 575

selectors, CSS, 282

_self, target names (frames), 233

Send to Back button, 389

sendreferer property (Go tag event), 476

Server Administration Web Access, 482-486, 490

Server Object, 445

Server setting (Available Servers dialog box), 574

server side code, Web applications, 506

servers
accessing (wireless devices), 468
application servers, 20, 496-497, 506
dynamic content, creating, 522
FTP servers, 573-574, 577
modifying, 484
multiple servers, Web Companion, 436
preconfigured, 502-503
preparing (building dynamic content), 515
proxy servers, ISPs, 572
remote servers, imported Web sites, 40-43
root directories, Windows (Lasso Suite installations), 434
starting/stopping (building dynamic content), 515-516
streaming servers, 363

WAP (Wireless Access Protocol), 468
Web servers, 108, 496, 536
Web Workgroup Server, site management, 19
WebDAV, 572, 578-580
Workgroup Server, 482
publishing sites, 490
Server Administration Web Access, 482-486, 490
settings, 484

Servers command (Edit menu), 573

servlets
Java servlets, 304, 507
JSP (JavaServer Pages), 498

set frames, 232

Set Margins to Zero command (Document menu), 127

sets, font sets, 166-167

setting
cookies, 332
keyboard shortcuts, 115
page properties, 80

settings
Directory setting (Available Servers dialog box), 574
Export settings, Smart Objects, 380
Form Inspector, 259-260
Nickname setting (Available Servers dialog box), 574
Password setting (Available Servers dialog box), 574
Server setting (Available Servers dialog box), 574
Username setting (Available Servers dialog box), 574
Web servers, 108
Workgroup Server, 484

Settings, Link Types command (Site menu), 56

Settings button, 377

Settings command, 60, 126, 521, 574

Settings dialog box, 390

Settings panel, 374, 390

Setup Wizard, 482

Setvar variable (WML), 477

Shared Lock, files, 579

Sharing command (File menu), 441

Sharing System Preferences panel, 435

shells, JavaScript shells, 14

Shipping fields, shipto screen, 551

shipping methods, Custom Merchant, 552

shipto screen, 551

ShockWave Flash. See SWF

shopping cart, 545-549

shortcuts. See keyboard shortcuts

Show Alternative HTML check box, 312

Show Controller (QuickTime), 353

Show Intro Screen command (At Launch menu), 25, 93

Show Link Warnings command (Edit menu), 565

Show List of Files to Sync check box (Sync Times Option box), 576

Show Options Dialog check box, 101

Show Rulers command (View menu), 131

Show Split Source command (View menu), 143

ShowHide command (Multimedia menu), 325

showing floating objects, 346

sibling pages, 62

single states, slices, rollover images, 393

Single User option (Site Wizard), 38

single user sites, converting, 486

.site, file extension, 26

Site Builder Target, 444-446

site design
anchoring, 52-53
annotations, 57-58
child pages, 54
creating, 50
design groups, 59
Design Section, 50
layout, 51
naming, 53
pending links, 55-56
recalls, 58-59
sections, 53-54
Site Design window, 51-52
submitting, 58
subsections, adding, 54-55
titles, 53
updates, 58-59
Web pages, 51, 54-56

Site Design command (Diagram menu), 53

Site Design window, 51-52

Site Document, managing, 26

Site Extras menu commands, Components, 292

Site Extras tab, 84, 292, 371, 377

Site Filename Constraints preferences, 59

Site folder, 65, 185, 292

Site Folder menu commands, Components, 292

Site menu commands
Clean Up Site, 568
FTP Server, Connect, 574
FTP Server, Server Nickname, 574
FTP Server, Sync Modification Times All, 576
FTP Server, Sync Modification Times Selection, 576
Get References Used, 211
Settings, 60, 521, 574
Settings, Link Types, 56
Site Report, 70
View, Navigation or Site, 45
WebDAV Server, Server Nickname, 579
Workgroup, Change Password, 490
Workgroup, Change User, 490
Workgroup, Convert to Workgroup, 486
Workgroup, Open Workgroup Administration, 490

Site Navigator command (Window menu), 67

Site preference, 99-102

Site Reporters, Accessibility Reporter, 16

Site Reports, 70-71

Site Settings
button, 60
Dynamic Content Tools, 511
window, 541

Site Specific Settings check box, 56, 60

Site tab, 53, 57-59, 83, 211-212, 567

Site Templates, 38, 43-45, 421

Site toolbar, 122

Site Trash, 63, 568

Site window, 26, 59, 65, 482, 486, 488-490
colors, 566
Colors tab, 566
components, 45
data, 564, 567
deleted files, 568
Diagrams tab, 566
Errors tab, 567
External tab, 566
Extras tab, 567
file transfer, 575
files, 563-565
Files tab, 562-565
Font Sets tab, 566
fonts, 566
FTP (File Transfer Protocol), 572-574
Library tab, 566
passwords, 489
searches, 567
site management, 18
Site tab, 567
Site Trash, 568
Smart Objects, 371
tabs, 45, 47, 562
troubleshooting, 569-570
users, 489
views, 564
Web pages, 45-47, 122

Site Wizard, 485
blank Web sites, creating, 38-40
Site Template (creating Web sites), 44
troubleshooting, 47
Web sites, 38, 41-42

sites. *See also* Web sites
administrators, 486
color, 102
data directories, 296
diagramming, 6-65
filenames, 59-61

files, 99-102
hierarchies, solving, 64-65
management, 65-69, 562.
See also Site window

planning, 477-478
prototype sites, building
(dynamic content),
517-519
sample sites, building
dynamic content, 515
static sites, 521-526
troubleshooting, 71
views, 66-70
Workgroup sites, publish-
ing, 490, 580

**Sites Section, Server
Administration Web Access,
482**

size, fonts, 167

**Size command (Type menu),
169**

size knobs, 95

**Size parameter (pop-up win-
dows), 328**

**size property (text input
field), 474**

sizing. *See also* resizing
bitmaps, 374
floating boxes, 317
grids, 128
horizontal lines, 186
image maps, 195
images, 185-187, 190
Java applets, 311
objects, 85
windows (Web pages), 126

**Slice, Make command (Object
menu), 397**

**Slice, Slice Options command
(Object menu), 397-399**

**Slice Options feature, 389,
397-399**

**Slice Select tool, 373, 389-390,
393, 397-399**

Slice tool, 387, 393, 397

slices
Auto slices, 388-389
background images, 392
bitmaps, 373
concatenating, 392
creating, 387-388
dividing, 389
exporting, 390-393, 400
font formatting (Illustrator),
399
hiding/showing, 389
HTML table data cells, 388
Illustrator mockups, 396-404
images (Photoshop),
387-390
integration, troubleshooting, 415
LiveMotion, 405-408
moving (Illustrator), 397
naming, 390
optimizing, 390, 399
options, 388
Photoshop, 386-408
previewing, browsers
(Illustrator), 399
saving (Illustrator), 401
selecting (Photoshop), 390
single states (rollover
images), 393
stacking order, 389
SVGs (Scalable Vector
Graphics), 412
tracing images, 409
User Slices, 389

**Slices from Guides option
(image slices), 388**

Slices menu commands, 392

**slide shows, QuickTime
movies, 356**

Slideshow tab, 357

Smart Objects, 17, 83, 370
application integration, 384
bitmaps, 372
categorizing, 371
Generic Smart Objects, 371
inserting, 371
bitmaps, 372-377
Export settings, 380
*opening original files,
380*
*SVG (Scalar Vector
Graphics) files, 377-379*
managing (Object palette),
29
Photoshop, 390
Site Window, 371
tracing images, slicing, 409
troubleshooting, 380
types, 372

Smart tab, 210, 223, 326, 371

**SmartObjects, directory or
folder, 371**

**SMIL (Synchronized
Multimedia Integration
Language), 20, 123**

Snap, grids, 129

snapshot files, 432, 445

snippets, 290-291, 298, 413

**software, middleware
software (Lasso Studio), 432**

**Software Development Kit
(SDK), 15, 21, 420**

**Solve Hierarchy command
(Diagram menu), 65**

Sort button, 87, 250

Sort Table
dialog box, 87
window, 250

sorting
data, Site window, 564
table data, 87, 250-251

sound. *See* audio

source, tracing images, 409

Source Code
color, 106-107
displaying (line breaks), 142
fonts, 106-107
HTML, translating, 88
managing, 31, 143
palette, 31-32, 144
printing, 107
SWF files, 378
view, 79, 514
viewing, 105, 143
window, 88-89

Source Code Editor, 140-143

Source command (Default Mode menu), 94

Source Editor, 12, 142, 411-412

Source heading (CSS Definitions panel), 284

Source menu commands, Colors, 141

Source preferences, 105-107, 143

Source Split view, 78, 143, 151

Source tab, 26, 140, 424

sources
Content Sources, Custom Merchant, 543
Data Sources, 508-509
creating dynamic content, 525
Custom Merchant, 540-542
encrypting, 541
Windows (Lasso Suite installations), 433

space
horizontal space, Java applets, 311
images, 190
vertical space, creating, 177
vspace, Java applets, 311

Spacer Cells option (HTML Tables), 392

spacer files, 16

span, classes (applying), 289

spanning bitmaps (Smart Objects), 373

Special, Document Statistics (GoLive menu), 224

Special, Table command (GoLive menu), 241-243

special characters, 163-164

Special menu commands
Insert Index, 422
New Link, 206-207
Start Tabulator Indexing, 274
Stop Tabulator Indexing, 274

Special tab, 580

speed, floating objects, 345

Spell Checker preferences, 104

SpellCheck, words (adding), 164

Split View. See Source Split View

Spotlight Family command (Navigation tab menu), 68

Spotlight Incoming command (Navigation tab menu), 68

Spotlight Outgoing command (Navigation tab menu), 68

spotlighting page groupings (Navigation view), 67

spring-loaded folders, 99

Sprite (QuickTime Editor), 356

sprites, streaming movies, 363

Square (unnumbered list), 179

squares, grids (sizing), 129

SSL, Custom Merchant (troubleshooting), 557

stacking order
images, 190
objects, 85
slices, 389

Staging tab, 51-52, 58

Stair Step icon, 78

stamps, date stamps or time stamps, 223

Start Tabulator Indexing command (Special menu), 274

Start/Stop Indexing button, 274

starting servers (building dynamic content), 515-516

states
rollover images, 394
single states (slices), 393

static sites, 499, 502, 521-526

static text, floating boxes, 322

stationery, 297
creating, 294
editable regions, 294-296
files, index pages, 478
inline selections, 294
modifying, 294-296
objects, 294
opening, 296
paragraphs, 294
storing, 296
styles, 280
troubleshooting, 298
updates, 294
Web pages
creating, 123-124, 296
locking, 295
saving, 135-137

Stationery directories, 296

Stationery folder, 135

Stationery menu commands, 297

status, files (Errors tab), 46

Status (Site preferences), 100

Status Bar, 78, 353

Status column (Error tab), 46

Status Field (RealMedia Control), 353

Status heading (CSS Definitions panel), 284

Status Messages (Network Status preference), 105

Status parameter (pop-up windows), 329

Stop Tabulator Indexing command (Special menu), 274

stopping servers (building dynamic content), 515-516

storing
custom objects, 115
data (Site window), 567
Data Sources, 508
diagrams, 566
extensions, 421, 427
images, 185
JavaScript, 307
objects, 305
plug-ins, 427
Slice Options (Illustrator), 397
snippets, 290-291
stationery, 296
SVGs (Scalable Vector Graphics), 413
templates, 296
variables, cookies, 332
Workgroup Sites, 485

Straight alpha (QuickTime mode), 362

streaming movies, 363-365

streaming servers, 363

Strikeout style (text), 170

String Object (Lasso Programming), 445

Strip HTML code for, Publishing Section (Server Administration Web Access), 484

stripping media files, 484

strips, background images, 133

Strong (Font Structures), 171

structure
file structure (Server Administration Web Access), 484
sites, Navigation view, 66

Structure command (Type menu), 170

Structure tab, 71

Structure view, site views, 66

Style (Table palette), 87

Style, Blink command (Type menu), 170

Style, Bold command (Type menu), 169-170

Style, Italic command (Type menu), 169

Style, Plain Text command (Type menu), 169

Style, Srikeout command (Type menu), 170

Style, Superscript command (Type menu), 170

Style, Teletype command (Type menu), 170

Style, Underline command (Type menu), 170

Style command (Type menu), 169

style definitions, 281-283
copying, 287
floating boxes, 289

Style option (image slices), 388

style sheets
custom classes, 288
external style sheets, 281, 284-288
internal style sheets, 281, 287

Style tab, 249-250

styles, 280. *See also* CSS (Cascading Style Sheets)
adding (Style tab), 250
clearing (tables), 249
components, 280
custom library objects, 280
custom library snippets, 280
fonts, 169-170
HTML Styles, 17
ID styles, CSS implementation, 289-290
Stationery, 280, 294-297
Table palette, 249-250
templates, 280, 294-297
troubleshooting, 298

Styles mode, tables (managing), 31

subject, annotations (site design), 57

submenus
creating (DHTML), 334-336
DHTML, 334
hiding, 335
links, 336
testing, 336
visibility, 335
z-index, 335

Submit button, 258-260, 543, 547, 550, 554

Submit Design button, 58

Submit Order Form button, 554

Subscript style (text), 170

subsections, site design (adding), 54-55

Sun, JSP (Java Server Pages), 507

Sun Microsystems, JSP (JavaServer Pages), 498

Superscript style (text), 170

SVG (Scalable Vector Graphics)
benefits, 409-410
code, 411-412
creating, 412
errors, 412
extensions, 378
files, 377-379, 411-412
HTML pages, embedding, 410
integration, 410-413
nested elements, 411
slicing, 412
storing, 413
tab, 351, 411
troubleshooting, 415

SVGZ compression, 411

swatches
Color swatch, 130-132, 172
Link, 188

SWF (ShockWave Flash), 350, 378
creating, 350, 386
LiveMotion, 405
source code, 378
streaming movies, 363
tab, 350

Switch Line Break Mode popup menu, 78

Sync Referenced Files Only check box (Sync Times Option box), 576

Sync Times Option box, 576

Synchronize Site, Maintenance Section (Server Administration Web Access), 485

Synchronized Multimedia Integration Language (SMIL), 20, 123

synchronizing
file transfer, 575
files (Workgroup Server), 485
time stamps, 576

syntax. *See* code

Syntax Checker, 14
button, 140
Highlight palette, 149

T

Tab check box, 195

tab order, image maps, 195-197

tabbing chains, form navigation, 273

tabindex properties, 474-475

Table icon, 87, 240, 251, 258

Table Inspector, 240-248, 252

Table of Contents, frames, 234

Table palette, 30-31, 241, 249-251

Table tab, 240, 244-248, 251-252

tables
aligning, 247-248
anchors, placing, 208
background color, 245
background images, 246
benefits, 240
borders, creating, 244
captions, 248
cells, 242-245
columns, 241-244
converting (grids), 252
creating, 87, 240
data, sorting, 87
form alignment, 258
grids, placing, 131
HTML tables, 396, 401
invisible tables, creating, 244
Layout Grid, 16
line breaks, 177
managing, 31
member searches, 459
nesting, 131, 251
Replace Rows, 545
resizing, 244
rows, 241-244
sorting data, 250-251
Table palette, 249-251
troubleshooting, 252
Web pages, 87

Tables palette, 87

tabs
2-up, 390
4-up, 390
Alt tab, 312
Annotations, 51, 57-58
Attribs, 350-351
Attribute, 411
Basic, 83, 184-186, 194, 251, 258, 311, 350-351, 410
Browsers, 470
Cell, 241-244, 247-248
Characters, 163
Color, 46, 114, 149, 562, 566
Design, 51, 53, 58
Diagram, 50-51, 84, 562, 566
Dynamic Bindings, 509
Dynamic Content, 83, 507, 511
Element, 150
Errors, 47, 567
Events, 307-309

External, 46, 203, 211-213, 562, 566
Extras, 46, 50, 136, 291, 567
Files, 46, 52, 71, 122, 136, 203, 489, 562-566, 580
Font Sets, 47, 562, 566
Forms, 83, 257, 261-264
Frame, 83, 231
Frame Editor, 231
Frame Preview, 225, 233
FTP, 47, 574
Head, 83, 151-153
Image Size, 375, 400
Images, 82, 356
Lasso Data Access, 443, 452
Lasso Form, 443, 446
Lasso Programming, 443, 451
Layout, 354, 411
Layout Preview, 79, 225
Library, 84, 291, 562, 566
Link, 82, 194, 207
Lock, 580
Master, 51
More, 191, 194, 222, 262, 350-351, 411
Navigation, 71
Object, 53, 307
Optimized, 373, 390
Original tab (Save for Web dialog box), 373
Outline Editor, 411
Params, 311
Plug-ins, 437
Preview, 26, 76, 354, 399
QuickTime, 84, 356-361
Report, 71
Rollover, 82, 194, 197
Row, 246-247
Script, 307
Section, 54
Select, 250
Sign, 59

Site, 53, 57, 83, 211-212, 567
Site Design window, 51
Site Extras, 84, 292, 371, 377
Site Reports, 70
Site Window, 45-47, 562
Slideshow, 357
Smart, 210, 223, 326, 371
Source, 26, 140, 424
Source Editor, 411
Special, 580
Staging, 51-52, 58
Structure, 71
Style, 249-250
SVG, 351, 411
SWF, 350
Table, 240, 244-248, 251-252
User Activity, 488-489
View, 68, 225, 478
WebDAV (Site Window), 47
WML Elements (Objects palette), 84

Tag Editor, 453

Tag tag (Head tab), 152

tags
Base tag (Head tab), 152
code, 140
Comment tag, 152, 218-220
Encode tag (Head tab), 152
extensions, nesting, 424
Form tag, 258-260
Generator tag, 94
head tags, adding, 151-153
IsIndex tag (Head tab), 151
<jsxitem> tag, 428
<jsxmenu> tag, 425, 428
<jsxmenubar> tag, 425
<jsxmenuitem> tag, 425
Keywords tag (Head tab), 152
LDML, 461
Link tag (Head tab), 152
managing, 146, 150

Meta tag (Head tab), 152
Outline Editor, 145
<p> tag, 173
<pre>, 174
Refresh tag (Head tab), 152
Script tag (Head tab), 152
Tag (Head tab), 152

Tags Case, HTML option (exporting slices), 391

tall orientation, 64, 68

Target
files, bitmaps, 375
folders, child pages (site design), 54
frames, 81, 233, 329
option (Slice Options dialog box), 398
parameter (pop-up windows), 328
setting (Form Inspector), 260

Target2Frames, frames (displaying), 234

TD W&H option (HTML Tables), 392

technologies, Web technologies, 20

Teletype style (text), 170

Template, Web pages (creating), 124

Template menu commands
Lock Page, 297
Lock Page or Stationery, Lock Page, 295
Unlock Page, 297

Template option, 78

Template Regions, 295

templates, 297. *See also* stationery
cards (WML decks), 472
creating, 294

editable regions, 294-296
inline selections, 294
Integration Templates, 421
modifying, 294-296
objects, 294
opening, 296
paragraphs, 294
Site Templates, 43-45, 421
storing, 296
styles, 280
troubleshooting, 298
updates, 294
Web pages, 123, 135, 295-296

Templates directories, 296

Term (unnumbered list), 179

Test Content Source button, 529

test data, Custom Merchant (troubleshooting), 556

testing
dynamic detail pages, 535
dynamic search pages, 527
submenus, 336

text, 160, 166
alignments, 175-176
alternate text, 188, 312, 377
annotations, site design, 57
blink text, 170
bold text, 169
clearing, 163
color, 171-172
copying, 162
cutting, 162
deleting, 163
dragging, 163
duplicating, 163
entering, 160-161, 472
Find & Replace, 164
floating boxes, 322
Font Structure, 170-171
fonts, 166-170
formatting, 166, 172-174
forms, 257, 266

headers, 175
highlighting, 162
italic text, 169
line breaks, 176-178
lists, 178-180
modifying, 161
pasting, 162
placeholder text
checkout screen, 551
databases, 510
dynamic pages, 529, 533
shipping methods, 552
shopping cart, 548
plain text, 169
selecting, 162
special characters, 163-164
Spellcheck, 164
strikeout text, 170
subscript text, 170
superscript text, 170
teletype text, 170
troubleshooting, 180
underline text, 170

Text Areas, 265-266

text boxes
entering text, 161
Key, 275
labels, 263
Reference text box, 264
Selected Constraints, 61

text color, Web pages, 132

Text color swatch, 132, 172

Text Document option (New Page), 123

Text Field icon, 264

text fields, 263-266, 331

text input fields, 474

Text Input object (Lasso Form), 444

text links, 206-207

Text toolbar, 161, 248

tiles, menu items, 425

time stamps, 223, 575-576

Timeline Editor, 343-345, 354

Timers, WML development, 476

titles, site design, 53

title card attribute (WML deck), 472

title properties, 474-475

To Be Edited (Files tab), 489

to child and back links, 62

Toggle Orientation button, 69

Toggle Slices Visibility tool, 373

toggles, Page window, 78

Token Input object (Lasso Form), 444

Token Object (Lasso Programming), 445

Tomcat, 498, 515

Toolbar parameter (pop-up windows), 329

toolbars, 76
Dynamic Content toolbar, 499, 509
JavaScript Editor toolbar, 306
Objects toolbar, 187, 190
Outline Editor toolbar, 147-149
Site toolbar, 122
Text toolbar, 161, 248
Type toolbar, Size, 169
Workgroup toolbar, 487

tools
Create Circle tool, 194
Create Sample tool, 358
Cut Out tool, 193
drawing tools (ImageReady), 393
Dynamic Content tools, 509-514

Eyedropper Swatch tool, 373
Eyedropper tool, 373
Hand tool, 373
Hide Content tool, 548
Move Image tool, 192
Polygon Hot Spot Drawing tool, 194
Rectangle tool, 194
Select Region tool, 194
Site Builder Target tool, 446
Slice Select tool, 373, 389-390, 393, 397-399
Slice tool, 387, 393, 397
Toggle Slices Visibility tool, 373
troubleshooting (dynamic content), 503
Undo tool, 86

Tools panel (Photoshop), 393

Tools parameter (pop-up windows), 329

_top, target names (frames), 233

Top property (floating boxes), 318

Tour links, pending links, 55

Tracing Images
command (Window menu), 192, 409
cutting, 193
deleting, 194
Illustrator, 409-410
importing, 192
mockups, 384
opacity, 409
palette, 192, 409
Photoshop, 386, 409-410
positioning, 409
slicing, 409
source, 409
SVG (Scalable Vector Graphics), 409-410

Track (QuickTime Editor), 356

tracks, video tracks (mode), 362

transferring files, 575, 577

Transform palette, 32, 84, 186, 189

transforming objects, 84

translating HTML source code, 88

transparency, jpegs, 185

Transparent (QuickTime mode), 362

Trash icon, 574

trees, markup trees (objects), 323

triggering
floating objects, 346
scenes, 350

troubleshooting, 21, 562
actions, 337
animations, 364
code, 154
content sources, 537
Custom Merchant, 556
database connections, 536
desktop customizations, 116
dynamic content, 536
dynamic site design, 518
extensions, 429-430
floating boxes, 337-338
fonts, 181
forms, 277
frames, 236
grids, 137
image maps, 199
integration, 413-415
JavaScript, 312
keyboard shortcuts, 116
Lasso Studio, 462-463
links, 89, 213
marquees, 226
movie clips, 364

palettes, 34, 90
plug-ins, 429-430
preconfigured servers, 503
preferences, 109
publishing, 580
Server Administration Web Access, 490
Site window, 569-570
Site Wizard, 47
sites, 71
Smart Objects, 380
snippets, 298
stationery, 298
streaming movies, 365
styles, 298
SVGs (Scalable Vector Graphics), 415
tables, 252
templates, 298
text, 180
tools (dynamic content), 503
Web pages, 137, 226
Web sites, creating, 47
windows, 34
wireless devices, 480

turning off IIS, 433

Tutorials, 421

Type Color button, 172

Type menu
commands
Alignment, Center, 175
Alignment, Increase Block Indent, 173
Alignment, Left, 175
Alignment, Right, 175
Font, Edit Font Sets, 167
List, 180
MySQL Database Query, 528
NoBreak, 178
Paragraph Format, 175
Paragraph Format, Paragraph, 173
Size, 169

Structure, 170
Style, 169
Style, Blink, 170
Style, Bold, 169
Style, Italic, 169
Style, Plain Text, 169
Style, Strikeout, 170
Style, Subscript, 170
Style, Superscript, 170
Style, Teletype, 170
Style, Underline, 170
formatting text, 166
Type pop-up menu commands, Custom Merchant Shopping Cart, 543
type property (Do event), 476
Type toolbar, Size, 169
types
buttons, 261
Page window, 94
pending links, 55
Smart Objects, 372

U

Underline style (text), 170
Undo Check Out (Workgroup toolbar), 487
Undo Cleanup Site command (Undo menu), 569
Undo menu commands, Undo Cleanup Site, 569
Undo tool, 86
Ungroup command (Edit menu), 59
Universal button, 261
Unlock Page command, 297
unlocking files, 485, 580
unnumbered lists, 179

Up state, slices (rollover images), 394
Update All command (Site window), 575
Update button, 438
Update Cart button, 545-547
Update check box, 438
updates
date/time stamps, 223
preferences, 92
site design, 58-59
stationeries, 294
templates, 294
Upload button, 575
Upload/Sync Times (Site preferences), 102
uploading
files, 577-579
site files, 102
Upper Alpha (numbered list), 178
Upper Roman (numbered list), 178
URL Character Encoding (Site Wizard), 41
URL check box, 202
URL Handling preferences, 94
URL icon, 211
URL option (Slice Options dialog box), 398
URL pop-up menus, 209
URL Popup icon, 210
URLs
anchors, WML decks, 473
base URLs, 152
navigational links, 203
providers, Custom Merchant, 542
Use Always check box, 105

Use Legend setting (Fieldset icon), 276
Use Map check box, 194
Used column (Error tab), 46
User Activity, 488-489
User Interface preferences, 95
User Slices, 389
Username setting (Available Servers dialog box), 574
usernames
Workgroup Sites, 486
Xchange, 421
users
accounts, 482, 486
events, 323, 330
identifying (Lasso Studio), 451
Server Administration Web Access, 482
Site Window, 489
UTF 8 (URL Handling preference), 94

V

validation, form validation, 278, 329-332
value properties, 474-475
Value setting, 267-268, 272
Variable (Font Structures), 171
variable frames, 232-233
Variable Object (Lasso Programming), 445
variables
content sources, 528
integration, 17
Lasso Studio, 454
storing (cookies), 332
WML development, 477
Variables button, 377

vector objects, Illustrator or Photoshop, 385

verifying code, 14

vertical space, creating, 177

vertical strips, background images, 133

video, 351-353

video tracks, mode (QuickTime), 362

view, site views (peripheral panes), 67

View, Navigation or Site command (Site menu), 45

View command (Window menu), 281, 478

View Inspector, 147

View menu commands
Hide Rulers, 131
Layout Mode, 442
Show Rulers, 131
Show Split Source, 143

View palette, 281, 564

View tab, 68, 225, 478

View window, 68

viewing. *See also* previewing
actions, 325
code, 12
comments, 219
images (Outline Editor), 147
links, 89, 213
media (plug-ins), 104
shopping cart, 545-549
Site Reports, 70-71
source code, 105, 143
special characters, 163
Web pages, 143, 468

views
Design view, 18, 51-52
Diagram, 58

Frame Preview, 80
Frame view, 79
Layout Preview, 79
Layout view, 76-79, 153
link view, 52
Navigation view, 52, 58, 61, 65-67
orientations, modifying, 69
Outline view, 79
site views, 66, 69-70
Site window, 564
sites, troubleshooting, 71
Source Code view, 79, 514
Source Split view, 78, 143

virtual links, 17

Visibility
grids, 129
submenus, 335

Visible
check box, 346
property (floating boxes), 318
setting (File Browser icon), 271

Visted Link color swatch, 132, 172

Volume (QuickTime), 353

volumes, scratch volumes, 108

Vspace, 191, 222, 311

W

WAP (Wireless Access Protocol), 468

Warning Messages (Network Status preference), 105

WBMP (Wireless Bitmap) images, 473

WDE (Web Data Engine), installing, 432

Web applications, 506-508

Web color, 84

Web Companion, 436, 441

Web Data Engine (WDE), installing, 432

Web images, 184-185

Web pages
addresses, adding, 211
background images, 133-134
blank Web pages (creating), 122
byte counts, 224
character counts, 224
color, 29, 84, 132-133
comments, 218-220
content, CSS, 281
creating, 26, 76, 122-124, 231, 296
date stamps, 223
dimensions, 125-126
displaying, 52
Document Statistics, 224
Frame Preview, 225
frames, 230
grids, 128-131
groupings, spotlighting (Navigation view), 67
Head Scripts, 152-153
hierarchies, 53
layout, 76
Layout Preview, 225
Layout Rulers, 131
link lines, 56
linking (external style sheets), 285
locking, 78, 295
managing, 27, 45-47
margins, 127
marquees, 221-222
objects, 82
opening, 122, 205
pop-up windows, 328
previewing, 225

refreshing, 152
saving, 134-137
scratch pages, 52
site design, 51, 54-56
Site Reports, modifying, 71
tables, 87
time stamps, 223
troubleshooting, 137, 226
viewing, 143, 468
WML (Wireless Markup Language), 468
word counts, 224

Web servers, 108, 496, 536

Web Settings command (Edit menu), 163

Web Sharing, Mac OS X, Lasso Suite installations, 435

Web sites
AdHost, 502
Adobe, 21
Apache, 498, 515
blank Web sites, creating (Site Wizard), 38, 40
Blue World Communications, 432
commerce sites, creating, 501
creating, 38-40, 43
diagrams, 566
dynamic Web sites, 496-498
errors, 565
Evocative Software, 501
importing, 40-43
Jakarta, 515
managing, 18-19, 482
MySQL, 498
navigating (In & Out palette), 565
PHP, 498, 515
planning, 25
Plug 'n Play, 501
Server Administration, 482

single user sites, converting, 486
static Web sites, 499, 502
Tomcat, 498
Workgroup Sites, 485-486

Web technologies, 20

Web Workgroup Server
publishing sites, 490
Server Administration Web Access, 482-486, 490
settings, 484
site management, 19
Site Window, 486-490

WebDAV (Web-based Distributed Authoring and Versioning), 47, 572, 575-580

wide orientation, 64, 68

Width property (floating boxes), 318

widths, Web pages, 126

Window menu commands
Actions, 323
Export, 406
Floating Boxes, 320
In & Out Links, 565
Inspector, 194, 307, 330
Optimize, 393
Rollovers, 393-394
Save as, Save as Stationery, 478
Site Navigator, 67
Template Regions, 295
Tracing Image, 192, 409
View, 281, 478
Workgroup toolbar, 487
Workspace, Default Workspace, 29, 82
Workspace, Manage Workspace, 114
Workspace, Save Workspace, 114

Window Settings box, 126

Window Size menu commands, Settings, 126

Window Size Popup menu, 79

windows. *See also* palettes; Page window; Site window
Add Data Source, 525, 541
browser windows, opening Web pages, 205
Check Spelling, 164
Data Source, 525
databases, building (dynamic content), 516
Document Statistics, 224
Document window, 294-296, 312, 372
Dynamic Bindings window, 543
Edit URL window, 204
Find window, 150
Highlight, 479
Images window, 95, 352
In & Out Links window, 89
Lasso Suite installation, 433-435
Network Status, 105, 577
pop-up windows, 328-329
Preferences, 92
QuickTime, 109
Site Design, 51-52
Site Settings, 541
sizing (Web pages), 126
Sort Table, 250
Source Code window, 88-89
Source Editor Windows, cursors, 142
Syntax Check window, 141
troubleshooting, 34
View window, 68

Windows (Microsoft), ASP (Active Server Pages), 498

Windows Character Map, 163

Wipe Transition command (Multimedia menu), 325-327

Wireless Bitmap (WBMP) images, 473

wireless devices
CHTML (Compact Hypertext Markup Language), 468-470
CHTML development, 477-479
troubleshooting, 480
WML (Wireless Markup Language), 468-477
XHTML-Basic (Extensible Hypertext Markup Language, Basic), 468-470, 477-479

Wireless Markup Language (WML). *See* WML

wizards, 15
Dynamic Site Wizard, 499, 509-510, 522
importing, 38, 41-42
Lasso Configuration Wizard, 445
Setup Wizard, 482
Site Wizard, 485
blank Web sites (creating), 38-40
Site Template (creating Web sites), 44
troubleshooting, 47

WML (Wireless Markup Language), 20, 468-470
decks, 471-473
developing, 469-477
emulators, 470
palettes, 469-470
preferences, 469-470
XML, 470

WML Deck option (New Page), 123

WML Elements tab (Objects palette), 84

word counts, 224

Word Wrap, Source Code, 32, 89, 141, 144

Workflow palette, 489

Workgroup, Change Password command (Site menu), 490

Workgroup, Change User command (Site menu), 490

Workgroup, Convert to Workgroup command (Site menu), 486

Workgroup, Open Workgroup Administration command (Site menu), 490

Workgroup Server. *See* Web Workgroup Server

Workgroup Sites, 485-486

Workgroup toolbar, 487

Workgroup toolbar command (Window menu), 487

Workspace, Default Workspace command (Window menu), 29, 82

Workspace, Manage Workspace command (Window menu), 114

Workspace, Save Workspace command (Window menu), 114

workspaces, 82, 114

wrapping
code, 141
text, forms, 266

Write Generator (General preference), 94

X-Z

Xchange, 421

.xds, Data Source database, 509

XHTML (eXtensible Hypertext Markup Language), 153-154

XHTML-Basic (eXtensible Hypertext Markup Language, Basic), 468-470

XHTML-Basic 1.0 command (Doctype menu), 477

XHTML-Basic option (New Page), 123

XHTML Page option (New Page), 123

XML (eXtensible Markup Language), 14, 20, 470

XML Data Source, content source, 501

xml: lang card attribute (WML deck), 472

z-index
multiple floating objects, 347-348
property (floating boxes), 318
submenus, 335

WHAT'S ON THE DISC

The companion CD-ROM contains many useful third-party tools and utilities, plus the source code and JavaScript samples from the book.

If Windows is installed on your computer, and you have the AutoPlay feature enabled, the START.EXE program starts automatically whenever you insert the disc into your CD-ROM drive.

WINDOWS 9X/2000/XP INSTALLATION INSTRUCTIONS

1. Insert the CD-ROM disc into your CD-ROM drive.

2. From the Windows desktop, double-click on the My Computer icon.

3. Double-click on the icon representing your CD-ROM drive.

4. Double-click on the icon titled START.EXE to run the installation program.

WINDOWS NT INSTALLATION INSTRUCTIONS

1. Insert the CD-ROM disc into your CD-ROM drive.

2. In File Manager or Program Manager, choose Run from the File menu.

3. Type *<drive>*\START.EXE and press Enter, where *<drive>* corresponds to the drive letter of your CD-ROM. For example, if your CD-ROM is drive D:, type D:\START.EXE and press Enter.

Macintosh Installation Instructions

1. Insert the CD-ROM disc into your CD-ROM drive.

2. When an icon for the CD appears on your desktop, open the disc by double-clicking on its icon.

3. Double-click on the icon named Guide to the CD-ROM, and follow the directions which appear.

Technical Support from Que Publishing

We can't help you with Windows or Macintosh problems or software from third parties, but we can assist you if a problem arises with the CD-ROM itself.